THE HALF-CLOSED DOOR.

THE HALF-CLOSED DOOR

Alan Tritton

Book Guild Publishing
Sussex, England

First published in Great Britain in 2008 by
The Book Guild Ltd
Pavilion View
19 New Road
Brighton, BN1 1UF

Typesetting in Times by
Keyboard Services, Luton, Bedfordshire

Printed and bound in Great Britain by
Athenaeum Press Ltd, Gateshead

A catalogue record for this book is available from
The British Library

ISBN 978 1 84624 271 7

Contents

Preface

When I first started writing this book, it was for the benefit of my children, grandchildren and subsequent generations. It never really occurred to me that it could have an appeal to a wider readership, but having finished it, I now feel that this could well be the case.

The first question that could be asked is where did I get the title of the book from. It comes from the introduction to Jan Morris's book, *Farewell the Trumpets* and the quotation is as follows:

> Say farewell to the Trumpets
> You will hear them no more
> But their sweet sad silvery echo
> Will call to you still
> Through the half-closed door.

My mother's family, the Baillies and the Roses, were all in their day imperial soldiers and although the Empire has gone now, these were the families who served it and I believe they took pride in serving it, despite their heavy casualties. They thought it was their duty to serve it and they did.

I therefore wanted my family and now also a wider readership not only to know about my life such as it has been, but also to learn about those soldiers, and in learning about them to appreciate them, and in appreciating them to feel proud of them as I feel proud of them.

And as the door starts to close on my life, these echoes of a once great imperial past call to me still, because I was once myself a small part of that imperial past and I can still hear the pipes and drums and bugles of my Regiment when I was on active service in the Far East sixty years ago.

I dedicate this book to my wife Diana. She has stood by me through thick and thin and particularly when, for four long years, I had to fight the evil of legal blackmail. I am hugely grateful to her and also to my eldest son, Guy, for the unstinting support they afforded me during that terrible time.

I must record my most grateful thanks to two remarkable women, because without them, this book would not have seen the light of day – they are the only two people in the country who can read my writing and therefore could type out the script. The first is Filomena de Souza, whose family come from Goa, and who was for many years my secretary in the Bank. She also continued to help me, long after I retired, with all the administrative work of the Calcutta Tercentenary Trust. The second is Joyce Elgar, who came to me for one year when I was High Sheriff of Essex and stayed on as my secretary for 15 years. I salute them and thank them both from the bottom of my heart.

In conclusion I would like to mention that most of this book has been written from memory. I have only once kept a Journal and that was in the Antarctic. Recollections of events with the passage of time can turn into reconstructions. If there are some inaccuracies – and there are bound to be – then I would please ask the reader to forgive me and blame it on a faulty, but I would hope not too faulty, memory.

1

My Tritton Family

I was born on 2nd October 1931. My father George Henton died on 6th March 1934 – he was only 28 years old.

My father, who I never knew, was the younger son of Herbert Leslie Melville Tritton and his wife Gertrude, née Gosset, always known as Gaga.

My grandfather was the eldest son of Joseph Herbert Tritton who wrote a book entitled *Tritton: The Place and the Family* which someone described as the dull chronicle of an Essex bourgeois family. I have always thought this was somewhat unfair. Nevertheless there could be said to be some truth in it, although things changed with the events of my life, which has been anything but dull.

The founder on my side of the family fortune, such as it was, was John Henton Tritton. He was born in 1755. His maternal grandfather, Henton Brown, after whom he was named, was a Quaker banker who lived next door to Barclay & Co. in Lombard Street, London. Henton Brown in his will nominated his grandson to be a partner in his firm and directed that he should have a quarter share in the business when he came of age, and when he did so this became known as Brown, Collinson & Tritton. It was a family firm. James Brown was the son of Henton Brown, Collinson was his son-in-law and John Henton Tritton was his grandson. That was in 1778. However, shortly after he joined, there seems to have been a series of defalcations with the result that the partnership became insolvent and John Henton, along with his two partners, was made bankrupt – an experience he never forgot. Bankruptcy was something not easily forgiven in Quaker banking circles but when Mary, daughter of John Barclay, the banker next door, heard of his failure she is reported to have said, 'I had rather lean on

1

John Henton's arm than ride in a coach and four.' Her strong belief in him was well founded. He paid off all his debts and won his discharge from bankruptcy.

He was then taken on as a clerk by Barclay, Bevan & Co. and he was able successfully to introduce some of the bankrupt bank's clients to that partnership. For these introductions he was paid £500, made a partner, and shortly afterwards Mary Barclay married him and they lived together over the shop (or rather the bank) for many years. This became the founding partnership of Barclays Bank which went on to become one of the largest and most successful banks in the world. The partnership prospered and, judging by the rate of return on the partnership capital, was phenomenally successful, particularly in the 1870s when the annual rates of return were well in excess of 40 per cent. John Henton became a rich man and in 1812, which I always remember as the year of Napoleon's invasion of Russia, he purchased a farm in Great Leighs, Essex which was enlarged by successive generations and became known as the Lyons Hall Estate.

Prior to the Reformation the Trittons, who were then living in Kent, were, one assumes, good practising Catholics as is evidenced by their wills, but like many other families during the Elizabethan period, they conformed to the new reformed religion.

However, later on they came under the influence of George Fox, the founder of the Quaker movement, and became Quakers themselves. How long they remained practising Quakers I do not know – it was probably until the early nineteenth century, when they became fervent Baptist evangelicals. It is perhaps worth noting that banking was not regarded as a profession in those days. If it had been, as practising Quakers, they would not have been allowed to undertake it. Banking, in fact, was never really regarded as a profession and, in my day, it was more often described as an industry.

As evangelicals, the Tritton family in the nineteenth century and, as it happens, into the early twentieth century, employed a Scripture Reader whose job it was, as the term implies, to read out the Scriptures to the long-suffering and presumably illiterate villagers of Great Leighs in their homes. This practice started the long war of religious attrition between the Anglican Rectors of Great Leighs and the evangelical Trittons.

To counterbalance the so-called 'High services' of the parish church opposite Lyons Hall, my great-grandfather, Joseph Herbert

2

Tritton, constructed a chapel close by on his property at Cole Hill. The official name of this chapel was the Mission Room. Furthermore, right next door to the Rectory he constructed a house known as the Manse for the mission teacher. This meant that the Rector, to get to his church opposite our house, had first to pass the Manse and then pass the Mission Room. To make matters worse, my great-grandfather in the summer organised a series of evangelical meetings in the garden of Lyons Hall under the cedar tree, which all employees and their families were expected to attend. These were referred to by the Anglican Rector as the 'Under the Cedar Tree Meetings'. These meetings were addressed by my great-grandfather and I expect, as an added attraction, tea and cakes were provided.

The Mission Room, like the cedar tree, has long since gone. There was once a rumour that the Catholics wanted to take over the Mission Room, as a place where Holy Mass could be celebrated, and that when this became known to the then Tritton family – I think it was probably my grandmother and her daughter Dore – they pulled it down.

There is one more twist to this unceasing religious guerrilla war and this was when the Reverend John Franklin, who had been a Chaplain with the 8th Army in North Africa, became the Rector of Great Leighs. He put up a small but attractive icon of Our Lady – after all the church is dedicated to St Mary the Virgin – but this was regarded by my aunt as idolatrous popery and she never again attended the church, except for her funeral in 1970. The icon is still there, as it should be.

If I have written at some length on my Tritton family's religious fervours, then it is because later on in my life, they became a subject of great difficulty to me which, as this book proceeds, will become apparent.

Now before leaving my great-grandfather, who turned down the offer of a baronetcy as it was not compatible with his religious beliefs, I must tell you a story about his expansive and expensive religious activities. As an example of these activities, in September 1884 he wrote a book for the London Baptist Missionary Society entitled *Rise and Progress of the Work on the Congo River*. He was Treasurer of the Society and the implication is that he personally financed a lot of its missionary activities in the Congo. The book was dedicated: 'To the Committee of the Society in grateful remembrance of their valued sympathy during a time of deep personal affliction and in warm appreciation of their unfailing efforts for the extension of the Redeemer's Kingdom, the following pages are affectionately inscribed by their friend and colleague, Joseph Tritton.'

The King of the Congo at that time was Dom Pedro V. He warmly welcomed the first Baptist missionaries and had full liberty accorded to them 'to teach and preach Jesus Christ'. From then on it was not too easy and the reason for this was the Portuguese opposition. In his book Joseph Tritton described the country as being originally 'discovered' by the Portuguese; he said that the name of San Salvador was given by them to the chief town; that the King ruled under their auspices; and that a 'nominal' Christianity was forced upon him and his subjects. He then went on to state that, 'the monuments of European civilisation are still recognised in the materials and ruins scattered about' and 'in the relics of an idolatrous faith, which sought with bell, book and candle, with priestly absolution and Church Authority, backed by persecution and oppression, determined and prolonged to make of the people of the Congo a nation professedly Christian'.

He went on to write:

Who can tell the woes of these unhappy natives under this so-called Christian rule of Portugal? The sword – the cannon – the slave whip – the various instruments of torture – the strong hand of power and the reigning lust of gain – these were the influences which marked the path of the invaders, these the weapons which pierced with a thousand wounds the victims of his iron rule.

And so on and so forth.

However, no sooner had the news of the Protestant missionaries arriving in the Congo reached Lisbon, than a party of Catholic priests was despatched, supported and escorted by a naval and military force. Faced with a Portuguese gunboat in the river opposite his palace, King Dom Pedro V capitulated, and turned his back upon the missionaries whose ministry he had encouraged and whose prayer meetings he had attended.

'There was one chief,' the missionaries wrote to the Society in London, 'who used to gobble up Portuguese' (as you can see he was a cannibal) 'to indicate his hatred for them.' But they also wrote – indicating how strongly and how long the influence of superstition prevails – that 'although the first Catholic mission had been abandoned, the memory of the Catholic missionaries is revered in the country to this day.'

The missionaries wrote that 'their graves are carefully tended and preserved with every sign of respect and their missals, books, letters and chalices still exist and the natives would not part with them.' To this, Joseph Tritton observed that he did not think all this represented a reverence for Romish relics but was actually associated with fetish superstition.

And so the book goes on like this for 60 pages. The Baptist missionaries had a hard time of it; they either died of malaria or other diseases, or they ended up in the stewpots of the cannibals, or they were evicted by the King at the behest of the Jesuits.

Towards the end of the book a missionary reports to the Society in London that, 'the great objective placed before me is to effect the moral conquest of Africa in such wise that the Christian Church can command the entire Continent and proclaim the Gospel over the whole of Africa and associated with that was to destroy the terribly cruel slave trade.'

I am not sure I would have liked my great-grandfather, and I am not sure he would have liked me either. He certainly would not have liked my conversion to Catholicism which, as you will see above, he described as an idolatrous faith enforced in Africa by the sword, the cannon and the slave whip. Perhaps it was as well we never met.

To give you a little more sense of the Trittons' religious fervour, it is helpful to go back to the Great War when there was a large encampment of soldiers in the Park. My great-grandmother, Mrs Joseph Herbert Tritton, called the Rector, the Reverend Andrew Clark, to say that she 'was very disappointed that they do not have evening prayers in the YMCA canteen when it closes every night at 9.30 p.m.' She said that she herself would be quite happy to undertake this 'duty', but that her husband would not hear of it.

One Sunday, she said, she was having Mr Hayes, the YMCA secretary from Terling, to tea and also some of the officers to tea and supper, and that she was going to broach the subject. She was very gratified that 22 men put down their names for these prayer meetings. She had twice asked them for tea. 'Sergeant Hunter, a

5

very dear man, had been so very kind in going round with tea invitations, but it was so hard on the poor dear fellows that, on each occasion, they had been unexpectedly called out on military duty and so had been unable to come'!*

She then erected on her own, at the end of the YMCA tent in Lyons Hall Park, another tent which she called 'The Quiet Tent' to which the men could withdraw to say their prayers. She hoped to have a Bible class there once a week. The Reverend Andrew Clark wrote in his diary that 'she often went there to chat with the men but generally, when she got there, a nice boy came along with a polite message that, just at present, the men in camp were very much occupied with their duties and could not come.'

My grandfather – who was the eldest son of Joseph Henry Tritton – had four brothers and four sisters. The sisters Elizabeth – known as Aunt Diddy, Olive, Violet and Annette – always known affectionately as Aunt Nettie, never married and like my Baillie great-aunts in Scotland all lived together in the same house, Brent Hall near Finchingfield, which they rented off the Ruggles-Brise family. I never particularly liked going there as they kept bantams, which chased me in my short schoolboy trousers round the garden. The sisters were fervent Anglicans and devoted themselves to good works, perhaps with the exception of Aunt Nettie, who was an accomplished artist until she became riddled with arthritis.

To me, with the exception of Aunt Nettie, who was my favourite, they were all rather forbidding, tall, old ladies, heavy-boned and rather hairy with deep somewhat masculine voices. They were good, conscientious and upright great-aunts but, after I took my first wife over to Brent Hall to introduce her to them, I never saw them again and I remember Aunt Diddy's last words to me as we departed were to the effect of how intensely they disapproved of her Catholicism. This, with the benefit of hindsight, is not surprising, because after my marriage – where none of the Trittons looked at all happy, in fact positively grumpy and glowering as they were taken through the Nuptial Mass – my Aunt Dore, the aunt who was then the life tenant of the Lyons Hall Estate and who was the one who flounced out of the church of St Mary the Virgin after seeing the icon of our Lady, never invited us again to her house;

---

* From *Echoes of the Great War: The Diary of the Reverend Andrew Clark, 1914–19* by Andrew Clark (OUP, 1985).

and I was then heir to the estate. It was as if she wished we did not exist. I find it curious, this dislike and distrust of Catholics, and there was always the suspicion in my mind that it was the thought of the Lyons Hall Estate falling into the hands of the Jesuits that brought on the stroke which seriously afflicted my aunt in 1963.

And then, of course, there were my grandfather's younger brothers. The eldest of these was Charles, born in 1871, and of whom I know little. I believe he was a local Director of Barclays Bank at Kinnaird House in Pall Mall. There is a story that one day he received what he regarded as an exceptionally irritating instruction from Head Office. He was so infuriated by it that he told his colleagues he would leave the Bank that day, and indeed he did, never to return. No one seems quite sure whether he was married or not, but he certainly developed a close relationship with Gladys, the barmaid at his club, where he used to lunch every day. I believe he went to live in the West Country where he indulged himself in his favourite sport of otter-hunting. He had no children.

The next brother was Arthur Francis, who was born in 1873. He married Beatrice May Lawrence – Aunt B, in 1905. They had five children. Arthur was a successful stockbroker who made a lot of money but lost it in the 1929 market crash and died shortly afterwards. He left his family in quite severe financial difficulties. His eldest son was Patrick Arthur, born in 1905, but more of him later.

The third brother was Claude Henry, born in 1874, who married Evelyn, the daughter of the Hon. Edward Strutt of Terling in July 1906. Claude was tall, good-looking, a born raconteur, and loved the ladies. He was a member of White's. I remember some years ago having a drink there at the bar with an elderly member, and when he asked my name and I told him, he asked if I was related to Claude, I said yes, he was a great-uncle. He then went on to ask if he had inherited the Lyons Hall Estate, to which my answer was no – I had. He looked thoughtful for a moment and then came out with the words: 'Well! That's lucky – if Claude had inherited it, it would probably have all gone by now.'

Claude lived in British East Africa for some time and made a living there as a big game hunter, and I believe he was at one time in the Yukon looking for gold. When the First World War broke out in 1914 he joined the Army Service Corps (which was not Royal then), being eventually promoted to major in France and decorated with an OBE. There were two sons of the marriage, Ronald and John. The former, whom we loved dearly, worked for the Savoy Group and British Petroleum, whilst John was a regular Army officer with the Royal Artillery, retiring as a Colonel. He subsequently became a Director of Strutt & Parker Farms Limited. This side of the family had shareholdings in the company inherited from their mother, Evelyn Strutt.

Then there was the youngest son, Alan George, after whom I am named. Alan George, who was born in 1882, served with the Coldstream Guards both in South Africa during the Boer War in 1900 to 1902, and then in France as a Captain, where he was twice mentioned in despatches. On 1st September 1914, he was involved in a desperate rearguard action protecting the retreat from Mons to the Marne. The Guards were heavily outnumbered by the Germans and they suffered heavy casualties, including Alan George, who was wounded in the hand and quite possibly in the leg. He was seen riding on his horse, deathly pale with his leg saturated in blood.

However, he quickly recovered from his wounds, which could not have been too serious, and by 24th September he was back in action again. He was killed on Boxing Day 1914 fighting near Bethune, and his body was laid to rest in a soldier's grave near the village of Le Touret. Alan George never married.

It was said that on his last leave before returning to the Front, he had a premonition that he was going to be killed and he was – by a sniper's bullet. Every year at the Remembrance Day Service at Great Leighs, his name is read out, as one who fell in the Great War and gave his life for his country. His name is, of course, my name, and as the bugles sound and his name is read out, we will and do remember him.

My grandfather, whose full name was Herbert Leslie Melville, was the eldest of the five sons and was born in 1870. He went to Eton and then on to Trinity College, Cambridge. He joined the family banking partnership of Barclay, Bevan & Tritton before it became a limited joint stock bank in 1896. In 1894 he married Gertrude Gosset, the daughter of the Clerk to the House of Commons, and had four children by her, two sons and two daughters. After his father's death in 1923, he moved to Lyons Hall and then, at the outbreak of the Second World War, when Lyons Hall was requisitioned by the Army, he moved to the Hole Farm where he died shortly afterwards in 1940, aged 69.

The eldest daughter was Lucy – Aunt Lucy – who was born in 1895. She married Reginald Bevan who had been badly wounded and gassed in the First World War, and I always remember him as an invalid – he was very good-looking. They had two beautiful daughters, my first cousins. The eldest was Rosemary, who became an air stewardess with British European Airways; in those days being an air stewardess was regarded as a glamorous job. She was killed when an Italian fighter crashed into her plane over Naples. Only recently did her sister Veronica become aware that she had an illegitimate daughter during the war. Rosemary was sent by her mother, Lucy Bevan, to Yorkshire for her pregnancy and the daughter was adopted. She made a happy and successful marriage and has two sons and two daughters.

Aunt Lucy and Reginald's second daughter was Veronica. She married John Lewis, a lieutenant commander in the Royal Navy, in Hong Kong and she adopted three children. She is still astonishingly good-looking.

Both Aunt Lucy and Reginald became Catholics, and this conversion resulted in an estrangement between Lucy and her parents. I believe that, to all intents and purposes, she was cut out of her father's will. She was, however, left some money by a Catholic friend, which enabled her to live in some reasonable but not affluent comfort. To me she was always kind and generous, and when I became a Catholic myself in July 1963, she almost went wild with joy, as my conversion represented her revenge against her parents and their treatment of her.

My grandfather's second daughter was Marjorie, always known as Aunt Dore. She was born in 1897 and was married in 1928 (the same year as my mother and father) to Cecil Garnett, who was a serving officer with the Rifle Brigade. He had a 'good' war, as they say, and was awarded the Military Cross for his fighting exploits in Normandy in 1944. After the war he became a stockbroker with funds provided to him by my grandfather. Very sadly he died in 1949 at the age of 49, from cancer. With his death, the family lost his benign influence over my Aunt Dore, who seemed to me to become increasingly embittered.

She had no children and I always used to think she was jealous of my mother. She lived at the Hole Farm and died in 1970. She

9

was the life tenant of the Lyons Hall Estate, and after her death, I discovered some letters she had written to Paddy, hers and my trustee. She wrote that she had never trusted me and never would, and as far as she was concerned I could go to hell – her words, and I will come back to this later.

The eldest son was Ralph Leslie, always known as Tim. He was born in 1900. He was great fun, loved parties and the girls, and was rather wild. He was never able to hold down a job. He was, however, commissioned into the Grenadier Guards, but that ended badly. The story is that he had been to a very late-night party – so late that he was unable to dress properly to mount Guard outside Buckingham Palace, and was discovered wearing his pyjamas under his dress uniform, so he was dismissed. I am not sure this story is totally true, but that is what I was told.

Despite all this, his parents loved him – he was after all their eldest son – and forgave him. Eventually, however, they despaired and sent him off to New Zealand, but what to do, I do not know. At Waterloo Station when he was boarding the boat train for Southampton, he was seen off by numerous beautiful ladies of the night and also his taxi-drivers, who he used to breakfast with, still dressed in white tie and tails.

In New Zealand, no sooner had he arrived there, than he met an extremely attractive girl, Alys. He returned with her and they got married in London. Five months later he was killed in a car crash on the Great North Road. He was only 28.

And this brings me on to the younger son, my father George Henton, who was very different to his elder brother Tim. What can I say about my father? He was born in 1905, he was tall, thin, bespectacled and probably a worrier like me. I have always hoped that he would be proud, or is proud, of me as his only son.

After Eton and Trinity College Cambridge he joined Barclays Bank like his father. In due course he became a local Director of the bank in Lombard Street, in the same room as his father. He was additionally appointed a member of the London Committee of Barclays Bank (Dominion, Colonial & Overseas).

It was in 1928 at St Pauls, Knightsbridge that he married my mother, Iris Mary Baillie – she was five years older than him. In November 1928, Marigold was born and in October 1931, I was born.

In 1934 my father was out hunting with the East Essex Hunt

when he suddenly developed an agonising pain in his stomach. It was diagnosed as a burst appendix and he was taken to Sister Agnes's hospital in London, where his father was also seriously ill. It all turned gangrenous, and without any antibiotics in those days, there was nothing the doctors could do. He died on 6th March 1934. Like his brother he was only 28 when he died, leaving Mummy a widow aged 33.

Now going back to my grandfather, he was appointed a Director of the Bank in 1914, at the outbreak of the First World War, and a Director of the Colonial Bank as well. The First World War showed that there did not exist any means of banking and financial cooperation between member states of the British Empire. This was partially remedied by the creation of Reserve Banks in South Africa, India and Australia, but no steps had been taken towards the creation of an Imperial commercial bank. The Colonial Bank had originally confined its business to the West Indies, but in 1916 it decided to start commercial banking in West Africa. It was this expansion which put some strain on its balance sheet. Also in 1916 the Charter of the Colonial Bank was amended to permit it to operate anywhere throughout the British Empire.

It was at this point that the Chairman of Barclays Bank and the Directors of the Colonial Bank considered that it could be advantageous to form some sort of association, as firstly the Colonial Bank needed more capital, and secondly because Barclays could direct a lot of business to the Colonial Bank branches. In doing this, it was considered that this would improve the standing of the Colonial Bank with the business community both at home and overseas.

To cut a very long story short, the Colonial Bank in 1925 changed its name to Barclays Bank (Dominion, Colonial & Overseas) (DCO), which simultaneously amalgamated with the National Bank of South Africa and the Anglo-Egyptian Bank.

My grandfather was elected to the Board of this new bank and in 1932 he was appointed Deputy Chairman and in 1934 Chairman – the year of my father's death. He started travelling extensively to visit the overseas branches together with his wife. In 1935 he visited Egypt, Palestine and West Africa, where my grandmother told me she had to change her clothes seven times a day because of the heat and humidity. In 1931 he had visited East Africa, and I have a wonderful group photograph of him with the staff of the Mombasa branch. He is dressed in a white linen suit with a white solar topee resting on his knees and is sporting a bow tie. All the British and Indian staff are named in the photograph, and there are four African messengers squatting at his feet but they have no names.

In 1936 he visited South Africa, but when he was in Johannesburg he had a heart attack, possibly caused by the altitude. He was unable to complete his tour programme and sailed home from Cape Town. He returned to work but it is doubtful whether he was ever fit again. In 1937 he retired as Chairman of DCO although he remained a Director until his death three years later in 1940.

When he retired as Chairman he was presented by the staff of the bank with a very large silver tray on which is inscribed the following words:

Dear Mr Tritton
We send you this tray and lamp bearing our names as a token of our abiding regard and affection.
Yours sincerely,
The Members of Staff of Barclays Bank
(Dominion, Colonial and Overseas)

I think that says it all.

He was a keen fox-hunter and for a time was Chairman of the East Essex Hunt. He served for many years in the Essex Yeomanry. He was a Deputy Lieutenant of the County of Essex and was High Sheriff in 1933. My grandfather was a good, upright and conscientious man. As was said in his obituary, he endeared himself to all who knew him, and his natural kindliness of disposition won him the affection of all those who worked for him.

I cannot say I knew him, although my sister Marigold and my first cousin Veronica did. I was eight when he died. His portrait, painted by Eve in 1940 shows an inexpressible sadness in his eyes. Ill health, the loss of two sons, the estrangement from his elder daughter Lucy, the declaration of what became the Second World War in 1939, his eviction that year from Lyons Hall when it was requisitioned by the Army, and having his beloved stables burnt down by them, must have all contributed to this terrible sadness – he deserved better.

2

My Baillie Family

It was once said to me of my mother's and father's marriage in 1928 that the Tritton family were disappointed that their son was marrying into an aristocratic but impoverished Highland military family and that the Baillie family were disappointed that my mother was marrying into trade or, as the Anglo-Indians would have put it, that she was marrying 'a box wallah'. There was, as usual, some truth in these remarks, but of course it was not the whole truth.

The two families were in fact very different, and during the course of this chapter I need to go back not only to my mother's family, the Baillies, but also to her mother's family, the Roses of Kilravock. I also need to go back even further to my great-grandmother's family, the Burnabys. She was Anna Burnaby, the sister of Fred and Evelyn Burnaby, and she married my great-grandfather General Duncan Baillie, who was born in 1826.

Duncan Baillie had an elder brother, Colonel Hugh Smith Baillie – Smith being his mother's name – and he was born in 1822. In 1847 Hugh married Eve Maria Viscountess Glentworth, the widow of Lord Glentworth, who if he had not died would have become the Earl of Limerick. She was the daughter of Henry Villebois of Marham House, Downham Market, Norfolk. On her marriage she refused to change her name from Lady Glentworth to Mrs Baillie. My Baillie great-aunts always used to call her Aunt Glentworth and they used to stay for long periods of time at the then enormous Marham House.

Before going on I must tell you a little about Aunt Glentworth, whose portrait hangs in Lyons Hall. She was born in 1803, the daughter of Henry Villebois. He was always known as the 'old

13

squire'. The last member of this family died in 1886. During his lifetime he stood for all that was best in Norfolk sport. He hunted in the Vale of the White Horse and Hertfordshire from 1842 to 1854. He then joined Lord Suffield in Norfolk, taking over first the West Norfolk hunt and then the whole County of Norfolk until three years later Lord Hastings took over the East Norfolk hunt from him. Furthermore, the Prince of Wales used to come over from Sandringham to shoot with him at Marham.

Aunt Glentworth must have been a remarkable woman – she lived for one hundred years, dying in 1903. There were two stories my great-aunts used to tell me about her. The first was that she used to tell them how she watched the Guards marching off to Waterloo from the doorway of the family house in Pall Mall – this was in 1815; the second was when she was invited to the Coronation of Queen Victoria in 1837, and remembered both the girlish grace and the dignity of the young Queen, who kept on trying to shift the oppressively heavy weight of her Coronation train throughout the service.

And of Marham, that great Villebois country house and estate, nothing very much remains: most of the huge house was demolished in the 1930s and the estate is now RAF Marham.

Now we must leave the Villebois family, which died out, and visit the Burnaby family. It was Aunt Glentworth's sister who married the Reverend Gustavus Burnaby and it was his daughter Anna who married my great-grandfather Duncan James Baillie.

The Reverend Gustavus Burnaby was a fine example of what Bishop Wilberforce used to describe as a 'squarson', that is to say a squire and a parson. He was well known in Bedfordshire, where he lived, for both his hospitality and his hard riding. He hunted three days a week with the Oakley. Judges on circuit at Bedford always dined with him and the Duke and Duchess of Bedford stayed with him on their visits to Bedford. He was, I believe, a generous man, but he was also autocratic and I think it is fair to say that he was usually but not always respected. It is possible that you would call him a snob, and it probably pleased him to have been appointed chaplain to the Duke of Cambridge.

As well as my great-grandmother Anna, he had two sons, Fred and Evelyn. Evelyn went into the church like his father. He married twice, his second wife being the Hon. Margaret Catherine Erskine, the one surviving daughter of Lord and Lady Erskine. He died at the age of 76 at Middleton. His only child and daughter was Ruby, who I looked after in her old age. She liked to tell me that her father's greatest difficulty was that he never knew the difference between capital and income. Poor dearest Cousin Ruby, she went stone deaf at the age of 18 and she used to tell me how she longed to go up in an aeroplane as the noise of the engines would drown out the perpetual tinnitus ringing in her ears. I have kept all her scrapbooks and photograph albums – she was an extensive traveller and a good skier.

I will write later about the other son, Colonel Fred Burnaby, but I now want to introduce you to the Baillie family. The Baliols according to the late James Baillie in his *Lives of the Baillies* were of French origin. Their name is derived from Bailleul in Flanders and they came over with William the Conqueror in 1066, as appears from a list of 'Les Compagnons de Guillaume à la conquete d'Angleterre AD 1066 par Leopold de Lisle Member de l'Institut, Paris'.

That is where the family tree starts.

However, what I want to do is skip many generations and rejoin the tree with the birth of Evan Baillie in 1740, who succeeded to Dochfour under the will of his elder brother Alexander, who died in 1798 and who never married. Evan had to make his own way in the world and died at the age of 95, reputedly the richest commoner in Scotland. He married a Mary Gurley from the Island of St Vincent in the West Indies – reputedly an heiress – and made his own fortune there. He served in the Army during the American War of Independence and became the Member of Parliament for Bristol, the main port for the West Indian trade.

Evan Baillie's second son was Colonel Hugh Duncan Baillie, of Redcastle and Tarradale, and he was married twice. His first marriage in 1796 was to Elizabeth Reynett, daughter of the Reverend Henry Reynett, a Doctor of Divinity. His second wife was Mary, the daughter and co-heiress of Thomas Smith of Castleton, Lancashire. The son and heir of the first marriage was Henry Baillie, who was born in 1803. This Henry Baillie had a distinguished career. He was Member of Parliament for Inverness from 1840 to 1868 and from 1858 to 1859 he was Under-Secretary for India during the Mutiny. In 1866 he was made a privy councillor.

This son and heir, Henry Baillie, had three sons but they all predeceased him and there were no children by his second marriage

15

to Clarissa Rush of Elsenham Hall, Essex. Thus there was no surviving heir from either marriage. Hugh Duncan Baillie, as I have mentioned earlier, did marry again.

The eldest son of this second marriage was Colonel Hugh Smith Baillie, a Colonel of the Royal Horse Guards, whom I have already mentioned. His wife was 45 when he married her, and there were no children.

The second son was my great-grandfather Duncan James Baillie. He became a general after having commanded the Royal Horse Guards, as it happens succeeding his brother Hugh Smith, and he had five sons and six daughters (the Lochloy aunts). My grandfather was the eldest son, so why did he not inherit that beautiful Redcastle Estate situated on the shores of the Black Isle as he perhaps should have done, and as he might reasonably have expected?

What happened as far as I know was this. The Redcastle and Tarradale estates were left back to James Baillie of Dochfour, my cousin Michael Baillie's grandfather, although, and this is the mystery, the estates had been entailed on Hugh Duncan's male heirs and the heir was my grandfather. The Lord Advocate of Edinburgh at the time urged my grandfather Ronald to challenge the will, but he was a penniless young advocate in Edinburgh at the time and he felt he could not take the risk of losing. It could possibly have been the case, however, that the eldest son, Colonel Hugh Smith Baillie, was not regarded as a safe pair of hands. He was the one, you remember, who at the age of 25 married Aunt Glentworth, the Villebois heiress who was then 45, and there were always stories that he did so because of gambling debts.

But what about my grandfather? The latter missed out on both Redcastle and Lochloy, which with its small but beautiful estate overlooking the Moray Firth was left to the six unmarried daughters. The upshot of all this is that Redcastle has been neglected by the Dochfour Baillies, there being no separate heir, and is now in danger of falling down, the roof having been taken off. Lochloy, which was left to the six great-aunts, was then left in turn to my first cousin Peter Wise who sold it, presumably as he was divorced and childless. Not only that, but he also sold all the contents. How sad we all were – another family house and all its contents sold.

16

3

Colonel Fred Burnaby

Now what I want to do is to introduce you to my great-great-uncle, Colonel Fred Burnaby, and follow his somewhat unusual career before he was killed at the Battle of Abu Klea, aged 43. He became a Victorian hero and I will leave you to judge whether this was deserved. However, remember that he was my great-grandmother's brother. After this Burnaby excursion I will come back again to the Baillies.

Uncle Fred was born on 3rd March 1842 and was educated at Harrow, but after two years he was threatened with expulsion for writing an article for *Punch* magazine entitled 'The Toad under the Harrow', referring to the headmaster of the school, and he was removed by his father and sent to Oswestry School. It is said that his career at Harrow reflected little credit on the school or on himself. After leaving Oswestry he was sent to Dresden to study languages before taking his Army entrance examination. Like his father and his brother, he had been destined to go into the Church, but one day when he saw his father conducting a funeral service he burst into tears and exclaimed that he did not want to be a soldier of God, but that he would prefer to be a soldier of the Queen.

He passed the Army examination with tolerable credit and in 1859 he was gazetted a cornet in the Royal Horse Guards, also known as the Blues. The purchase of this commission cost his father the huge sum of £1,250.

The Royal Horse Guards was the smartest regiment in the Army, but he was neither rich and nor did he come from a grand family. His pay was 8 shillings a day and he had to provide for himself, out of his own pocket, two chargers and a civilian groom to look after them. It was also the case that the Queen in those days did not provide her officers with their uniform, so, once again, out of his own pocket he had to provide himself with a cuirass, a tunic, a helmet, jackboots, white breeches, frockcoat and overalls, a patrol jacket, a stable jacket and so on, all to be purchased out of his tiny bank account at Cox's.

Uncle Fred was a quite extraordinary man. He rose by seniority to command his regiment. His political, journalistic and literary interests led him in 1868, when he was only 26, to found with his friend Tommy Bowles the journal *Vanity Fair*, described as a weekly show of 'Political, Social and Literary Ware'. It was Tommy Bowles who introduced him to his great friend, the painter Tissot, and it was Tissot who painted the famous portrait of Uncle Fred which now hangs in the National Portrait Gallery in London. Just as a footnote, Tommy Bowles had met Tissot when they had both been members of the 'Eclaireurs de la Seine', an elite band of sharpshooters in the Siege of Paris.

In 1874 he joined the Carlist forces in Spain as correspondent for the *Times* newspaper – as a royalist he was sympathetic to the Carlist cause. It was his first war and although he wished to take part in the fighting, he was restrained by Prince Carlos – it would have been, apart from anything else, a serious breach of Queen's Regulations.

In the same year Uncle Fred, who had five months leave every year, decided that an interesting way to spend this leave would be to pay a visit to Colonel Charles Gordon in Central Africa. It should be recalled that Colonel Gordon of the Royal Engineers, who was internationally renowned for his exploits in China, where he had subdued the powerful warlords with his cane and the extraordinary magnetism of his light blue eyes, had recently accepted the invitation of Ismail, the Khedive of Egypt, to succeed Sir Samuel Baker as Governor of the Equatorial Province of the Sudan.

The *Times* newspaper once again commissioned him as its correspondent, having been impressed with his despatches from Spain. He set off with the Earl of Ranfurly, the Earl of Mayo, Lord Russell and Sir William Gordon Cumming, and after a comfortable voyage to Suez on board a P&O liner, had to exchange this for a verminous old pilgrim ship for the six-day voyage to Suakin.

He left his titled friends at Suakin as they were going on for a shooting expedition in Somaliland and Abyssinia, and with a caravan of 20 camels set off into the interior. In due course he reached Khartoum, which had been impoverished by Gordon's suppression of the slave trade.

He met Gordon and they did not take to each other. Gordon disliked the intrusion of this young cavalry officer who was also doubling up as the *Times* correspondent and, in any case, he disliked journalists.

Uncle Fred had his own views about this extraordinary Colonel of the Royal Engineers, regarding him as either 'Mad or Methodist',* but probably both. The upshot was that Gordon refused him permission to write freely, except on descriptions of the country and what Gordon called 'dead objects', meaning antiquities.

There are many stories about Gordon, but I will relate just one. In June 1880 he accepted the appointment of Military Secretary to Lord Ripon, Viceroy and Governor-General of India. Everybody was astonished by his acceptance of such a subordinate position. Moreover Lord Ripon was a liberal and a convert to Catholism, whilst Gordon was a conservative and a very evangelical Protestant. Nobody expected they would get on, and indeed they fell out only 48 hours after Gordon arrived in Bombay and he almost immediately resigned his appointment. The *casus belli* was that the Parsee poet Malabari had presented one of his books to Lord Ripon and he had handed the book over to Gordon, telling him to convey to the author how much he had enjoyed reading the book. Gordon took the book and when he found that its pages had not been cut, he handed it back to His Lordship, telling him that he could not write such an atrocious lie. This led to a huge row and Gordon resigned his Military Secretaryship.

All this was a disappointment to Uncle Fred, but it was during his stay in Khartoum that he read an old newspaper which happened to report that the Russian Government had issued an order to the effect that no foreigner was allowed to travel in Russian Asia. Reading this, Uncle Fred resolved immediately to ride to Khiva in Russian Asia and, if possible, on to Merv and so through Afghanistan to India.

Clearly in this book it is not possible for me to write at any length at all about the Great Game between England and Russia

---

*From *The True Blue* by Michael Alexander.

over India and its North-West Frontier Province, but it is interesting to read an excerpt from the Russian Terentyeff's book entitled *Russia and England in the East*. Terentyeff wrote:

> Another advantage which we have gained [this was the capture of Khiva by the Russians] lies in the fact that from our present position our power of threatening British India has now become real and not visionary. In this respect our Central Asian possession serves only as an étape on the road to further advance. If in the time of Czar Paul an overland expedition to India was considered feasible, it is certainly much more so at this present time, when we have shortened the distance by such an immense stretch of territory.
>
> Asia will not, of course, ever form the avowed object of a dispute between England and Russia but, in the event of a war produced by European 'complications', we shall clearly be obliged to take advantage of our proximity to India, which is now afforded us by our present position.
>
> Besides the English there is another nation whose attitude is one of expectation from the Russians – namely the Indians themselves. The East India Company is nothing less than a poisonous unnatural plant engrafted on the splendid soil of India – a parasite which saps away the life of the most fertile and wealthy country in the world. This plant can only be uprooted by forcible means: such an attempt was made by the natives in 1857 [a reference to the Indian Mutiny]. Sick to death, the natives are now awaiting a physician from the North.

Such a controversial political background added dramatic interest to Uncle Fred's plan to visit Khiva and, in particular, to investigate the extent of Russian infiltration into Turkestan.

Uncle Fred duly reached Khiva and his extraordinary journey there in the middle of winter is recounted in his book *A Ride to Khiva*.

Whilst he was still at Khiva, hoping to move on, he was surprised to receive a telegram, duly presented by a Russian officer, from no less a person than the Duke of Cambridge himself, ordering his immediate return to European Russia. In fact what had happened was that the great Duke whose Chaplain was Uncle Fred's father, had been requested by the Foreign Office to send the telegram, following representations made to the Foreign Office by the Imperial Russian government which had stated that the presence of Captain Burnaby in Central Asia might lead to 'complications'.

And now we must move to Uncle Fred's next exploit. It was in May 1875, it will be recalled, that a rebellion broke out in the then Turkish province of Herzegovina, whose Christian Slavs were exasperated by a Muslim administration that gave no representation to the large Christian population. This rebellion, which was supported by Russian Pan-Slavists, spread to Bosnia and looked like becoming a major international problem. The rebels, supported by a division of Russian 'Volunteers' and the armies of Serbia and Montenegro and even the Bulgars, now increased their demands.

It was on 8th May 1876 that a band of Turkish irregulars entered the small Bulgarian town of Batak and perpetrated what the British investigating commissioner, Walter Baring, described as 'perhaps the most heinous crime that has stained the history of the present century'. There were plenty more to come in the twentieth century. Five thousand inhabitants – men, women and children – were put to death; some were butchered in the streets; some were burned alive in the school and others in the oil-soaked church. During that month 12,000 Christians were massacred throughout that Turkish province alone.

The massacre caused an outrage and the country was split into those who wanted to support 'Holy Russia' in a crusade against the 'Cursed Crescent', and those who preferred to defend 'Misunderstood Turkey' against the 'Russian Tartar'. In this very controversial and highly charged atmosphere, Uncle Fred decided to visit Turkey and see for himself. So, once again, he set off in November, not the best time to make this journey, across the plains of Anatolia and into the snowy mountains of Armenia.

On Horseback through Asia Minor is the book Uncle Fred wrote about his journey, and he was still writing it when in April 1877 Russia declared war on Turkey. This war was well reported, but it was the Russian siege of Plevna and its Turkish defence which made up Uncle Fred's mind to use his winter leave (all these long leaves...) to make his way through the Russian lines into Plevna. He went as the 'travelling agent' of the Stafford House Committee, which had been formed by the Duke of Sutherland and others to provide medical services for the Turks.

In the event he was dissuaded by the Turkish Commander-in-

Chief, Mehemet Ali, from making the attempt to enter Plevna and shortly afterwards, after a valiant sortie, the garrison surrendered and 120,000 Russians were released for service elsewhere. Uncle Fred took part in the battle of Tashkessan in which the Turks temporarily defeated the Russians, and in the subsequent long Turkish retreat over the Rhodope mountains. It was written by Captain Hozier, the War Office historian of the Russo-Turkish War, that of the battle of Tashkessan, 'It would be difficult to find in all records of history, whether ancient or modern, a more brilliant act of military heroism.'

In 1878 Uncle Fred was adopted as the Tory candidate for the constituency of Birmingham. In fact it was not unusual in those days to combine soldiering with politics: the Household Brigade was represented in the Commons by eleven serving officers – indeed in 1870 the Household Brigade numbered 82 in the House of Lords and 41 in the House of Commons. But in the general election he was defeated and so was the Tory party, and Gladstone became the new Prime Minister.

In 1879 Uncle Fred married Elizabeth Hawkins-Whitshed, the only child of Sir St Vincent Hawkins-Whitshed, the 3rd Baronet of Killoncarrick in Ireland. Her family was well connected and she was fond of pointing out that her ancestry could be traced back to Catherine the Great. She was aged 18 as opposed to his age 36, and she was the sole heiress to some 1,310 acres in West Tallaght and nearly 600 acres in Killoncarrick. Many people thought that Fred had married her for her land and money.

The wedding took place at St Peters, Cranley Gardens, and the bride was given away by her cousin Arthur Bentinck, later the Duke of Portland. A Guard of Honour was provided by the Blues and afterwards they all repaired to Bailey's Hotel in Gloucester Road for a fork luncheon.

It was not a happy marriage. She was found to be suffering from lung trouble and they went abroad to North Africa for the warmer climate. She was soon down with a bad attack, but they were able to return home for the birth of her first and only child, Harry St Vincent Augustus. She was then ordered by the doctors to live in Interlaken in Switzerland, where she lived for a number of years.

The trouble was that Elizabeth was an extremely competitive lady, not only generally but also particularly in relation to Fred.

He was a balloonist and best-selling author, and if he was a balloonist, she was going to be a high-altitude mountaineer, and an author in her own right, and all this she did. She became the first President of the Ladies' Alpine Club, wrote several books on mountaineering, and became an expert Alpine camera artist. She was the first person to film bobsleigh racing and skating.

Nothing indeed escaped her, and she said, 'The world has no secrets before my eyes.' The *Alpine Journal* view was that her most striking characteristic was 'an exceptional faculty of judgement which was never surpassed by any climber of the so-called stronger sex'. She exuded self-confidence. She worked in the Service Sauté Militaire in the First World War and was made a Chevalier de la Légion d'Honneur in 1933, two years after I was born. After Fred was killed in action at the battle of Abu Klea in the Sudan in 1885, only six years into his marriage, most of which they spent apart, she married Dr Main, who died in 1892. After his death she married Mr Aubrey Le Blond. She was not universally popular. Lady Bentinck took a dim view of her success and wrote that 'she is scandalising all London and looks like a Red Indian'.

So that was Fred's wife. Probably she was too much for him, in more senses than one. The result was that Harry, the only son, but now heir to the so-called Burnaby Estate in Ireland, was left in the care of his grandmother, whilst Uncle Fred was left on his own in his bachelor chambers in Charles Street.

In 1882 Uncle Fred, who was now commanding his regiment, renewed his interest in ballooning. His ambition was to be the first man to cross the English Channel solo in an air balloon, and on 23rd March 1882, that is what he did.

Uncle Fred, wearing a striped blazer and a pillbox cap, stepped into the little wicker basket and the balloon ascended. England soon vanished behind a large, thick black cloud – he was flying at about 12 miles an hour and at an altitude of 5,500 feet. But then something went wrong. The balloon started to deflate and began to descend. Uncle Fred threw out more and more ballast and at long last, when he had descended to 500 feet, the balloon slowly began to rise. Although he had stabilised the height of the balloon, he found that the coast of France was receding and he then discovered that he was drifting rapidly down the Channel in the wrong direction. The French coast faded away, the wind dropped, and at 1,400 feet the balloon hung motionless over the water.

After an hour of being becalmed, he decided that he must try his theory of varying winds at different altitudes. More ballast went out – the balloon rose to 3,000 feet. No wind. More ballast out and up to 6,500 feet – still no wind. More ballast out, and the balloon rose to 10,000 feet and here he found the wind and it was from the right direction. Soon he was over France where he began to descend, and eventually crash-landed near the Chateau of Montigny, Envermeu in Normandy. Thus ended the first solo balloon air crossing of the English Channel. Uncle Fred never flew again. The Duke of Cambridge, the Commander-in-Chief of the Army, first rebuked him for leaving England without permission, and secondly told him that he did not approve of him going up in balloons whilst he was on full pay.

In 1881 back in the Sudan, a certain Mohammed Achmed, the son of a carpenter from Dongola and a man with the reputation for the strictest piety, announced that he was the awaited 'Mahdi', the expected one of God, and that his divine mission was to free the Sudan from its oppressors, then having conquered Egypt, to establish his headquarters at Mecca and from there to convert the whole world to the true faith. Many people took him at his word and he soon became a force to reckon with in Southern Sudan.

Since Gordon's departure from Khartoum in 1879, the authority of the Egyptian government over its enormous southern territories had deteriorated. The garrisons were undermanned, the Turkish officials were corrupt, the tax collectors were ruthless and the slave-hunting tribes were bewailing their loss of livelihood. The Egyptian authorities had made a number of attempts to beat the Mahdi's forces, with varying degrees of success, and in 1883 the Khedive appointed a retired Indian Army colonel called Hicks – Hicks Pasha – as the Chief of Staff of the Army of the Sudan.

In April Hicks Pasha won a notable victory at Marabia on the White Nile and this so encouraged the authorities that they decided to beat the Mahdi for good. Hicks Pasha was put in command of a substantial force: 7,000 Egyptian infantrymen, 5,500 camels, 500 horses and various guns and machine-guns. Unfortunately, this force was led astray by guides in the Mahdi's pay and got utterly lost in the Kordofan Desert, one of the driest parts of the Sudan, where they were attacked by the Mahdi's forces and massacred.

While the Mahdi so effectively reasserted his authority in the south, his lieutenant Osman Digna – a former slave trader and dealer in ostrich feathers – was defying the government in his own neck of the woods, namely the Hadendowa country around Suakin, which was the place you will remember where Uncle Fred had landed from his pilgrim ship to cross the desert and meet Gordon.

On the same day that the Mahdi was massacring Hicks Pasha's army, 500 Egyptian soldiers were massacred by Osman Digna's men whilst on their way to relieve the Egyptian garrison at Tokar, and when news of the massacres reached Cairo it was realised that something had to be done. That something was the despatch of an expedition composed of the Egyptian gendarmerie commanded by General Valentine Baker Pasha, Uncle Fred's old comrade-in-arms during the Russo-Turkish War.

Baker Pasha, who had been dismissed from the British Army for molesting a young lady called Miss Dickinson on a train from Midhurst to London (as a result of which the railways brought in corridor trains), had been taken on by the Sultan of Turkey. His job was to act as military adviser to the Turkish Commander-in-Chief on the River Danube front facing the Russians. After the war there, and after the British takeover of Egypt, Lord Dufferin had recommended that the Egyptian Army, which was in a chaotic state, should be run by a majority of British officers under the command of a British general. On Lord Dufferin's advice, the Khedive offered the post of Commander-in-Chief to Baker Pasha, who was then at Istanbul running the Sultan's gendarmerie. Baker Pasha accepted the appointment, but before taking it up, Wolseley, who had just arrived from England, announced that 'with the greatest possible regret' he had been instructed to oppose the nomination. These instructions had come from Mr Gladstone, or quite possibly from the Queen via Gladstone, the former having declared earlier 'that Her Majesty had no further use for his services' as a result of the train incident.*

Baker Pasha was then put in charge of raising an Egyptian gendarmerie, and as a final indignity for a professional soldier, Baker was ordered to change the name of his force to a constabulary and it was this force that was ordered out to deal with Osman Digna. Baker was so upset by all this that he called for his old comrade-in-arms, Uncle Fred, to assist him. So on 20th January 1885, Uncle Fred set off for Egypt and joined Baker at Suakin.

---

*From *The True Blue* by Michael Alexander.

Baker's ramshackle army was then moved down to Trinkitat, which lay on a low stretch of the coast separated from the mainland by a salty swamp. There the troops disembarked and set off on 3rd February 1884 for the wells of El Teb, 8 miles away in the direction of the beleaguered garrison at Tokar.

As the forces moved forward, they were confronted by some Arabs. The Egyptian cavalry suddenly went out of control and the Egyptian soldiers also panicked and then fled, some 4,000 men running for their lives, with only a few hundred Arabs behind them spearing everyone in reach. It was a shambles. Nearly 2,500 officers and men were killed out of a total force of 3,746, and the following day Baker Pasha and Uncle Fred and what was left of the force re-embarked at Trinkitat and left for Suakin.

Meanwhile, General Gordon arrived at Khartoum with instructions to evacuate the Egyptian garrison from the Sudan and to establish a government. In a moment of aberration or irresponsibility the British Government had sent out one man to compete with the Mahdi – Gordon's personal magnetism was supposed to save the situation without the support of a single soldier.

Nevertheless, as a precaution, three British battalions stationed in Cairo were brought together to form the nucleus of an expeditionary force, and on 18th February this force sailed for Suakin.

Both Baker and Burnaby were given jobs as intelligence officers and once more they sailed down to Trinkitat and set off towards Fort Baker, although by this time news had come through that the Tokar garrison had surrendered to Osman Digna's forces. Nevertheless, they decided to continue, and the confidence with which the British square advanced across the desert was in marked contrast to the shaky progress of Baker's Egyptians whose bodies lay rotting on the nearby battleground.

As they went forward towards the wells of El Teb, they found them heavily defended. The Arabs opened fire and Uncle Fred's horse was shot under him and a bullet pierced his left arm above the elbow, furrowing the bone before emerging. The square continued to move forward, and as they reached the defences a vast number of tribesmen rushed over the parapets and tore into the square. But they could not stand up to the rifles and machine-guns and they started to fall back. Uncle Fred wrote that the Arabs gave as splendid an exhibition of courage as the world has ever seen, and those English officers who had been at Ulundi said that great as the courage of the Zulus undoubtedly was, it was nothing in comparison with these Arabs, armed only with spears and shields and inspired by fanaticism and love for their Mahdi.

Before leaving for England, Uncle Fred was presented to the Khedive who gave him the Sudan Medal and clasp and Khedival Star. He had been away for three months.

When Uncle Fred got back it was clear that Gordon's position in Khartoum was the most burning issue in the public conscience. He was boxed in and could not get out, but even when the Mahdi captured Berber, Gladstone continued to prevaricate and temporise.

In June that year Uncle Fred had a breakdown. He had a bad liver, a bad heart and a congested lung, and in addition, he had been sent to Coventry by the officers of his own regiment of which he was colonel, for making a remark about one of his brother officers whom he had met on that officer's way to meet up with a certain lady in the Temple – a *rencontre* which had been picked up by the press. Nobody is quite certain who this brother officer was, but the *on dit* at the time was that it was Lord Edward Somerset with whom he had quarrelled. Matters went further when Prince Edward was invited to dine with the regiment and the officers notified Uncle Fred that, if he appeared, no other officer would come to the table.

In spite of his continuing illness and now unpopularity, he continued his campaign for the relief of Gordon at Khartoum. But the Army, now without the encouragement of the government, was quietly making its own preparations against eventualities. In the end, the mounting force of public opinion (considerably influenced by Uncle Fred's speeches and the determination of Queen Victoria) forced the government to act, and Wolseley was appointed Commander-in-Chief in Egypt.

Wolseley duly invited Uncle Fred to accompany him as one of his intelligence officers, but his letter to the War Office requesting permission was rejected. However Uncle Fred was not discouraged by this rejection and decided to make his own way to Egypt. He had asked for permission to take six months' leave to go to South Africa, which the Duke of Cambridge may or may not have believed. He was granted five months' leave and the War Office, thinking that he might be planning to join General Warren's expedition to Bechuanaland, sent a wire to Cape Town ordering that he was on no account to be allowed to take part in any military operations in South Africa.

Uncle Fred, however, left for Egypt in November. He passed quickly through Cairo, lest he should receive a telegram from the War Office ordering his recall. He turned up at rear headquarters at Wadi Halfa in December, where he was offered the job of inspecting staff officer by Lord Wolseley, which he accepted.

On 28th December 1884, he received orders to move on to Korti, a place between Pebbah and Merani where Colonel Stewart, Gordon's assistant in Khartoum, was murdered by Arabs when the boat in which he had left Khartoum ran aground. When he arrived there, the main column of the army had left, but he was put in charge of a grain caravan with orders to overtake the main column as soon as possible. On the back of one of those camels were two red coats, to be worn by the first British soldiers to approach Khartoum so as to give immediate encouragement to the anxious watchers on Gordon's palace.

Uncle Fred and his grain caravan reached the rocky pools of Gakdul on the 14th where he met up with the main force. They left the next day. There would be no more water until they reached the wells of Abu Klea, two days' march away.

Uncle Fred rode along with General Sir Herbert Stewart, the commander of the Camel Corps, together with Lord Airlie and Lord Charles Beresford, two of his close friends, and various 'specials', that is, war correspondents and war artists.

It soon became apparent that the Arabs would contest the approach to the wells of Abu Klea and, of course, if they did so successfully the force would be entirely without water and would face annihilation, like the army of Hicks Pasha. Having ascertained that this was indeed the case, the army encamped for that night. It was that night that Uncle Fred went out on his own to pay a visit to the enemy territory. Why did he do this? It was an extraordinary irresponsible outing for a field officer to undertake, and he was suitably admonished by General Stewart on his return.

The next morning Uncle Fred went out again, this time with General Stewart, but of course they immediately came under fire and Uncle Fred had his horse shot under him. To me, as a soldier, these forays both at night and in the morning are baffling and downright inexplicable unless Uncle Fred had some sort of death wish, and that he may have had.

It was decided that the main force should form up into a square and move along the valley which was broken up by boulders and rocks. It was a dreadful position as the ridges on either side of the valley were held by the Arabs, who fired straight down at the moving square. Again, this was inexplicable: why did not the columns secure the ridges before moving? The result was that the square incurred heavy casualties, and frequent halts had to be made to enable the doctors to attend the wounded. It was also the case that many of the camels were wounded and were unable to keep pace with the square, with the result that the rear of the square was thrown into confusion.

At this point something like 15,000 Arabs suddenly appeared. They had concealed themselves in a deep gully in the valley floor and they now appeared before the square in full battle array. Rushing forward, they came in utter silence towards the leading corner of the square, but seeing the confusion in the rear, they suddenly wheeled and ran towards the rear of the square.

At the same time as all this was happening – and it all happened very quickly – the gap in the rear left of the square was used by Lord Charles Beresford to run out his Gatling machine-gun with a crew of eight blue jackets about 30 yards out of the square ranks. Beresford, who was a friend of Uncle Fred, was apparently obsessed with his new gun, which he wanted to fire himself.

When Uncle Fred saw Beresford out of the square he ordered 3 and 4 companies of the Heavy Camel Regiment, who were acting as infantry, to wheel out of the already distressed square to protect Beresford. It was an order which no infantry officer trained to appreciate that in battle, an unbroken front was a basic definition of a square formation, would have dreamt of giving. It was in fact an unforgivable order, because Uncle Fred had been sent to the rear not to give orders but to oversee matters, and the reason for this was that he had never commanded in a battle despite his lengthy service in the Army. It was also highly irresponsible of Lord Charles Beresford to have run out of the square with his gun – a pointless exercise as it turned out, because the gun jammed and Beresford was caught out in the open and his party was over-whelmed, although he survived.

Uncle Fred was himself caught out of the square on his borrowed horse, and he was riding backwards and forwards shouting at the men to fall back quickly to within the square. But he himself seemed to make no attempt to get back. While he was fighting, an Arab ran his spear into Uncle Fred's shoulder. It did not do much damage, but it forced him to turn in his saddle and his brief sideways glance gave his opponent the opening he had been waiting for. He drove his spear straight into Uncle Fred's now unguarded throat. He fell out of his saddle onto the ground, and as he did so half a dozen Arabs fell on him. He died from three mortal wounds: a spear wound in the throat, a bullet in the forehead and a sword stroke which cut half his head away.

Lord Binning, who was with him when he died, reported that his face was entirely composed and that he wore the placid smile of one who had been suddenly called away in the middle of a congenial and favourite occupation. It was this composure and placid smile, together with his lone excursions into enemy territory and his mad rush from the square, which gave rise to the story that he wanted to die in action. After all, he was in poor health, his marriage had failed, and the Army authorities were talking about court-martialling him for having gone to the Sudan without permission and not to South Africa.

Wolseley laid the blame for the 'square that broke' on the unsteady behaviour of the Heavy Camel Regiment, but this seems unfair to them – the blame lies perhaps on Lord Charles Beresford for running his Gatling gun out of the square, and Uncle Fred for opening up the square to protect him.

Uncle Fred was buried that same day, 17th January 1885, under a cairn on a lonely hillside in the Bayunda desert. Later on the British government raised a monument there with a brass plate inscribed with the names of Uncle Fred and the eight other officers killed in the engagement. The monument is still there, but there is no mention of the 79 other ranks who were also killed.

Uncle Fred was an excellent writer and journalist, but I am not sure how good a soldier and officer he was. He was a superb linguist – he spoke French, German, Italian, Turkish and Russian – and he was undoubtedly very brave, sometimes to the point of foolhardiness.

When the Victorian press heard of his death, they decided to make him a hero – the Victorians had need of heroes. The obituary in the *Telegraph* described him thus:

> The Queen had no more loyal a subject, the Army no finer officer, the country no truer patriot than Frederick Gustavus Burnaby *mort sur le champ d'honneur*. His name will live in

the annals of this Empire and the memories of his companions as long as valour, devotion to duty and faithfulness until death, shall remain the watchwords of the Sons of the Island Queen.

He was killed aged 43. He was brother to my great-grandmother, and as children we were brought up by his nieces – our Baillie great-aunts – on his exploits.

4

The Baillies and Lochloy

So now, to all intents and purposes, I have set out how the Burnaby and Villebois families fit into my mother's family, and so we must move on to my great-grandfather, General Duncan James Baillie. Before going on I would just like to remind you that he was the second son of Colonel Hugh Duncan Baillie of Redcastle and Tarradale, who was the second son of Evan Baillie of Dochfour.

My great-grandfather was born in 1826. At an early age he joined the Royal Horse Guards, the Blues, which as you will now know was the regiment of his brother-in-law Fred Burnaby. He became the Colonel of that regiment, succeeding his elder brother Colonel Hugh Smith Baillie.

During his service with the Blues he held various posts of honour and responsibility in connection with the Court of Queen Victoria and the Household Brigade. He was a very good-looking man, quite charming, and a great favourite of Queen Victoria and members of the Royal Family. My great-grandfather was very dark, and one of his daughters, Aunt Eila, inherited these same dark good looks. In fact, Cousin Albert Baillie, a former Dean of Windsor who wrote a book entitled *My First 80 Years*, said of her that she was more attractive than her sisters. She was in fact quite striking when she was young and, when she was at Court with her father, the Prince of Wales is said to have greatly admired her. She was a favourite great-aunt of mine and she was, besides, also an excellent pianist. Like all her sisters, she did not marry.

After his Colonelcy of the Blues, my great-grandfather was promoted to Major-General when he was appointed to command the 72nd and 79th Regimental Districts whose depot was at Fort George on the Moray Firth. Shortly before his death in 1890, he

33

had succeeded by right of seniority to the rank of Lieutenant General. He died quite suddenly at Lochloy aged 63.

My great-grandfather also involved himself in politics. He was a Conservative and leader of the party in the counties of Moray and Nairn, and as Chairman of the Conservative Association for these two counties he rendered many important services to the Unionist cause in the North of Scotland.

It is interesting to reflect that, at his funeral at Nairn in 1890, the entire Nairn County Council turned out en masse and led the procession from Lochloy to Nairn. As the procession got close to Nairn itself the Provost, the Magistrate and Nairn Town Council joined it and the cortege passed along the High Street to the Episcopal Church. Every shop and business in Nairn was closed, all the blinds of the private houses were drawn and the streets were lined with the inhabitants of Nairn. The bells of the Episcopal Church tolled, but so did the bells of the other denomination churches. It was, in fact, the longest cortege ever to have been seen in the county.

His widow, my great-grandmother, lived for another 50 years at Lochloy and attained her one hundredth birthday in 1940 when she died – the second year of the Second World War.

And now we must turn to the eleven children, the five sons and six daughters. The latter all seemed to live relatively uneventful lives. They moved in a triangle: between the London house in Queensgate, Kensington, London where their father commanded the Household Brigade; Lochloy, which was their main residence; and Marham House in Norfolk which was, of course, the home of their Aunt Glentworth. As we all know, none of them ever married, and various explanations have been put forward for this including the one that all the eligible husbands had been killed in the First World War. This was, of course, not the case. Aunt Eila and Aunt Ida for instance had been born in 1867 and 1868 respectively, and the youngest, Aunt Effie, had been born in 1877, so Aunt Effie would have been 23 at the time of the Boer War and aunts Eila and Ida would have been 33 and 32 at the time of that war.

No, there has to be another explanation, and I am sure that explanation is not that they were put off sex by their nanny, which has sometimes been put forward as some sort of traditional reason. I think the more likely explanation is that they did not have the really beautiful looks which would have offset their lack of money in the rich society circles in which they moved. So there were no attractive dowries about, their father being a professional soldier and not having any landed estate. It was also the case that their father died quite young at the age of 63 in 1890 when Aunt Effie, for instance, was only 13. There has always been the story that Aunt Effie wanted to marry, but that she was deterred by her other sisters.

It is interesting to read about the clothes they wore. For instance, Aunt May was presented at Court in March 1893. She wore a petticoat and bodice of white corded bengaline, trimmed with crepe and bunches of white lilac, and a Court train from the shoulders of white striped satin and moire. Aunt Rona was presented at Court in 1902. She was described as being an extremely pretty debutante (so perhaps I was wrong about the looks) dressed in a charming gown of satin, the skirt opening over a panel finely embroidered in silver, the bodice prettily draped with chiffon edged with tiny ribbons and having shoulder-straps of silver. A train of satin was folded back at one side and fastened with a garniture of lilies.

And then there were the clothes of her mother, a widow, presenting her. A handsome gown of black satin imperiale, the bodice appliquéd with fine jet, opening over white folded lisse, and a train of very fine black velvet, turned back at the corners, with large plumes.

I have mentioned aunts Eila and Ida. They lived together at a house called The Manse, Jamestown, Strathpeffer, and then later on in Nairn. I remember them both very well. To me, of course, at the time they seemed very old, very Victorian, but despite their age very upright. They both died when they were 88 years old.

I do not remember very much about Aunt May. She was a teacher, and I have a feeling she did not get on very well with her sisters, although she returned to Lochloy when she was older and died in 1960.

The three sisters who lived at Lochloy all their lives were Lillie, Effie and Rona. Of these three Aunt Lillie ran the household whilst Aunt Rona, who was sweet and pretty but not very bright, busied herself with her bees and garden. She was a superb apiarist and made the most delicious honey, which was of course such a treat in the war years when food was so short.

It was, however, Aunt Effie who lived longest. She was born, as I have mentioned, in 1877 and died in 1980 aged 103. I once asked her what her two best memories were during her long and what always seemed to be tranquil life. She answered with hardly any hesitation that these were the arrival of the Highland railway line at Inverness, and seeing men walking about on the moon – truly a transport revolution in her life.

I must tell you a little more about Lochloy. It was originally a farmhouse, which was leased from the Brodies of Brodie Castle and then later bought. To accommodate eleven children and all the servants, a large Victorian wing was added which fronted the house. It was not really a comfortable house, with something like 22 bedrooms and, I recall, only one bathroom. Aunt Effie used to tell me that when she had difficulty going to sleep she used to count how many fires had to be lit by the servants before breakfast – she never got beyond 20.

To get to Lochloy from Nairn you had to take the Brodie road then pass the golf course, pass the Drum, an old farmhouse, and then turn right up the long drive shaded by Scots pine trees, pass the old farm buildings, and there you were. And what a glorious view presented itself.

Below the house on its terrace were fields in which we worked during the war, stooking the sheaves of barley and wheat mingled with sharp thistles which constantly pricked our bodies as we clasped them and stooked them upright. Then there was the Carse, running down to the sea, and the Long Bar, an island which had been created by the currents, which you could reach at low tide. The Carse had been covered by trees but during the war these were all felled by Canadian lumberjacks who had also built a small railway line on which the logs were carried to the Brodie road. During the war, the huge sands leading up to the Long Bar were covered in wooden poles to deter German gliders from landing. Then there were the waters of the Moray Firth, looking across to Cromarty, and mountains covered in snow in winter, of which the highest was Ben Wyvis. Sometimes, when we looked out, we could see the naval fleet sailing up to Cromarty, huge grey battleships and cruisers and destroyers, reminding us that a war was on. It was always a thrill and excitement arriving at Lochloy.

When we lived there during the war, there was no electricity and we used Aladdin lamps and candles. During the day all the oil lamps were kept in the lamp room where the wicks were cleaned and trimmed daily.

When you entered the house through the front door, you arrived first in the hall, on the walls of which there hung helmets and cuirasses which had been used by my great-grandfather. There were fishing rods and whips on the left and right of the inner door. To the right was the dining-room, part of the Victorian addition, with a huge table and sideboard. There was also a brightly polished iron fireplace, but a fire was never lit there and in winter the room was so cold that the Scotch broth congealed over between leaving the sideboard and arriving on the dining table. This room had a glorious view over the Carse and the sea and the mountains beyond.

To the left was the drawing-room packed full of furniture, paintings and bric-a-brac, and old curtains and carpets – the house had never been redecorated since the Victorian front was added in 1877. Leaving the Victorian addition you entered a small room on the right, which was the room we always used, always known as the school room. It had a small whitewashed fireplace in which, during the winter, a few twigs were set alight and that was that. The room had also a large wind-up gramophone, the first we had ever used, and on the walls were hunting horns. This room once again faced north, overlooking the Moray Firth.

Beyond on the right was the kitchen where the cook, Mary, used to make the most delicious oatcakes, and adjacent to it was the large pantry, with everything immaculately clean. On the other side was the honey room where Aunt Rona used to make her delicious honey. Going back still in the old farmhouse area were two quite small and very dark rooms, again full of books, bric-a-brac and guns, either side of the garden door which faced south. These looked out on to a huge lawn in the middle of which stood a large monkey puzzle tree, whilst to the right was the large Scottish kitchen garden full of fruit and vegetables in season. There was even a large greenhouse in which grew the most delicious grapes we had ever tasted.

Upstairs on the right in the Victorian addition was our bedroom, which Marigold and I shared with Nanny. We had an open fireplace, a washbasin – no running water, of course – and the dressing table was an old converted spinet. We had potties under our beds and sometimes it was so cold during the night that it was a huge effort to struggle out of bed, find the matchbox and light the candle to find the potty. It was always somewhat frightening doing this as well, as the candlelight cast all sorts of shadows round the room and, as we had always been brought up to believe in ghosts, I was usually torn between the overwhelming necessity to pee and an overwhelming reluctance to light the candle.

Still upstairs, and now going back into the old part of the house, was a long corridor on the walls of which were prints of the battles of the Crimean War. On the right were six bedrooms which faced north. Each great-aunt had one of these bedrooms and when one of them died, the door was shut and nothing inside the room was touched until my cousin, Peter Wise, following Aunt Effie's death in 1980, sold the house, all the contents and the farm and estate. And so another family property and nearly all its contents were lost – it was unbearably sad.

And what did we do at Lochloy? The answer is that we walked and played and rode and bicycled, and at harvest time worked in the fields, stooking and pitching sheaves onto the top of the horse-drawn wagons. In those days there was no car, so sometimes, as a special treat, Aunt Lillie used to take us in the pony-cart to do the shopping in Nairn where, for the first time, I saw *Snow White and the Seven Dwarfs*, which gave me nightmares. Another film which I remember seeing was *The Drum*, a film which I have never seen again, although I have always wanted to. It was all about a Scottish regiment fighting on the North-West Frontier of India.

We went for long walks down to the Old Bar island, and through the Lochloy woods to the Loch itself where, in the winter, we skated. I built a bivouac in the woods which was nearly watertight. Perhaps we went to the odd children's party. We helped sometimes with the WI Canteen at Ardersier, to which soldiers from Fort George used to come – a cup of tea was a penny, an old penny in those days. From that price it has now risen 240 times: a cup of tea at Chelmsford Station now costs £1. It was a happy, innocent childhood and the only real reminders of the war were the poles on the sandy beaches and the ships of the Fleet sailing up the Moray Firth to Cromarty. It was truly a paradise for children.

Lochloy was a very old place and it had centuries of history behind it. It comes into view for the first time with the military exploits of King William the Lion when he came north to subdue the rebellious Norsemen. One of his knights was Sir William Hay who greatly distinguished himself in these royal campaigns, so much so that, as a token of his appreciation, the King granted him all the Lochloy land and there the Hay family stayed for the next six centuries until it was acquired first by the Brodies and then the Baillies.

And what about Lochloy and its fairies? The home of the fairies was in the thick wood above the Loch and they loved dancing on the seashore. If the fishermen saw them dancing in the early morning they knew they were going to have a good day's fishing. Have you heard the story of the fairies and the crofter who had a parcel of land on the high ground about a mile south of the Loch, and who suffered great misfortunes?

What happened was that his wife and only child died, his horse and his cow and all his belongings were seized for debt and taken away, and he was left miserable, lonely, desolate and poor. The fairies knew what had happened to him and they took pity on him and supplied him with food. But he began to take it all for granted, and there is a law amongst fairies that when the recipient ceases to be grateful for their gifts, then they must be withheld, although they did not wish to do this. However, one night a knock came on the crofter's door and he refused to open it, even after several knocks. Eventually the messenger disclosed his identity – a fairy sent by the Queen of Fairies to get a little cup of milk for the Prince of the Fairies who was very ill, having fallen into the Loch. The crofter relented, gave them a bottle which he had firmly corked, and sent them away. When the fairy got back to her home above Lochloy the bottle was opened and it was found to contain water not milk. So the fairies took their revenge and filled up the crofter's land with water. Thus when he woke up the next morning he saw all his land covered with water and there it still is – the Black Loch – the name the crofter gave it. And that was how the Black Loch came to be formed on the bleak moor on the high ground above Lochloy.

Before we leave Lochloy for the moment – we will be returning later – there is just one more story, not this time about Lochloy but about the Culbin Sands which lie to the east of Lochloy.

The Culbin Sands in those days were great extensive sand-dunes – now I believe forested – and when the wind blew, the sand-dunes shifted and drifted. Many years ago there was a small village there and the villagers liked to play cards in the evening, but occasionally they used to play cards on the Sabbath. Now, in those days, if you played cards on a Sunday, you were thought to be playing cards with the Devil. One night in 1695 when they were playing cards on the Sabbath a great storm blew up and the wind started to shift and drift the sand, and before long the sand overwhelmed the village and they all died. So, of course, the moral is never to play cards on the Sabbath, because it is the Devil you will be playing with.

It was at Lochloy that all the eleven children of my great-grandfather and great-grandmother were brought up, and it was a happy place in those days.

5

My Regimental Baillie Great-Uncles

We have looked briefly at the great-aunts, but now we must turn to the great-uncles, leaving my grandfather, who was the eldest son, to later.

After my grandfather the next son was Alan Charles Duncan, who was born in 1865. It is after him and also my Tritton great-uncle Alan George that I am named. Both died of their wounds.

Alan Charles Duncan joined the Seaforth Highlanders in 1887 and was promoted to Captain in 1895. The bare bones of his career with the Seaforth Highlanders is that he was sent out to India to join his battalion. He took part in the 1888 and the 1891 Hazara Expeditions, and in the Chitral Relief Force Expedition in 1895 under Sir Robert Low. He also fought in the engagement at Mamungai. For all these battles he received the campaign medals with clasps, and they are now in Lyons Hall.

He served with the regiment in Crete and Malta and it was from there that his battalion left to join Kitchener's expedition to the Sudan. He was badly wounded at the Battle of Atbara while leading his company's charge into the zareba, and his leg had to be amputated above the knee. He just survived the long journey down the Nile to Cairo, but he died shortly before his brother Duncan and sister Ida arrived to see him at the Citadel Hospital there.

The Battle of Atbara, which took place on Good Friday, 8th April 1898, is not particularly well known. It was a short, sharp, vicious engagement between an Anglo-Egyptian force commanded by Kitchener, and a Dervish army commanded by Emir Mahmoud, who had 4,000 cavalry and 14,000 infantry. Kitchener's force numbered 13,000 men with 24 guns under Colonel Long.

At 1.15 a.m. in the middle of the night, the British, Egyptian and Sudanese brigades formed up in squares and began marching towards Mahmoud's encampment, which was protected by a strong zareba and deep trenches. It was a strongly fortified and naturally difficult position to carry, and the soldiers knew that casualties would not be light.

As the brigades, marching in darkness and in their squares, approached the Mahmoud position the order was given to wheel into attack formation. The regiments involved were the Cameron Highlanders, the Warwickshire Regiment, the Seaforth Highlanders, the Lincolnshire Regiment and the Sudanese Regiment of Macdonald's Brigade, with the 2nd Egyptian battalion in support. On Macdonald's right was Maxwell's Brigade and the 14th and 12th Sudanese Regiment battalions and the 15th and 8th Egyptian battalions. The artillery and Maxim guns accompanied the infantry just in the rear, whilst the cavalry and the horse artillery were way over to the left, their responsibility being to protect the left flank from the Dervish cavalry. Lewis Bey's 4th and 3rd Egyptian battalions were in support also to protect the left flank from Mahmoud's 4,000 mounted Baggara. Finally two companies of the Camel Corps and the 7th Egyptian Brigade occupied a position near the centre but to the rear of the infantry.

At 6.15 a.m. at first light the artillery bombardment began and the line of British, Egyptian and Sudanese brigades began edging very slowly towards the zareba. Shortly after 8 a.m. the bombardment stopped, the bugles sounded the general advance, and off they went. The bands of the Khedival battalions began playing, the bugles sounded again, the drums started beating, the pipes and drums of the Scottish regiments skirled and beat, while the Queen's Colours and Battle Colours of the British regiments fluttered in the breeze. It must have been quite a sight.

Shortly after 8.15, under heavy fire from the Dervishes, the zareba was rushed and the hand-to-hand fighting was intense with heavy casualties on both sides. It was all over in half an hour. Casualties were over 500 and of the British troops, the Seaforths and the Camerons had the heaviest. Lieutenant Gore, Captain Alan Baillie's subaltern, was shot dead close to him and five other Seaforth officers were wounded including Alan Baillie, who later succumbed to his knee wound after his leg was amputated above the knee.

It is reported that his patience and fortitude amid his terrible suffering were the wonder and admiration of the doctors and his soldiers. He never grumbled or complained, but remained cheerful throughout.

He was an exceedingly popular man with both his brother officers and men. He had never been known to say any unkind word, while the officers of the battalion in Egypt said that no man was more beloved – his good nature, his readiness to do anything and everything for everybody, and his lovable disposition endeared him to all.

After he died one of his soldiers in his company wrote a memorial poem to him. It reads as follows:

Sad news for dear auld Scotland
Speeds to the misty north.
We've lost our brave young Captain of the gallant old Seaforth.
That day we stormed Atbara and saw our leader fall
Our heavy hearts were heedless of spear or sword or ball,
To the rear we gently bore him
He bade us join the fight.
Careless, though all untended
If but his men were all right.
We hoped the desert over
If t'were but Heaven's will,
Again his lead to follow
But vain was human skill.
The gloamin grey was falling,
When we, a mournful band,
With pibroch sadly wailing
Left him on foreign strand.
We'll march no more together
We'll miss his kindly care
Until we meet our Captain
In yonder land so fair.

This was written by Private Thomas Robertson Clarke, 1st Battalion Seaforth Highlanders in the Sudan. For a private soldier to write such an emotional epigram for his captain says everything about my great-uncle Alan.

Alan was a gifted artist, and he was fluent in French. In fact many of his letters home from India were written in French, and when he was dying but still hoped to recover, he said that he wanted to enter the Diplomatic Service where his French would have been useful.

In some curious way I have always felt an affinity with my two great uncles Alan and Ian. All three were severely wounded in action and subsequently died of their wounds. All of them went through the shock and agony of being wounded in action – it is a terrible experience, as I will relate later, it happened to me in Malaya.

The third brother was Duncan Gustavus. He was born in 1872 and in January 1900 he became a member of the Edinburgh party of the mounted infantry contingent of the Queen's Volunteer Brigade which, in its turn, formed part of the mounted infantry detachment of the City of London Imperial Volunteer Corps.

All this, of course, sounds rather strange: that is to say, the decision of the Edinburgh volunteers to go to South Africa as members of the Lord Mayor of London's Corps. Here is the story. When the War Office agreed to accept volunteers for service in South Africa, the 20 mounted men, including Duncan Baillie, offered themselves for South Africa and suggested that they might be allowed to go as a section of the mounted infantry company of the Royal Scots, the territorial regiment then serving in South Africa. The War Office did not like this suggestion. The suggestion was then made that the men should endeavour to get out to South Africa via the Imperial Yeomanry. But, of course, the men were mounted infantry and not yeomen, and were unwilling to relinquish the particular branch of the service in which they had been trained. The War Office was again approached but did not respond. The result is that the 20 men made their own arrangement to go as mounted infantrymen with the City (of London) Imperial Volunteers (CIV).

Duncan Baillie was immediately promoted from 'gentleman' to Lieutenant on 12th March 1900. The CIV fought at Jacobsdal, Britstown, Paardeberg, Klip River, Roodepoort and in Johannesburg, and in one of these battles he was wounded, although not severely. He returned from Cape Town on 7th October 1900 on the *Aurania*, so it was a short war for him.

He also took part in the First World War, commanding the Lovat Scouts throughout the war. In 1917 he was awarded the DSO for his conspicuous gallantry and devotion to duty at the Battle of

Salonika. The citation goes on to say that 'he commanded his battalion with great skill and determination during a night attack and showed great coolness and courage. He set a splendid example of pluck and initiative to which the success of the operation was largely due.'

He also fought earlier at Gallipoli, but I do not know what part he took in that expedition.

In 1919 he was awarded the CMG, and in the same year he married Mary Cochrane, the daughter of Mr and Mrs Blair Cochran of St John's, Ryde, Isle of Wight. The wedding was attended by Princess Beatrice, Governor of the Island, and the Marquess and Marchioness of Milford Haven. Unfortunately there was a railway strike that day, so the numbers attending the wedding were less than anticipated.

There was one son of the marriage, Hugh, who was born on 12th October 1920, in London. Sadly Hugh, who is still alive at this moment of writing in 2008, went deaf and never married.

The fourth son, who was born in 1874, was Hugh Frederick who was educated at Wellington and the Royal Military College at Sandhurst where he came fourth in the passing-out examination. In 1898 he was commissioned into the 2nd Battalion Seaforth Highlanders and in October 1899 he sailed from Glasgow to South Africa where he took part in the advance on Kimberley and was wounded at the Battle of Magersfontein. This was probably the most desperate battle which took place in the South African war and one in which the Highland Brigade suffered severe casualties and was forced by the Boers to retire.

What happened was this. Both the British and the Boer forces numbered approximately 12,000 but the Boers had an extremely strong position which consisted of a series of kopjes which they had for the past six to seven weeks been fortifying with trenches and embankments. This Boer position was well concealed and the British reconnaissance was ineffective.

The Magersfontein kopje was $6^{1}/_{2}$ miles from the British camp, and the job of the Highland Brigade was to storm this strongpoint with the bayonet at first light. On Sunday afternoon the five artillery batteries set off across the plain. Behind them marched the Highland Brigade, consisting of 3,500 men. They were dressed in khaki, with khaki aprons to hide the front of their kilts, but no sporrans, claymores or coat buttons.

45

By the early evening sleety rain began to fall, but the men had no greatcoats, only a blanket and a groundsheet. About 3 miles from the Kopje they halted and bivouacked, except there was neither food nor shelter.

Meanwhile the Boers were being shelled by field guns, howitzers and a 4.7-inch naval gun. This bombardment, one of the biggest since Sebastopol, was awe-inspiring but apparently the wrong hill was shelled. There were very few Boer casualties, but what it did was to prepare the Boers for the British attack.

The heavy, icy rain continued to fall all night and a violent wind arose. No fires were allowed, no smoking, and there was no food. At midnight the order 'Quarter column' was given and the four battalions, including the Seaforth Highlanders and Hugh Baillie, lined up in the most compact formation in the drill book: 3,500 men, 30 companies, 90 files, all compressed into a column 45 yards wide and 160 yards long. A night march by compass in an unknown territory is a delicate and dangerous manoeuvre – I myself achieved it successfully on my battle training course on Dartmoor, when I commanded my company.

But now disaster loomed for the Highland Brigade. Major Benson, who was the navigator and ADC to General Wauchope and who was killed in action, succeeded in getting the brigade into more or less the right position and, having done so, told Wauchope that this was as far as it was safe to go in a massed formation. However, Wauchope told him to go on a little further. To extend the 90 lines of men marching shoulder to shoulder, to three lines of men extended at 5 yards apart, would take about a quarter of an hour, and it could and should have been done there and then, but the column continued to march as the massed formation with Wauchope marching in front with his unauthorised claymore. Suddenly the Boers opened up an intense rifle fire, and the Highland Brigade was caught out in massed formation in the open, with any movement attracting a bullet. Day broke and various attacks were made without success. The men were exhausted – they had had no breakfast and they had been soaked to the skin during the night march. The day had now become very hot and they had no water and they could not move without being fired at.

And then suddenly their nerve failed and they found they could take no more. At about 1 p.m. the Colonels of both the Seaforth and Gordon Highlanders ordered two companies to trickle back, but the trickle became a flood and the flood an avalanche of retreating Highlanders. It was a terrible sight – the Highland Brigade retreating in complete disorder, with officers running about with revolvers threatening to shoot them and, at the same time, giving out incoherent and impractical orders. It was a disaster.

Hugh Baillie was wounded but he survived to take part in a number of operations and actions in South Africa.

We must try and move on, but before we do so, I must mention what happened to him after South Africa. In 1903 he had gone to West Africa where he had been specially selected for duty with the 3rd Northern Nigerian Regiment attached to the West African Frontier Force.

What was happening there that needed the services of Hugh Baillie as well as some other British officers? It appears that for some time the British administration had intended to dispatch a strong expedition of some 300 troops to visit the warlike tribes to the south of the Benue and to penetrate up to the Munshi country, and in the course of their operations the Okpotos of the Bassa Province of Northern Nigeria would have been visited. But unbeknown to the British administration, a party led by a Captain O'Riordan and a Mr C. Amyatt, took it upon themselves to try and reinstate a chieftain who had been driven out by another tribe which was hostile to the British. This party, consisting of some 90 men, was ambushed and nearly all the men were killed or sold into slavery.

It was reported by the native interpreter who had survived the ambush that, after leaving Dekina, the chief port of the Bassa Province, the column proceeded for three days and during that time had actually succeeded in restoring the ousted chieftain to his position. But in doing this a great deal of fighting had taken place, ammunition was running low, and the two British officers were attacked while they were having breakfast. A running battle took place, made far worse by swarms of bees which also attacked them. They put up a good fight but eventually they were all killed except the native interpreter, who escaped.

The British administration therefore decided to send a punitive expedition up country and it was this expedition which Hugh Baillie joined.

The reports of this punitive expedition against the Okpoto tribe, who had ambushed and killed Captain O'Riordan's column, show that the operations were very severe and far worse than expected.

The nature of this country, which was dense bush and unmapped, and the confidence given to the natives by their success over the ambushed force (they had captured all their guns) made the operation the most difficult that, up to that time, had ever taken place in Northern Nigeria. The expedition suffered 70 casualties out of a total force of 300.

This punitive expedition, under the command of Major Merrick, had eight British officers, one of them Hugh Baillie, and consisted of 300 West African Frontier Force men composed of one company of the 1st Northern Nigerian Regiment and one company of the 2nd Northern Nigerian Regiment, together with two Maxims and a gun detachment and 400 carriers.

The force concentrated at Lokoja, and disembarking at the village of Mozun, made a night march to Dekina, the headquarters of the Bassa Province. After 48 hours' hard marching through dense bush and difficult country and deserted villages, they had their first encounter with the Okpotos at a village called Kirmin Awuru. From then on, for the next three months, they had a running fight on their hands.

The most important engagement took place at Ogedo, a main Okpoto town, and for some time it was a close-run thing for the West African Frontier Force. Fighting continued daily and often nightly for several weeks but, in the end, the Okpotos got tired of fighting and decided to comply with the terms imposed by the British. They agreed to pay the heavy fines, to surrender the hostile chieftain and to give up the bodies and kits of the murdered officers and the captured guns.

The reader may very well ask why I have gone to such lengths to describe a military event in Northern Nigeria in 1903, and my response must be that it was one of those bloody bitter colonial engagements which have now been almost entirely forgotten, but importantly for me, it was one in which my great-uncle Hugh took part.

In 1904 he rejoined the 2nd Battalion but in 1907 he went to Staff College, being subsequently in a senior staff position with the 51st Highland Division. He then rejoined the 2nd Seaforth in 1914 and went to France with his regiment. He took part in the retreat from Mons and was wounded near Armentières in October. He was awarded the DSO after the battle of Soissons, and here again it is interesting to record what happened.

The Seaforths went up the line in single file to the heights and arrived there at three o'clock in the morning. A-Company was in the firing line and the rest were in reserve. Soon the German shelling started and all hell was let loose. Colonel Bradford, the Commanding Officer, was the first man to be killed. Casualties were very heavy and the shelling and firing continued all day. The Seaforths managed to stay cool despite the murderous fire and a sergeant reported as follows:

Captain Hugh Baillie, who commanded my company, set a very fine example. He walked about in the firing line while shells were falling incessantly around him, as if he was on manoeuvres. The remarkable thing was that men lying in the trenches, apparently well protected from the enemy, were being hit left, right and centre. The Captain, however, went calmly about giving instructions and advice, exposing himself quite openly to enemy fire, yet he came through without a scratch.

Subsequently he had a succession of Staff appointments: in 1919 he was GSO Scottish Division Army of the Rhine. For his services he received the DSO Brevet rank and was five times mentioned in despatches. In 1921 he was appointed to command the 1st Battalion Seaforth Highlanders and during his tenure he led the battalion in Belfast during the most difficult times of the Irish troubles. It was his example and the work done by him in this period which did a great deal to ensure the successes and efficiency of the battalion under most difficult peacetime conditions.

Hugh Baillie married Hilda Kemble, the second daughter of Mr Kemble of Knoch, Isle of Skye, in 1920. There were no children of the marriage and he died in 1941. I never met him.

And so we come to the last son, Ian Henry Baillie. He was educated at Wellington. He first held a commission in the 1st Lanarkshire Rifle Volunteers before 1914 but in the outbreak of war, he joined the Cameron Highlanders, first at Inverness and later the 1/4th Battalion in France. He was promoted Captain in 1914.

He went out to the front along with eight other officers to fill the gaps and blanks caused by the heavy casualties sustained at Neuve Chappelle. He was severely wounded at the Battle of Festubert in May 1915 and, like his brother Alan, died shortly afterwards.

What happened seems to have been this. The 4th Battalion

Cameron Highlanders advanced at 7.30 p.m. on 17th May 1915 and they soon found themselves faced by a deep ditch which could not be jumped. Some swam it, some got over planks left by the Germans and all the while they were heavily shelled from some houses on their left. One company lost direction altogether, another company on the right was virtually wiped out, losing all its officers, but one company struggled on and took the furthest back communication trench, when the appearance of an unexpected deep stream threw out the whole movement.

At about 9 p.m. the advance company was in a desperate position with both its flanks up in the air so to speak. At about midnight, two platoons were moved up in support but no machine-guns could be got across the stream, and the Germans from left and right were bombing the trench while their Maxim and rifle fire 'watered' all the hinterland.

In the small hours, the Commanding Officer, seeing that the position was hopeless, ordered a retirement. It was no light task for the parapet behind was very high, there were no communication trenches, and the whole area was being swept by fire from the Germans. Some of the company pulled up the coverings of the ditches which ran across the trench and crawled down them. One officer managed to slither over the parapet with his men and got them away to safety. Nevertheless the battalion was reduced to half its strength, its gallant commanding officer Lieutenant Colonel Fraser was killed and so were 12 other officers. Some were drowned in the ditches and when the men returned they were covered in mud from head to foot. This was the bloody vicious engagement in which Ian subsequently died of his wounds.

My grandfather, Ronald Hugh Baillie, was born in 1863. Unlike his military brothers he went to the Scottish Bar and in due course became Sheriff of Roxburghshire. He lived in a large Victorian house called Jedbank just outside Jedburgh, and it was in that house that my sister Marigold and I, together with our first cousins Ursula, Caroline and Peter Wise lived when our house in Kent was requisitioned by the Army and when the Wise's house in Tor Gardens, just off Church Street, Kensington, was bombed and destroyed during the Blitz in 1940. We had nowhere else to live – Lyons Hall had also been requisitioned by the Army.

Jedbank was, like Lochloy, cold and devoid of electricity. However, unlike Lochloy the servants' quarters had gas lighting whilst we had the usual candles and Aladdin lamps. When I once asked my mother why the servants were advantaged by having gas whilst we were disadvantaged, the answer came back that gas was not considered socially acceptable, so it was all right for 'them' but not for 'us'. It was a gloomy house with many bedrooms, all unheated, and again only one bathroom. Like at Lochloy we used to go up to our bedrooms by candlelight, but we enjoyed night lights, a great advantage when looking for the potty under the bed. Jedbank had beautiful grounds, a large vegetable garden and a tennis court. There was also a comfortable gardener's cottage in which Mr Wilkie lived, who was very religious.

For many years my grandfather had been 'seeing' Elizabeth Rose of Kilravock but he had no money and could not afford to get married. It was not until he was appointed Sheriff of Roxburghshire in February 1897 that he could afford to get married, and this he did three months later on 3rd April.

6

My Rose Family

By now we have had a good run through the Baillie family and we now have to turn to the Rose family. Like the Baillies they were a military and landowning family.

The original patrimony of the Roses appears to have been the lands of Geddes in the County of Inverness. In the days of King Alexander II, as early as 1219, Hugh Rose appears as a witness to the founding of the Priory of Beaulieu, now Beauly. The founders of that Priory were the Byssets, at that time among the great houses of the north and the downfall of that family forms one of the strangest stories of King Alexander's reign. In 1242, after a great tournament at Haddington, Patrick, the young Earl of Atholl, was treacherously murdered and 'burnt to coals' in his lodgings in that town. Suspicion fell on the Byssets, who had a bitter feud with the House of Atholl. Sir William Bysset had just entertained the King and Queen at his Castle of Aboyne and on the night of the murder had sat late at supper with the Queen in Forfar. In vain the Queen offered to swear his innocence. In vain Bysset himself had the murderers cursed, and offered to prove his innocence in battle. However, everybody believed he was guilty. The Byssets saw all their lands, goods and cattle confiscated, and before the fury of the powerful kinsmen of Atholl, they were eventually banished from the Kingdom.

Sir John de Bysset however left three daughters, the eldest of whom inherited the lands of Lovat at Beaufort and became ancestress of the Frasers, whilst the youngest inherited Redcastle on the Black Isle and Kilravock on the River Nairn, and married Sir Andrew de Bosco. Mary, one of the daughters of this marriage, married Hugh Rose of Geddes and brought him the lands of Kilravock and Culcowie on the Black Isle as her marriage portion.

53

This was at the latter end of the reign of Alexander III and from that day until recently the Roses have been lairds of Kilravock in unbroken succession. From an early time, there is evidence of their lands having been erected into a feudal barony: the Roses were known as Barons of Kilravock. The Roses always kept a low profile and though by marriage and otherwise they acquired and held for many generations considerable land in Ross-shire and in the valleys of the Nairn and the Findhorn, they only emerged occasionally into the limelight of history.

It was a Hugh Rose – all the sons were called Hugh – who built the still existing Tower of Kilravock in 1460, and his energy or his urgent need for protection is shown by the fact, recorded as marvellous, that he finished it within a year.

The Rose family at this time was at serious variance with the Thane of Cawdor – their next-door neighbour. It was this Thane's father who six years earlier had built Cawdor Castle, and Thane William himself had made one of the best matches of his time by marrying a daughter of Alexander Sutherland of Dunbeath, whose wife was a daughter of one of the Lords of the Isles. Thane William was an ambitious man: he had his estates changed into a Crown holding by resigning them into the hands of the King and procuring a new charter, and to make sure of the permanence of his family, he set aside with a pension his eldest son, William, who had something wrong with him, and settled the entire thanedom and heritage of the family on his second son, John, who, to close the feud between the two families, married Isabella, daughter of Rose of Kilravock. Unfortunately it was not a happy marriage, but out of it and at the risk of some digression arose one of the more curious stories of the North.

The young Thane John did not long survive his marriage; he died in 1498, leaving as sole heiress to the Cawdor Estates an infant daughter Muriel. The old Thane William and his four sons were naturally furious and they did their best to have Muriel declared illegitimate, but to no avail.

By reason of the new Charter, the child was a ward of the Crown and the Earl of Argyll, who was then Justician of Scotland, procured her wardship and marriage from King James IV. The Rose family were no doubt glad to have the keeping of the child entrusted to so powerful a guardian, but old Lady Rose of Kilravock was suspicious as to the good faith of Muriel's new protector. When the Earl's emissary, Campbell of Innerlives, arrived at Kilravock to convey the child south to Loch Awe, Lady Rose is said to have thrust the key of her coffer into the fire and branded Muriel with it on the thigh.

Innerlives had not gone far on his way to the south when he began to be overtaken by the child's four uncles and their followers. With shrewd ability he devised a stratagem. Sending Muriel off as quickly as possible with a small guard, he dressed a sheaf of corn in her clothes and proceeded to give battle with the greater part of his force. Seven of his sons, it is said, fell before he gave way, and even then he only retired when he felt sure the child was far beyond pursuit. When someone afterwards asked whether he thought the child was worth such a sacrifice, and even suggested the heiress might die before reaching womanhood, he is said to have replied, 'Muriel of Cawdor will never die as long as there is a red-haired lassie on the shores of Loch Awe.' She did indeed survive, and lived to a good old age. The Earl of Argyll married her when she was 12 years old to his second son, Sir John Campbell, and the Earls of Cawdor of the present day are directly descended from the pair.

Hugh Rose, grandson of he who had built the tower, for some reason now unknown seized William Galbraith, the Abbot of Kinloss, and imprisoned him at Kilravock. For this he was himself arrested and kept for a long time a prisoner in Dumbarton Castle, then commanded by Sir George Stirling of Glorat.

The next laird was known as the Black Baron. He lived in the very difficult time of the Reformation and in his youth he fought and was made prisoner at Pinkie Cleugh. Yet he managed to pay his ransom, 100 angels, and to provide portions for his 17 sisters and daughters. He also built the house at Kilravock, adjacent to the tower. He reigned as laird of Kilravock for more than 50 years.

It was during his period as laird that Mary, Queen of Scots, paid her visit to Kilravock. The Castle of Inverness, of which the Earl of Huntly was keeper, had closed its gates against her and her half-brother, whom she had just made Earl of Moray, and the Queen, while preparing to take the castle by storm, took up her quarters at Kilravock. It was at Kilravock that it is reputed she made the famous remark that: 'she repented she was not a man to know what life it was to lie all night in the fields, or walk the rounds with a jack and knapscull'. A few days later the Captain of Inverness Castle surrendered, overawed by her preparation, and was hanged. Shortly afterwards the Queen defeated Huntly himself at Carrichie and thus brought the great rebellion in the north to an end.

The Black Baron of Kilravock was 'justice depute' of the north under Argyll, Sheriff of Inverness and Constable of its castle under Queen Mary, and also commissioner for the Regent Moray. He lived to be summoned to Parliament by King James VI in 1593.

Hugh, the 14th Baron, lived through the difficult times of King Charles II and James II but, though sharing his wife's warm sympathy with the persecuted Covenanters, managed himself to avoid the persecution of his time. The 15th Baron began life as a supporter of the divine right of kings, but later admitted what he thought as the justice and necessity of the revolution. He voted against the Act of Union but declared for the Protestant succession, but after the Union was appointed one of the Scottish Commissioners to the first Parliament of Great Britain. On the outbreak of the Earl of Mar's rebellion in 1715 he stood firm for King George's government, armed 200 men of his clan, kept the peace in his countryside and maintained Kilravock Castle as a refuge for persons frightened by the Jacobites. He even planned to reduce the Jacobite garrison at Inverness and, along with Forbes of Culloden and Lord Lovat, blockaded the town.

His brother, Arthur Rose, who had recently been ransomed from slavery with the pirates of Algiers and whose portrait in Turkish dress used to hang in the dining room at Kilravock, tried to seize the garrison. At the head of a small party he made his way to the tolbooth but he was betrayed by his guide. As Arthur Rose pushed past the door, his guide shouted that he was an enemy and he was then shot and crushed to death between the door and the wall. On hearing of his brother's death, Kilravock sent a message to the garrison ordering them to leave or, if they did not, he would burn down the town. Frightened by his threat, the Governor and the magistrates evacuated the town and castle during the night and Kilravock entered and took possession of it the following day.

In 1734 the 16th Baron was returned to Parliament for Ross-shire. He built the house of Coulmonis on the Findhorn and married Elizabeth Clephane, daughter of a soldier of fortune and a friend of the Countess of Sutherland.

He was engaged in the quiet life of a county gentleman, hawking, shooting and fishing, when in 1745 the Jacobite rebellion broke out. Two days before the Battle of Culloden, Prince Charles Edward rode out from Inverness to bring in his outposts on the Spey, who were retreating before the Duke of Cumberland's army and he spent an hour or two at Kilravock. He kissed the children, begged a tune on the violin from the laird, and walked out with him to see one of his plantations. Before leaving, he said that he greatly envied the laird's peaceful life in the middle of a country wrecked by war.

Next day the Duke of Cumberland arrived at the castle and spent the night. In the course of talking to the laird the Duke remarked to him, 'You have had my cousin here?' to which Kilravock explained that he could not refuse to entertain him, and the Duke remarked that he had done quite right. The laird was the Provost of Nairn and when we used to stay there Ruth Rose, our great-aunt, always used to show us a silver-mounted drinking cup of coconut. This cup bears the inscription: 'This cup belongs to the Provost of Nairn 1746, the year of our deliverance. A bumper to the Duke of Cumberland.' Not everybody was on the side of the Jacobites.

In 1787 Burns visited Kilravock and found a sympathetic friend in the person of the then Mrs Rose. In his thank-you letter he wrote: 'The beautifully wild scenery of Kilravock, the venerable grandeur of the castle, the spreading woods, the winding river, gladly leaving its healthy source and lingering with apparent delight as it passes the fairy walk at the bottom of the garden.' Kilravock like Lochloy had its fairies. Like Cawdor Kilravock had its Lia Fail. For hundreds of years a gooseberry bush grew on the outer wall of the upper rampart of the tower and it had always been the tradition of Kilravock that, so long as it flourished, the family would also flourish.

My great-grandfather was Major James Rose. He was born in 1820 and succeeded his father in 1854 as the 23rd Baron. James Rose was the eldest son of a second family. India and the Crimea wiped out his elders and some of his juniors too. He entered one of the Honourable East India Company's cavalry regiments and fought in the Indian Mutiny. He married Anna Maria Twemlow with whom he had four children, of which my grandmother Elizabeth was the second-eldest. The eldest had been born in India during the Mutiny and was always known in the family as 'the Mutiny baby'.

He was appointed Lord Lieutenant of Nairnshire and there is a wonderful photograph of him at my grandfather's wedding in 1897 and, looking at him, one is quite surprised that he lived another 12 years. In 1909 he was succeeded by his son Hugh Rose, my great-uncle. Colonel Hugh Rose, as he was always known, became baron.

He too had an interesting military career with the Black Watch. He served in the Egyptian Campaign of the 1880s and received the Egyptian Medal 1882–89 with bars. He also received the Khedive's Egyptian Star. Later he served in the Boer War with the 1st Battalion and received the South African Medal with various bars. He was awarded the CMG. He died at Kilravock on 22nd February 1946.

I do not remember him all that well, although we stayed at Kilravock both before and during the war. He was, I believe, a gifted water diviner. He also (or it may have been his father) believed that the Ark of the Covenant was buried beneath the castle, and he had the interior of the drawing room redesigned so that it resembled the Ark. I also remember when we stayed at Kilravock being told to look out for the old grey lady – the Kilravock ghost – who was well known and liked, so much so that I believe a place at the dining room table was usually set for her; but I never saw her. Like Jedbank and Lochloy, Kilravock had no electricity. Our bedroom was usually in the fifteenth-century tower. It had very narrow windows for shooting arrows out of and the bedroom walls were at least six feet thick. To get to this tower bedroom you had to appropriate a candle from the lamp-room, light it and, with one hand shakily shielding the flame from the draught, you set forth past the old dining-hall, whose underfloor was covered with at least a foot of sawdust to keep out the screams of the prisoners in the dungeons below. Up the 500-year-old stone spiral staircase you went until you arrived in the bedroom, by which time you were so frightened that you dived straight under the bedclothes to escape the shadows which the candle cast on the old grey stone walls. Of course, getting up at night, like at Lochloy, was a refined form of torture.

After Great-Uncle Hugh died in 1946, his widow Ruth, née Guillemard, took over the estate and died in 1965. Some years later I was appointed, along with Jim Stubbs, a Kilravock trustee.

Colonel Hugh Rose, my great-uncle, had one son, also called

Hugh Rose in conformity with the family tradition. He was a page at my mother's wedding and you can see him in my mother's wedding photographs. At the beginning of the Second World War, he was called to the Colours and, following in his father's footsteps, joined the Black Watch, being given an emergency commission in March 1942, with the 1st Battalion. The battalion embarked in June 1942, at Avonmouth for North Africa. But before he left, Hugh knew that the gooseberry bush had died, and he knew that if the prophecy was correct he would not return.

The huge convoy which was carrying the Highland Division sailed without incident via West Africa round the Cape of Good Hope and north again through the Indian Ocean and Red Sea. No enemy aircraft or submarines were seen.

The 51st Highland Division moved up to the El-Alamein line with the 9th Australian Division to their right and the New Zealand Division to the left. The Black Watch were positioned on the far right of the Highland Division. It was a night attack and each platoon officer was accompanied by his piper so that throughout the night as the attack went in 'the skirls of the most eerie, exhilarating and frightening music the battlefield knows would pierce the din of shells and mines exploding and the hoarse racket of gunfire'.* One Highland officer, hearing his piper playing 'The Road to the Isles', asked himself, 'I wonder if it is'. He knew, of course, that the isles were the celestial isles of the Blessed whence none returned.

The Black Watch kept so close to the artillery barrage that they had to pause several times during the night to wait for it to lift. Their objective was some 6,500 yards from the start line, a distance far greater than had ever been previously attempted for a night attack. 'Control over such distances was hard but keeping direction was even harder and it was an awful problem to know where you were. We were working on dead reckoning by compass, pacing and taping over distances but, even so, it was not easy as members of the navigation party kept on getting hit.' So wrote Hugh Rose's Commanding Officer, Lieutenant-Colonel Roper-Caldwell.

Trouble began at the second German minefield, which was both extensive and elaborate, tripwired and booby-trapped, but they got through and the battalion reached its objective exactly on time at

---

*From *Alamein* by Jon Latimer (John Murray, 2002).

11.45 p.m. The last few yards were disputed by machine-guns, but they were charged and silenced. Then as the Colonel turned round to congratulate Hugh Rose – he was the youngest officer in the battalion – he was shot in the neck and killed instantly.

So the prophecy was true. The gooseberry bush had died, the son and heir had been killed, and that was the end of the family and Kilravock.

Hugh Rose had two sisters, the eldest being Elizabeth and the youngest Madeleine. Madeleine married a Baird and had four sons, the eldest of whom was David, who returned from Australia on the mistaken assumption, as it turned out, that his Aunt Elizabeth would leave him the Kilravock Estate with its 8,000 acres. He married my sister Marigold's third daughter Rosie, with whom he had four girls. Sadly the marriage did not work out.

After the death of her mother Ruth Rose in 1966, my great-aunt, Elizabeth, the eldest daughter, who had become the life tenant of the Kilravock Estate after her husband Hugh's death, inherited. It was a tragic succession because, with the death of her mother, the estate had come out of trust and Elizabeth went 'religious'. The contents of the castle were sold, including the priceless library and its documents and archives, and the castle was turned into a Christian guest house and given along with the estate to a Christian sect.

So of the family houses: Woodlands, my mother's and stepfather's house in Kent, was requisitioned by the Army and after the war was demolished and became a housing development – I wonder whether they found all the petrol gallon tanks we had buried in the garden when petrol rationing came in. Jedbank was sold and demolished. Lochloy was sold. Kilkravock was turned into a Christian guest house and is managed and owned by some religious sect based in Edinburgh. Marham House was mainly demolished in the 1930s and sold with the estate, now consumed by RAF Marham, a huge Air Force base. Our father's house in Sloane Court East was destroyed by a landmine during the war. And all this in one generation. How sad it all is. Only Lyons Hall has survived, just, having been requisitioned by the Army during the war and then turned into an Italian prisoner-of-war camp and then converted into flats. In 1980 it was reconverted into a family house by my wife and myself.

Now going back to 3rd April 1897, that was the day my

grandfather, Ronald Hugh Baillie of Lochloy, married Elizabeth Rose of Kilravock. The wedding was held at St Columbas Church, Nairn, and the wedding day was signalled by the hoisting of the town flag on the municipal buildings and many other buildings were similarly decorated with flags and bunting. Furthermore, to celebrate the wedding, my Baillie great-grandmother gave a party for the inmates of the Poorhouse in Nairn. The local newspaper reported that Colonel Clarke, the Chairman of the Union Board, presided and at the close made a few appropriate and felicitous remarks, and called for a hearty note of thanks to Mrs Baillie of Lochloy and cheers for the newly married couple, which were heartily accorded.

It is interesting to note some of the gifts to the bride and bridegroom – no lists in those days, you got what you were given. The Villebois gave a china lamp; Aunt Glentworth gave them a cheque; Mr and Mrs Braugham gave them a copper breakfast heater; Mr and Mrs D. Cameron gave them a copper coal scuttle; Mr Paul Campbell a pair of shoes; the Hon. Helen Dillon a book; Sir William Fraser another book; Miss Grant and Mr Wilfred Grant gave them another copper coal scuttle. The Kilravock tenantry gave the bride a massive silver epergne and the bridegroom a meerschaum pipe, whilst the Kilravock servants gave the bride a set of silver fish knives and forks and the bridegroom a shepherd's crook. The Lochloy servants gave them a dining-room clock. The bride's father gave them a cheque and a chiming musical box, which is now at Lyons Hall, and so on.

The *Highland News* gave the wedding a lavish write-up, the headlines being a 'fashionable marriage, the bride and bridegroom representatives of our old Highland nobility and all the guests both rich and poor alike showing the love and affection for the ancient houses of Kilravock and Lochloy'.

Again, it is interesting to read of the clothes worn by the bride and the bridesmaids, who were Rona Baillie and Muriel Pope. The bride wore a skirt of drab cashmere, trimmed in front with ribbon velvet. The bodice was velvet of the same shade, showing a white silk front, draped with costly lace, while the sleeves were of velvet made in the bolero style. Her hat had a brim of drab straw, with crown and trimmings of white accordion-pleated silk, with rosettes and sprays of lily of the valley, whilst she carried a bouquet of white lilies and tulips with satin streamers.

Rona Baillie, my great-aunt, and Muriel Pope, a Rose first cousin, were dressed in white lustre with zouaves, edged with cream embroidery and with folded silk waistbands. Their hats were of white chip, with a frill of white chiffon falling over the brim (an effective background to their pretty faces, as the *Highland News* put it) with chiffon rosettes and white tips.

And my great-grandmother, who had now been widowed seven years and was to live another 43 years – remember she was the sister of Uncle Fred – wore a gown of black silk with embroidered jet front, a black silk cape edged with squirrel tail fur, and a black lace bonnet with violets. So she was still in mourning, and I think remained in mourning clothes for the rest of her life.

My grandfather was 34 when he married. He had to wait until he was appointed Sheriff of Roxburghshire before he could afford to marry and keep his wife in the style to which she was accustomed – a large house and servants. It has to be said that neither the bride nor the bridegroom look very happy in their wedding photographs and I remember Aunt Effie telling me that right up to the wedding, the family tried to dissuade him from going ahead. But they did, and they had two daughters: my mother, Iris Mary, born in 1900, and her sister Eve Glentworth a little later. Apart from Hugh, the son of Uncle Duncan and Aunt Mary Baillie, who went deaf and never married, these two daughters were the only offspring of the five sons and six daughters of my great-grandfather and great-grandmother.

I know very little of the lives of my grandfather – always known as Gubby – and his wife Elizabeth. They were lucky to live in the same house, Jedbank, all their lives. Both were awarded the OBE, Elizabeth first in 1918 and Gubby in 1920. At that time he was, inter alia, the Chairman of the Roxburghshire Local War Pensions Committee and he also gave valuable service in other departments of war work. My grandmother was very religious and was always much involved in good works. She used to write articles for the *Scottish Mothers Magazine*, and there was one she wrote entitled, 'Thoughts on the War'.

I quote part of what she wrote:

I am going to write a little about this War-time, this time of stress and storm, which occupies all our minds to the exclusion of almost everything else and all one's little daily business and pleasures and plans seem to have receded and become matters of very little importance under the strain of this colossal struggle for existence as a nation.

When too our brave men are called to die, there is this consolation for the bereaved mother or wife that she can feel that the death of a soldier is a death of self-sacrifice and in this way is strangely like the death of the God-man who for us surrendered His life on the Cross of Mount Calvary.

My grandmother died in 1934, so that in that terrible year, my mother lost both her husband and her mother. My grandfather survived the War and died in 1949.

7

Early Days

Mummy and Daddy were married in 1928 at St Paul's Church, Knightsbridge, by Cousin Albert Baillie, the Dean of Windsor, a cousin. As the press put it, the bride came from a well-known old Highland family, but there was no mention of Daddy's family.

Mummy, who was several years older than Daddy, wore an ankle-length dress of oyster-coloured satin, the long straight lines of which were caught at the side by a lovely ornament of gold beads and pearls. Her bouquet was of lilies of the valley, white heather and roses. The long train was composed of gold lamé edged with old Brussels lace and was carried by Hugh Rose of Kilravock and Hugh Robin Baillie – who was, as I have stated earlier, the only son of Colonel Duncan Baillie. Mummy's long tulle veil was held in place by orange blossoms and gold leaves and her ornaments were a diamond and sapphire brooch and necklace. For going away Mummy wore a sapphire blue satin dress with a velvet coat trimmed with grey fox fur. The honeymoon was spent in the South of France.

Marigold, my sister, was born on 13th November 1928 at Lyons Hall and, as I have said earlier, I was born on 2nd October 1931 in Knutsford, Cheshire, when my father was attached from Barclays to the Union Bank of Manchester. We were then living at Ollerton House, Ollerton, near Knutsford from which he commuted to Manchester. We then moved to a village called Shelford, near Cambridge, where my father was working at the Local Head Office of the Bank at Cambridge. We did not stay there long before my father was appointed a Local Director of the Lombard Street District of the Bank and we then moved from Cambridge to London and lived in a house at Sloane Court East, where my earliest memories begin.

It was a large Victorian house on six floors and Marigold and I lived on the top floor with Nanny, Doris Lambert, who stayed with the family for 50 years from 1928 to 1978 when she died. She was the one constant in our lives, but perhaps more in my life than my sister's.

Nanny Lambert, I came to realise later, was illegitimate and was fostered in Essex. Her mother lived in a small cottage in a village called Shingham, near Swaffham in Norfolk, and we occasionally went to stay with her there during the War. My main memories of this cottage were that it had no electricity, no water except that which we obtained from the local pump, and no telephone. The toilet facilities consisted of a thunderbox at the end of the garden, and it was to there that we had to repair with newspapers.

I remember once when we were staying there, there was a big thunderstorm with vast amounts of lightning. Nanny's mother had a great fear of lightning and when the lightning started all the cutlery was hidden away and the mirrors were turned round – all this to prevent the lightning from being attracted to the cottage.

Our bedroom at the top of the house in Sloane Court East was on the street side and I always remember listening to the cries of the street hawkers, those who sold muffins, those who mended wicker chairs and those who sharpened knives.

Every evening Nanny took us down to the drawing room on the first floor to play games with Mummy for an hour, and then it was back again to the nursery. Once, I remember, I was presented to Queen Mary at the Albert Hall. She wore, as she always did, a long dress and on her head she wore what I now think was a toque with an aigrette. She was very stiff and upright and very awe-inspiring to a little boy like me, even though I was dressed in my best blue satin suit.

One day I remember I swallowed a small curtain ring. Everybody was desperate with worry, the ambulance was called, and then, just as it arrived, Nanny who was holding me upside down and banging away at me, managed to get it to fall out and it dropped out of my throat.

One memory was going to see the Coronation of King George VI in 1936. We were in the Mall with Nanny and it was pouring with rain. I went to shelter myself under the huge horse of a mounted policeman. Nanny was petrified that the horse would rear up with me underneath, and pulled me away as soon as she could.

My father died in May 1934. I have no memory of this terrible event, but I did find out afterwards what happened. He was out hunting with the East Essex Foxhounds – I have a photograph of him in his hunting clothes at Lyons Hall. Apparently he experienced a terrible pain, which was diagnosed as a burst appendix. In those days there was no such thing as penicillin, which saved my life when I was badly wounded in the Malayan jungle. As a result gangrene set in, and after enduring excruciating agony, he died in St Agnes' Hospital in London. He was 28 and my mother was 34.

Mummy, in her middle thirties, thus became a widow and a very attractive one – she was much in demand. She was great fun, very good-looking and an excellent listener. However, she was left very badly off. She had a small pension from the Bank, a small income from her marriage settlement and a few shares. I do not think that personally she got any help from the Tritton family. They may have paid for the costs of our education and that was all, except they bought Nanny a small car to ferry us around. There is no record in the Visitors' Book of her ever staying again either at Lyons Hall or the Hole Farm after Daddy's death and one wonders why.

In the event, two years after Daddy's death, Mummy met and married a man called Robin Barnes-Gorell. I know very little about his family but I understood they came from Derbyshire where, at one point I believe, they owned coal mines. Whether it was the demise of the coal mines or the stock market crash in the late 1920s or a combination of both, the position was that by the time he married my mother he had very little money, and moreover he did not work. I think it was Nanny who said – and she often got things wrong – that Mummy married Uncle Robin thinking he had money and he had done the same, thinking Mummy had money. In effect, there was very little.

In the event, Uncle Robin, as I will call him from now on, managed to get a job with Wingets in Rochester through the intervention of a friend, and they bought what always seemed to me to be a large house called Woodlands in the village of Shorne in Kent. All this was in 1936. Here we lived with Nanny until 1940 when the house was requisitioned by the Army following the outbreak of war in 1939.

Marigold went to school at Gad's Hill nearby – Charles Dickens's old house – whilst Nanny took me in the little car to Miss Snowden

Smith's school in Rochester. It was a good school and I learnt a lot, especially spelling. If I ever spelt a word wrong I had to hold my hand out for it to be smitten painfully with a ruler. I recall that, even at the age of seven, I was able to spell diarrhoea correctly – no mean feat.

At Woodlands we had our spaniels and bunnies, which we used to feed with tea-leaves and bran. There was also a large walnut tree in the garden, which not only produced beautiful large walnuts but also had a particular structure which enabled us to build a very comfortable tree house.

I also remember our visits to the Chatham Naval Dockyards during Navy Week – all those big grey battleships, cruisers and destroyers, and even a submarine in which I got claustrophobia. It was wonderful to see the pride of the British Fleet and immensely exciting to me as a young boy and to all the other hundreds and thousands of visitors. What pride we all took in those wonderful ships and their crews, and the power they represented. And where did they all go? I don't know, but I suppose most of them ended up at the bottom of the sea during the war. One great ship I admired – I think it was called HMS *Southampton*. What happened to her? Was she sunk during the Malta convoys?

And so we used to divide our time up between Woodlands and Lyons Hall with Nanny. Then Marigold and I had whooping cough and we were exiled to Whoopy Cottage where I am now writing these lines, Frinton, Cromer, Sheringham and elsewhere, including Scotland. It was at one of these seaside resorts that Nanny took us to stay as paying guests in a small little villa near the beach. Breakfast in the villa, then all day at the beach hut playing on the sands. My chief memories are of Heinz Sandwich Spread, a cold north-east wind whipping off the grey North Sea, and digging deeper and deeper into the sand to get out of the wind as Nanny, in her uniform, watched us benignly and sometimes not so benignly to see we did not get into too much mischief.

It was at Lyons Hall that I had my first operation. I had been suffering from adenoids for some time and it was decided to operate. But where? Certainly not at a hospital – no! – on the dining room table. In due course the surgeon, anaesthetist and nurses arrived from London. I was upstairs and was brought down by Nanny. They tried to chloroform me but did not succeed as I jumped off the table and escaped. They inveigled me back and suggested I blow my nose with a handkerchief. I did. It was impregnated with chloroform and I went out. A real cheat, I thought, as I went under.

And then came September 1939; and we were at war with Germany. I was nearly eight years old.

Nothing immediately changed for us. We were still at Woodlands, but Uncle Robin started buying up gallon cans of petrol and burying them in the garden in anticipation of petrol rationing. He also, with the help of others, dug a huge air-raid shelter in the vegetable garden but we never really liked it and preferred the shelter built by the ladies next door. But then Uncle Robin was called up and joined the Coldstream Guards in London. We hardly saw him again until towards the end of the war when he went down with tuberculosis.

A little later on an anti-aircraft gun battery was established in the wood adjacent to our garden and soon all hell was let loose – the Battle of Britain had begun. The house, which was not far from the River Thames, used by the Germans as a navigation line, was situated between Rochester and Gravesend and at Gravesend there was an airfield. The sirens started. The alarm was terrifying but the all-clear was so calm, peaceful and sustained.

Between the alarms and the all-clears Marigold and I used initially to rush out into the garden during that glorious summer weather of 1940 and watch the dogfights overhead. But then it all began somehow to get closer and closer, and we had increasingly to run to the air-raid shelter or, if there was not time to get there, to the cupboard under the stairs with all the house crockery shaking and rattling above, as the bombs whistled down and the battery of anti-aircraft guns opened up and fired repeatedly.

There was one very bad night I remember when a screaming bomb came down when we were lying in bed. Those screaming bombs were really frightening and we thought it was going to hit the house. It landed nearby with a huge explosion.

There was a very bad day when we were out in the car with the roof open. Suddenly, without any warning, some German bombers and fighters came over and the anti-aircraft guns started off and we couldn't get the roof shut as all the jagged lumps of shrapnel fell all around us and onto the car. We saw a house and with our heads covered rushed to the porch of this house, banging on the door to be allowed in, out of the bombs and shrapnel. We were allowed in and actually it was all over very quickly. Some blood, not much, and we were safe.

I think it was about this time that the London House in Sloane Court East received a direct hit from a landmine which also destroyed three or four of the adjacent houses.

It was too dangerous to stay where we were and, in any case, Woodlands was in the course of being requisitioned by the Army. Instead we went with Nanny to Lyons Hall which was itself also being requisitioned by the Army. So we had to leave there, and we ended up for several months at the County Hotel in Chelmsford, itself and the surrounding countryside being bombed by the Germans, aiming for the Hoffmann and Marconi factories. Sometimes the German bombers, under hot pursuit by RAF fighters, dropped their bombs in open countryside to lighten their load and to this day you can see a line of bomb craters between Fuller Street, Aycroats and Flexhill. I always remember the huge searchlight situated just above Goodmans Farm and the dugout shelter in Dead Man Hole up Cutthroat Lane, from which the Leighs Home Guard were supposed to emerge after the German Panzers had invaded and attack them in the rear – a wonderful example of Dad's Army potentially in operation.

At night we used to listen to the engine noise of the planes droning overhead and wonder whether they were German or ours. In fact, after a time, one's ears were so attuned to the different pitches of the engines that it was not long before we could tell the difference between friend and foe.

Meanwhile, at the County Hotel life proceeded. I went to school at King Edward VI Grammar School close to the hotel, whilst Marigold went to a girls' school nearby. The County Hotel had two very good recommendations in those days: one was the breakfast – eggs, bacon, sausages and tomato sauce – remember rationing had started; and the other was a very good table tennis board. The sweetie shop close to the school where I used to buy my sherbet has gone, and so has my classical tutor, Mr Becket, with whom I used to take extra Latin lessons as I was having difficulty with that language. I always recall his name as I had the impertinence to ask him whether he was descended from St Thomas à Becket. My education had not so far extended to priestly celibacy and chastity.

Meanwhile the requisitioning of Lyons Hall by the Army was more or less completed. Many huts, shower rooms and ablution facilities were constructed in the garden, and soon a Scottish regiment moved in, one of whose first acts was to burn down the beautiful Edwardian stables opposite the house. I remember seeing them on fire. We were told a boiler had overheated and set the chimney on fire.

By this time my grandfather and grandmother (Gaga) had moved out down the road to the Hole Farm where Aunt Dore lived. Her husband, Major Cecil Garnett, was away at the war. Soon after this move, my grandfather died – he was 69. I remember him just before he died, sitting in a comfortable armchair beside the drawing-room fire. He had lost both his two sons; he was estranged from his eldest daughter, my Aunt Lucy; another World War had started and his home had been taken from him. I think he died of a broken heart. After his death his body was set out in his bedroom at the Hole Farm and all the farm and estate workers and their wives had to file past his body and pray for him.

By this time, spring 1940, life was getting dangerous even at Chelmsford and King Edward VI Grammar School, where we had started to spend considerable periods of time in the bomb shelters.

We now had no home, and Mummy had decided we had to go north and spend the war with her father, Ronald Baillie, at his house Jedbank, just outside Jedburgh in the Scottish Borders. At the same time my proposed preparatory school, Stone House, Broadstairs, had evacuated to the borders of Lancashire and Yorkshire, to a house owned by the school Headmaster's family, the Farrers. Enemy action was disrupting life at Broadstairs, and besides it was thought that a German invasion was imminent. It is interesting to note that I was told that during the war most of Essex was under 24 hours' notice to evacuate in the event of a German invasion.

Although this never happened in this country, *Deo gratias*, it happened countless times in Europe and I remember talking to a German landed family to which this did indeed happen. They lived, I recall, in Silesia where they had a large comfortable house with farms and woodlands and, of course, servants even during the war. In 1944 they were hoping that the retreating Germans would be able to stop the advancing Russians. Hope began to evaporate, and then one day they heard for the first time the distant rumble of great guns in the east. The noise of the guns got nearer and nearer and soon, very soon, they were told by the Germans to leave within 24 hours. They did manage to get away themselves in that terrible winter of 1944, but they had to leave everything behind them, all their possessions, and they never saw them again. As a side note, I still do not know where most of the Lyons Hall furniture, china, linen, cutlery and so on, went to when the house was requisitioned. Most of it was never seen again.

In those days there used to be a school train. Whether or not they still exist, I do not know, but I doubt it. Everybody has cars now, but in those days, even if you had a car, there was no petrol.

One day in 1940, while the Blitz was still on, although the all-clear had sounded, I paraded at St Pancras Station as a very nervous seven-year-old boy with my school trunk, my tuck box, my gas mask and my identity card. Nanny was there to see me off. I boarded the carriage specially reserved for Stone House boys, none of whom I had ever seen in my life before, and the train left. Eventually we arrived at Clapham Station, via Hellifield, and Ingleborough Hall, the Farrer home now taken over by the school was just up the road through some imposing gates. The Hall seemed huge to me then, but today it seems to have shrunk. It is still a school – the Farrers never returned – a school for backward children run by the council.

It had a most beautiful garden, full of the most wonderful trees, plants and shrubs – in fact just what you would expect from the renowned botanical Farrer family. A little way above the house was an artificial lake created by the Farrers, which was fed by Clapham Beck. This beck full of tumbling glacial water continued on, having plunged down the spectacular waterfalls, also created by the Farrers. But before you got to the lake, there was on the right a large steading where we used to cut up wood for the house fires. And just below the steading was an icehouse, the first I had ever seen.

The house was deliberately detached from public view by huge tunnels and embankments and bridges. For instance, tradesmen had to come through a large dark tunnel, several hundred yards long, to arrive quite rightly at the back of the house, whilst other tunnels had been created for walkers and farm vehicles to prevent them from being seen by people in the Hall. Those long dark tunnels were quite spooky when you were on your own, but great fun to play games in.

It is curious how well one remembers the names of our teachers 65 years later. There was Major Farrer, a tall kindly man. He was the Headmaster, or perhaps he was just the proprietor. There was

J.L. Richardson, always known as JLR, who seemed to run the school. He got married when we were there and we christened his wife Peach Blossom – she was lovely. There was Mr Sharp, a clergyman, very athletic but small, and Mr Duckworth, who never stopped smoking, very irascible but with a kind heart. There was Miss Sandberg who taught us languages; Patrick Williams who taught us music and Commander Holmes, both of whom I shall mention later; and others.

We did, of course, have a matron, Miss Allerton, who was quite severe and used to 'conduct' us when we were brushing our teeth and she was assisted by a lovely young assistant matron. Whenever I had nightmares she always used to comfort me and say that nightmares were always the precursor of something nice happening.

What do I remember most about my school days there? I remember the ice-cold compulsory showers in the morning and the glacial lake in which we learnt to swim by being towed by a sheet from the back of a rowing boat which was suddenly let go. I remember the terrible shortage of food. It was served on those horrible little green rubber mats which had a dreadful smell. Supper was always particularly meagre and I remember one dreadful occasion when all we were served with was one sardine on dry toast and a mug of tepid cocoa for our supper. Sweets were tightly rationed in those days and all we were allowed were two sweets a week after lunch on Sunday. Sunday was also the day – and again I think it was after lunch – when we were given a weekly lecture or review of the progress or lack of progress of the war, complete with a huge map of the world on which the positions of the German, Russian, British, American and Japanese armies were displayed using special large, coloured drawing pins. I remember listening to the radio news in June 1944, and hearing about the Allied forces landing on D-Day in Normandy, and what excitement that was.

Most of us suffered from chilblains, and some were afflicted far worse than others. Nobody seems to have heard of chilblains these days but for the incognoscenti they were extremely itchy inflammations of the fingers and hands and toes and feet, due to the cold. The itchiness and soreness used to drive us nearly mad, particularly at night in bed.

I recall that at one point I went through a special sort of religious conversion and was given special lessons by the clergyman, Mr Sharp, who told me always to remember that 'I can do all things through Christ, which strengtheneth me'. I had two such religious conversions later in my life: the first was at the time of my confirmation in Eton College Chapel in 1948 – I have still kept the order of service – and the second was when I was received into the Catholic Church by the Benedictine monks at Ampleforth Abbey in July 1963.

Patrick Williams was an excellent music master and we often used to play duets. It was on these occasions that I found it difficult to take my eyes off his nicotine-stained fingers playing alongside mine when I should have been reading the music. He told me that I must get to the point where I enjoyed practising the piano, and so I did. It was an instrument I enjoyed enormously, and I am always thrilled that Guy, my eldest son, is himself such an excellent pianist.

On Saturday evenings a film projector was set up in the dining-room and we used to watch films. I always remember that there was a very special smell about the spools of film. One evening we were shown a film by Hitchcock called *The Lady Vanishes*. I have never been so frightened in my life and, once again, when the nightmares came on, the beautiful young assistant matron was called out to calm me.

Once a day we were lined up to take one spoonful of Radio-Malt – far nicer than Virol – and once a week we had to expose our small, white, naked bodies to the ultra-violet lamp. This was a lamp standing in the middle of a room. We had to put goggles on and spend a few minutes facing it and a few minutes with our backs to it. It was supposed to do us good, given the lack of sunshine in the winter. The ultra-violet lamps emitted a curious metallic smell which I have never forgotten. Nowadays I doubt that it would pass the Health and Safety Executive.

And so, at long last, I must come to the education. We learned the usual subjects but, in my case, I was enormously fortunate in having a geography master called Commander Holmes He had prominent protruding eyes and I think he had been in the Navy during the First World War as a submariner. He was responsible for me taking a huge interest in the subject, including geology and glaciology, and here I must digress for a few lines.

Ingleborough Hall is situated in one of the most interesting geological areas in the country. It lies in the Carboniferous limestone district of North-West England on to which have been deposited many erratics from the last Ice Age. These limestones have developed a peculiar type of topography from the weathering they have undergone. In particular, because of the solubility of calcium carbonate in natural rainwater and the highly developed system of joints in these limestones, this means that the greater part of the water circulation is underground and this led to the formation of fissures and caverns, often on an enormous scale. For instance, on Mount Ingleborough, just above Clapham Beck, can be found Gaping Ghyll which is nearly 400 feet deep, while at the bottom of this hole there is this huge cavernous chamber 480 feet long and 100 feet wide and 100 feet high. This Gaping Ghyll hole was unfenced when we used to visit it but I cannot remember ever descending into the chamber nearly 400 feet down. In any case, I have always had a mild form of claustrophobia and I could never have been a speleologist.

At the same time the absence of surface water has had a peculiar effect on the landscape since it causes limestone to behave as if it were a hard rock and to form conspicuous plateaus bounded by steep escarpments. These were all around us but a good example is provided by Ingleborough itself with its plateau, on which I believe the Romans used to have a fort. The middle of this mountain consists of the thick limestone of the Lower Carboniferous series surmounted by a mass of Yordale rocks, most shales and grits with a capping of millstone grit on the summit. The surface of the plateau has an extraordinary appearance: the limestone is so pure that there is no soil and the whole consists of a bare and corrugated surface of smooth rocks with a huge number of joint fissures in which ferns grow luxuriantly. These fissures are locally called 'grikes'.

It was Commander Holmes who introduced me to all this – the geology, the glaciology and the erratics – and he opened up a whole new world to me, and I am forever grateful to him.

I was a great reader of books when I was at Stone House and I remember reading all of Charles Dickens's books, those of Marryat, Merriman, Henty and so on, but I could never get on with Thackeray and Trollope which I decided to leave for my old age. I am old now, but I still have not read them.

Two more short stories, but both indicative in their own way. Mumps. Towards the end of one term I contracted mumps and I knew I was doomed to stay on after everyone had left for the holidays. I awoke early in the morning. Everybody was getting ready to leave. Soon they went down to have breakfast. They did not come back. And then I heard the buses arrive, laughter and loading, the farewell shouts, and then the buses went down the drive. Silence. I was the only boy left behind. Oh, what misery!

When we left the school to go to our public schools, having taken the Common Entrance Examination, we were required to give a lecture on a subject of our own choice. I still do not know exactly why but my choice was the 1924 British Mount Everest Expedition in which Mallory and Irvine lost their lives.

Nobody knows whether one or both of them reached the summit. A few days before their summit attempt, Colonel Norton had traversed right across the North Face into the Great Couloir and had climbed to a spot only about 750 feet from the summit. He was not using oxygen, but he always insisted afterwards that oxygen, or rather the lack of it, was not the limiting factor: it was the steeply shelving, snow-covered rocks on the far side of the couloir which deterred him. If he had gone on – and he could have gone on to the summit – he knew that he would never get back alive.

It was a fine expedition but for the loss of Mallory and Irvine, but accidents do happen on mountains and mountaineers do really have to be objective about the risks they undertake.

Why did I give this lecture? I really do not know. All I know is that 30 years later I was a member of Chris Bonington's 1975 British Everest South West Face Expedition. This expedition was successful, a new route was climbed, and I do not think it has been climbed again – it is very dangerous. But we too lost a man, Mick Burke, the BBC photographer, somewhere between the summit and the South Summit, and I was carrying letters for him which I never delivered.

8

My War and Post-War Years

At the same time as our house, Woodlands in Kent, was being requisitioned by the Army, the house of my mother's sister, Aunt Eve and her husband Tony, in Tor Gardens, just off Church Street, Kensington, received a direct hit from a German bomb and so, like us, they were homeless. Mercifully there was no one in the house at the time.

Aunt Eve and Uncle Tony moved to a flat in Winchester Court, Vicarage Gate nearby, but the three children, Ursula, Caroline and Peter and their nanny, Margaret, also descended, like us, onto Jedbank. Mummy, of course, stayed south with her husband, now Captain Robin Barnes-Gorell, Coldstream Guards. So there were five first cousins and two nannies living in our grandfather's house.

It was a fine large Victorian house and although I have mentioned it earlier, I will do so again because after all I did spend four years of my life there. It had, of course, no central heating and no gas our side of the baize door. Marigold and I slept in the left-hand side top-floor bedroom and Nanny did too. We went to bed with candles but we had to snuff these out before we went to sleep. As I was frightened by the dark, Nanny occasionally allowed us to have nightlights, which were comparatively safe. The Wises slept in the right-hand-side top-floor bedroom. Below them was our mother's bedroom when she was there, and below us was Aunt Eve's bedroom, when she was there. I cannot remember either my stepfather or Uncle Tony ever coming to Jedbank when we were there. So we never saw them during the war.

The drawing-room was full of Aunt Glentworth's beautiful furniture, whilst the dining-room was very dark and gloomy. The large entrance hall was full of cuirasses and helmets from my grandfather's father, General Duncan James Baillie of the Royal Horse Guards. Towards the rear of the house was the kitchen over which Jeannie the cook presided – or rather did not preside, as we hated her food – but the rear quarters of the house were illuminated by gas, a luxury denied us. My grandfather approved of gas lighting for the servants but not for his the gentleman's side of the house – in other words, according to my mother it was socially incorrect and therefore non-'U'.

Our grandfather, who was in his late seventies, put up with this invasion very well indeed. Most of the time he spent in his large bed-sitting room smoking his pipe and playing Patience, at which he tended to cheat. Occasionally we used to sit with him and try to talk to him although he was not all that communicative – but he always used to say 'Boo' to us when we met on the stairs. He always wore a kilt and walked to church every Sunday.

Behind our little room where we all sat and in the winter tried to keep warm, was the library full of the most wonderful books and here we used to play Murder. Oh dear, oh dear, what happened to all those lovely books? I suppose they were all sold when he died.

I did, however, manage to keep five, the Jules Verne Captain Nemo trilogy and copies of *With the Flag to Pretoria* and *After Pretoria the Guerilla War*. It has to be remembered that two of my grandfather's brothers fought in the South African wars, and both were wounded and both were decorated. They were Hugh and Duncan.

Every Sunday we went to the Episcopalian church at the bottom of our hill which was presided over by Mr Pettifer, although I think he would have preferred to have been called Father Pettifer. He was, I think, a little 'that way inclined' but he always made a great fuss over any children and we all liked him and helped him out at the church fetes and bazaars.

Also once a week we went to the cinema at which all the audience seemed to smoke incessantly. It was a distraction, but there was one film which always has stood out in my memory and that was *Anthony Adverse*. If you can see it, go and see it. It thrilled me.

We had no car so we had to go everywhere on our bicycles, even venturing on occasions all the way up to Carter Bar, on the border between England and Scotland. It was a long, hard but beautiful cycle ride, but coming back was virtually all downhill. In those wartime days there was no traffic on the roads, and there were no predatory men. In fact we were all brought up to believe that nothing really nasty happened in life in spite of the most brutal world war in history being fought out beyond our shores in Europe, North Africa and the Pacific. Our life was placid and serene at Jedbank. However, I have to say that the way we were brought up by our mothers, nannies, aunts and great-aunts did not equip us at all well for the vicissitudes and misfortunes we were all to experience in later life.

From time to time, during the war, we left Jedbank and went to stay at Lochloy with the great-aunts and at Kilravock with great-aunt Ruth Rose and great fun it was too, but that was the limit of our holidays except the odd isolated expedition to Ullapool and, closer to home, North Berwick where we stayed at a guest house with Nanny. Occasionally we went out to tea, providing it was within bicycling distance, but otherwise we were socially marooned, and thus it went on for four long years.

Was all this normal? I really do not know – it seemed normal to us at the time, but writing this makes me feel it was somehow not normal, although nothing in wartime can be normal and, in any case, we did not have any money. Even if we had had a car, which we didn't, we would not have been able to use it due to petrol rationing. What I do think was possibly abnormal now, reflecting on this period in our lives and those of the Wise first cousins, was that there was no male influence whatsoever in our lives – we were entirely brought up by women. There again, that was nobody's fault, it just happened like that, but I do feel it left some sort of mark on all of us. I do not know what this mark really was, but if I had to guess it, it would be lack of self-confidence and, in fact, in virtually all of my school reports this lack of self-confidence seems to be the one constant, not by way of criticism but of concern.

What I do remember particularly were the beautiful, cold, snowy winters. This sort of weather, with global warming, seems to have disappeared now, but in those days we did have freezing winters and we all went skating, tobogganing and snowballing. There was something about the air which was exhilarating – an exhilaration you can only get in the high mountains or the polar regions. There was no noise, no pollution and the best adjective I can use to describe it all is pristine. It was pristine; it was exhilarating – a pointer perhaps to the Antarctic.

One winter was so severe that the railway line south was blocked by snow for a week or so, with the result that I could not return to school. What bliss to have a few more days at home before re-entering that world of cold dormitories, cold beds, cold showers and chilblains.

In 1944 I was coming up to my thirteenth birthday and a decision had to be made as to where I went on to public school: Eton was chosen. But there was one disadvantage to Eton, which was that it was still being bombed and doodlebugged, and later rocketed by the German V2s. However I took my Eton College entrance examination and passed quite respectably.

By this time my stepfather had gone down with tuberculosis and was seriously ill. He had a terrible operation to collapse one of his lungs, but I think that all came a little later. As I never saw him, the dates have got mixed up.

What I do remember in 1944, before presumably he became ill, is that he was Captain on Guard at Buckingham Palace when the Guards Chapel was bombed. He had invited my mother and Marigold to the service because I believe there was always a good lunch afterwards in the Mess. However my mother, who was always fey, had a premonition of a disaster, and declined along with Marigold. Due to this decline Uncle Robin also did not attend the service – he was not in the least bit religious – and then suddenly as he was looking out of the window in Wellington Barracks he saw the doodlebug crash into the Guards Chapel. Hundreds of people were killed and wounded, and so would have been my family, except for Mummy's premonition.

Writing about being fey, she once told me a story about the Tay Bridge disaster when the bridge collapsed and a passing train fell into the water. Apparently what happened was this. An old lady was travelling on that train, and she realised she should not have been on it because she had always been told that it was a sin to travel on the Sabbath. However, she continued, but then at the last station, before the train ran on to the bridge, she also had a premonition of disaster and alighted from the train. If she had gone on she would almost certainly have been drowned.

I left Stone House in the summer of 1944. The war was still on, but the Allies were now fighting on the mainland of Europe;

General Slim was beginning to turn the Burma campaign round and the Americans were forcing back the Japanese in the Pacific. Even the Local Defence Volunteers were less active in the village of Clapham.

It was about this time that my mother and Uncle Robin, who was now an invalid, started renting houses or part-houses or flats. The first was called the Tannery, in which Mr Strauss, a bachelor, lived. Mr Strauss was a writer and a book critic, so his house, which we rented part of, was filled with books and, as it happens, with smoke – he was an inveterate pipe smoker. This house was close to Woodlands in the village of Shorne. It could not have been a very successful ménage – a family occupying a bachelor's house – and it did not last long.

Later we moved to a rented house in Rudgwick in Sussex, and it was here that I remember hearing that the war against the Japanese had come to an end. We were aware that the Americans had dropped those two atomic bombs on Hiroshima and Nagasaki, but to us it was the best thing that could have happened because, firstly, they brought the war to an end and, secondly, they had obviated the need to invade Japan at the cost of millions of casualties.

A little later on, after the war ended, we moved into an upper-floor flat in Argyll Road, off Kensington High Street. I cannot remember very much about this flat, but we were there during the great freeze of 1947 when, to all intents and purposes, coal supplies ran out and thus gas supplies, which we relied upon for heating and cooking. That was the year Marigold came out as a debutante, had her season and was presented at Court. To me Buckingham Palace and the glittering (even in those days) debutante balls were a world away from our rather grotty upper-floor flat in Argyll Road. Marigold will remember it all better than I.

In September 1944, I was taken down by train to Eton for my first half by my mother and Uncle Robin. We found our way to my house, Manor House, where Mr A.H.G. Kerry was the housemaster. Then I was shown into a small narrow long room, overlooking the School Library, with a tip-up bed, a wash basin, a 'burry' (Eton slang for a bureau-desk), an ottoman and a chair and not much else.

I was left behind alone in this dark little room thinking gloomy thoughts, and went to bed. Next morning, when I was woken up by the boys' maid bringing in hot water for the basin, I realised to my consternation that Uncle Robin, who had been to Eton himself, had either failed or forgotten to tell me how to put on a stiff white collar and tie with all the studs. I was mortified, and I don't think I ever forgave my stepfather for this because it meant that on my very first day at Eton I had to go out in the corridor and seek help from an older boy, who could not understand why my stepfather had failed to teach me this most important and necessary technique for a young Eton boy. So on my first day at Eton I had, or so I thought, lost face.

At this stage of my life, I cannot remember much about my life at Eton and my days there. I became a fag; I learned how to light fires for my fag master. We were only allowed two open fires a week due to the shortage of coal and we had no central heating, so it was back again to chilblains. I cooked for my fag master and I was fagged round on errands to other houses. When a senior boy shouted, 'Hey Hammersley here', we all had to run as fast as we could to where he was shouting and the last to arrive was given the fag job.

Early school was at 7.30 and usually some distance away. At about 6.45 the boys' maid came in to wake us up and give us hot water in our basins to wash, and by 7.15 or 7.20 or even sometimes earlier, you had to be dressed and out of the house and on your way to your division. If you were late you were put on the 'Tardy' book, and three of these and you ended up in front of the Lower Master and given a 'Task'. Occasionally, and it did not happen very often, the 'beak', your master, was late and if he was 15 minutes late you were given a 'run', i.e. you could go back to your house.

After early school there was breakfast and then Morning Chapel, first at Lower Chapel and then later on at College Chapel and then divisions all the way through to 'Boys Lunch', quite late at 1.30 p.m. When I became a Director of Barclays, lunch for the Directors and General Managers was always at 1.30 p.m., a practice inherited from Eton days. And so on.

I learnt to shave; I learnt how to grow tomatoes in my window box; I played games reluctantly; I joined the Musical Society and continued with my piano lessons under Thomas Dunhill and then later Dr Ley and, even later, Doctor Watson, the Precentors of Music at Eton. 'Precentor' is an old monastic title.

Occasionally we spent the night in the shelters – the war was not over yet. The doodlebugs still came over, their engines shut off, and down they would come with a huge explosion. At least, with these so-called VIs you knew when they were coming, whereas with the V2 rockets, they just descended without warning and blew everybody and everything to bits when they landed. I remember hearing their colossal explosions when we were in division.

I progressed up the school satisfactorily and successfully. I worked hard and was known as a sap. Occasionally I did 'EWs', extra work, for my friends for which they were very grateful. When I moved to the Upper School I was allowed to buy a wireless of which I was inordinately proud and I used to listen in bed to late-night concerts, both orchestral and jazz.

I became a 'wet-bob' and rowed up the river. I would have liked to have rowed in an Eight but when I went out for Eight trials, I was turned down. What sadness! There is nothing to beat the rhythm and energy of an Eight.

I joined the Eton Corps and went out on field days. We used to disembark out of our lorries at Combermere Barracks in Windsor and then the whole corps marched through Windsor and Eton following a fife band, which was so far away at the front that you could not hear it, or the drum beat, at the rear. The result was that we could not keep step and the resultant shuffle was painful to an extreme. I always thought we were the laughing stock of Windsor and the watching, giggling girls.

Once a half, Mummy came down to see me, usually on the Green Line Bus and we used to go out to lunch in Windsor. Occasionally I went up to see the Dean of Windsor, Albert Baillie – what a comfortable house he had. It was Cousin Albert who later on had the temerity to write a book entitled *My First 80 Years* which could be described slightly better as the 'Memoirs of a Victorian Clerical Snob'. It was Cousin Albert who, once when feeling ill, summoned the doctor, who prescribed him cigars and brandy. And thus he lived on well into his nineties.

I took up smoking secretly, up the chimney of my room. You could not buy cigarettes but we bribed the handymen to get them for us. They were, I remember, Victory V cigarettes. I was never caught, but the boy in the room next to mine was. His name was Noble. He was a heavy smoker and he always left his fag-ends on his chimney ledge. One night there was a great storm and as the Housemaster came into his room to say goodnight, there was a sound of a rushing, mighty wind, and lo and behold the draught created by the opening door propelled hundreds of fag-ends down from the chimney ledge onto the grate in front of the Housemaster. This Pentecostal wind, however, did not affect his career. The Housemaster looked at him, looked at the grate covered in fag-ends, walked out of the room and never said a word.

One day in May 1945, it was VE Day and we all went mad with excitement. The war was over: no more bombs and doodlebugs. We had a pitched battle on the roof of our house with the house next door. We commandeered bicycles and went off into Windsor. We had got so used to the war that its end seemed to fall flat.

Later I went up to London, staying at the Royal Court Hotel in Sloane Square, to watch the great victory parade. How exciting to see all those troops from all over the world marching past with bands playing. An historic day but, in a way, quite frightening as the crowds were immense and a lot of jostling took place. That was the day I recall when I was told that to keep alive in a tight crowded mass of people, you had at all times to keep your arms above your head, which enabled you to 'swim' over the crowd. If your arms were pinioned to your side, you were trapped and quite likely to go down – so keep your arms up at all times.

The winter of 1947 was quite exceptionally cold and parts of the Thames froze over – and we were only allowed two fires a week in our rooms. Spring brought flooding on a huge scale and a fortnight before the half ended, the school had to evacuate. That half we missed trials – the Eton term for examinations.

I took my School Certificate examinations, obtained distinctions in all subjects except maths, and then had to decide what subjects I should take for Higher School Certificate examinations. I cannot remember these now except one – the New Testament in Greek. This was by far the easiest paper I had ever been presented with and therefore my easiest distinction. There was one subject that defeated me and that was logic. Logic became illogical to me.

I made a serious mistake in choosing my Higher School Certificate subjects because I did not realise until too late that the subjects I wanted to read at university, if I did indeed go, were geography and geology – especially oil geology. But I recall that for these subjects you required maths, physics and chemistry, and I did not have them nor, I have to say, was I particularly interested in them.

After I left the Army in 1952, I did try to go to university –

Trinity College, Cambridge, where my father and grandfather had been. But I had no money, my mother did not have any money, and a request to the Tritton trustees in the form of Patrick Tritton, a first cousin of my father, for money to go to university was declined instantly – the first of many actions by that man against me, which in the end so embittered me against him.

Two things happened in 1948. The first was a showing in School Hall of the film *Scott of the Antarctic*, which had been mainly filmed in the British sector of the Antarctic, namely the Falkland Islands Dependencies. The scenery was the most beautiful I had ever seen and I always remember thinking then that that was where I wanted to go.

The second happening in that same year was that I coached my house choir to victory in the house choir competition, and was duly given the coveted cup, which I bore proudly back to M'Tutors, my house. Unfortunately, that was the year that Eton won the Ladies Plate at Henley and the Captain of Boats, David Callender, also happened to be Captain of my House. The Ladies Plate was a huge, beautiful plate, which everyone admired. I say 'unfortunately', because this huge Ladies Plate completely overshadowed my House Choir Cup and I was left feeling very much the poor relation, which I suppose I was – my house, in any case, was not very musical.

By this time I had indeed made a lot of progress with my music and I had now moved on to come under the tutelage of Dr Ley, the Precentor of Music at Eton, always known as Daddy Ley. He was a superb pianist and organist despite having very short legs. He it was who undertook to teach me to play the organ, and I started on the organ in Lower Chapel. It has to be remembered that the touch required for playing the organ and piano is entirely different: for the latter you have to strike the note but, for the former, you have to slide your fingers across the keys, taking immense care not to hit a wrong note, which would reverberate lethally around the Chapel. It also needs to be remembered that you have three to four manuals; you are surrounded by stops whilst in addition you have to play with your feet, using them also to control the level of sound.

In due course I progressed to playing the organ in both College Chapel and School Hall, and it was in the former while playing once for Evensong Vespers that the new Precentor of Music decided to put his hand down my shirt. I recall I was playing the *Nunc Dimittis* and the concentration required to do this while this hand was wandering around under my shirt became almost too much for me to bear.

I also started what was, I think, Eton's first jazz band, although perhaps Humphrey Lyttleton preceded me. We were proscribed almost immediately, but gradually the authorities relented and we were eventually allowed to play in School Hall. I played the piano, Jeremy Sandford the clarinet, Christopher Mayhew the drums and somebody else, whose name I cannot now remember, played the double bass. It was glorious fun. We played entirely traditional jazz.

I am not sure I look back on Eton as my happy schooldays – put it this way, I was not sorry to leave. I still really do not know why this should have been the case. Perhaps there was this unease that everybody and their families seemed to be much richer than we ever were: of course, it would have been different if my father had lived. I was always very conscious of the lack of money, and our comparatively lowly cottage in Suffolk in which we were then living. So perhaps it was a combination of a number of factors in my upbringing: lack of a father and lack of any male influence; lack of money and lack of a settled home for many years; lack of physical prowess in the field; all these perhaps led to a lack of self-confidence and sometimes a feeling of pervasive insecurity.

It was in 1947 that my mother and stepfather, after seven years of homelessness, finally bought a house called The Cottage, near Woodbridge in Suffolk. The reason for living in East Suffolk was that my stepfather, following his operation to collapse a lung, had to all intents and purposes become an invalid. The doctors had told him that for the sake of his one remaining lung, he must live on a dry sandy soil.

The Cottage, Eyke, which was to become their home for the remaining 20 years of their lives was, as its name implies, an old cottage, or perhaps two with a modern addition. It faced directly onto the road, which was becoming increasingly busy as it was used by American Air Force personnel stationed at both Bentwaters and Woodbridge. The back of the house had a glorious view over the Deben Valley, looking across to water meadows, the river itself and the railway line to Lowestoft. The house itself, apart from being very cottagey in the kitchen quarters where the hot water boiler fuelled by coke was positioned, did not have any mains water and this had to be pumped up daily into the house water tank from a well by means of a small generator. There was, of course, no central heating, but some Dimplex electric radiators were purchased. The cost of this house was £5,000 and when it was sold 20 years later to June and Henry Fooks they paid the same price, so there must have been very little or no house price inflation during that period.

Even so, it was felt by the doctors that the winters were too cold for Uncle Robin's one remaining lung, and not so very long afterwards they were advised to spend the winters in the Mediterranean. They chose to go to Palma, Majorca, where they stayed at the hotel Majorica. All this was not as easy as it sounds because, in those days, foreign currency was tightly rationed and all you were allowed to take out was about £50–£100, details of which had to be entered into the back of your passport by the bank from which you bought the currency.

Now clearly Mummy and Uncle Robin could not live for several months in a Majorcan hotel on merely the sum of £50, so a special application had to be filed with the Bank of England explaining the position, requesting on compassionate and health grounds a foreign currency allowance to cover their hotel and other costs. This was usually forthcoming, but all this is indicative of the tightness of the foreign exchange controls exercised by the Bank of England in those days.

At the Cottage, Eyke, Mummy and Uncle Robin did have daily help both in the kitchen and the garden. The cook was Dorothy Nunn, who lived opposite across the road. She was enormously fat and jolly and a very good plain cook. Tanner the gardener bicycled over from a nearby hamlet and kept the garden in good order.

Uncle Robin, shortly after acquiring the house, decided he would set himself up as a chicken farmer, so he acquired some chickens, but somehow it all went wrong. There were quite a large number of so-called gentlemen farmers around us in those days – most of them had been in the armed forces during the war, did not want a sedentary office job, so used their gratuities to buy a small farm. The house was often the main attraction rather than the farm. Most of them were unsuccessful and later had to sell up.

There were two landed families nearby, the Sheepshanks and the

87

Bunburys, and both seemed to own large areas of land. The then Sir Charles Bunbury allowed me to shoot rabbits on his land, but his gamekeeper made life difficult for me and in the end I desisted. In any case, for some reason I disliked having to go to Sir Charles to ask him for permission to shoot. It would, of course, have been quite normal for me to be invited to shoot at Lyons Hall, but this never happened even though I was the heir to the estate. Many years later Geoffrey Ratcliff, the main tenant farmer of the Lyons Hall Estate and to whom the shooting rights had been rented out, invited me once a year to shoot on what I regarded as my own land. In any case, once again, I felt uncomfortable that I was put into the position of having to be invited to shoot by a tenant. It therefore gave me enormous pleasure when my Aunt Dore, the life tenant of the estate, died and I was able to take the shoot in hand and build it up into a very creditable family shoot once again, as it had been before the war.

The other family were the Sheepshanks, Robin and Lilius, who lived at The Rookery nearby. They were enormously kind to us and to Mummy and Uncle Robin and, along with June and Henry Fooks, looked after them when they were both dying in 1966 and 1967. We, that is to say Marigold and myself, could not be more grateful to them.

Uncle Robin, who was unable to work and could well have been unwilling to work in any case, led a curious life. He had just a sufficiency of money to get by, which was greatly assisted by his total disability pension. He was always given breakfast in bed, where he read the newspapers; he then shaved with an old cut-throat razor and emerged at around 11 a.m. pottering around the car and the garden for the next hour. He then walked along the road to the Elephant and Castle pub which was presided over by Les Wallace, who also provided a taxi service for us. Here he drank gin until nearly 2 p.m. when he returned for lunch, which was always far too late for us and drove Nanny almost mad. After lunch he went to sleep in his study until the evening, when he either returned to the pub or drank gin again, all the time smoking endless cigarettes, inhaling into his one good lung. All this made dinner once again very late. He usually went to bed near to midnight.

In some curious way, which I never really understood, my mother and Uncle Robin were very fond of each other and made each other happy, despite the terrible illnesses they endured. I think they were probably happiest in Majorca, where there were a number of expatriates and where they had parties and fun.

Uncle Robin had contracted tuberculosis in 1944, as I have mentioned. Mummy had her first brush with breast cancer in 1947. She was unwilling, however, to have a mastectomy and underwent radiotherapy treatment. From then on until' 1961, the disease was either in remission or had left her, but in that year it reappeared.

But I am running too far ahead and I must now go back to my last days at Eton. These were very relaxed: trials were over, Higher School Certificate had been taken without difficulty. We gave our friends leaving presents in the form of photographs of ourselves and we had our last meeting with the Headmaster, Claude Aurelius Elliott, who gave us a lesson on the perils facing young men in the world which ended with the long-anticipated admonition 'not to fornicate in Old Etonian braces'.

Before I left I had made two arrangements: the first was to apply to join the British Schools Exploring Society's Expedition to Arctic Norway, leaving that summer of 1949. I was accepted. The second was to write to my old Stone House Headmaster, J.L. Richardson, and ask him if I could teach for the Michaelmas term before being called up by the Army for my National Service. JLR accepted me and told me that my salary for the three-month term would be £50, but this would include board and lodging. So that was my salary, £4 per week – less now than the minimum hourly wage rate.

9

My First Expedition

The British Schools Exploring Society had been founded by Surgeon Commander Murray Levick who had taken part in Scott's last expedition, and so when the members of the expedition assembled at King's Cross Station on 3rd August with all their Arctic equipment, we were privileged as he spoke to each of us in turn. I was later to be elected as a member of the Antarctic Club, and I had the great good fortune to meet, at our annual dinners in London, many of the survivors from what was later to be called 'the heroic age' of expeditions – a wonderful link with the past.

The leaders of the expedition were all Army officers, with the exception of the two medical officers. The leader was Major Spooner of the Parachute Regiment with Captain Gavin Murray of the Dragoon Guards as the second in command. There were two Captains from the Royal Engineers as Survey Officers, a Major from the Royal Signals who was Wireless Officer, and a Captain of the Royal Tank Regiment and the Royal Artillery.

At Newcastle we embarked on the MS *Venus*, always known as 'the vomiting *Venus*', and for that crossing to Bergen she certainly lived up to her reputation. We arrived very much overdue after what became known as one of the worst crossings in recent times.

We spent three days in Bergen awaiting a boat to take us up the coast to Bodo. We had three days of absolutely filthy weather in Bergen. During this time we sorted ourselves out in groups – each group had a leader. We paid a visit to King Haakon's summer residence and we also went out on a launch trip through the nearby fjords. During this trip we had a very close view of the enormous U-boat pens built by the Germans during the war, their network of land-based torpedo batteries sighted across the harbour mouth and the huge concrete mooring blocks which held the German battleship *Bismarck* so close to the cliffs that camouflaging net could be draped over her from the land. What a truly magnificent ship she was.

In due course we embarked in an ancient coal-burning coastal steamer called the *Kong Harald* and left port at one o'clock in the morning. The voyage to Bodo took two and a half days. Bodo had been very extensively damaged by the Germans during the war but arrangements had been made for us to eat here before leaving for Finneid through some wonderfully mountainous country. At Finneid we picked up a huge barge and a tug which took us through a deep inland fjord to Skjonsta where we found a small railway line which served the copper mines at Sulitjelma.

The next day we got to a lake called Risvann where our camp had been prepared by the advance party. All the tents were pitched, the equipment and camp stores, food supplies and medical stores were all stacked and ready for us, all 8 tons of them.

This base camp was sited on the banks of the Douroelna River, flowing from Lake Douro at the foot of Mt Nord Saulo to the east into Lake Risvnann. To the east lay three main waterways of Lake Peskejaure, Lake Mavasjaure and Lake Ikisjaure. To the north lay the Sulitjelma mountain range, mainly glacierised at that time, and for me it was enormously exciting to be in a land of glaciers and mountains. Generally the terrain was scrubby birch at the lower levels but very soon you rose above this to much more extensive tundra country with increasing amounts of old and sometimes new snow. Even further up, the terrain was heavily glaciated and became much more interesting. The first night we were at base camp, the temperature dropped to –6°F.

As I have said earlier, we divided up into groups and we each carried out some long extensive journeys up to ten days at a time. Everything on these march journeys had to be carried: tents, food, clothing, sleeping bags and cooking utensils, etcetera, with loads varying in weight of up to 70 lbs – which was, interestingly enough, the average weight we carried when we were fighting in the jungle in Malaya.

Generally the climbing and marching was not difficult, except on steep snow slopes. It was, of course, on the other hand extremely tiring and at the end of each day we ached with pain until we got used to it.

One of the doctors was Doctor J.C. Hawksley who must have been a most eminent man as he had been awarded the CBE and was also a fellow of the Royal College of Physicians. He was, in a way, very similar to Commander Holmes. He undertook with me the glaciological survey work, whilst I carried out with him the geological survey work. We worked extremely well together and I greatly admired him. He it was who used to say, 'Interesting glacial scratches', as we wandered around with our geological hammers.

Generally the areas we were working in had surface features moulded by Pleistocene glaciation, the ground being of boulder clay, with erratics scattered indiscriminately. There were many moraines and drumlins. Most of the erratics were of igneous rock. The glaciers on the south-eastern side of the Sulitjelma massif were stationary or receding. Overall our impression was that of a recent ice-cap, gradually receding to a stage of valley glaciation. The snowline was at about 2,000 feet, just 200 feet above the altitude of our base camp.

The geological topography of the area we surveyed results from the great period of diastrophism, mountain-building and igneous activity during the Old Red Sandstone Age. The whole area had been hugely altered by dynamic metamorphism and igneous intrusions on a large scale and had subsequently been completely glaciated during the Pleistocene period as mentioned above.

However the real interest in the area is its history of glaciation and the subsequent retreat of the ice which, as it happens, is not yet fully complete, or was not when I was there, as witness the ice-cap to the north of Sulitjelma. The journey to Sulitjelma from Bodo revealed many examples of glacial action, hanging valleys, truncated spurs, cirques, roche moutonnees, striations etcetera. It was a good introduction to the Antarctic and the Himalayas.

We had excellent food in the march journeys, mainly consisting of pemmican (60 per cent dried powdered beef and 40 per cent fat) and biscuits, cheese, margarine, sugar, dried peas, chocolate, oatmeal, raisins and tea. All this amounted to just short of 4,000 calories on the march journeys. In base camp it was, of course, different – food was more plentiful and supplemented by some very excellent rainbow trout which abounded in the lakes and rivers. Before we left, bilberries were available in profusion and they were delicious.

The real curse of the expedition was the mosquitoes at the lower levels of base camp. Once you got to a higher level they fell away and so, in a way, it was much more comfortable to be away from this camp and in the mountains. We tried every remedy, from cream to wearing mosquito nets over our faces, but as everybody knows, mosquito nets are hell to work with. I cannot remember if we smoked on this expedition – we probably did; apart from anything else, Dr Hawksley was an inveterate pipe smoker. Cigarettes I have always found invaluable in deterring mosquitoes and midges.

In the middle of September we returned to Sulitjelma where we enjoyed the luxury of a hot bath. Then we moved on to Bodo where once again we embarked on the old coal-burner *Kong Harald*. This time the voyage south was not uneventful. In a thick fog, but mercifully in a flat calm, the ship ran onto the rocks not far from the entrance to Trondheim fjord. I was sitting in a cabin which I shared with three others and I remember looking out of the porthole and instead of seeing fog I suddenly saw water, which brought me up on deck very sharply. What had happened was that the crew were drunk, and seemed to be hopeless at dealing with the position. There were, of course, ugly rumours about the likelihood of the boat breaking its back if the wind and sea got up. But it did not, and in the end kedge anchors were swung astern and we managed to pull ourselves off the rocks. There was a great sigh of relief all round, but it did mean that I had to send a telegram to JLR at Stone House stating that, due to being shipwrecked off the Norwegian coast, I would be arriving at the school days late. I was a hero when I eventually arrived.

So ended the expedition. What had we achieved, and what had I personally achieved? We had carried out a topographical survey of an area of about 100 square miles. We had carried out three more surveys – geological, glaciological and botanical – and had maintained a continuous series of meteorological observations. We had trekked long distances with heavy packs and had associated ourselves with young men drawn from all walks of life, most of whom I never saw again; the exception in my case was John Chapple, who became Chief of the Defence Staff.

But for me it was all that and more. I had crossed the Arctic Circle – not a great feat admittedly but I now had a certificate to that effect. I had proved myself in the field, so to speak, to my own satisfaction, although I had not been chosen for the Long March. But for the first time since my geological glaciological scrambles around Ingleborough with Commander Holmes, I had discovered what I wanted. That was the thrill, the excitement and exhilaration of climbing in those wonderful snowfields in the mountains to the south of Lake Balvatnet, with all around those dark, almost menacing peaks with the clouds scudding along and the wind soaring over the frozen lake of the col. And then in the evening pitching the tent, weighing down the skirting with rocks and snow, crawling inside, lighting the Primus stove, sipping a mug of piping hot pemmican hoosh, and then lying snug and warm in one's sleeping bag, listening to the wind flying along, the clack, clack of the tent flaps, and sometimes the howl of a lone wolf far away. All this created a very powerful impression on me and I resolved to undertake another expedition to the frozen wastes of the polar regions.

I spent three months as an assistant master at Stone House School and for these three months I was paid the princely sum of £50, although this included board and lodging as I have mentioned before. By and large the masters were almost the same as when I had left five years ago. I cannot now remember what I taught but it was probably classics, English and geography. Mercifully, in those days, you had the ultimate sanction of the cane to enforce discipline but, generally, I was able to do this without such a relatively extreme sanction. My class were aged ten and eleven, a fairly rough lot and you had to be on top of them all the time – you could not show any sign of weakness.

The one thing I remember about my teaching days, apart from the dreadful lack of money, was that at the end of each day I usually felt drained, and most teachers will find this familiar. From the moment you enter the school, whether it be in the class, at mealtimes, supervising games in the afternoon, setting papers, marking them and correcting them, usually in the evening, you have continually to give out of yourself without really expecting much in return. Natural authority helps, but I am not sure at my age then, 17, I carried much of that. I was not much older, for instance, than the older boys – only four to five years. I recollect I enjoyed my three months but, of course, I was only marking time before I joined the Army and this I did on Friday, 13th January 1950 – an unlucky combination.

10

My Early Army Days

In those days you were conscripted for National Service: the Navy, the Army or the Air Force or even, I believe the coal mines. Before you joined up you had to establish where you were going and in my case my stepfather, who had had a wartime commission in the Coldstream Guards, arranged for me to join that regiment. In those days there was something called the Brigade Squad. This squad was made up of young men who had been at public school and were thought as having potential for being considered for a commission as a Guards officer. Basic training at Caterham Barracks for this Brigade Squad was considered to be the toughest in the Army and this basic training went on for about four months with a break at Pirbright where there were extensive firing ranges. During that time you had to undergo what was called a WOSB, that is to say a War Office Selection Board, which ultimately determined whether you were officer material and could therefore go on to an Officer Cadet Training School for another period of around four months at the end of which you were hopefully commissioned.

So on Friday, 13th January 1950, I took the train from Woodbridge in Suffolk to Liverpool Street, crossed over to Waterloo, and there took the suburban train to Caterham. Carrying my small suitcase I walked up to the guard room where the Guardsmen sniggered and sneered at me and, shortly afterwards, having formally reported for duty, I was led across to my barrack room, which I would share with 20 others. The barracks themselves looked like some grim Victorian institution with high windows; there was a washroom and toilets, and a fireplace at one end of the room.

The first day we were provided with our uniforms and boots and equipment, including blankets, pillows and three biscuits –

three individual mattresses underneath which we placed our trousers every night for pressing.

We were assigned to a trained soldier – in our case Guardsman Ross, a short, brutal man who liked his drink. We were also assigned to a Sergeant Withers – another bully, but whom I eventually liked.

The same day we had our hair cut off: short back and sides, the shortest in my life, and it greatly embarrassed me when I had to give away my sister Marigold in marriage in March 1950, dressed in Guardsman's uniform and with virtually no hair.

The Major in command of the Brigade Squad was Major White, an officer in the Irish Guards, who had red hair and a thick luxuriant moustache. Like all Guards officers and men, his hat was pulled down very low over his face so that it was almost impossible to see his cold blue eyes. He was a remote man, and he intended it that way.

It was, of course, a very alien world to us, and to me it was some sort of Kafkaesque nightmare. Somehow we survived, and it is true to say that in surviving we became soldiers. We were drilled mercilessly, often at the double; we were inspected continuously; we were shouted at and instructed; we cleaned and polished our boots so that we could see our faces in them. We also had to clean the soles of our boots; we cleaned and polished all our brass including our cap badge; we blancoed all our webbing; and every morning we had to lay out for inspection our biscuits, blankets, sheets, pillows, our uniform and shaving material – everything, in fact, we were not wearing. Everything had to be laid out meticulously in the correct position and order on our beds. When the officer and Sergeant came round for the inspection, we had to stand rigidly at attention by our beds until the inspection was over. If anything was out of order you were put on a 'charge', and in fact you were put on a charge for any so-called misdemeanour, imaginary or otherwise.

A 'charge' necessitated you being marched up at the double by the Sergeant to Major White in front of whom you stood rigidly to attention. The Sergeant read out your 'offence', the Major listened and then asked if you had anything to say in your defence – to which the answer was always 'No' – and then you were sentenced to some fatigue.

I recall that, in the end, the drilling and the marching became enjoyable, especially when the military band was on parade. We marched up and down, we presented arms, we were inspected yet again, and our 303 rifles were peered at for any sign of dirt. To this day I have always enjoyed marching along with the military or pipe band leading us: keeping step, swinging our arms, and heeling and toeing our boots and feeling the rhythm and beat of the band.

For all this we were paid 27s 6d a week, less breakages, and this we received at pay parade.

On Saturday evenings there was usually a dance in the Drill Hall. Lots of girls came up from the town. They sat on one side of the hall and we sat on the other. When the band started up you left your seat and went over to the other side of the hall and invited a girl to dance with you. When the band stopped, which it did every three minutes, you and the girl returned to your respective side of the hall and waited for the band to start up again. We in the Brigade Squad, or at least most of us, felt embarrassed by these brief meetings with the girls from the town – a social gulf seemed to separate us and I always felt awkward and did not really enjoy these dances, although they were a pleasant break from the cold monasticism of the barrack room.

One day we were given an aptitude test to test our mechanical abilities. This consisted of being given a bicycle pump, and we were told to take it to bits and put it together again. When I had completed this task, I found I had two pieces left over which seemed surplus to requirements, so I put them in my pocket. I was never found out and I was passed A1 for mechanical ability – something I have never possessed.

Towards the middle of our time at Caterham, we were sent off to a War Office Selection Board which, over a two-day period, assessed whether we were worthy or not to go on to Officer Cadet School. I cannot now remember the tests we underwent, although one consisted of getting one's men across a river with ropes and logs. My attempt to do this was not successful so I asked my sergeant to carry on with the exercise. This was considered as having the right sort of initiative. At the final interview I was able to talk about my leadership of one of the survey parties on the British Schools Exploring Society Expedition to Arctic Norway. This got me through, and I was now on track to go to Eaton Hall Officer Cadet School in Cheshire.

However, before I left Caterham, I was asked by Major White

to undergo an eyesight test, which consisted of a number of Guardsmen of differing Guards regiments marching up and down in front of me. I was asked to say to which regiments they belonged, and I was not able to see sufficiently well to do this. The result was that I was told I could not get a commission in a Guards regiment because there was a ruling that you could not wear spectacles under a bearskin. I am not sure that this was totally true, but this is what I was told. So I now had to find another regiment to join – provided, of course, that I received a commission. Here Mummy came to my rescue. She wrote to the Colonel of the Seaforth Highlanders requesting him to accept me in view of her family's connection with the regiment. He agreed. I was, of course, disappointed not to be destined to become a Guards officer, which I probably could not afford anyway, having no private income but, as things turned out in the end, I was hugely glad I joined the Seaforth Highlanders as they were on active service in the Far East. If I had remained with the Guards, all I probably would have done would have been involved with ceremonial duties in London. That is not something I would have enjoyed.

And now one short final incident before leaving Caterham. One night Trained Soldier Ross came back drunk to our barrack room. His bed was adjacent to the bed belonging to Trooper the Earl of Bective. For some reason Ross, in his drunkenness, decided to pick a fight with the Earl, who decided he had no alternative but to fight back. It was a most unpleasant, ugly scene and soon we all had to join in to separate them. Neither the Earl nor the Trained Soldier was the victor and I do not know whether the Trained Soldier apologised or not – he should have done.

So the next stage in my life was a four-month training period at the Eaton Hall Officer Cadet School, at the end of which I would hopefully be commissioned into the 1st Battalion Seaforth Highlanders.

Eaton Hall was a huge gothic mansion near Chester owned by the Duke of Westminster. It has now been pulled down – sadly. I loved its magnificence and, in particular, I loved the private chapel and its organ adjacent to the huge square stable yard – shades of *Brideshead Revisited*. This still remains.

Our first barrack room was a Nissen hut, among many others, which lay alongside the main driveway to the Hall. Here we settled down before being 'promoted' to the rooms above the stables.

At Eaton Hall we were instructed in how to be officers, not guardsmen. In many ways it was quite enjoyable compared to the horrors of Caterham. At this distance I am afraid I cannot remember all the exercises we carried out – sometimes called TEWTS – Tactical Exercise Without Troops – but it was very efficient, interesting and enjoyable.

Two exercises do stand out in my memory. The first was called Operation Marathon. We were required to spend 48 hours in the open on a remote hill in Wales, pretending we were on the front line, digging trenches, camping out, eating from a field kitchen. In a way it was not far from the real thing – although we did not use live ammunition. We were wet and weary by the time we returned.

The second was on Dartmoor. We went to a place near Okehampton for a week which was used as a battle school with, in this case, live ammunition being used over our heads. The battle school was a particularly dreary place and the weather for that week was foul, wet and cloudy. There was an unpleasant episode leading up to the night exercise which I will tell you about. We were being trained in throwing live grenades. You queued in a trench leading to the throwing pit, you then stood there alone and threw your grenade, which then exploded. Unfortunately, as I neared the throwing pit – that is to say, I was the next man to throw – the officer cadet in front of me got his throw wrong. He took the pin out of the grenade, threw it, but released it too early, with the result that the grenade, instead of being thrown forward went straight up in the air and landed back in the throwing pit. I cannot remember whether the detonator was four or seven seconds, but both he and myself had to move as quickly as we could away from the throwing pit and throw ourselves flat on the ground, while the grenade blew up with a devastating explosion in the confines of the pit – a dangerous episode.

Now going back to the night exercise on the boggy wet moors of Dartmoor. Here I was ordered to command the company which was to undertake the night attack. This meant an all-night march in the rain across the moor by some 90 men – that is, three platoons – and I was responsible both as Company Commander and Navigating Officer to get the men across the moor so that they would be in exactly the right position to mount an attack at first light against the 'enemy'.

The march took several hours in pitch darkness and, amazingly enough, nobody got lost or sank into a bog without trace, and we arrived on the start line in good order at first light to start the attack. I say it myself – it was a very creditable performance.

When I returned to Eaton Hall, I received an instruction to see the Commanding Officer – one always dreaded these occasions. I marched up to him, saluted, and I was put at ease. He then told me he was so impressed with my leadership of the successful night attack that he was promoting me to be an under-officer, which entitled me, apart from anything else, to wear appropriate emblazons on my uniform. I was immensely chuffed, but less than chuffed when he took a look at my trousers, which had not been properly pressed between those bloody biscuits, and said that he was minded to put me on a charge for being improperly dressed. He did not, but it was a very uncomfortable moment and for a time took away the joy of my promotion.

Eventually we were, or at least most of us were, commissioned as second lieutenants, and we duly had a passing out parade with the military band playing happily away. It was a good day and the way was now forward for me to join my regiment, the Seaforth Highlanders, as Second Lieutenant A.G. Tritton. I had 'made' it. I was now a fully fledged second lieutenant in the Seaforth Highlanders. But first of all, like my great-uncle Fred in 1859, I had to buy my own uniform. For this I repaired to the regimental tailors, Meyer & Mortimer in Sackville Street off Piccadilly in London.

Here I ordered my kilt and trews, which I still wear from time to time 55 years later, my officer's coat, my belt, regimental stockings, sporran, my Glengarry and TOS (tam-o'-shanter). It was all quite expensive but worth every penny and my coat had those wonderful single pips on each shoulder signifying that I was a Second Lieutenant, and I was only 18. I was asked whether I was going to buy a claymore as that was on the list, but I told the tailor I could not afford it and, indeed, whenever I was on a ceremonial parade or officer on duty when they were obligatory, I was always able to borrow one.

Before learning the history of what I am proud to call my regiment, I must tell you the origin of the regimental badge. This is a stag's Head (*cabar feidh*) with the motto 'Cuidich'n Righ' (Save the King). When King Alexander III was hunting in Kintail with a large retinue of Highland chiefs, he came up with the hounds as they pulled down an immense royal stag. The King, drawing his 'skean dhu' (I had to buy one at Meyer & Mortimer), ran up just as the stag shook off the hounds, and turning on the King hurled him to the ground with its antlers. The Chief of the Mackenzies shouted 'Cuidich'n Righ' and, grasping the stag by its antlers, killed it with his hunting spear and thus saved the King's life. Ever since, the stag's head and antlers have been the cognisance of the Clan Mackenzie and thus the Seaforth Highlanders. The old battle cry of the regiment was and still is 'Cabar Feidh gu Brath' (the Stag's Head for Ever), and always at the annual dinner of the Cuidich'n Righ Club – our regimental club and the oldest in the British Army – the chairman of the dinner speaks these words out with the regimental piper standing by his side – an emotional occasion.

And lastly, why the elephant on our sporran? I will tell you. For this we now go to India in the year 1803. The then Governor-General in Calcutta was the Earl of Mornington, whose deliberate policy was to bring the whole of India under the control of the Honourable East India Company. The Directors of the Company in London were very averse to war and Mornington continued to assure them that war was very improbable. However, despite these assurances, he began issuing orders for the assembly of the Bengal Army against Sindhia.

Everything had been carefully thought out: the plan of campaign, the organisation and disposition of the armies, the military and political objectives to be secured, and also the terms to be imposed on a defeated army. Castlereagh described the whole campaign as 'a chef d'oeuvre of military energy, foresight and science'. Of all the wars fought by the British in India, this was the most uniformly successful.

The major operation took place in the Deccan under Arthur Wellesley, the brother of the Governor-General and later on to be the Duke of Wellington. The operation was against the combined armies of Sindhia and the Raja of Berar. General Lake was in northern India fighting forces of Sindhia's army, who were trained and commanded by the French. Both generals Wellesley and Lake were invested with full political and military powers.

Arthur Wellesley's brilliant five-month campaign, which included the Battle of Assaye, was reckoned by him the finest victory of all his career including Waterloo. Under his direct command he had units of the Madras Army, numbering at full strength 11,000 men of whom 1,600 were British and some 5,000 Mysore and Maratha horse. A contingent of about 9,000 men from Hyderabad under Colonel Stevenson consisting of the Nizam's subsidiary force was also under Wellesley's command but it mainly operated separately.

Having captured the fortress of Ahmadnagar, he spent some time heading off an attempt by Sindhia and the Raja of Berar to strike south into the Nizam's territory. They were deflected and turned north. On 22nd September Wellesley and Stevenson separated to avoid the delay of passing all their forces through a single defile. They planned to reunite on 24th September to make a joint attack on the Marathas but on the 23rd, after a night march of 18 miles, the Maratha armies were spotted only 6 miles distant and seemed about to move off. Fearing that they might escape, Wellesley decided to attack without waiting for Stevenson to join him. Leaving his baggage behind, with only a single battalion of sepoys to guard it, he marched forward with the rest of his troops, including the 78th Regiment, the Seaforth Highlanders and found the Maratha Army, not as he had hoped, already on the move, so that he could attack them in the disorder of march but drawn up in a strong position with the River Kaitna in their front and its tributary the Juah a short distance behind.

Wellesley was outnumbered six to one: 30,000 Mahratta horses in one magnificent mass were waiting for him on his left; a dense array of infantry, dressed armed and accoutred like British sepoys, occupied the centre and left, which was resting on the village of Assaye. In all there were 17 battalions of Mahrattan infantry, formerly commanded by British officers but now commanded by French officers, numbering some 10,000 men in an admirable state of discipline. And in front of them there were 100 cannons with the gunners standing ready beside their field pieces – again extremely well trained by the British, and their fire was both as quick and well directed as that of the British artillery.

Against this force of some 40,000, Wellesley had about 5,000 men of whom 1,500 were Europeans, including artillery, with 26 field pieces, of which only 12 were used during the action – the rest being guns of the cavalry and the battalions of the second line, which could not be used.

Without hesitation he moved to attack their left, and having found an unguarded ford of the Kaitna river, he managed to get most of his infantry across, although they were under constant and direct fire from the enemy's artillery. Once across they formed up across the neck of the land between the Kaitna and Juah rivers, with the first line now strengthened by artillery, with the British rear now resting on the village of Assaye and with the Peishwa's and Mysore cavalry remaining south of the Kaitna and protecting the British left flank.

The British first line consisted of The Picquets, four 12-pounders, the 1st Battalion of both the 8th and 10th Native Infantry and the Seaforth Highlanders (the 78th). Behind them were the 74th Highlanders and two battalions of Native Infantry – the second line. The third line comprised three Native Cavalry regiments and the 19th Light Dragoons.

Once in position they were only 500 yards away from their enemy. The order was given to advance and after a false start due to the Picquets not moving forward as directed, they charged at about 150 yards distance, where upon the French officers jumped onto their horses and disappeared. So the enemy's first line was defeated, and now it was the turn of the second line. Although shelled from the front, right, and now their rear, and with the enemy cavalry threatening their flank, the British ceased fire and not a word was heard or a shot fired until Wellesley gave the order to attack the second line with bayonets. This second attack was successful and victory was now assured.

At 4.30 p.m. it was all over. Wellesley had two horses killed under him and for some time the issue had been very much in doubt 'I can assure you,' he wrote, 'that the fire was so heavy that at one time I much doubted whether I could prevail upon the troops to advance and all agree that the battle was the fiercest that I have ever seen in India. Our troops behaved admirably and the Sepoys astonished me.'

As a footnote, Wellesley's brigadier major in the battle was Colin Campbell, a Seaforth, and he like Wellesley had two horses shot under him and was badly wounded. He served on Wellesley's (now the Duke of Wellington) staff throughout the Peninsular Campaign and was awarded the Gold Cross with six clasps. He took part in the Battle of Waterloo and later became General Sir Colin Campbell KCB and Governor and Commander-in-Chief of Ceylon. To cap all this he was a Knight of the Order of Maria Theresa of Austria, St George of Russia, Maximilian Joseph of Bavaria and the Tower and Sword of Portugal. He died in his bed 44 years after the Battle of Assaye. How's that for a career!

The Seaforth Highlanders carved a great name for themselves by their very gallant conduct in the battle, and to mark this King George III ordered that the regiment should bear on its colours an elephant and the name 'Assaye'. So you now know why I wore an elephant on my sporran.

But there is one more campaign, among innumerable others, which I should like to tell you about. In 1857 war was declared by the British on Persia and in this war the regiment had the good fortune to serve under Havelock and Outram, whose names used to resound across British India. From both these men the regiment earned high praise and 'Persia' and 'Kooshab' were added to the regiment's colours.

They then moved on to Bombay in May 1857, where they received the news of the outbreak of what was to be called the Indian Mutiny. Under Havelock again, they took part in a series of brilliant engagements against the mutineers, including the historic Relief of Lucknow, earning for themselves the fitting distinction, not the Seaforths of India, but 'the Saviours of India'. After Cawnpore they were specially complimented by Havelock, who said that in the whole of his long career as a soldier he had never seen troops behave so well under fire as the 78th Highlanders.

Sir James Outram addressed the regiment in January 1858, which he subsequently put in writing, lest the regiment attribute what he said as being in the excitement of the moment:

Your exemplary conduct, 78th, in every respect throughout the last most eventful year, I can truly say and I do most emphatically declare has never been surpassed by any troops of any nation in any age, whether for indomitable valour in the field, or steady discipline in the camp, under an amount of fighting and privation such as British troops have seldom or ever heretofore been exposed to. The cheerfulness with which you have gone through all this has excited my admiration as much as the undaunted pluck with which you always close with the enemy, whenever you can get at him, no matter what the odds are against you or what the advantages of his position.

So spoke the famous Sir James Outram.

I wondered whether I would be able to live up to all this. I had my doubts, but I did not express them and in any case, who would I express them to? Perhaps Mummy or Nanny – but I did not. Later on I will tell what it felt like to go into action against the enemy for the first time.

I now had to report to the Regimental Depot at Fort George and this I did in the early autumn of 1950. Fort George was planned as an impregnable bastion for King George III's army. There are huge ranges of buildings on a monumental scale to accommodate the erstwhile Governor and his officers, an artillery regiment and two infantry battalions – some 2,000 men all told. There were barrack blocks, powder magazines, ordnance stores, a bakehouse, a brewhouse, a chapel and all sorts of provision stores.

When I arrived there in 1950 it had not yet been restored – this was carried out in the 1990s – and although it did stand in this most beautiful of all positions, it was run down as well as being bleak, windy and cold. If you faced north from the principal gate and guardroom across the main square to the left, you espied the old artillery block and Governor's House, and this was where the Officers' Mess was situated.

I have to say I had rather a slow and somewhat perfunctory introduction to the Officers' Mess – nobody took any notice of me. But at least I was there, I had my room, and my short-term duties were explained to me. This consisted of training recruits until the regiment and the War Office decided what to do with them and me. I thoroughly enjoyed training the recruits – I had only just ceased being trained myself. The highlights were when I route-marched my recruits up to my grandmother's Kilravock Castle, a round trip of 10 miles, where we were welcomed with tea and scones. I became quite popular.

Of course, it was not to last and in truth I did not want it to last – I wanted to join the battalion then fighting in Malaya against the Communist Chinese, although somehow I doubted whether I would be drafted. But I was and shortly afterwards I was sent on embarkation leave and left the fort.

I have always thought of the expression 'embarkation leave' as being somewhat sinister. There is some sort of implication that you are to embark for somewhere, quite often very far away, but that you might well not return, as indeed quite a few of us did not. So the expression does have the connotation of your last leave at home before you embark for active service overseas from which the return is uncertain.

Before I joined my troopship I was given a huge long list of items to buy out of my own pocket which I would need in both the jungle and the tropics. I bought a tin trunk which could be sealed against ants, I had all my tropical uniform made for me. I even bought a canvas washing bowl and a small canvas seat, but the most important item I bought was a very lightweight collapsible camp bed which I could carry below or above my pack in the jungle. This was without doubt one of my best buys because it meant that when I was fighting on patrol in the jungle, at night under my basha (shelter) I could sleep comfortably raised about 6 inches off the ground, with my mosquito net nicely tucked round me and, of paramount importance, I would not be overrun by ants, insects, snakes, all those horrible creepy-crawlies which can make jungle camping a nightmare.

So now I had two uniforms, one for a temperate climate and one for the tropics, although I had only one kilt – there were no lightweight kilts. I was given a small 38 revolver and six rounds of ammunition. I was also asked to make a will in my Army Book. None of us knew what to do; none of us had any money, so we asked an officer, recently returned from overseas, what we should do. He replied, 'All to Mum', so that is what we wrote and signed.

In early October 1950 I woke up at The Cottage, Eyke, and realised this was my last day at home for some time and could conceivably be the last time ever – I was both apprehensive and excited. I dressed up in my uniform, packed my last bits and pieces and I was driven to Woodbridge Station with Nanny; Mummy was far too upset to go with me. The old steam train came in and off we left for Liverpool Street Station and took a taxi to Waterloo. As the train left Waterloo Station, Nanny and I, both with tears in our eyes, waved at each other until we could see each other no longer.

At Southampton I took a taxi to the dock where the British India ship, the *Dilwara*, was moored along the quayside. There were huge numbers of troops everywhere, many of them with relatives on the dock, but gradually everything sorted itself out and we prepared to sail. The band played away, followed by the pipes and drums, 'Will ye no come back again?' And some of us did not come back again. Streamers were strung from the ship's decks to the shore. The ship sounded its siren, the mooring ropes were loosened and gradually we began to edge away from the dock. The waving and shouting never stopped as the streamers tore apart and fell into the sea, and the sound of the pipes and drums got fainter and fainter. The ship gathered speed and soon we were in the grey murkiness of the English Channel and on our way to Singapore, Malaya and Pusan in Korea.

But what was going on in Malaya that required my presence there in 1950? I will tell you and I hope you will be patient with me as it does require some background information.

11

Malaya, Troopship and Arrival

The Malayan Peninsula is, as we all know, attached to the mainland of South-East Asia by a 500-mile-long isthmus which also comprises southern Burma (Myanmar) and southern Siam (Thailand). Geographically it consists of parallel mountain ranges with peaks rising to just over 7,000 feet which, as they approach the sea, lessen in height to foothills that in the west merge into shallow estuaries and mangrove swamps, and in the east, where I was for a time, to a very different coastline of rocky headlands, sandy beaches and casuarinas trees. When I was there – it has changed since – four-fifths of the country was thick, unbroken, evergreen jungle.

Malaya is very near the Equator – Singapore is only just north by a few miles and this means there are practically no seasons and the sun sets and rises at about the same time all the year round. The day temperatures average just over 90°F, but there is generally a welcome drop to about 70°F later in the night. The continuous combination of high temperatures and high humidity gets on the nerves.

About 50 years ago before I arrived, the Malayan Peninsula was reckoned as one of the world's unhealthiest regions. Port Swettenham narrowly escaped being closed two months after its opening because the mortality from malaria and its associated diseases proved so high, and the death rate on the rubber estates was estimated at 20 per cent. However, under the British it had become one of the most healthy countries in the East and had won international fame for its pioneering work in tropical hygiene.

The original Straits Settlements comprised, firstly, Penang, the island having been ceded by the Sultan of Kedah to the Honourable

East India Company. To this island there had been added some land on the peninsula mainland and the whole was known as Province Wellesley, named after the then Governor General in Calcutta. Secondly, Malacca, which had had a chequered history. Captured from the Malaccan Sultanate by the Portuguese in 1511, the latter enforced a system of monopoly which ruined Malay international commerce for a very long time. It passed by conquest to the Dutch in 1641, to the British in 1795, back again to the Dutch in 1818 and was finally ceded to the East India Company in 1824.

The third settlement was Singapore, which had been founded by Sir Stamford Raffles in 1819, by a treaty which allowed a trading post to be established on the island which was then more or less uninhabited.

In 1826 the three settlements were combined to form the fourth Presidency of the British Indian Empire under the East India Company. In 1858 the Company was abolished, following the Indian Mutiny the previous year, and control of the settlements passed to the India Office and then to the Colonial Office in 1867.

The British at first did not wish to get involved in the political affairs of the Malay States and wanted no political responsibility. However, trade in tin and other Malayan products was increasing in importance and defence of this trade demanded increasing political control. However, if the affairs of the Straits Settlements were marked at this time by the ordered niceties of a Victorian imperial outpost, this was far from the case in the hinterland of the peninsula which was largely inaccessible except on foot.

The increasing political control of the British led to four states – namely Perak, Selangor, Negri Sembilan and Pahang – this latter state was permanently bankrupt – being federated in 1895. Siam in 1909 ceded to the British her sovereignty over the states of Kedah, Kelantan, Trengganu and Perlis. In 1914 the southern state Johore accepted a British adviser. These five states were known as the Unfederated Malay States.

Thus by the early 1900s, all of what was called British Malaya was drawn into the British sphere, the Crown Colony of the Straits Settlements, the Federated Malay States and the Unfederated Malay States. It needs to be emphasised that the Malay States were protectorates and not British territory. By treaty agreement, the Malay Sultans governed in accordance with the advice of their

British Residents and Advisers, except of course in matters of Malay religion and customs.

In the middle of the nineteenth century, two events changed the face of the country. The first was the development of the tin industry, which resulted in large-scale Chinese immigration – in 1937 Malaya produced nearly 40 per cent of the world's output of tin. The second was the introduction of rubber. Para-rubber is not indigenous to Asia. The first seedlings were taken to Malaya, after having been smuggled out of Brazil and germinated at the Royal Botanical Gardens at Kew. By 1937 there were well over 3 million acres under rubber and Malaya produced more than 40 per cent of the world's rubber.

By the time I arrived in Malaya in 1950 nearly half the population was Chinese, of which only about one-third had been born in the country, the remainder having varying degrees of political, economic and family connection with China. The Chinese, whose enterprise and industry had contributed so much to the commercial development of the country, were mainly based in the towns and in the villages where the middle-class shop keeper-cum-moneylender were both the economic backbone of the country and the economic scourge of the country.

The Chinese, in a foreign land, always retain their family and national customs, and when they came to Malaya they brought their own political groups and secret societies with them. When the Kuomintang in China was formed it soon had its adherents in Malaya and by 1927 there was a strong and well-organised KMT – short for Kuomintang – among the younger Chinese in Malaya, which gave financial and moral support to the revolution in China. In 1930 the Malayan Communist Party (MCP) was established and existed not only alongside the KMT but also often in conflict with it. In 1937, when the Japanese–Chinese War broke out, immediate sympathy with China was shown by all sections of the Chinese community in Malaya, and the MCP began to organise all the local independent Chinese associations into an anti-Japanese organisation. In this purely patriotic guise, it became very powerful. For instance, it collected voluntary or enforced contributions throughout the country, administered its own justice in dealing with those who infringed the anti-Japanese boycott, and established well-run administrative branches for Communist propaganda, organisation and particularly communication.

When Russia signed her pact with Germany in 1939, the entire flood of propaganda turned against Britain and the local government and it was then that the organisation proved its strength. Mass demonstrations were staged all over the country, which culminated in an attempt to stage a general strike, which succeeded in paralysing the local war effort for several months.

When Germany declared war on Russia, the whole of the MCP effort changed abruptly and turned to the support of Russia and her allies. All anti-British propaganda was stopped and the British Government in Malaya was offered full cooperation in the war effort by all sections of the Chinese population in the event of an extension of the war to the Far East.

On 8th December 1941 the Japanese attacked Pearl Harbour and on the same day they landed at Kota Bahru in north-east Malaya. On the same day they also invaded Siam, but the Siamese forces packed up after fighting a 'prolonged' battle of 90 minutes, shortly after the Japanese invaded!

On 15th February 1942, the Japanese captured Singapore, only just over two months after having invaded Malaya. It was the worst imperial defeat in the history of the British Empire.

While all this was going on, the Communists together with other British, Chinese and Malay guerrillas started moving into the jungle. Gradually the MCP headquarters regained contact and, importantly, control over its members who were guerrillas. They were organised into groups with 'State' (headquarters) and 'District' and 'Branch' units. MCP regiments were formed in every state. Couriers blazed communication trails through the jungle. Camps were built; supply lines extended; agents trained in towns and villages to spy on the Japanese and their collaborators, and later on the British; other agents looked after finances for the MCP, collecting subscriptions and purchasing the supplies needed by those in the jungle.

The party executives were delighted that the Japanese war was providing them with the kind of training that would be useful against the next enemy, the British – for they were certain that the Japanese would be defeated, and the British via their Force 136 was providing them with weapons.

So in the jungle, a fairly disciplined Communist-dominated guerrilla force, formed out of rubber-tappers, mine workers, vegetable gardeners, squatters, woodcutters, barbers, shop assistants and house-servants, had become established.

The MCP central executive never for a moment lost sight of the ultimate objective which was to take over the country. In 1943 it drew up a long-term programme which declared as its first objective: 'Drive the Japanese Fascists out of Malaya and establish the Malayan Republic'. The party planned to combine with Russia and China to support the struggle for independence under a Communist regime. In 1945 when the MCP saw the possibility of an invasion by the Allies and the end of the war, the party began to select good fighters to form a secret force. Dumps of weapons and ammunition were established for later use by this 'secret' army in an anti-British struggle after the war.

Then the atomic bombs were dropped on Hiroshima and Nagasaki, and the Japanese surrendered. By then the British Force 136 had handed more than 2,000 weapons to the MPAJA, the Malayan People's Anti-Japanese Army, which was now some 7,000 strong.

The troops who appeared in the streets of many towns and villages in Malaya in September 1945, almost immediately after the surrender of Japan, were not British or Allied soldiers – these were still on the high seas – but the Communist Chinese guerrillas. Wearing their new British jungle-green uniform that had arrived in airdrops, they emerged from their jungle camps and were cheered by the population. They took control of towns and villages from the Japanese, and raised the red hammer and sickle flag.

Surprisingly, the Communists made no attempt to seize control of the country, even though the situation was in their favour: they, the MCP, were the only power in the interior. Slowly the whole of Malaya was reoccupied as a British military administration took over; it handed over to a civil government a few months later. Victory parades were staged and the MPAJA took part.

In 1947 Russia started a new policy of aggression in Asia. A common pattern of rebellion began to develop in the Far East. In China, the Communist Party opened a push against the national government; in Indo-China the French were opposed by the Vietminh; in Burma a Communist party waited until the British had granted independence to the country before it started operating; in Indonesia the Communist Party became violently active against the Dutch colonial government.

Then in 1948 the MCP turned to violence and bloodshed. It murdered contractors of labour on estates and mines; it threatened British planters and miners with death, and several were killed; it

115

attacked isolated police stations and terrorised the countryside. All these acts were carried out by what were described as 'mobile killing corps' formed from the MCP'S 'secret army' in the jungle.

Then on 16th June 1948, three British planters in the rubber-growing district of Sungei Siput in Perak which, before the war, had been a Communist stronghold, were murdered with great deliberation. A State of Emergency was declared. Police leave was cancelled, officers recalled, the police were armed and in the time honoured-tradition, the army was called in to 'assist the Civil power'. Planters and miners armed themselves and they knew they faced death by day and night. The war, or emergency, had begun.

The administration expected to control the rebellion within a few weeks. The MCP thought in terms of ten years. They had a blueprint for victory and success. First they planned to cripple the economic system of the country and harass the police and the army. Secondly, by increased guerrilla activity, they expected to take over rural areas, which would then be declared 'liberated areas'. Finally, from their jungle bases and from these 'liberated areas' they planned to extend their control over the rest of the country. I arrived during the first and second phase.

It transpired much later from captured documents that the MCP had actually planned to open their revolt in September 1948 but undisciplined members in Johore and Perak, in which were based most units of the so-called 'Inner Force', had gone on the rampage before the meticulous plans of the MCP could be finalised.

This was fortunate for the country, and for a host of British and Asian civil servants, policemen, planters, miners and others who had been earmarked for assassination during a quick country-wide paroxysm of killing. The party had assumed that these killings would have created such fear and chaos that they would have helped them to gain their objective more swiftly.

The Seaforth Highlanders had crossed the causeway from Singapore to Malaya in 1948 to fight the MCP in Johore. Later on they moved up to Pahang and it was there in October 1950, that I joined them.

But now, dear reader, having introduced the country of my destination, I must revert to the HMT *Dilwara* and our voyage out to the Far East in October in that year of 1950.

The ship, a former British India liner converted to a troopship, was comfortable for the officers but less so for the other ranks who slept below decks in hammocks. It was so swelteringly hot down there in the tropics that they were allowed to take turns to sleep on deck.

Long voyages become, after a time, a sort of mesmeric routine: walks round the decks; leaning over the rails watching the porpoises; waiting for the regular meals served by perfectly mannered Goans; singing hymns at the Sunday Church Service; the inspections, the training exercises – remember we were on a troopship; and again leaning over the rails in the evening as the sun set, and always always hoping to see the green flash – and only once did I see it much later on.

Not everybody seems to know about the green flash, and it is indeed quite rare for it to be seen. The weather conditions have to be absolutely right: as Jules Verne put it, 'the instant of the last ray of light when the sky is perfectly clear'. You also need a calm atmosphere, so that the layers of air of different temperatures separate out. This sort of sandwich effect in the atmosphere creates a lens that bends and distorts light, rather like a mirage, and this also explains why the top of the setting sun seems slightly flattened. As the top edge of the sun slips below the horizon, it sinks through these various layers of air and these layers tease out the component colours of sunlight, running through the spectrum from orange to yellow, and then maybe for a second or two comes the green flash. When you see it you will shout with joy as you will be one of those few people who have seen it, so rejoice.

Occasionally I was asked to take training exercises on the decks, as I was an unaccompanied officer and supposed to have little to do – which was, of course, quite correct. One training exercise I was asked to undertake was for me to demonstrate how to de-assemble a Bren machine-gun and, having done this, to reassemble it again. Like the bicycle pump test at Caterham Barracks, I had four bits left over when I finished, and no obvious places where they should fit. I had always been told that when you get in a mess like that, you had to order your sergeant to 'Carry on, please', and, deeply embarrassed, for the second time in my life, I had to do just that. I was still only eighteen.

We took ten days to get to Port Said, the entrance to the Suez Canal, and here for the first time we met the East. It was unforgettable. The smell, the noise, the gully-gully men, the hawkers, the ships' bunkers being filled with coal by coolies carrying the bags on their shoulders, the boys diving for pennies, the veiled women in their long dresses, the dirt, the squalor, the dark faces everywhere and again, above all, the smell of the East.

I went ashore feeling incongruous in my kilt, and curiously enough somewhat ashamed of my white face and white knees. In quick succession I was offered Spanish Fly, a so-called aphrodisiac, a piano, a set of erotic pictures (rather exciting but how could a young officer in a kilt let the side down by buying such 'filthy' pictures) and, finally, the man's sister – all politely and not so politely declined. We walked about in dirty, shabby streets, and partook of coffee and beer in a cafe where we were served by a waiter in a fez. We ventured into the famous emporium Simon Arzt, found nothing to buy, and soon it was time to go back on board ship.

We left in the evening and sailed through the Suez Canal to Port Suez and then out into the Red Sea. It got hotter and hotter, the prickly heat got worse, and every now and again we put the scuttles out of the portholes to scoop up the air as the ship turned in circles to get fresh air on board. We passed Jeddah and Hodeida and then we left the Red Sea behind as we passed through the Straits of Bab-el-Mandeb and headed north-east to Aden, the British possession on the south coast of the Yemen, originally part of the British Indian Empire. We arrived off Steamer Port, we went ashore, we rode on a camel, we had a drink in the RAF Officers' Club, looked at the unique water catchment areas, and then went back on board ship, which was still bunkering up with coal.

We then sailed close to the north coast of the Island of Socotra and then we were in the Arabian sea en route for Colombo, the capital of Ceylon. What a beautiful island, and what a beautiful capital and what lovely and graceful people. I was entranced, and what a contrast with England, grimy, dirty old England, impoverished after the war, city centres wrecked by bombs and rationing – it was five years after the war ended and there was still food rationing!

I took myself off with some friends to the Mount Lavinia Hotel for a swim and a delicious colonial curry tiffin. It was the first time I had swum in the tropics: what a change from Frinton, Cromer and Sheringham. I was a young man in those days; I was very innocent, impressionable and very self-conscious. I came from a long line of imperial soldiers; I was kilted; I was white, very white and here I was on a most beautiful island with mountains and jungle, long white sandy beaches with waving palm trees coming down to the sea's edge, and all around me were beautiful dark women in their saris, barefoot, flashing their large dark eyes at me. It was intoxicating – I wished I could stay – but if I had come back after leaving the Army what could I have done? A tea planter? But the tea plantations were all being nationalised after independence. The Colonial Service? But the writing was on the wall for that, and I never wanted to go to Africa. I was perplexed as always, but I knew that Kipling's temple bells were calling and I hoped one day there might be a neater, sweeter maiden in a cleaner, greener land. Why could we not stay longer? But we could not and after a stay of 24 hours we embarked over again, this time for Singapore.

We passed the north-west coast of Sumatra and headed down the Straits of Malacca to Singapore where our four-week voyage came to an end, although the ship was going on to Pusan in South Korea.

There was a band to greet us, as there had been a band to see us off in Southampton. It was all very orderly and efficient. I had orders to join my battalion headquarters at Temerloh in Pahang and I had wondered how to get there. That would be all right said battalion headquarters, we will send someone down to meet you and take you 'up country' as it was called.

I went straight from the dockside to the railway station to board the night train to Kuala Lumpur, except that I was to disembark at Gemas junction where the East Coast railway line branched off to Pahang. The station I was aiming for was Mentakab where I would be met and taken to battalion headquarters at Temerloh.

At the railway station I looked for the Seaforth to meet me and was glad to see him on the platform; his name was Corporal Moran. I knew there was something wrong before I moved up to meet him. I was right, there was something wrong. He managed to salute me and then fell down dead drunk at my feet. I had to get the Royal Military Police to remove him. So now I was completely on my own and I would have to find my own way to Mentakab.

It was a darkened train – no lights were allowed to show so as to avoid affording the Communists a target and indeed, when I was standing by the window in the bar, I opened the curtain over the window very slightly but shut it again very quickly when I noticed that there were two bullet holes in the glass.

The train went slowly. The slower it went, in a sense the better, because if the line was blown up the carnage at a slow speed would be far less than at a high speed. It was insufferably hot – there were little fans but they did not do much good. And then suddenly we arrived at Gemas. It was still in the middle of the night.

Still very self-conscious – but at least I was not wearing a kilt – I found myself the only European to leave the train and once more I was on my own. I asked the stationmaster if there was a private or a semi-private room I could use. He said 'Yes', and there I sat sweltering in a room with the electric light almost totally obscured by moths of every description. I was conscious that I did not have any anti-malaria pills on me and I just prayed that I would not be stung by any of the thousands of mosquitoes around me as I felt sure I would get malaria. I was stung, but I did not get malaria.

The hours went by slowly. I had been in Malaya less than 18 hours and here I was alone on this station in the middle of Malaya surrounded, apparently, by Communist guerrillas and I was only armed with a 38 revolver and six rounds of ammunition – not much use in an emergency. Eventually, the dawn broke and a little later on the up train arrived (or was it the down train?) – there was only one up and one down train a day.

I got to know these trains very well, and so a description of them is worthwhile. The engine was always in the middle. Either side of the engine were two armoured carriages, more like goods wagons, and at each corner there were projecting loopholes for use when the train was ambushed, which was not an infrequent occurrence. Either side of these armoured goods wagons were carriages for passengers, although these were dispensed with if the train was being solely used by the military.

On either side of the passenger carriages or armoured cars were a number of flats, wagons with no sides or very low sides. The object of these flats was that when the train was blown up it was hopefully only the flats which would go over the embankment, and not the carriages, armoured cars and, most importantly not the engine – although even this happened on occasion.

The armoured cars were manned by Malay policemen with a Malay sergeant in charge. Most of the passengers tended to be Chinese, although there were always some Malays and Indian Tamils, whilst the engine driver was always Indian. In one of the

120

luggage vans, a Chinese cook always lit a fire and he produced some of the best Chinese food I have ever eaten. What about that? An open fire in a railway carriage and a Chinaman cooking the most delicious food. It was quite an experience.

The train left. The top permitted speed was 15 miles per hour – a little higher in open country – but of course you did not want to be going too fast when you were blown up and went over. As I have said earlier, the slower the better. It was an interminable journey. But then something happened: the train came to a halt. I asked what had happened and I was told the bridge in front had been blown up. We started going back, and then suddenly there was a big boom and the bridge behind us was blown up. We were caught and I was the only European on board. What should I do? I supposed as an officer I should do something, but all the soldiers or police were Malay and I did not speak Malay. In any case, I had never fought in action.

In the end it did not matter. We stayed there all afternoon with our fingers on the trigger, tense, expectant, sweating. The jungle edge was only 100 yards away. Finally, in the early evening, a company of Gurkhas came out of that self-same jungle edge and relieved us. The train could not go forwards but nor could it go back, so I left it and went with the British officer commanding the Gurkha company and stayed with them until the bridges were repaired. I had been just 24 hours in Malaya.

The Gurkhas were most hospitable and welcoming. They made me feel very much at ease. I was even asked to attend one of their ghastly celebrations which seemed to consist of slitting the throats of every goat they could find. But there was one thing I enjoyed, and that was the sound of the pipes playing reveille and the last post. It was a curious feeling hearing the pipes in the jungle – they did not quite seem to fit.

After several days the bridges were temporarily repaired and the train was able to move again; this time without further misadventure I arrived at Mentakab, the station for Temerloh. There a jeep was waiting to take me to battalion headquarters at Temerloh. Here everything was orderly and efficient and highly organised.

Everybody was very smartly dressed in their jungle green uniform, with knife-like creases in their trousers, polished Scottish brogue shoes, tartan belts, green stockings, skean dhus and red flashes. In the morning and the evening, the pipes played.

121

The Officers' Mess was in a most attractive and comfortable house which had previously been owned by a European – and possibly still was – and here the officers foregathered for their meals and refreshments. It was all very civilised and somehow familiar.

The Lieutenant-Colonel commanding the battalion was Patrick Johnson. He had a difficult job. The area for which he was militarily responsible was essentially central and east Pahang and extended between 100 and 150 miles north to south and a similar distance west to east. Most of Pahang was covered with wild mountainous jungle. To the north lay the huge area that was then called King George V National Park, and when we were operating there, our maps were extremely inaccurate and quite a number of the rivers ran uphill. There were some very large rivers, of which the biggest was Sungei Pahang on which Temerloh was situated, and these were difficult to cross as there were no bridges. Communications were very poor. There was only one road, which went from Jerantut via Maran and Gambang to Kuantan – a road which was ambushed many times – and there was the single-line East Coast railway, which started off at Gemas and ended at Jerantut, although before the war it had gone on to Kota Bahru in Kelantan, which you will recall is where the Japanese landed in December 1941, only eight and a half years previously.

For this responsibility, Colonel Johnson had something like 800 troops, with one company stationed at Kuantan on the East Coast 150 miles away by rail or road, one company at Jerantut at the end of the railway line, about 90 miles north, one company at the railway village of Kuala Krau, and the remaining company at Kerdau, also on the railway line. You will see from this that we were very widely dispersed and as a result not very effective. Against us were two Communist regiments.

There seemed very little for our Commanding Officer and his company commanders to do – it was very much a Lieutenants' war in the jungle and we bore the brunt of it. It is perhaps worth mentioning that our Commanding Officer, who, as it happens I liked very much, never once visited my company either in Kuantan, Kerdau or Kuala Krau. There would have been nothing for him to do if he had.

Pehaps therefore to pass the time at battalian headquarters he instituted the dartboard tactic, which may or may not have emanated out of Staff College. For those of you who are not particularly familiar with this tactic, the CO stood well back from a map of Pahang, where there were large white blank spaces indicating that these were unmapped areas – a particuarly white area was the King George V National Park, where what rivers were shown usually ran up-hill – and threw a dart at the map. The idea was that we would fight our way through the jungle to where we had assumed the dart had landed and report back in the time-honoured way. Mercifully this only happened to me once. It took me 10 days to get through some very swampy jungle to get to the impact point of the dart, but there was nothing there and nothing on the way there or the way back. However, it could be said the absence of enemy activity in the area covered by my patrol was in a sense useful information so perhaps it was not such a bad tactic after all!

12

Jungle Fighting

At that time the Communists completely dominated the Pahang jungle and moved about in regiments numbering up to 300. Indeed, at the beginning of what was always euphemistically called the Emergency, both Kuala Krau and Jerantut had been raided by the Communists and later on, just before I arrived, 300 Communists once again had attacked Kuala Krau and declared it a 'liberated' area, having killed four policemen and two British railway engineers. If you were, as I was, a platoon commander with about 20 soldiers and you bumped really hard into a Communist regiment, the chances of your coming out of it alive were nil. They did not take prisoners; and I have to say we did not take prisoners either. There was one time near Gambang that I came across a large Communist ambush position into which we were supposed to enter. By the time we got there, they had mercifully given up hope and left; their fires were still warm.

Essentially, our operations in Pahang were carried out normally on a fire-brigade basis, although this changed whilst I was there and I did carry out a number of deep jungle penetration patrols as they were called. In those days we did achieve a number of 'eliminations' as they were called, but there was nothing very positive to show. The local Communist units just brought in fresh recruits, regrouped and carried on as before. Very few people visited the state by motor car; in any case there was only one road, and this road was regarded as being very dangerous – for we military it was a road on which you were not allowed to travel with under six vehicles, of which two had to be armoured.

I did not stay long at Temerloh but I did have one untoward experience. I was sleeping in a tent under my mosquito net. The tent had two upright poles and one crossbar. One morning I woke up at the sound of the pipes, looked up and saw an enormous python wrapped round the crossbar. It seemed to be asleep but I was certainly not asleep and I remember wondering whether it would be better to stay where I was, immobile, or to fight my way out of the mosquito net and run for it. I chose the latter, and the python was killed.

Before I leave Temerloh and Mentakab, there is one thing I wanted to mention as it became important to me later on, and this was that during the war against the Japanese there had been near Mentakab a large camp of Communists, forming part of the 6th Independent Anti-Japanese Regiment, and it was here that Freddie Spencer-Chapman, a Seaforth Highlander like me and a member of the British Force 136 operating in the jungle against the Japanese, had spent a year. His book the *Jungle is Neutral* was a sort of jungle Bible to me and was invaluable.

At the same time, Kuantan to which I had been posted had formed part of the 7th Independent Anti-Japanese Regiment and their successors. Because of the vastness of the East Pahang jungle, they were able to make large clearings right inside the jungle and grow enough rice and vegetables to be self-supporting. Their camps were indeed quite comfortable, with parade grounds, barracks, a hospital and so on, and a pole on which the Red Star was flown. Not a place to turn up in by accident, with 20 men.

And so it was back to Mentakab to catch the one up train of the day to Jerantut via Kerdau and Kuala Krau. At Jerantut I was met by Major Lynch, a Canadian Seaforth Highlander, who commanded the Seaforth company there. He looked very shaky and smelt of whisky, perhaps understandably as Jerantut had recently been raided. I stayed there for a day or so while a six-vehicle convoy was assembled, and then I left on one of the most dangerous roads in Malaya to Kuantan. But first of all we had to cross the very wide Sungei Pahang River on an old clanking chain ferry – very exciting and we were all relieved to get across safely. River crossings in Malaya were always dangerous because, as you neared the far bank, you were completely exposed to enemy fire from concealed positions on the river bank where the jungle came down to the water's edge.

Virtually every mile of this long, narrow, twisting road was ambushable, as the jungle came right down to the edge and often overlooked the road. Later on when I was not too busy I occasionally used to command these convoys; we were very rarely ambushed, but the Malayan police were. They once accused me of being in league with the Communists on this account because, on one occasion, after I had passed a particularly dangerous stretch of the road, the police behind me were ambushed. My reply to this was: 'Next time you go in front and see what happens'.

Many of the British officers and sergeants of the police force – we were 'in aid of the civil power' – had been members of the Palestine police force, who had been demobilised when the Jews defeated the Palestinian Arabs. They were extremely tough, often rough, and they had fixed violent notions (nurtured in Palestine, when handling Jews and Arabs alike) of how to treat anybody who was under suspicion. One often saw hockey sticks and cricket bats in their offices which were used to obtain information, the *sine qua non* of defeating the terrorists.

They were in fact a tower of strength, and a large number transferred to jungle police squads, where many of them were to be killed. In time the 'Specials' as they were called were, as one Army officer put it, 'to prove their value one hundred times over'.

The half-way point between Jerantut and Kuantan was a small nondescript village called Maran, and it was then on to Gambang – a hotbed of Chinese Communists – and then finally Kuantan on the East Coast. What an attractive place, with, just outside the town, lovely beaches washed by the China Sea, beautiful rocky headlands and palm trees everywhere. A heaven, and it was called Chempedak beach. Now there is a Hyatt hotel, but when we were there, there was nothing.

I was duly introduced to my Company Commander, John Davie; James Nairn, the second in command, whose brother became Chancellor of Essex University; and three lieutenants, Robin Campbell, Graham Dunnett, who has just retired as Lord Lieutenant of Caithness, and Jock McLeod, whose family were well known to my mother. There was also a medical officer, Dr Copley.

For some reason the Officers' Mess where we lived, slept and ate, when not in the jungle, was a Chinese shop in the middle of town. For some strange reason also, given our vulnerability, there was never a sentry on guard nor any sort of protection. I never understood this, but we were never attacked, although seven British officers sleeping in one room must have been a tempting target.

Shortly after my arrival, I was taken out on my first patrol as an officer under instruction. We were to be away for a week and we were to base ourselves at Gambang, which as I mentioned earlier was a hotbed of Communists. Here we took over the local school and commenced patrolling both day and night. To the north was a large area of what was called tin-tails where the Chinese had removed about 10 feet of soil to get at the underlying tin. This was quite open country and, after one large sweep, we left it alone. The south was more interesting: it was *belukar*, i.e. secondary jungle, merging into *ulu*, primary jungle. There were a number of small Chinese allotments, for want of a better word, and we usually called them 'squatters' as they had no title to the land.

But what did I look like? What were my clothes and what arms did I carry? Starting from the bottom, I wore jungle boots. As these were always wet, they did not last long and constantly had to be replaced. Then I wore jungle trousers tucked into my boots, a shirt and a jungle hat. I initially carried a 303 rifle but I found that this was too heavy in the jungle, particularly when cutting your way through *belukar* and bamboo. Later on I changed it for a silent De Lisle rifle and a light American Mark Two carbine. I carried a parang, a sharp Malay sword and a machete, the latter for cutting my way through jungle. I carried a water bottle into which I placed sterilisers. I carried a map, a compass and a notebook, which I used to navigate in the jungle. I usually wore six live grenades on my belt and two large ammunition packs or pouches. On my back I carried a heavy pack – around 60 to 70 pounds, in which I placed some clean dry clothing, my food rations and so on. Below my pack I carried my precious lightweight bed. And, of course, I had a supply of anti-malaria tablets. Every morning I had to oversee the men taking these tablets – it was a court-martial offence if you went down with malaria.

The worst thing about the jungle and the swamps was the leeches, which latched onto every part of your body and got more and more swollen with your blood. There was only one effective way to deal with them, and that was to light up a cigarette and apply it to the leeches until they fell off. Depending on the circumstances, you could gather in one hour up to something like ten. This meant that every hour we stopped not only for a rest, but also for a cigarette, hence the immense importance of cigarettes to soldiers operating in the jungle: not only for one's nerves – we all suffered from nerves – but also for those leeches.

Among the many other problems of fighting in the jungle was

this problem of being wet. From the moment you set out on a patrol until the day you got back – maybe a week or a fortnight later, or whatever – you were soaked all the time, from sweat, from swamps, from rivers, from often monsoon-like rain. During the day you were soaked, and during the night you usually remained soaked. We all suffered from skin disease, jungle sores, fevers and so on. One never felt well in the jungle.

Besides the jungle itself you had to cope with the animals. There were insects and snakes everywhere. There were small white ants, great red ants – thousands of them marching in military formation through the jungle. There were little black soldier ants, centipedes, scorpions, beetles of every size and shape. There were monkeys everywhere, water buffalo, deer, seladang (large Malayan wild ox), even elephants, tigers and bears, although we only very infrequently saw these. A herd of water buffalo wandering around a night ambush position was exceptionally unpleasant – if you were lying down, as you usually were, a water buffalo became absolutely vast and if panicked would trample you even to death.

Fighting in the jungle was heat, steam, greenness, sweat, rotting wood, pallor, silence during the day, a huge clamorous noise in the morning and evening, cutting, paranging, feeling sick, nerves, fear – but surprisingly enough, we got used to it. Secondary jungle *belukar* was always hell, but primary jungle, the *ulu*, made you feel relatively safe and cool. And we always had to remember: he who shoots first may live longest.

Stealth and cunning were essential weapons to both sides, but first you had to know how to track. Initially, we used Iban headhunters from Sarawak to help us. They were good, but after a time we, I think, became almost as good. Most of the Ibans had joined the British security forces not only for the money and the chance of a decapitation (after all they were headhunters), but also because they were promised a rifle as a present on their return to Sarawak. My headhunter was called Oogas – I always called him Mr Oogas. He had heavily stretched ears and he was not what I would call an attractive man. As a tracker I always made him go first – he might also be shot first – but he was of inestimable value in cutting a track through the jungle, a wretched job, and even worse when cutting your way through *belukar*.

Behind him I positioned a man with one of our two heavy Bren machine-guns and behind him myself – I had to be right up front as I had to do all the jungle navigating; it was particularly important to know where you were when calling for airdrops. I never got lost, but therein lies a story. I was always afraid that if anything happened to me my soldiers would not know, firstly, where they were, and secondly, how to get out. So one day I started to instruct my men on jungle navigation. Soon afterwards my company commander came up to me and asked me what I was doing. I told him. He looked at me – he was a singularly unattractive man, a Gordon from Aberdeen – and told me quietly to stop. Later I asked him why, and he replied, 'If they know where they are, laddie, they might not follow you.' Perhaps he had a point, but I disregarded his advice.

Now, what sort of day and night did we have when we were out on patrol in the jungle? Obviously before we left the men were briefed as to our objectives, and how long we would be out; usually our Chinese police officer added in his views and so did anyone else who wished to.

There was very little 'we' and 'they' in the jungle, we were all in it together – I relied on my men just as much as they relied on me; we were entirely interdependent, to use what I think is a fairly modern word. Once we had left the confines of the company camp, we were entirely on our own – nobody could come to our rescue, nobody could reinforce us, and if somebody was wounded we would have to prepare a makeshift stretcher, probably out of bamboo and webbing, and carry him out. A casualty usually meant the end of the patrol as well as a significant imbibing of rum.

We usually entered the jungle through a rubber estate – some were neglected and overgrown, providing a lot of cover for potential ambushes. Others were kept fairly clean and open, where we were clearly visible. Consequently we adopted a very open order until we got to the jungle–rubber edge. This edge was usually *belukar* – that is to say, jungle which had been cut down and regrown. It was always difficult to get through and it was always with a sigh of relief that we eventually entered primary jungle – *ulu* – which was cool and with the tree canopy often something like 100–200 feet over our heads. During the day it was very quiet but the dawn and evening chorus was almost deafening.

During the entire length of the patrol I was continuously checking our position with the map and compass. Every change in direction had to be noted down and also the length of travel after each change of direction. If we were being supplied by air I had to give the exact coordinates to the Royal Australian Air Force.

Every hour, as I have mentioned, we stopped for a rest of say five minutes, well away from the track we were on. We de-leeched with our cigarette ends. Before stopping and resting, I put out sentries to guard the approaches to our halt. No talking was allowed, only whispers. I used these rests to check my position and write up my notes on the terrain.

The loads we were carrying became increasingly heavy during the day, and those most affected by the weight were the Bren machine-gunners and the wireless operator. Generally I liked to keep radio silence – I did not wish to give away our position to the Communist guerrillas. This radio silence infuriated my second company commander – the Gordon – as he never knew where I was. Even if he had known, it would not have made the slightest difference because there was nothing he could do. I have to say, I took an almost childish delight in this radio silence because it meant that, apart from anything else, when battalion headquarters telephoned him if the lines were not cut, or radioed him as to Tritton's movements, successes or failures in the jungle, he always had to admit (if he was truthful) that he didn't know, and this always bucked me up no end, although it led to trouble in the end.

Every time we came across a track we examined it with great care. We never took much interest in old tracks, but a track which had relatively recently been used was a source of great excitement, in the sense that there was some sort of prospect of action. It was particularly important not only to know whether the track had been recently used, but also to know how many Communist guerrillas had trod it and, of course, the direction in which they were travelling.

At about 4 p.m. we stopped, once again well away from the track. Sentries were posted at either end of our camp position and these sentries were relieved every two hours. Everybody else set up their basha and made themselves as comfortable as possible, while the volunteer cook tried to get a fire going – not easy as the jungle was always so wet, particularly in the monsoon. We usually had some sort of stew and, amazingly, plum duff, which the Jocks loved, but I found too heavy. And of course we had mugs and mugs of piping hot tea laced with condensed milk, beautifully sweet.

As night time approached – and it did at exactly the same time every day, we were only a short distance north of the Equator – the sergeant and I 'stood to' the men and this lasted until it was completely dark when they were 'stood down' and retired to their bashas. I have mentioned that the sentries were changed every two hours and these were changed either by me or my sergeant. The reason for this was that the first six hours of the watch, that is, from 6 p.m. to midnight was usually taken by the sergeant. At midnight I relieved him and this meant I had to be wide awake from midnight to dawn when, once again, I 'stood to' the patrol until we had full light. As it happens I never felt sleepy in the jungle as my nerves were so tense and taut that sleep was a relatively minor consideration.

Once it was light, the cook relit the fire if he could, and we enjoyed porridge, baked beans and bacon from our tin supplies which we carried so laboriously on our backs.

Airdrops were always a great excitement. For these, obviously, the wireless was made to splutter into life and our position given. For airdrops it was imperative to find an open area – usually quite difficult – and we had to mark out on the ground the two letters 'DZ' which stood for dropping zone. To make sure, fires were lit onto which wet leaves were placed so that there was a good smoke, showing our position as well. It was always slightly nerve-racking for me as I was never entirely sure with my map and compass navigation and my log book that I had got my positioning right but, mercifully, I never had a failure.

A contact, an elimination, a Communist jungle camp or food depot find was always immensely exciting as it relieved the tedium of endless days of patrolling. When that happened, the wireless was coaxed into life and I reported in. Quite often I was not where I was supposed to be, but how do you cope with a company commander who never went into the jungle?

At the end of the day, as I have said earlier, this jungle war was a lieutenant's war – the lieutenant and his men. You patrolled with your men and they patrolled with you; they ate and drank with you and you ate and drank with them; they relied on you and you relied on them; they fought with you and you fought with them. They were young, I was young, we were all in it together. When we 'bumped into' Chinese Communist guerrillas and we had a fight on our hands, you knew you would have their full support and bloody-minded determination.

Before going back to Gambang let me mention our Chinese police officers. Remember that the security forces apart from the British and Gurkhas were comprised almost entirely of Malays, whilst the terrorists were comprised again almost entirely of Chinese. To be, therefore, a Chinese police officer acting in support of the security forces required enormous courage, bravery and determination. I salute them. They had a huge price on their heads, larger than the price on our heads. Although I did not exactly admire their methods of obtaining information from suspects, they were invaluable – apart from anything else they were our interpreters, as none of us spoke Chinese or knew any of the various dialects.

During our period at Gambang, we carried out large sweeps. When we found huts which we thought were being used by the terrorists, we burnt them. Once we surrounded a small Chinese village in the middle of the night and went through it house by house searching and interrogating. I went into one small house and found a Chinaman surrounded by matchboxes. I asked him what he was doing. He replied that he was taking a few matches out of each box to make up a new box to sell. That's a Chinese businessman for you.

The last day of that first Gambang patrol, we were patrolling on the jungle-rubber edge. The rubber plantation was overgrown, providing plenty of cover. The Jocks (Scottish soldiers) were moving across the plantation in a very wide formation, 20 to 30 yards between each man. Suddenly we came under fire from the jungle-rubber edge and the bullets started whistling over our heads. I instinctively moved behind a tree but, to my consternation the Jocks were running forward firing. I was behind, and they were in front. I thought of *The Four Feathers*, ran out and forward, and got out in front of them. We raced forward. There was heavy firing for about five minutes and then it stopped. The terrorists had fled. There were no casualties, but it was my baptism of fire. I felt sick, and I remembered later what Hemingway said of cowardice in the face of the enemy. He wrote that this resulted from an inability to suspend one's imagination – so when you are in action, try and remember this. One thing I remember was that when one was in action, fear disappeared.

We carried out a series of small, generally unsuccessful jungle operations. We knew that the Communist terrorists were around in large numbers; they had several companies and regiments in Pahang, which they regarded as safe.

Christmas 1950 and the New Year arrived (the latter more important to a Scottish regiment than Christmas) and early in 1951 the company was transferred to Kerdau, the first station on the East Coast railway line up from Mentakab. John Davie, our superb company commander, left us and his place was taken by Major Petrie, a huge overweight Gordon Highlander, who had, as it happens, a successful Second World War career and gained, I think, the Military Cross for bravery in crossing the Rhine in 1944–45.

Whenever he got into his cups in our little mess tent on the jungle edge, he used to order sardines on toast covered with vinegar. Once these had arrived, he used to relive his crossing of the Rhine and these recollections went on interminably.

There was one ghastly occasion when he was in his cups that a Lance-Corporal Docherty, who liked his drink and was also drunk, suddenly appeared from behind the tent flap with what turned out to be a loaded 303 rifle. He pointed it as straight as he could at the Major with his finger twitching on the trigger. The rifle wobbled around quite a lot but, at one of his more unsteady moments, he was rushed by the company Sergeant Major, who had heard the altercation. He was rugger-tackled and relieved of his rifle. He was then put into manacles and leg chains and the last I saw of him he was being bundled into the armoured train to be court-martialled at battalion headquarters. I should not have felt sorry for him, but I did.

I took this Company Commander out on his first and, as it turned out, last patrol. It was not a success – he hated the jungle and never went back into it again. But he did have this infuriating habit of ordering my platoon out on patrol to areas which, because of my knowledge of those areas, I knew were never used by the terrorists.

There was one occasion when I had been sent out every night for a week of night ambushes. We had had no success, nor did we expect to have any as, once again, we were always ordered to ambush tracks which were not used. On the last night I decided to ignore my orders and set out my ambush position by a track which I knew was used. This track, however, was quite close to the company jungle camp, which was fortified by barbed wire and trenches and was unfortunately overlooked by a hill, from which the terrorists could fire down on us. In the early morning, before first light, some terrorists did come along the track and we opened fire with some success.

Unfortunately, as we were so close to the camp – about 500 yards away – the camp and the Company Commander thought that they were being attacked and all hell was let loose, with bullets from our own side whistling over our heads. Eventually it all died down and at first light I went back to the camp and explained what had happened. Major Petrie was furious, and accused me of disobeying orders in the field. I explained tactfully to him that because he never went into the jungle, he was forever sending me to ambush tracks which were not used. He refused to accept this and sent me down the line to be interviewed by the Battalion Commander, with a view, as he put it, of being court-martialled. I was almost sick with nerves. I was marched into the Battalion Commander's presence, mercifully not under close arrest, and explained to him what had happened. He took a benign view of what I had done and his last words to me were, 'Don't do it again.' My relief was intense.

One day a newly commissioned second lieutenant joined us. He was a very pleasant young man but, like all of us, nervous. One night I was picket officer and doing my rounds when suddenly I heard a cry of 'Help', which was repeated several times. I traced the call to the officers' toilet, which was a one-holer hard up against the barbed wire, which meant that there was access only from the front, which was open. This young officer with his trousers down was sitting on the one-holer and immediately in front of him was a king cobra swaying backwards and forwards waiting to strike him. Mercifully I had my parang with me, and stepping up closely behind the cobra, I managed to decapitate it. It was a horrible creature, One bite and he would have been dead. The poor man was in a terrible state and I tried to calm him down. Unfortunately he lost his nerve and had to be sent back to the UK.

The company camp was situated by Kerdau station with the actual village across the line. This was now protected and guarded in an endeavour to stop food and supplies being given to the terrorists. Further down the line there was a small Malay house in which lived the most beautiful Eurasian woman, who used to walk up and down in front of us. We all lusted after her, but nobody knew if she was available or not. One early morning just before first light, a sentry thought he detected some movement by the barbed wire and opened fire and the company was 'stood to' until full dawn, when we were stood down. Later on the company cook reported sick and said that he had gashed his right shoulder. He was sent down the line to the medical officer at battalion headquarters, who advised us that it was a flesh wound occasioned by a bullet. What had happened was that the company cook was overcome with lust and had gone down the line to see the beautiful Eurasian woman and, in returning in the dark, he had stumbled against the barbed wire and had got shot. Still, it might have been worth it.

It was in the *belukar* near Kerdau that we bumped into a terrorist camp. They must have heard us coming and fled just as we were coming in – all the fires were lit and the cooking pots were still on top of the fires with hot food in them. It was a very comfortable, well equipped camp and my success was regarded as quite a coup, so much so that I was asked to re-enact an attack for the benefit of the newsreels. This we did with much gusto, and you can see me leading my men in a photograph used by Arthur Campbell in his book *Jungle Green*. For some reason I was hatless, unlike all my men, and I remembered later that I greatly disliked my jungle hat and often wore a deerstalker instead, which was more absorbent of sweat.

It was while I was stationed at Kerdau that I took my platoon to a large rubber estate, British owned, and managed by – I hope I recall his name correctly – Pat Daintry. He was experiencing a number of serious incidents, including ambushing, intimidation and shootings. He had a number of 'Specials' – short for Special Constabulary. These were all Malay. They were given a beret, a sort of khaki uniform, a pair of rubber shoes and a rifle. Ammunition was initially in very short supply and these 'Specials' were rationed to five bullets a month and the manager had to account for every bullet fired.

He had a very comfortable house on a small hill. This was surrounded by barbed wire, trenches and searchlights, in other words it was well fortified, and it had to be. Below was the rubber or latex factory and further away were the coolie lines – long rows of houses for the Indian, mainly Tamil, labour force, for whom medical and educational services were provided. Indians had originally come to Malaya as indentured labourers and in general provided cheap labour on the rubber estates as well as in the public works, railways and telephone services. They comprised 10 per cent of the population of Malaya.

Pat Daintry was a very genial, hospitable man and I greatly enjoyed our patrolling on his estate, and he often came with us.

The fact that he had a platoon of Scottish soldiers on his estate allowed him to relax and while we were there, not unnaturally, there were no incidents. He used to play records for us on his gramophone and that was the first time I heard the Polovtsian Dances. To this day, when I hear that music, it always reminds me of that lovely rubber estate bungalow in Pahang.

My final patrol at Kerdau was one of the longest and hardest I had to carry out. It was in a sense a reconnaissance expedition to ascertain if there were any terrorists in the area between Kerdau and the Sungei Pahang at Temerloh. After leaving the railway line, where unfortunately I slipped and fell and broke my one surviving pair of spectacles, we were in broken jungle and swamp – the worst combination. Our progress was painfully slow and most of us were ill from some sort of swamp fever. The leeches were atrocious and we all wondered what we were doing there. I was sick with nerves, and the only food I could eat was boiled sweets. Eventually, like all things, it did come to an end when, after a jungle bash of some 14 days, we finally reached the Sungei Pahang where most of us slept under Malayan kampong houses with the chickens and pigs. The Sungei Pahang – a very broad river at the best of times – was in full spate and somehow we had to cross it. In the end we found some *prahus* – little native canoes – which we commandeered, as the Malays were unwilling to take us across. They said it was too dangerous. We had used *prahus* before but never to cross a river such as the Sungei Pahang which was full of crocodiles and poisonous snakes.

Weighed down with all our equipment, guns and ammunition the freeboard was only about two inches – the *prahus* were not made for Europeans – we started going backwards and forwards across the river which was about a quarter of a mile wide at that point, and miraculously we all got across without mishap. The Temerloh Mentakab road ran just along the south side of the river and as this was used by military vehicles, it was not long before we were picked up and I walked into the Officers' Mess unshaven, haggard, in torn dirty clothes and smelling of swamp. What had we achieved? Nothing very much. We were able to confirm that there were no tracks in that area which had been used recently by the terrorists, no camps, and that was about all. But the journey was our achievement, and I was so proud of my men. We were close after that.

Sometime that year – we are now in 1951 – the 1st Battalion Seaforth Highlanders was relieved by the 1st Battalion Gordon Highlanders. I was told to stay on with them, so I changed my TOS (tam-o'-shanter) badge and my tartan belt. The company was moved up the railway line to Kuala Krau which, as I have mentioned earlier, had at one time been 'liberated' by the Communists. The camp was situated on a small hill overlooking the railway station. It was a pleasant spot, and being slightly elevated was refreshed from time to time with gentle breezes and, of course, also swamped from time to time with torrential monsoon deluges.

We used railway sleepers as floors for our tents but these had a disadvantage – and that was that they became home to scorpions. I have always hated scorpions, and the fact that every morning one had to shake out one's boots to ensure there were no scorpions hiding there, or anything else for that matter, made them particularly unattractive. Every month we took the sleepers up, killed the scorpions and replaced the sleepers. I used to torture them by sprinkling petrol in a circle around them, setting the petrol alight and then watch them sting themselves to death.

Once again the officers' toilet attracted attention. This was very much a home-made contraption – basically a shelter covered with atap leaves. It was close to the Officers' Mess where we used to eat when we were in camp. One evening I had to take myself off there. A storm was brewing, there were dark threatening clouds everywhere, the lightning flickered and the rain started to fall. I had just left *la petite place*, as my grandmother used to call it, when there was a blue fizzling light, an almighty crack like a thunderbolt, and *la petite place* disappeared – literally disappeared in front of me. I was so glad; ten seconds earlier and I would not have been writing this book.

The Officer Commanding Police District Kuala Krau was a singularly unattractive man – he was a short, fat, ugly brute and I recall he came from the North of England. We were, as I have mentioned before, technically in aid of the civil power and therefore acting technically in support of him. However, there was always a state of undeclared war between him and my Seaforth company, which was made much worse by the fact that he had acquired an attractive Eurasian mistress and for that we regarded him as having let the side down – the British side. We were, of course, also slightly or perhaps greatly jealous of him as we led our celibate existence near to him and his house. I remember that once, in order to repair the fences between us, he asked me to accompany him on a night wild pig shoot using strong torches. However, I felt I could not let my side down so I declined and so we continued our policy of non-cooperation. It was all ridiculously stupid, of course, but it reminded me of my great-uncle's letters from India – a huge number of them – and in those letters there was not a single mention of Indian women. There were 40 officers in his battalion, of which only two were married, so what did they do? The answer was nothing, and shooting and games took the place of women.

At Kuala Krau we started undertaking deep jungle penetration patrols in a more serious fashion, and for these we used to be supplied by air; the planes used were Dakotas of the Royal Australian Air Force. Sometimes it was difficult to find large enough clearings in the jungle for these to proceed, but they had to proceed somehow, as we usually carried rations for only a week to ten days. It was, of course, enormously important to know where you were, so that you gave the correct coordinates to the Australians. Mercifully we never suffered any really serious mishaps – the worst one was when we had to have a free fall and all the tins of rum broke on impact. That nearly did cause a mutiny, as we regularly drank rum, particularly after an engagement. As I have said earlier, we always used to receive large supplies of tinned cigarettes, partly for smoking but mainly for leeches.

It was at Kuala Krau that for the first time I came across the Sakai, who were aborigines living deep in the jungle. There were about 50,000 aborigines of a variety of tribes and these roamed their tribal grounds along the central mountain range in Pahang. For many years the Communists had given them patronage, cultivated and nurtured them, and helped them with funds and vegetable seeds. Some believed that the Communists were really their only true friends and everyone else was an enemy. In return for this help, the Communists were using them as guides, porters, food suppliers and cultivators.

There was a Sakai settlement some miles along the river to the north-west of Kuala Krau, and sometime in 1951 it was decided that they should be resettled near Kuala Krau under our protection. So a camp of wood and atap thatched huts was built for them on the assumption that they would accept settlement, but nobody was sure – we could not force them to leave the jungle; on the other hand they were being forced to provide food to the terrorists and we wanted to stop that.

So in due course we went on a mission to persuade them to come in and live near us. It took about a week to get to their camps. They were little men, naked except for a loincloth, and they still used blowpipes with poisoned darts to hunt their game in the jungle. We were greeted cordially and in the evening they gave a dinner in our honour, which consisted mainly of roast jungle rat, which was surprisingly good. Then the interpreters got to work and eventually they decided to come in. This they did, and we became friends.

One day I was commanding the crash platoon – a platoon which was always on standby for emergencies. Early that morning two Sakai came into our camp and using our interpreter they told us that the terrorists had approached them and asked them to leave food in a certain place by a certain time, and pointing up at the sun we deduced they meant by midday. So, accompanied by the Sakai and our interpreter, I set off with my platoon, and two or three hours later the Sakai told us we were there, and accordingly I laid my ambush position some way back from the track which they were to use. At midday, according to schedule, they came along the track. What happened after that is a bit vague in my memory. But it seems that the Bren-gunner on the left of my ambush line opened up prematurely, allowing the terrorists to scatter. But they scattered only temporarily, and then started to fight back – they might have been desperate for the food. Faced with this situation behind my tree in the jungle, where I could see nothing through the deep undergrowth, I decided we had better charge them and see where we went from there. Shouting 'Follow me', I stood up, ran out from behind the tree, and almost instantaneously I was struck down, with my right arm flapping uselessly. The bullet had gone straight through my upper right arm close to the shoulder, fracturing the bone and severing the main artery. Blood was everywhere and I started to faint. The medical orderly came up, and when he saw me he also fainted at the sight of my blood. When he woke up and I came round, I asked him for morphia, but he had forgotten that in a rush to leave the camp. The most important thing was to get a tourniquet on the arm as quickly as possible to stop the bleeding, or rather reduce it, and this gradually became effective and I started looking around me. Some terrorists were wounded – none were thought to be dead – so it was time to leave.

At that time I believe there were only something like three helicopters in Malaya and from the radio we were told they were all busy; in any case, we were out of range. So there was nothing for it but to resign myself to walking out of the jungle, which I did, but it was extremely painful and every hundred yards or so I had to sit down before I fainted. Eventually I got to the railway line where a train had come up for me, and I was placed on one of the flats. Once I got to the camp, I was administered the necessary morphia and I cheered up and had a cup of tea, which was extremely welcome.

The next thing was to get me down to Mentakab where there was a casualty clearing station, and here I stayed for several days – which was nearly fatal. The reason for this delay was that I had to get to the British Military Hospital at Kinrara, Kuala Lumpur where they would be able to operate on my wounded arm and shoulder, but for this I had to take the heavily ambushed road from Mentakab via Karak and Bentong to Kuala Lumpur. An emergency convoy took several days to organise and meanwhile, because the wound had not been properly cleaned out, infection had started in the bone and was spreading. Eventually a convoy was organised, and still in great pain, I was taken by ambulance to the British Military Hospital in Kinrara.

At Kinrara I was immediately operated on by a wonderful Canadian Army surgeon, Dr Taylor, and he fixed the arm. But because of the infection, I was placed on a high dose of penicillin for no less than six weeks. If penicillin had not been around, I would have died from the infection. Meanwhile, I was extremely uncomfortable in the heat covered as I was in plaster all over my right arm and shoulder, and then all round my body to the waist, leaving only my left arm and shoulder free. But the Queen Alexandra's Royal Army Nursing Corps nurses were wonderful and looked after me superbly, writing letters for me and looking after me tenderly. I loved their uniforms, beautifully starched and spotless.

Meanwhile the news of my wounds had reached the War Office in London, who decided to telephone Mummy at The Cottage, Eyke. The telephone rang, she lifted it and then suddenly fainted when she heard the words 'War Office'. It was the news she had been dreading, and she did not know whether I was dead, dying or wounded severely – it was, of course, the latter. My stepfather, Uncle Robin, came to see what was the matter, picked up the telephone and was given the information as to what had happened. Mummy recovered and was told I was alive; not well, but expected to pull through. And pull through I did, although it took several months.

After six weeks at the British Military Hospital, Kinrara, it was decided to move me down to the British Military Hospital, Singapore, preparatory to getting a boat back to the UK. That should have been all right except that the casualty evacuation plane, a converted DC3, went up in the late afternoon and everybody knows that in the tropics you sometimes have huge build-ups of cumulonimbus and torrential thunderstorms. This was my first flight, but at least I felt secure on my stretcher strapped to the floor of the plane. But then we hit the 'cu-nim' and we were tossed up and around so violently that I thought my last hour had come. Indeed, it was nearly the case, as we had to make a forced landing on a grass airstrip short of Singapore. Eventually we took off again and reached Singapore safely.

I never saw all my notes and maps again. The notes were highly detailed and contained descriptions of each jungle patrol I had been on, with notes as to the geology, the fauna and flora and the track conditions etcetera. What a loss – I minded it so much. Meanwhile in the British Military Hospital, Singapore, I waited until one day it was announced to me that I would be joining the British Indian Steam Navigation Company's motor vessel *Dunera*, another liner converted to military use. I was going home.

The voyage home was long and boring. We were not allowed to land in Colombo, and because of what the Victorians would have called 'complications with the natives', we were not allowed to land at Aden.

This only left Port Said, and here, I have to say, I was very foolish and this foolishness nearly cost me my life. I went ashore in my kilt, still swathed in plaster from neck to waist with only my good arm, my left arm, free. I wanted to go for a long walk after having been cooped up in hospitals and troopships for so long. I went further than I should have and I discovered later that the area was out of bounds to British troops. There were a number of ramshackle buildings about, surrounded by ramshackle bamboo scaffolding. As I walked along the so-called pavement, a brick fell down, narrowly missing me. I did not take much notice, but when several bricks began falling around me, I realised I was the object of some intention and that intention was my death.

The sight of a kilted British officer swathed in plaster with bricks falling down around him attracted the attention of a crowd, and they began to pick up stones to throw at me. I considered discretion was the better part of valour, so I took to my heels, feeling very white, stupid and incongruous. It was an ignominious retreat, running along as best as I could in my plaster, pursued by children throwing stones at me. It was, for a short time, an unpleasant experience and it shook me up, particularly when I realised I had risked death entirely unnecessarily. Eventually I regained the dockside and my attackers left me.

When I reached Southampton I was taken firstly to the nearby Netley Hospital, a large Florence Nightingale establishment. I stayed there for a short time before being moved to the Military Hospital at Millbank and then finally to the Military Hospital at Colchester, from which I was discharged fit and ready to return to duty. I therefore rejoined my battalion at Cavalry Barracks Redford in Edinburgh, and spent the rest of my time training soldiers for the war in Korea. I shared a room with Robin Douglas-Home – he was a better pianist than I was. He eventually married Sandra Paul, and committed suicide when she left him. She finally married, fourth time round, Michael Howard, who later became the leader of the Conservative Party.

I had enjoyed my soldiering except for the first and last periods, and that was because I went out to the Far East. Soldiering in the UK or Ireland was not for me – it would have been utterly boring. I was asked to stay on and I declined, but I did sign on, as I had to for a period of eleven years, with the Territorial Army the 11th Battalion Seaforth Highlanders based at Dingwall north of Inverness. I also became, unknown to me at the time, a Z Reservist and later on, when I was living in Paris and some international incident with the Russians blew up, I received a letter from Edinburgh reminding me that I was a Z Reservist and that, on the receipt of a first-class single ticket to Edinburgh, I was to proceed directly there and await instructions. But I never received the ticket.

So now I was a civilian again. What was I going to do? I was restless, I did not want to settle down, I was only 20. I considered university and taking a degree in geography and glaciology, but I had no money and my mother had no money. That left the Lyons Hall Estate trustees. Bear in mind that provided I survived to the age of 25, then my interest therein could not be defeated – in other words, I was the heir to the estate. I therefore got in touch with Paddy Tritton, who rejoiced in the title of managing trustee, and asked him if I could be provided with some funds to enable me to go to university. His reply was in the negative, and from then on he was about as awkward and difficult as any man could be. He also had a foul temper – no wonder his first wife left him, but that may have soured him for life.

Whenever he was refusing me something, as he always did, he reminded me that my grandfather, his Uncle Leslie, had been his benefactor. I longed to point out to him that this was a totally contradictory position to take, but I am afraid it was the case that I was frightened of him. He had the cheque book and the authority, and I had no weapons or ammunition at all.

My grandfather had been his benefactor, and that of his brothers and sisters, because when Paddy's father, my great-uncle Arthur Tritton, lost all his money in the Crash of 1929, my grandfather helped them financially; to what extent I obviously did not know. But refusing me everything was a gross abuse of my grandfather's generosity to his family. This was the first of his many truly inimical acts, and his first cousin, my Aunt Dore Garnett, who was to become the life tenant of the Lyons Hall Estate following the death of my grandmother, adopted a similar attitude.

Many people are jealous of the next generation – I have never been – and this may have been the case with my aunt. But there were other factors at work, one of which was that if I had not been born, the estate could have gone to Paddy. There were no other grandsons.

For many years the hostility shown to me by my Tritton family both perplexed and horrified me, and it became implacable when I married a Catholic. To this day I still wonder why. What really was the origin of this antipathy? And why did my aunt, who was chairbound and later bedridden as a result of a stroke, look at me just before she died with real hatred in her eyes? Actually, her last words to me were, 'I hate you'. Why? Why? Why?

So Paddy Tritton put an end to my university plans – or perhaps it was Aunt Dore – and I have never forgiven them for that.

Later on I found a letter from Cousin Paddy to a lawyer describing me as a fairly stupid and extremely tactless young man, who had antagonised his Aunt Dore by marrying a Roman Catholic girl and it was because of this that he had such difficulty in getting her to make over any money to me.

13

The Falkland Islands and its Dependencies

So, again, what could I do? I now decided I wanted to go to the Polar regions, preferably the Antarctic, but the Arctic as a second choice. Therefore I wrote to Commander Simpson who was both leading and organising the British North Greenland Expedition, applying to join his expedition. However, I was too late as he had already made up his numbers. So I began thinking seriously about the Falkland Islands Dependencies Survey – in any case I had always wanted to go south not north.

Before going any further I must introduce you, first of all, to the Falkland Islands, secondly, the Falkland Islands Dependencies and, thirdly, the Falkland Islands Dependencies Survey, which later became known as the British Antarctic Survey.

In 1950 the Falkland Islands were almost unknown. In 1940 even the Admiralty, which should have known better, sent out a signal following the German invasion of Norway, warning the Orkneys, Shetlands and the Falkland Islands that, as a result of this invasion, they were to expect German canoeists. As somebody said at the time, that would be some canoe trip – several thousands of miles down across the North Atlantic and the South Atlantic, virtually all the way to Cape Horn – some 8,000 miles. The islands lie in the South Atlantic Ocean between 51 degrees and 53 degrees South and 57 degrees and 62 degrees West – that is to say about 250 miles to the east and somewhat to the north of Cape Horn. The islands are in the same latitude south as London is north. They comprise two large islands – East Falkland and West Falkland separated by the Falkland Sound – and about 200 smaller islands ranging in size from a few acres to 82 square miles.

The two main islands have a very deeply indented coastline,

147

providing many excellent harbours and anchorages but, as we all know, the seas can be exceptionally rough and tides and currents treacherous, so that they have provided a graveyard for a large number of sailing ships – as I recall, something in the order of 130 wrecks. The country is hilly and can best be described as wild moorland with frequent rocky outcrops and those peculiar stretches of angular rocks which look just as if they had been poured down from the hills and which are known as stone runs or stone rivers. The soil is chiefly peat and much of this is waterlogged and, as I found to my cost, quite difficult to negotiate in winter. The islands are exceptionally beautiful, but it does take a fine sunny day to appreciate them fully.

Except where they have been planted, there are no trees. Apart from Stanley, where every home has its garden, there is no cultivation except in the immediate vicinity of the farm settlements, which are all situated on the coast for access to shipping. There is an enormous wealth of bird and marine life, prevalent among the former being the penguins and albatrosses, and among the latter the sea lions and elephant seals.

The one thing one always remembers about the islands is the wind, which often blows at gale force and maintains an average of 15 knots – half a gale – throughout the year.

The islands were discovered by Captain John Davis when his ship, the *Desire*, was driven by storms among the islands. Captain Davis, second in command of Sir Thomas Cavendish's second expedition to the South Seas, had lost contact with the other ships when the fleet was forced by bad weather in the Strait of Magellan to put back into the South Atlantic. The *Desire* and the *Pinnace Black* reached the agreed regrouping point, Port Desire on the Patagonian coast, where Davis had to carry out extensive repairs.

Davis was making his way from Port Desire to the Strait in the hope of finding Cavendish there when, as John Jane who travelled on the Desire and chronicled the voyage records:

On the 9th we had a sore storme so that we were constrained to hull, for our sails were not to endure any force. The 14th we were driven among certain islands never before discovered by any known relation, lying fifty leagues or better from the shore, easterly and northerly from the Strait, in which place unless it had pleased God of his wonderful mercy to have ceased the winds, we must of necessity have perished.

The first landing of which there is certain knowledge was made in 1690 from the English sloop *Welfare* commanded by John Strong who, on a privateering cruise against the French – who were then at war with England – was driven by westerly winds among the islands. Captain Strong identified and sailed along the sound between East and West Falkland, naming it Falkland Sound after the then First Lord of the Admiralty.

Captain Davis's discovery of the islands had in fact been confirmed in 1594 when Sir Richard Hawkins sailed along the north coast. However, he did not land: 'The want of a pinnace disabled us from finding a port, not being discretion with a ship of charge in an unknown coast to come near the shore, before it was sounded.' He did, however, give the first description of the islands: 'a goodly champion country much of the disposition of England and as temperate'.

Later, that is to say in the eighteenth century, many French ships started trading with the Spanish Pacific ports, later both legally and illegally under the Assiento, which was the contract to supply slaves to Buenos Aires which the French acquired in 1706. Many of these ships resorted to the Islands to take on water and revive their scurvy-ridden crews – perhaps they did not bother about the slaves – the islands being a rich source of the plant (scurvy grass) that made this possible. The French also gave the islands a new name, Isles Malouines, after St Malo, the port from which most of the French ships came. This was corrupted by the Spanish into Islas Malvinas, which is the name the Argentinians use. It has nothing to do with 'bad winds', a common misconception.

It was in 1764 that the French, under the command of Louis de Bougainville with the permission of the French foreign minister the Duc de Choiseul, established a settlement in the islands, naming it Port Louis in honour of the French King.

It was in 1765 that Captain Byron, who had been sent out by the Admiralty to survey the islands, landed at what is now known as Saunders Island. Naming the harbour Port Egmont, the then First Lord of the Admiralty, he took possession of the islands in the name of King George III. He did this not knowing that in the previous year they had also been claimed in the name of the King of France.

Shortly afterwards the French colony passed into Spanish hands. The Spanish government, on learning of the colony from its agents in Montevideo, instructed its ambassador in Paris to inform the French Government that the Bourbon Pacte de Famille – the French and Spanish Kings were cousins – which had recently been concluded did not authorise such a one-sided action. At the same time, Spain not only invoked the Bourbon Pacte de Famille but also the Treaty of Tordesillas under which Pope Alexander VI had awarded to Spain all the land in those waters.

On 10th June 1770 the Spanish made a surprise attack on Port Egmont and forced the British garrison to surrender, and although the settlement was soon restored, it was abandoned in 1774.

There is a fascinating story behind the Spanish attack on Port Egmont and its subsequent restoration. Following the attack and surrender, the British Government issued an ultimatum to the King of Spain demanding restitution of the colony. Encouraged by the French foreign minister, the Duc de Choiseul, the Spanish now attempted once again to invoke the Bourbon Pacte de Famille (which had, as it happens, been established by Choiseul himself), stipulating that if necessary the Bourbon thrones of France and Spain would come to the support of each other.

In the meantime those in Paris who were against Choiseul were horrified at the thought of a war between England on one side and France and Spain on the other – a war which could be disastrous to France. After considerable discussion it was decided that the secret weapon to be launched against Choiseul was the King of France's new mistress, the beautiful Madame du Barry. Under pressure from Madame du Barry, the King, who usually found it impossible to make up his mind about anything, pulled himself together to write a letter to Choiseul dismissing him as chief minister.

On the 23rd December 1770 the King, who still had not sent the letter of dismissal to Choiseul, met up with him only to be told by him that war was now inevitable and that Spain, France and England were now mobilising their troops. The King immediately told Choiseul to inform Madrid that there would be no French support for a war with Spain over the Falkland Islands, and he requested Spain to accede to the British demands.

It was decided to follow this up with a personal letter from the King of France to his cousin the King of Spain, explaining to him why France would not come to the assistance of Spain. According to Talleyrand, who is usually very reliable in such matters, it was Madame du Barry who, after a long night of love in bed with the

King, drafted and then wrote the letter in the King's name, once again telling his cousin to accede to the British demands.

It all seems very likely. The anti-Choiseul faction would never have sent his mistress to give the King the night of his life without fully briefing her on what sort of letter was required. It worked, and the King of Spain immediately wrote to his cousin with the words, among others, 'I will do everything possible to prevent war'. Thus the war was averted and Port Egmont on West Falkland restored to the British.

So very grateful thanks are due to that lovely lady who, in one of those ironies of fate, was betrayed and denounced by the Englishman George Grieve and guillotined in Paris during the French Revolution.

It is certainly not for me in this book to set out the history of the Falkland Islands, which has been excellently chronicled by Mary Cawkell in her book the *Falkland Story 1592–1982* – 1982 being the year the Argentinians invaded the islands – and now I must move on to the Dependencies and the Survey.

The territory covered by the Dependencies is essentially a triangle, with the South Pole at its southernmost point or apex. Their principal geographical features are South Georgia, the South Sandwich Islands, the South Orkney Islands, the South Shetland Islands and Graham Land, now more commonly known as the Antarctic Peninsula. The area was annexed to the Crown by Letters Patent in 1908.

Although South Georgia is supposed to have been first sighted by Amerigo Vespucci in 1502, it is certain nobody set foot on its shores until 1775 when it was visited, charted and claimed for the Crown by Captain Cook in the course of his historic circumnavigation of the Southern Ocean. Reports of the vast number of whales and seals aroused the interest of British and American sealers, and it was their voyages which led to the discovery of many of the Antarctic islands and in 1820 to the discovery of the Antarctic mainland itself – as it happens, the same year as King George IV's accession and coronation.

Until 1925 no other nation challenged or, for that matter, commented on the British claim. It was, however, in that year that Argentina suddenly and very surprisingly formulated claims to the South Orkney Islands. More audaciously, in 1927, the Argentinians extended their claim to include South Georgia, and by 1937 had claimed the right to all the Dependencies.

When war broke out in 1939, the early course of hostilities no doubt encouraged the Argentinians to hope that Britain would be defeated and that the Dependencies would fall to Argentina without further argument. The Argentine claim, as I understand it, was based on geographical proximity and the papal decree of 1494 embodied in the Treaty of Tordesillas mentioned earlier, allocating to Spain all lands west of a meridian thought to run south from the southern tip of Greenland – the title to which Argentina had declared she had inherited.

All this was complicated by the fact that in 1940 Chile, unwilling to miss out on any pickings, also put forward a claim to a nearly identical area which included all the Falkland Islands Dependencies. Her grounds were based not only on geographical proximity but also on the somewhat specious claim that geologically the Antarctic Peninsula is a continuation of the Andes and thus part of the motherland.

In 1942 an Argentinian expedition visited Deception Island and on 8th February purported to take possession of the sector between 25°W and 68°34'W. This was formally reported to the British Government, as a result of which HMS *Carnarvon Castle* was ordered to Deception and, in January 1943, Argentina's marks of sovereignty were obliterated, the Union Jack hoisted, and a record of the visit left behind.

This then was the political background which led to the British Government, even in time of war, to take action to preserve the country's existing rights by establishing a small number of survey stations. This is how the British Antarctic Survey started, although for the first two years it was a naval exercise mounted under Admiralty auspices and code-named Operation Tabarin, the name of a London nightclub being thought very suitable for a detachment which was to winter in the Antarctic darkness. Not only had the activities of German commerce raiders brought home the strategic importance of Antarctica, but political developments within Argentina made it highly undesirable that that country should be in a position to control the southern side of Drake Passage, the only sea route to the Pacific Ocean if the Panama Canal was put out of action. The original intention was for two bases to be established, one to guard Deception Island and the other to occupy a position on the Antarctic Peninsula. The detachment at Deception, while doing what it could to deny the use of this harbour to enemy commerce raiders – quite impossible – would be in a position to provide information on the activities of both enemy and neutral vessels. Deception Island is appropriately named, for it is only from a narrow angle that one can see where the coastline is breached by a gap known as Neptune's Bellows; so small and narrow is it that it almost seems you can reach out and touch the rocks either side, when you enter the water-filled volcanic crater. Suddenly you are in the calm waters of a huge landlocked harbour 7 miles across. This magnificent sheltered harbour was first seen some time after 1819 when the South Shetlands were discovered by Captain William Smith in the brig *Williams*. It provided shelter for many of the sealing ships during the nineteenth century but it was not until 1910 that it became a major whaling station, the shore-based operations continuing until 1931 when it was abandoned.

The other base was intended to be sited at Hope Bay at the northernmost tip of the Antarctic Peninsula. The two ships SS *Scoresby* and SS *Fitzroy* entered Antarctic Sound between Trinity Peninsula and Joinville Island but there was too much ice about and the *Fitzroy* was not equipped to sail in ice. Later they sailed south through Gerlache Strait to a small sheltered bay surrounded by high ice-cliffs. This was Port Lockroy on Wiencke Island, which had been used in the past by whaling ships.

Thus was born my Survey – I have always been proprietorial. Once again, as with the islands, I will not write at any length about the Dependencies and history of the British Antarctic Survey: for this I will pass you on to the book entitled *Of Ice and Men* by Sir Vivian Fuchs – Bunny to all of us who knew him.

It was this Survey that I decided to apply for in the summer of 1952. I was duly called for an interview at the Crown Agents' office near Westminster Abbey and shortly afterwards, to my great joy, I learnt that I had been accepted. This joy was not, I am afraid, shared by Mummy – after all I had only recently returned from Malaya – and I am pretty sure it was not shared by members of the Tritton family. Why were they always so negative about me? All this was in the summer of 1952 and thereafter the pace of events hotted up. I had a medical and there was a lot of discussion as to whether I should have my appendix out before I sailed south. After all, they said, your father died of appendicitis and only one of the Survey stations has a doctor, and no ship can get through

153

to your station during the Antarctic winter and, in any case, the relief vessel will not go south until the austral spring, November or December.

All these seemed to be formidable reasons as to why I should have my appendix out; in the event, however, I decided against it and I had no problems then or, as it happens, ever since. The next item was the dentist. There were no dentists at all down south, so it was very important that my teeth were in very good order. I recall I was given some protection for them from very cold weather during the Antarctic winter, but I cannot remember what this was. We were given a plentiful supply of cloves, these being considered the best antidote for toothache. In the event I had no dental problems. Curiously enough I never worried about health problems whilst I was down south and, indeed, I have never felt fitter in all my life than when I was in the Antarctic.

As I had no professional qualifications – I really was too young to have any, being not yet 21 – the Survey sent me on a three months' meteorological course at the Met Office which was then under the Air Ministry up at Stanmore in Middlesex. So every day I commuted from my bedsitter to Stanmore to learn how to be a meteorologist, and particularly a meteorologist in the Antarctic.

As a result of decisions taken by the Government of the Falkland Islands and the Dependencies, a meteorological organisation had been established without precedent in the Antarctic and I was to be part of this. Essentially the general functions of the service were: the provision of forecasting services for the whaling fleets, then operating in South Atlantic and Antarctic waters; the organisation of meteorological observations and the broadcasting of this information in the form of collective messages to be used by South American countries, South Africa and ships operating in the area; the collection and publication of climatic data and investigations into the meteorology of the Falkland Islands and the Dependencies. To me all this was pretty heady stuff.

The meteorological instruments we were to use were of the then latest type used in the British Meteorological Service and included the following as standard:

i) Temperature and Humidity: Dry and Wet – bulb, maximum and minimum thermometers, psychrometer, thermograph and hygrograph.

   ii)   Atmospheric pressure: barometer (marine type) and barograph.

  iii) Wind: electrically controlled wind vane and cup anemometer.

  iv) Cloud: cloud searchlight and nephoscope.

   v) Precipitation: rain-gauge.

  vi) Sunshine: sunshine recorder.

 vii) Upper winds: pilot balloon equipment.

Owing to the extreme nature of Antarctic weather our observations were subject to special difficulties, which included: the failure of instruments affected by very low temperatures, heavy snowdrifts and icing; cases of the anemometer being blown away by strong winds; the observational programme being interrupted by the inability of the observer to reach the instruments during blizzard conditions – there were several occasions when the winds were so strong that I was lifted up into the air trying to reach my instruments; humidity values derived at low temperatures from dry and wet bulb thermometers being subject to large errors; owing to the 'pumping action ' caused by gusty winds, difficulty in assessing the atmospheric pressure accurately; the association of cloud types at certain height ranges in temperate climates not being applicable in the polar regions.

The daily and nightly carrying out of synoptic observation kept us always very close to the weather, and apart from the snow and ice, my main memory of the Antarctic is almost continual wind interspersed by periods of calm sunny weather, making the Antarctic the most beautiful place on earth.

But I have moved on a little too far and I now need to go back to October 1952, when the Royal Research Ship, the *John Biscoe*, departed from Southampton Docks for Stanley and the far South. Prior to my departure I gave my twenty-first birthday party at the house of a friend of mine, George Cooper, in Ennismore Gardens Mews. There were lots of beautiful girls there and I suddenly became very conscious that after leaving for the Falkland Islands, I would not see another girl for something like 18 months – a sobering thought in the midst of the champagne. In fact, I had a very protracted celibate life, what with fighting in the Far East and a long-extended period in the Antarctic. I always remember, going back to Kuala Krau in Pahang, that I was quite jealous of our local OCPD (Officer Commanding Police District), a small ugly fat brute of a man who had acquired a very attractive Eurasian mistress. Such a relationship was of course impossible for an officer in a fighting regiment, because of the honour of the regiment and fears of 'conduct unbecoming'. And this reminded me that when I was talking with my sister's mother-in-law, Lady Phyllis MacRae, who had accompanied her husband, a serving officer in the Seaforth Highlanders, to India in 1925, she mentioned that nearly all the officers were unmarried. I think there was only one other officer accompanied by his wife. Bearing in mind that most Indian women are extremely attractive, did they not feel tempted? Or were they afraid, like me to 'let the side down' by consorting with a 'native' woman? Would this have been considered 'conduct unbecoming'? Almost certainly. Reading the letters of my great-uncle, who served in India with the Seaforth Highlanders on the North-West Frontier, there is not a single mention of Indians of the female sex. How sad! And how huge their sacrifice for the British Empire, including, in his case, his life.

Many years later I asked a very old friend of mine, who had served in India in the olden pre-war days, whether the temptation ever came over him at his station. He answered yes and the signal to the servants was to leave the bathroom door open and a lady would appear. However, he said, it was imperative that she left his bed before his servants brought him his early morning tea. It was very different for us, young commissioned officers of the imperial Army in the Far East, as any such native alliance would have not only hopelessly compromised my position, but also that of the regiment. In fact, I would probably have been dismissed from the regiment.

14

Southern Voyage

On 20th October 1952, having said goodbye, I boarded my train at Woodbridge Station and set off for Southampton. At the station I got a taxi and told the driver to go to Berth 37 in the docks. I duly arrived but there was no ship – or that was how it appeared. And then I noticed a crow's nest sticking up just above the dock wall and realised the RRS *John Biscoe* was so small that it lay well below the dock wall. For a 10,000 mile voyage, she was not hugely encouraging.

The Survey had originally relied on chartered vessels for the relief of the Survey stations but this was not satisfactory and before I arrived in the Antarctic, Sir James Wordie, who had been a member of Shackleton's *Endurance* expedition, found a wooden-hulled harbour net-layer, built in America, but which during the war had seen service with the Royal Navy as HMS *Prefect*. After the war she had been returned to the Americans, as she formed part of the Lend-Lease Agreement.

She was built of pitch pine, but amidships and fore and aft, up to the waterline, she was sheathed in greenheart, the toughest wood, as a protection against the ice. She displaced about 1,000 tons, had a length of just under 200 feet, a beam of 30 feet and a draft of 14 feet. Her twin diesel electric engines developed 1,200 horsepower and her maximum speed was about 10 knots. She had been renamed the Royal Research Ship *John Biscoe* in honour of an Enderby Brothers sealing skipper who circumnavigated the Antarctic and annexed Graham Land on the Antarctic Peninsula for the Crown in 1832.

I climbed down, not up, to the ship, where I was greeted and told to sign on as a member of the ship's crew at a rate of pay of a shilling a month – I believe that being signed on as a supernumerary was for the purpose of marine insurance. I then went down a stairway so steep and narrow that one would never forget to refer to it as a companionway. There I found 'Expedition Wardroom' written over the bulkhead – at last I was a member again of another expedition.

We had canvas bunks, chained in tiers of three, and we each had a small locker. In the wardroom was a table, a locker for drinks, a few chairs chained to the floor, and of all things a red rexine settee. Opposite the small galley up top was a washroom and shower – salt water only. There were no portholes because there were no openings of any sort in the hull – the ship was built for strength and the ice.

There was a ventilator on deck but this was clamped shut in heavy seas. Our quarters extended across the ship just forward of the engine room bulkhead and we were always warm – too warm in the tropics, when I chose to sleep on the open deck and watched the mast and crow's nest swing gently backwards and forwards across the dark starlit sky. It was heavenly, peaceful and spiritual.

So there we were on board on 20th October 1952. There were meteorologists, surveyors, scientists, geologists, engineers, radio operators and carpenters. I think it would have been hard to find a more dissimilar crowd – we came from all walks of life – but we soon settled down and looked forward to the long voyage south.

Our departure was an occasion for a television outside broadcast and the reporters milled about on the dockside trying to pick up human interest stories. At last, at 3 p.m., the pilot came on board and we sailed amidst cheers, tears, streamers and 'Auld Lang Syne'. And now we were on our own. There was a slight sea, a low swell, and it was cloudy with poor visibility, as the boat, heavily laden with a huge deck cargo, rolled sluggishly at the beginning of its 8,000-mile voyage to Stanley.

On the second day we ran into a severe storm, the worst the Bay of Biscay can produce. There was a huge sea running and a heavy, short swell making the ship roll and pitch alarmingly. At the same time we were shipping seas forward with heavy spray all over the ship and poor visibility.

It was an experience which was to be repeated many times: the ship with horrible regularity rising to dizzy heights, then crashing down and falling on its beam ends. I spent some time on the bridge with the Captain and the officer of the watch carrying out my meteorological duties. As I did so, I watched the pendulum as roughly three times a minute the ship rolled through an arc of nearly 90 degrees. These huge swings and rolls were only surpassed during a violent storm that we experienced in 1954 when we were sailing north-westwards from Thule, the southernmost island in the South Sandwich Islands group. Once again, I was on the bridge watching the pendulum when suddenly the ship swung through a total arc of 112 degrees – 56 degrees on either side. It is almost impossible to describe a storm at sea in a small ship: the convulsive crashing of the ship, the screaming of the wind in the rigging, the huge seas towering above the ship threatening to overwhelm us with each successive wave, the loss of boundary between the sea and the air, the seawater surging over the decks and the spray flying over all.

At midnight on the third day we were still hove-to when suddenly the lashings on the foredeck cargo carried away and all the hydrogen cylinders on deck broke away and crashed into the scow which was also lashed to the foredeck. A scow is a large flat-bottomed boat with squarish ends, which we used to relieve the survey stations. At 2.30 a.m. we shipped a particularly heavy sea which carried our life-rafts overboard and at about the same time the clamps on our weather door broke away and suddenly huge amounts of water were pouring down our companionway. The lights went out, and the engines stopped. The water kept on pouring down, and with each successive roll surged backwards and forwards and deeper and deeper, flooding our wardroom and bunks and lockers.

At long last the bosun and the mate arrived and after a lot of metallic hammering managed to secure the weather door; and for the next 24 hours we had to bale out our quarters. The lights came on, the engines restarted and we felt we were going to survive. At the height of the storm I used to go down to the engine room where the motion of the ship was less violent, preferring the smell of the diesel oil to the instability of the deck. Mercifully, I have never been seasick in my life.

The following day the wind dropped from hurricane force to a steady 40-mile-an-hour gale, but there was such a huge sea running that it really made very little difference to the motion of the ship. At last, however, we could leave our wet fug-hole and venture out onto the deck, which was only a few feet above the sea and

159

frequently under it. It was an exhilarating sight – the mountainous waves even larger now because their crests were no longer whipped off in spray. And as the ship slid down in a deep trough, each wave appeared as a wall of green marble, beautifully veined with skeins of white lacy foam, then as the ship started wallowing, the wave lifted up its towering side and for a moment hung high, oh so high, translucent against the sky, that each time I thought it would crash down on to the stern and poop us. Some time later a German four-masted sailing barque, carrying a large crew of cadets and grain from Buenos Aires to Hamburg, was pooped in the South Atlantic and went down with all hands.

By the fifth day the weather improved, the wind force decreased and we sighted the Island of Madeira to the east. Then days later we arrived at St Vincent in the Cape Verde Islands where the ship was watered and bunkered, but we had no time to go ashore – anyway it was night-time.

What did we do while we were at sea? We made our regular weather observations, we holystoned the decks, we washed our clothes, we peeled potatoes, we stood in the bows watching the porpoises race in front of the ship, and at night, as I lay on the deck and before I went to sleep, each gentle roll of the ship brought the phosphorescent waves level with my eyes and the dark silhouette of the crow's nest swayed to and fro against the starlit heavens far overhead. A great peace came over me and I was very, very happy.

After three weeks at sea the wind changed, the temperature started to drop, and then one day there rose up in the distance a plume of spray, which stood for a moment before it disappeared – it was a whale spouting. And then one day again there was a great bird, now floating aloft above the crow's nest and now skimming down over the tops of the waves on motionless outstretched wings – our first sight of the wandering albatross. The flight of the great albatross is a lovely poem in motion. He takes the wind in huge arcs and circles, sometimes close to the ship, sometimes far off, sometimes gliding down so that the tips of his wings almost touch the water and then rushing upwards into the sky without moving his wings at all. Don't fall overboard when the albatrosses are around as they will be on to you at once, and they will go straight for your eyes. On 13th November, 20 days out from Southampton, we sighted Cabo Polonio on the Uruguayan coast. Later we took on the Montevideo pilot and an hour later we docked and we were all off the ship like a flash of lightning – aiming for the bars, nightclubs and restaurants (food was still rationed in England), and our last chance to see a pretty girl for nearly two years.

Three days later the pilot came on board again, a tug edged us out and we were on our way south to Port Stanley. Two days later we were in the Roaring Forties, the sky overcast with hurrying masses of grey cloud under which the sea was iron-grey and sullen, the waves rushing forward before a driving wind and creaming at their tops into masses of foam which slid down their backs, the ship rolling and pitching heavily with spray over all – the Forties were living up to their reputation.

In the old sailing days when the grain ships used to fight their way round Cape Horn from Australia to England, the sailors knew that before they reached the trade winds and the blue tropical seas, the Southern Ocean between the latitudes of 40 and 50 degrees South lay in wait for them with furious gales, fog and icebergs drifting forlorn and lonely up from the south. They gave the name 'Roaring Forties' to this part of the South Atlantic Ocean for these are, I suppose, the most terrible and dangerous seas in the world. Across these seas great blustery gales and depressions rush shrieking one after another, and there is nothing to stop them. The elements rage together in a welter of grey nothingness, hundreds of miles from land, whilst further south are the 'furious fifties', the 'shrieking sixties' and, even further south, the 'frigid seventies' – the home of the pack ice.

But now in these southern seas we saw more and more life: wandering albatross, sooty albatross, the speckled Cape pigeons with their quick, busy flight, continuously settling on the water and then hurrying on again. Flocks of whale birds skimmed about and Mother Carey's chickens rode on the backs of the waves. The spoutings of the whales became more frequent, followed by their long curving backs. For this part of the sea swarms with minute life which every southern spring bursts into swarming activity forming the food of all these birds and whales who live here.

As we came up to the Falkland Islands, which are in the same latitude south as London is north, the wind dropped, the ship rolled easier, the sun came out and it was a beautiful bright day with a gloriously clear blue sky as we entered the Stanley Narrows, came through into the harbour and berthed alongside the jetty. It was 31 days since we had left Southampton. It had been a long voyage, and I had put on weight.

Stanley from the seaward, and particularly on that fine sunny day, is attractive with its clusters of clapboard houses overlooking the harbour, the blue waters of the harbour providing a beautiful background to their coloured walls and roofs, neat garden plots, and all the glass porches and verandahs full of flowers. And, of course, the famous hideous Jubilee villas built of brick immediately up from the jetty. All the houses had electricity, plumbing and peat fires, although in my experience peat fires never give out much heat – they merely smoulder. There were five pubs in Stanley – the best known were The Globe and The Upland Goose – and to complement the five pubs there were five churches, a large number for a population of around 1,000 people. The most significant of these was the Anglican Cathedral with its whalebone entrance. There was a school, a hospital and a Government House, and beyond that a road leading westwards for 5 miles – the only road in the colony, and it was on that road I renewed my driving licence, so that I became the proud possessor of a Falkland Islands driving licence.

In those days the colony was quite poor, unlike now, except for the sheep farmers who were still riding high on the prices received during the Korean War wool boom – but all this came to an end. When I first visited the islands the total island flock amounted to some 600,000 head of which a third were owned by the Falkland Islands Company. Most of these were Romney and Corriedale with pedigree rams being imported occasionally from Patagonia and New Zealand. It was a hard life for the men who worked on the sheep stations and many wanted to get away to Australia and New Zealand.

Stanley was fun, but there was a lot of work to do, including an interview with the Governor, Sir Miles Clifford. During the course of this interview, I was asked to lead the Survey station at Signy Island in the South Orkneys. Initially I demurred – I really wanted to go to Hope Bay on the Antarctic Peninsula from which the main survey journeys were being undertaken, down mainly the East Coast of the Peninsula, but the monocled, autocratic colonial Governor had decided that the South Orkneys was the Survey station for me and I was just the man to lead it. I did not feel I could refuse, so I accepted it.

On 24th November at 10 p.m. we let go forward and aft and

by 10.30 p.m. we were under way for Hope Bay and the Antarctic on a slight sea and swell. It was exciting to be on the final leg south and south was where I had wanted to go for a long time. On the second day out the sea got up, the temperature dropped to freezing and it started to snow. And then we saw our first icebergs drifting lonely and forlorn up from the south. On 27th November in the afternoon we sighted Cape Dubouzet and shortly afterwards entered Hope Bay. At 6 p.m. Doctor George Marsh, the leader of the station, came on board. He was to become a good friend of mine and some years later on he was appointed consultant haematologist at the Hammersmith Hospital.

The weather then deteriorated with frequent snow showers and a heavy swell from the north-east, which made unloading impossible. However, next day the weather improved and for the next 14 hours we loaded stores into the scow and ferried them to the ice-cliff above which the station was situated at Hut Point. The following day we resumed landing stores at Hut Point and once again worked until ten o'clock at night and, at midnight, weighed anchor, having taken on board three FIDS (members of the Falkland Islands Dependencies Survey): Bruce Hill, Brian Hunt and Max Unwin.

Just after midnight, we cleared Cape Doubouzet and set off for Deception Island, avoiding numerous icebergs and growlers. Nine hours later we entered Neptune's Bellows and sailed into the harbour. The island is in fact a volcano, which has now sunk, letting the sea into the crater. The volcano is not yet extinct so that, inside the harbour, there is an unpleasant sulphurous stench and steam continually rising from the beach. In spite of the ice that during the winter and spring choke the harbour, the black volcanic sand and the shallows of the sea's margin are steaming and warm. Deception Island is both an insecure and a depressing place, which I was glad to leave. Several years later, the volcano reactivated itself and there was a massive eruption – I am glad I was not there.

The glory of Deception Island, if it can be described as such, has long since departed. In the boom years of the whaling industry 1927–30, dozens of whaling factory ships used to make fast to the shore during the summer, while their fleets of catchers spread slaughter in the seas outside, which abounded in whales. There was also a whaling station in the harbour and a small hut containing an office where a British official carried out the duties of a magistrate, whatever they may have been, to the community of Norwegian whalers.

The whalers used to arrive at Deception Island in November when the ice cleared. In the early years before the introduction of whaling regulations, the catchers used to bring in whales at such a speed that the factories only stripped off the blubber and let the rest of the carcass, the skrott, float away, so that the shores became littered with rotting corpses. Long after the regulations obliged the factories to use up the whole carcass, the bleached skeletons remained, giant vertebrae, ribs and skulls testifying to the ruthless slaughter which had taken place only 20 years before I visited the island.

When I arrived there in 1952, Deception Harbour was silent and deserted except for the British station situated amid the rusting machinery, tanks and boilers and the wind-shattered factory building. The station itself was an old whalers' dormitory which had been left in good condition. We reprovisioned the base and this only took eight hours. We were thankful to leave this depressing, unstable island where one of the Survey personnel had committed suicide following receipt of a letter from his ex-wife.

We set sail for Admiralty Bay in the South Shetlands, having completed watering, and we arrived there at midnight on 3rd December. Two days later, we had completed the relief of the base and reprovisioned it for another year.

We now set sail for my new home Signy Island. We had a rough following sea and there were numerous icebergs and growlers about for which we first had to reduce to half-speed and then later on to slow speed as we navigated our way through them. Visibility was poor and there were frequent snow showers. At 5 a.m. we came up to the Island and entered Borge Bay, where our little hut was situated on Bernsten Point. There was a rough sea running, it was snowing continuously, there was a strong westerly wind blowing and it seemed bitterly cold.

I was the first ashore and such was my hurry that I left my heavy-duty gloves and inners behind. Without them I could not do any work as my fingers went numb with cold. So I had to borrow a pair of sledging gloves. It took two days to reprovision the base. On the last day the *John Biscoe* was due to leave at 5 p.m. At 4 p.m. the last motorboat left us and I found it strange that my life on the *John Biscoe* had ended for the time being. She had been my home for seven weeks and had become part of my life. Meanwhile the ship had forgotten the outward mail and soon Arthur Mansfield, Ray Tanton and myself had got the heavy Norwegian pram launched and, swept on by a strong following wind, we soon reached the *Biscoe* and climbed aboard. We walked about saying goodbye, and I remember feeling overwhelmed by the heartfelt farewells which were extended to me.

We got back into the pram but, due to the strong west wind, we went backwards rather than forwards and for several minutes it seemed we were about to be swept out to sea. Not that that would have mattered, as the *Biscoe* was on standby, although it would have had to have launched the motorboat. We drifted slowly behind the stern to the taunts of the ship's crew and the clicking of cameras. By the time we had eventually winched the pram up on the shore, the *Biscoe* had weighed anchor and was moving off out of the bay. Faintly but quite distinctly we heard the ship's siren sound three times, and knew she was on her way to South Georgia. We all scrambled up to the wind-tower on top of Bernsten Point and watched her getting smaller and smaller as she sailed down the Orwell Channel, the cream of her wash sparkling bright in the sunshine, and beyond her the magnificent snow-covered mountains of Coronation Island. The wind grew bitter – we hauled down the Union Jack and walked quickly and quietly back to our hut. We were on our own.

15

The South Orkney Islands, Antarctica

The South Orkneys were discovered by George Powell aboard *Dove* on a British sealing expedition from London, and Nathaniel Brown Palmer aboard *James Monroe* on a US sealing expedition from Stonington. According to Powell, he came to the channel separating Spine Island from Coronation Island and at the northernmost point of the channel, a boat was put ashore to the mainland. He wrote that: 'at this place we landed and took possession of the land in the name of King George the Fourth and as I imagined it to be the first land discovered since the Coronation of our most gracious Sovereign I have named it Coronation Island'.

Six days later Michael McLeod, sailing in *Beaufoy*, discovered the islands independently; he returned in 1822 with James Weddell aboard the brig *Jane* and landed on the north coast. On a further voyage aboard *Jane*, Weddell returned to the South Orkneys and surveyed the north coast of Coronation Island. Matthew Brisbane, who was in command of *Beaufoy* and who was accompanying Weddell, discovered Signy but did not name it. A Scotsman, William Bruce, established the first station on the islands when he brought the Scottish National Antarctic Expedition on board *Scotia* to Laurie Island in 1903. The meteorological station was later transferred to Argentina.

The start of whaling at the islands can be dated to 1907–08 when the Newfoundland Whaling Company deployed a whale factory ship there. The whaling was not a success as the ice conditions were particularly bad. Floating whaling factories visited the islands annually until 1914–15 and over 2,000 whales were taken. In 1913 the *Tioga* under Captain Moe – an island is named after him to the south of Signy – found shelter on the exposed west coast at Port Tioga, but she was blown ashore and wrecked. Whaling resumed after the First World War and a licence was granted to Tonsberg Hvalfangeri to establish a shore whaling station at Factory Cove just below Bernsten Point. This station ran for four years, principally processing skrotts from floating factories, but it was a failure and it ceased to operate in 1925–26. Floating factories operated from the same cove off Borge Bay and below Bernsten Point and approximately 3,500 whales were taken over the period 1921–29, a mass slaughter. When I arrived there were still a number of steel and wooden barges and the remainder of the whaling equipment comprised of five digesters, a boiler, winches and a tank.

The original hut, slightly enlarged by the time I got there, was built in five days in March 1947. There was also a Nissen hut which had been transferred from Cape Geddes – this was used for stores, its solid wooden floor having been built of materials from the whaling house ruins. I liked the main hut from the start, and I had a bunk from which I could look at the weather and sky without moving my head.

And now for a description of the hut itself. You entered by the outer porch which led straight into the coal hole – not a very impressive entrance but then we only had visitors once or twice a year. Then there was the inner porch with hooks for our anoraks, wind proofs, sledging gloves, etcetera. The third door led into the hut proper. On the left was the bunkroom where we lived, slept and worked. We had a stove there which was never let out on fear of instant death, a survey desk, a gramophone and a small polar library. Straight ahead was the radio room with its transmitters and receivers. To the right of the radio room was the met office with all its instruments, and opposite that was the kitchen, which had a wonderful Esse cooker which never went out, and adjacent to that was the water tank which had to be laboriously filled up daily with blocks of snow – and a block of snow makes very little water when melted. Continuing to the right was a passage way where we kept a lot of stores; the bulk of the stores were, for safety reasons (mainly fire), kept in the Nissen hut. Going on further there was a laboratory on the left; adjacent to that was a greenhouse, but that blew away in a blizzard; and on the right a darkroom and a workshop, and that was that.

There was a small shed outside housing the diesel engine which had to be cranked up every morning, sometimes with difficulty. Also outside there was a toilet built to the specifications of Surgeon-

Commander Bingham, and therefore always called the 'Bingham Bog' with the admonitory sign: 'No micturition before defaecation'. This was actually extremely important, because the biscuit tin underneath the bog seat became unbearably heavy if this practice was not observed. This was because it had to be carried a hundred yards or so down to the tide crack and emptied – the tide crack is the point where the sea ice meets the land ice. To be taken short at night was almost unbearable as you had to find a torch, dress if you had the time and run out into usually a blizzard in minus temperatures to the Bingham Bog.

Outside again was the hydrogen balloon shed from which we sent up our pilot balloons to ascertain the upper air currents. And then finally there was a small emergency hut just above the tide crack where, if the hut burnt down or blew away, we could shelter until the relief ship arrived – probably a year later.

The main hut was deliberately situated on a very exposed point so that it did not drift up with snow on all sides and we could get out if there was a fire – the greatest of all concerns in the Antarctic. It was so exposed that at times during the frequent gales and blizzards the roof tended to lift up, and to reduce the danger of the roof blowing away, we fixed cables over it. And that was my home for 15 months.

Soon after my arrival I made my first attempt at dog-driving: one of the more difficult skills in the world. Here I will have to give you some background information about not only the dogs themselves, but also their harnesses, their traces, their hitches, not forgetting the types of sledges they pulled.

Our huskies originally came from Greenland. They are a distinct breed, very hardy with a strong, stocky build, with a dense inner fur and a coarse outer thatch that allows them to survive in exceptionally cold weather. The husky is, in fact, a descendant of the wolf and they have a wolf-like appearance, but they are much larger boned, with a broader head, a shorter snout and a tightly curved tail. Some of them were very large and when they stood they could easily rest their paws on my shoulders. Generally, however, they come in all shapes and sizes, and nearly all could be ferocious fighters. They could, of course, be affectionate, but what mattered most was their spirit and their willingness to pull our sledges. They have a notorious flaw in their character and that is the propensity to fight whenever an opportunity arises; not because

169

they are naturally vicious but, because like their ancestors the wolf, they have a need to exert their authority or, at least, maintain their position in the pack.

One of their most wonderful habits was their singing when they were happy, and particularly when there was a full moon. One dog would begin a low woo-ing and gradually they would all come in, all 50 of them, each with a slightly different pitch and the bitches with their higher, lilting pitch. After they had all got going, there was a huge crescendo followed by an abrupt silence as if a conductor had told them to stop. And then they would start all over again. To me it was an extraordinary experience, standing out there on the snow and ice in a full moon surrounded by all the glaciers and mountains, listening to that long-drawn-out wolf-like singing – it was both beautiful and eerie as the crags echoed back their singing, and there was a great peaceful harmony between me, the dogs, and the ice and mountains.

The dog harnesses we used were of a very simple design. They were made, or rather we made them, from lamp-wick, the tubular cotton webbing we used in our oil-lamps, and their harnesses stayed reasonably soft, even when frozen. Most of the pulling pressure was taken by the breastplate of the chest, leaving the shoulders to move freely and the windpipe free from pressure. Each dog had his own individual harness specially made for him and the dog's name was sewn on the harness – this was an occupation that whiled away the long dark winter evenings. Their harnesses were hung up close to the kitchen and there was always that smell of sweaty harnesses, seal oil, blubber, tarred rope and much-used leather collars, which I will never forget.

We had two types of sledges – the Greenland and the Nansen. The Greenland was a short, solid and rigid sledge used, as its name implies, by Greenlanders. Generally we used it for relatively short local journeys, particularly in the summer when a lot of the snow had disappeared and there were exposed rocky outcrops everywhere. It was a sledge that required no more than five dogs.

The Nansen sledge was quite different and it was so called because Nansen himself had adapted it from various Eskimo designs. It was a light sledge, flexible and resilient, and could carry 1,000 lbs over pretty rough terrain. It was constructed of selected aircraft grade ash, was 12 feet long and had 4-inch-wide runners that curved up at both ends. The runners were held apart by five bridges and were covered with a smooth resin-based laminate to reduce friction. The Nansen had handlebars to hang on to and there was a footbrake. If you were walking or perhaps running alongside the sledge, it was, of course, not a problem putting your foot on the brake. On the other hand, if you were skiing alongside, it was necessary to slip your boot out of its loose binder, cross the two skis over so that you did not lose the now loose ski, and then stamp on the brake. There was also a semicircular bamboo 'cow-catcher' at the front end, which acted as a buffer in the event that the sledge ran into the dogs. The dogs were attached to the sledge with a rope bridge that we spliced onto the base of the middle bridge and then wrapped around the second and first bridges.

There is no right way for hitching a dog team to the main hauling trace of a sledge. Essentially there are two systems. The first, and the one we most frequently used, was the centre trace. This comprises a long central rope to which short links of thinner rope are attached, picking up the harness rings of the individual dogs. With centre trace you had a lead dog out in front and four, six or eight pairs of dogs behind the leader.

The other system was the fan trace which was an adaptation of the Inuit Eskimo fan. Each dog is hitched onto a separate trace, the traces being of varying lengths, with obviously the lead dog having the longest. The lead dog was always chosen for his or her brains, while the remaining dogs were chosen for their strength. The lead dog was often a bitch – they were more sensitive, more alert and, dare I say it, more intelligent and less inclined to fight. Having a lead bitch dog on heat, which once happened to me, was an extraordinary experience, with six lusty huskies behind her, pulling away for all they were worth, and our mileage that day was the greatest I ever achieved.

The first day of the sledging season was the most difficult. The dogs were full of enthusiasm, longing to get away, and sometimes their impatience was too much and a fight occurred. We had to separate them, generally by their tails if you could get at them, and by the time you had finished all the traces were almost inextricably muddled up and had to be disentangled. These fights were the only occasion during which I was bitten by mistake, and the dog who did it looked suitably crestfallen when he realised what he had done. There is, in fact, nothing quite like the semi-chaotic yet exhilarating take-off at the beginning of a day's sledging.

Back in my day, we had a 40-foot-long rawhide whip – the object being to flick this along the left or the right of the lead dog in order to make him or her change direction. The flicking and cracking of a 40-foot rawhide whip is not as easy as it sounds, and the first few times I tried I managed to curl it round my head and this was exceedingly painful. Gradually I mastered it – however, later on we used it less and less frequently as the lead dog learnt to respond to our instructions.

The dogs were spanned out on chains on the snow and ice below our hut, but in summer this snow and ice melted, and in the occasionally wet conditions the dogs looked anything but happy. They were fed every other day, and when they were not working they needed less food. This took the form of two frozen penguins which we had either sledged back from Gourlay Peninsula using the Greenland sledge or, alternatively, brought back on our pram boat, which was hardly seaworthy at the best of times, using the Seagull outboard engine, which was not known for its reliability. The over-all sea journey was, or seemed to be, about five miles and it was along a very exposed and rocky coast. We always used to say that the required complement of our pram was four. One to steer and work the outboard engine, one to row when that did not work, one to bale and one to pray. It was no use shouting for help – the nearest person was 400 miles away.

Of course, in late summer the penguins disappear with the onset of the pack ice and that is the most difficult period: when the penguins have gone and the sea ice is not strong enough to bear the weight of a sledge loaded with seal meat. During that period, the frozen seal meat had to be carried up and down some very steep and tricky slopes.

When the sea ice formed in April or May, we killed a lot of seals – a horrible job, to be repeated time and time again. I made a real mistake here when we did not quarter the seals after gutting them, as this would have made their transport easier. All these dead seals were marked with bamboo canes and these proved indispensable as, otherwise, they would have been lost under the heavy snowfall.

The dogs were fed every other day – we could not feed them every day, there were too many dogs and the effort and energy required to cut up the frozen seal carcasses was too much. I was not too certain how much to feed them but, in the end, we fed them about 10 or 12 lbs of seal meat – as I have said, every other day. Initially we tried to use felling axes to cut up the frozen carcasses, but these proved useless and, in the end, we had to use cross-saws. We then loaded these on to the sledge to take them up to the dogs.

Most evenings I held a canine surgery at the hut. Mostly these were puncture wounds – sometimes severe – which had to be treated, and I used Dettol and sulphanilamide which was usually successful.

The greatest worry we had was over a dog called Castor. He developed a huge swelling under his jaw, as big as two cupped hands, and his hind right leg was also affected. His temperature rose to over 103°F and I had to inject him with large quantities of penicillin. However, his condition deteriorated and the swelling spread into his head and face. I got on the blower to George Marsh at Hope Bay and his advice was to increase the penicillin dosage to 250,000 units and hope that his temperature would subside. I had wanted to incise the swelling but I was told on no account to do this. At long last the temperature came down, the swelling subsided, and Castor recovered.

We had several litters but one of the bitches, Betty, was a hopeless mother. Most of her puppies died, but I managed to save two by feeding them every three hours with warmed but diluted Ideal milk by way of a pipette. Between feeds, I placed them in a box over the kitchen stove and they survived. I always thought that Betty should be ashamed of herself, but she wasn't.

My first sledge journey with dogs was to go over to Gourlay Peninsula to sledge back penguin carcasses. Ray Tanton accompanied me and we took the Greenland. We crossed the ice-cap col in good weather, but by the time we started to get back, the wind had suddenly got up to gale force and we had a full blizzard to contend with and visibility down to a few yards. The load was too heavy for the dogs to pull and after about a few hundred yards, we jettisoned our load of corpses by an ice-cliff and covered them with rocks and ice so that the scavenging paddies and skuas could not get at them.

With the load off the sledge the dogs started to move fast, but they would not go up the slope, so that we were running along the edge of the ice-cliff with, in my case, one foot on the top of the ice-cliff and the other sometimes dangling over the cliff with the sea below. The next hour was appalling. The blizzard was williwawing down from the ice-col – we could not see anything as our goggles frosted over, and these we had to discard. Eventually we reached the top of the ice-col. My colleague got down onto the now empty sledge, covered his face with his gloves, and I took on the job of brakeman as we descended from the col down the steep ice-slope and gully towards Bernsten Point and our hut. And so ended my first journey driving dogs.

And now, 40 years later, what happened to the descendants of our beloved huskies? Well the answer is that they were either killed, or evicted and evacuated back to Greenland. All this was a great and entirely unnecessary tragedy committed by the environmentalists who, when nobody seemed to be looking, inserted a clause into the Antarctic Treaty which read as follows: 'Introduction of non-native species, parasites and diseases. Dogs shall not be introduced on to land or ice-shelves and dogs currently in those areas shall be removed by 1st April 1994.' If ever there was a non-native species in the Antarctic it was human beings, and they also are the biggest polluters with their mechanical vehicles. Logically, they should also be removed from the Antarctic. Few, if any, of the bureaucratic environmentalists had any idea or appreciation of the value of that special relationship which existed in the Antarctic between man and husky in that lonely white continent. The death sentence on the huskies pronounced by the environmentalists was unforgivable as well as being an entirely unnecessary crime, and should be held against them for all time.

We were five young men and our average age was in the early twenties. There were two meteorologists apart from myself and their names were Derek Parsons and Arthur Berry, who were both professional meteorologists. Ray Tanton was an engineer and an excellent mountaineer, and Gwilym Owen was a very capable wireless operator. We were all very dependent on Ray because it was he who was responsible for our power, and without power, quite apart from lighting, we could not transmit or receive messages. Of course, we were enormously dependent on Gwilym Owen because, without him, we were entirely cut off from the outside world. We were already geographically cut off from the outside world – Hope Bay was the nearest survey station and that was 400 miles away, and we were not about to do a Shackleton against the prevailing westerly winds and ice. So there we were, entirely interdependent, no doctor or dentist, but with sufficient food stores to last two years in case the relief ship failed to get through the ice. It was a sobering thought, but I cannot remember ever worrying about it – which is strange, because later I became quite a worrier.

The daily and, for that matter, nocturnal regime was very demanding. For the duty meteorologist the day started at 6 a.m. when he undertook his first synoptic observations of the day. These continued throughout the day, every three hours, until 3 a.m. the following morning, that is, a 21-hour day, when he was allowed to rest until midday. Wireless transmissions were carried out regularly and we were in frequent contact not only with the other survey stations but also with Stanley, and sometimes Heard and Macquarie islands in the Australian Antarctic sector. We were also able to communicate directly with the Admiralty in London and they with us, using the secret four-figure naval code, which was a devil to decode. The Admiralty, of course, were primarily interested in the movements of Argentinian naval ships – more about that later.

We also took it in turns to cook – one week on and four weeks off. We had to cook three meals a day, trying to make them as varied as possible, and every other day we had to bake bread – not as simple as it sounds in a cold draughty hut. I even made hot cross buns and puff pastry. We had brought down with us from Stanley a number of mutton carcasses, which we deposited in a crevasse in a glacier – a useful deep freeze – and during the season we ate penguins and occasionally seal meat, of which the best by far was leopard seal – the only carnivorous seal, and very fast and dangerous on land or ice. We had a variety of recipes for cooking penguins and when Bee Nilson brought out the *Penguin Cookery Book*, somewhat facetiously I wrote to her and mentioned to her that her *Penguin Cookery Book* did not include any recipes for cooking penguins. Somewhat to my astonishment she replied from New Zealand, and I sent her all my recipes, for which she wrote to thank me. Of course, they never appeared in her book. I enjoyed cooking and I continue to enjoy it. Apart from the regular met observations, the wireless transmissions, the cooking, the maintenance of the generators and equipment, there was always a myriad of other jobs to be undertaken, including looking after the dogs, the geological and glaciological surveys (both of which I undertook myself), the seal, penguin and bird counts (these took a great deal of time), and of course all the preparations and undertaking of the sledge and boat journeys to Coronation Island. There was, in fact, so much to do that sometimes there never seemed enough time in the day and night to do it all.

Every spring we made visits to the penguin rookery to collect their eggs. We then sledged these back to the Survey station and, to keep them from spoiling, we used to store them in flour, which was the way we were told to keep them fresh. It worked! We had fresh penguin eggs throughout the year. Penguin eggs are not delicious, and when boiled the white does not go white: it remains opaque, and it is all somewhat disconcerting. We therefore scrambled or omeletted them.

We got used to cooking penguins – all we used were the breasts, having skinned and gutted them. Penguin meat is slightly fishy and therefore needs a lot of onion, herbs, tomatoes, Lea & Perrins etcetera to disguise it. Having done this remedial work, it is usually very tasty. A point to note is that penguin meat goes black when you cook it. Don't be put off.

The best seal meat I ever had was the liver of a leopard seal. The meat is excellent but the liver is superb, and with fried dried onions and tinned bacon, it was a culinary delight and savoured by all.

I seem not to have mentioned our washing arrangements. To all intents and purposes, although we washed our clothes, we did not wash ourselves and I think that the main reason for this was the sheer fatigue of cutting snowblock after snowblock, hauling these snowblocks up to the hut and hoisting them into our hot water tank – and I have mentioned before that a snowblock produces very little water. We never shaved, but I remember that once a month I did treat myself to a bath. We did not have, as it happens, a bath, but we did have an old whale oil barrel in which it was possible to immerse oneself – just. However, this process did, of course, entail a huge number of snowblocks so it was very much a one-off event. This monthly immersion in the whale oil barrel was of enormous efficacy and to emerge clean and soaped was always a great morale-booster (it was a pity the water got cold so quickly). Then after one had dried and dressed, the whale oil barrel, now full of its cold water, had to be manoeuvred through our three doors onto the pee glacier, so entitled because micturition was not allowed in the Bingham Bog. In summer, of course, this pee glacier melted, but to stray far from the hut when wanting a pee in the middle of a blizzard would be to court disaster. I remember once many years later when the RAF had flown me to the United States Air Force Station in Thule in north-west Greenland from Resolute, the DEW Station in north Canada – DEW is the acronym for Distant Early Warning System Station of a possible nuclear attack for Soviet Russia across the North Pole. I lost my way in mid-winter between the Officers' Mess and my bunkhouse. There was a huge blizzard blowing, it was pitch dark and at one time I thought I had had it, but then I found the marking ropes and all was well. The outside temperature was –50°F and the inside temperature was +70°F.

Whilst writing this I have read Sir Vivian Fuchs's book *Ice and Men*. In it he refers to me undertaking, at the request of the Scientific Bureau, the measurements of Weddell seals and collecting skulls from seals killed for dog food. He also states that I was frustrated as I was unable to make much contribution to the knowledge of Coronation Island, particularly the mountains, which were unknown. Nevertheless, he states that, although not really equipped for long sledging journeys, my companions and I initiated a number of very useful journeys to Coronation Island when the sea ice froze over, and that these ventures included a number of 'first ascents' and that I brought back a large collection of rock specimens which were valuable in demonstrating the geology of Coronation Island.

As I was so interested in the geology of Signy and Coronation Islands and my reports were used in the Falkland Islands Dependencies Survey Scientific Reports on the geology of the South Orkneys by D.H. Matthews and Derek Maling, who preceded me, I am going to give you a paragraph or two on the geology of the islands.

Signy is formed entirely of metamorphic rocks which means that the rocks were changed from their original form by an intense period of heat and pressure. Similar rocks occur along the westward margin of the Antarctic Peninsula and thus form part of the Scotia metamorphic complex. As well as being metamorphosed, the rocks are intensely folded and faulted and up to four different fold episodes can be observed. During metamorphism it has been calculated that the rocks reached temperatures of up to 550°C.

The association of the different rock types, the metamorphism and the style of deformation are all characteristics of active plate margins where the oceanic crust is sub-ducted beneath a continental

177

margin, similar to the Andes. In this sort of environment ocean islands containing ocean floor basalts and limestone are scraped off the descending plate, mixed with sandstones, metamorphosed, deformed and accreted on to the continental margin and probably occurred against the Antarctic Peninsula. The age of this event is uncertain but the metamorphism is thought to be a minimum of 200 million years ago. Finally, during the last 25 million years, the South Orkney group of islands including Signy moved away from the peninsula to their present position.

Now I must turn to the wildlife which is prolific in summer and virtually non-existent during the winter. Here I must trouble you with some facts and figures.

First, the penguins. Comparison with earlier counts shows that the number of Adelie and chinstrap penguins doubled between 1948 and 1958 and, since then, the number of Adelies has again doubled, whilst that of the chinstrap has multiplied five times, all due to increased food availability. The most recent counts I have seen are for Adelies 37,200 pairs, Chinstraps 80,000 pairs, Gentoos 300 pairs and Macaronis only 11 pairs. Second, the petrels. The Southern Giant Petrel was originally estimated at 500 pairs, but their numbers are decreasing, mainly I fear because of research activity. The Cape Pigeon: about 1,200 pairs, the Snow Petrel: about 300 pairs. the Antarctic Prion: the enormous number of 50,000 pairs; Wilson's Storm Petrel: the even more enormous number of 200,000 pairs, that is, 400,000 birds – wonderful – particularly as Wilson's Petrel is almost my favourite bird. Black-bellied Storm Petrel: about 100–200 pairs. Other birds breeding on Signy are the blue-eyed Shag, about 800 pairs; the Sheathbill, about 150 pairs; the Antarctic and sub-Antarctic Skua, about 150 nests – surprising as the population seems much larger; the Antarctic Tern, about 200 pairs.

The population of whales around the South Orkney Islands never recovered from the mass slaughter in earlier years, and Signy in any case is a poor area for whale spotting because many species fed well offshore. It is dreadful to report that between 1920 and 1930 nearly 100,000 whales were harpooned and killed, of which 40,000 were Blue Whales and over 30,000 were Fin Whales, the rest being Right, Sei, Humpback and Sperm. And then there were the seals in the South Orkneys and Signy. The islands were never as rich a sealing ground as the South Shetland Islands where more than a million were 'collected' between 1819 and 1830. When I was at Signy I saw only one fur seal and, when I first saw it, I really did not know what it was – I had never seen one before. But by 1987 there were over 13,000 fur seals on the island and, when I last went to South Georgia, there were hundreds and thousands of fur seals, probably well over a million, making it sometimes extremely difficult to land on beaches. The elephant seal is common on Signy and the total population must be very large, but possibly not so common as the Weddell seal, my favourite. We all fell in love with the pups, who are quite quite beautiful – and I emphasise that word 'beautiful'. And then there were the crabeater seals, the estimated population in the Antarctic being around 50 million. During the winter many hundreds if not thousands of crabeater seals haul out on to the fast ice around Signy. And finally, the leopard seals, which are about 10 or 11 feet long with that impressive and sinister snake-like head. Although they do mainly eat krill – *Euphausia superba* – they are opportunists and they lie in wait for penguins jumping off the ice. Penguins are, as it happens, extremely wary of leopard seals – and, for that matter, killer whales – when leaving the ice for the sea to fish, and they always wait to see what happens to the brave one, the first to jump from the floe.

So there we have it – an island teeming with life during the summer and the breeding season. Now I am going to give you a short description of a penguin rookery which I have partly borrowed from Ommaney's book *South Latitude*. The two main rookery areas at Signy were Gourlay Peninsula and Cape North.

In the Austral summer these areas are teeming with thousands of penguins, mainly Adelie and Chinstrap. They make a black and white shifting mass on the cape and snow-covered land, and a continual movement seems to cover the ground. Though the whole multitude looks in a sense stationary yet whenever you look there is a coming and going, a shifting, a movement of little black and white shapes.

There is all the time the sound of multitudinous chattering and over all an ammonia stench. This smell and the noise increases as you enter the rookery and soon becomes overpowering, choking and deafening. Although I always love pictures of penguins, nevertheless I recall the powerful choking stench of the rookeries, the birds' bodies smeared and their feathers clotted with their own ordure.

179

As you penetrate further into the rookery, a chatter of indignation arises and their beaks are raised in a chorus of protest, rage and horrified expostulation. They stab at your boots with their sharp beaks and attack your legs with their stiff flippers. Some would run at you, bristling with fury and then, after a few thrusts and smacks at your legs, they suddenly forget or cannot be bothered, and waddle back to their nests as if nothing had happened. No one worried until I had become an immediate and impending crisis, and then when I had gone, they forgot me.

If you sit among the Chinstrap penguins, as I frequently did, you see in front of you a black coat and a white waistcoat and eyes islanded in a triangle of white, divided by a black line from the whiteness of the throat. The eyes gaze at you, totally expressionless, blinking without shutting, veiling themselves for a split second in that disconcerting way they have. They make little contented hissing noises to themselves, nuzzling their beaks into their breasts and under their flippers, and suddenly they would, through sheer lightness of heart, lift their beaks and squawk. Or they would stretch their necks vertically upwards until they looked like bottles and then, with their flippers held out, they would make a high ecstatic gurgling noise, expressing unparalleled joie de vivre, as though life in that stony snowy waste was the most infinitely desirable form of existence in the world. And every now and then they raised their tails and shot a creamy jet over the foul stones.

The place where I used to sit was near one of their pathways of this rookery city that wound through and down to the sea. Up and down these pathways they passed continually, singly or in groups. Sometimes those going in opposite directions would stop and pass the time of the day, bowing and chattering, and then pass on. They moved awkwardly and with a waddling gait, their heads pushed forward as if they were short-sighted and uncertain of the ground, their flippers held out stiffly behind them.

In the springtime, even on the stony barren and snow wastes of Signy, they get down to that fundamental process, to which in the end all activities boil down. The penguins were now in pairs and one member was wandering purposefully about, intent on some kind of search. He seemed to be searching the ground and presently, after a great deal of careful consideration, he would pick up a little stone in his beak and carry it back to his consort. He would always place it with great pride at her feet – an object of great price, an offering, a tribute, and there would be more rejoicing over it than over the sixpence that was lost and is found. They bowed to each other, lifted their beaks upward, then swayed their heads in semicircles from side to side alternately, shaking their flippers and squawking with pleasure. The hen would then bend down and nose the stone with her beak on to the ring of stones with which she was already surrounded, and then suddenly both forgot and just stood around with expressionless eyes or doing vague things with their beaks in their feathers. And soon he would be off again, receiving indignant pecks and buffets from his unfriendly neighbours, searching for another treasured gift for his lady. Occasionally he saw an enormous penguin which was me, and dropped his stone in front of me, awaiting the response. But there was none and he soon forgot about me, waddling away to his consort who received him with bows and ecstatic lifting of the head, his momentary faithlessness unnoticed.

In this way, thousands and thousands of homes were being built throughout the rookery city and thus were being laid the foundation of a family life. In many cases the stone home was already built and the hen sitting full length upon her white breast in her uncomfortable circle of stones. Under her, warm and alive, dirty but infinitely precious, was her egg. Her whole bearing expressed desire fulfilled, and her husband stood by proud and satisfied.

Later on, when the eggs are hatched, life begins to get too much for the anxious parents. The chick grows fast and clamours louder and louder to be fed. It stretches its beak upwards in endless expectancy and if not yielded to immediately, it importunes its parents without mercy, yelling up into their faces for food. Both husband and wife now take it in turns to go away to sea and return with gorged crops which, after a little feigned refusal, they disgorge for the benefit of their offspring. This is a horrible business. The parent bends down, vomiting in its throat and the chick pushes its beak and sometimes half its beak into its parent's beak. The chick gobbles away and directly the meal is over, shrieks for more.

The chick grows into a dirty, dark grey object – quite unlovely – and its demands on its parents become too much for them and so all the parents in the community take collective action against the aggression of their children. They band the younger generation together in groups, each under supervision of a few grown-ups, who act as guardians and nurses. This allows the rest of the parents to go away to sea and return continually with their pulpy vomit of krill.

But the sea represents danger as well as food, and where the sea laps the rocks or the ice cliffs, you will see the penguins bowing and chattering because down there there may be a leopard seal – and a leopard seal, as we all know, makes a single mouthful of a penguin. So while they think he is down there, no penguin will dive in and, even when the coast is clear, you will see them try to coax or force each other, with true gallantry, to enter the water first lest he is there after all, because that, of course, means death.

So the season marches on and we get into late summer. The young die in thousands, killed by the skuas, who swoop incessantly overhead, and also from exposure and starvation, and the colonies are strewn with tiny skeletons which the 'paddies' – the sheathbills – flutter about picking clean. The parents get tired, they go to sea less, and they stand about in groups moulting. The chicks start taking to the waters, the days grow shorter, the snow storms start to howl and the pack ice starts to come up from the south. Then the penguins leave with the onset of the pack, swimming hundreds of miles north. In the spring when the ice has gone, or sometimes when it has not gone out, they return to their snowy and stony cities which they left in the autumn and, once again, the gentlemen start searching for those hard and cold but infinitely desirable stones, which, bowing, they proudly present as tributes to their ladies.

I have mentioned before that we had to kill seals to feed to our dogs, but we were also under orders to kill seals to feed the dogs at Hope Bay. So we used to go out in the spring for Weddell seals. We used to see them on the ice sleeping motionless all day and all night. The storms that raged round them meant nothing to them, and the wind howled round them and the snow piled up against them. The trails they made, smeared with their own excrement, curved through the snow from the ice-edge. When you approached them they raised their heads from their snowy pillows and looked at you with their lovely sad lambent eyes along the barrels of their bodies. If you touched them they writhed suddenly as though in agony and gave a hoarse cry, and their shining sorrowful eyes filled with tears. These we shot, and then cut their throats, every time feeling like murderers, which indeed we were, as the hot red blood rushed and flowed onto to the white pristine snow about them.

We eviscerated them with our sharp sealing knives and warmed our hands and fingers in the warm guts which still moved. And then we brought the huskies and sledges around, loaded the carcasses and moved them to the cache. The extraordinary thing was that the seals which we had allowed to live took no notice. They raised their heads, opened their mouths, reproached us with their eyes for what we had done and then went back to sleep with sighs of slothful comfort. And then lazily they raised their tail flippers aloft and then rubbed them one against the other, as if they were washing their hands of the whole bloody murderous business.

In a way this all sounds uneventful, but there are, of course, stories and stories and anecdotes too numerous to mention. Some I will mention, before moving to my next enterprise and adventure, the 1954 Antarctic relief voyage, which took many months.

I remember once in the late Antarctic summer before the pack ice set in, we were all sitting in our bunkhouse living-room, doing whatever we were doing. There was a gale blowing, probably from the north-west, and the hut was shaking – it was all perfectly normal. But then suddenly we all – and I emphasise the words 'we all' – heard a ship's siren sound, and not sounding once, but repeatedly. At that time there were no reported ships in our vicinity but, of course, clearly something was wrong. We all rushed out to the Point with our strong torches – it was nearly dark – and waved and waved them around, as we were all quite certain that a ship was in distress. And then we heard the ship's siren again and, once again, we waved our torches and stared into the flying snow as it whipped along to the Point. But nothing – absolutely nothing. We all agreed we had all heard a ship's siren, that it had repeated itself several times and, although the visibility was bad, it was not all that bad. So what had happened? We were all rather un-nerved. None of us could quite believe that it was a ghost ship's siren we had heard – after all it was quite close, and we had rushed out because it sounded as if the ship was close to the rocks, and we wanted to signal it away. But nothing. So perhaps it was a ghost ship, perhaps an old whaling trawler which had come to grief or near to grief on some long-past day. We will never now know; it seems a mystery, but we all heard it quite distinctly and that was not imagined.

Then there were two visits of Her Britannic Majesty's warships to our bay. I think they were called HMS *Nereide* and HMS *Snipe*, respectively, but don't hold me to that. These ships were frigates – frigates of the South Atlantic Squadron. In those days we had a South Atlantic Squadron. These frigates had very thin steel hulls – something like a quarter of an inch I believe – and so they were totally unsuitable for operating in ice and their Captains were very nervous. Here you must remember that as leader of the Survey Station I had been sworn in as a Magistrate of the Falkland Islands Dependencies – in this case the South Orkneys – and not only was I a Magistrate but I was also the Customs officer, the postmaster and anything else official you could think of. From the first ship the Colonial Secretary, His Honour Colin Campbell, who had sworn me in as a Magistrate, came ashore. I liked him very much, but I do not think he was very happy being 'Col. Sec.', as the expression was in those days, in the Falkland Islands, having been sent there from Kenya. I always rather understood in those days (perhaps not now, as we have flogged off very nearly all our colonies), that being posted to the Falkland Islands was not far off being a punishment posting. I would have loved it.

Our pram was, as usual, inoperable that day – that is to say, it needed repairs which we had not got round to doing, and also the outboard engine was out of action. (Why were Seagull outboard engines so unreliable in contrast with those engines made in Japan?) So we were relieved that His Honour came ashore in the frigate's boat.

After a short inspection of the quarters – there was not much to see – and the dogs, we wondered what to do with him and his naval entourage. So we suggested Gourlay Peninsula and the huge Adelie penguin rookery there. So off we set. The weather was beautiful, the sea was calm and Coronation and Signy were looking as lovely as I ever can remember them. And nothing untoward happened, nothing at all. We had a picnic at Gourlay – the ship's

184

The Seaforth Highlanders marching past the Viceroy at the Lahore Durbar, 1905.

Officers of the Seaforth Highlanders in India, Captain Alan Baillie in uniform standing rear right.

Vanity Fair cartoons of Uncle Fred Burnaby and Henry Villebois of Marham. Uncle Fred and Tommy Bowles founded the journal *Vanity Fair*.

Uncle Fred Burnaby in his Royal Horse Guards uniform. Killed in action at the battle of Abu Klea in the Sudan in 1885.

Captain Alan Baillie, Seaforth Highlanders, killed in action at the battle of Atbara in the Sudan 1897. Photograph taken in Rawalpindi, India.

Above: Red Castle on the Black Isle. This is the castle which my Grandfather as the eldest Baillie son might have inherited. It is now empty, uninhabited and its roof removed.

Left: My Baillie Great Grandfather as a young officer in the Royal Horse Guards, which he went on to command.

The Baillie brothers at Lochloy. Left to right: Ronald, Alan, Hugh, Duncan and Ian.

The Baillie family at Lochloy. Standing, left to right: Alan, Rona, Ronald, Ida, Duncan. Seated, left to right: Lily, Ian, my Great Grandmother, Eila, May. In front: Effie and Hugh.

Officers of the City Imperial Volunteers during the South African war, Duncan Baillie extreme right.

Lochloy, Nairn, Scotland. The home of my Mother's Baillie family and where all the Baillie Great Uncles and Great Aunts lived, and where we often used to stay as children. It was sold by my first cousin Peter Wise.

Kilravock Castle, near Nairn, Scotland. Home of the Rose family for five hundred years. This was where my Grandmother Elizabeth Rose was brought up and where we often used to stay as children.

Marham Hall near Downham Market, Norfolk. The home of Colonel Hugh Smith Baillie and his wife, always known as Aunt Glentworth nee Villebois. The house was almost totally demolished in the 1930s and the estate is now RAF Marham.

Left: Colonel Hugh Rose C.M.G. of Kilravock, my Rose Great Uncle. He served with the Black Watch in the Nile Expedition, 1884, the Boer War and the First World War, where he was mentioned in despatches four times.

Above: My Grandfather Ronald Baillie.

Left: My Baillie grandmother's brother Colonel Hugh Rose. Both cartoons from *The Tatler*.

The wedding at St. Paul's Church, Knightsbridge of Mummy and Daddy in 1928. Hugh Rose, killed at El Alamein, and Hugh Robin Baillie were pages. Rosemary Bevan, my first cousin, was bridesmaid. She was killed when an Italian fighter crashed into her British European Airways flight over Naples.

The Royal Research Ship *John Biscoe* caught in the pack-ice off the west coast of Graham Land, Antarctica. Note the crow's nest used for pack ice navigation.

AGT in the Antarctic in 1952.

The Signy Island hut in winter 1953. The wireless masts blew away in a blizzard, as did the greenhouse. The 'Bingham Bog' is on the right of this photograph. This was my home for 15 months.

Galindez Island, Argentine Islands, 1954. Construction of the FIDS/IGY (International Geophysical Year) station looking eastwards to the Antarctic peninsula.

AGT taking it easy on the Signy icecap. Note the Greenland sledge and the small five-dog team of huskies.

AGT at the summit of one of the Cuillin peaks on Coronation Island. This particular peak had not been climbed before.

The south coast of Coronation Island, South Orkneys in summer - note the 200 feet high ice-cliffs of Sunshine Glacier.

AGT newly commissioned as a Second Lieutenant in the Seaforth Highlanders. Later I was promoted in the field (jungle) to First Lieutenant.

Above: Charging a terrorist camp in Pahang, Malaya, 1951. You can see me hatless leading the charge with my map case over my shoulder. The photo was a re-enactment for the benefit of the newsreels.

Left: The start of Operation Echo at Kerdau, Pahang. Moving along the railway line before entering the jungle.

My armoured train, otherwise known as the Fort George Pug, standing at Kuala Krau station. Note the rifle projections.

Diana at a dinner party
in London.

The 1975 British Everest South West Face Expedition, embarking at Heathrow Airport.
Chris Bonington in centre, AGT on his right, Lord Hunt, Chairman of the organising
committee, on his left. Extreme left Dougal Haston and extreme right Doug Scott, both
of whom achieved the summit.

Nanny Lambert on the terrace of the flat I bought her in Stanhope Gardens in Kensington. For fifty years from 1928 to 1978 she was nanny, confidante and helper to the Tritton family.

Collecting my CBE at Buckingham Palace in 1999. The citation read for Anglo-Indian relations and preserving the cultural heritage of India.

officers took photographs of the penguins – and we returned in record time in a boat which did not look as if it was going to sink.

The second visit was by the Governor himself, Sir Miles Clifford. For him we had constructed a jetty, which had taken an enormous amount of energy and effort to build, but which later on was swept away by the ice. The Governor was piped ashore – I greeted him in my boating jacket and as I was being inspected I had shined my regimental buttons as well. I have to say that at the time I was somewhat wary of the Governor. The reason for this is that when we were sledging on Coronation Island in the winter, I had suddenly realised that it was the Coronation day of Her Majesty Queen Elizabeth II. So using our wireless I sent a message to Her Majesty saying that: 'We members of the Falkland Islands Dependencies Survey, sledging and surveying on Coronation Island in the Antarctic – so named after the Coronation of King George the Fourth, send our warmest felicitations to Her Majesty on her Coronation Day.' This message indeed got through and we received a very warm and grateful acknowledgment from Her Majesty the Queen, and later on a signed photograph. However, the Governor had been very upset at my sending this message without his agreement and told me I had 'usurped his authority'. Nobody likes to be ticked off by his Commanding Officer, and I did not either, but to this day I cannot see that I did anything wrong – but those were different days.

Later that year 1953, the Argentinians constructed a military station on Deception Island. When we heard about this, Sir Winston Churchill, the then Prime Minister, sent a cruiser down to the island with Royal Marines on board, to eject them – which they did very efficiently. However, it was as a result of that visitation that I received my first message from the Admiralty in the dreaded four-figure naval code. This took me a long time to decode, but it was quite clear what the message was: 'Expect reprisals as a result of the Royal Marines action at Deception Island'. I radioed back in the four-figure naval code and I asked what I should do in the event that an Argentinian ship appeared in the bay. The answer to that was that I was to deliver a formal protest as Magistrate of the South Orkneys that he, the Captain of the Argentinian ship, was infringing Her Britannic Majesty's sovereign waters and that he must depart immediately. I acknowledged receipt of this message but radioed back that I thought it would be difficult for me to deliver such a protest to the Captain of the Argentinian ship as I had only a leaking old pram and one 12-bore shotgun – my own – with a limited number of cartridges. I did not say that I thought it was very likely that the pram would sink well before I was able to instruct the Captain to depart Her Britannic Majesty's sovereign waters. The reply was that I was to do my best in the circumstances, and this indeed is what happened. An Argentinian frigate did appear. I got out the pram and got the outboard engine working to deliver my protest. But, as forecast, the pram started to sink about halfway out to the ship, the outboard engine spluttered and stopped, and we were left rowing along with two men baling.

Eventually, we were rescued by the Argentinians. We climbed up the rigging ropes, dirty, unshaven and stinking of seal meat. Once on the deck I demanded to see the Captain – who, as it happens, had been at Dartmouth – and I delivered to him my formal letter of protest – typed out by me in accordance with the regulations, and advised him that he had to depart forthwith. He then delivered his formal letter of protest to me, advising me that I was infringing the President of Argentina's sovereign territory and that I had to depart. So we looked at each other, exchanged protests – and then he invited us in for a drink. It suddenly became all very enjoyable but, after an hour or so of toasting each other's health, we departed and went back to the Survey station, our pram towed by the Argentinian motorboat. It was, of course, both farcical and ridiculous, but slightly uncomfortable at the same time, because it would have been perfectly possible for them to have ejected us just as we had ejected them from Deception Island – but that, fortunately, did not occur. I recall I wirelessed the Admiralty – at least I hope I did – 'Protest submitted and lodged'. I never got a reply and for that I was grateful as I would have had to decode yet another four-figure naval message.

In 1953 we had a relatively poor year for sea ice in the sense that there was fast ice between Signy and Coronation. In 1953 it started to go out towards the end of August, whereas in previous and subsequent years it usually – and I emphasise the word usually – went out much later. For instance, in 1966 the pack ice was sighted on 16th April, the ice became walkable on 9th May and it did not leave until Christmas, thus giving the surveyors eight months of travel as opposed to our only four months. All this meant that our planned survey sledging journeys had to be severely constrained – the last thing one wants is to be on a diminishing ice floe as it moves out into the Southern Ocean. However, to give you a taste of the sort of journeys we undertook on Coronation, I will give you two examples.

On 8th July 1953 Ray Tanton, our engineer, skied over to Cape Vik on a reconnaissance journey by himself – always risky – and got within 300 feet of the summit of the peak to the north of Cape Dallman in the Cuillin Range on Coronation Island. The Cuillins are so called because they resemble in appearance the Cuillin range in Skye.

The next day, with the weather fair and fine and the fahrenheit temperature at zero, we sledged over to Cape Vik with a small team of five huskies, as we were carrying a minimal load of supplies. About 1 mile this side of the Cape, the fast ice in Normanna Strait ended and its place was taken by hummocky pack ice which had newly arrived. The water between these floes was well frozen.

At Cape Vik, Derek Parsons turned back with the sledge and Ray Tanton and I proceeded on foot to the Cape – it was not possible to use skis. We crossed the tide crack well west of the Cape and put on crampons. Down by the sea ice the air seemed very much colder than a few hundred feet above it – this was probably caused by a temperature inversion as there was a well-defined layer of fog on the range of mountains. Immediately to our west was a heavily crevassed corrie glacier which separated the eastern ridge, which we were about to climb, from the two southernmost peaks of the range. A series of steep snow-slopes led up to the ridge, and there was an ideal hard ice crust.

Once on the ridge we roped up. To the east the ground fell away precipitously to the Marshall Bay sea ice, whilst to our west the snow fell steeply to the glacier below. Higher up, the incline increased to very steep. From now on we belayed with ice-axes. The next few pitches were difficult as we had to traverse out onto a rock-face, which was very steep. but Ray found a good ice-axe belay and shortly afterwards we got to the top – it had not been climbed before.

On the summit we had a magnificent view of the heavily glacierised Sandefjord Plateau – Deacon Hill was particularly prominent. To the south we had a superb unobstructed view of the whole of the west coast of Signy. Pack ice was ten-tenths to the south of the group of islands. Icebergs trapped in the pack ice were very numerous and were mainly tabular, indicating that they had broken away from the ice-shelves in the Weddell Sea. The glacierisation of the eastern part of the Norway Bight, which is mainly taken up by the Cuillin Range, was in marked contrast to the western part. The Sandefjord ice-plateau spills over the land in an all-embracing mantle and reaches the sea in a continuous heavily crevassed ice-cliff.

At the top I experienced some sort of very spiritual emotion. It was a glorious day, a bright blue clear sky, not a breath of wind, no noise, no birds, no animals, nothing and stretching all around us was this most beautiful panorama of mountains, islands, glaciers, ice-cliffs, ice-caps, pack ice, icebergs, all frozen into an astonishing immobility and stretching for what seemed hundreds of miles. It was not only beautiful, it was also sublime, and there was only one Person who could have created such sublime beauty and that was our Creator. And in all this we were the only humans, except for our three companions many miles away in Borge Bay. Truly the Antarctic is a paradise, and I felt so enormously privileged to have been able to see and experience this sublime beauty and, at the same time, deeply humbled by this magnificence.

We could have stayed there for hours but, sadly as ever, time marches on and we descended, crossed the tide crack and worked our way back through the pack ice. And to cap it all, we were treated to one of the most beautiful sunsets I have ever seen. I think it was one of the happiest days of my life.

Later that month we had been given permission to carry out a geological sledge journey to the Divide, a short narrow isthmus at the south-eastern end of Coronation Island. We had been waiting for some time for some good weather to appear. It did not, but getting impatient to get under way, we set off at the end of July in a snowstorm with the wind averaging 30 knots. We took the Nansen sledge, with only five dogs instead of the usual nine, and we drove them centre track, i.e. a lead dog with the other dogs harnessed in pairs behind.

Due to the thaw-like temperatures, the sea ice was sticky and Ray had to ski out in front of us to give the dogs some incentive to get a move on. Once, however, we were on the old fast ice, the surface greatly improved and we were able to make good progress. The Pyramid tent had been pitched by Derek and myself by Shingle Cove on the south coast of Coronation only two days previously. It was still standing despite the gales, but we had to repitch it, not easy in a gale-force wind. The dogs were spanned out and we walked over the sea ice to the Sunshine and Syncline glaciers where the huge ice-cliffs collided with the sea ice.

That night the temperature dropped to 0°F but the following morning we woke to find the temperature up to 24°F with heavy drifting snow. It was so bad that it took us two and a half hours to get away. We reached Cape Olivine in 40 minutes, by which time I had gone up to my waist in seawater, having fallen through a crack in the sea ice which was lightly covered with snow. Every now and again I collected rocks and marked them.

Still going east along the south coast of Coronation, we moved out of the old fast ice and entered very heavily hummocked pack ice. Progress became very slow as a path through the ice had to be reconnoitred before we could take the dogs and the sledge through. It was immensely frustrating. Indeed, halfway along, the sledge runner collapsed under the front bridge, partly because of the conditions and pressure, and partly because the runner was in fact very worn. It was clear we could not go on. It took us a long time to retrace our steps to the Sunshine Glacier ice-cliffs as the sledge capsized several times and the broken end of the runner kept on catching on ice-blocks.

During the night the temperature soared into the high thirties, whilst a strong gale came on and it started to pour with rain. We could not stay where we were – the sea ice was rapidly becoming flooded and we feared it would start to go out, although it had been able to stand up to several strong gales. The water above the ice, which had become bare, was already ankle-deep. The dogs could hardly get any grip on the ice, the sledge often side-slipped, and I had to hang onto the sledge with all my strength as I was wearing mukluks not boots as I thought it was going to be cold. Ray Tanton had to put on crampons. Eventually, after having had to jump floes – at which the dogs were magnificent – we made our way back to Shingle Bay where we had left a depot of food.

Mercifully, the sea ice between Shingle Bay and Borge Bay was hardly flooded at all, but in two days' time, the entire sea ice was a sheet of water. We were glad we were back: if we had gone on – which we could not have done with the broken sledge runner –

we might not have been able to get back. Perhaps we should bless that broken runner – it could well have saved our lives.

The greatest day in the Antarctic is midwinter's day, 21st June, because from then on one can look forward to the sun returning and some daylight at midday, with this daylight lengthening day by day. It is a great turning point, so a celebration is held with much food and drink – although as we hardly ever drank alcohol at all throughout the year, it seemed somewhat artificial and unpalatable. We had a six-course meal cooked by Gwilym, our radio operator. He excelled himself and the trifle weighed a stone – no less than 14 pounds. It was delicious. After this great meal we got on to the blower and talked with the other bases until half past three in the morning. Outside there was the usual gale with heavy snow and drift.

Some people feel depressed by the seemingly endless Antarctic winter nights. These are usually accompanied by seemingly endless blizzards, which got me down, and I remember one lasting ten days around midwinter, which was too long. It became a huge effort to dress and go out in these dark, howling blizzards to carry out the met observations and feed the dogs. So that we would not get lost we rigged up rope-lines, and you ventured away from these at your peril. Sometimes the wind was so strong that we were physically lifted up by it and deposited rudely and roughly some distance away. It is indeed a curious experience to find yourself propelled through the air by a wind so strong that you can do nothing about it.

Normally I am exhilarated by the excitement of wind, but during a long blizzard you just long for the noise to stop. The snow and the wind permeate everything; it is relentless and uncaring, and when it does stop the relief is enormous, as if a great load has been lifted away from you and a great peace comes over you.

When I wrote my first long letter from the Antarctic to my mother, I wrote: 'Darling Mummy, First of all I would like to say how wonderfully happy I am down here in the Antarctic and what a wonderful life it is' and I signed off: 'From your ever loving Alan'. When I wrote my final report entry in my Station journal, I wrote these words: 'I think it can be said in all truthfulness that we have all had a very happy year here in the South Orkneys', and signed off with these words: ' I have the honour to be, Sir, your obedient servant Alan Tritton, Clifford House, Signy Island'. I think that that word 'happy' says it all.

16

The 1954 Antarctic Relief Voyage

Was I sad to leave Signy after such a long time – 16 months? The answer is no, because I was now about to embark on the *John Biscoe* for the main 1954 Antarctic relief voyage for the Survey stations, so there was a huge amount to look forward to, including the construction of a brand new scientific survey station in the southern Argentine Islands which was to assist the 1956 International Geographical Year observations. And, anyway, when I left Signy there was a thick fog.

In due course, on 1st February 1954, the *John Biscoe* came in through Normanna Strait, having cleared the Inaccessible Islands which lie about 23 miles westward of Sandefjord Bay on Coronation Island. At 1.30 she dropped anchor and by 3.30 she weighed anchor and we were away for Joinville Island in thick fog and amid frequent icebergs – an unpleasant combination. As we got further west we encountered a lot of brash which led to pack ice, but this was initially quite loose. Nevertheless, we constantly had to change direction to avoid the worst of it, but we did not have too many bumps and anyway you get used to the crashing of the ship in pack ice, although the first few times are disconcerting. Apart from anything else, it is very difficult to concentrate in pack ice as you are always bracing yourself for the next crash. In fact, it is really far better to be on the bridge where you can see what is going on, rather than down in the wardroom. There used to be a story about our Captain Bill Johnston who was a very experienced ice-master. Bill Johnston liked his pink gin, and when he was on the bridge navigating in pack ice, he seemed to like it more – so much so that it was said that the ice progressively got pinker and pinker until it was all suffused in pinkness. Actually, you do need a strong nerve in pack ice, and pink gin can be of considerable assistance.

Later on with the pack ice easing we sighted Bransfield Island and shortly afterwards Joinville Island, which together with Dundee and D'Urville Islands make up the Joinville group. Joinville Island had been surveyed by George Marsh, David Stratton and Ken Blaiklock and we picked them up together with their dogs and sledging equipment. Joinville Island is covered almost entirely by an ice-cap through which protrudes the 2,500-foot summit, which terminates at its north-western end with two remarkable peaks, although these are not visible from Antarctic Sound.

George Marsh, a doctor, was the leader of the Hope Bay Survey station, David Stratton and Ken Blaiklock were surveyors. They were all to take part in the successful Commonwealth Trans-Antarctic Expedition under the leadership of Bunny Fuchs, but more about them later.

Shortly after we had picked up the Survey party, we were full away for Hope Bay for a short visit before again getting full away for Port Lockroy. Down the west coast of the Antarctic Peninsula we sailed, through the Gerlache Strait, coasting Brabant Island, and then entering the renowned Neumayer Channel before dropping anchor at Port Lockroy. Port Lockroy, surrounded by high ice-cliffs, lies on the western end of Wiencke Island and north-eastward of Doumer Island. It is one of the best small harbours in the area and in the past had frequently been visited by past expeditions and whaling vessels. The base had been established in 1944 on Goudier Island and was now conducting an ionospheric and meteorological programme. We stayed overnight in Port Lockroy and then the following morning set off for the Argentine Islands.

The western coast of the Antarctic Peninsula is magnificent, spectacular and dramatic. I find it very difficult to describe it, so I have looked at my old *Antarctic Pilot* and in a few sentences this is what it says:

The western coast southward of Cape Renard is backed by an extensive ice plateau, as much as 7,000 feet high, the western edge of which lies close to the coast, but it is only at some of the headlands that the rugged mountains reach the sea as rocky spurs and ridges. The bays are filled with extensive glaciers, which descend from the plateau and terminate seawards in ice-cliffs. At the edges of the glaciers, the moving ice merges with the ice that fringes the rocky promontories and continues almost unbroken round the points to the adjacent valley glaciers. The ice-cliffs are continuous except at some of the more prominent headlands where the rocky cliffs rise sheer from the sea. The whole of this coast is steep and affords no anchorage but it is bordered by numerous islands, islets and reefs extending as much as 30 miles seawards, affording several small harbours into which a small vessel can be warped and secured to the shore.

The *Antarctic Pilot* then goes on to say that, 'owing to the existence of numerous islets, rocks, sunken rocks and reefs, many of which are uncharted and the position of many others approximate, a vessel in the area should be navigated with great caution, particularly when in pack ice. Some of these dangers rise sheer out of deep water so that, in those cases, sounding gives little warning; many of the islets and rocks are no higher than ice floes and could easily be mistaken for them. Experience has shown that radar, although of invaluable help, is by no means infallible in its ability to detect icebergs, bergy bits or ice and snow-covered land correctly. An efficient and keen lookout is absolutely essential for safe navigation.' Just so.

At 6 a.m. we weighed anchor at Port Lockroy and steamed through the dramatic Le Maire Channel. Coming up to the Channel it is almost impossible to see it as the lower parts of the cliffs appear to join, and it is only on a near approach that the Channel can be made out. On the eastern side of the Channel is Mount Scott, nearly 4,000 feet high, and at about 8 miles south of the famous Dureberg buttress stands Mount Peary, well over 6,000 feet high – one of the most conspicuous massifs in this part of the Peninsula.

The Argentine Islands are what the *Antarctic Pilot* describes as a picturesque archipelago of which Galindez Island is the highest, just under 200 feet, and it was on Galindez Island that we constructed the new scientific and survey station.

To get to Galindez Island we had to navigate the narrow Meek Channel and, in doing so, we collided with an ice-cliff, the bows of the ship biting into the overhang. The starboard rails peeled off, but we managed to get away, leaving a graze of red paint and the imprint of her bows in the ice. We all cheered and made wry faces at the officers on the bridge. At 9.30 we moored – three cables port, four cables starboard – and here we stayed and worked for seven weeks surrounded by the most beautiful scenery in the world and blessed with the most perfect, sunny, calm weather.

There was a sheltered cove in a corner of the anchorage, where exposed rock strata inclined to the sea in an unbroken slab and afforded a natural slipway for unloading the stores. Behind the snow free area assigned for the hut was a snowfield covering several acres, and further on rose the little ice-cap of Galindez. It was truly a glorious place with wonderful views extending what seemed like hundreds of miles south down the Antarctic Peninsula and north to Le Maire.

What were we doing at Galindez Island in the Argentine Islands just off the Antarctic Peninsula? For this I have to refer you to the plans to hold a Third Polar Year during 1957–58 (following those held in 1882–83 and 1932–33), but this time the scientific studies were to be part of a global investigation, not confined to the polar regions. The period was to be known as the International Geophysical Year (IGY).

For this year, 12 nations agreed to maintain stations in the Antarctic and there was a huge planned scientific programme coordinated by the Special Committee for Antarctic Research working under the aegis of the International Council of Scientific Unions. The principal objectives of the IGY year were the examination of the earth and its atmosphere and the effect of the sun upon them. Studies were to be made of aurorae, cosmic rays, geomagnetism, glaciology, ionospheric physics, meteorology, seismology and gravity. Particular attention was to be paid to meteorology, for the wide, although sparse distribution of scientific stations in the Antarctic made it possible for the first time to gain a comprehensive picture of the southern weather system.

All FIDS stations were geared to contribute to this IGY programme but we were there in the Argentine Islands to construct a new geophysical observatory, handling geo-magnetism, seismology, upper air observation, ozone measurements etcetera.

Ralph Lenton, a very experienced FID who was later also to take part in the Commonwealth Trans-Antarctic Expedition led by Bunny Fuchs, was put in charge of the building work. He was faced with the complex problems of constructing a non-magnetic hut and installing a Dobson ozone spectrophotometer and a seismograph. By 1955 all these were operational and a little later the ionospheric programme was transferred to Galindez Island from Port Lockroy.

We were extraordinarily fortunate with the weather as this made unloading the several hundred tons of stores much easier and, as the decks were cleared of timber and it became possible for the first time to walk freely about on board, the stacks of timber grew on shore.

We did initially have a problem, and this was with the Antarctic skuas who were nesting on our site. They, of course, thought we were about to nest on their site – which, of course, we were. The parent birds swooped down on us, screeching at us in mounting agitation as we neared the mossed depression which held their two precious eggs. This went on for several days until it became clear to them that we intended to stay, and then they gradually accepted us and settled down to incubate their eggs. But on Signy it was different and when I was walking alone I always carried aloft a ski-stick to protect me from these birds, and even this precaution did not always work.

Let me describe a skua attack, or rather attacks of skuas. As I said, you are walking along when suddenly there is a dark rushing shape of wings, the shape of sharp claws and the shape of a curved beak rushing down close to your head and then sharply moving away – it is the first dive-bombing attack. You see all around you these large brown birds, standing and staring at you intently.

And then the attacks begin in earnest. They swoop down on you, each time getting closer and closer until you see at close quarters the talons, the sharp curved beak and the bright, hard, wicked eyes, and then they see your ski-stick and they rush upwards and away – but not always. There was one time when I lowered my guard and suddenly felt a sharp blow on my exposed head which drew blood. Skuas are not small birds, they have a wing span of 6 feet; they are scavengers and marauders, robbing other birds of their chicks and eggs.

In victimising young penguins they try to cut one off when it gets separated from its parents and gradually worry it to death, whereupon they pick out their eyes and make two holes in the back through which the tissues of the kidneys can be removed. In a penguin rookery you can see hundreds of bodies of young penguins mutilated in this way by skuas, who are also quite happy to eat their own kin. Sailors, sealers and whalers have always hated skuas and I have always thought this was due to their terrifying appearance – very much in the same way sailors have always hated sharks. In some ways they are similar to the caracara birds which are unique to the Falkland Islands.

But now, after this diversion to the skuas, I return to Galindez and the construction of the new station. First of all we had to build concrete piers which would carry the weight of the hut. However these had to be grouted on to solid rock and this necessitated digging down and down through the loose rock and ice until we found this solid rock at different levels, so that all the concrete piers had to be constructed to deal with this difference.

Mixing concrete in the Antarctic in those days was not easy. First you had to get freshwater ice and then melt it in an oil drum over a fire. Then you had to get hold of shingle and sand in sufficient quantity and in the correct proportion to mix it with Fondu, which is a cement with a quick-drying action that generates sufficient heat to prevent it freezing before it sets. The proportions were four buckets of shingle, two buckets of sand and one bucket of cement. You turned this all onto the staging, making certain that there are no large stones in the mix, and then you started mixing and manoeuvred it in a dry saucer shape in which you poured the water from the oil drum, where the ice had now melted. You then shovelled and mixed it into a consistency which had the approval of Chippy Raymond, the carpenter. Meanwhile Chippy had been setting the wooden staging into which the concrete mix would be poured to form the piers of the hut. At night – or I would rather call it something else as we had 24 hours daylight and the sun hardly set below the horizon until the time came for our departure – we now swathed our work in sacking, with coke braziers burning nearby if the frost promised to be intense. So every morning Chippy would test the concrete piers to see if they were sound, and he did this with a hammer. Sometimes he would find a pier already beginning to crumble and then we would have to start all over again. When we had finished, I think we worked out that we had mixed by hand no less than 300 tons of cement – an extraordinary achievement of which we were all proud.

I have mentioned that the fine anticyclonic weather held for nearly all the time we were there. The place, compounded of sun, virgin snow, a multitude of birds and a sapphire sea set off against the beautiful magnificence of the mainland, produced such an intense consciousness of being alive that it was almost impossible to bring one's spirit under some sort of bearable control. And I remember one evening, after the day's work was done, going alone up to the little ice-cone of Galindez, and there before me and all around me was this panorama of such unbelievable beauty that I was quite overcome with emotion. There were the great mountains and glaciers stretching for what seemed like hundreds of miles to the south towards the Pole, and there was the pack ice, the ice floes, the islands, the islets, all suffused in the evening colours of mauve, pink, green and blue. And then there was this incredible peace, calm and serenity – not a sound, not a breath of wind, just beauty. I was overwhelmed.

I think that most of us realised that the building of this hut was one of those periods of enchantment and unalloyed happiness that seldom if ever occur in a lifetime. The pervading harmony owed little to conscious effort within, nor entirely to the beauty of the world without, but was rather an extension into something immeasurably greater, and at the same time more delicately fine and deeply part of the place and of ourselves. It was to me a divine revelation of the beauty of the Creation.

Day after day we toiled at constructing the hut – ten hours a day on site and, as you will have realised by now, we had the most beautiful weather. The sun circled through a cloudless sky, skimming the horizon at midnight, then climbing in the heat of noon to the north, and when we took off our shirts our skin went brown in the rays.

Each morning we would go directly to the site as soon as the motorboat touched the rocky slipway, and gradually we finished establishing the piers and levelling out the reinforced concrete bed for the diesel generators. Now we turned our hands to building the hut itself. We carried the joists and lifted them into position, tacking the battens and hardboard to stop snow drifting up from below. We insulated the floor, and by now we had several feet of flooring in place. When we thought we had finished the floor, we had to repeat the work all over again as it had been ordained that we should have another floor laid diagonally for extra strength.

The frame of the hut had been previously cut and labelled alphabetically so, with the floor as a working space, we were able

197

to assemble the gable ends and then, with all hands on the ropes, pull them upright in an erect position. To assemble the complicated framework of the hut, we were organised into two teams to build the walls and join them by a complicated system of roof trusses. We then moved on to the roof itself and the necessary insulation of ruberoid and fibreglass – then suddenly it was all finished, the weather changed and the sea began to freeze over. It was time to move on.

But there was one terrible thing we had to do before we left – we had to slaughter some 180 crabeater seals and transport them to Hope Bay, where the Survey station was short of seals for their sledging dogs. So we set about yet another murderous slaughter, covered in slime, blood and guts and stinking of blubber. It was a loathsome job, made the worse for the fact that we had to live with all the corpses on the decks all the way to Hope Bay. The night before we left we had a farewell party. It was not enjoyable – there was a forced hilarity about it all – and in any case we were all exhausted. Too much drink was drunk and there were various renditions of bawdy songs, which did not amuse me.

The harmony of the previous weeks had gone and it was time now to get away. So on the 2nd March 1954, we hauled in the cables mooring the ship to the shore, the anchor came up, and slowly – but ever so slowly – we edged our way down the Meek Channel, past the red paint on the ice-cliffs and then out into Penola Strait towards the Maire and Neumayer channels and Port Lockroy and Deception where we paid brief visits.

But at Deception we received orders to return to the Argentine Islands. I do not know why, and meanwhile the seals were putrefying on our decks. So it was back again and once more we moored in the Meek Channel, renewing our work on the new hut, so perhaps it had been less ready than we thought. And here we stayed another fortnight before finally departing on Monday, 22nd March 1954.

This time we stopped in the Neumayer Channel and went ashore on to Anvers Island where there is the remarkable Copper Peak from which we gathered geological specimens. The copper veins were large and noticeable. There had been some talk of a possible base on this island, but this was never established. Meanwhile, apart from collecting geological specimens, I took the opportunity to have a solo climb up the steep snow-covered slope of the peak, but it became too steep and I desisted. It was a pleasant change, but by the late afternoon we were off again to anchor in Port Lockroy for the night.

At 6 a.m. we were away for Deception, still a miserable place, but we stayed there only four hours before sailing for Admiralty Bay and Hope Bay. Between these two bases we ran into heavy pack ice but we were able to avoid the worst and soon we ran into Antarctic Sound, and an hour or so later dropped anchor at Hope Bay. Here we stayed for two days unloading all those poor wretched putrefying seals – all 180 of them.

In the afternoon the wind got up and increased to gale force and we started dragging our anchor, so we had to get under way. The wind moved to force 8 with some very strong katabatic gusts all night, making the ship yaw on both anchors. It was a dangerous time, but by midnight the wind decreased and at 8 a.m. the following day we were full away to Signy, which we reached on 29th March after a rough voyage.

Two days later, when we were about to get away, the port anchor fouled an old Norwegian mooring cable, but an hour later we were again full away for South Georgia in a heavy sea and numerous icebergs.

Now I will have to divert here a little to tell you something more about South Georgia which, after Coronation Island, is the second most beautiful island in the world. In 1948, the Colonial Office published a book entitled the *Colonial Empire 1947–48*. On page 40, there was a two-paragraph reference to the Falkland Islands and the Dependencies, mentioning that, 'as a result of the Argentinian and Chilean activities which have infringed British sovereignty, formal notes of protest have been exchanged between His Majesty's Government and their Governments.' My next port of call is another Colonial Office book entitled *British Islands in the Southern Hemisphere 1945–1951* in which South Georgia gets an honourable mention.

It notes that South Georgia is about 116 miles long and 20 miles wide at its greatest width, has a floating population of some 1,500 workers engaged in whaling during the summer and less than half that number – actually much less – in the winter when they are engaged in maintaining ships and plant, etcetera. South Georgia, although possibly discovered by Amerigo Vespucci in 1502 and possibly again by Antonio de la Roche in 1673, was nevertheless properly discovered by Captain Cook in 1775, who visited it, charted it and set foot on it, and above all claimed it for the Crown. This was in the course of his historic circumnavigation of the world.

It was Captain Cook's report of the fur seal colonies that created so much commercial excitement. Soon American and British sealers were making annual voyages to South Georgia, where these fur seals were slaughtered almost to the point of extinction. Today they have recovered to such an extent that it is almost impossible to land on any South Georgia beach, so numerous are they.

There have been many good books written about South Georgia but by far the best is Bob Headland's *The Island of South Georgia*, first published in 1984. Bob Headland is now the Archivist of the Scott Polar Research Institute in Cambridge and I number him among my good friends. The second book is *Logbook for Grace* written by Robert Cushman Murphy, who compiled the two world-famous volumes on the *Oceanic Birds of South America*, including the Antarctic. Robert Murphy, an American, went south in 1912 on the sealing and whaling brig *Daisy* out of New Bedford. Before he left he became engaged to Miss Grace Barstow and his book *Log-book for Grace* was written for her. It was eventually published many years later in 1948. In his preface Robert Murphy wrote: 'Grace is both the subject and object of this tale and she has been my recourse in countless problems of judgement, whilst her matchless vitality has often revived me. She has read the proof with me, just as for 35 years we have read all our proofs together.' Read *Log-book for Grace*, you will never forget it.

The book was written when sealing was sealing and whaling was whaling and by that I mean it was carried out by men from a sailing ship in open boats and hand harpoons. And if you go to Mystic Seaport on the eastern coast of the United States just north of Newhaven, you will see a restored whaling port and a restored whaler, just like the brig Robert Murphy embarked on to sail to South Georgia. And what do I mean by all this? The answer is that South Georgia represents the history of land-based whaling and sealing, and, although it was bloody, murderous and filthy, yet for the people engaged in it, it conjured up stories of great bravery, great dangers, great vicissitudes endured by men: pack ice, storms, icebergs and fog. And, of course, there were the ships they sailed in – in the early days these were sailing ships, and for many of the crew they were away from their homes (if they had a home) for up to five years. There was, dare I say it, a certain romance about whaling. This, of course, did not apply to the whaling itself but to the whalers themselves: those who captained the catchers, the harpoonists, the men who flensed the whales on the 'plan'. These were men, real men. They left home for long dangerous journeys south, and many died – witness the cemeteries at Grytviken, Husvik, Stromness, Leith and Prince Olav Harbour – and for many it became a way of life; but of course a life for them was a death to the innocent whale.

Let me tell you about a short whaling trip I joined. A whale catcher does not roll, she bounces. She does not pitch, she bucks, she dances and kicks her heels, and she is always awash with water midships. If she does a skid turn, quite normal practice when hunting whales, she may well go over, so you hang on and when you next look at the Norwegian crew you look bravely at them and pretend that you have been doing this sort of thing all your life – and not for just one day, never to be repeated.

You watch the young man on the wheel and you watch the men on the gun-platform in the bows loading the harpoon gun, a deadly, vicious-looking instrument. You watch the men ramming a harpoon down the muzzle. If you have never seen a harpoon, it is like a spear about 6 feet long with a swivelled head. Three barbs each with a swivelled head are kept in place by lashings, which when the harpoon strikes, will break so that the barbs stick outwards and prevent the harpoon being withdrawn. On the front of the head is a pointed conical bomb which is exploded inside the whale by a time-fuse. A long line is attached to the harpoon and a length of this is coiled down on the platform on which the harpoon is mounted. The rest runs up the foremast over pulleys, over the drum of a winch on the foredeck and down into the hold. This is the harpoon line, the fishing line and the mast is the rod.

Suddenly you hear a whistling, rushing explosion and a little way off a great burst of spray shoots into the air and then you see a great flat grinning head, followed by a broad curving back, turning and turning and turning. Suddenly a back bursts through the water ahead. The harpooner swings his gun, fires, and the black streak of the harpoon flies out and hits. And then the line goes down and down and down, and then a long way away in the depths there is a horrible thrashing disturbance and the terrible, lonely and titanic death struggle has begun. And now he comes up, wheeling and thrashing, and suddenly a red fountain bursts upwards – the whale is spouting blood. It is the end. So the whale fought for his life and his harmless, free, joyful life had been suddenly taken away from him by Man, in an explosion of agony. Damn you, Man, for what you have done to the innocent wildlife of this world.

Now, when you go to South Georgia and the southern Antarctic Ocean, you see no whales. Hundreds and thousands of beautiful innocent whales were murdered off the coast of South Georgia all the way up to the 1960s, and then suddenly there were no more – they had killed them all. The whalers did not believe this, and so much did they expect to come south again that, for instance at Leith, everything was left to await their return. But they never returned and nor did the whales – they were all dead.

We had a rough journey to South Georgia: a mean gale, a heavy swell and driving snow with the ship rolling heavily. Due to numerous icebergs and the poor visibility due to the snow, we reduced to half speed. Overnight the wind increased to force 9, more a storm than a gale, and the ship pitched and rolled heavily with the sea pouring onto the main deck. It was seriously uncomfortable and sometimes it was almost frightening to be on the bridge. But we weathered the storm and on 2nd April 1954, at 9 o'clock in the morning, we entered Cumberland Bay – at the head of which lies the Grytviken whaling station – and drew alongside Government Jetty at King Edward Point, above which is the Memorial Cross to Shackleton who died here at King Edward Point in January 1922. The last words in his diary were: 'A wonderful evening. In the darkening twilight I saw a lone star hover, gemlike above the bay.'

South Georgia is in many senses Shackleton's own island, and his name is virtually twinned with the island. Everybody has heard of, if not read, the tale of the 1914–1917 Imperial Trans-Antarctic Expedition and their ship the *Endurance* which was crushed by the ice in the Weddell Sea; the survivors on the disintegrating ice floes; the boat journey to Elephant Island; and the greatest achievement, the journey in the open lifeboat *James Caird* from Elephant Island to King Haakon Bay on the south coast of South Georgia and the three-day journey over the mountains and glaciers from the bay to the whaling station at Stromness, from which Shackleton organised the rescue of the members of the expedition still marooned on Elephant Island.

I was brought up on this story of great courage and endurance, and here I was in South Georgia, following – dare I say it – in his footsteps. South Georgia is so beautiful with its mountains and glaciers, its ice-caps and high soaring peaks, its islands and islets and its huge abundance of wildlife – including even reindeer, introduced by the Norwegian whalers for food. I have referred earlier to the romance of the sealers and whalers and their astonishing bravery and endurance in earning their living in the Antarctic and, in many cases, earning their deaths, as whaling and sealing are dangerous occupations. But there is also another romance, and that is the romance of the island itself, because South Georgia calls people to itself – it is uniquely beautiful. I remember once, many years ago, whilst sailing south from Stanley to Grytviken in autumn in a near-calm sea and bright, bright moonlight, watching South Georgia come into view, a completely white mountainous island covered in snow and ice to the water's edge, a beautiful white virgin goddess calling sailors to its shores.

In those days Grytviken was a working whaling station although, by the time I got there, it was beginning to close down for the winter. We were royally entertained by both the Norwegians and the British at King Edward Point. I took the opportunity to go off on my own to climb the local peaks around Grytviken and I paid my homage, like all visitors, to Shackleton's grave in the Whalers' Cemetery. I was deeply moved.

Meanwhile the ship bunkered, and a few days later we were full away to another whaling station, Leith, where we tied up alongside the huge factory ship the *Southern Opal*, where we took on more oil and water, the former in drums, as being the end of the season most of the oil tanks were empty.

That evening I and one or two others were invited by the whaling station doctor to have a drink with him. Whaling stations were supposed to be 'dry' and so I was curious to know what beverage we were to be given. The doctor turned out to be German; we all thought he was an SS doctor, hiding from the authorities in South Georgia, but this may have been maligning him.

At any rate he gave us what looked like whisky, but it did not taste of whisky. But I thought, well here goes, and I did. About an hour later I was almost paralytic and in leaving I fell down the stairs. However, with the help of my two friends, I clambered up on to the deck of the *Southern Opal*, crossed it, avoiding all the

203

digesters, and then managed to get down onto the *Biscoe* and into my bunk.

I found out afterwards what this so-called drink was. It was this. You know that shoe polish has a certain alcohol content to make your shoes shine? If you boil up shoe polish, you can drain it through a loaf of bread (or perhaps, rather, a slice of bread) and pure alcohol will appear. You then colour this with diluted prune juice and lo, it looks like whisky. So I had been drinking neat alcohol; no wonder I fell down the stairs. Many years later I went back to Leith and went to visit the remains of the doctor's quarters and there still were the stairs, just as steep as they had been that night over 50 years ago.

On 4th April, following my night out, we were full away for the South Sandwich Islands, which lie to the south-east of South Georgia and, once again, I will have to divert here and tell you a little about these islands, which were then virtually unknown and were not surveyed until 1964 – ten years later.

These South Sandwich Islands form a volcanic arc of eleven islands. There is a deep sea-trench on the convex side of the arc and this has a depth of about 21,000 feet. Nearly all the islands are volcanically active but, despite that, away from such activity, the islands are ice-covered. There is, like most Antarctic islands, an abundance of wildlife, large colonies of chinstrap penguins, lesser colonies of macaroni, Adelie and gentoo penguins and an abundance of silver-grey fulmars, snow petrels and Cape pigeons. These penguins and other birds, and the elephant, fur and Weddell seals, have the islands all to themselves – they are, of course, all uninhabited.

It was once again the famous Captain Cook who discovered the islands, in January 1775. In 1819, the Imperial Russian Navy Expedition under the command of Captain Bellinghausen sighted the islands, and that is why a number of the islands have Russian names like Leskov (Bellinghausen's first lieutenant), Visokoi and Zavodovski. Further south in the Southern Thule group of islands, an island was named after Bellinghausen himself, whilst he in deference to Captain Cook called one of the islands Cook Island.

Now what were we doing visiting the South Sandwich islands in late autumn, when the weather is universally appalling? The answer to this is, briefly, that we were looking for any sign of Argentine occupation because, if there were, we were going to lodge a formal protest in the time-honoured way: that is, to say that the Argentinians were infringing Her Britannic Majesty's sovereign waters and land and were to depart forthwith. There were no signs, as we discovered, but later on the Argentinians did establish a station on Thule, which was destroyed by the Royal Navy in 1982.

We laid course for Zavodovski Island. There was a slight sea, a low swell, and it was overcast. We cleared Cape Disappointment, so called by Captain Cook as he then realised that South Georgia was not part of the Antarctic continent for which he was searching, and then Clerke Rocks, named after the officer who first sighted them, who wrote in his journal about South Georgia: 'I did flatter myself from the distant soundings and high hills about it, we had got hold of the Southern Continent but alas these pleasing dreams are reduced to a small isle and that a very poor one too – as to its appearance in general, I think it exceeds in wretchedness Tierra del Fuelgo and Staten Island.' In this he is, of course, referring to South Georgia, not Clerke Rocks, whose two main rocks are called Nobbly and Office Boys – and why that is I do not know!

Two days later we were in a full gale with a heavy swell and driving snow. We edged up to the north-east coast of Zavodovski where we wanted to land. However, our anchorage was very unstable and we feared to put the boat out. Zavodovski – the northernmost of the South Sandwich Islands group – is essentially a single active volcano flanked by lava flows, and it smells. The island's points are named, for instance, Noxious Bluff, Stench Point, Acrid Point, Reek Point, Pungent Point and Fume Point, and close up you can smell sulphur. Not the most attractive island, and after a day and night there we weighed anchor at 6 a.m. and we were full away for Leskov and Visokoi islands.

Leskov is the surviving part of a once much larger volcanic cone, and Crater Bay on the east of the island is the site of the principal eruptive centre. When we were passing it, we could see some active fumaroles emitting steam. It is impossible to land on the island except, presumably, by helicopter, and we saw no penguins or seals – not a place to dwell on.

Visokoi, which lies about 40 miles east of Leskov, is slightly larger. It is again volcanic. The last time the summit crater was seen to be active was in 1930. There is very little fumarolic activity. Essentially, therefore, Visokoi is a latent volcano constructed of lava infected by dykes. It is also much eroded but the coastline is magnificent, huge high rock cliffs alternating with precipitous ice-falls.

Candlemas and Vindication Islands lie about 23 miles south-east of Visokoi. They are separated by Nelson Strait, which is about 2 miles wide. We went extremely slowly through this Strait and so we had a good opportunity to examine the two islands – visibility was excellent.

Candlemas is almost two islands but they are just joined by a low-lying area of volcanic sand with two lagoons, one called Medusa, the other called Gorgon. These two lagoons are separated by Chimera Flats, so clearly a Greek scholar was at work here. The northern part of the island is actively volcanic – it consists of a mass of lava flows which surround a group of scoria cones, and this northern mass falls to the sea in spectacular vertical cliffs and rises to the reddish volcanic cone called Mount Lucifer, after the rebel archangel.

There were many active fumaroles. We saw no penguins or seals. The southern part of the island is very different: heavily glaciated with two peaks called Mount Perseus and Andromeda, so continuing the Greek theme. The ice-cap cascades directly to the sea in the east and south parts of the island, but in the west the long ice foot is flanked by extensive moraines and ice-free areas.

Vindication Island, by contrast with Candlemas, is not very interesting and is only remarkable for the continuity and steepness of the high rocky cliffs which surround it. We saw no signs of volcanic activity.

Once clear of Nelson Strait we set course for Saunders Island and in a freshening gale from the north-west, we reached the island four hours later and anchored in Cordelia Bay on the east coast. We had a very anxious time in the bay – there was a very rough sea, the *Biscoe* was swinging on the anchor, there were persistent snow squalls and visibility was poor. In addition the sulphurous fumes from the active volcano, Mount Michael, blew directly down on us and soon the ship was stinking and we all started to cough. It was most unpleasant. And here we waited for the weather to improve.

Twenty-four hours later, the wind decreased. We weighed anchor and were soon full away from that ghastly sulphurous bay to Southern Thule. This is the southernmost of the South Sandwich

Islands. Like all the islands in this group it is volcanic, and a large active cone occupies the centre of the island – the rest is glaciated.

We arrived there in thick fog but, mercifully, it cleared and we were able to drop anchor in Ferguson Bay – not a particularly good anchorage as it is exposed to the westerly and south-westerly swells and gives little shelter. By the morning, we had not a gale on our hands, but a full storm, and even worse it developed into a hurricane from the north-north-west. Nevertheless, it was decided to get away from Ferguson Bay and try our luck in open water. We cleared Herd Point and then we were in it. The sea was appallingly rough. The ship was pounding, pitching and rolling, we were shipping water forward and there was spray over all. There were also numerous icebergs about. It was on this day that I was up on the bridge when the ship rolled through an arc of 112 degrees and the captain, Bill Johnston, said to me, if she goes further than that, she won't come back. She did come back, but shortly afterwards we hove to.

By late afternoon on 10th April there was a temporary lull in the storm and we got under way again but we soon had to reduce speed as the wind force once again moved up from gale force 9 to storm force 10 – it was all very uncomfortable. The best place was in one's bunk, strapped in, but the constant pitching, rolling, pounding and crashing got one down in the end and this was when a retreat to the engine-room became necessary, as the motion was less violent there. No food could be cooked and we lived off corned beef and Spam. However, we did manage to get cups of hot tea and that helped. But being hove to did not help, because it meant we were going backwards and we were all anxious to get to Port Stanley, our next destination.

It took us over a week to get to Stanley – the wind was never less than half a gale from the north-west and then, at last, on Thursday, 15th April, we arrived at the Government Jetty in Stanley and suddenly there was no movement and it was like going from hell to heaven. I had been on the ship continuously for two and a half months.

17

Return to the Falklands

In Stanley I was invited to stay at the very comfortable home of Señor Ernesto Rowe. Señor Rowe was a bachelor, a businessman with good links to the mainland and the Agent, I think for Hambros Bank. There were no banks on the islands.

From here I got in touch with Norman Keith-Cameron, who had invited me to stay at his sheep station at Port San Carlos. He had been a good friend of my Uncle Tim and indeed they had gone out to New Zealand together in the mid-1920s. This was when Uncle Tim was seen off by his beautiful ladies of the night. At the outbreak of war in 1939, he had immediately volunteered for service and he was accepted into the Coldstream Guards, where he had met Cuthbert Fitzherbert, who was later to become a Vice-Chairman of Barclays Bank, in charge of personnel as they were called in those days. I believe that he had been asked to report on me.

The *Biscoe* was due to stay in Stanley for a month so this afforded enough time to get out to Port San Carlos and work with his family on their sheep station. So one morning I went down to the jetty and got a boat out to the FIGAS seaplane moored in the harbour. FIGAS stands for Falkland Islands Government Air Service, and this air service had recently been started by Sir Miles Clifford and was invaluable. The seaplane was a Norseman, equipped to carry up to eight passengers. I clambered aboard and shortly after a choppy take-off we were airborne and heading west for Port San Carlos. It was a beautiful day – the islands were looking their loveliest and it was somehow reassuring to know that if anything happened to the plane, we could land almost anywhere, given all the water around. In about half an hour or so, the Norseman landed at Port San Carlos. Norman Keith-Cameron came out in his boat to pick me up and then it was up to his house, which very much resembled a farmhouse in the Highlands of Scotland. His wife and three children were there and I was immediately made an honorary member of the family.

For three weeks I had a most wonderful life there working on the sheep station. Most days I spent in the saddle, and occasionally I made forays on my own in the direction of Cape Dolphin. It was beautiful country, with lovely sandy beaches and the sea a deep Mediterranean blue. Once we sailed over to the San Carlos settlement, the home of the Bonner family, chatted, had a drink and then lunch. It is astonishing to think that nearly 30 years later this almost completely unknown place would be overrun with soldiers and sailors, ships and aeroplanes, bombing and shelling and death. It now has a War Memorial, including the grave of Colonel Jones who was awarded, posthumously, the Victoria Cross, at Goose Green some way to the South of San Carlos.

I remember telephoning the War Office twice in 1982. The first was when the Argentinians landed on South Georgia and I told them that without any doubt, due to the announced withdrawal of HMS *Endurance*, the next invasion would be the Falkland Islands. The second call was when British forces landed at San Carlos and I told them that I knew the area very well – I asked if I could be of any help as I had a lot of photographs of the area, taken with my Box Brownie. They were extremely polite, thanked me profusely for my offer of assistance, but ended up by saying that they had a complete set of photographic images of the area taken by satellite. There was no contest between a Box Brownie and a satellite.

Clearly this idyllic existence could not go on forever – and, of course, it did not. But now a problem arose. The weather had deteriorated to such an extent that the FIGAS Norseman could not fly, and meanwhile the *Biscoe* was signalling that if I could not get back soon, in the next two or three days, the ship would leave without me. The weather forecast was dire and so there was only one course of action to take and that was to ride to Port Stanley.

So one morning, with a gaucho as a guide, an extra horse and a mule to carry my belongings, we set forth. The weather was dismal in the extreme: a gale, pouring rain, low cloud and very poor visibility – no wonder the Norseman could not fly. In those days there was no track between Port San Carlos and Stanley, all communication being either by boat, or more recently, by air. So my reliance on the gaucho was absolute, although for safety's sake I took a compass with me.

The treeless moorland was saturated with water and before long we were soaked to the skin, but the horses kept going and we started to make good progress. We had a scare when about ten gauchos emerged out of the mist, riding across our front some way ahead. The gaucho told me that they were from the Douglas Settlement, that they were bad men and that we needed to keep out of their sight as they were dangerous. We kept out of their sight and later proceeded. Having crossed a number of swollen rivers – the water coming up to well above our stirrups – we eventually reached the settlement at Teal Inlet where we were given tea and cakes.

We left, and some time later stopped for the night in a shepherd's shanty, where we were able to cook up some mutton and potatoes – the staple diet of the Falkland Islands. It is a pity now, writing this 50 years later, that I cannot remember much about my gaucho or even his name. He was a rough man, tough as all gauchos are, but he looked after me and he did not lose the way. The first day we must have travelled about 30 or 40 miles and by the end I was wet, saddle sore and weary.

The next morning we rose early, saddled up and loaded the horses and mule, and set off after a breakfast of mutton and potatoes. After a short time we had to cross the flooded Arroya Malo. I was reluctant to do this but the gaucho urged me on and I entered the water. It was soon well above my stirrups and then came up to my knees but my horse persevered and after a shaky moment in mid-river, we reached the far bank – we had got through.

Our next stop was Top Malo House where we were provided with coffee, mutton and potatoes and we were able to stand in front of a good fire which warmed us through. We continued our journey. There was still a gale-force wind, driving rain and low cloud. We crossed the flooded Paso Maneas Brook and edged round many creeks before we got to Estancia House, north-west of Mount Kent. By this time we had only 20 miles to go before we reached Stanley, and we were doing well. Finally, we reached the point where the 5-mile road west of Stanley stopped – the only road in the islands – and soon we were in Stanley itself. It had been quite an experience; and the *Biscoe* had not yet left.

Was I at any time frightened? Only twice: once when we were fording the Arroya Malo and once when we sighted the Douglas men, who mercifully did not see us – or if they did, they took no notice of us.

On Friday, 14th May, after a farewell visit by His Excellency the Governor to the ship, we sailed at 9 a.m., went through the Narrows, and sailed south leaving Cape Pembroke to starboard. Our destination was Goose Green, which lies at the top of Choiseul Sound which is some 25 miles long and named after the Duc de Choiseul who has been mentioned earlier. Here we discharged one car, ten bags of mail and took on 250 mutton carcasses. We left the following day at noon, dropped some mail off at the Lively Island Settlement, and at 4 p.m. we were again full away for South Georgia in a slight sea, which got up as we once again headed south, the temperature dropping steadily and visibility worsening. Four days after leaving Stanley we secured alongside the whaling station at Leith. The following day we discharged the mail and 100 mutton carcasses and we were soon away for the Grytviken whaling station where we arrived an hour and a half later. Here we discharged the remaining carcasses, all 150 of them, and the following day we were full away in a north-westerly gale bound for Montevideo.

I have looked at the ship's log for this voyage to Montevideo – it was a winter voyage and the weather was consistently bad and at times atrocious. The log states, day after day: vessel rolling heavily ... vessel rolling and pitching very heavily ... very rough sea and heavy swell ... vessel shipping water forward ... vessel rolling and pitching violently and pounding at times ... signal projector from port wing carried away and lost overboard ... vessel shipping water on main deck ... heavy rain storm ... distant lightning. However, the temperature gradually rose from freezing in South Georgia until, as we neared Montevideo it rose to the mid-sixties and the wind shifted at last to the north-east.

A week after leaving Grytviken in the evening we entered the River Plate. We were all urging the boat on as we wanted to dock at Montevideo before the port closed at midnight. If we were later than that, or so we thought, we would not be allowed to dock until the morning and we would have missed a night in the bars and nightclubs. Remember, we had not seen girls for nearly two years – and some longer than that – and our testosterone levels were exceptionally high.

At 9.30 p.m. we picked up the pilot and at 11.30 p.m. we docked, and at 11.31 p.m. we were all off the boat and heading into town along with the Captain and crew except one officer and the night watchman.

I headed off with David Stratton to a nightclub called Aquila d'Oro, etched in my memory forever, and there I met a most lovely French-Uruguayan girl called Rita – whether that was really her name did not matter in the least – but anyway I immediately fell passionately in love with her. Unfortunately she could not speak English, but mercifully my French was reasonably good and, of course, she spoke excellent French, and so we managed all right. She was enormously attractive and fun as well as beautiful, and for many months we used to write to each other.

The following day I found myself with no money – I had spent it all. So I went to the Captain and asked him if I could have an advance on my pay, which was sitting in my London bank account, or alternatively whether he could lend me some money. He refused, so the following night I went back to the Aquila d'Oro and Rita and explained to the owner that I had no money, but I could play the piano and if he would let me play in the intervals when the band was resting I would do so, and the only recompense I needed was free drinks and Rita. Surprisingly enough he agreed, and so every night we were in Montevideo, I spent at the Aquila d'Oro, playing the piano, supplied with free drinks with Rita by my side. All this was intoxicating for a young man who had never experienced anything like this before, and I think it all went to my head – so much so that 50 years later, I can remember the place vividly and, of course, darling beautiful dark Rita.

But once again this other sort of idyll could not last and the time came for me to say a tearful goodbye to the lovely Rita and a grateful goodbye to the owner of the Aquila d'Oro, rejoin my ship and head back north to the grey dreariness and drabness of post-war England.

An outward-bound journey on a polar expedition vessel to the Antarctic is full of anticipation and excitement. In contrast the return journey is full of feelings of déjà vu, and even a sense of foreboding and depression as one headed back to the grim reality and monotony of everyday existence in England, with its awful pervading greyness and poverty and its bomb-shattered cities.

The journey home was uneventful and monotonous but there

213

was one occasion when early one morning I saw from the bridge one of the most beautiful sights in the world – a four-masted barque under full sail belting through the early morning mist. It was just like the *Flying Dutchman* as it appeared, disappeared and reappeared in and out of the mist, rapidly overtaking us. It passed to our port, and then this vision of pure loveliness left our sight and one marvelled at the sheer beauty of a great four-masted barque under full sail. It transpired later that it was the *Pamir*, carrying grain from Buenos Aires to Hamburg and mainly manned and crewed by young German cadets. And here it is so sad to relate that this beautiful ship on one of its subsequent voyages was pooped and went down with all hands. Pooping, even with us, was an ever-present fear in dangerous seas when those large terrifyingly high waves threatened to break over our stern.

My journey came to an end when at half past six on the morning of 22nd June 1954, on a typical grey dull day, the Needles pilot boarded the ship, and at 9.30 we berthed. Then the grey officials came on board, customs officers, immigration officers, followed by the stevedores. We were asked whether we had anything to declare. 'What!' we said, 'From the Antarctic?' How different from Montevideo, where we were off the ship without any questions or papers.

I took one last look at my bunk, which had been my bed for something like six or seven months. I paused to look round the expedition wardroom, now empty, and took a last walk round the deck and up to the bridge where I had spent so many hours carrying out my weather observations. Then a final glance at the crow's nest, which showed to the world that we were an ice-ship.

The goodbyes were said, hands were shaken, and then it was up the gangplank to the quayside.

Nothing had changed since my departure nearly two years before. I took the train to Waterloo, crossed London to Liverpool Street Station, and caught the steam train to Woodbridge. I was home. I was happy to see Mummy again and happy to be in a comfortable bed again, but all this began to pall, and in a few days' time I was once again restless, perhaps even bored. But what was I going to do, after all these years of adventure, danger and excitement?

18

Bank Clerk and Engagement

It was to be Barclays Bank. And even now, thinking about it all again all these years later, I did not really have much alternative without a degree and, of course, I did not have any money, except the money I had saved from my £300 per annum salary whilst down south, and that would soon go.

There had indeed been much pressure for me to go into the bank, particularly from my grandmother Gaga, the widow of my grandfather, the Chairman of Barclays Bank (Dominion, Colonial & Overseas), and also from my godfather Emlyn Bevan who was a Director of the Bank and who had been a good friend of my father when they both worked together as local directors of the Bank at 54 Lombard Street, in the office always known as 'The Room'.

First of all I had to go through a series of interviews, particularly intense, because if I entered the bank's service I would be placed on the Special List of entrants who, if they survived, were earmarked for management at an early age – early in those days being something around about the 30-year-old mark.

The most difficult interview I had was with the Chairman, Sir Anthony Tuke, who had been a banker all his life and was formidable in both appearance and intellect. He asked me how interested I was in commercial banking. I felt that I had to be honest and replied that after fighting in the Far East and surveying in the Antarctic, I was not too sure how interested I was in banking, but I was willing to give it a try. I did tell him that I had read a book called *Modern Banking* – not the most exciting book I have ever read, but I had read it diligently. This seemed to strike a happier note, and I walked out of his office, past the tailcoated messengers, into the lift and down to the ground floor and went home. Unfortunately, I had forgotten my appointment with my godfather after my interview with the Chairman as he wanted to know how it had gone. My first black mark, and I was not yet even in the bank.

I started in the bank in October 1954. My first branch was the British Museum branch which is now, I think, a Tibetan Centre. It was what they called in those days a manual branch – that is to say there were no accounting machines, only one adding machine, which two charming girls manipulated. Otherwise all the ledgers and statements were written up by hand and every calculation was made manually. I had to learn the double-entry bookkeeping system – I learnt how to do the post, I learned how to work out the decimals for calculating interest and any number of mindlessly boring chores. I felt it was rather like being a recruit in the Army again.

It was all very hierarchical. There was the Manager, Mr Heath. He came from the East End, was sharp, shrewd and volatile – he was a good Manager and got on well with his numerous Jewish customers. Then there was Mr Dowdeswell, the Chief Clerk, grey – how often do I use that word – bespectacled and a fountain of banking wisdom, etiquette and discipline. Then there was Mr Barnes, the security clerk, who wrote up all his securities ledgers and dealt in allotment letters, share certificates, bonus entitlements and charges. He was always very smartly dressed in a black coat and dark pin-striped trousers. He was affable and very helpful.

Then there were the cashiers, one of whom had been a Squadron Leader in the War, perhaps a Group Captain. I still do not know to this day how this wonderful man, after a brilliant war record in which he had won the DFC, who was at the same time an excellent church organist – he played at St George's Church, Bloomsbury, nearby – could endure being a bank cashier. But here you must remember that for many servicemen returning after the war to Civvy Street, a job – any job – was of paramount importance, particularly if you were middle-aged and married.

Another cashier, a grey, sad thin man, I recall once wore a cardigan when he was on the till, as we called it. This cardigan broke the Bank's dress rules and he was told by Mr Heath to take it off. And then behind the till were the waste-clerks on high wooden office stools, processing the waste, writing up the ledgers as if nothing except the dress had changed since the days of Dickens.

I used to arrive at about 8.30 to 8.45. I was let in by the branch messenger, Tommy, went down to the restroom, where I had a cup of tea and a fag, and emerged at about 9 a.m. The branch opened to the public at 10 a.m. I had an hour's lunch break – a pint of beer and a sandwich – which always made me feel sleepy if I had been out the night before, and then at 3 p.m. the doors were slammed shut. At that point there was always a sort of a flash of lightning as everyone lit up their cigarettes.

During my early years there were three courses which we had to attend at the Bank's training school at Wimbledon, which was run in my day by, first of all, the redoubtable and energetic John Tonkin and, secondly, by Mr Wheeler who I think had been a Colonel in the Army during the war. He is what I would describe as a kind disciplinarian, that is to say he exercised firm discipline in a kind and understanding manner – the best way.

The first course was instruction in the Bank's basic bookkeeping systems. I am afraid I did not really excel in this course and I came very near to the bottom of the class. The second course was called the mechanisation course and was designed for the position in the bank known as 'OC Mech', that is, a branch officer in charge of mechanisation: the mechanised bookkeeping system as opposed to the manual system. I did better in this course. The third course was called the securities course, which basically dealt with the mechanics of taking security for the Bank's lendings. Here I distinguished myself by becoming very nearly top.

There was rather later a course dealing with balance sheets, their interpretation and so on, which, of course, included accountancy and audit. Here I really did excel myself and came top of the class, so from bottom of bookkeeping to top of balance sheet interpretation I was making progress.

Now going back to the British Museum branch, the great day came on 31st December – balance day, when all the ledgers and statements had to be balanced manually and the six months profit of the branch ascertained from the rates provided to us by the Chief Accountant. These rates were always a fiddle, but they were a useful guide to the branch's profitability and the bank's margins, which were what they broadly represented.

We worked as hard as we could to get the figures balanced and right before the pubs shut. If we went out to the pub before they balanced we were usually there in the branch until midnight. For this great effort we were given 5 shillings, always known as 'balance money', and if we were truly late, then the bank in its munificent generosity gave us the taxi fare home.

In 1955 I was transferred to the Chancery Lane branch, a much bigger outfit with a Manager, Assistant Manager and a Chief Clerk. It was also a mechanised branch, that is to say the ledgers, statements and waste were produced by machines – made by Burroughs. The branch had a large number of barristers and solicitors, partnership accounts and curiously enough, advertising accounts among which I recall was W.S. Crawford. It was a good business because the advertising agencies always got their money in from their clients before paying it out to the newspapers and magazines, and these accounts generated large current account balances on which, of course in those days, no interest was paid.

The Manager was Mr Bradley – how well one remembers all these names 50 years later. The Assistant Manager was Mr White and the Chief Clerk Mr Ingrey, the youngest Chief Clerk in the Bank with a career full of promise in front of him. Sadly this did not materialise; he was enormously energetic and highly intelligent, but he had what they call an 'unfortunate manner' with the staff and came to be thoroughly disliked.

Following on my OC Mech course, I was moved up to be assistant OC Mech at the branch. All the machinists were girls from the East End and Essex and were all bright as a button, cheerful, hard-working and intelligent – such a contrast to the men, who were often sad and bitter. Here it must be remembered that without achieving an appointment in the Bank, you were condemned to a life of dreary drudgery and annual salary scale increases until you reached the top of the scale, with occasional merit rises thereafter – sometimes as low as £10 or £15 for the year, rather exceptionally £50 for good work and initiative. And they were all trapped by the Bank's Staff Housing Loan scheme, which provided a mortgage rate of $2^{1}/_{2}$ per cent, which in those days was less tax. This Staff Housing Loan Scheme was the Staff Handcuff and made it almost impossible to change jobs. Loans to staff were rigorously controlled in those days and all applications had to be sanctioned by Staff Department, who were always on the look-out for staff overspending as this could have led (and quite often did) to what were known as staff defalcations.

So your staff bank account was watched like a hawk, and you were not allowed to borrow money from anywhere else and, of course, in those days there were no credit cards.

So now it was time to move on to another branch, this time Portman Square, to learn about securities and foreign work. Here the Manager was Mr Bernard Louis Cripps, one of the most talented managers in the Bank, with a formidable intellect. I learnt a lot from him. The business was mixed, predominately Jewish. I forget the name of the Assistant Manager but the Chief Clerk's name was Mr Salter. He was a large florid man with rather a leer about him. Somehow he got into trouble, I think it started off as marital trouble but, like all such trouble, it led quite quickly to financial trouble and then possibly a defalcation. One day at three o'clock in the afternoon, just as the branch door was slammed shut – it was always slammed – and the cigarette flare of lightning lit up the premises, the Inspectors arrived, all wearing bowler hats. The girls burst into tears, so formidable did they seem – and were. The Inspectors took over all the keys – I had a key myself in those days and there was nearly trouble as they could not find me; I was dozing in the lavatory after a pub lunch. Mr Salter was put under interrogation and he disappeared, never to be seen again.

When I first came to London I rented a bed-sitting room in Flood Street, Chelsea, for £5 a week. It had been advertised in some paper by someone called Richard Bourdon-Smith, a surveyor, whose brother became a well-known silver merchant. It was a dark poky room on the ground floor of Rossetti Garden Mansions and it became insufferably suffocating when those dreadful London smogs came along and one had to shut all the windows. The stale air was better than the smog. I remember one day when the smog was so bad that I lost my way walking up Flood Street, among the cars and buses that were about – very few of them – with their headlights full on, wandering around the road. My two associations with Flood Street were not happy ones. First, this horrible dark bed-sitting room, and secondly, the large six-bedroomed house up the smart end of the street, which I bought in 1964 and was where my first marriage ended in disaster.

From Flood Street I moved to some bachelor chambers in Petty France in Westminster. At least one's chamber there was serviced and breakfast was provided, but it was not an exciting sight to see all those young impoverished bachelors hunched over their individual breakfast tables. Later on I moved in to David Stratton's flat at 5 Onslow Square near South Kensington Station. This was a large flat on two floors owned by his mother and I was much happier there. I had met David Stratton in the Antarctic. He was an old Harrovian surveyor and was number 2 at Hope Bay. Later on he became second-in-command of the Commonwealth Trans-Antarctic Expedition under Bunny Fuchs. We became good friends, and remained so until his very early death.

After he left the Antarctic for the last time, he took up a job with British Petroleum, which had greatly assisted the expedition, and eventually was promoted manager for the Eastern Mediterranean. It was while he was there that he decided to climb Mount Ararat in Eastern Turkey, which he did very successfully, but on the way down a progressive paralysis overcame him until he was neither able to walk nor stand nor hardly breathe – he had contracted polio. Apparently if you have the polio bug without knowing it, and at the same time undertake severe physical exercise, the paralysis is much worse, and this is what happened to David. He was flown home to the Radcliffe Infirmary in Oxford where he was put in an iron lung. David was quite extraordinary. When he was in the iron lung – he was never out of it – he fell in love with his nurse and decided, totally paralysed as he was, to divorce his wife, which he did. I think he had been considering divorce for some time before his paralysis. In the end I believe he asked his sister to turn the machine off, and he died in his early forties, a ghastly end to an enormously brave man who had distinguished himself in the Royal Navy, the Falkland Islands Dependencies Survey, the Commonwealth Trans-Antarctic Expedition and lastly in British Petroleum. He was a great companion and friend.

Eventually we comprised a quartet of bachelors in the flat, Kenneth Anderson who came from a shipping family, and Nick Holloway, an insurance broker. They were all Harrovians and we had lots of fun.

The rent was again £5 a week which, in those days, was also roughly the price of a restaurant dinner for two without wine. Also in those days there were hardly any restaurants outside Soho – nobody had any spare money. There was one in Fulham Road called Salamis and one in the King's Road called Unity, a Greek restaurant, and that was about it, apart from a restaurant in Knightsbridge called Esperanza but that was quite expensive.

The great trouble I had during the winters was deciding where to go for the weekend, and the reason for this was that my mother and stepfather lived in Majorca in their hotel all winter, and The Cottage at Eyke was shut up. I did invite myself to the Hole Farm where the life tenant of the Lyons Hall Estate lived (my aunt, Mrs Garnett, always known as Dore), but I always felt persona non grata there, which indeed I probably was. She had a nephew living there, Henry Garnett, who started off working in a brewery and then left that and went into the Church of England where he seemed very happy. It was lucky that when I was 25, under my grandfather's will, I became the eventual heir of the Lyons Hall Estate – my aunt, if she had had a free hand would have left it to her Anglican nephew. There always seemed to be some sort of conspiracy between her and him on which I could never lay my hands, until after her death when certain correspondence came to light. As I have written earlier, her last stroke-riddled words to me before she died were 'I hate you', and I think she did – there was always a malevolent tension about when I was staying there at the Hole Farm. Effectively, I was homeless every winter.

By this time I had bought a new car, a green and white Ford Zodiac with white-walled tyres. I had fallen in love with it when I saw it in the showroom, and it cost £600. Of course, I did not have £600, but I had found out that when I was born my father had taken out an insurance on my life. The policy was held by Ian Mitchell-Innes, a solicitor with a firm called Caprons & Crosse, and my father's best friend and best man at his wedding. I asked him to surrender it for me and he did not approve, but in the end he had no alternative, and I had no other recourse if I was to buy the car. A car was becoming a necessity – apart from anything else, no girl would go out with a boy without a car (or if she did it would not be for very long); and in the circles in which I lived, carlessness was a signal of poverty and ineligibility.

It was in the year 1955 that I disgraced myself, and I shudder even now to think about it. Over the years my grandmother had been kind to me: she sent me cold cooked pheasants to Eton; she gave me an allowance of £200 per annum which enabled my annual income to creep up to the £1,000 per annum mark, less tax of course; she was the one who wanted me to go into the bank and, although I resisted her at first, nevertheless it has to be said at this distance of time that in the end I had many enjoyable and successful years in the bank.

Now it happened like this. My grandmother died and the funeral was to be at St Mary's the Virgin. I was asked to read the Lesson. Coincidentally, the *John Biscoe* was arriving back from the Antarctic the day before the funeral at Southampton and I was invited down for a party on board the ship to see all my old friends. Well, it was a party, but I had promised myself that I would leave it early to get back to London and then go on to the funeral in Essex. But I am afraid to say it did not work out like that. I arrived at Liverpool Street Station to see the train which was going to be met at Chelmsford just leaving the platform. I tried to get onto it, but it was moving too fast. And as I stood on the platform watching the train go by, I saw the ashen face of my Great-Uncle Claude look at me as the train gathered steam. I had been asked to accompany him. Oh dear, oh dear, oh dear. I got the next train down, took a taxi to the church where the funeral service was just under way. Shaking with nerves and, truth to say, with alcohol also, I read the Lesson. To this day I shudder at the awfulness and embarrassment of it all and all I hope is that she has forgiven me. Great-Uncle Claude did, as he gave me his Lyons Hall silver when I married three years later.

Now the Bank in its infinite wisdom decided to send me to learn banking in the provinces and of all places they sent me to the branch at Leamington Spa, Warwickshire, where I knew absolutely nobody at all. I motored up there and checked in at a small hotel on the outskirts of the town full of grey old sniffling ladies with dripping noses eking out their widows' pensions. It was not the place for me but I had to survive there a few weeks before I found a pub in Henley-in-Arden where I could rent a room.

Leamington Spa branch had a Manager, Mr Geoffrey Weller, who was always very pleased with himself and wore a gold watch-chain on his waistcoat. At lunchtime he disappeared to his local hostelry and sometimes came back quite late. But he was a good and honest Branch Manager, he knew his business, and his customers liked him.

His Chief Clerk was Mr Lacey, who always looked as if he was on the edge of a nervous breakdown. He was thin and grey and had spectacles with particularly thick lenses, which perched on the end of his nose and he was always knocking them back. He was not unlike a modern Uriah Heep but he had a heart of gold and we became good friends; he often invited me to meet his wife and

222

family at his flat – and whilst doing so he always rubbed his hands with invisible soap.

The branch was entirely manual – not even one adding machine. By this time I had been promoted to being a cashier, two years after entry, but something went wrong and I was demoted to writing up manually ledgers and statements. Not many of the customers found it easy to read my writing which had deteriorated after I nearly lost my arm in the jungle. Indeed I still have very little feeling in my right hand. I have to say I loathed Leamington Spa with its fading Georgian gentility and pretences and, in particular, I disliked the departmental store nearby called Bobby's with its dull, tasteless English food and equally dull brittle English waitresses whose Brummy nasal accents I could neither accept nor sometimes understand. I was glad to get out of there and I have always looked upon Leamington Spa as the utter nadir of my banking career.

I was now transferred to the main branch in Birmingham, namely 63 Colmore Row, which was in the same building as the local head office whose Senior Local Director was Guy Bryan – a very tall man with large bulging eyes and an Adam's apple which wobbled constantly. He had been in the same regiment as the Chairman of the bank during the war and had made good, as they say. I think it was true to say that we all stood in awe of him – if not sheer terror – but underneath this unprepossessing aggressive exterior he had a kind and generous heart.

Once again the problem of accommodation arose and without knowing anybody in Birmingham at all, I started off once again in a bed-sitting room, at 18 Clarendon Road, Edgbaston. This room had a gas fire and a gas ring which you had to feed with sixpences. There was one very nice young Swiss there who enlivened the house with his amatory noises and manoeuvres, but otherwise the house was once again full of old, grey, sad men, who looked at breakfast as if they were crying over their cornflakes, and at high tea over their powdered green pea soup. The landlady, who was a widow, was not very nice either. Many times I used to go down to The Plough and Harrow at the end of the road and have a good steak.

Gradually I became aware that across the road in the top-floor flat were three young men, one of whom turned out to be Mark Thompson-McCausland who had been at Eton with me. The others were Harry Hodgson and John Biffen who later became Leader of the House of Commons. They agreed to invite me to join their entourage, and it was with enormous relief that I moved across the road from my bedsitter to their bachelors' chummery, albeit a chummery without servants. Clarendon Road, both the bedsitter and also the bachelors' flat, have always been etched in my memory.

It was in 1956, just before I went up to Birmingham, when I received a letter from a man called Klaus Helberg, who turned out to be the Director of the Norwegian Tourist Office. He also turned out to have been the wireless operator for the team who had blown up the German heavy water factory in Norway during the war, and as a result he had spent many months eluding the German search parties in the Hardanger and Jotunheim. In his letter he explained that he knew I had been in the Antarctic and that I had sledged huskies. His letter went on to say that he wanted to popularise dog-sledging in the winter in Norway as a tourist attraction and that he wanted a trial run, so to speak, to see if it would work. He and I would be the leaders, it would take about ten days to a fortnight, and the Norwegian Tourist Office would pay my expenses. This seemed to be a wonderful opportunity, so naturally I accepted.

In due course, having crossed over from Newcastle to Bergen on the familiar 'vomiting *Venus*' I found myself at Finse where Scott had trained for his ill-fated, as it turned out, last Antarctic expedition. So for the next fortnight, with two teams of huskies and a number of interested tourists, we skied and sledged from hut to hut, sometimes in beautiful weather but more often in terrrible blizzard conditions. Some of these huts had been used by Klaus Helberg when he had been escaping from the Germans, so each time we arrived at a hut he was given a hero's welcome and a lot of aquavit was consumed. It was the greatest fun, and I think my daughter Christina has a photograph of me, sent by Klaus Helberg, dancing with an enormously fat Norwegian lady, looking very happy! Klaus Helberg took part in a television documentary film re-enacting the successful raid on the German heavy water factory.

In the autumn of 1957, my mother and stepfather, Uncle Robin, left to spend the winter in Majorca as usual. This meant as always that I had the prospect of something like six months without anywhere to go at the weekend and Birmingham at the weekend was not a place for any of us expatriates to linger. Other friends had their parents' homes to go to, but I did not, and if I went to the Hole Farm to stay with my aunt, I was always made to feel unwelcome.

The Birmingham expatriates had to make their own social life. There were only two or three Birmingham families who invited us to their homes so we were very much on our own but in the autumn of 1957 something happened and I fell tumultuously, hopelessly and I think helplessly in love with a girl called Clare d'Abreu. It happened like this. She and her sisters were living with their parents at a house called The Leys, Alvechurch, just outside Birmingham. Their father, Alphonsus Ligouri d'Abreu, was Professor of Surgery at the Queen Elizabeth Hospital in Birmingham: he had pioneered thoracic surgery in this country and he was also Dean of the Medical School in Birmingham. He was very dark and I was told he was Portuguese. His wife Betty, on the other hand, was a sister of Sir Robert Throckmorton who lived at Coughton Court, Alcester, in Warwickshire. I was always devoted to her, and she was to become a wonderful mother-in-law to me.

To be invited to a party at a private house at the weekend, when the alternative was moping in the bachelor flat in Birmingham, was an opportunity too good to miss. The invitation came vicariously through a friend, Richard Lethbridge, who was like me a Birmingham expatriate. He knew the family and was very attracted to Clare's younger sister, Felicity, who later married Charles Crosland. That marriage ended in divorce and the second time around she married Roald Dahl, the famous children's author, having supplanted his wife, Patricia Neal the actress, in his affections. I had in fact been invited to make up the numbers for the party, as they were short of men. So I went to the party, met Clare, and was quite overwhelmed by her dark beauty.

And here I must digress a little to tell you, dear reader, about these two families, the Throckmortons and the d'Abreus.

The Throckmortons were an old Catholic landed family, who first came into prominence when a previous Sir Robert Throckmorton became a member of King Henry VII's Privy Council and thus began a long association with the Tudor monarch. His son George was returned to the Reformation parliament in 1529 as Knight of the Shire of Worcestershire. It was this parliament which began the religious rift with Rome and also saw the beginning of the Throckmorton family's conspicuous adherence to the Catholic faith despite all the hardships it brought.

225

The house itself, Coughton Court, was twice sacked in the seventeenth century: in 1644 by Royalist troops, and in 1688 when a Protestant mob destroyed what was called the 'newly erected Catholic church' and the east side of the house. The 4th Baronet, who lived until 1791, had three magnificent landed estates, at Buckland, at Weston Underwood and at Coughton. The family went into decline thereafter. Weston Underwood was demolished in 1826 and the estate sold in the 1890s, Buckland was sold in 1909, and in 1934 most of the Coughton Estate was sold. However, the Molland Estate on Exmoor was retained and this estate had come to the family by an eighteenth-century marriage. It had been a Courtenay estate, and hence for continuity's sake Charles Tritton's second name is Courtenay. After the death of Sir Robert Throckmorton in 1989 – who had become a very good friend – Clare inherited Coughton and the Molland Estate, but this was long after we divorced.

Now we move on to the d'Abreus, and here I think it is sensible to start off with Clare's grandfather, John Francis d'Abreu. He was born in 1893 in Mangalore, India, which was then in the Presidency of Madras. He was the youngest of seven children of Antony Abreo, who was a merchant, and Catherine Lobo. The Abreos and the Lobos were part of an enormous family within a successful and established community of Mangalorean Catholics. He went to the Grant Medical College in Bombay and subsequently left India for Scotland and seems to have changed his name from Abreo to d'Abreu.

In 1891 he qualified as a doctor by obtaining the prestigious triple licentiate from the Royal College of Physicians in Edinburgh, the Royal College of Surgeons, Glasgow, and the Faculty of Physicians and Surgeons of Glasgow.

In 1895 he married Teresa Noonan and there were seven children of the marriage, of which, as I have mentioned, Alphonsus Ligouri, always known as Pon, was the youngest. Why was he christened Alphonsus Ligouri? The answer here seems to be that he being the seventh child, his parents had run out of names and looked up the Saint's name for that day of his birth, i.e. 1st August 1906.

So this was Clare's family: on her mother's side, an old Catholic English landed family, and on her father's side, an immigrant Indian medical family from the Carnatic who were Indian–Goan–Portuguese. I did not know this as my father-in-law Pon was always referred to as being of Portuguese origin. But would it have made any difference if I had known this? The answer is, of course, no.

And so it came to pass that I asked Clare to marry me and she accepted. Looking back on all this 50 years later, I sometimes feel I should not have asked her to marry me; I had very little money, although I had prospects of inheriting the Lyons Hall Estate one day; the Bank was still moving me around all over the place and in the first seven years of our marriage we were moved by the Bank seven times, enough to destabilise any marriage, and most of the moves were entirely unnecessary; and then, of course, my family were anti-Catholic and the thought of future Trittons being Catholic and the Lyons Hall Estate ending up in Catholic hands drove them to apoplexy.

In the end all this cost me a huge sum of money because my Aunt Dore, the life tenant of the estate, delayed and delayed making over the estate until it was too late. I had hoped that the estate might be made over to me as a gift in marriage, because in those days such gifts were free of inheritance tax, but that was not to be and, as I have said earlier, I still cannot really understand the hostility shown to me by the Tritton family. If, of course, my father had lived it might have all been very different – but, as they say, diagonal relationships are usually more difficult than direct relationships. Most families are supportive of their children – in my case I was, of course, a nephew – but my family could not have been less supportive excepting, of course, my mother. Sometimes I felt that they were quite actively trying to destroy my marriage and, at the end of the day, one can say that certainly they helped to achieve that.

19

Marriage and Money

As I have said earlier Mummy and Uncle Robin were at that time in Majorca. The engagement happened so quickly – many people would say far too quickly – that I had no time to forewarn Mummy and the first she heard about the engagement was from my letter. In those days telephones did not work very well, and in any case I did not feel it right to jump it on her over the telephone – all my life I have had an aversion to the telephone. Mummy wrote back saying how pleased she was. She said she hoped I would be very happy – and she was looking forward to meeting Clare.

The Trittons' reaction was, of course, very different. It was one of intense disapproval, if not downright hostility and the main reason was Clare's Catholicism. All this dispirited me and, as a result, I cleaved to the d'Abreu family where I enjoyed the feeling of being part of the family home – it was, in other words, all normal, whereas my life without a home except in the summer was anything but normal. I think for all my life I have craved for the security and stability of a family home.

Now I had to turn my mind as to where we should live in Birmingham, bearing in mind it would not be very long before the bank would start moving me again. In the end we alighted on a small cottage, the lodge of one of those large grand houses in Edgbaston. The rent was £5 a week, the same as I was paying for my share of the bachelor flat in Clarendon Road.

The wedding took place at Coughton Court in March 1958, but before that I had to be indoctrinated into the Catholic faith, and I have to say now how greatly I resented that at the time – perhaps I was then too much of an Anglican. The first priest I was sent to see was a Jesuit at Farm Street in London, to whom I instantly took a violent dislike, so much so that I refused to see him again. After that debacle I was introduced to a charming Oratorian in Birmingham, who I think was as equally embarassed about the whole thing as I was, but he was kind and gentle and I liked him.

The wedding went off well except for the Tritton brigade glowering at me, and we then went up to London by train and stayed the first nuptial night at Claridges. The following day we flew to Gibraltar in an old plane, arrived at the Rock Hotel where my sister had honeymooned, and that night Clare had some sort of collapse and the doctor had to be called. We eventually set off for the Marbella Club, then the only hotel on what came later to be called the Costa Del Sol. There, to cut a long story short, Clare went down with pneumonia. The doctor refused to allow us to travel back by air, I had no money, and we had to return steerage in a P&O liner from Gibraltar to Tilbury, all arranged by my best man, Kenneth Anderson.

By the time the ship got to Tilbury I also had gone down with pneumonia and we both had to be taken to the Queen Elizabeth Hospital in Birmingham, where as the result of the intervention of my father-in-law, the Matron relented and allowed us to convalesce in the same room. It was not really an auspicious beginning.

Later that year I was moved down to the Exeter branch of the Bank where I was appointed a securities clerk with a special brief to understand the vagaries of agricultural banking. And a year later I was moved up to London, where I was attached to London Inspection and particularly to the team known as the 'Vice Squad' as we dealt with branches and branch managers where there were difficulties – and I will leave it at that.

Prior to an inspection we all congregated in a nearby coffee shop, usually Lyons, and then smartly on the dot of three o'clock, with our bowler hats on, we presented ourselves at the door of the branch and demanded the keys – it was the prelude to a full inspection. I always remember one of the most boring jobs I ever had to do was to tick off all the travellers cheques paid to the travellers cheques issued register. How is that for learning about commercial banking!

The next bombshell was the instruction that I should go out to Nairobi, Kenya, to learn about colonial banking with Barclays Bank (Dominion, Colonial & Overseas). We would go out by boat and spend a year there. But here a problem presented itself: Clare was enceinte (I refuse always to use that ugly word 'pregnant'), and the doctors did not think it was advisable for her to travel out to and live in Kenya. Prior to that we had had a lot of difficulty in conceiving and we were both loath to take any chances.

If I could not go to Kenya, what was the Bank going to do with me? In their infinite wisdom they decided I should go out alone to the New York Agency of the bank, without Clare, although she was expecting our first baby. And I was not only to go out there on my own but I was to stay there for six months, i.e. almost to the due date of the birth. It seems inconceivable now, writing this 45 years later, that anybody should have issued such an instruction, particularly as I was only, once again, going to carry out relatively routine clerical work at the agency, which could have been done anywhere. But in those days we did as we were told.

I quite enjoyed New York. I lived in a downtown hotel, but later on, when Clare came out to join me for a few weeks, we were lent a splendid apartment by Jack Leib, a Wall Street broker, and then later on another apartment by the Bank's representative, Guy Meek, a bachelor. It was a lovely apartment but, as befits a bachelor, very fussy. In due course, Clare flew back on a British Airways VC10, and seeing that plane take off with Clare and our precious unborn baby was too much for my emotions.

In due course my spell in New York came to an end and I was told I had to report to the Foreign branch at Birmingham to learn all about foreign work, which as it happens was exactly what I had been doing in the New York Agency. But, of course, this entailed yet one more move – our fourth in two and a half years. Clare had been able to rent a small house near Henley-in-Arden (remember that I had been in digs there when I was working at the Leamington branch), and on 24th September 1960 Christina was born in Birmingham. She was a great joy.

Of course the Bank would not leave me alone, and early next year 1961, I was instructed to go to Paris and work for Barclays France for up to a year. That was easier said than done. No help was going to be given me in finding accommodation for Clare and Christina, so once again I left them behind in Warwickshire – Christina was only three months old then – and went to Paris where I stayed at the Travellers' Club on the Champs D'Elysées. I had a tiny room at the top of the club, where every morning I was served coffee, *oeuf à la coq* and toast in bed by an elderly retainer.

Barclays France in those days was presided over by Francis Fairfax-Cholmeley and his wife Meta. Francis knew my father and they had both been together at Cambridge, so I had a warm welcome, but the overwhelming necessity was to find 'une apartement' and every day I scanned the rental advertisements in the *Herald Tribune*. Eventually, after many false starts and cul-de-sacs, I found a walk-up apartment on the second floor of a nineteenth-century apartment building. It was owned by an ancient White Russian called Monsieur Eliacheff, who had presumably fled from the 1917 Revolution or perhaps even earlier. It was furnished in that typical nineteenth-century faded ancient grandeur, but it had two bedrooms, a large drawing-room, a small dining-room, a kitchen, and a geyser to heat the water. It was at 12 Rue de Quatre Septembre – the same street as the bank, and near the Bourse.

In due course we ferried over our belongings in our new Hillman Minx and despatched our bed in a removal van. I have to say I hated that apartment. I felt imprisoned in its faded confines and I used to go for long walks in the evening just to get out of it. In two and a half years of marriage this was our sixth – repeat, sixth – home, and there were two more to come.

And now I must shortly digress and tell you a little about the history of Barclays Bank (France) Limited. When the British Expeditionary Force was sent to France in 1914, Cox & Co. and the Army agents followed them to Paris, at a time when von Klicks's great strategic attack might still have caused the fall of the city and perhaps decided the outcome of that dreadful war.

The London & South Western Bank had a shareholding in Cox & Co., and when in 1918 Barclays amalgamated with that bank, Barclays took over that shareholding. When the war was over – that is to say the 1914–18 war – the bank had seven branches in France and one in Cologne, the headquarters of the British Army on the Rhine. A little later two branches were opened in Algeria – in Algiers and Oran; and at that time Algeria was part of metropolitan France and was enormously wealthy through its agricultural exports.

In September 1939 the Second World War broke out. Nothing very much happened until May 1940, when the Germans' bold use of their overwhelming armoured forces – the Blitzkrieg – defeated the Allies in six weeks and they occupied Paris. It became very difficult for the Bank to operate. The Riviera branches were now threatened by the Italians, who had allied themselves with Germany, and France itself was divided into the Occupied and Unoccupied zones.

It was the duty of the German Controller of Enemy Banks in Paris to ensure that financial arrangements were provided for German enterprises in France. This was difficult as it suggested cooperation with the enemy. However a solution was found in the acceptance by the Bank of two large accounts, one for the Custodian of Enemy Property and the other for the Raw Materials Purchasing Agency. The possession of the Custodian account enabled the Bank to keep records and defend the interests of the absent Allied owners while the figures passing over the Raw Materials account were of great value to the French government, to which they were secretly communicated. These two very large accounts provided an excuse to support the Bank's refusal to take other German business, and the German Controller reluctantly accepted this compromise.

Subsequently this German Controller was captured and, in his prisoner-of-war camp, he was interrogated at length by a British intelligence officer who appeared to be fully aware of all his past activity. He could not know that the British officer happened to be a member of the staff of Barclays Bank France. His name was Colonel E.K. Stewart-Smith and he was the father of Christopher Stewart-Smith, who lives near us in Essex at Stanley Hall, near Halstead.

The Local Director resident in Paris was, as I have mentioned, Francis Fairfax-Cholmeley; the General Manager was Monsieur Sollogoub who was, I believe, a White Russian; while the Manager of the main branch was Michael Pringle. The Manager of the Securities Department was a Mr Innes-Firkins, who had served in the Royal Navy during the war and was married to a French woman. Sadly he came to a sticky end. As Manager he was responsible for his clients' stock exchange transactions. He was not paid at all well – nobody was – and as his expenditure exceeded his income he got into the habit of placing profitable stock exchange transactions to his own account and less profitable ones to his clients' accounts. He was found out and sent to prison, I believe.

As a stagiare, I worked in all the departments of the branch at the Siege Local – the head office – and learnt to speak French tolerably well. I even served as a cashier. For some time I joined the local French inspection team. My first French inspection was

Agence Biarritz, where Clare joined me. Here again there was trouble – the local British Consul was a member of the staff of the Bank, and he was found doing the same thing as Innes-Firkins, so not only was he sacked from the Bank, but he was also sacked as British Consul in Biarritz. I cannot say I look back on my days with Barclays France with any particular fondness. As I have said I hated our apartment; the work was hardly of any interest; and we found it very difficult to make French friends – indeed we did not make any.

There were two frights during our time in France. And for the first I will have to digress and delve into the French–Algerian War, which started on All Saints Day 1954 when a young honeymooning couple – they were French schoolteachers, dedicated to their work among underprivileged schoolchildren – were dragged off a bus and shot dead. Their murder by the Muslim mujahedin, alias the National Liberation Front of Algeria (FLN), marked the beginning of the revolt against the French colonial 'occupiers'; although technically Algeria was part of metropolitan France. It was a horrible war. There was the rebellion itself; a civil war between the Algerians; a struggle between the *pieds noirs* and Paris which culminated in a mutiny of the French Army; and this was followed by open French terrorism under the aegis of the brutal killers of the OAS (Organisation armée secrète).

In 1958 General Massu's paratroops broke the FLN hold on Algiers by the widespread use of torture. The French won the Battle of Algiers but they went on to lose the war through the revulsion which dominated French and foreign public opinion.

In 1961, the year we were in Paris, the Army in Algeria mutinied. This mutiny was led by the elite paras under four dissident generals, and the troops together with their tanks reached as far as Rambouillet near Paris before the mutiny collapsed. It was while the paratroops were marching on Paris that a panic started and the barricades started to go up; the shops were closed, the streets deserted, nobody moved and an eerie silence came over the city. There was nothing we could do. Evacuation was out of the question – if indeed it was necessary. So we stayed put and hoped for the best.

Then General de Gaulle made one of his most impassioned speeches, heard by French conscripts all over Algeria. The mutiny collapsed, but the political unreliability of the French Army made it necessary for France to devise an exit strategy from her proudest colony – a part of France. The end came in 1962, shortly after we returned to the UK, when de Gaulle surrendered unconditionally to the Muslim mujahedin. All French oil assets in the Sahara went, and no less than a million *pieds noirs* – French colonials, families who had lived in Algeria for three generations or more, fled to France.

And what of Algeria? It should have prospered as an independent state, rich in oil reserves and agricultural products. Instead it became a typical failed Muslim state with rampant corruption and abysmal inefficiency. And as a footnote, the horrors suffered in Algeria over the past 50 years read like a paradigm, a microcosm of Islam's frustrated inability to meet the challenges of the modern world, which leads it to lash out against the rich, successful West. The French had half a million troops in Algeria, yet they were defeated.

The second fright we had, also in 1961, was when there was another stand-off between the West and the Soviet Union over Berlin. I had forgotten that I had remained a Z Reservist in the Army. After leaving the Army in 1952, I was required to become a Territorial Army Officer for eleven years – why eleven? – and in so doing I had also become a Z Reservist: as I understand it, the first to be called up in an emergency. To the Army this was an emergency, and greatly to my surprise, therefore, I received a letter from the Army reminding me I was a Z reservist and enclosing an open single (not return) first-class ticket warrant from Paris to Edinburgh where I was to report for duty on receipt of a telegram from the War Office and, as they say in the Army, await further instructions. Imagine my consternation – I had a young wife and baby, Christina, and the prospect of leaving them alone in Paris without any support or money was appalling. Fortunately, like the French mutiny, this East–West crisis came to an end and I never needed my single ticket to Edinburgh.

In due course France came to an end. Although I hated the apartment, I had begun to enjoy my work. I had progressed through all the departments of the branch and the Bank itself – that is to say its Head Office – and I had learned how the bank as an entity worked. Above all, I had enjoyed working with the French staff, who were all highly individualistic and talented and who all seemed to have 'affaires d'amour' on the side. So much so that the time between 5 p.m. and 7 p.m. was always known as 'cinq à sept', because that was when all these affairs were consummated in the *petit maisons* near the branch – from closing time of the branch to taking the train home. I enjoyed it all, the camaraderie, the gossip, the practical jokes, the sharp and cynical humour, the drinking in the bars, the smoking – everyone smoked – the flirtations, the naughtiness. It was a great and exciting change from the grey drabness of the bank in England. How often have I used that expression, but it was like that until the mid-1960s when the English started to come alive – and probably too alive.

But before I left I had to deal with Monsieur Eliacheff, the owner of the apartment. The reason for this is that I had had to take a year's lease and now the Bank was sending me back early. The lease was in my name. I mentioned this to the Bank and told them that the money for the remaining part of the lease was their responsibility, not mine, as I had been instructed to leave. It was a responsibility they felt, curiously, disinclined to accept. I went back to Monsieur Eliacheff and pleaded *'force majeure'* – there was such a clause in the lease allowing me to break it. As expected, he said it was not a case of *force majeure* at all and that the Bank was responsible, and I said that in that case he should write to Monsieur Portier, the chef de service of the Service Contentieux, who dealt with litigious and legal matters. I assume that Monsieur Eliacheff, who was of Russian Jewish extraction, eventually got his money, as I heard nothing more. But to this day I have always been amazed that not only did the Bank in Paris not help me find accommodation but also, when I was instructed to leave earlier than originally intended, it felt initially no responsibility for the cost to me of this somewhat earlier termination – and I had no extra allowance for working in Paris to help me. I was aggrieved at the time and now, writing this 45 years later, I still feel aggrieved.

The reason for my removal from Paris was that I was to be seconded to York local head office with the intention that, if I performed well, I would be appointed a Local Director's Assistant – the first real step on the ladder if I was so appointed. To date I had seen no rhyme or reason in my Bank peregrinations. There was no sensible reason for transferring me from London to Leamington Spa, to Birmingham, to Exeter, to London again, to New York to Birmingham again, to Paris, and now to North Yorkshire. There seemed no sensible connection, and indeed there wasn't – it was merely a question of filling up time, being reported on by different Directors and Managers. The work itself could have been learnt in no more than three places – London, New York and Paris – and if I had followed my original instinct, which was not to go into the Bank until later, then I could have gone back to the Antarctic and possibly joined the Commonwealth Trans-Antarctic Expedition. 'Following the Flag' as do many wives with military husbands is understandable – it's called the exigencies of the Service – but following the Barclays flag for no apparent reason or necessity, that is hard for a wife and in a sense even harder for a husband because I had no sensible reason to offer my wife for this continuous moving, which by this time had got on my nerves.

In the meantime Clare had gone ahead and had found and purchased a charming small Georgian house near Malton, with no less than 4 acres of ground, and all this for a figure of £4,500 or thereabouts. It was a lovely house – however rather too close to the main York-Scarborough railway line, which ran at the bottom of the garden, and the River Derwent the other side. So the river and the railway line were a worry for us with Christina, but there were no accidents.

I must have performed well because, in due course, I was appointed a Local Director's Assistant; my salary was raised from £1,000 per annum to £1,600, and the greatest joy was a bank car, which you could choose yourself. I chose a green Humber Vogue Estate Car, which had a lovely smart wooden facia and panelling. After all the long years of clerical drudgery, I felt I had at last arrived, and the car proved it.

The York district of the Bank covered East Yorkshire and some of North Lincolnshire. There was a range of branches – the northernmost being Whitby and the southernmost Louth. The largest branches were in York, Scarborough, Hull and Grimsby. The senior Local Director was Andrew Gibbs and he was supported by Basil Niven, a first-class banker who had been Manager of the main branch in Hull, whilst the District Manager was Owen Cloke, who had been Manager of the Staines branch. It was a mixed agricultural, commercial and industrial business and as far as I can recall after these many years, produced profits of about £1 million a year.

My job as Local Director's Assistant was really to act as a sort of conduit between the Branch Managers and the Local Directors. What they thought of me I really do not know, but they were always invariably polite and we got on well.

It was all quite hierarchical. For this position I was allowed to share a room with the District Manager, who was always extremely kind and forbearing. I had a very limited lending discretion and an equally low discretion for repairs expenditure on Bank premises. But it was the freedom to visit branches in my new car that I enjoyed so much, and also the ability to visit and meet customers and talk business with them. And also, as a very special privilege, to lunch with the Local Directors and District Manager in their little attic dining-room in Parliament Street, York.

I enjoyed working in the York District, we had a lovely house and garden – even a house in a tree – we made friends through other friends and, of course, the Bank, but I had constant money worries as our expenditure always exceeded our income. This made life difficult as Bank officials were required to live within their income. You were not allowed to borrow from the Bank or, if you did, this was an exceptional matter and you had to get your loan sanctioned by Staff Department, who also controlled your Staff Housing Loan. It was at this time that I had to sell my reversion in my mother's and father's marriage settlement, which was in trust for me. I sold it through a firm called Foster & Cranfield in Cheapside, London, where I had to climb some rickety stairs to get to the office, where I was made to feel like a pauper and debtor which, of course, I was. All my banking instinct told me not to do it, but I had to, as the Bank was beginning to notice our continuous overexpenditure and it was getting on my nerves.

I had always hoped for some help from the Tritton family, but this was never forthcoming even though I was the heir and my interest could not be defeated as I had reached the age of 25. Indeed it transpired later that the Trittons, namely my Aunt Dore Garnett and the managing trustee Paddy Tritton, were concerned that I would borrow against a charge on my reversion to the Lyons Hall Estate; but it never occurred to me to do this – I could not have repaid it anyway and, of course, could not forecast the date of my aunt's death.

It was on our way back from France to Yorkshire that Clare and I together with Christina called in, at our own request, at my aunt's house – the Hole Farm. We had never been invited there and we were never to be invited again. We rather wanted to show her we were still alive, and to show off Christina. We were given a cup of tea, but the tension was so palpable that we fled. I had never before felt such hatred. Was it simply because Clare was a Catholic, or was it more? It must have been.

One of the customers of the Bank at York was Ampleforth Abbey, and I was asked to meet Father Robert Coverdale who was the Father Procurator of the Benedictine Abbey and its school. The Father Procurator, I should explain, looks after the finances of the community. He was an exceptionally nice man, although I would like to think of a better expression than 'nice'. He was the first Catholic priest I liked and, interestingly enough, he had links with Essex in that the Coverdales were hereditary land agents to the Petre family at Ingatestone, an old Catholic recusant family. His sister was a nun at New Hall, Boreham, near to Great Leighs.

I had begun to hate the religious divisions in my family. I had always resented the fact that I had to undergo instruction in the Catholic faith prior to my marriage and I had always hoped that, whereas I used from time to time attend a Catholic church, Clare might occasionally attend an Anglican church, but this never occurred and it became the source of a festering tension. In a way, therefore, it came as a huge relief to meet a monk to whom I could talk – a sort of auricular confession.

In due course, he invited me to his study at Ampleforth – I think this was after Vespers and before Compline. I was very nervous because I had come to some sort of decision that I wished to become a Catholic and, in a sense, it was now or never. When I touched on my possible conversion he seemed quite taken aback – quite genuinely as I afterwards discovered – so much so that he got a bottle of sherry out of his cupboard and we both had a very generous glass. He then mentioned in a remarkably disarming manner that he had never before had to try and instruct a potential convert, and that he did not really know where to start, but start he did. Afterwards he went to Compline and I sat in the body of the abbey and for the first time in my life I listened to the monks' Gregorian chant and all those wondrous cadences rising and falling, and it filled me with a marvellous feeling of joy and peace. I felt an extraordinary feeling that after all those years of religious wandering, I had come back to the one true Church and that I wished to return to the beauty, unity and authority of the old Church and its monastic traditions which had been so brutally destroyed by King Henry VIII. To this day, whenever I see an old ruined monastery or abbey like Glastonbury, Rievaulx and Fountains ruined by that king, the sight fills me with an inexpressible sadness that not only had these beautiful buildings been deliberately destroyed, but also the beauty of the Opus Dei and the Hours – the Mattins, the Lauds, Prime Terce, Sext, None, Vespers and Compline – had also been brutally destroyed and swept away, and that something most wondrous and precious had been lost in the stripping of the altars of the old faith. And my sadness gradually turns to anger that such an unforgivable act had been perpetrated.

Every fortnight or so I used to be invited to supper in the monks' refectory. This was held in silence, and a monk read a book of religious significance whilst we ate. At this distance in time I cannot remember the food, but I recall we were served with ale. There is something attractive about a community of monks, their lives devoted to praying and singing the Offices and dedicating themselves to an unseen God. It is easy to stand somewhat in awe of them, these monks who had given their lives to God, and as priests were men apart. I always found with priests that however friendly and affable they were – and they were – they never talked, at least to me, about their inner spiritual life. 'And why should they?' one might ask. But I always remained curious, perhaps if only to bring out in the open my own doubts and see if they shared them. Or was their faith so much stronger than mine? Perhaps it was, and I suppose now I will never find out.

And so it happened that one day in July 1963, after my six months of instruction was over, I was received into the Church. It is a decision I have never regretted, and the best way I can describe it is as a coming home; after all those years of searching, I had found my harbour, and my religious ship was now berthed securely and safely for the rest of my life. Sadly, however, this conversion upset Mummy a great deal. As I have mentioned, Mummy was a devout Anglican, and at that time she was suffering from cancer, from which she eventually died. To have hurt my mother was a source of great anguish to me and I have always wanted to make amends for that but, of course, the effect on the Tritton family was catastrophic.

Many people have said to me that, of course, I only became a Catholic because of Clare, and in a sense you could say that was partly true, but it was only part of the truth. The real ignition was Father Robert and my accidental meeting with him when he introduced me to something I had never encountered before, and that was the life of the Benedictines, the Opus Dei and the sheer beauty and emotion of the High Mass and the wondrous Gregorian chant of the monks.

Although I have never regretted my conversion, I have two serious complaints. The first is the abandonment of the Latin Mass, to which as a classical scholar at Eton I was devoted. However, I comforted myself with the knowledge that the Anglicans, in their less than infinite wisdom, abandoned the beautiful words of Cranmer for the miserable pedestrian and prosaic English of the modern prayer book. The second complaint is the turning of the altar towards the congregation, which the Anglicans have copied.

The Mass is a mystery and to try to deprive it of its mystery is an error. On the contrary, everything that can be done to enhance the Mass as a mystery is devoutly to be desired; and here I take off my proverbial religious hat to the Orthodox Church which has never changed its traditions and rituals and any question of removing the iconostasis would trigger a religious revolt. So well done to the Orthodox Church for not changing – and all their churches are packed.

In 1963 Mummy and Uncle Robin came to visit us in Yorkshire; both were ill, but managed to survive the car journey. Of course, the great joy in November was the birth of Guy, christened Robert Guy Henton. He was born at the Children's Hospital in Birmingham and I experienced a real feeling of terror and dread when I went to see him at the hospital and found him in an oxygen tent and yellow with jaundice. But all my prayers were successful – he recovered, and we set off on the car journey from Birmingham to Malton.

As we drove on the fog got thicker and thicker until in the end we could not only not see where we were driving, but we were also lost. We had to find somewhere to spend the night and we eventually found a small hostelry and here we uncomfortably lodged for the night with Guy being fed regularly. Luckily there was room at the inn as I did not want to find ourselves in the stable like Joseph and Mary. Next day the fog had lifted and we arrived home safe and sound.

It was that year, 1963, that we experienced an exceptionally cold and icy winter, not only in Yorkshire but also all over the country. The pipes were frozen and the roads became impassable, although the little train still ran from Malton to York on its picturesque journey down the Derwent river valley, past the old ruined abbey of Kirkham.

York as a Local Director's Assistant was only a stepping stone to the next appointment, Local Director, to which all the successful Special Entrants aspired and for most of them, although not all, this position was the summit of their aspiration. To be a Local Director in a place like York represented an interesting and comfortable lifestyle in particularly attractive country. But it was also not a place where, for instance, ambition seemed to reign supreme, and I had always been both competitive and ambitious, which may or may not have stemmed from my lack of self-confidence on which all my schoolmasters reported. Confidence is gained by success, although there are many people who are naturally self-confident and successful – I have always envied them. A public school education should breed self-confidence, but it never did with me.

I was summoned to Head Office at 54 Lombard Street to learn my fate. I was interviewed by a Vice-Chairman and later by the Staff General Manager. They seemed to think reasonably highly of me and told me they were promoting me to be a Local Director at 54 Lombard Street itself – the holy of holies, where nearly 200 years ago John Henton Tritton, having married a Miss Barclay, had been made a partner in the banking firm which was to be called Barclay, Bevan, Tritton. I had the temerity to ask what my new salary was to be and they told me £3,000 per annum – nearly double my present salary and, of course, with central London allowances on top. I was thrilled, but when I returned back to Yorkshire and told Clare what I thought was the glad news, after what seemed a stunned silence she burst into such prolonged tears that I thought I had done something wrong in accepting this treasured and devoutly to be desired promotion and appointment.

Thinking about all this many years later, I feel she had a point. This was going to be our eighth move in six years. We had a lovely house in Yorkshire. The two children were still very young – Christina was three and Guy was only a few months old. A move would be very expensive and difficult, and London house prices seemed to us sky high, even on my somewhat higher salary of £3,000 per annum. But what was I to do? If I turned down this appointment it would effectively be the end of my career in the bank, so I had to accept.

Before I start describing my work in the holy of holies, always known as the Room – the old Partners' Room – we had to look for a house. My godfather Emlyn Bevan, who was not only a

Director of the Bank but also senior Local Director of 54 Lombard Street, wanted us to live in London. Being a wealthy bachelor, he had little knowledge of either family life or the expenses related to it. We certainly did not want to live in the suburbs, so that meant either central London or the country. I preferred the country and commuting, but a lot of pressure was applied and we ended by looking in central London. It was almost impossible to find anything and gradually I very reluctantly had to raise the price range. Staff Department had always decreed that four times your salary was the maximum amount you were allowed to borrow for house purchase. The interest rate of $2^1/2$ per cent was, of course, a very attractive concession, and so attractive was it that it stopped most married members of staff from leaving the bank. This mortgage interest rate of $2^1/2$ per cent was reduced by full tax relief, so that the effective rate was to me about $1^1/4$ per cent although, of course, monthly repayments had to be made. The trouble, of course, was the multiple, since on a salary of £3,000 the maximum I would be allowed to borrow was £12,000, and even in those days you could not buy a house in Central London for that. One also needs to remember that places like Fulham, Battersea or for that matter anywhere South of the River were terra incognita and therefore beyond the pale. Curiously enough this also applied to north of Hyde Park – we had no friends living north of the Park. All this meant we were confined to a choice of houses in three areas – namely Chelsea, Kensington and Pimlico – and it was in these three areas that we looked. It was also exceptionally difficult to look together for a property because Christina was only three and Guy was only three months and it was a long way in those days between Yorkshire and London.

However, I was of course aware that I had a vested interest in the Lyons Hall Estate: that is to say I had an absolute reversion on the death of my aunt, and the previous year, in 1963, she had had a stroke. She suffered this stroke, as I have mentioned, when under the dryer at the hairdressers and the cause of it was rumoured to be her horror that the Lyons Hall Estate would be inherited by her newly converted Catholic nephew.

It therefore seemed to me that the trustees could, and indeed should, assist me with a house purchase. So I have to say with some reluctance we committed ourselves to buying 23 Flood Street in Chelsea, a large family house, at a price of £24,000 against which would be set the net proceeds of the sale of the Yorkshire house.

Looking back on all this, it was clearly foolish of me to rely on Paddy Tritton, the Lyons Hall Estate managing trustee. Even when he managed to obtain the signature of the stricken Aunt Dore on a trust deed in which my reversionary interest was merged with the Aunt's life interest – this was on 31st March 1965, nearly a year after we had moved into 23 Flood Street – he refused to provide me with any income or capital from the trust, and I by that time was the only beneficiary.

I have never really understood his motives in refusing to give me a penny, but I think it was because he may well have given an undertaking to Aunt Dore that, as long as she was alive, although now bedridden with her stroke, I would enjoy no benefit from the estate; and that included being barred from going anywhere near it. I was therefore in the extraordinary position of being legally entitled to the estate and farm, but this was deliberately withheld from me, and not only that, I was denied any benefit or enjoyment from the trust and from the estate. The reasons for this undertaking I really do not know, but it must have been partly the Catholic position, and partly because she had always been jealous of my mother who had children, while she did not. After Aunt Dore's death, I found a letter addressed to Paddy in which she wrote that she had never trusted me and never would and, as far as she was concerned, I could 'go to hell' – her words. So what was it? Who knows, but it still hurts today as I write this.

All this was happening during Clare's pregnancy with Charles – he was born on 12th May 1965. The expenses of that birth and also the expenditure Clare had incurred on the house and continuing financial problems put me in a very difficult position with the bank, as I frequently had to go and see the Vice-Chairman to ask him to help me. So much so that I began to be told that if I did not get control of my finances, it would affect my career in the bank. The problem was that I could not control our finances and I was caught between our expenditure rate and Paddy's continual refusals, acting on behalf of Aunt Dore, and I could not stand up to either. The result was that I, for the first time in my life, went into a spiralling depression and had to have time off work.

At the same time as all this was going on, the endless arguments over money, the threats about my career, the tensions, my mother was dying of cancer. Uncle Robin had died the year before in June 1966, and my mother was left alone in The Cottage at Eyke, ill and in great pain. It was really too far for Marigold with her five children in Scotland to come south to look after her, and I could not, beset as I was by what was now a collapsing marriage, a 'trial' separation, financial worries and a depressive illness. Oh how I regret not being able to help Mummy more in her final months of disease, pain and sickness, but essentially I had lost control of my life, and I was only 34.

On 16th February 1967, Mummy died in Ipswich Hospital. I had managed to go down and see her for a few times, both at The Cottage, Eyke, and also in the hospital, but she was wasting away. To herself she never admitted she had cancer, and I always wanted to believe that – she said she had brittle bones. For a long time I could not accept her death, not at the funeral, nor even when her coffin was set down in the grave, surrounded by bright spring flowers. Mummy had asked me just before she died whether Clare and I had got together again and I was able to say truthfully at the time that the answer was yes; but it was not to last long despite all my prayers and those of Mummy.

Mummy was buried in the graveyard of the church at Eyke and she was buried with Uncle Robin. I always remember them telling me that they wondered who would 'go' first – they were both so ill. In the end it was Uncle Robin followed by Mummy eight months later. The church was packed for the funeral and I have never seen so many beautiful flowers. I was in almost continual tears and hardly able to cope but I managed to do so and so that was the end of The Cottage, Eyke, 20 years after Mummy and Uncle Robin bought it for £5,000.

By September of that dreadful year, the marriage was over and it took me nearly five years to come to terms with the reality that this had actually happened to me. For a long time I always thought we would get back together again, but it was not to be.

Mummy's life had not been an easy one. She had married when she was twenty-eight – her younger sister Eve had married before her. She had expected Daddy to inherit Lyons Hall Estate, and thereby to live at Lyons Hall. Daddy was, of course, the younger son but his elder brother Tim had been killed in a car crash on the Great North Road, only five months after he had married. Daddy was an exceptionally able man and was destined to become a Director of the Bank, like his father and grandfather. But, of course, none of this happened. Daddy had died in 1934; his father was also at that time, like Daddy, in St Agnes' hospital, but was so ill he was not able to see him. I believe he said that he should have been the one who died, not Daddy.

After Daddy's death and funeral at Great Leighs, Mummy was never invited again to Lyons Hall, although my stepfather did go there, but that was only to plead for money for the upkeep and education of Marigold and myself. Quite shortly after, she married Uncle Robin in 1936.

Their house, Woodlands, was requisitioned by the Army in 1940 and Uncle Robin went off to the war so to speak, although he never served abroad. We, as I have mentioned, went off to Scotland, whilst Mummy and Uncle Robin had to live in a series of hotels or flats near to where he was stationed.

It was in one of these hotels near, I believe, the Guards Depot at Caterham, where Mummy and Uncle Robin had a very narrow escape from death. The hotel caught fire. Their bedroom was on the second or third floor – they could not go down the stairs and there was no fire escape. In the event Uncle Robin was able to knot some sheets together, and tying one end to a fixed point in the bedroom, they slid down the sheets and managed to escape.

Although Mummy and Uncle Robin had very little money, Mummy was a great enjoyer of life – she was gregarious, amusing and fun and everybody loved her except, of course, the Trittons. She was a devout Anglican and towards the end of her life made a long auricular confession. I was, as a son, devoted to my mother and it is true to say that I loved her. I remember her daily in my prayers and long sometimes to see her again with Daddy in my next life and to tell her about my own life. God bless Mummy and Daddy.

At this time I had become so short of money that not only was I beginning to sell some of the family silver, but I also had to borrow money from Nanny and, before Mummy died, I had to ask her to sign a blank cheque payable to myself, onto which, feeling extremely guilty, I inserted a figure of £750. I felt as if I was sinking into some financial and marital abyss, but despite this my overriding concern was to keep my career going at the Bank and to be able to provide for, support and educate the children, as I had promised my mother-in-law, Betty d'Abreu, to whom I always felt very close.

The trial separation and the trial reconciliation had not worked. To all intents and purposes the marriage had broken down irretrievably, and all my marital daydreams of a happy marriage, a happy home and happy children disintegrated in front of me. I was on my own again, and once again I found it almost impossible to believe that this was the reality of my life. In 12 years I had gone from a bedsitter in Rossetti Garden Mansions, Flood Street, via a very circuitous route to an expensive six-bedroomed house in Flood Street, and now back to a bedsitter – it was unbelievable.

After Mummy died I was able to persuade Paddy Tritton to rent a cottage to Nanny at Lyons Hall. This cottage, where I am now writing, was the cottage then attached to Lyons Hall where Marigold and I had been isolated with whooping cough, hence its name Whoopy Cottage. It consisted of two bedrooms, a downstairs bathroom and two small rooms separated by the kitchen. Here I sought refuge and started to commute. However, Paddy again let me down. He knew that Nanny could not afford the rent of some £350 per annum – the lease was in her name – and that I would therefore have to pay it. But, of course, as the then life tenant of the estate, if I did pay the rent I would be paying it to myself, which was absurd. The rent would come out of my taxed income and would then go into my trust income account where it would be taxed again. But Paddy was adamant about that and I used to get rent reminders, reminding me to pay, effectively, rent to myself! It was a Kafkaesque world, seemingly divorced from reality, but nevertheless I had to keep reminding myself that this was reality and not a temporary nightmare.

I gradually came to the conclusion that I could not commute forever from a rented cottage in the country and so I bought the tail-end of a lease of a flat at 99 Cadogan Gardens, SW3. It was a walk-up flat on the third floor but it had three bedrooms, one for Nanny, who was looking after me, one for myself and one spare. It also had two lovely rooms overlooking Cadogan Gardens. It was very old-fashioned and in anything but immaculate condition, but I changed all that. It was, nevertheless, a time of living in complete limbo, working, wondering what was going to happen next – did Clare really want a divorce? – going round to see the children once a week, fortified by gin and pretending that everything was sort of normal, which of course it wasn't and, by now, getting letters from solicitors. Mummy's death had, however, temporarily

20

Banking Anecdotes

Now going back to 1964, 23 Flood Street was purchased and I entered the Partners' Room at 54 Lombard Street. The Room was very hierarchical. At one end of the Room sat my godfather Emlyn Bevan and Theodore Barclay. In the middle of the Room sat Tim Bevan, later to be Chairman of the Bank, and Richard Barclay followed by me, and behind us sat Peter Forrester whose father had been I believe, General Manager of the Union Bank of Manchester, taken over by Barclays. Remember that in the late 1920s and early 1930s, my father had been seconded to the Union Bank of Manchester, which is why I was born at Knutsford just outside Manchester.

The Lombard Street District of the Bank managed the City business, by far the most interesting business of the Bank, inasmuch as we dealt not only with the large domestic and international corporations, but also with the great markets of the City. These were the money markets, the foreign exchange markets, the commodities markets, the insurance markets, the shipping markets, the securities markets, that is to say the jobbers and brokers, and included in the secured money markets in those days were the discount houses and the bill brokers and the money brokers, all of whom put on black top hats to see us, which they did every day. Surrounded by all the great portraits of our predecessors, the Barclays, the Bevans and the Trittons, we were ruthlessly kept in order by Theodore Barclay and Emlyn Bevan, who liked to overhear us – so we always talked in a whisper. Outside the Room were the messengers in tailcoats, effectively our menservants. They were all loyal and conscientious, and I remember in the old days that whenever my grandmother and I went up to the City from Chelmsford, at Liverpool

Street Station we were always met on the platform by a Lombard Street messenger wearing a tailcoat and a top hat and escorted to a bank car – and it is quite extraordinary to think that this was really not so long ago.

The managers of the City always presented their advance applications to us personally; no appointment was needed and these were all dealt with immediately, so that the customer had always a very quick response – unless, of course, it was particularly complicated or beyond our lending discretion, in which case it had to go upstairs to the General Managers. Immediate access to the General Managers was exceptionally useful and, of course, we did have access to the Chairman and Vice-Chairmen, which was usually a good thing but not always – and here I refer to my financial difficulties which were the responsibility, unhappily for me, of a Vice-Chairman. How I dreaded those occasions when I was called up to see him and sat waiting to see him in the magnificence of the Chairman's suite, surrounded by tailcoated messengers and secretaries.

Theodore Barclay and Emlyn Bevan always made a great point that we were there to serve the managers and not to see customers, which I preferred, although we could give lunches in a private dining-room for them. One day I was invited to attend a cricket match between the staff of the district and the staff of British Overseas Airways Corporation, who were customers. I accepted, but failed to get Theodore Barclay's approval for the event. I duly attended the cricket match, which the Bank lost because BOAC had produced some of the finest West Indian bowlers for their side, and then I returned to the office. On my return I was given a thorough dressing-down for being absent from the Room by Theodore Barclay. He did indeed rule the Room in a despotic fashion and, to a lesser extent, so did my godfather, who was the senior of the two. The former would always ask extremely searching questions if you had the temerity to ask his approval for anything beyond your fairly limited discretion. But if you gave him the absolutely right answers consistently over a period of time, he gradually gained confidence in you and then usually, but not always, accepted what you said. Of the two, Theodore Barclay was the better banker. Emlyn Bevan was the better diplomat, and both skills were a requirement in those days and presumably still are.

From time to time, for special family banking anniversaries, we had a Room dinner. These were quite extraordinary events and sometimes even wives were invited. In the middle of the Room a long table was set up, all the desks having been pushed to the walls. On this table all the banking families' silver was placed, together with little lamps with candles. The main lights were switched off, so that only the illuminated portraits of the banking ancestors were lit up, including that of my great-grandfather, Joseph Herbert Tritton. The food was always simply superb and the wines the best in the bank's cellars. These were unbelievably privileged occasions and nobody thought then that within a few years it would all vanish, never to be seen or experienced again.

An enormous privilege for local directors in the Room was that they were allowed to lunch in the Chairman's Mess. This was the Chairman of Barclays Bank Limited not the Chairman of Barclays Bank (Dominion, Colonial & Overseas) who had his own mess, although once a month, I think on board days, they all lunched together. These lunches were surprisingly informal and became more informal as time went on. When I first was allowed to attend – and I suppose 'attend' is the right word – there were no pre-lunch drinks except sherry. And I always remember that on my first day when Byers the butler, always dressed in a tailcoat as were all the messengers, came up to me and asked me if I would like a sherry, I had the temerity to ask for a gin and tonic instead. I remember to this day his look of immense disapproval, his leaving me and going behind a screen to bring me this avant-garde drink. You always helped yourself at these lunches which were quite delicious. I cannot remember wine being served except at board dinners – we were always given lemonade, but there was a glass of vintage port available at the end of lunch.

There was never a seating order or placement, it was far too informal for that, but I always took care to avoid sitting next to the Chairman. This was the Tuke who interviewed me for the Bank and told me he had never been interested in anything else but banking. One day there was no alternative, I had to sit next to him. I sat down in fear and trembling, and do you know what he asked me? He asked me whether I had read some recent banking report, and what I thought of it. The short answer is, I had not read it, and he turned away to speak to his neighbour. I thought that was almost the end of my career.

Before leaving the Room, I should mention why the bill brokers, the money brokers and the discount houses came to see us every day in their top hats. The reason for this is that going back to the old partnership days of Barclay, Bevan, Tritton & Co., the Lombard Street partners always managed the liquidity of the bank and this practice had continued. In those days, which are really not so long ago, there was no unsecured inter-bank market and all money deals were done on a strictly secured basis with a margin. Very briefly, what happened every morning, and this included Saturday morning in the old days, was this. The Local Director 'doing the money', as it was called, used to be brought the 'book' by the Manager of the Brokers Loan Department. He would tell you the Bank's liquidity position and how much you were required to 'get out' into the market by way of loans or the purchase of bills – you got a better rate by the use of 'fixtures' loans not provided overnight, but fixed for a certain period of time. This was advantageous both for the Bank, because of the better rate, and for the broker who had the certainty of funds for that fixed period of time. In addition, the Manager told you what target balance you had to lend down to. This target was the Bank's required balance at the Bank of England.

The top-hatted gentlemen queued outside and at 11 a.m. the book was opened and the door of the Room opened and they entered one by one and you did the required business – we were all friends. They had to balance their books by the close of business – this was the close-off time for the Large Town Clearing in the afternoon. Very often some houses had difficulty in doing this and, when you got back from lunch, there were a few worried brokers waiting for you to borrow last-minute or, rather, late money, for which if you had it you were able to charge a penal rate. But more often than not you sent them away as you were unwilling to face the wrath of the Bank of England and the general management if you reduced the Bank's balance at the Bank of England below the target level.

There was one occasion when I was doing the money when I ran into trouble – not my fault I assure you, but because of the monetary convulsions leading up to Harold Wilson's devaluation of sterling in the autumn of 1967. What happened was this. The Bank of England was supporting sterling very heavily in the foreign exchange markets but, of course, I had no idea how much and how much it would impact on the Large Town Clearing and, thereby, our position at the Bank of England. So the afternoon before the devaluation, the decision for which was taken overnight, I made up to the correct target balance at the Bank of England and went home. Imagine my consternation the following morning when I arrived at the Bank and was immediately summoned to the Chairman and the General Managers to be told that I had overdrawn the Bank's account at the Bank of England – an unprecedented event, and I was responsible. I told them it was simply not possible, as I had made up to the required target. I then made enquiries and soon found out that it was not my fault. The reason was that the frenzy of the speculation against the pound was reaching its peak and the Bank of England was engaged in a massive support operation, that is, buying the pound and selling its foreign exchange reserves. The result of this was a huge movement of funds away from the banks to the Bank of England in the late afternoon, and the swing was such that my target credit balance at the Bank of England had completely evaporated and instead a huge overdraft appeared. I was exonerated, but after this I made arrangements with the Bank of England to tell us the extent of their support operations and how much was expected to impact on Barclays, so that I could judge the effect on our position. This worked, and I never got into trouble again.

Once a year we invited what we called the 'Market' to a champagne party in the Room. This was a splendid occasion. Once again the desks were pushed up against the walls of the Room and the most sumptuous smoked salmon sandwiches were set out and the Bank's best champagne provided. The Chairman of the Bank and general management were invited along with the Bank's Chief Accountant, later the Treasurer of the Bank, and all the bill brokers, money brokers, gilt-edged jobbers, together with the representatives of the Bank of England, including hopefully the Governor, but more particularly the Principal of the Discount Office. The origin of this outstandingly successful party – always known as the party of the year in the City – was that Peter Forrester, the bank's doyen of the discount market as well as a 54 Lombard Street local director, although brilliant (he was a student of Keynes), disliked entertaining the market to lunch and instead organised this party to kill them all off once a year. So it suited everybody. Sadly, like most good things in the City it died, and the cause of death was the growth of the unsecured markets and the introduction of computers and technology in the City's markets, when all deals were transacted via the screen and telephone. It

21

The British Trans-Arctic Expedition

Despite all my marital and financial travails, life did go on and in 1966 I was asked by Sir Miles Clifford, the Chairman of the British Trans-Arctic Expedition Committee and also former Governor of the Falkland Islands, to join his Committee. He had also been a Vice-President of the Royal Geographical Society and a member of the Committee of Management of the Commonwealth Trans-Antarctic Expedition – an expedition, as I have mentioned earlier, that I had dearly wanted to join and with the benefit of hindsight I perhaps could have. Miles Clifford had also been Chairman of the British National Committee on Antarctic Research and had just given up being Director of the Leverhulme Trust. Other members of the committee included Colonel Andrew Croft, the Commandant of the Metropolitan Police Cadet Corps, a member of the Trans-Greenland Expedition 1933–34 and Deputy Leader of the Oxford University Arctic Expedition 1935–36. Also Sir Vivian Fuchs (Bunny), Director of the British Antarctic Survey, formerly the Falkland Islands Dependencies Survey and its leader from 1947–52. He had also been leader of the Commonwealth Trans-Antarctic Expedition 1955–58 on which my great great friend David Stratton, whom I met in the Antarctic and subsequently shared a flat with, was Deputy Leader. Then there was Lord Hunt, who had been leader of the British Mount Everest Expedition in 1953 – the first expedition to make the ascent of the mountain. He was also a former Vice-President of the Royal Geographical Society – a position which I eventually attained myself.

In addition we had Rear-Admiral Edmund Irving, a former Hydographer of the Royal Navy, a President of the Institute of Navigation and once again a former Vice-President of the Royal

Geographical Society; Sir Arthur Porritt, who was to become Governor-General of New Zealand and was Sergeant Surgeon to the Queen as well as being a member of the International Olympic Committee. Finally there was Patrick Pirie-Gordon, a Director of Glyn Mills and Honorary Treasurer to the Royal Geographical Society and formerly to the Commonwealth Trans-Antarctic Expedition. I was there as a Director of Barclays Bank, actually Local Director, and a former member of the Falkland Islands Dependencies Survey.

So it was a fairly high-powered Committee and I felt honoured to be invited to join it, although I had no idea of the amount of work in which I would be involved.

The leader of the expedition was Wally Herbert – now Sir Walter Herbert – who had been a member of the Falkland Islands Dependencies Survey 1955–58, a member of the Scottish Spitzbergen Expedition in 1960, and a member of the New Zealand Antarctic Expedition 1960–62 during which he completed one of the finest and longest sledging survey journeys in the Antarctic. Wally very belatedly received a knighthood for our British Trans-Arctic Expedition.

The objectives of the expedition were to make the first surface crossing of the Arctic Ocean from Point Barrow in Alaska to Spitzbergen via the North Pole; to carry out a study of the pack ice environment, and to make regular synoptic weather reports from the central Arctic basin via a relay station set up on the drifting ice-island T3; in addition, a climatological programme and sea ice studies complementary to the under-ice profiles recorded by nuclear submarines and the more precise sea ice investigations carried out at the American and Russian drifting ice-stations; and finally, a geographical traverse during the winter drift across the submarine Lomonosov Ridge which would include ocean depth soundings, magnetometer and gravity measurement.

So a high-powered Committee and some very ambitious objectives of which the most important was the surface crossing from Alaska to Spitzbergen.

Prince Philip very kindly agreed to be Patron of the Expedition, but what about the all-important funding of such an enterprise? It would cost in the region of £50,000 – remember this is 40 years ago as I write this. In order to assist us with this, we engaged George Greenfield, a well-known literary agent, whose clients included Bunny Fuchs, Ed Hillary, John Hunt, Chris Bonington etcetera – in short, explorers, adventurers and mountaineers, as well as many other clients.

The plan was for George Greenfield to arrange and enter into publishing and media contracts on behalf of the expedition, now a company with charitable status limited by guarantee. Once these contracts, dependent on certain objectives such as reaching the North Pole and making land, were signed, sealed and delivered and equally importantly insured, the banks (in this case Glyn Mills and Barclays) would lend against them. In the case of Barclays I myself would do the lending as the limit would be within my discretion. It was all very risky as anything could happen, but the insurance which I had arranged with Lloyds of London gave me comfort, although we had to pay a premium of £7,000 for this comfort. To this day I really do not know why Lloyds took on these risks, but knowing the Chairman, Mr Mance, helped. In the event, there were no claims except for a movie-camera value £150 which disappeared through the sea ice into the water below. Lloyds of London were so pleased with us that at the end of the expedition the Chairman not only gave a lunch for us, but also generously refunded some of the premium, a very pleasant surprise.

This plan worked on the whole very well, so much so that George Greenfield and I financed many more expeditions like this, including Chris Bonington's 1975 British Everest South West Face Expedition in which both of us took part; but more about that later.

The operational plan of the expedition was to be carried out in two main phases. The first was a training programme in north-west Greenland which George and I financed by way of advances on the sale of copyrights for stories and films resulting from the completion of this programme.

This training programme extended to 1,350 miles and was actually one of considerable historical interest in that the expedition retraced the route taken by the American explorer, Dr Frederick Cook, who in 1908 claimed to have been the first to reach the North Pole. Cook's claim was discredited by the supporters of Robert Peary who claimed that he reached the North Pole in 1909. This is still the subject of controversy.

To undertake this programme three members of the expedition wintered in 1966–67 at Qanak at latitude 78 degrees North (the northernmost Eskimo settlement in Greenland). At the end of

February 1967 they sledged across Smith Sound, the sound between Greenland and Ellesmere Island where the ice, I recollect, was not much more than a mile wide. Sledging on sea ice, as I know in my own experience, is or can be extremely risky and they were lucky to get across intact. Having crossed Ellesmere Island, which was even then, in winter, hardly snow-covered, they made for the northern tip of Axel Heiberg Island and from there west and south to Resolute. The last 100 miles was open water so they and the dogs were airlifted to Resolute.

The Royal Air Force had kindly agreed to undertake, without charge, two so-called polar training flights to carry the expedition stores to Resolute and then on to Point Barrow in Alaska, the starting point of the expedition. I was asked to accompany this flight which was to be undertaken during midwinter. At midwinter in the polar regions it is well known there is almost complete darkness at midday, there is intense cold with frequent blizzards and flying conditions are difficult.

Wally Herbert and I drove to RAF Lyneham, Wiltshire, in the early hours of 27th December 1967, and boarded the plane, a Hercules C130 of RAF Supply Command, which was already on the runway crammed with ration boxes and 45-gallon kerosene drums. Two pilots – one reassuringly well versed in polar flying, a meteorologist, an engineer, three navigators (two extra to bring themselves up to date with gyro steering), a quartermaster and an Army air despatch officer made up the flight crew.

Our accommodation was collapsible canvas seats around the aircraft. These seats did not prove tenable for long. The cold inside our part of the aircraft was so intense that, on the theory that even a little heat rises, we made nests for ourselves on top of the ration boxes. Our breath sparkled in glittering white ice crystals on the portholes, whilst the noise – the plane was not soundproofed – and the vibration of the four propellers hammered us into a form of insensibility.

Not long after we had taken off we learnt that our two destinations, Thule and Resolute, were reporting impossible landing conditions due to severe blizzards, which left only Sondestrom and Frobisher in Canada as alternative landing strips. By now we realised we could not get back to Keflavik in Iceland as we had insufficient fuel. However, except for the 90-knot headwind, which cut our ground speed to 260 knots, the weather conditions remained benign and by 1530 GMT we could just see, in that unbelievably eerie polar ice-glow, the dark serrated edges of nunataks rising up through the Greenland ice-cap and the ice-falls on their sides plunging down to merge with the crevassed glaciers below. By now Frobisher had also closed down and we touched down at Sondestrom in the nick of time before that too closed down.

Sondestrom, far up the Davis Strait on the west coast of Greenland, was first laid down as an airstrip in the Second World War II. In those days the bigger aircraft were able to carry sufficient fuel to make the hop between Newfoundland and Keflavik, but the fighter aircraft being ferried to England from the USA needed a number of airstrips at intermediate stages, and this was one of them. It became a small USAF air base manned by Danes and Americans.

Across the runway was a small new hotel where we could stay but for the moment we stayed at the base operations office, hoping for the weather to improve both at Sondestrom and at Thule; but there was no such luck. Three hours later we checked in at the Arctic Hotel – the bedroom price was $2 a night with service included and the heat was stifling. While we were at Sondestrom the Americans were extremely generous to us and at the Officers' Club we were given cocktails and canapés, three-course meals with wine and, as a special treat, a Swedish pop group complete with go-go girls in varying stages of undress. It all seemed unbelievably incongruous for this to be happening only 50 years after the Scott and Shackleton expeditions and the heroic age of polar exploration.

It snowed heavily in the night and in the morning the snowflakes were still eddying down obliquely, white in the glare of the station lights against the pitch blackness of the morning. It was exceptionally cold – –40°F – and out there on the runway our aircraft sat looking like a crouching beast, dark and inert, covered in snow and frozen into immobility. But although it was still snowing with us, the blizzards had cleared Thule and Resolute and we were given permission to leave. The aircraft had to be de-iced by a machine, but this did not work and meanwhile we set to work with brooms and brushes clearing the snow until the de-icing machine was coaxed into working.

Two hours later we were flying over Thule and in the midday polar twilight we could see the pack ice, the frozen leads showing up black and irregular, whilst here and there we could see icebergs stranded in the pack, halted on their long, lonely journey to the south. Later on we touched down on the ice runway at Resolute – the temperature –45°F. Resolute is so called because of HMS *Resolute*, one of the search ships looking for survivors of the ill-fated Franklin expedition. It is a small cluster of huts on the southern end of Cornwallis Island close to the North Magnetic Pole.

We started to unload the aircraft and as I did so, I saw to my horror what looked like the plane's life blood ebbing away. Under each wheel, a widening pool of dark red liquid stained the fresh whiteness of the snow. What had happened was that the cold was so intense on the flight from Thule that the brake drums had contracted, allowing the brake fluid to escape.

At Resolute I had the extraordinary feeling of being home again, and by that I mean my Antarctic home. It was all so familiar, the noiseless tread on the soft snow drifting and swirling along the ground, the wind flying along, booming and braking like waves on a seashore, the clacking of the aerials on the wireless masts, the dull ache of the cold on the face, the frozen breath and the greenish-bluish glimmers of light far away to the south, and over all the magnificent desolate isolation and the lingering polar ice-glow. I turned back to the aircraft; I had not felt so happy for a long time. I think many people will find it difficult to understand this – and it is not easy to explain – but all those who have lived and worked in the polar regions will know what I mean, and I would think that many people who are working and living in an increasingly crowded South-East England with its stresses and strains, overcrowded trains, light pollution, noise, pollution from cars, lorries and aircraft and the whole rat race, will agree with me. Humans are not meant to live in such conditions and there will be an increasing number of people fighting to escape from this rat-hole.

We flew on to Thule – not a long flight, but a difficult one for the navigators. Apart from the problem with the compass and high latitude, due to the proximity of the magnetic pole, the other problem was the convergence of the meridians of longitude at these latitudes, involving in any conventional method of navigation, continual changes of heading. At that time, 1967, we had special polar grid maps, which ignored the usual longitudinal presentation. But the problem with this is that grid north continued straight over the North Pole towards the Pacific, so that the aircraft is apparently flying south when it is in fact flying north.

The navigators told me that the airborne gyro compass did not solve all the problems created by magnetic conditions. Even the best gyro compasses precess due to friction, air resistance and the earth's rotation. This is not a worry when you can get an astro or a radio fix, but if you cannot do this when a magnetic storm brews up and prevents a radio fix and your periscopic sextant freezes up and prevents an astro fix, then you are in trouble, and this is precisely what happened to us on that flight from Resolute to Thule. So it was an awkward and anxious flight. Eventually, we wheeled over North Star Bay, the scene of the ill-fated B52 crash and its nuclear bombs, and landed on the long runway at Thule.

For those who are still not quite sure where Thule is, its position is at 76°30'N and 68°30'W. It is 700 miles north of the Arctic Circle and 700 miles south of the North Pole. It is or was one of the three Ballistic Missile Early Warning System stations in the world, the others are or were at Clear, Alaska, and Fylingdales, Yorkshire. At that time there was constant military air activity at Thule whilst the big B52 planes with their hydrogen bombs cruised the air ready for instant retaliation. Again, at that time, Thule was manned by 3,000 US personnel who, as usual, had their cinemas, bowling alleys, TV station and one-armed bandits, and like at Sondestrom, go-go girls were flown up to entertain these 3,000 men; the girls had to be protected from them by barbed wire.

The Base Commander was there to greet us, along with the Royal Greenland Trade Department representative. They told us that the bay ice had been firm enough for the huskies to be driven down the coast and they were now at Dundas with two members of the expedition. We put our special Christmas hamper in the back of a truck driven by Jens Zinglersen, the trade representative, jumped in after reading our special winter storm instructions, and drove off to Dundas where Zinglersen lived with his Eskimo wife.

Down below his house the huskies were happy. There was a glint of moonlight on the bay-ice and over to the east a ridge of rock sheered up into the dark sky and echoed back the huskies' welcome. Suddenly they burst into song and their long wolf-like howl stirred up memories of calm evenings in the far south, when the blizzards had died down and a tranquil moon rose high in the starry heavens and my huskies burst into song in sheer delight and joy at the beauty of it all.

I walked back to the house and Zinglersen's wife gave us dinner.

We broke open the Christmas hamper and the talk got down to dog-driving, the virtues of different types of dog sledges – the Nansen and the Greenland – and the different types of dog harness, fans, traces and tackle. And then we moved on to the different types of ice conditions, and once again it was all familiar.

Then we left Dundas, drove the ice road and as we came over the last hill, we marvelled at the myriad glittering lights of Thule below us and the bombers and fighters, some of whom had been flown down from Nord, the American Air Force base on the north coast of Greenland. And I marvelled then, and I do now, at the extraordinary bravery of these 'right stuff' pilots who were constantly in the air, protecting us from the missile systems of our then enemies, the Russians, during the Cold War. They have my respect and admiration and their bravery should not be forgotten.

In the early hours of the morning I left the Officers' Club and promptly lost my way. I had, as they say, slightly (or perhaps more than slightly) overindulged. However, a wind of 40 miles per hour and a temperature of –50°F sobered me up immediately. But I did not know where I was and all the hut doors seemed to be locked, and if I did not find my hut within a few minutes I would be dead. Of course, all the huts were exactly the same and indistinguishable. To this day I cannot quite remember how I found my visitor's hut, but I did.

It was only a short sleep, and at 7 a.m. I was up. I called a cab – yes, they had cabs at Thule – and at 8 a.m. I found the RAF Hercules all prepared for departure. At 9 a.m. we took off, banked to the south-west as we cleared the land and then set off for the long journey down the coast and then over the Greenland ice-cap. At 26,000 feet we picked up a 140-knot jet stream and sped along at 500 knots. The light increased, the sun again appeared to the south, slinking along the horizon. The East Greenland coastal range came into sight and then dropped behind us. The pack ice opened up and then we were over open sea. At 8 p.m., touchdown at RAF Lyneham and the trip was over. I was home again, but of course I was homeless, and I stayed the night at the Royal Court Hotel in Sloane Square in London where 23 years before I had stayed with Mummy and Marigold to watch the Victory Parade in London in May 1945.

The expedition left Point Barrow in February 1968, heading for the North Pole. The ice conditions were atrociously difficult to start with, but as the daylight increased they started to make good progress and the airdrops by both the Royal Canadian Air Force and the Arctic Research Laboratories in Barrow were all successful.

In September 1968, Alan Gill damaged his back manhandling his heavy sledge. Nobody knew, including the doctor, Ken Hedges, whether it was severe muscle strain or an acute slipped disc. Messages started to fly backwards and forwards between the expedition and the committee in London. Winter was approaching, and with the advent of total darkness and unbelievable cold in a few weeks' time, the team would have to halt on a suitably large ice floe, erect their hut and stay there until the following spring. Wally Herbert, Fritz Koerner and Alan Gill himself wanted him to winter over and give his back a chance to recover. Even if, when the time came, his back had not improved, he could remain under Ken Hedges' care until March, when some Canadian geophysicists were due to take over the hut for their polar observations. Alan Gill and Ken Hedges would then fly out on the geophysicists aircraft. Meanwhile, Wally Herbert and Fritz Koerner, the two most experienced polar travellers, would make a dash for Spizbergen.

When this plan was put to the committee we strongly opposed it. We felt that the onward journey of more than 1,000 miles over the sea ice of the Arctic Ocean was extremely hazardous in any event – anybody who has sledged on sea ice knows this. For such a journey to be undertaken by only two men on their own, however tough and experienced they might be, was asking not only for trouble but also death. The reason for this is that if an accident occurred, or one or both of them got ill or the weather deteriorated, or the sea ice started to break up early – which, as a matter of fact, it did – then it could well be impossible to get a light aircraft in to rescue them. And if a rescue could not be effected by a light aircraft, whose pilot would also be risking his own life, then we would end up with two dead explorers, and it was extremely unlikely that their bodies would ever be found.

Unfortunately, the press got wind of all this altercation and was having a field day. Wally Herbert, thinking he was talking privately to Freddie Church, our RAF Signals Officer, on the radio link and feeling frustrated as well he might with the committee's tendency (as he put it in a formal message back to London) to issue him 'directions' instead of 'recommendations', blew his top. Unfortunately the public address system was accidentally left on and Peter Dunn, who was then at Barrow as the correspondent for the *Sunday Times*, which was the newspaper which part financed the expedition, overheard Wally's remarks. He published the story and the other newspapers picked it up and then, as is their wont, falsified it, coming out with such headlines as 'Arctic Hero's Lonely Battle against Chairborne Committee' and 'We Think Mr Herbert is Not Himself', *Daily Mail*, 26th September 1968, with a photograph of the committee including myself at the British Antarctic Survey, two standing – I was – and two seated. The reference to Wally not being himself arose because someone said or may have said that he must be suffering from 'winteritis', which is polar slang for the psychological and depressive effect which the long dark polar winters can have on a man, although I never suffered from it myself.

At the same time there was the worry that if we the Committee changed our mind and approved Wally's plan and there was a disaster, then the press would swiftly forget that it had been Wally's idea in the first place, and we would have been the culprits for sending Wally and his men to their doom. We therefore stood our ground, that is to say the previous instruction that Alan Gill should be airlifted out for medical attention, and the remaining three should winter over and continue their journey in the spring, was confirmed by the Chairman, Sir Miles Clifford.

In the event, the sea ice did break up in the area where the Twin Otter aircraft would have had to land, and the flight was abandoned. Alan Gill remained with the other three in their winter quarters and recovered. In the spring of 1969 the expedition reached the North Pole and then went on to complete the first and only successful crossing of the Arctic ice-cap. With global warming, such a journey could not now be repeated.

It may well be asked how we managed to get HMS *Endurance* up to Spitzbergen and to therefore provide standby facilities between 20th May and 20th June 1969, to pick up the expedition after its crossing, at no cost to the expedition. Earlier we had explained to the Royal Navy that the expedition would attempt to approach Spitzbergen from an easterly direction in order to minimise the risk of being caught out by large stretches of open water, or being swept down a south-westerly stream on an ice floe. Furthermore, that Wally would be radioing reports which would be relayed from Spitzbergen to the British Antarctic Survey in London, which would enable the latter to give the Royal Navy sufficient time of any requirement to rescue the party from the ice.

HMS *Endurance*, specially strengthened in the ice, would accordingly be coming back earlier from the Antarctic, where she was acting in support of the British Antarctic Survey, and to assist the expedition the Royal Navy agreed that the ship would be given some naval tasks in the Spitzbrgen area, so she would thus be in a convenient position to assist the expedition. These naval tasks meant that we would not have to pay the Navy for this assistance, for which we were truly grateful.

In due course HMS *Endurance* did pick up the expedition and arrived at Portsmouth on Monday, 23rd June. We all went down to meet her in the early morning and there was an elaborate protocol of arrival: the Commander-in-Chief being the first to board the ship, followed by the families, followed by the press and the photographers, followed by ourselves. It was a joyful occasion and it was to be followed by a Civic Lunch at the Guildhall, given but not paid for by the Lord Mayor of Portsmouth. The reason for this is that we had persuaded the *Sunday Times* and the International Wool Secretariat to sponsor the lunch and reception, at a cost to each of these organisations of £75 – or so we thought. They duly sent their cheques to me – the budget as submitted to me by the Portsmouth Lord Mayor's Office for lunch was £150. But when I eventually got the bill from the Portsmouth Corporation, they included an extra figure for staff labour; they then included an extra figure for staff lunches; and they then included an extra figure for the pre-lunch reception drinks. I felt it was a gross impertinence for the expedition to be charged in this way, particularly for staff lunches, and clearly we had been taken for a very big ride by the Lord Mayor and the Portsmouth Corporation for which they will not be forgiven. Later on the members of the expedition and ourselves were feted by Lloyds of London, the Westminster City Council and many other organisations.

In summary, the expedition was a success, although when Wally Herbert inscribed his book *Across the Top of the World* to me he wrote: 'For Alan – a book of eloquent omissions', a reference to a major incompatibility problem which occurred during the expedition. The total cost of the expedition was around £70,000 including some unbudgeted expenditure, including the sum of £3,041 being the cost of extra flying incurred by the Royal Air Force for the transport of extra supplies for the expedition. This was itemised as 17 hours 47 minutes' flying, so a cost to ourselves of about £180 per flying hour. This and other unbudgeted expenditure produced a shortfall for the bank of about £5,000, which under my discretion I conveniently wrote off – there was no hope of getting it back.

Finally, I would say one thing about this expedition. It involved me in a huge amount of work as both joint treasurer and organising secretary, but it also set a pattern of how in future I should fund both polar and mountaineering expeditions, and for this George Greenfield was essential and this partnership of ours continued successfully for many years – the culmination being the funding of the successful 1975 British Everest South West Face Expedition and Ran Fiennes's Transglobe Expedition.

22

Domestic and Foreign Banking

I mentioned earlier that in 1969 I had purchased the fag-end of lease of a flat at 99 Cadogan Gardens. I redecorated the flat and moved in there and as Nanny was more or less homeless, she moved in as well. It certainly was not an ideal position for either of us, but we managed.

This moving in entailed the removal of most of my belongings from 23 Flood Street – an exquisite agony. It also represented my entry into the twilight world of divorced men and women and also, in my case, unmarried women. The former were all obsessed with their marital break-up, the fights over the children and, of course, above all else, money. Most of the men in my position had to deal with divorce settlements, two household expenses and, of course, school fees – let alone one's wife's new partner occupying your house.

I have to say I hated this horrible twilight world. There was a restless instability about it all and there were all those shifty, usually unhappy relationships whereby people were constantly trying to reassure themselves with endless and usually unsatisfactory sexual liaisons. It was a rudderless and hopeless world and there I was, a divorced Catholic with three children and one ex-wife to support – it was the absolute nadir of my life. But I kept my promise to my mother-in-law Betty, and my priority, apart from keeping my job upon which everything depended, was to try and ensure that my children were, as far as possible, protected from the mayhem going on round them; but it was all extremely difficult.

Now turning away again from all these marital and financial travails, it was in the late 1960s that I was promoted in the Bank and appointed a Local Director of the Bank's Foreign branches in the UK and of the bank's overseas representative offices. These so-called Foreign branches – you would now call them international branches – were the branches which carried out all the foreign work for all the Barclays domestic branches in the UK. These Foreign branches were sometimes confused with the branches of Barclays Bank (Dominion, Colonial & Overseas) – DCO for short – but that was a separate bank in those days.

Here I must digress a bit and go back to the war years and, in particular, to what happened when war was declared in September 1939. The mood of optimism that had arisen in the 1920s following the end of the First World War disappeared with the Wall Street Crash and the subsequent depression which reached its nadir in Europe with the failure of the Creditanstalt in Vienna in 1931 – the year of my birth – which was followed by the failure of another bank in Berlin. The following conference drew up the famous stand-still agreement by which the world banks agreed to maintain the pre-crisis credit lines at the disposal of the German banks. It is interesting to note that the several millions of pounds which Barclays had lent to these German banks were not repaid until after the Second World War.

By this time the markets were in a chaotic state and the gold standard was suspended in the UK in September 1931. In 1933 a large number of American banks failed and the dollar was no longer backed with gold. The collapse in world trade and financial markets greatly reduced the work of the Foreign branches, which were then controlled by an Assistant General Manager.

By 1935 there was some slight improvement in world trade but by then war fears were rising and the general uncertainty meant that there was little foreign business. In September 1939, even this came to an end and for the duration of the war and afterwards there was rigid foreign exchange control with fixed exchange rates and the foreign exchange and commodity markets in London closed. The staff of the Foreign branches reduced by two-thirds and the business was severely restricted.

In 1949 the pound was devalued against the dollar from the fixed rate of £4.03 to £2.80 and this was part of the inexorable decline of the pound as a world currency. It is interesting to note that, despite this, by the end of the 1960s, some 25 per cent of all world trade was still transacted in sterling. In 1951 the foreign exchange markets were reopened 12 years after they had closed.

Despite the Bank of England controls, the foreign exchange market re-established its international importance, particularly so with the establishment of the Eurodollar markets – Eurodollars were dollars held outside the United States.

In 1959, about eight years before I joined the Foreign as I used to call it, the Bank decided to expand its Foreign business – once again, I reiterate that this was the UK bank's foreign business not that of Barclays Bank (DCO). Of the many recommendations, the first to be implemented was really a quite radical reshaping of the management structure of this Foreign business, which was designed to compete for a much higher level of this business.

We opened offices in Zurich, Brussels, Beirut, Tokyo, Frankfurt and Milan in addition to those already established in New York and San Francisco, and all these were administered and controlled by the Foreign branch local directors, of which I was one. During the same time we opened eight additional Foreign branches in the UK. By the end of my Foreign tenure there had been a huge increase in business and the numbers of staff increased commensurately, notably at the Chief Foreign branch at 168 Fenchurch Street, which had originally been the Head Office of the old London & South Western Bank. This building had a relatively attractive façade but the interior, which included the City Office business, was Dickensian and I remember being taken to the vaults where there were pile upon pile of rotting bags of copper coins.

One more slight digression here. The City Office business of the Bank at 168 Fenchurch Street had been as I said the Head Office of the London & South Western Bank. By rights, of course, it should have been controlled by the Lombard Street Directors – it was after all a City business – but the General Managers never allowed this to happen, mainly because they felt that the Lombard Street Local Directors, led by Emlyn Bevan and Theodore Barclay, were too orthodox in their banking approach and not sufficiently entrepreneurial. The result was that the City Office became known as the 'General Managers' bank' because advances which might not have been agreed by the Lombard Street Local Directors were domiciled there instead. All of this came to an end when I returned to Lombard Street to take overall control of the Bank's City business, and insisted that City Office came under my control and also, as it happens, the former Barclays Bank (DCO) business in Old Broad Street and Gracechurch Street. Thus the whole of the Bank's domestic and international business in the City came eventually under my control.

Meanwhile the predominant features of our business were the constant expansion of the Eurocurrency markets, the growth of the great multinational corporations, the increasing competition from the huge influx of foreign banks into the City, and the increasing sophistication of finance directors who became adept at finding other sources of funding, as government credit restrictions became tighter.

The second major sterling devaluation in 1967 reduced the value of the pound from £2.80 to £2.40. Up to that day the Bank of England had been heavily supporting sterling in the market to protect the £2.80 rate and it was this huge late outflow of money which caused me unwittingly to overdraw the Bank's sterling account at the Bank of England and which almost caused a temporary shadow over my career. It was at my insistence thereafter that the Bank of England provided us with information as to the extent they were supporting sterling in the market.

This devaluation further reduced confidence in sterling – the sterling area gradually disappeared with the disbandment of the Empire. However, the City was as inventive as ever and has flourished as one of the three most important financial centres in the world along with New York and Tokyo.

It was during my time with the 'Foreign' that I first started travelling for the Bank overseas, something I enjoyed enormously. As the result of the Bank having despatched me to Paris for a year, I was virtually bilingual and this was a huge help. The foreign management began regular visits abroad to maintain their existing ties with correspondent banks and develop new ones, and this included the USSR, many of the Middle and Far East countries, and South and Central American nations. Occasionally on these 'trips' as we used to call them, the foreign management were accompanied by Board Directors to add both '*ton*' and 'weight' and it was on one of such trips that I first went to India with Bill Wedge. By that time I was a Director of the Bank, and after that I took India under my wing. That first trip of course enabled me to join up with the British Everest South West Face expedition in Nepal.

At the same time as all this was going on, I was appointed by the Bank of England as a Commissioner of the Public Works Loan

Board, which was essentially a conduit for funnelling government money into local authority projects. Like all government bureaucracies, there was a formula for these loans, and by the time they got to me there was very little I could usefully add. I think that, with the benefit of hindsight, I was somewhat too critical of the bureaucracy, and at the end of four years my contract was not renewed. I had not been paid anything for this extra responsibility, but nevertheless I was sorry that, as they say, my services on this Public Works Loan Board were no longer required. I was never very good at diplomacy.

At about this time in the mid-1960s I was also very fortunate to be involved in what became known as Barclaycard. There was an ad hoc committee, of which I was a member, established to consider this under the chairmanship of Derek Wilde, one of the very best and visionary Senior General Managers the Bank has ever produced and also one of the kindest men I ever came across in the Bank. He and I later were to become closely involved in the acquisition of Mercantile Credit.

What had happened was this. In San Francisco the Bank had a Representative's Office under the control of the new so-called Foreign branches Local Directors of which I was by now one. At the end of 1965, this office was upgraded to become a subsidiary bank in its own right. Derek Wilde was at the opening of the new bank, and whilst he was there he struck up an agreement in principle with the management of the Bank of America to enlist their assistance in establishing Britain's first credit card. We did have, through the chief Foreign branch, a close banking correspondent relationship with the Bank of America.

Once the concept had been agreed and accepted by the Board, I dropped out of this ad hoc committee and my involvement was now over. But it is interesting to recall some details of the launch of the card and what subsequently happened. The launch was in 1966. One million cards were issued unsolicited to customers of the Bank through the recommendation of the branch Managers. Something like 30,000 merchants were signed up – these so-called merchants again recommended by the branch Managers – who were willing to accept the card. Three years later there were 1,250,000 Barclaycard holders able to use their cards, and some 600,000 merchant outlets round the world – it was truly a consumer revolution.

Profitability of the card was, however, another matter and regulatory restrictions on credit were particularly tight in the 1960s. Although the Bank of England in 1967 permitted extended credit, Barclaycard credit was only allowed to be revolving rather than cumulative. It is, of course, the case that although you might just about cover your costs by the commission charged to the merchant outlets, you will almost by definition not make any money unless you are in a position to permit extended credit, and this is what the Bank of England did not allow.

There was a brief period of credit freedom inaugurated by Competition and Credit Control but this came to an end in 1973. The previous year Barclaycard had crept into profit, but in 1973 it again became loss-making. However, as we all know, the Bank persisted. There was no way really it could now withdraw. Later on Barclaycard became a major contributor to the Bank's profits: something like £800 million in 2004.

It was an exciting time also for me because in 1968 the Bank acquired Martins Bank and the major City business of Martins came under my control. It was quite difficult for the senior City management of Martins Bank to adjust to this loss of independence and change of control. There was a lot of resentment and although we always used the word 'merger', to try and deal with these sensitivities, everybody knew that it was, of course, an acquisition.

At that time Martins Bank had a powerful City Board although the main Board was domiciled in Liverpool: Martins Bank had originally been the Bank of Liverpool. Somehow this City Board of Martins was reconstituted to accommodate the acquirer. I joined the Board as an executive Director and this Board was chaired by John Keswick, a Martins non-executive Director, who also joined the main Board of Barclays. Most of the Martins Bank non-executive Directors on this Board seemed to be much more interested in finding out from the advances applications just what sort of financial shape their business competitors were in, rather than making a positive contribution to the board and the business. I have to say that I resented that.

However this was certainly not the case with the Chairman, John Keswick. He and I became good friends and our paths frequently crossed later on. I admired him. This also happened with Sir John Nicholson, who was I recall Chairman of Martins Bank before the acquisition. Both he and I also became good friends. I believe this all happened when, with Chris Bonington and Lord Hunt, I became heavily involved with the 1975 British Everest South West Face Expedition, in which I participated but also, more importantly, for which I arranged the necessary funding. I think that after all this they saw me in a new light and this involvement earned me their respect and friendship.

I believe we paid much more than we should have for that Martins business. They had expanded their business to obtain market share at relatively low margins, and certainly in the City their business was not as clean as ours. But, as I have said before, our business was perhaps too clean – hence the unwillingness of the General Managers to domicile business at Lombard Street. Nevertheless, their City business was a huge boost to ours in terms of the size of deposits and assets, although it added relatively little to our profitability.

In the late 1960s – remember I was living with Nanny in my flat in Chelsea, separated from my wife and children – another thing went right for me. I was asked to represent the British Bankers' Association on the Council of the International Chamber of Commerce based in Paris. This had a considerable number of National Committees in the various countries which were members. The International Chamber of Commerce is reasonably well known to large companies, both here and abroad, but is hardly known at all to the public at large so, at the risk of another digression, I will tell you a little more about it as I was part of it for more than 20 years.

The International Chamber of Commerce (ICC) can be said to be the only private sector organisation which makes rules that companies everywhere use daily. The ICC was founded in 1919 in the aftermath of the First World War. In those days there was no world system of rules which governed trade, investment, finance and commercial relations. The founders of the ICC considered that the private sector itself was best qualified to establish voluntary global rules and standards of business.

One of the most important achievements of the ICC was in 1922 when it established the International Court of Arbitration which has enabled many thousands of business disputes to be settled. In this the ICC rules allow parties to choose the arbitrators, the rules of law that apply and the language in which the arbitration is conducted. The ICC was a prime mover in bringing about the New

York Convention, which helps to ensure the independent enforcement of ICC arbitration awards in more than 130 countries. It has many other commercial activities, and over the years the ICC has become the largest, most representative business organisation in the world.

In addition, it works closely with the United Nations where it has top-level consultative status. It also maintains close relations with the World Trade Organization, the Organisation for Economic Co-operation and Development (OECD), the European Union and many other intergovernmental and non-governmental bodies. It is also politically active and each year the President of the ICC has an annual meeting with the head of the host government at the Group of Eight economic summit. So it is quite an impressive organisation, although comparatively unknown.

One of the attractions of the ICC was that every two years it held an international business conference in a different country. As the representative of the British Bankers' Association I was invited to these conferences, and the British Bankers' Association kindly agreed to pay not only my expenses but also those of my wife. This therefore meant that in addition to my normal overseas travel as a Foreign Branch Local Director, I visited many other countries. These included France, Turkey, Brazil, America, India, Sweden, Germany, the Philippines, Austria and so on. Here I have to confess that I did not take a very active part in the working parties underlying these conferences, but it did enable me to meet a huge number of top international businessmen, which was very useful. At the end of each trip overseas I wrote a long report on the content and decisions of these conferences and sent it off to the British Bankers' Association, together with a note of my expenses. I am not sure whether anyone read these reports but I found it all fascinating and full of interest, and it particularly helped me in India.

In 1969 another thing went right for me. Paddy Tritton relented and allowed me to use the Hole Farm rent and rates free. I say rent free as previously he had made me pay rent to myself via the trust, which I have mentioned earlier. The house was fully furnished in a sort of 1930s style favoured by Aunt Dore. It was not particularly comfortable but nor was it particularly uncomfortable; at least it represented a less ignominious entry into my inheritance. It also came with a gardener and his wife, who mucked me out from time to time.

So by 1969 I had been promoted in the Bank to what was called 'the Foreign'; I had been appointed a Commissioner of the Public Works Loan Board; I had been appointed the British Bankers' Association representative on the Council of the International Chamber of Commerce; I had bought the fag-end of a lease of a flat in Cadogan Gardens; and I had been given rent and rates free the Hole Farm in Essex. So things were looking up, although any prospects of a reconciliation were looking down and, in fact, with the benefit of hindsight were probably never there. Indeed Betty d'Abreu used to come and see me in the flat before she died in 1970, depressed that two out of her three daughters were seeking divorces – she was, of course, a devout Catholic and most years went on a pilgrimage to Lourdes as a nursing sister. I do not feel I can divulge what she said to me; I always respected her confidence, and as I have said earlier, she was a wonderful mother-in-law to me and to this day, every day, I always pray for her and her husband Pon. I was extraordinarily lucky to have such in-laws.

And now I must move on with what is becoming a somewhat lengthy chronicle and turn away from the Public Works Loan Board, the introduction of Barclaycard, the Martins Bank acquisition by Barclays and the International Chamber of Commerce, and back to Great Leighs.

In 1970 my Aunt Dore died, hating me to the last. As I have said before, I have never understood this hatred, and it was palpable hatred. The funeral was at St Mary's church opposite Lyons Hall, a church she had never attended since a former rector had put up that charming little wooden icon of Our Lady – after all the church was dedicated to Our Lady. Paddy Tritton came down for the funeral and although he had been invited to a small reception at the Hole Farm, organised by Nanny and myself, he did not deign to attend. Henry Garnett came but as he had always been a protégé of Aunt Dore as well as being her nephew, I felt uncomfortable in his presence and I was glad when he left.

Aunt Dore had had her stroke under the hairdresser's drying machine in 1963. On 31st March 1965, she put a rather shaky signature to the trust deed by which her life interest and my reversionary interest were subsumed into a new trust. I think I may have mentioned earlier that in 1965 the *inter vivos* period was five years but in 1968 that appalling Labour Chancellor of the Exchequer, Roy Jenkins, extended this *inter vivos* period retrospectively to seven years and I was caught for death duties for about £100,000. In 1970 that was a very large sum of money against an asset of about £265,000, that is, the Lyons Hall Estate and farm. This thus came under threat, although I was allowed seven years to pay it off plus, of course, interest.

Following Aunt Dore's death Paddy Tritton resigned as trustee and so at long last I was mercifully rid of him. Before he retired he asked me one question, and that was how I intended to pay off the estate duty, a sensible question because as a trustee at her death, he was liable for the payment of her estate duty. He told me that in his view I had three choices: one was to sell the whole estate, one was to sell half the estate, and the last one, which he did not favour, was to try and retain the estate. I told him that I would try the latter.

Now it so happened that my former wife, as part of a financial settlement prior to the divorce she was set on, began trying to get the Lyons Hall Trust varied in her favour. It was at this point that Paddy stepped in and told me that I had to go to a top lawyer to save the estate from falling into her hands. My divorce lawyer – a nice man – was simply not up to dealing with this sort of thing. Accordingly I went to Theodore Goddard and as a result I took Counsel's opinion who stated that, in his view, the trust could not be varied in her favour. I cannot say what a relief this was. This was passed back to the other side and I heard no more about it, as they say, *Deo gratias*.

Nevertheless Aunt Dore's death did allow some movement towards a settlement as Paddy Tritton was not in situ any longer. However a major problem presented itself on the way to a settlement and it was this. Paddy had never allowed me to receive any income from the estate and farm, even though it was technically mine for tax purposes. He did this on the basis that the farm's only source of capital was retained income or profit, and there was a long expensive backlog of maintenance and improvement work to be carried out. It was difficult not to agree with this but, of course, in declaring my income for divorce purposes, what figure could I place on this? I received nothing, but of course I was deemed by the divorce lawyers to receive it, and I entered in a sort of Kafkaesque world where nothing was something. I cannot now remember how this was solved.

The Farm Account did have some money in it and this plus a

loan enabled me to pay off the £30,000 mortgage on 23 Flood Street. I had considered putting it into a trust for the children, but I could not face the endless arguments that this would entail over maintenance expenses, so in the end I gave it to my former wife as part of the settlement.

So ended this unhappy marital saga but, of course, what it did do was to leave me and the estate in debt, whilst at the same time I had the death duty debt of £100,000 hanging over me, together with full liability for the children's school fees.

So in 1971 I was divorced with substantial debts and liabilities. However, I was now free to run the estate without Paddy Tritton. To 'run it' is really a misnomer: it was managed by Strutt & Parker, but they now reported to me, not Paddy.

Despite these debts I decided with the help of Virginia Menzies to update the Hole Farm and bring it into the twentieth century. It was expensive, but worth it, and I was now proud of the house and its stables; before, I used to apologise for its dowdy appearance.

I remember one extraordinary night at about this time. There was deep snow everywhere and the taxi-driver taking me home from Chelmsford Station dropped me at the top end of Goodmans Lane as the snow was too deep for him to venture down the lane. There was complete silence, the moon and the stars were shining brilliantly in the dark sky, the snow was everywhere – it was just like a Russian winter landscape painting. I got out of the car and set off down Goodmans Lane to the Hole Farm and suddenly I was extraordinarily happy, with the beauty of it all around me and, of course, the silence. It was like stepping into another world, and moreover a world which seemed safe, secure and natural, and it was my land, my home, and I felt very possessive – I was going to keep it, and make a success of it.

In 1971 I met a tall, fair-haired American girl at a party. Not only was Diana beautiful, but there was also a feeling of stability and security about her, which attracted me. She was also highly intelligent and a graduate of the University of California in Los Angeles, where she had majored in English Literature and English History. She had left the United States to work in London as a copy-writer in an advertising firm and had no intention of returning. To cut a long story short, we decided to get married and, of course, in so doing she acquired not only a husband but also three stepchildren, not to mention Nanny for whom I acquired a small flat in Stanhope Gardens in South Kensington. A stepmother's position and role is not an easy one, and she used to tell me that it was strange that there were no books on the subject, particularly as this was becoming more frequent. However, she persevered and writing this 35 years later, I feel I can say quite truthfully that she has a very good relationship not only with her stepchildren and their husbands and wives, but also with the ten grandchildren.

We married in January 1972 – it was a registry office wedding followed by an Anglican church blessing in the Boltons. I have to say, being a Catholic convert getting remarried in an Anglican church following a registry office ceremony required me to have a tight grip on my emotions, firstly because in the eyes of Holy Mother the church, I was still married to my first wife, and secondly because I seemed to have broken my vows to my first wife, and now I was repeating the same vows to my second wife. I found it all very disturbing and I remember my emotions being very confused.

But two things happened to me in 1972 apart from my marriage to Diana. The first was that I was promoted to be the Senior Local Director and Regional Director of the Bank's central London business, known as Pall Mall district. The main office was 1 Pall Mall. This was a very important and significant lift-up for me because this central London business was one of the Bank's most important businesses and it carried, as it happens, a good deal of risk, for which we required high margins. In recognition of this responsibility, I was in that same year appointed a Director of Barclays Bank UK Management Ltd, which had recently been established to direct and manage, as its name implies, the UK domestic bank business.

Prior to all this the minority shareholding in Barclays Bank (DCO) was bought out and that bank – my favourite bank – changed its name to Barclays Bank International as a wholly owned subsidiary of Barclays Bank Ltd. In the course of these changes, my old job as a Local Director Foreign branches disappeared: 'Local' and 'Foreign' never seemed quite to fit together and these so-called Foreign branches were renamed Barclays Bank International Bank branches, as they now came under the control of Barclays Bank International as it began to be called.

In being appointed Senior Local Director and then Regional Director of the Pall Mall District, I alighted on the remains of an old family partnership bank, namely Ransom, Bouverie & Co. This bank was founded in 1786 in Pall Mall and after various overtures they amalgamated with Barclay, Bevan, Tritton & Co. under the extremely lengthy title of Barclay, Bevan, Tritton, Ransom, Bouverie & Co., always known as 'the long firm'. The reason for this amalgamation was the desire of the Barclay–Bevan–Tritton partnership to have a presence in the West End of London. They had been reluctant to open a branch there as they did not wish to compete with what they called their friend – the friend being a member of the Bevan family.

Following the November 1967 devaluation of sterling, in which you will know now that I played a somewhat curious part by overdrawing the bank's account at the Bank of England, they imposed very strict lending restrictions on the commercial banks. These restrictions became extremely irksome and they were one of the main reasons why it took Barclaycard so long to get into profit. At the same time, and I was very conscious of this in central London, there started burgeoning a growing number of wholesale banks. These were merchant banks, foreign banks and what were called secondary and tertiary banks. These were licensed by the Bank of England and funded themselves through the inter-bank sterling deposit markets, which were unsecured, and they started eating into the clearing banks' corporate market business.

In 1969 the Bank of England and the Treasury established a Committee to consider a more effective monetary policy framework to accommodate the financial strains which were then beginning to appear. In 1970 a Conservative Government was elected under the premiership of Ted Heath and this Government decided to adopt a more so-called free market approach to monetary policy. The result of all this was that in 1971 the Bank of England presented a radical set of proposals entitled 'Competition and Credit Control' which we called 'Competition and No Credit Control'. Essentially, and without going into too much detail, this abolished the clearing banks' interest rate cartel, so that each bank was able to set its own rates. This did not work out in practice, because if a bank set its own rate too high it lost business, and if it set the rate too low it was swamped by customers arbitraging. At the same time the convention whereby the clearing banks kept 28 per cent of their assets in cash and liquid instruments was replaced by a system of reserve assets as a percentage of deposits – namely 12.5 per cent. Suddenly, therefore, the multiplier for advances was significantly increased. More importantly, lending ceiling restrictions were removed and all this left just interest rates as the Treasury's only instrument of monetary control. In other words, the floodgates of credit were opened.

To be fair, when these changes were being considered, the economy was sluggish, essentially because of these ceiling restrictions. But now, with their removal, an uncontrollable demand for credit set in, particularly as this had been suppressed for so long, and a boom developed in which money was poured into the property and stock markets, particularly by these new secondary and tertiary banks. Now it so happened, as I have mentioned earlier, that a majority of the bank's property customers were domiciled in central London and, of course, were now my responsibility. Requests for property advances started pouring in and I even had a number of requests from stockbroking firms in the City for loans for their stock market operations. All these I turned aside, and I almost accused them of trying to take advantage of the clearing system. In the City the Large Town Clearing system operated on a same-day basis, and this was because of the City's money markets and also the foreign exchange, securities, commodities markets, which ran into billions of pounds daily with all the attendant same-day clearing risks. In central London and elsewhere the usual three days' clearing applied, which for the less scrupulous enabled a system known as cross-firing to be undertaken, i.e. using this period for raising credit. So all these requests were turned aside.

The property boom developed at an increased pace. In June 1973 interest rates were around the 6 per cent mark but by November they had increased to 13 per cent. About two-thirds of our lendings were for property, but the word 'property' covers a multitude of property-related transactions such as industrial and commercial development, residential development, property trading, property investment, and so on. In 1973 I began to take fright, not only because of our property exposure, but also because of our property companies' exposure to the secondary and tertiary banks, and at one remove their exposure to property companies, particularly as they were relying on volatile short-term funding from the wholesale money markets. They all were making the classic mistake of borrowing short and lending long. And, of course, as interest rates rose, property valuations began to fall and the security margins narrowed or fell away completely.

By the end of 1973 there was a whiff of financial panic in the air in central London and I was in the middle of it. At the same time as interest rates were rapidly rising, so was inflation. Oil prices were in the process of being quadrupled by OPEC and the coal miners were threatening to strike. In 1973 a company known as Cedar Holdings, which borrowed money short term and lent long term on second mortgages, of all things, began to have difficulty in renewing its borrowings from the market. As it happened these borrowings had risen from £3 million to £67 million in three years and Barclays was the lead banker, although their accounts were not domiciled with me. It was also awkward in that Barclays had brought the company's shares to the market, its first effort as an issuing house. Just before Christmas 1973 the Bank of England had organised a rescue for the company, with Barclays contributing £22 million.

The Bank of England's fear and ours too was that there would be a systemic run on the banks, triggered by defaults, the like of which had not been experienced since the nineteenth century but of which every bank was terrified: a 'run on the bank' or a 'run on the funds'. They therefore organised what came to be called the 'lifeboat', an open-ended albeit terminable agreement by all the clearing banks to support all solvent but illiquid banks by recycling their deposits as they fell due and were not renewed.

Now it so happened that I was able to see all this from both sides. When Barclays acquired Martins Bank it also acquired its 18 per cent shareholding in Mercantile Credit which specialised in consumer finance, mainly motor hire purchase. The Chairman of the Bank asked me to represent this 18 per cent shareholding interest as a Director of Mercantile Credit, and this I accepted. At that time Daniel Meinertzhagen of Lazards was non-executive Chairman – Lazards had an interest as well – and the Managing Director was Victor Adie (who I recall was an inveterate smoker; there were cigarette boxes all over the boardroom table).

Even Mercantile Credit was not immune to the general financial panic and increasingly its deposits were not renewed on maturity despite the Bank's 18 per cent shareholding interest. It was very disconcerting to note at every Board meeting, the company's life blood of deposits being eroded and removed. To cut a long story short, Barclays, because of its interest, became the recycler so to speak, and in due course the company fell into Barclays' hands and was taken over in 1975. Derek Wilde was then the Bank's senior General Manager, the one who had pioneered Barclaycard. He and Derek Weyer were two of the best Directors and General Managers I ever worked with in Barclays. Derek Wilde and I spent a considerable amount of time working out what price we should offer to pay for the Mercantile Credit shares held by outside shareholders, and eventually we came out with a figure which was accepted reluctantly although, truth to tell, they had little alternative. One final short comment on Mercantile Credit. As a Director I had perforce to buy a qualifying number of shares. For these I paid out of my own pocket. Naturally, by the time Barclays took the company over, they had fallen in value and so I was left out of pocket but the Bank did not reimburse me for the shortfall.

Meanwhile, while all this was going on, a number of our property companies lendings began to look sick. Rates were rising, values were falling and, although all our lendings were secured with a margin, these margins were falling as values fell, and we started every month to update our valuations to see where we were and more importantly whether we needed to make provisions – either precautionary or actual. We had, of course, the cushion of suspense interest, that is to say, when we knew we would not get the interest paid and therefore suspended it. Actual provisions were, of course, another matter, but by and large we had lent sensibly and had never got carried away. These provisions were not hugely significant and, as it happens, most of them were recovered by a later inflation of property values. However, it was not a happy experience. But I must have done something right because, in 1974 when I was still aged 43, I was appointed a Group Director of the Bank.

23

The 1975 British Everest South West Face Expedition

And now, as they say, for something completely different. You will, I know, remember the name of George Greenfield, the literary agent for the British Trans-Arctic Expedition and how we had together financed that expedition and in a similar way other smaller expeditions. George and I had become good friends, and not only was this because he was the doyen of the literary agents corps in London, counting among his clients such eminent names as David Niven, Enid Blyton, Sir Francis Chichester, Jilly Cooper, John Le Carré, Sidney Sheldon, George MacDonald Fraser and many others, but it was also because he had specialised either accidentally or on purpose in polar explorers, mountaineers and adventurers. I have mentioned Sir Francis Chichester but I should include Ed Hillary, Bunny Fuchs, Chris Bonington, Doug Scott, Ran Fiennes and Robin Knox-Johnston. So we had a natural friendship and mutual interest.

Today it seems not only that everybody knows about Mount Everest, but also that a large number of people have climbed it via the normal South Col route. But not all that many people have heard about the South West Face route, which I believe has only once been climbed successfully, and that was in 1975. Prior to 1975, there had been a Japanese reconnaissance expedition in 1969, followed by another expedition in 1970, an international expedition in 1971, Chris Bonington's expedition in 1972, and another Japanese expedition in 1973, but none had been successful. Both the 1972 and the 1973 expeditions reached the height of 27,300 feet, but were not able to establish camp there. So there had been five strong expeditions which had all tried the South West Face route and all had failed. All these expeditions had been stopped at more or less the same place, the foot of the 'Rock Band' which is a wall of rock stretching across the face of Everest with its base at 27,300 feet.

It was in early December 1973 that Mike Cheney, who ran a trekking business called Mountain Travel in Kathmandu, sent a cable to Chris Bonington. Mountain Travel had been founded by Jimmy Roberts and he had been the leader of the first Himalayan expedition to Annapurna II in 1960. Mike Cheney had always been the backroom boy, doing all the detailed work of arranging documentation, booking Sherpas and porters and getting equipment through Nepalese Customs. This cable read: 'Canadians cancelled for Autumn 1975. Do you want to apply? Reply urgent. Cheney'.

It was a difficult decision for Chris. In a significant sense it was the wrong time of the year. He had already found that it could be almost too cold and windy to climb the South West Face in the autumn and he was hesitant, not only because of the weather conditions and the problems of leadership and organisation, but also because of the money needed to finance a large expedition to climb a route where success seemed very unlikely.

Nevertheless, Chris found it impossible to turn down this opportunity and so therefore applied for the slot in the autumn of 1975. Mike Cheney pushed his cause in Kathmandu and so did the Foreign Office. In April 1974, very much to his surprise, he received permission from the Nepalese Government and a cable confirming this reached him when he was staying at the Indian Officers' Club in Delhi en route to the Garhwal Himalaya.

Even so, Chris was cautious in his reply, insisting that before he made a firm decision he had first to find a single sponsor to fund the cost, and this seemed to him virtually impossible. On his return from the Garhwal Himalaya, where he had been heartened by his success, he telephoned George Greenfield to see if he could help. When Chris told George of the likely cost – in excess of £100,000 – he winced, but then made the suggestion that they should approach me (we were all mutual friends) as a director of Barclays Bank.

We all met together in my office in Pall Mall. Chris had prepared a paper for me on his chances of success and the probable cost. I was, as usual, sympathetic but non-committal, but I agreed to take the proposal to the Chairman, Anthony Tuke. I cannot now find my letter to the Chairman but he, in his turn, took it to the General

Management Committee of Barclays Bank International with his full recommendation, and it was agreed. The story I heard afterwards was that the General Managers had recently turned down his proposal for sponsoring a cricket team and they did not want the Chairman to be turned down twice. In my letter to the Chairman I had also made the point that it was an underwriting rather than a sponsorship, in the sense that all the media rights, books and television rights worldwide would be assigned to the Bank and that actually, provided the expedition was successful (a huge proviso because most of the climbers did not rate their chances at all high – well below 50 per cent) then the Bank could make a surplus and that surplus should be donated to the Mount Everest Foundation. It was, of course, an open-ended underwriting: the Bank could not back out if costs went seriously over budget.

Chris was forever afterwards enormously grateful for my conviction and enthusiasm for the expedition but, of course, I told him that at the end of the day it was Anthony Tuke's decision, not mine. We announced our support for the expedition on 18th October 1974, at a press conference at 54 Lombard Street, and I have to say we were rather taken back by the number of questions and comments as to why the Bank was undertaking this commitment. There were comments as to how the Bank could possibly justify spending so much money on such a pointless venture, which seemed to have little chance of success, at a time of grave financial and economic crisis. All these were, in a sense, fair comments, but I had not bargained for the number of letters from customers who had been refused overdraft facilities, asking how the Bank could justify refusing them when they had just given this mountaineering expedition so much money. The word 'given' was not, of course, correct – although it would be more correct if the expedition failed and one or more climbers died in the attempt. All that would take some explaining to an increasingly destructive and sceptical press, let alone frustrated customers.

I preferred to look at it all in a positive, constructive light. I had no idea, nor did anybody else, whether the expedition would be successful but I would do everything to ensure that it was successful and that my conscience should be absolutely clear in this respect. Curiously enough I cannot recall my having serious doubts about the climb. If I had had, I do not think I would have stuck my head out so high above the parapet.

The next stage was for Chris to select his climbers and for us to establish a Committee of Management in view of the size of the enterprise. Lord Hunt, who had been the leader of the first successful British Everest Expedition in 1953, agreed to be Chairman, Sir Jack Longland, who had been on Everest before the war, also agreed to join the committee and so did Ian McNaught Davis, Colonel Wylie who had also been on Everest, Doug Scott, who was there to represent the feelings of the expedition members, and myself. It was a workable size.

The first meeting of this committee was held in my office (as were all subsequent meetings), on 26th September 1974. Chris proposed the names of the lead climbers and the support climbers. They all had responsibilities. Martin Boysen was in charge of the food; Peter Boardman, communications; Mick Burke, mountain cameraman; Paul Braithwaite, equipment; Nick Estcourt, treasurer and insurance; Doug Scott shared the responsibility for equipment with Paul Braithwaite. Charles Clarke was the doctor, Dave Clark the equipment organiser, Mike Cheney organisation in Nepal and base camp manager, Ronnie Richards transport and Mike Thompson food organiser. Then Chris proposed the names of the three main Sherpas – Pertemba as the sirdar, An Phu the climbing sirdar and Phurkippa as the Ice Fall sirdar. In addition there were to be 32 high-altitude Sherpas, 15 Ice Fall Sherpas, 4 mail runners and a various assortment of cook boys and liaison officers.

We agreed an outline programme of events and a timetable. We agreed the assault rations, the advance base camp rations, the base camp rations and what we called 'goodies', that is, Fortnum & Mason hampers, hams and bacon. We had an initial stab at the budget, which came out at £96,250. This included a figure of £32,000 for Sherpas, local transport and food in Nepal, £8,000 for insurance, £5,000 for oxygen and a contingency allowance of £10,000.

Meanwhile George Greenfield, who attended most committee meetings, reported to us on media contacts which he had started to negotiate. As it happened the BBC, Yorkshire and Granada Television expressed interest; so did the *Times*, *Observer* and *Telegraph* for the newspaper news and feature rights; whilst for the book rights, Heinemann, Michael Joseph and Hodder & Stoughton wanted to bid for these. In the end Hodder & Stoughton got the contract. That left foreign book rights and overseas newspapers rights, but we decided to leave these for the time being.

In very general terms my experience with the media was to arrange for a minimum guaranteed payment, or advances in the case of book rights with an additional, substantial, if possible, bonus if the expedition was successful. We also had to consider the newspapers and television rights in the context of those organisations agreeing to publicise the Bank, and I remember we noted that the BBC can sometimes be 'very sticky' when mentioning the names of sponsors. Personally speaking, I intensely disliked the use of the word 'sponsors', and I would have preferred the usage of the word 'underwriting'. I was extremely sensitive to the possibility that, in the event of a climber being killed – and one was, namely Mick Burke the BBC cameraman – the Bank would be accused of, in a sense, sponsoring his death. Perhaps I was too sensitive on this point. Meanwhile preparations started going ahead: food, ration lists, oxygen equipment, transport, contract terms with members of the expedition, insurance cover (which was, for instance, obligatory for the liaison officers and all the porters) – the list was endless and all this occupied a great deal of time.

In February 1975 we had an expedition 'Meet' at the Beech Hill Hotel at Windermere. All the members of the committee were there and so were all the climbers, together with Chris Ralling and Ned Kelly representing the BBC film team. So also was Bob Stoodley. Now Bob was the chairman of Manchester Garages and he played a key part in organising the transport for the expedition. It had been decided in November 1974 that the expedition equipment was going to have to be transported overland to Kathmandu. Bob had agreed with Chris that he should undertake this. He was ideally suited for the job and he threw himself into it with quite astonishing enthusiasm. He told us of the deal he had arranged with Godfrey Davis, the vehicle hire company, whereby the Ford Motor Company, via Godfrey Davis, had agreed to supply two 16-ton heavy-duty trucks, suitably modified for driving overland to Nepal, which would each carry a load of 10 tons – all for the total cost of £1,000. All this in return for full publicity, and so this offer was gratefully agreed.

The journey route for the transport was also agreed, and for those of you who might be interested – I certainly was – the route which was nearly 7,000 miles was as follows: London – Zeebrugge – Brussels – Nuremberg – Graz – Belgrade – Sofia – Istanbul – Ankara – Sivas – Erzurum – Tabriz – Teheran – Masshad – Herat

– Kandahar – Kabul – Rawalpindi – Lahore – Delhi – Cawnpore – Benares – Rexaul – Birganj – Kathmandu.

In all, 12 countries were traversed and the journey took three and a half weeks. The 6.2-litre lorries each averaged 5.9 miles per gallon at a fuel cost of 3p per mile. Diesel costs ranged from 70p a gallon in Germany to 6p a gallon in Iran. The trucks departed from Barclays Bank, 33 Old Broad Street, London, on 9th April. I took the children to see them off and I photographed them all in the driver's cabin. It was an emotional send-off. They reached Kathmandu on 3rd May: Nanny's seventieth birthday! It was a magnificent effort and grateful thanks are due evermore to Bob Stoodley.

When the lorries reached Kathmandu, they were unloaded in Mike Cheney's garden and the next three weeks were spent in shuttling the loads to the airport and waiting for the right kind of weather to fly the planes into Lukla, and from there ferrying them by Sherpa porters to Khunde. All this was arranged by Mike Cheney working through the new Sherpa Co-operative, which he had helped them form, leaving them responsible for the contracts with the light aircraft, and the organisation and payment of porters from Lukla to Khunde.

On 29th July 1975, the expedition team left London by Air India for Delhi. Lord Hunt and I were there to see them off and we were all granted permission to stand on the tarmac at the foot of this huge Air India jumbo jet to be photographed. I recently had another look at this photograph, and was sad to note how many of the climbers in that photograph had been killed in accidents.

All this was an exhilarating time for me, but something else also intrigued and exhilarated me, and that was the Air India jumbo jet. In a very curious way there was a whiff of mystery, excitement and intrigue in the interior of that aircraft. There was a different smell, the smell of incense. There was a different sound, the sound of the raga, and then, of course, there were the lovely Indian stewardesses in their saris. It was a witching moment and it was to alter my life.

Before he left for Kathmandu, Chris told us he wanted to formulate a policy with regard to visitors to base camp and he suggested that if friends or wives of the team arrived at base camp, they would be welcome for a couple of days and would then be asked to move on. If wives or friends arrived towards the end of the expedition, they would be welcome to join the expedition and accompany it back. I asked Chris whether that included myself and perhaps my wife, Diana, and he replied, 'Yes, of course'. So I made up my mind to do precisely that.

In this chronicle I have no wish to describe the expedition in detail – in any case you can read that in Chris's book *Everest the Hard Way – the First Ascent of the South West Face* – but I do just want to mention a few highlights so that you can keep them in your mind.

In August 1975, the expedition walked in from Kathmandu to Khunde to assist acclimatisation. On 21st August Nick Estcourt and Dougal Haston reached and sited base camp, with the rest of the team arriving the following day. Later that month good progress was made with the ice-fall and Camp 1 was established.

On 2nd September 1975, Camp 2 was established at a height of 21,800 feet and the South West Face was stood upon four days later. Camp 3 was established at a height of 23,000 feet. Camp 4 was established at a lower point than intended as it was the last spot giving real protection from avalanches and rock falls from above. The expedition was by now well ahead of schedule. Camp 5 was established at 25,000 feet and a fixed rope was run up to the foot of the left-hand gully leading up into the Rock Band.

On 20th September the problem of climbing the 1,000-foot-high Rock Band, the main obstacle on the South West Face, was solved following the discovery of a ramp that led out of the deep cut gully towards the top of the Band. Two days later Camp 6 was established and next day Dougal Haston and Doug Scott prepared for the first assault on the Summit, running 1,500 feet of fixed rope across the Upper Ice Field towards the South Summit Gully.

Next day, 24th September, they reached the Summit at 1800 hours, having bivouacked and brewed up at the South Summit. They bivouacked on the way down and had what they described as the coldest bivouac of their lives. Two days later – 26th September – a second attempt was made by Peter Boardman, Sherpa Pertemba, Martin Boysen and Mick Burke. Boysen turned back as one of his crampons had fallen off; Boardman and Pertemba went on without difficulty to the Summit. As they descended they were surprised to see Mick continuing on up on his own.

It is assumed he went on to the Summit. Boardman and Pertemba waited for him at the South Summit before attempting the long traverse back to Camp 6. They waited for him for some time. Meanwhile the weather deteriorated with violent gale conditions and a white-out. Mick did not arrive and they assumed he must have slipped on the way down in the white-out. Boardman and Pertemba managed to get safely back to camp after taking the agonising decision to continue down. The next day the weather was impossible and there was, therefore, no question of a search being undertaken and in the interests of safety, which was now paramount, Chris ordered the mountain to be cleared. By 30th September all the expedition was back in base camp, by 11th October they were all back in Kathmandu and on 17th October we all flew back to London.

Now you will recall that Chris had told me we would be very welcome to climb up to base camp and, of course, having spent such a huge amount of time and effort in helping with the expedition, I was very keen to go. But, of course, somehow it had to fit in with all my other duties and responsibilities. Accordingly I went to the Chairman of the Bank, Anthony Tuke, and told him of my desire. He was very sympathetic but said that if the Bank was going to pay, which it was, I would have to work in India before I went up the mountain. Accordingly it was arranged that, as a Director of the Bank, I would go out to assist the line manager with his Indian business. Thus the purpose of this trip was to foster and develop existing banking relationships, to establish new ones and investigate the current economic and political conditions in India. In those days we had no presence in India, and all we had were correspondent banking relationships, which were maintained by the Chief Foreign Branch.

Now, I feel I owe my readers some sort of explanation as to why Barclays had no presence in India nor, indeed, east of Suez. Here I had always been brought up to believe – and I think it must be true – that soon after Barclays established Barclays Bank (Dominion, Colonial & Overseas) – formed, as I have mentioned, from the Colonial Bank, the Anglo-Egyptian Bank and the National Bank of South Africa – that some sort of agreement was made with the Chartered Bank. This agreement was to the effect that Barclays would concentrate on the West Indies, Africa and the Levant, allowing the Chartered Bank to concentrate on all the territories east of Suez. Here it must be mentioned that nearly all these countries were members of the British Empire. This line was always described to me as the equivalent of a banking papal line. It worked, but whereas the African territories following independence went backward, the Asian territories went forward. Barclays was very late into Asia and only started in the 1970s or even later. It had been the case that Barclays had bought an interest in the Chartered Bank in 1959. It was particularly interested in its strong Indian branch network but found this important interest more or less valueless when this merged with the Standard Bank in 1969; the Bank then sold its holding.

Meanwhile, although the Chairman had given his agreement in principle to the trip, Tim Bevan who was then Vice-Chairman asked me to cut it short, as the banking and property crisis was in full swing and he wanted me to be here rather than there travelling through India and Nepal and climbing on Everest. So the India trip was reduced to one week and the Nepal trip from four weeks to three weeks. I had no alternative but to agree, although I pointed out that part of the Nepal trip represented a major part of my holiday entitlement.

So on 20th September 1975, laden with all our Everest equipment as well as all our tropical clothes – mercifully we were travelling first class – we took the British Airways night flight to Bombay; that is to say, myself, Diana and Bill Wedge, the Chief Foreign Branch Manager. How exciting it all was – my first visit to the subcontinent. We arrived in Bombay at 6.30 in the morning.

Now I would like to make a short digression and tell you a little about banking in India at that time. In spite of its huge economic problems, India did actually provide us with some business. There were 16 nationalised banks, all of whom competed vigorously with each other, and there were a number of private banks who were challenging the nationalised banks and who appeared to us to be making excellent progress. Some of them had foreign exchange licences and several more were about to enter the international field. Our visit provided us with the opportunity of calling on most of these with a view to a banking relationship with Barclays.

The Government of India used the banks comprehensively to achieve its social objectives and, although some concessions had recently been made, lendings had to be mainly concentrated on agriculture and small-scale industry where concessionary interest rates applied. Branches had to open in rural areas as quickly as possible with, I recall, a target of 6,000 a year – an enormous number. Rates of interest for what the Indians called the priority sector were low (4 per cent in some cases) but these loans were refinanceable with the Reserve Bank of India. Costs, of course, were high and I learned with interest that a great many of the loans to farmers were for as little as 200 rupees – say £10 then. Of course, for the banks to make a profit the larger borrowers in the private sector were charged up to 18 per cent or 19 per cent, and to judge by the number and apparent prosperity of the industrialists we met, this did not seem a problem. Most of the banks had very low ratios of capital and reserves to deposits, sometimes as low as 1 per cent, which would frighten most of us. On the other hand a 40 per cent liquidity ratio was required, and hidden reserves were allowed.

The one thing they all seemed to ask us for were loans for shipping under Indian bank guarantees, underwritten by the Government, and we promised to look at some of these proposals. Meanwhile we also looked at the possibilities of opening a branch in India, something which later became very dear to my heart, but at that time the bureaucracy and the regulatory environment was so severe and the projected costs so high that it seemed that such a branch would take an extremely long time to get into profit. But the possibility was kept on the agenda.

When we got out of the plane we had our first sniff of India – a smell one can never forget – and then we entered the airport. Indian airports in those days were indescribably awful and the heat and the smell and the humidity I can only describe as appalling. We took a taxi into the centre of the city – the driver never for one moment took his hand off the horn. There were no traffic rules, hardly any traffic lights, and even if there were, nobody paid much attention to them. There were cows, children, rickshaws, bullocks, carts, bicycles, pedestrians and buses wandering all over the streets and roads, and everywhere there were slums, people sleeping on the pavements, people searching the rubbish tips, people hauling huge loads, people begging, all competing to somehow survive in an atmosphere giving rise to severe doubts about the sewage system (if it did indeed exist). I was overwhelmed by the sheer number of people everywhere and our temporary white isolation from all these dark faces in our Ambassador car. And woe betide you if you have an accident as it is extremely likely that the crowd will assume its your fault and will go for you.

This once happened to me in Calcutta many years later. I had been to visit the Governor of West Bengal in Raj Bhavan – Government House, built by Lord Wellesley in around 1800 at the then huge cost of £70,000 – and I was on my way back to the Tollygunge Club in southern Calcutta. I was in a Land Rover driven by a Gurkha. At the roundabout at the northern end of the Maidan, where there was a bus stop with a large crowd of Bengalis waiting for the buses to come, a man on a scooter clipped the Land Rover and fell off. The bus stop crowd immediately assumed it was our fault – which it was not – and surged towards the Land Rover and in a moment they were all over the car on the roof and on the bonnet everywhere trying to get hold of me, but probably more particularly the Nepali driver, who should not have stopped. For a time, and it seemed a very long time, he was frozen by fear into immobility. I had to kick him very hard and I told him to drive like hell, which he did with bodies flying off the bonnet and roof. A policeman tried to stop us but we went straight past him and eventually got to Chowringhee, where I got out of the car and told the driver to get back to the club. I did not want to be in the car if the police stopped it. So the answer is that, if you have an accident, do not stop and only report it when you arrive at a police checkpoint. And essentially this advice holds good in most Eastern countries.

Later that morning we eventually arrived at the Taj Hotel, next to the Gateway of India monument. It was an oasis. We stayed in the Old Wing and from one window of our bedroom we looked out on the luxury swimming pool of the hotel and from the other window we looked out onto something completely different. This was a ruined block of flats at the top of which we saw an old woman coming out to hang her laundry on the balcony. Below her in the street were men in turbans and robes either squatting on the ground or sleeping on the pavements, or lighting little fires on which they were cooking their rice.

That evening we were collected by a most lovely Parsee girl in an equally lovely sari and were taken by her driver to her parents' apartment. Her father was the Chairman of one of the nationalised banks. It was a very modest apartment – we went straight into the front reception room. On one side was a settee, a TV and a coffee table, and on the other side of this room was a dining table and a huge refrigerator, which they had bought from England – nothing else. After two hours or more of drinking whisky and conversing, supper was served buffet-style as is common in India. And it was interesting to talk to the daughters, both of whom were brilliant as well as beautiful: one had just taken a degree in London and the other was studying English at the University of Bombay with a view to going to law school. In general, in those days, I was enormously impressed with the Indian standard of education for girls. I think almost without exception during my 30 years of working in India, the girls I met had all been to university or were going on to Indian, American or British universities. We left at midnight and they gave me a beautiful pair of cuff-links and Diana a lovely straw shoulder bag. We were overwhelmed.

The following day I worked, but we were able to fit in a visit to the Tower of Silence which is where the Parsees bring their dead. They place the bodies in one of three towers which are open to the sky. The bodies are, of course, naked. Within half an hour the vultures pick the bones clean, and these are then burnt to a fine ash. The Parsees believe that you must not defile the elements – earth, fire, water and air – and so it is very much dust to dust, ashes to ashes. Of course, I could go on a huge digression about the Parsees and the Zoroastrians who originally, as the name implies, came from Persia, but I will leave you, dear reader, to research all this yourself. But one matter I must mention is that the Parsees, apart from being highly religious and devout as well as commercial – very much like, in fact, my Tritton family – had also been great shipbuilders for the British Navy, and many ships were constructed by them in Bombay. Nowadays the Parsees have a problem and the problem is some sort of epidemic among vultures which kills them – meaning, of course, there is a profound shortage of vultures to peck the bones.

But enough of the Parsees for the moment. There were endless engagements, commercial discussions with the Chairmen of the major banks, discussions with the Governor of the Reserve Bank of India – equivalent to the Bank of England – discussions with the British Deputy High Commissioners, and dinners. So many dinners, at which the Indian wives stood out in their beautiful saris, lovely jewels, lovely dark hair and, as I have mentioned before, all highly intelligent, cosmopolitan, well travelled and well read – somehow the European women at these dinner engagements always looked pale and dowdy and badly dressed, it was an astonishing comparison. On the other hand, they were all overwhelmed by Diana, tall, beautiful, blond and a graduate of the University of California, Los Angeles. The men seemed to lust after her, while I lusted after these beautiful women.

I always remember when many years later Prince Charles and Princess Diana came on an official visit to India, and it was not successful as their marriage was breaking up at the time. Everyone remembers the sad picture of Princess Diana sitting alone and forlorn at the Taj Mahal – a deliberate photograph to bring attention to herself. Prince Charles had gone up to Kathmandu.

Now it so happened on that trip she had agreed to come to Calcutta, where I was working with quite a number of young restorers and conservators at the Victoria Memorial Hall there. I had very much wanted to introduce these young restorers and conservators to her, but she refused. However, later one day, the Indians gave a reception for her and now I cannot remember where, but it was somewhere in Calcutta. She arrived in a sleeveless white blouse and a rather short black skirt and, I always remember, no stockings; it was, of course, as usual extremely hot and humid in Calcutta and there was no air-conditioning – I think the electricity supply had failed, a familiar occurrence in those days. The contrast between the Indian women in their beautiful saris, heavily bejewelled, looking beautiful, cool and elegant, and Princess Diana perspiring, with her long white bare legs was surprising. And the other astonishing fact was that all the Indian women had been to university, whereas, I believe, Princess Diana had only attained an E in her O levels for domestic economy. I never really knew what domestic economy means, but it must mean housework and cooking. I found the contrast deeply upsetting, particularly bearing in mind that in the olden days if she had become Queen, she would also have been Empress of India, but in no way would she have matched up to these Indian subjects.

And while writing about Indian subjects of the Crown, I remember meeting a number of older high-caste women at parties in Delhi, Calcutta and Bombay who had experienced life under the Raj and, again, these women were highly intelligent. Sometimes I used to ask them about their experiences, because I have never ever felt superior to an Indian, although I have often felt uncomfortable with Africans. These Indian women nearly always told me that, by and large, the British officers were polite and courteous, but always rather distant as if they felt embarrassed and uncomfortable talking with them. They did not have much time for the non-commissioned-officers' wives, who they said were often fat and ugly, coarse, rude and uneducated. In a way such a comment is not surprising coming from high-caste women, but a number of them did say that if there had been no other reason for India to gain its independence, it would have been to get rid of these women.

On 25th September we flew from Bombay to Delhi in a very cramped and shaky Boeing 737 of Indian Airlines. There were turbans all around us, smells of spice and saffron, and tinkling Indian raga music, which I have always liked. It has always been a never-ending surprise to me how reluctant the Indian Government has been to invest in new aeroplanes, not only for Indian Airlines, the domestic airline but also for Air India, the international carrier, with the result that now private airlines are taking much of their market. Air India could be, and at one stage was, a highly acclaimed airline, but it allowed itself, or rather the Government allowed it, to become almost a has-been compared with Singapore Airlines and British Airways which, freed from the yoke of government, have been remarkably successful. The same applies to Indian Airports which are run by the Government Airports Authority. Here again most of these airports are 'Abandon hope all ye who enter here' places and remain monuments to Nehru's statist and socialist politics whereby nearly everything was owned and managed, or rather mismanaged, by the Government. It is only since 1991 when India ran out of foreign exchange reserves that the policy began to change, and it is now catching up fast.

In Delhi we were treated to a rapturous welcome. We were garlanded, Diana was given a huge bouquet of flowers, the Central Bank of India's Chairman was there to meet us with his wife, and we were provided with two AC (air-conditioned) Ambassador cars which took us to the huge Ashoka Hotel. The Ashoka Hotel was Government owned and when we first entered the colossal foyer there was an additional smell which I did not at first recognise. It was, however, urine – not a good start.

Once again a busy round of business visits, commercial lunches and dinners commenced, but one day we were invited to drive down to Agra for the day to see the Taj Mahal. The journey there was not without incident. The first test was driving long distance on an Indian road. This road started off as a sort of motorway, what we would call a dual carriageway, but there were no dual carriageway rules. The Indian drivers, particularly those of the lorries and buses, used all four lanes for both directions so it was all quite exciting, but nerve-wracking for Diana who was suffering from a combined Bombay and Delhi belly.

The Taj Mahal is astonishing and it exhausts all adjectives. Its builder, Shah Jahan, had been married twice before he met Mumtaz and neither of these two wives bore him children, but the beautiful Mumtaz gave him 14. Sadly, she died in childbirth at the age of 37. Before dying she made two requests to Shah Jahan: the first was that he would never marry again, and the second was that he should build her a tomb that all the world would come to see. He fulfilled both her wishes, but died a prisoner of his son.

Like Bombay, Delhi was frenetic – we met most of the elite of India, businessmen, bankers, Government ministers. Everyone was enormously kind to us, incredibly helpful, and invariably courteous and polite. I seemed to be given a status far beyond what I deserved, but it was all genuine and they all seemed to be pleased that a Director of the Bank should have come to India and I returned every year and sometimes several times a year.

Three days later we were up at five o'clock in the morning to catch the Royal Nepali Airlines' only jet aircraft, a Boeing 737 flight to Kathmandu. Emigration from Delhi was a nightmare and the flight was delayed due to bad weather – it had been a late monsoon.

Diana was still ill with her Delhi belly and I went down with it between the departure lounge and the aircraft, while I was walking towards it. All very difficult and embarrassing but thank heavens after the heat of the tarmac, the plane's air conditioning revived me, although I spent most of the flight in the loo. But not all, and through the monsoon clouds I was able to catch a glimpse of the Terai and some of the Himalayan peaks. We touched down at the airport; it was midday and the first thing we heard was that four climbers had reached the Summit – I was almost too late.

In those days in 1975 Nepal was charming and tranquil, a veritable Shangri La, but all this changed in later years and I am glad we got there before it changed. Of course, it changed for the worst, and for that a large part of the blame attaches itself to the Nepali Royal Family, particularly recently.

Now, before we move on, I want to tell you a very short story about this one and only Royal Nepal Airlines Boeing 737 jet aircraft. On our return from Everest whilst we were staying in the Shankar Hotel a festival of some sort took place, which seemed entirely to consist of cutting the throats of goats. You will remember that I experienced something similar when I was rescued in Malaya from my ambushed train by a company of Gurkhas and witnessed a mass slaughter of goats. Now it so happened that I had to go down to the airport, and there was the Royal Nepali jet sitting on the runway splattered with blood. I asked why, and the answer was that this was an additional insurance protection in case the Lloyds of London insurance of the aircraft was somehow deficient!

Once again we met businessmen, bankers, Government ministers. Once again we were given luncheons and dinners. Once we were driven out of the valley into the nearby hills. It was a beautiful warm day, cooler in the hills with all the green rice terraces around us. Suddenly we saw a Hercules 130 aircraft flying overhead from which a company of Nepali Gurkha paratroopers were jumping out. To my astonished amazement, when the parachutes opened, the Gurkhas started ascending rather than descending and some went so high that we lost sight of them. Did they come down eventually? Yes, of course they did, but the upward lifting thermals were exceptionally strong that day; I have never seen such a sight again before or since.

In Kathmandu we stayed at the wonderful Soaltee Oberoi Hotel. There we met two of my greatest friends, Rex and Pansy Cooper – he had been with the Seaforth Highlanders in Malaya and his wife Pansy's brother was Alec Mackintosh, who had also been in the Seaforth. You may remember it was at Rex's brother's house in Ennismore Garden Mews that I gave my champagne twenty-first birthday party before departing for the Antarctic. I believe they got engaged at around about that time. They had been trekking in the Himalayas and were about to depart for the UK.

There was a huge amount to do in Kathmandu. We were assigned a Sherpa, Ang Kami; we went to Mike Cheney's house to drop off and collect supplies; we went to Mountain Travel; we went to the airport to meet George Greenfield but he was not on the plane; we applied for a trekking permit at the Immigration Office, which should also have had a sign over the doorway stating 'Abandon hope all ye who enter here'. I collected the money for the Sherpas who had been promised a bonus if the Summit was reached, and we went to a dinner organised by the Nepal Rastra Bank at the Yak and Yeti Hotel which was run by a White Russian, Boris Lissanovich.

Boris was an enigmatic and quite extraordinary character. His family came from Odessa on the Black Sea. He was the youngest of four sons who had gone into the Imperial Navy. His father had a home on the outskirts of Odessa between the racecourse and the cadet school. He also had a country home where he bred racehorses. At the age of nine Boris went to the Cadet School and four years later the Russian Revolution began. The Reds captured Odessa in 1917, but Boris's family were able to escape, and crossing Rumania and the Balkans they managed to get to Warsaw, having ridden all the way. However, no sooner had they reached Warsaw when they were advised that Odessa had been liberated by the White Army. So they returned, but no sooner had they returned, than the Reds reoccupied the City. Boris was a member of the Defence Corps and was also a cadet of the Imperial Army, so he could expect no mercy. He had to escape.

Now it so happened that a relative was the ballet mistress at the Odessa Opera House. She arranged for him to have an alibi – he became a member of the corps de ballet of the Opera House, and he was given a certificate to that effect. He thus became a ballet dancer and after many privations and difficulties he managed to receive a contract to dance at the Alhambra Theatre in Paris. He became a ballet dancer not because he wanted to, but because it was the only means of securing food in revolutionary Odessa. He toured France and Germany and secured a contract with the Theatre Romantique Russe, which was headed by Boris Romanoff who was to become the ballet master at the Metropolitan in New York. Back in Paris, after a stint as a works foreman in the Renault automobile works to supplement his pay, he heard that Diaghilev was in town and importuned to be auditioned by the grand master at the Sarah Bernhardt Theatre. So good was he that Diaghilev took him on. This became Boris's life, and until Diaghilev's death he was a member of one of the most distinguished ballet companies of all times. With his death the Ballet Russe was disbanded and Boris was out of a job. But he survived and danced at La Scala in Milan and at the Lyceum in London, and began co-starring with Diana Manners (Lady Diana Duff-Cooper), daughter of the Duke of Rutland.

The British now failed to renew his working permit, and with his wife Kira he went to entertain clients of the Taj Hotel in Bombay and then went on to Burma, China, Java and Ceylon, but it was in Calcutta that he founded the famous 300 Club – 300 to demonstrate that it was even more elite than the 400 Club in London. The club was financed and supported by the Maharajah of Cooch Behar and was a huge success.

But then the war came. In 1942 came the 'Quit India' riots and Boris, who was then in Simla, returned to Calcutta by rail through a country devastated by the riots. After the Maharajah died, the club rather fell apart and Boris took off for Kathmandu where he took over an old palace and ran it as the Royal Hotel. He was always in and out of prison for something or other, but he survived, and when we arrived in Kathmandu in 1975 he was running his restaurant and bar called the Yak and Yeti and there he used to regale us with stories of the old days, as he called them.

The barman at the 300 Club was John Freddie Bowles, who had formerly been the barman in the Rivoli Bar in the Ritz Hotel in London. He had been 'pinched' by the Maharajah of Cooch Behar who loved his famous martinis. When the 300 Club closed, he also went to Kathmandu where he became the barman at the Soaltee Oberoi Hotel where we stayed. John Freddie was a wonderful man, a great poet, and he became passionately involved in the expedition, so much so that when we left we gave him a signed photograph of all the members of the expedition.

It was at a bankers' dinner in Kathmandu that news came to me that Mick Burke had been killed between the Summit and the South Summit, and I left immediately. I was carrying letters for him from his wife. The next day, 30th September, I was woken very early with the news that Hamish MacInnes, one of the climbers, was being helicoptered off the mountain. I went straight down to the airport to see how he was. What had happened was that on the climb up from Camp 4 to Camp 5 he had been overwhelmed by a powder snow avalanche. He told me it was like breathing fine, white smoke, which went straight down into his lungs and there melted, so the sensation was one of drowning, which of course it was. In the end he decided to leave the expedition.

Later that day I collected our trekking permits and various pills. The following day, 1st October, we got up at four o'clock in the morning to catch our Twin Otter flight to Lukla. Lukla was where we would be meeting our Sherpa guides and porters who would carry all our tents and cooking equipment. But the flight was cancelled due to bad weather. We returned to Soaltee. Later that day two members of the BBC film crew were helicoptered in from the mountain suffering from frostbite and they came with mail for us from Chris. Their names were Chris Ralling and Ned Kelly and they were both splendid men and fine film producers. Ned Kelly specialised in mountain photography and had been on the Everest International Expedition four years earlier. Chris Ralling specialised in producing television documentary films and was an experienced climber and ski mountaineer. In the end they produced the finest film of an Everest expedition that I have ever seen and it was shown throughout the world. (And, as a footnote, you will remember that I had got assigned to the bank the film and the television rights to this film.)

2nd October 1975 was my forty-fourth birthday. Up once again at 4 a.m. and to the airport; the flight was cancelled. And the same thing happened the next day. By this time we were getting extremely irritated and, by way of diversion, we went to see a seventeenth-century temple of Kali, about an hour's drive from Kathmandu. It was one of the most sinister and evil places I have ever visited. Here chickens and goats were regularly sacrificed and the blood smeared over the Kali images – it was truly barbaric.

The next morning once again we were up at 4 a.m. to go to the airport and this time we took off. They said it would be a half-hour flight. We climbed above the clouds and there towering above us were the Himalayas, snow-covered, pristine and beautiful. And below us was Lukla, but we could not land – the cloud was too thick and, even at that time in the morning, the katabatic winds were too strong. So it was back to Kathmandu, but not back to the Soaltee which was now fully booked. So we moved to the Shankar Hotel, an old Rana palace. We survived.

On our fifth day of trying to fly to Lukla, 5th October, we succeeded in getting onto the plane and we set off once again in our little Twin Otter, and this time we made it. The Lukla grass airstrip is inclined at quite a steep angle and the runway ends in a steep wall of rock so the pilot has to stop before he hits it, but as the plane is going uphill this is not too difficult. Taking off is more dangerous as the runway, going downhill, ends abruptly, overlooking a deep chasm of 1,000 feet or so. Thus the trick is to be airborne before you reach the chasm, but then the pilot has to turn very sharply to the left to avoid hitting the vertical wall of rock dead ahead! To add to the exclamation mark, if one was needed, several crashed aircraft which had been dragged off the runway littered both sides of the airstrip. But the landing was smooth. The Sherpas were there to meet us and so it was then up rucksacks and away to the north towards Tibet, the sun beating down on our heads, the Dudh Khosi river cascading and thundering down from the high glaciers. Then into the cool of the pine forests, the prayer-flags flying in the breeze, the lammergeyers soaring in the sky above us and all around the steep green closeness of this most lovely of valleys.

Everything had to be carried: food, tents, camping gear. I was ashamed to see our Sherpa girls, aged 12 or 13, putting a couple of full rucksacks into a wicker basket and then hoisting it onto their backs by means of a leather strap which they placed across their foreheads. They walked barefoot on the rough track and, as they did so, they leaned forward to take the weight on their heads and necks and all the time they smiled and giggled.

I would have liked to have thought we were in no hurry, but we were: to meet the climbers coming off the mountain. So quick had the climb been that they were two to three weeks ahead of plan and so they were coming down as we were going up, and our intention had been to meet them at base camp. So we were in a hurry, but the last thing you should be is in a hurry at that altitude and I was starting prematurely to get a bout of altitude sickness, which continued until I came off the mountain.

In reality the climb up was quite pleasant; we woke with the light and were given mugs of tea by the Sherpas. We had a light breakfast and broke camp with the Sherpas going quickly on in front of us to prepare lunch. A short rest, and then the Sherpas went on ahead again to find a convenient spot to pitch camp and light a fire. By the time we arrived the tents were pitched, the yakburgers and rice were cooked and ready and then, as the sun set, the temperature dropped like a stone and it was into our sleeping bags.

And so we moved on past the villages of Ghat and Phakding, across the swaying Hillary bridges, and then we started the steep 45-degree climb to Namche Bazaar. This took us nearly five hours and it was 20 steps up and sit down for five minutes or even longer on occasions. It was enlivened by the yaks coming down the track, loaded with goods and driven by traders from Tibet. They had come over one of the high passes between Nepal and Tibet, and as they trod down, their bells tinkled merrily and happily. And then on the climb up we suddenly saw for the first time the Summit of Everest in the distance, framed in a notch of closer mountains, with its eternal plume of snow drifting away from the Summit. The Sherpas went down on their knees, saying in a devout tone 'Sagarmatha, Sagarmatha', the region's name, holy to Sherpas. And then we were above the Dudh Khosi valley and over to the east we could see the great soaring peaks of Tamserku and Kantega, 22,000 feet high and big, and away to the north-east one of the most beautiful mountains in the world, Ama Dablam, and then to the north Lhotse, Everest and Nuptse. Along the track were the prayer-flags and the stupas, the yaks with their bells tinkling away, the lammergeyers soaring in the sky.

Finally we reached Namche Bazaar where we were going to encamp. But this was not to be because the entire expedition was higher up waiting for us, and they had sent Charles Clarke and Doug Scott down to take us up with Ang Kami, our personal Sherpa. Meanwhile a thick mist had come down, and Diana and I were exhausted. Diana even entreated a Tibetan trader to load me on to one of his yaks and take me north, but he demurred – he was also in a hurry. We nearly got lost; for Ang Kami it was a half-hour climb, for us and George Greenfield it took three hours before we reached Khumjung as it was getting dark and the mist was still down.

Chris Bonington came out to meet us and then we settled down, all 19 of us, in a large, red, box-like tent and were given a celebration dinner by the Sherpas: soup, mutton, three vegetables, jelly and cream, tea and coffee, and that most ghastly of all drinks, chang, a sort of thin milky-looking native drink which is quite alcoholic but which has a disgusting taste. Not for me, but nearly a gallon of it was drunk that night. After dinner we played Poker and then finally we retired to our down-filled sleeping bags. As I went to sleep I felt full of pride that the expedition had been successful and that, in my own way, I had helped make it all possible – and this was indeed how Chris inscribed his book to me.

Being part of an expedition, even though I was not on the

climbing team, is something peculiarly satisfying, and the atmosphere of camaraderie and shared experiences in an encampment in the high Himalayas was exhilarating. And, of course, I was popular with the Sherpas and porters as I had trudged up the mountain with their success bonus in nice new Nepali notes.

Next morning we were awoken at 5.45 a.m. with a mug of tea. We were racked with muscular pains in our legs, panting in the thin air, and I was struggling with an altitude sickness headache, so much so that Charles Clarke, the doctor, gave me a once-over looking for any signs of pulmonary or cerebral oedema which is common in the Khumbu valley, but there weren't any.

Now I want to sing the praises of one particular man: his name was Mike Cheney, the base camp manager, who was aged 46 and was director of Mountain Travel in Kathmandu. Mountain Travel was a trekking business which had been founded by Jimmy Roberts who had been the leader of the first Himalayan expedition to Annapurna in 1960, and had been deputy leader of Chris Bonington's Everest expedition in 1972.

Mike Cheney had always been the backroom boy, doing all the work of arranging documentation, booking porters and helping with clearing climbing equipment through Nepal customs. But Mike had never been a full member of an expedition. It was Mike who alerted Chris to the effect that the Canadians had cancelled their 1975 autumn booking of Everest. He asked Chris whether he wanted to apply, adding that a reply was urgent. And it was Mike who had superbly master-minded the organisation of the approach march to base camp. But Mike was not well – he had been in hospital only a few weeks before our arrival. He was very frail, but he was determined to join the approach march and so he did, starting several hours before everybody else and arriving in camp always the last. When I met up with him at Khumjung he was very grey, very frail and in severe pain. But Mike went all the way to base camp, organised and managed the camp with all its stores and equipment, and marched all the way back again to Khumjung from where he was portered down to the small airstrip at Syangboche above Namche Bazaar, on which a Pilatus Porter aircraft can land.

The last time I saw Mike Cheney was in Hammersmith Hospital. He was as usual full of enthusiasm and *joie de vivre*, looking forward to getting back to Kathmandu. There are some people who, as you journey through life, have a remarkable effect upon you.

In my view he was the great unsung hero of the expedition, for whom I had the greatest admiration and respect, not only for his brilliant management and organisation of the approach march and base camp, but also for his bravery and tenacity in fighting his continuous pain.

Although the bulk of the expedition was now on its way down, Chris decided with our full agreement to go back as far as we could in the time available and so we left Khumjung on a beautiful day and made the long ascent to Thyhangboche Monastery, past the stupas, past the prayer wheels, past the prayer-flags and past the yaks with their bells tinkling away, and all around us once again the huge peaks of Amadablam, Nuptse, Lhotse and Everest and, as always, the lammergeyers soaring and wheeling high in the sky. At the monastery we were introduced to the wizened old Buddhist Abbot, whose piety and benevolence were matched only by his commercial instinct for money.

We went on to Pangboche but decided that was the furthest we could go in the time available and so we returned to our encampment at Thyangboche above the Imja Kola river. That night we had rain which turned to snow in the early morning.

And now it was time to return. We had gone as far as we could and we were only a few miles short of the Khumbu glacier on which base camp is situated at 18,000 feet. We had an easy walk down to Phunki where the monks had established two waterwheels, except that the waterwheels were prayer wheels continuously turned by the water so as to avoid the necessity of manually turning them – a nice touch.

That evening we arrived at the Everest View Hotel. This had been built by the Japanese who had also built the nearby airstrip at Syangboche. It was very Japanese – the bedrooms had mats on the floor – and before we arrived there we had been told that instead of hot and cold water in every room, there was oxygen in every room for all those visitors suffering from altitude sickness. Its foundations were stone and all the rest of it was glass and wood. I say 'was', because some time later it burnt down. All the water had to be taken up in buckets every day from Khumjung by Sherpa girls and porters – this was not men's work.

We left after tea but in the meantime a thick mist had come down and the track was extremely narrow, with a 1,000-foot drop to our left. We came to a fork, but as we could not see which way to go, we climbed back to the hotel. Mercifully we found a Sherpa, and offered him 20 rupees to show us the way down to our new camp by the Syangboche airstrip. If we had taken the left fork, which was the one we would have preferred, we would either have gone down to Namche or gone over the edge. So in the end we found our camp.

The reason for the site of this camp was that it was adjacent to the airstrip and we would not have to move far when a plane did eventually arrive and if we could get on to it, as a queue had formed. We had no commissary tent, only a junior cook, and we had to eat outside around a fire over which were placed two cauldrons. So there we sat day after day, night after night, waiting for a flight and waiting for the thick cloud to clear.

Once we saw a helicopter making its way to the hotel – someone had gone down with acute altitude sickness and had to be got down to Kathmandu. The pilot must have been incredibly brave, flying at 15,000 feet in virtually nil visibility with mountains all about him. But he saw a small hole in the cloud, got hold of the patient and then had to wait for another hole to appear. We all laughed. Here was a tourist paying the hotel $100 a night and then having to pay $1,000 for a rescue helicopter.

On 11th October we were still encamped at Syangboche. Two small planes did get in, but they were taken by the hotel people. Our plane, which should have arrived, had been sent elsewhere. And so we stayed yet another day and night, but the following day we were advised that a Twin Otter would be waiting for us at Lukla and that a special UNICEF Pilatus Porter, piloted by the famous Swiss aviator Emil Wick, would fly us down to Lukla. Beside the pilot it could only take four passengers, the rest of the space being taken up with expedition gear. We shoved our gear on board and we were about to say a temporary farewell to the others who would be flying out hopefully the next day.

At the last minute, an Indian couple arrived. The wife was a rather formidable lady and she formed up to Emil Wick, saying, 'My husband is the Indian Ambassador to Nepal and on his behalf I am commandeering this aircraft. We have an important engagement in Kathmandu this evening at the British Residency.' Emil pointed out to her that we had already booked it, but she said that made no difference. There was then a discussion. Emil started to look worried and he took us aside. India had great clout in landlocked

Nepal; it could easily close the land and air routes, and this had happened not so long ago. Nepal would be commercially throttled, and Emil and his co-pilots drew their flying licences from the Nepalese Government. If he refused to take the Indian Ambassador, and his wife were to get her husband to lodge a formal complaint, then there would be trouble. So Emil asked Chris and ourselves to get off the aircraft and stand down.

Emil Wick had been a good friend for a long time – not only to Chris's and other British Himalayan expeditions, but to all nationalities. In an emergency his skills and experience in taking off and touching down on rugged airstrips in difficult conditions in the high Himalayas could mean the difference between life and death for an injured climber. So Chris, Doug Scott and ourselves shrugged our shoulders, smiled rather wanly, got out of the tiny plane and unloaded our gear.

We then saw a triumphant smile on the face of the Ambassador's wife as she got ready to board the aircraft; the husband had the good grace to look away. As the last rucksack was lifted off, Doug Scott turned to her and in a mild voice asked her if she would mind telling us what business called her and her husband so urgently back to Kathmandu. 'Not at all,' she replied. 'There is to be a special party at the British Residency tonight and His Excellency and I have been invited to meet the leader of the British Everest expedition and the climbers who reached the top.' Chris Bonington and Doug Scott, who had reached the top, both murmured that that should be interesting. She had therefore thrown the chief guests off the plane.

This 'hijacking' of our seats did have its aftermath. A week later George Greenfield flew back to London to help prepare for the expedition's return. At Delhi airport, in the early hours of the morning, he met up with the *Daily Mail* reporter who had covered the Everest ascent, and told him the story of the Ambassador's wife. The reporter wrote it up on his return for the *Daily Mail* and the London correspondents of Indian newspapers picked it up and reported back. The Ambassador was given a formal reprimand and his career prospects may well have been reduced. Poor man! And all because of his forceful wife.

Emil Wick did come back for Diana and myself, and we took off in his tiny Pilatus Porter. Now Syangboche is not dissimilar to Lukla. It is a downhill grass strip at the end of which, like Lukla, there is a deep river gorge beyond which there is a sheer mountain wall dead ahead. Being at 14,000 feet, the aircraft can only get airborne towards the end of the strip, by which time you feel you are only a short distance away from the mountain. This means that we had to climb and wheel very sharply: either to starboard in the general direction of Lukla and Kathmandu, or to port in the direction of Everest. For the first and only time Diana made some noises as we were taking off – to the effect that she wanted to get out, but of course it was too late. We bounced around in the thermal updraft, and in a light aircraft like the Pilatus Porter this sensation verges on the indescribable, but we made it to Lukla where the Twin Otter was waiting for us to take us to Kathmandu.

Meanwhile, Emil Wick had gone back to Syangboche to pick up Chris and George and then, because Chris wanted to get some better photographs of the mountain, Emil took them up to 24,000 feet. Because the Pilatus Porter is a high-wing monoplane, it made it very difficult for Chris to get his vertical tracking shots. So he shouted his predicament to Emil, who then pulled the aircraft over so that it was virtually flying on its side with the starboard wing upright in the air and the mountain only a few hundred feet away. George was never quite the same after that. They then flew back to Kathmandu and arrived at the same time as we did.

At the airport there was a press conference, where there were lots of photographers. We all looked awful – dirty, dishevelled, sunburnt and haggard. Diana kept her sunglasses on to make herself unrecognisable. Despite this there was an article about her in the *Rising Nepal* newspaper, as she had done the climb for charity. We stayed at the Shankar, and had dinners at the Soaltee, Annapurna and Yak and Yeti hotels.

On 14th October we flew with all the expedition members to Delhi but, before we did so, we went to say goodbye to Mike Cheney – what a wonderfully brave man. And we went to say goodbye also to Freddy Bowles, the barman at the Soaltee, and gave him a paper with all the climbers' signatures on it – he was thrilled.

At the airport before we left we were seen off by the Sherpas and their wives and we were presented with white scarves (tokens of honour). Mine is in my bathroom at home. On the plane the pilot announced that the plane was carrying the members of the successful British Everest South West Face Expedition and all the passengers clapped and applauded us. It was all quite heady stuff.

In Delhi we stayed at the Akbar Hotel – far better than the Ashoka. I was going down with a heavy Himalayan chest cold, and Charles Clarke, our doctor, gave me some pills.

We went to a large reception at the High Commission and then on to another one at his Residence. What a lovely house and garden. And here Diana fell in love with the most handsome Sikh, who was in a wheelchair. He had been the first Indian to climb Everest but had been badly wounded in the spine during the 1971 war with Pakistan and he was now paralysed below the waist. What a tragedy! And he had a most lovely wife. I thought they had been married a long time, but it turned out that they had married after he was paralysed. They told Diana that in Delhi they had read all about her in the *Hindustan Times*, and that she had become quite a celebrity.

My health improved following a strong dose of antibiotics. We went to lunch with the Naval Attaché and his wife in the High Commission Compound; we went to lunch with the President's Bodyguard – formerly they were, of course, the Viceroy's Bodyguard – the equivalent to our Life Guards. All the mess silver was put out for us and all around were portraits of British Governors, Generals and Viceroys. We were a scruffy bunch, still bearded and in our mountaineering clothes, and our hosts were immaculate in their Presidential uniforms. The curry lunch was too hot for Diana so she ate very little, but I loved it.

Later we were taken round the former Viceroy's house, now the President's house, by one of his ADCs and then into the garden. And so I must tell you a little bit about the building. The palace, for that is what it is really, represents an extraordinary synthesis between Western and Eastern architectural styles. It was, as we all know, designed by Lutyens and he created a building of what I can only describe as superb Anglo-Indian architecture. It has an extraordinary feeling of powerful serenity about it, brooding as it does on the highest point of Raisina Hill flanked by the twin Secretariat buildings designed by Baker, a concession which Lutyens later bitterly regretted, although I am not sure why – they seem fine enough to me. To me this great palace is one of the finest and most beautiful creations in the architectural world.

When I look at the modern architectural abortions like the

eviscerated Lloyds of London building in the City and the crouching, mosque-like Barclays building, also in the City, I always remember a saying of one of my old Indian friends, when he said that the worst modern architects in the world were the Indians closely followed by the British – neither seem now capable of designing a beautiful building. I have always been ashamed of the new Barclays building. As a Director of the Bank I was appointed to the Board Committee to supervise the design of the new building at 54 Lombard Street. I told the Committee that I was there to ensure that we constructed a beautiful building with the emphasis on soaring vertical lines of which we could be justifiably proud. Instead we were betrayed both by the architects and, I am afraid to say, also by the Deputy Chairman, Andrew Buxton, who seemed to take no interest in the conceptual design of the building and, indeed, adopted what I can only describe as a philistine attitude to the whole project. He even placed the Chairman's Mess in the dungeons of the building where there was no natural light.

The palace is indeed a masterpiece, and it is larger than Versailles. It is built of the same red sandstone that the Moghuls had used at Fatehpur Sikri and this red sandstone is interspersed with cream stone from Dholpur, Bharatpur and Agra in brilliant horizontal bands of colour. Outside there is an immense courtyard at the centre of which stands the Jaipur Column, a thin needle of red sandstone carrying a white egg and bronze lotus, from which arises the six-pointed glass star of India.

If the exterior is magnificent, then the interior, which we were taken around, is sheer genius. The principal floor consists of a wonderful series of state apartments at the centre of which, beneath the great dome, lies the circular Durbar Hall – the innermost sanctum of the old Indian Empire – and here you see that the eye of the dome is open to allow sunshine to flood the hall, bathing what were the vice-regal thrones in imperial light. A dazzling array of Indian marbles completes the effect – white from Makrana, green from Baroda, pink from Alwar, black from Bhaislana, grey from Marwar, and most splendid of all, the yellow marble from Jaisalmer.

Then there are the huge state rooms, the State Drawing-Room, the State Dining-Room, the State Library, the State Ballroom. They all give an extraordinary feeling of the old imperial order and hierarchy of the British Indian Empire, particularly with all the portraits of Queen Victoria, created Empress of India in 1876 by Disraeli, Queen Mary, Queen Alexandra, King Edward, the Viceroys and Governor-Generals and lastly portraits of the Mountbattens, the last Viceroy and Vicereine. It was a wonderful privileged tour and we were enormously grateful to be shown round personally by the President's aide-de-camp.

Later that day there was a reception for us at the Himalayan Mountaineering Club followed by a reception by Air India, who were the official carriers for the expedition – they had given us free seats. From there we went straight to the airport. As usual it took hours to get through immigration and customs but, finally, we boarded the plane.

The journey via Kuwait, Rome and Frankfurt took us 16 hours. When we arrived at Heathrow there were about 50 reporters and photographers waiting for us and we were all interviewed. They were all delighted to meet Diana as they had all heard of her charity climb. Later on we all got into a special bus and were taken to Barclays, 54 Lombard Street, for the press conference in the Great Hall. All of us were on the stage. It was a great success, and at the end the Chairman told me that, as a Director of the Bank, I had to shave off my beard – I was once again to become respectable.

Before finally leaving Everest, I must tell you about Dougal Haston, who reached the Summit and who was one of our best climbers, if not the best. He was tall, immensely strong with extraordinary long arms, a Scottish university graduate, and he climbed the North Face of the Eiger in winter and made the first ever ascent of Annapurna, together with Don Williams. He was also a writer, and George Greenfield encouraged him to write a novel with a climbing background. One day he telephoned George from Leysin in Switzerland, where he ran a mountaineering school, to tell him that the novel was ready and he would post the typescript to him over the weekend.

On the Monday George was telephoned and told that Dougal had been killed while skiing by himself. It was terrible, but George set himself down to read the novel – he was after all Dougal's literary agent. The main character of the book was a man who ran a Swiss mountaineering school. This man was an expert skier and climber, and in the warm afternoons when the sun had loosened the deep snow high up on the mountains, this man would deliberately

24

City Banking Memories

I came back from India. The difficult banking position in the City and central London had eased and the whiff of financial panic had disappeared. At its height Sir John Prideaux, the Chairman of Westminster Bank, had to make a statement to the effect that the Bank was not in trouble, although I had noticed that they were losing deposits to us. An element of normality had reappeared but, of course, nothing in banking is ever normal for long and here I would like to go back to that Competition and Credit Control paper issued by the Bank of England in 1971. We all know what happened to the Credit Control element, which ended up with the banking and property crisis, but the Competition element was very different and here the position was beginning to change very rapidly and margins were coming under increasing pressure.

The profit strength of the clearing banks was derived from the protected and essentially uncompetitive nature of their branch networks. For instance, when I joined the Bank as a clerk, something like 75 per cent of the Bank's deposits were interest-free, current account credit balances; the remaining 25 per cent were on deposit at fixed cartel rates. Competition and Credit Control ended this practice and the competitive position of the Bank in the marketplace became a matter of continuous concern and attention. In particular, the building societies were offering higher deposit rates; not only that, their branches were much more user friendly, to use a modern expression, than ours. Our branches were designed to give an impression of stability to our middle-class customers, but to the affluent working class they represented a relatively disdainful detachment. Of course, in those days, most working people were paid in cash and never went near a bank in any case. However, they did represent an increasingly interesting market, but the structural costs of the banks were then too high to access it. In fact it was only possible to access this market with the state-of-the-art technology which was just beginning to come on stream, and it was only with this technology that you could begin to hope to make a profit. The technology of the building societies was better than ours but it has to be remembered that theirs was a very simple business focusing almost entirely on mortgage lending and raising deposits for that purpose. Furthermore they were all mutuals, which meant that they did not have shareholders to whom dividends had to be paid. Competition and Credit Control also ended the clearing banks' monopoly over the money transmission system and it started to become a free-for-all.

It was about this time that I proposed to the General Management – the particular General Manager was Mr F.S. Bedford, who had taken some interest in my Foreign business – that we should enter the mortgage market by acquiring a demutualised building society. Demutualisation was, I have to admit, almost unheard of in those days, but my suggestion was turned down flat and it was many years later that the Bank acquired the Woolwich Building Society for a vast sum of money. In any case, at the time I made my proposal, it was more than likely that the Bank of England would have vetoed it. Mr Bedford was a tall, bespectacled, North Country man who always seemed to me to be full of swagger and self-confidence. This all disappeared, however, when he was taken ill on a foreign trip to India. India did not seem to suit him and he had to be repatriated home.

With 75 per cent of the Bank's deposits repayable on demand, the Bank was understandably reluctant to lend long, or what we liked to describe as medium-term lending, particularly as, in those days, it was difficult to get matching funds from the market. However, our customers were pushing us in that direction and eventually Barclays London & International was established under the very able management of Frank Weir to engage in sterling and foreign currency medium-term lending, which of course required an entry into the foreign exchange markets.

However, all this meant that in the City I now had to contend with no less than three Barclays Banks: Barclays Bank Ltd, Barclays Bank (DCO), subsequently International, and Barclays London & International, all of which had different sterling and foreign currency and foreign exchange positions – all of which impacted upon my City business. Because these positions were different, customers could take advantage of these to arbitrage between one bank and another, usually to the clearing banks' detriment in the late Large Town Clearing, whereby overdraft facilities were misused.

But, of course, it was not only the building societies which were becoming a real competitive threat to the commercial banks: so also were the foreign banks, particularly the American and later the Japanese and the European banks. Their activities hugely impacted on the business I was managing in central London and the City, and the reason for this is that their activities were almost entirely wholesale and were directed at the large British and London based multinational corporates of which the overwhelming majority had accounts at offices which came under my control.

Furthermore, many of these multinational corporates had accounts not only with me, but also with Barclays International all over the world and, of course, now Barclays Merchant Bank, formerly Barclays London & International. In other words, my business was beginning to be unlike any other business in the UK bank in as much as I was increasingly having to manage an international business within the confines of the domestic bank and to control it worldwide.

Something, of course, had to give and the first 'give' was my taking control of all the Barclays International business based in the City, and this occurred when the minority interests in that Bank were bought out and the two balance sheets merged. This was a huge help but it did not solve all my problems, because nearly all of these companies were engaged in the worldwide money, commodities, insurances and securities business, and were becoming increasingly sophisticated and could not be managed by generalist local Directors and branch managers within the confines of the UK Bank. They required instead to be managed by specialised corporate finance Directors who were well versed in the Euromarkets, the new commercial paper markets, foreign exchange and so on, as well as the new esoteric products such as swaps, collars, caps and derivatives and so on, and who also understood the dynamics and specialist requirements of these companies.

So something had to change and I introduced to what was still known as 'The Room' three corporate finance Directors. One was Ted Foster, an outstanding banker, who went on to General

Management and then on to be the head of the Corporate Division; one was Laurence Grand, and the other man was Richard Steel. The latter two had both been to Eton with me and had come into the Bank from careers in merchant banking. Eventually, however, even this became illogical and in due course they went to form part of the new Group Corporate Division which was able to operate across group boundaries.

As some sort of corollary to this, it became apparent to me that the senior branch Managers, who were managing and developing huge businesses and who later I appointed as branch Directors, were sadly becoming redundant. The reason for this was that if you had senior corporate Managers reporting direct to corporate finance Directors, whether based in my office or the Corporate Division, branch Directors were being continually bypassed, and even more so when administration Managers in those large offices began reporting direct to an administration Director in my office. This was all quite evolutionary and revolutionary, but effectively it was dictated by the market, and the management structure could not stand in the way of providing the Bank's best services to this market.

My position, therefore, as City Director and a Group Director at the same time during this period of extremely rapid change, was exceptionally interesting and stimulating and I was fortunate to be so closely involved in all this development. It was a far cry from writing up manual ledgers in the old British Museum branch.

Now, once again I have to go back to this word 'Competition' because when I started off in the Bank the banking market in the UK was one of the most protected in the world and when I left the Bank it had become one of the most competitive markets in the world, all over a relatively short period of time. To give you some sort of illustration of this, the margins on the Bank's business actually halved between 1970 and 1990 from 4 per cent to 2 per cent, while the entire group's margins fell from 2.6 per cent to 1.7 per cent. All this meant that profits could only rise if the Bank did considerably more business, not only with all the risks that that implies, but also with the consequent strain on the balance sheet; or if it substantially reduced its costs, most of which were fixed; or if competitors were driven out; or if the Bank ventured into new markets where the returns were assumed to be higher. The Bank in fact did all four, not all of them successfully, and this will bring me on to Barclays de Zoete Wedd – BZW – in due course.

There was one particular area which engaged my attention, and that was the provision of global custodian settlement and foreign exchange services to our customers engaged in the worldwide global securities markets. This was an intensely competitive business, but if you got the technology right then you could make a lot of money out of it. We laboured long and hard at this. We had a dedicated team of specialist managers and computer technicians and we were full of hope when, after a long gestation, we proudly announced our new Barclays Global Securities Services. Unfortunately the General Managers were never fully convinced that we would earn a proper return on the capital expenditure incurred in all this, and although we started off well, we were starved of the capital investment required to develop and upgrade the specialist technology required and we became an also-ran instead of a forerunner, and started to lose business.

There was one American bank which particularly specialised in this sort of business: it was the State Street Bank of Boston, and the Board was seriously considering making a bid for this Bank but, in the event, there was, I think, some sort of leak. The share price started moving against us and the proposed bid was abandoned; a pity, because it was a good profitable business and because of its superior technology, most of its customers were embedded, so to speak, which made it almost impossible for them to leave even if they wanted to.

Now among our customers were not only the discount houses, the bill brokers, the money brokers, the stockjobbers and stockbrokers but also, as I have already mentioned, the major (and minor for that matter) American, European and Japanese securities firms. But the one thing that distinguished the British securities firms from their counterparts in New York, Paris, Frankfurt and Tokyo was that they were hopelessly undercapitalised – most of them were partnerships. This was all very nice for the partners as long as the party lasted so to speak, but the writing was on the wall for these partnerships. But not, as it happened, for the individual partners, and the reason for this is what eventually came to be called the Big Bang. Now for those of you who cannot recall what Big Bang was all about, it was this. In 1983 during Mrs Thatcher's premiership her government, and in particular the Office of Fair Trading led by the redoubtable Gordon Borrie, saw the Stock Exchange quite rightly as a bastion of protected self-interest, inimical to fair trade, while coincidentally the Bank of England was becoming more and more concerned that the City would lose out to New York and elsewhere unless all these old-fashioned partnerships were done away with and their capital positions subsequently strengthened.

The Big Bang was a deal done in 1983 between the then Secretary of State for Trade and Nicholas Goodison, the then Chairman of the London Stock Exchange, whereby members of the Exchange would do away with the demarcation line between stockjobbers and stockbrokers and in particular the barrier to entry which protected them both. Fixed commissions were also abolished, and in return for all this – and this was the point – then the Government would drop its case against the Exchange which it had recently launched in the Restrictive Practices Court.

The result of all this was that as far as the Bank was concerned – and I was very involved in all this – Barclays Merchant Bank saw the Big Bang as an opportunity to spread its wings into this new global securities market and aspire to become a major player with the Bank's capital behind it. This aspiration was put to the group board and, as usual with such proposals, a Board Committee was established on which I as the City Director was asked to serve.

Now, of course, all the major American, Japanese and European banks and securities firms also saw the Big Bang as an opportunity – one in a lifetime – to enter this new market in London and to gain a competitive advantage by flexing their financial muscles. The result, as you can imagine, was a mad scramble to buy out the British partnerships and to pour money into them. Their delighted partners all became millionaires overnight and all this resulted in a huge excess capacity, with all that implies.

So the question was put to the committee whether we wanted to enter this market and if so how, and how much it would cost us, as the partners, sensing a bonanza, were inclined to prostitute themselves to the highest bidder. But this price could only be for goodwill – that is to say for the partners themselves, because in reality there was nothing else, only a list of the partnerships' clients.

To be frank, a detailed investment and strategic appraisal was not made, the feeling on behalf of some, including the Chairman, being that all this was somehow a strategic imperative and you were either in it or out of it, and if you delayed then you might have missed a once-and-for-all opportunity. In general, I agreed with this. However, the strategic imperative seemed to be a jobbing business first and a broking business second, whereas I was not interested in the jobbing business, a recipe for a large capital requirement and a very dodgy return. I wanted a broking business: it required relatively little capital but with its client list could lead to many banking and investment management opportunities.

I am afraid I was in a minority on the committee and in 1984 the Bank, at a hastily convened meeting, decided to purchase a minority interest in Wedd Durlacher, a well-known firm of stockjobbers. A 29.9 per cent interest was purchased and it was agreed that this minority interest would be converted into a majority interest when the Stock Exchange regulations permitted. As it happens Wedd Durlacher had already approached De Zoete, Bevan and it was made clear that both firms were to be included in the necessary discussions and negotiations. De Zoete, Bevan had already two suitors, namely Kleinwort Benson and the Bank of America, but Barclays was the preferred partner. To both Wedd Durlacher and De Zoete, Barclays had three advantages. Firstly, we were a British bank; secondly, we had a large capital base; and thirdly, we offered them a large degree of management autonomy – which may or may not have been a mistake.

In the end we paid too much for Wedds, and in my view the Bank made a bad deal for its shareholders. Not only was it a bad deal in financial terms, but it was also a bad deal in the sense that stockjobbing is a major-risk business calling for large amounts of capital if the jobbing positions go wrong. In any case, in my view it was an acquisition without any obvious merits.

It is not for me in this book to write about the death of BZW – I was in at the birth but I had retired well before the funeral rites. Suffice it to say that BZW was too ambitious – it overtraded, overexpanded, overpaid its staff and failed to get control of its costs; in fact everything a clearing bank branch manager used to warn his customers about. In the end the business got to that point where an agonising decision had to be made, that is to say, whether to go on, with all the implications for a continuing high capital requirement or whether to cut losses and get out and sell the business for the best terms available, bearing in mind the Bank was a forced seller. The decision was made to sell, and the exit must in reality have cost the Bank's shareholders a huge amount of money.

25

India

There was a major event in my life in 1976: this was a personal invitation to me as representative of the British Bankers' Association from the Indian National Committee of the International Chamber of Commerce to attend a conference in New Delhi. I accepted, and having received the approval of the Association, which would pay for the trip, and also the approval of the Bank, to whom I suggested that it would be opportune to renew my relationship with the Indian banks in Delhi, I left.

I stayed at the Ashoka Hotel, where the lobby still smelt of urine, where the food was still indescribable and where cockroaches still roamed at will. The Conference, attended by representatives from all over the world, including delegates from the Soviet Union and Communist East European states as well as China, was like all conferences. Endless speeches, plenary meetings, committee meetings, council meetings took place, and it is so long ago now that I cannot remember the theme, but probably it was to do with a defence of multinational corporations against state intervention and nationalisation. In those days the multinational corporation was under constant attack, and indeed in India, apart from Unilever, they were effectively barred from operating.

This state of affairs was engineered by the Indian authorities who, under the Foreign Exchange Regulation Act – FERA for short – required companies, mainly British, to divest themselves of 60 per cent of the company's shares to Indian entrepreneurs or institutions, the former mainly Marwaris who picked up these shares on the cheap as the British were, in effect, forced sellers. The remaining 40 per cent gave the management responsibility without power, with the result that over time this remaining 40 per cent was sold off again, usually to the Marwaris, who became very rich as a result.

The Prime Minister and Government Ministers turned up in droves to the conference, together with all the senior Secretaries of the Government departments, and we listened to them politely because they as socialists, and indeed the then British socialist government, believed in state institutions commanding the heights of the economy and they wanted to show it worked. Of course, it didn't, and it is interesting to note that both India and the Soviet Union almost went bankrupt in the same year, 1991, when in the case of India their foreign exchange reserves fell to the equivalent of cover for two weeks' worth of imports only.

At this conference I met, and indeed he invited me to lunch, a most impressive Sikh, who was then the Chairman of the Planning Commission. His name was Manmohan Singh and he is now, in 2008, the Prime Minister of India, a man of the utmost integrity commanding great respect – a Prime Minister who one longs to get in this country.

We were dined and lunched, we were invited to receptions and parties, the Indians were enormously welcoming and hospitable and I enjoyed every second of it. But now I wanted to get out of Delhi. The State Bank of India kindly lent me a car and a driver and off we drove to Jaipur, where I had been invited to stay with the Rajmata of Jaipur – that is to say, the Queen Mother – at her house called Lily Pool which is adjacent to the Rambagh Palace. She was the third wife – now widow – of the former Maharaja Jai, who had died whilst playing polo at Cirencester in 1970.

Now why had I been invited to stay with the Rajmata of Jaipur? The answer to this is that her husband Jai had been for many years a great friend of my first wife's uncle, Sir Robert Throckmorton, and he had very kindly written a letter to her about me. So here I was at Lilypool, the house of the Queen Mother of Jaipur, and this brings me naturally on to my next digression – the Jaipur family.

Jai had been adopted – his real name was Mor Mukut – and he was one of the two sons of the Thakur of Isada. Maharajas who did not have sons were fully entitled to adopt a male heir but, in British times, this adoption had to be confirmed by the Viceroy and there were difficulties over this and to these difficulties was added the opposition of the Maharaja of Bikaner. In the event he was formally adopted as the heir to Maharaja Madho Singh on 21st April 1921. Now Jai was married three times. His first wife was Marudhar Kanwar, always known as First Her Highness, who he married when he was thirteen in 1924, and by that marriage there were two children, Princess Prem Kumari and Bhawari Singh, always known as Bubbles because of his fondness for champagne. In 1932 he married again, this time to Kishore Kanwar, the niece of First Her Highness. And so now there was a Second Her Highness, by whom he had two sons, Jai Singh always known as Joey, and Prithviraj Singh always known as Pat. So now there were four children.

While all this was going on, Jai had become enamoured of Ayesha Cooch Behar. She was a woman of quite exceptional beauty, and throughout the years has remained so. Jai and Ayesha married and so she became Third Her Highness. There was one son by the marriage, Jagat, who married a Thai princess by whom he had two children. Sadly they divorced, and I believe the Thai Royal Family refused to allow him to travel to Thailand to see his children – it was all very sad, and not so long afterwards Jagat died.

Now what I would like to do is draw your attention, in particular, to the timing of my visit in 1976. In 1970, shortly after Jai had died, the Government of India brought in the bill to abolish the princely purses, which had been guaranteed by the Government of India at Independence when the princely states including, of course, Jaipur, acceded to the Republic of India and had surrendered their income as Heads of State to the Government in return for this princely purse – that is to say, pension. This abolition was forced through by Mrs Indira Gandhi of unblessed memory, who it was rumoured had once been spurned by Jai. However the bill was turned down by the Supreme Court and in 1971 Mrs Gandhi called an election which she won. Mrs Gandhi then forced through the bill once again, and this time she was successful. Princely India came to an end.

In 1975, just before I went on my Everest expedition, the Indian Income Tax Department started probing into the Rajmata's affairs and produced a search warrant. They did not allow her to telephone either her accountant or her lawyer. Later that year she was arrested, and she was told that it was to do with her supposed contravention of the fearsome foreign exchange regulations. Once again she was not allowed to telephone her lawyer, and Bubbles the Maharaja was also arrested. They were both taken to Tihar jail in Delhi, one of the most terrible prisons in the world, and Ayesha the Rajmata was thrown into a cell together with the Delhi prostitutes. There were no washing facilities, but she was allowed to use the so-called bathroom of the condemned cell, which had no running water.

Ayesha was never charged with anything, but because the dreaded Mrs Gandhi had by now declared a State of Emergency she was able to ignore all the laws which should have protected Ayesha and Bubbles from this terrible treatment. At that time Mrs Gandhi imprisoned any powerful member of the opposition; she fostered informers and rewarded those who had denounced others, and many Indians assumed that Mrs Gandhi had, in effect, taken leave of her senses and gone mad. Bubbles was released after two and a half months, but no reason was given; Ayesha remained incarcerated.

She fell ill and her lawyers petitioned the High Court. The Government counter affidavit was a masterpiece of dishonesty claiming that her detention was necessary for effectively dealing with the emergency in view of the serious impact of violations by the détenu on the economy of the country. It was all rubbish, of course, but eventually world opinion and protests brought about her release from prison, to be taken to hospital. She was allowed to return to Jaipur but she was obliged to tell the police about all her movements and to apply every two months for her parole to be renewed.

These conditions continued without any charge being brought until Mrs Gandhi called an election in 1977 and lost, and the new Government annulled all the orders against Ayesha. There must have been some strange streak of vengeance which drove Mrs Gandhi to hound Ayesha and the Jaipurs. Perhaps it was true that she had been spurned by the Jaipurs when she used to visit her aunt in Jaipur. Perhaps she thought that Jai should have supported her father, the Kashmiri Pandit Nehru, although that family had not lived in Kashmir for a long time. In the end, as we all know, she was assassinated by her Sikh bodyguard.

So this was the background to the lady I was staying with – still on parole, and her movements still monitored by the police, and she the Rajmata of Jaipur. It was a terrible story. To me she was enormously gracious, kind and hospitable, although I have to admit I was in considerable awe of her not only because she was very beautiful and dignified, but also because she came over as a very regal lady, which of course she was.

I had a lovely time staying with her at Lilypool, situated close to the Rambagh Palace, but now it was time to move on, and first to stay at Ajmer with Jack Gibson, the retired principal of Mayo College, the public school for the princely Rajput families. Lord Mayo, who founded the college, was the Viceroy who was assassinated in, I believe, the Andaman Islands. My driver and I eventually found his small house at Shanti Niwas near Ajmer. Jack Gibson had been a bachelor all his life and lived very simply in his sparsely furnished house. When I arrived there and unpacked, I found to my consternation and mortification that I had left my soiled smalls in a drawer at the Rajmata's house, and I wondered whether she would ever speak to me again. But of course it was not her who went through the drawers, it was the servants. They did eventually catch up with me in London, having been brought back by Sir Robert Throckmorton. So I had to borrow a set of underclothes from Jack, which had all been made locally and were therefore easily replaceable.

Jack Gibson could be said to have lived several lives since he came out to India in January 1937, as a housemaster for the Doon School in its formative years. I remember reading the first page of his memoirs, *As I Saw It* – which was published in India in 1976 and is well worth reading – where he wrote:

Yesterday I spent in the train through Central India, rather monotonous, but an experience. At tea time an Indian got in and we talked; most interesting but depressing. I am already shocked by the extremes of squalor and magnificence, of subservience and pride in the country but I think the English are hated. To start with there was what I myself noticed from the moment of landing in Bombay; the way the average Englishman but, much worse, the average Englishwoman treats the Indians. Any sensitive person would react to it and I don't wonder the ruling race is disliked.

All this, of course, echoes what I had been told myself about pre-war India.

During the war he served in the Royal Indian Naval Volunteer Reserve and was Principal of the Joint Services Wing of the National

Defence Academy from its founding till well after Independence. He became principal of Mayo College in 1954 and retired 15 years later. It is fair to say that many of his students at the Doon School, Mayo College and the National Defence Academy went on to become leading figures in Indian politics, business and the civil and military services – so much so that he was honoured with the Padma Shri by the President of India and was also honoured with an OBE by the Queen. The Padma Shri is equivalent to a knighthood.

Besides all that, he took up skiing at Gulmarg, which led to the Presidency of the Ski Club of India; he went climbing in the Himalayas which led to both the Presidency of the Himalayan Mountaineering Club and also the Presidency of the Indian Mountaineering Foundation (you will recall that the former gave a Reception for us when we returned from Everest). He paid regular visits to Sikkim and Bhutan where he advised the King on educational matters.

It was a real privilege to be invited to stay with him and I am always grateful to Doctor Charles Clarke, one of the two doctors on the Everest expedition, who had suggested I stay with him if I was passing through Ajmer. We toured round Ajmer and the surrounding countryside, and we paid a long visit to Mayo College where I attended morning assembly and had tea with the Principal, Mr Das. All in all it was a most interesting visit to me and I would have liked to have returned, but I did not, and I only once saw him again in London, when he was still thinking he should get married. He died aged 86 in 1994, 18 years after my visit. Do please read his book, *As I Saw It*.

Two days later my driver and I set forth once again, this time en route to Bundi. Shortly after we left Shanti Niwas, we passed the garrison town of Nasirabad and once again I must make a little historical digression.

In May 1857 the 15th Bengal Native Infantry mutinied here, when they heard the news of the mutiny at Meerut, and they were soon joined by the 30th Regiment. The 1st Bombay Cavalry were ordered to charge the mutineers but, as soon as they got within a few yards of them, they veered off, leaving their British officers to go on on their own and most were either killed or wounded. The Adjutant of the 15th Bengal Native Infantry Regiment had his horse – it was his own – shot under him, but it carried him out of danger before falling dead. Shortly afterwards this Adjutant was refused compensation for the loss of his horse by the Military Auditor-General on the grounds that the regiment having mutinied, he had no longer occasion to keep a charger and therefore it was not necessary to replace it! Some things never change.

Nasirabad was reoccupied by British troops in June but there was a further mutiny in August which led to the temporary disarmament of the 12th Bombay Native Infantry; this time there were no European casualties. How history comes alive when you visit the places where these events occurred.

We moved south-east, crossed the Berach River, passed through Deoli and later that afternoon arrived at Bundi where I had been invited to stay by the Maharajah. He lived in a minor palace called Phoolsagar at the edge of a tank – a reservoir – and underneath this minor palace was a waterfall as the tank emptied out into the river. It was consequently rather damp, dark and disconcerting. The name of the Maharajah was Bahadur Singh. During the Second World War, as a Lieutenant, he served in Burma in an Indian cavalry regiment equipped with tanks. He took part in the Meiktila drive against the Japanese as a tank troop commander and was severely wounded in the neck. While being taken to the rear, he recovered consciousness and insisted on returning to the battle, which he did, continuing to take an active part in operations. For this bravery in the field he was awarded the Military Cross. I am not sure of his personal history; he had been married, he had had two children, a boy and a girl, but I believe he was estranged from his son, and his daughter Kittens, who was estranged from her husband, lived near Madras where she had a stud farm.

But the one thing he said to me which I never forgot was that he wished he had died at Independence in 1947 because, at that point, everything started to change and he found it almost impossible to cope with the change. And, of course, life to all intents and purposes became even more impossible financially when Mrs Gandhi abolished the princely purses pensions in 1971, and suddenly he as Maharajah had no money. As I have written earlier, at Independence the princes were virtually obliged to surrender their state income on accession to the Republic of India in exchange for a guaranteed princely purse pension and this is what Mrs Gandhi reneged on. Furthermore, because most of the Maharajahs were suddenly left with virtually no income, there were forced sales of wonderful pictures, paintings, works of art and so on to raise money. At the same time most of the old servants and family retainers in the palaces were dismissed. It was indeed a terrible act of vengeance on the part of Mrs Gandhi.

Bundi is mediaeval: nothing seems to have changed since the fourteenth century, and there is an atmosphere of evil and cruelty about the place, which you can almost feel at times, not only in the narrow mediaeval streets but also in the sad crumbling palaces and fortresses. Bundi was founded in 1342 by the Hara Clan and all through Bundi runs a sense of sad past romance and brave suttee queens, of valour and chivalry. And wherever you go in Bundi you have the feeling of being watched, and sometimes it is overpowering and sinister. In one deserted pavilion it is said that a Bundi queen was walled up alive in retribution for some wrongdoing.

Every fortress in Rajputana has its share of legends. One of Bundi's most famous stories concerns a prophecy of centuries ago – not unlike the prophecy that when the gooseberry bush at Kilravock died so would the Rose family (and that turned out to be true). The Bundi prophecy was that if a Bundi prince and a Rana of Udaipur should meet, the death of one of them would result. And so it happened, four times in 300 years, that a prince of each house met, and four times one of them died at the hands of the other.

My host was enormously gracious, welcoming and kind, but oh so sad. I particularly wanted to visit one of the tanks where Rudyard Kipling had stayed when he visited Bundi in 1889. It was a most idyllic spot, with the lake and hills and forests all around, although further away most of the Maharajah's forest had been cut down by peasants following Independence. It was here that Kipling wrote 'The Last Suttee':

The black log crashed above the white;
The little flames and lean,
Red as slaughter and blue as steel,
Leaped up anew, for they found their meal
On the heart of – The Boondi Queen

I was glad to leave Bundi. The question now was which route to choose to drive to Chittorgarh and Udaipur. I wanted to go the shortest route possible, by admittedly a very minor road, but I was advised against this for several reasons: there were no telephone lines along this minor road, there were no petrol stations, but most of all it was a route well known for dacoit activity. I was told it was far better to go south to Kotah and then turn west to Udaipur. Of course, I should have chosen this route, but the first one sounded more exciting and had a piquancy of danger about it, so I chose it, but I should not have done so. It was indeed a horrible road and we made very slow progress, averaging about 20 miles per hour. Every now and again we came to a village, and once we went through a small town called Bejolia. But there were no dacoits. Although I was not particularly nervous, I was certainly very conscious of my colour, as I doubt if any of the villagers or peasants had ever seen a white face before – whenever we stopped I felt very conspicuous. Indeed, all Indians are very curious and I was always immediately surrounded by what seemed like hundreds of children and men and women, all staring at me and all quite silent. I was always glad when the engine started and we moved on, leaving the inhabitants still staring at me and the car. My driver, however, did a wonderful job and we eventually came onto a better road where there was at least some traffic. On my minor road I doubt if we saw, for the best part of 100 miles or so, more than two cars and three or four lorries and, of course, no petrol stations or telephones.

Eventually we passed by the great gloomy, brooding fortress of Chittorgarh whose walls are the finest mediaeval Hindi defence work to survive in any degree of completeness, and arrived at Udaipur where I stayed at the Lake Palace Hotel and visited all the sights around. Mercifully, the lake was full – I could think of nothing worse than staying at the hotel when a monsoon had failed and the lake had dried up. I believe this is often the case now, with so much water being abstracted as the population grows. I had wanted to go back to Chittorgarh which is so redolent of Rajpur history, if only because the heights of Chittoor are the military key to Rajputana and its occupation, the first objective of any invader.

In 1303 the Tartar Ala-Ud-Din laid siege to the fortress. After months of deadlock, the Sultan offered to lift the siege on one condition: namely that he be allowed a glimpse of the fabled beauty Padmini, the wife of the Rana's regent. The Rajputs agreed on one condition: that he was not allowed to gaze directly on Padmini, but that he could see her reflection only in water. The palace of Padmini stands in a pool of water within the fortress, and as the

329

water stilled, the Sultan was able to see her lovely face. But Ala-Ud-Din, as usual, played dirty and he laid an ambush by the outer gates where Maharana Bhim Singh was kidnapped. The price of his freedom was, of course, the hand of the fair Padmini. She agreed, provided she should come to him with her court of ladies. Under cover of their palanquins, a body of Rajputs entered the Sultan's camp. The Rana and Padmini escaped, but all the Rajputs were killed.

Once again, the Sultan besieged Chittor but, before his final assault, a great funeral pyre was lit within a great subterranean chamber and the defenders of Chittor walked in procession – the queens, their wives and daughters – to enter the chamber where they were immolated in Chittor's first jahar. And it happened again in 1535 when Bahadur Shah, the sultan of Gujarat, besieged Chittor. The Rajmata, the Queen Mother, led a cavalry attack on the Muslims and died fighting. This time a large number of women and children made Chittor's second jahar and all were immolated in the fire rather than, as Hindus, being taken by Muslims. It must have been awful. And it happened yet again when Akbar besieged Chittor, and it is recorded that the women all dressed up in their bridal finery. After they had sent their children before them to die, willing or not, the princesses and queens entered the flames and all that was vibrant and beautiful died with them. Akbar sacked the citadel. Everything was wrecked or defaced, and thousands of the country people who had either taken part in the defence or had taken refuge in this huge fortress were put to the sword by Akbar. Chittoor, the scene for a thousand years of heroic valour, romance and adventure, was left empty and desolate. And so it was when I visited it in 1976: it was completely empty, nobody there, and the sadness of those ruined walls, gates, temples and palaces was palpable as I walked round.

Like Bundi, I was glad to get away from Chittoor, and I vowed I would never return; although I did some years later with Diana and my sister Marigold.

Meanwhile, unbeknown to me, the State Bank of India was wondering where their driver and their car and their honoured guest, a Director of Barclays Bank, had got to, because to all intents and purposes we had disappeared into the Indian countryside. I had reverted to my old jungle habit of never telling anybody where I was except, of course, when I needed something such as an airdrop. So I telephoned from Udaipur to say that I would fly back, leaving the driver to find his own way back to Delhi. It had been an interesting trip and I hope I have done it justice here, but it was not quite over as the flight from Udaipur to Delhi, including stops at Jaipur and Jodhpur, proved quite dramatic.

We took to the air in a clapped-out Indian Airlines DC3 with its two propellers. Shortly afterwards there was a big bang and most of the cowling over the port engine was carried away and went crashing down to the earth. However, the pilot carried on and it was reassuring to me that he had his son with him in his cockpit. It was a turbulent, uncomfortable flight and every time I looked out at the port engine, I expected it to burst into flames. However, we duly arrived in Jodhpur and here a maintenance engineer came out with a stepladder to have a look at where the cowling had broken off. I thought for a moment that he was trying to repair the jagged edges with Elastoplast or something similar, but perhaps that was my imagination. The pilot with his son took a look at it, shrugged his shoulders and clambered back into the cockpit. We felt comforted by his confidence and eventually, very late, we crept into Delhi during a heavy thunderstorm. I had arrived back, and all that was left for me was to write a fulsome thank you letter to my hosts the State Bank of India and leave for the airport to take my overnight British Airways flight to London. It had been a memorable trip, and there were many more to come over the next 25–30 years.

Just before leaving this part of India, I can tell you of another journey I undertook with, this time, my wife to Kotah which lies about 40 miles south of Bundi. We had been staying with Joey and Vidya Jaipur – who had called their son Benny as, more than anything else, he loved watching Benny Hill films. Diana had been fascinated by the fact that their house – I think it was 12 The Civil Lines – had no kitchen. Our breakfast was prepared by a woman squatting on the floor in front of a old-fashioned electric toaster; that is to say, you put the bread in both sides of the machine and then, when one side was ready, you turned it over. She also had on the floor a little electric heater in which the eggs were boiled. That is all. But the mystery was solved, because we found out that all the meals they had in the house were brought in from the Rambagh Palace kitchen.

The private banquets we used to attend at the Rambagh were

magnificent, with separate tables on the palace terraces and, because it was during the cold weather season – never described as winter – there were wonderful hot braziers everywhere. Sometimes we used to be invited for dinner at the City Palace where everything was silver: silver tables, silver chairs and so on – the only trouble was that they never appeared to be polished, and with the many servants around, this was surprising.

One day when we were there Mr Taubman of Sotheby's appeared with his entourage, having arrived in his private jet aircraft – it was rumoured that this was the first time a private jet had been allowed to land in India. This was surprising because Sotheby's was regarded with deep suspicion in India, as I shall relate later. The Maharaja Bubbles gave a drinks party for them in the garden of the City Palace, followed by dinner. At the drinks party I was introduced to Mrs Taubman who, according to the pilot, had been Miss Israel. She was very attractive but I had no idea what to say to her, so in a rather hopeless sort of way I asked her where she lived. Her reply to this was that she lived in New York, Chicago, Florida, Paris and London – which one did I want her to talk about? This was too much for me, and that was the end of the conversation.

There was one elderly American lady staying there as well. She was one of those middle-aged American ladies to whom I generally have a strong aversion. She came down, actually up, to dinner – as the dining-room is at the top of the palace – and I remember her complaining about her bath. What had happened was that when she was lying naked in the bath she suddenly espied a dark eye looking down on her from a hole in the ceiling. She was affronted, but she was taken aside and told not to worry. There had been a hitch in the plumbing and the eye was there so that when she turned the hot or cold tap the servant with the eye was able to manipulate the pipes above; the actual taps did not work so a response was needed from above. I do not think she was particularly mollified by this answer, and when she got going again I told her she was lucky to have a bath – Jaipur is in the middle of the desert and water was desperately short.

We had received an invitation to stay with Brijraj Singh of Kotah and his wife Honey. They lived at the Brijraj Bhavan which, during the British period, was the Kotah Residency. It was quite a journey to Kotah from Jaipur and we went via Tonk, which used to be a

332

Muslim state surrounded by Hindi Rajput states. And here, dear reader, I must make one of my little digressions. Now not many people have heard of Tonk, but I had and I wanted to visit it if possible.

The old ruling family of the state were, as it happens, Afghans. The founder of the state was a certain Amir Khan who began life as a mercenary leader of Pathans on the North-West Frontier but went on to command a large army, which he used in alliance with Holkar and assisted him in levying tax contributions exacted by the Mahrattas. Then along came the British East India Company which had decided to take action against the Pindaris and needed help from Amir Khan and his forces. At first Amir Khan asked too much, but when he was offered a guarantee of all the lands he had obtained from Holkar on condition he disbanded his army – which then consisted of 52 infantry battalions, a horde of Pathan cavalry and a number of guns – he accepted. So the now Nawab Amir Khan built the then new town of Tonk. He was succeeded by his son who, in the Mutiny in 1857, distinguished himself by holding the Tonk fort against the mutineers who were led by Tantya Topi. In recognition of this achievement and his help to the government, his gun salute was raised from 15 to 17, and later to 19 guns.

This son of Amir Khan, whose name was Nawab Wazin-Ud-Daula, was also an eminent scholar of Muslim theology, literature and history, and was greatly esteemed by all the Muslim learned theologians in India. During his reign many Muslims moved to Tonk and settled there, and in his time Tonk was known throughout Muslim India as the Tower of Islam.

We drove south, stopping at an old Dak bungalow where we had a late lunch. However, as we neared Kotah, we came across a huge long tailback of lorries and cars waiting to cross the Chambal River bridge. In fact it was an octroi strike as the lorry drivers were refusing to pay octroi, the state customs tax. We could have been there all day and all night – time did not seem important. Eventually our driver lost patience, drove across fields to the embankment of a canal, which had a track not a road, and after various alarms and excursions we found a military bridge (or it might have been a military railway bridge), and thereafter, paying the guards the necessary hurry-up fee, we passed into Kotah just before nightfall. Like all journeys in India, it had been what they call an interesting experience.

Old Kotah is as charming and delightful as Bundi is sinister, brooding and mediaeval. Kotah had once belonged to Bundi but was separated in 1579 by a ruler who wanted to provide for his younger son. Kotah, like all India, was always vulnerable; it was impossible to choose the right side in every Moghul succession dispute; it was impossible to guess the intentions of Amber, Mewar or Bundi; and it was impossible to predict when or where the armies of marauding Mahratta would descend on the state. At one point the entire Kotah royal family was slaughtered in a battle that attended Aurangzeb's accession as Moghul emperor.

The city palace at Kotah is a dream. It is surrounded with high walls, strong bastions and ramparts, but there is much delicate stonework, domes and those wonderful elephant-shaped brackets to support its carved balustrades. 'The minarets and cupolas of the palace give it an air of light elegance,' as Lieutenant-Colonel James Tod put it, and the close association of Kotah with the politics of Moghul India has endowed the interiors with all the grace and decorative intricacy of Moghul design.

I have mentioned that Brijraj and Honey's house was the old British Residency; his father and mother were still living in the huge palace designed by Sir Swinton Jacob. Now, in the Residency where we were staying, a terrible triple murder took place in October 1857, and once again I am going to make one of my little digressions to tell you what happened.

On 13th October 1857, the political agent of Kotah, Major Burton, returned from Neemuch where there had been disturbances. He left most of his family there, mercifully, but brought back with him his two sons who were aged 19 and 21 respectively. He was received with great courtesy by the Maharajah and the usual ceremonial visits were duly exchanged the following day. Everything seemed normal and calm. But the following day two regiments of the Maharajah's contingent mutinied and arrived at the Residency where they stated that the political agent, Major Burton, had to be killed.

When he first saw them, he believed that they were some of the chief subordinates coming to pay him their usual visit of ceremony and respect. But he was quickly disillusioned as they rushed into the house and all his servants abandoned him except his camel driver. He and his two sons with their guns fled to the top floor of the house, where our bedrooms were. Here the mutineers were stopped temporarily as the youngest son had shot one of them. For five hours the three men were besieged on the top floor, but the mutineers brought up two guns and the building was set on fire. After these five long hours they began to hope, nevertheless, that the danger was over. They let down the camel driver on a mission to the Sikh soldiers, who were supposed to guard the Residency, to ask them to loosen the boat so that they could escape across the Chambal River – the house stands above the river to capture the morning and evening breezes. However, the Sikh soldiers responded that they had no orders to let them go, and at this moment scaling ladders were put up against the walls, the mutineers climbed up, and the father and his two sons were immediately put to the sword.

Nobody could understand why this should have happened. Major Burton was greatly respected by everyone – particularly the Maharajah. He had lived in Kotah for 13 years. He had hurried back from Neemuch at the Maharajah's request to see him, and Kotah wanted him and his family back. The reason for him being at Neemuch with his family was that the officer commanding that station had asked him over to deal with the Kotah contingent, who were restive and indeed had now been disbanded. It was all terrible, and here we were in the house where all this had happened.

Brijraj and his wife were wonderful hosts and we had a most interesting time exploring both Kotah and the surrounding countryside and, in particular, some temples some distance off which were beautifully carved. We were also pleased to have been staying at the same time as Lady Egremont, who had been visiting Mayo College. It was her grandfather Lord Mayo the Viceroy who had founded the College, and the Indian Principal had invited her to address the school as the granddaughter of the founder, a very kind and thoughtful action on the part of the Indian trustees of the school. I liked that very much.

Now it was time to leave Kotah and the hospitality of Brij and Honey. Despite Kotah having a nuclear power station there was no air service so we perforce had to take the Frontier Express train which went daily all the way from Bombay to Delhi, but in pre-Partition days, as the name implies, to Peshawar. There was a cavalcade of cars to the huge station and here we were met by the stationmaster in his full uniform who immediately took us to his private office where we were invited to partake of tea and scones. And then when the train arrived, on time, he saw us personally to our reserved compartment and bade us goodbye. I could see that it was all genuine, with no trace of 'I am doing this because the Maharajah asked me to do it' – what a wonderful man.

Later that evening we duly arrived in Delhi.

26

The Transglobe Expedition

In 1977 I was appointed City Director of the Bank which required a move from Pall Mall back again to 54 Lombard Street but it was in 1976, when I was resting on my laurels, or at least so-called laurels of the 1975 British Everest South West Face Expedition, that my good friend George Greenfield, with whom I had worked closely on Wally Herbert's Trans-Arctic Expedition and Chris Bonington's British Everest Expedition, asked me to meet Ran Fiennes, whose full name was Sir Ranulph Twisleton-Wykeham-Fiennes, 2nd Baronet. Now the reason for this was that dear Ginny, his first wife, who very sadly died in 2004, had a bright idea and the bright idea was this: to follow the Greenwich Meridian right round the world via the North and South poles – one of the most ambitious journeys ever to be proposed.

Ginny had met George shortly after the British Trans-Arctic Expedition had ended and, at that time, her name was Virginia Pepper and she was engaged to be married to the Baronet. She explained to George that Ran had recently completed a journey by jet boat towards the source of the Nile and wanted to write a book about it; would he, George Greenfield, be his literary agent? George replied yes, provided Ran dropped the first two 'barrels' of his name, distinguished lines of descent though they were, and to this Ran, somewhat reluctantly, agreed.

Ran had been an officer in the Royal Scots Greys. He had then passed through the exceptionally tough selection course of the SAS (Special Air Service), and had then fought the Yemeni invaders while seconded to the Sultan of Oman's forces. He was on good terms with this wealthy Sultan. In 1972 he took Ginny's idea to George, who explained to him that he faced three main problems:

337

one was time; the second was money; and the third was Government approval. He also explained that the only journey then made across Antarctica had taken four years of full-time planning, two years of sledging, and had cost about £1 million. This was the Commonwealth Trans-Antarctic Expedition led by Bunny Fuchs, whose deputy leader was my great friend David Stratton. George also went on to explain that Ran would need a committee of management, carefully picked from the exploring establishment, particularly the polar establishment, because he would need this committee to lend him its collective credibility and support and to use its many contacts to find outside sponsors. And, as the two poles would have to be negotiated, his first backer needed to be a polar expert and that, of course, was Sir Vivian Fuchs.

So Ran approached Sir Vivian to obtain his personal support. His advice was that no one would take him seriously until he had gained polar experience. Quite independently Ran came to see me at Pall Mall at the suggestion of George Greenfield, as I have mentioned, and this was because, unknown to me, I had apparently been elevated to the polar establishment and he also wanted my advice and support. As it happened what I said to Ran was exactly what Sir Vivian Fuchs (Bunny) had said to him. I told him that once he had carried out a polar journey in the Arctic, provided it was successful, he would then have the necessary credibility to seek the support of the Royal Geographical Society and what seemed now to be called the 'polar establishment', of which I was apparently now a member.

And so it came to pass. Ran and his colleagues, Oliver Shepherd and Charlie Burton, did precisely that. They spent four months in the Arctic getting within 167 miles of the North Pole and when the Twin Otter came to pick them off the by now melting ice, Ran received a message that the Prince of Wales had agreed to become Patron of the proposed expedition. Thereafter the main executive committee was established, to be chaired by Rear-Admiral Sir Edmund Irving, a former Hydrographer of the Royal Navy, who was very well known to me. The committee included a number of others who were equally well known to me, such as Colonel Andrew Croft, Sir Vivian Fuchs, George Greenfield, Tom Woodfield, and Sir Alexander Durie, who was or had been Chief Executive of the Automobile Association and who was, like me, a Board Director of Mercantile Credit. I was also appointed a member of this executive committee and was asked to assume the position of Honorary Treasurer.

So the duo of George Greenfield and myself once again swung into action: he was responsible for the media contracts and I was mainly responsible for the finance – as usual a difficult position, but made easier by the presence of Prince Charles as Patron of the expedition who had the ability to do what I used to call 'leaning on people' for funds. In this he was remarkably helpful and successful. For instance, we had a real problem with financing the fuel supplies for the expedition ship and aircraft. All British, French, German, Italian and Japanese oil companies turned us down, including ICI Petrochemicals and Phillips Petroleum who took four months to say no. In despair Ran Fiennes did what he had always promised himself never to do, and that was to ask Prince Charles for help. A week later the Prince's office telephoned and Ran Fiennes was instructed to telephone Dr Armand Hammer in Los Angeles. We had some concerns about Dr Hammer – he had been an old friend of Joe Stalin and he had been responsible for the very large, somewhat dubious Russian–American grain deals and so on. But he did own an oil company called Occidental, although as this company did not retail gasoline they could not help. However, Dr Hammer did persuade one of his competitors to agree to supply the necessary fuel, and this was Mobil Oil. This was curious, as we had already approached Mobil Oil in Europe, but then we were told that the supplies would be Mobil Oil USA and that Dr Hammer had spoken to that latter company's chairman. Thus we were to receive $1 million worth of fuel and all this was down to Prince Charles's powers of persuasion.

It is perhaps interesting to note here that Dr Hammer had apparently three ambitions in his lifetime: one was to live long enough to see a rapprochement between Russia and America – this never happened in his lifetime; the second was to live long enough for there to be found a cure for cancer, and this also never happened; and his third ambition was to be made a knight – this also never happened but hence, possibly, his willingness to accede to Prince Charles's wishes.

Now I am not going to write at any length about this expedition because you can read all about it in Ran Fiennes's book *To the Ends of the Earth*. However, I will say just this. Everything went well on the southern half, culminating in the traverse of Antarctica in 67 days by skidoo. Then a major problem arose. Oliver Shepherd's wife was not only desperately missing him. but also increasingly concerned about his safety. There was talk of the marriage breaking up. He decided to withdraw. The committee felt that a replacement should be recruited but Ran and Charlie Burton wanted to continue as a pair when the Arctic was reached. There was a lot of excitement at this impasse between the Committee of Management and those in the field, and this reminded me of the same position which had arisen with the British Trans-Arctic Expedition. In the event Sir Edmund Irving as Chairman flew out to New Zealand, together with Sir Vivian Fuchs and Brigadier Wingate-Gray, who had been Ran's Commanding Officer in the Special Air Service, hoping to influence Ran personally.

Now it so happened that after the Transglobe's trade exhibition in Auckland it was followed by one in Sydney, Australia, and it so happened that Prince Charles was there at the same time. And so when the Patron of the expedition went on board the *Benjamin Bowring* to meet the crew, it would be fair to say that Ran 'nobbled' him during a private discussion in the Captain's cabin. That is to say that if the Patron agreed that a party of two would suffice as I saw it for the much more dangerous Arctic sea ice crossing, the committee could not really gainsay him, but Ran was left in no doubt that if anything went wrong on this sea ice crossing, it would be on his own head. It was very difficult for the Rear-Admiral to accept that an instruction which had been given by the Committee of Management of which he was Chairman had been countermanded by the Royal Patron and for the rest of this expedition this rankled.

I think none of us fully understood and appreciated the enormous physical endurance, courage and determination of Ran Fiennes and Charles Burton as they threaded their way through the Northwest Passage and crossed Ellesmere Island on their way to the frozen Arctic Ocean. Eventually they reached the North Pole by skidoo in April 1982, and thus they had attained two of their main objectives, the North and South poles. But the journey was far from over as they still had to complete the traverse of the Greenwich Meridian on the earth's surface, and the last stage was going to be the most difficult – not only because they had to link up with the *Benjamin Bowring* on the edge of the pack ice near Spitzbergen, but also because the ship, although strengthened to operate in open pack ice, was not able to penetrate close pack ice. So Ran and

Charlie Burton had to reach her, and not by one way or another – it had to be on foot, and using the prevailing current to float them towards the ship, to safety and success.

By this time in May, the pack ice was breaking up and melting and it was felt by some people that they should be evacuated by air provided there was a suitable floe on which the aircraft, a Twin Otter, could land. So the Rear-Admiral ordered such an evacuation, with the agreement of most of the Committee of Management, but not by all. To those of us who had been on the British Trans-Arctic Expedition Committee, there was a strong feeling of déjà vu – we had all been here before. The batteries in Wally Herbert's radio set had suddenly become strangely weak when the instruction to prepare a landing strip to evacuate Alan Gill with his bad back had been transmitted, although these batteries made a remarkable recovery soon afterwards. Thus the strip was not prepared, the weather broke and Alan Gill stayed on to overwinter with the rest of the team, his back or slipped disc having recovered.

So now it happened all over again. Ginnie the wireless operator found it difficult to pass on the Chairman's instructions, and nor did a further instruction get through. In the end the message was reduced to a strong recommendation to call it quits and for the two men to be airlifted out. This time this recommendation (not an instruction) got through, but the two went on floating south somewhat erratically with the additional hazard of being pursued by polar bears. In any case, the possibility of any aircraft landing was by this time out of the question as extensive open water leads were opening up in the ice, and were becoming more and more frequent and wider and wider. In the event, they took to their kayaks and eventually reached the ship on 4th August 1982. On its return the ship was boarded in the Thames Estuary by Prince Charles, who helped steer the boat back to Greenwich, almost exactly three years since he had navigated her on the first few miles of her outward journey. But this time he did not go round in a circle in the middle of the Thames – intentionally – hardly! But it may have been because only a few days previously the IRA had murdered his great-uncle and close confidant Lord Mountbatten.

All this may sound like a very expensive and dangerous jolly and it has to be said that there is a certain amount of truth in that possible criticism, but offsetting this was the large amount of work undertaken in the scientific programme, which like Scott's last expedition is often overlooked. So there was a zoological programme, an oceanographical research programme, which included physical oceanography, and so on. A Ross Sea survey was undertaken together with a magnetosopheric research programme and, of course, a climatic and meteorological programme which was very much up my street, and finally a glaciological programme. All the results of these programmes can be found in the book *The Scientific Results of the Transglobe Research Programme*.

Now it was all over. It had taken up a great deal of my time and energy for a period of five years – a long time in retrospect – but it was a great help having a secretariat to support me and this made a lot of difference compared with the British Trans-Arctic Expedition.

27

Essex Farming and Activities

Now I would like to turn to something completely different, and this is the Lyons Hall Estate and farm. I am not sure it now qualifies as an estate because that implies that there are tenant farmers. There were, of course, but there are none now and the entirety is now farmed by the family. But before I embark on this, I think it would be helpful if I gave some background to farming in Essex, and what has happened over the last 100 years and what is happening now, because farming in Essex has always been a rollercoaster. As I have always said, farmers not only have the business risk, but they also have the weather risk, and there is very little you can do about the latter,

As the twentieth century dawned the inhabitants of Essex could look back on a hundred years that had seen many changes but which had not fundamentally altered the pattern of either village life or farm work. The countryside more or less still looked the same. The landscape still consisted of small fields and hedges, hay and corn stacks stood in relief against the skyline, farms and their barns still nestled on ancient sites, and churches and their towers still stood as reminders of some sort of timeless stability. Country lanes still meandered all over the place, muddy and rutted in winter and dusty in summer. You could hear the blacksmith's anvil and you could see the horses trudging towards the markets, pulling their heavy loads. Cattle grazed the marshes and meadows, sheep were folded on the arable fields and grazed the pastures. There were cows in the fields and each village had a number of small shops, which usually consisted of the front room of a cottage. The fields were ploughed with horses, the harvest was carted by horse waggons and later threshed. Even I, born in 1931, can remember

343

all this both before the Second World War, during the war and after the war.

Looking beyond this apparent rural idyll and apparent outward tranquillity, a lot of change was going on. Although the squires remained, and the Trittons were squires – 20 years of depression had forced out many of the old farming families – the yeomen, that is to say the owner-occupiers, had become far fewer in Essex and their places had been taken by the thrifty Scots.

The village still fed itself and Great Leighs was no exception. Practically everything that was eaten and drunk by the inhabitants came from the village. The bakeries used local flour; milk was produced from grass, mangel-wurzel, turnips and hay from the local fields; hops were still grown in Essex and every farm had its brewhouse, and so did Lyons Hall Farm. Vegetables were home-grown and delicious whilst gleanings from the harvest fields fed the chickens and produced the eggs. There were the wild fruits from the hedges, particularly blackberries of which we have an abundance, but nobody picks them now. Damsons, sloes, medlars, wild plums and crab apples were all gathered by the mothers and the children, and every farm had its orchard.

Everybody seemed very healthy and there was only one doctor for the whole of the Walthams and the Leighs. His name was Dr Robinson, he lived in Little Waltham, and not only did he deliver my sister Marigold at Lyons Hall in November 1928, but also he had quite an eye for Nanny who, at that time, was in her early thirties.

Farmers were pre-eminent in their villages and their powers over their labourers were immense. In economic terms the inhabitants of the village relied on the success of the farm to survive, and the farmer in his turn relied on his labourers to survive, but they were tied to the farmer by their tied cottage, and could not move. In any case, they could not ask for more money as most farmers were teetering on insolvency. As a matter of interest, about 56 per cent of the population of Essex was engaged in agriculture in 1800, but by 1900 it had gone down to 3.81 per cent and by 2005, the percentage was statistically insignificant.

But going back to 1900, a Felstead farmer, who farmed on heavy boulder clay, wrote as follows:

there are farms without sheep, farms without cattle or pigs, farms that are undermanned and under horsed, with overgrown hedges, ditches filled in, arable fields covered in twitch and thistles, farmhouses, buildings and cottages rapidly going to pieces. Many have fallen down and will never be rebuilt and, as the buildings and cottages disappear, so does the church go out of cultivation. Agricultural land is regarded as the worst possible investment for spare capital; landlords advertise their farms in vain.*

The nadir of the great depression was in 1894–1895 when the price of wheat per imperial quarter fell to 23 shillings, which was the lowest figure recorded for 150 years. But by 1920, farmers could look back on an unprecedented boom and this, of course, was the result of the war and indeed in 1917 the price of wheat reached its highest for 99 years and it is interesting to note that when in 1917 the Germans launched their unrestricted submarine warfare campaign, wheat stocks in this country were reduced to one week and five days bread supply for the whole of the country.

Going on from there, in 1920 wheat prices hit a high which was not to recur again for another 30 years. The wartime boom had been short-lived and the depression that followed was to be deeper and more severe than anything that had happened in the nineteenth century or even in the run-up to 1914. The inter-war period was a catastrophe for farmers and it was in 1924 that my grandfather gave up farming. On 30th September 1924, G.B. Hilliard & Sons held an auction of the valuable livestock and dead stock of Lyons Hall, Goodmans and Wakering farms.

The catalogue included: '15 active, young carthorses and a chestnut nag mare, quiet to ride and drive; 54 head of neat stock; 157 Suffolk ewes; 158 strong Suffolk lambs including 82 ewe lambs; 80 head of swine; 135 head of RIRC and Sussex poultry and a good assortment of agricultural implements including harnesses, a Cose tractor, four tractor ploughs, Clayton and Shuttleworth's Barnwork [what's that?], straw elevator and five knife chaff cutters' and so on. And all this was because my grandfather took the decision to get out of farming and instead let the farms.

My grandmother wrote down all the prices which each lot raised. The first lot was two dung cromes and two jets, but there is no price alongside this – perhaps she had not arrived in time. The

---

*From *Essex Farming* by Peter Wormell (Abberton Books).

first lot priced was lot 45 consisting of two barn shovels, two brooms, corn scuttle and six pails which raised 5 shillings, but the next item was a Ward's dressing machine which raised £5. Item 94 was range-nesting boxes which raised 2 shillings. A double-shaft iron-arch road wagon with ladders went for £44 10s and the Cose tractor, new in 1923, lot 307 went for £155.

And then there were the horses, Prince, Captain, Boxer, Bowler, Tinker, Short, Trimmer, Kitty, Brown, Blossom, Smiler, Shy, Tom and others, who were sold for 350 guineas. How sad to say goodbye to all those wonderful horses, particularly perhaps Captain, who reached the highest figure and went for 50 guineas. And finally, a pedigree Jersey heifer in full milk and due with second calf in March 1925, bred by A.W. Ruggles-Brise Esq. and in calf to Brigadier General J.T. Wigan's bull, sold for £25 10s.

So the Trittons went out of farming, but some time later they were back in it again and the farm size has now increased to approximately 2,500 acres as we have undertaken to contract farm two nearby farms with an acreage amounting to around 1,000 acres. We would not have been able to achieve this without the dynamic and energetic management of James Evans, our new farm manager, and his capable and hard working colleague Spencer Runnacles. Thus instead of 13 men required to work 300 acres, we now have two men to work 2,500 acres, plus, of course, contract staff required to bring in the harvest. So instead of one man to 23 acres it is now one man to 1,250 acres – an astonishing and extraordinary change in a single generation. Of course, the other side of the coin is that whereas the valuation of the machinery on the farm in 1965, when I took over, was £12,000, the value of this machinery is now at a figure of around £400,000.

As I am writing this book primarily for my family, I feel it would be interesting for them to learn what Strutt & Parker wrote to my great-grandfather about the harvest results for the year ending 29th September 1914. At that time there were three partners of Strutt & Parker, namely Edward Strutt, Charles Parker and John Strutt. They wrote in longhand as follows:

Dear Sir, Lyons Hall Farms.
    We have pleasure in forwarding you these accounts for the year ending September 29 1914. [This was just after the Great War had started.] Considering the dryness of the season, we

think you should consider them very satisfactory, though no doubt the valuation of the corn could not have been on so high a basis if it were not for the high prices which are now prevailing owing to the War.

As we predicted, last year's corn crop shows a surplus on valuation and we should expect the same to arise next year.

Livestock, considering the extremely dry summer we have gone through, have not done badly and the outlay for feeding stuffs has not been quite so large as in the previous year,

With reference to the expenses, labour again is slightly higher but not more so than in similar occupations, though it is still a high price per acre.

Horse expenses are less than in the previous year but are quite sufficient for the number kept.

We think it might possibly be wise to make a rather larger expenditure on artificial manure. This chiefly we would recommend in the Autumn and not in the Spring owing to the dry summers which we experience in Essex.

We suggest to you that it might be an opportunity for selling some of the middle-aged horses. There is a great demand for horses 9–12 years old and even a littler older if they are good sound animals. These horses seem now most in demand and between £40 and £60 can be realised for good workers of this description.

All the animals on the farm which we saw, seem well cared for and show that interest is taken in them.

We are, Yours very faithfully, Strutt & Parker

Letter to J.H. Tritton Esq., 14 Lowndes Square, London

This is the sole report on a year's farming in Essex in 1914. During the year in question the surplus amounted to £270 against a valuation of £6,593. No drawings were made against this profit and the value of the land was not included in the valuation; I do not know how much land the Trittons then farmed.

The then farm manager was a certain Mr Stoddart who lived in Wakerings Farmhouse and he was assisted by Mr Palmer who lived in the adjoining cottage. Mr Palmer was responsible for paying the wages and the farm labourers used to gather at his house on Saturday mornings to receive their pay.

John Wright, who lived and worked at the farm all his life, told me that when he was old enough to walk, he used to go round with his next-door neighbour Mrs Fuller at Cole Hill Cottages carrying tea cans to the men who were working on the fields or stackyards, and these tea cans were also used to carry milk from the farms. John Wright himself started working at Lowleys Farm in 1935. At that time it was mainly an arable farm and the land farmed comprised about 300 acres.

Barley and oats were the main cereals grown. Sheep, pigs and cattle were kept along with some chickens. The oats were harvested and fed to the horses mixed with chaff. There was also a mill driven by the tractor which rolled the oats flat, and this same mill ground the barley and beans into meal which was fed to the cattle.

They used to make hay every year with the grass grown on the meadows, and they also grew red clover, tares and lucerne, which were also used to feed the sheep, along with kale, turnips and swedes.

Mangels were also grown. They were harvested in the autumn, by pulling them up by hand, twisting the leaves on the top and throwing them into a horse-drawn tumbril – shades of the French Revolution. This tumbril had a small tailboard that could be removed and it could also be tipped up by removing a wooden rod in front attached to the shalves – a word I have not come across before. The mangels were then clamped for the winter and covered with a thick layer of straw to keep out the frost. They also used a grinder. The mangels were put in a container on top of the grinder and by turning a handle, a large wheel with spikes on it cut these up into slices which were then fed to the animals.

Potatoes were also grown and sold off the farm. Local women were engaged to pick them up after they had been ploughed out with a special horse-drawn plough. Like the mangels, these potatoes were clamped, although the mangel clamp was about 5 to 6 feet high, while that for the potatoes was only about 3 feet high. In the spring the potatoes were put through a riddle which was turned by hand and this sorted out the potatoes into their various sizes. They were then forked onto an elevator with two or three people standing by the machine, picking out the green ones, the rotten ones, stones and so on. They then went up another elevator and dropped into a bag where they were weighed up in 1 cwt bags and these bags were then tied up with string, ready for collection.

The most important machine on the farm was the binder. This was the machine that cut the corn and tied it up into sheaves. These sheaves, numbering eight to ten, were then stood up in traves – in Scotland we called this stooking as I have mentioned when writing about our times at Lochloy. When the sheaves were dry they were de-stooked and carted back to the farm in horse-drawn waggons. At either end ladders were attached, which extended the length of the waggon. The men, and this now included me, pitched the sheaves up to the person on the waggon who distributed them evenly around the waggon. The trick was to put the pitchfork exactly into the middle of the sheaf so that the weight was balanced. This did not matter so much when the load on the waggon was low, but it mattered more and more as the load got higher and higher and, in the end, you were pushing it up using both hands and arms at the base of the pitchfork – and you knew about this the next morning. Gradually, however, my muscles got tighter and harder.

When the load was so high that it was nearly out of reach, it was taken to the yard where another gang of men stacked it, and when finished the stack was made to a point and, in due course, it was thatched to keep out the rain. Later on the threshing machine men came along. The corn was threshed and it came out in front into sacks whilst the straw went out the back, and it was either stacked or made into a bale. The chaff came out of a chute at the side of the machine and it was then bagged up and placed in the barn and used as cattle and horse food.

In those days there was little machinery on the farm. There was a horse-drawn mower to cut the grass and a horse-drawn turner to turn the swathes of grass after it had been cut, and this helped to dry it. There was also a horse-drawn sweep which collected the hay and took it to the stack. The one tractor was used for both ploughing and cultivating, but both the seed-drill and the harrow were horse drawn.

I remember the bullocks were kept in various yards and fattened for slaughter. Some went to Mr Collier on the main road. He used to kill his animals on Mondays. Mr Collier's butcher's business has recently become a casualty of the supermarkets and his son now works for Humpheys, the adjacent farmers, who have also invested in an abattoir.

During the winter months attention was given to the woodlands, and about 1 acre of woodland was coppiced every year. At Haslers Farm and also at Lyons Hall Farm, which was then tenanted by Mr Ratcliff, there were long deep pits. A tree was rolled over it and then sawn up. Now this was hard work: one man stood in the pit and one man stood on top of the tree, and the crosscut saw was pulled backwards and forwards.

For all this in 1936 the rates of pay per week were 31s 6d; the overtime rate on weekdays, including Easter Monday, Whit Monday and Boxing Day was 9d and a farthing for one hour's work, and for Sundays and Christmas Day 10d and a farthing per hour. For women, however, to whom only the hourly rate applied, the corresponding rate if you were over 21 was 6d and a farthing per hour and if you were aged between 14 and 16 the hourly rate was $3^1/_2$d, so for an eight-hour day you earned 28 old pennies – and remember that there were 240 pennies to the old pound!

Now what about the farmers and the estate owners – what was happening to them? After 1921 farming went into a sharp decline and this, coupled with the severe drought in 1921 and his father's death in 1923, is what probably propelled my grandfather to give up farming, but not the land. To put this into some perspective, farm prices in 1922 were less than 50 per cent of what they had been two years previously. There was a mass exodus of Essex landowners with farm rents dropping from around £2 per acre to under £1 per acre, if indeed they could find a tenant. Some farms were offered for sale for as little as £5 per acre, although the usual price was between £10 and £15 per acre. Many farmers went bankrupt.

Between 1900 and 1937 the top 12 estates in Essex were reduced to nearly 50 per cent of their previous area. Between the wars nine major estates were split up and in total the major estates sold 43,000 acres, but during the period 1900 to 1943 over 406,000 acres went from landowners to farmers. So not only were the landed families selling, but they were also selling at virtually the bottom of the market. Putting all this another way, after 120 years 98 out of 110 landowning families who had substantial estates in Essex had gone and, as it happens, the turnover in Essex land during the century just ended exceeded any previous period with the exception of the Dissolution of the Monasteries.

So not only has there been a revolution in the ownership of land during the last century, but there has also been a revolution in the entrepreneurial ability of some farmers, like the Philpot family who started from scratch in 1937 but by now have built up a landholding of 3,700 acres and with tenancies farm another 8,500 acres. This is a substantial business all created in the last 50 years.

All this will give you some background to the Trittons' Lyons Hall Estate which I inherited in 1965. The estate was started with a purchase of some 400 acres in 1812 including Lyons Hall itself which dates back to 1535. The soil type is very variable and includes Hanslope, Hornbeam, Oak and Ludford association. These represent clay in the far south of the farm, a loamy clay in the east and to the north, and sand and gravel on either side of the River Ter which runs through the estate. This sand and gravel represents the run-off from the last Ice Age.

In the olden days there were a number of separate farms, all of which have now been bought and amalgamated into the estate, which is now all farmed in hand.

All told, eleven farms have been absorbed into what we now call Lowleys Farm. Again, for the record, when Mr Green of White House Farm gave up farming, my grandfather bought the land on the Wakerings side of the Boreham Road, whilst Lord Rayleigh bought the land on the other side.

Now what sort of shape was the farm in, which I was inheriting? As you will now know, I was not allowed to take part in the management, I was not allowed to take any money out of it, although it was my income for tax purposes and furthermore I was virtually debarred from going anywhere near the estate or the farm so that I should not be seen by my aunt or reported upon to her.

In essence the new trust in 1965 took over livestock and deadstock valued at £23,525. We took over land valued at about £233,000 – this was for 1,100 acres then, so the value was then about £200 per acre. We took over investments valued at £33,000 but, five years later, these had all gone to pay off the mortgage on 23 Flood Street, so that my former wife received the house – my house – unencumbered. The total profit for the year ended 31st March 1966 was £4,428 11s 3d, whilst we had a share in the Rabbit Clearance Society of 10 shillings and that was that.

And now to the Single Farm Payment. This is hard to compute, but to demonstrate the complexity of the calculation we start off as follows:

   i) The flat rate element is 15% rising to 100% in 2012 whilst the historic element is 85% falling to 0% in 2012 – this is called the dynamic apportionment.
  ii) The deductions are:
     a) UK modulation at 6% in 2006 rising to 10% in 2012
     b) National ceiling cutbacks at 1% flat
     c) European Union modulation 4% in 2006 rising to 5% in 2007 and then flat through to 2012
     d) National reserve at 5% in 2006 and staying at that figure
     e) Financial discipline 0% in 2006 rising to 8% in 2012.

In other words, the deductions are 16 per cent in 2006 rising to 29 per cent in 2012 – an over all deduction of nearly one-third.

Putting all this into figures, we come out with a set-aside entitlement of 1712; an ordinary entitlement of 168,027; plus a protein bonus of 668; but no Plus Energy Crop Bonus, total 177,407, less the deductions of 27,835. All this eventually comes out at a figure of 177,406 less deductions, that is to say Euros 149,571, which then has to be converted into sterling. This payment is effectively a reducing pension no longer related to production. This is what is described as decoupling – that is to say, as farmers we sell at the world price in accordance with the agreements reached with the World Trade Organization, which states that there should be no direct subsidies to farmers.

In March 1966 we bought 36 acres of the Bishops Hall Farm land for £8,250 – that is to say at £230 per acre. The following year we bought Longs Farm, 200 acres, from Mr Smith, who was giving up farming. I believe that just prior to that purchase, we had been offered Moulsham Hall Farm, but the trustees were too slow off the mark and this went to a Mr Thomassin-Foster. He made a fortune out of the Great Leighs bypass, selling the intervening land between the bypass and the village to David Wilson Homes for a horrible housing development.

In 1970, when my aunt died, Paddy Tritton asked me how I would cope with a swingeing death duty tax of around £100,000. He felt that I had essentially three choices: one was to sell the estate, the second was to sell off half the estate, and the third was to hang on and hope for the best and, against his advice, this was what I decided to do.

As it happens I never had any doubt that my decision was right, but the position was made much worse because, firstly, the availing liquidity had to be used to pay off my first wife to enable the divorce to be finalised; and secondly, because by now I was beginning to incur school fees, which as every middle-class family knows are crippling. Clare had tried to get the Lyons Hall Trust varied in her favour, which would have meant a sale, but I took Counsel's opinion, which was in my favour and this strategy of hers was mercifully defeated.

In the 1970s the farm produced good profits but here it needs to be remembered that these were the days of the Labour government. This appalling government raised the top earned income tax rate to 83 per cent and on top of that imposed a 15 per cent tax surcharge on unearned income, so my overall top tax rate ran up to 98 per cent, which in every sense of the word was confiscatory. It needs also to be remembered that inflation was rampant at that time which meant that retentions after tax were minimal, and after inflation were negative. So it was a very difficult time, and the only way to deal with this was to both borrow and sell assets.

Now when I arrived on the scene all the cottages were lived in either by farm workers or retired farm workers, who had all been promised a rent-free cottage for life in lieu of a pension. This was unsupportable, and something had to happen. This happening was twofold: the decline in the workforce as mechanisation took over, and death. This meant that over a number of years a number of cottages became free, and instead of reletting them, which in those days meant a statutory tenancy with no power of termination, I sold them. Of course, I intensely disliked doing this, but I had no other source of capital to pay not only school fees and death duties, but also to fund the increasing working capital requirements of the estate and farm from minimal or negative retentions due to the high tax rates and high inflation. So various cottages were sold including Fulbournes Cottage at the top of Palk Hall Lane, Valentine's, the Manse built next door to the Rectory by my great-grandfather to embarrass the Rector, Longs Farm Cottage, Shed's Cottage, and later more, until with the end of the death duties and school fees the financial position stabilised, since when there have been no more sales.

Against these sales and before my Aunt Dore died, we built two modern farm cottages next door to Lowleys Farm Cottages. In deference to my 'beloved' aunt these were called Garnett Cottages after her, but nearly 40 years later I changed their names to 3 and 4 Lowleys Farm Cottages.

As the position reversed itself and we started to have more liquidity, we started buying land again, of which the largest acreage was the Glebe Land of some 70 acres or so. In agricultural terms the cost price was barely viable, if viable at all, but the land was contiguous and available. The sale by the Church Commissioners was conducted on a tender basis and was spread over four lots, and although our price was not the highest for one or two of the lots, in its entirety ours was the highest and the Church Commissioners preferred to sell to one buyer to reduce their costs. So we took over this land and bought one or two adjacent fields as they came up for sale – thus the estate remains an integral whole, which was my intention.

In 1987 I started to worry about the succession – I was then 56. There were then still two tenancies: one was the Lyons Hall Farm, which was tenanted by Mr Ratcliff, and the other was Fulbournes Farm, which was tenanted by Bill Lagden in a joint tenancy with his sister Nora who had never married but who ran the riding school at Fulbournes.

Geoffrey Ratcliff, who farmed many other farms, had been a tenant since 1924 when my grandfather went out of farming. Nowadays there is a Tenancy Succession Act and although I thought it would not be exercised by the Ratcliff family, I wanted to get this farm over to the next generation at a low valuation for tax purposes and not at the high valuation created by vacant possession. I am not sure now that this reasoning was quite valid, but anyway it was transferred to a trust with a 15-year lease back to me at a nominal rate. In the event Geoffrey Ratcliff died after having been a tenant for over 60 years and the family did not – nor could they as it happens – exercise any rights under the Tenancy Succession Act, so this land came into possession for farming purposes.

Geoffrey Ratcliff was not the easiest man to deal with, and the last time I saw him was at a party given by Alan Jordan, a Great Bardfield farmer, at his house at Porters Farm, Rivenhall, where I believe he also farmed. At that party Geoffrey Ratcliff came up to me and told me that, in his view, he had been bullied all his life by the Tritton family. I replied that I was surprised at such a remark because I thought, as a member of the Tritton family, that we had been bullied all our lives by him. The word 'bullying' arose because he was always, quite naturally, trying to get his rent down because he farmed most of the light land on the estate, whereas we were always trying to raise his rent. Remember that in those days the net rent after expenses was taxed at 98 per cent – so perhaps it was really all unnecessary, as the tax man had it.

Now we need to turn to dear old Bill Lagden, who was not a good farmer and who seemed to spend most of his time in the pub St Anne's Castle. His acreage was an impossibly small one of 200 acres – manageable in the old days, but not now. In due course, we managed together with him and his sister to negotiate a sub-lease of his tenancy from the trustees so that we could farm the land ourselves. This worked well. Bill died and his sister was willing to surrender her tenancy, so that all the land came into our possession. In a sense then, at that point we were no longer an estate, having no tenants, and became a farm. All this was important for tax reasons because, when I started all this, only farming land 'in hand' was land qualified for death duties relief, whereas these duties were still levied on the value of tenanted farms. This I believe has changed now.

During my tenure, the size of the farm staff has dwindled. When John Wright started working on the farm in 1935, there were 13 men working on the then farm size of 300 acres, that is, one man to 23 acres. Most of the work was carried out by the horses and one tractor.

When mechanisation really started it was clear that most of the fields were too small, and a number had already been amalgamated before I came on the scene. At that time there were 75 fields all with their individual field names, which I have retained, and if we count the fields in the acquired land then the total of the fields, which were all surrounded by hedgerows, must have been numbered not far short of 100. Now I suppose there are roughly 45, so there has been quite a change in the scenery. Taking for example Whitehouse field, which now extends to about 35 acres, this I remember originally consisted of five fields, Whitehouse, Orchard, Paddock, Little Hands and Spiceleys. The Doole field, which again extends to some 35 acres, originally consisted of six fields, Meglands, Cocklands, Doole, Kingfield, Terling Crofts and Wood field. By the way, 'Doole' is the name of a grass path which runs through a field. In the end the average size of a field on the farm is 20 acres or, as they now like to call it, 8 hectares, which means nothing to me. Although I do like and enjoy hedges, once again I do not like too many of them and I do far prefer long distant vistas of fields and the feeling of space and distance they provide. Nowadays hedges are subject to controls before they can be removed. We have not removed any since the restrictions came in but, just before they did, an elm hedge crossing Wire Meadow field died from Dutch Elm Disease and was removed.

During my stewardship of the farm I planted eight small woods, all told. All these except one were planted for the benefit of the shoot, and it is this subject to which I will now turn. When I came into so-called possession, the shoot was let to Mr Ratcliff, the tenant of Lyons Hall Farm. One of his employees, namely Arthur Quilter – who lived in Church Cottage together with his wife Bessie, who had been a parlourmaid at Lyons Hall before the war and who kept the church immaculately clean – also carried out the gamekeeping for him. And all this continued for some years, with myself being invited once a year by the tenant, Mr Ratcliff, to shoot. I did not know any of his friends but I do remember the delicious lunches of roast beef cooked by Bessie which we ate in the dining-room.

Clearly all this was a most unsatisfactory position as far as I was concerned, but as long as my Aunt Dore was alive, nothing could be done. And then we were into death duties and money was short and I did not have sufficient money to employ a gamekeeper even if he was part-time.

All this, of course, was very well, but I now had a shoot and no keeper. In the event Ric Cole and Mark Poole, who had been my pickers-up, came along to me and said they wished to make me a proposal. The proposal was to undertake the keepering on the farm and estate on a voluntary basis, but in return for this to have free access to the estate and farm for shooting purposes and, of course, to have their own shoot at the end of the season in January. This sounded almost too good to be true and, ever since, the shoot has been a marvellous success story. Indeed Ric Cole and his family have now moved into a house on the estate and he now, in effect, our estate handyman.

Before leaving the farm, I should mention that I have always been very keen on conservation and so good was I at this that in 1982 I won the Essex Farming and Wildlife Competition. We were

356

deemed by the judges to have achieved the best balance between conservation and practical farming husbandry. They went on to say that I had demonstrated a high standard of commercial farming coupled with a wide scope for wildlife conservation. All this was music to my ears, and I looked forward to at least a week's free holiday in Majorca by way of a prize. Sadly, however, the prize was a bottle of whisky and a plaque of rather nondescript appearance with my name on it.

I had never really taken much part in Essex activities – I was too busy elsewhere, not only in this country but worldwide. However, someone noticed me and this was Julius Neave, a good friend. I remember him coming over to see me at my peg when we were shooting together, telling me he had it in mind that he wanted to put my name forward as a future High Sheriff of Essex. He asked if I would like to think about it, and he said he hoped I would accept. Well the answer to this was yes, particularly as 'my year' would coincide with the Millennium of the Shrievalty as it is called. 'My year' could fill a chapter in this book, but there really is not space here.

I became High Sheriff in 1992 and it certainly was a most unusual experience, but it was also exceptionally interesting, working as I did with the Essex police and the Essex magistracy. A major problem arose at the outset as to what uniform I should wear and I opted to wear my No. 1 regimental (Seaforth Highlanders) uniform. This could be either trews or a kilt. Even I felt that a kilt was a bit over the top for Essex, and this was reinforced by a remark made to me by the Lord Lieutenant that a kilt in Southend would get the inhabitants of that borough too excited. I agreed so on full ceremonial occasions I wore my No. 1 dress uniform and there is a photograph of me in this uniform in the hall. Unfortunately, when I was putting on my regimental belt for the photograph, I put it on upside down and when my old adjutant, John Whitelaw, came to stay to shoot, he immediately pounced on me and told me that I was improperly dressed – adjutants never change.

Following my retirement as High Sheriff, I was appointed a Deputy Lieutenant of the County of Essex and later President of the Essex Club and later trustee of Brentwood Cathedral, so I must have done something right.

I want to digress here for a moment, and this is on ladies' fashions, or rather lack of them. Bearing in mind that in every

357

newspaper shop there seems to be hundreds of fashion magazines, admittedly mainly for the younger market, it was all the more astonishing to me that when I was High Sheriff and going to endless official functions and making speeches and hobnobbing, I can recall that hardly any of the middle-class, middle-aged ladies took the slightest trouble about either their clothes or their appearance. They seemed to be universally grey and drab, with often their hair cut unattractively à la brosse. Why do these wonderfully worthy women deliberately disguise their femininity under such dreary clothes? What is wrong with them? When I went to similar parties in Bombay, Delhi, Calcutta and Madras, all the Indian women were brilliantly attired in their best saris; they were covered in jewellery and they all had beautifully long dark hair and many were radiantly beautiful. But in England, no, and the question is, why? Why don't they bother? There must be some reason, and I am sure it is not the climate. There were, of course, some women who were smartly dressed and made up, but they were always in a very small minority and usually came from South Essex, and that perhaps says something. My Indian secretary, Filomena de Souza, whose family came from Kenya and Goa, always told me that women are as old as they look, but men are only old when they stop looking – and by this she meant at women – and she is right. I have always adored looking at and admiring women and I even fell in love with a beautiful Egyptian waitress in the Airport Hotel in Cairo – I simply could not take my eyes off her. She was just as attractive as our Air Egypt air hostess on a flight from Aswan to Cairo, who was beautiful, but really should not have been an air hostess, because as we were taking off she made the sign of the Cross – nothing wrong in that – but then lit up a cigarette as the plane took off. Not the first time I have seen that but it is very unusual. So please, ladies, do smarten up and start looking and behaving feminine again.

28

The Victoria Memorial Hall, Calcutta

There have been endless books written about Calcutta so I am not going to take you on a conducted tour of that great city, extraordinarily interesting as it is, although Winston Churchill saw it otherwise. I could myself probably write a book about it, but what I want to do is to draw your attention to one great building, the Victoria Memorial Hall, which lies at the southern end of the Maidan, because it was with this building and its collections that I became involved for nearly 14 years of my life,

Now I also do not want to describe in any detail this remarkable and beautiful edifice, because it was the restoration and conservation of its collections which became a passion for me and enthused me to found and establish the Calcutta Tercentenary Trust (CTT) for that purpose.

But, first of all, a little bit of history, and let us now look at the Maidan: a very large open space in the middle of Calcutta, with to the north Government House, which I used to frequent with my many meetings with His Excellency the Governor, to the west the river, and to the south the old Dhee Birjoor prison which was demolished at about the turn of the last century and on whose site the Victoria Memorial Hall now stands. This huge open space known as the Maidan was never designed as a park, but essentially as a sort of glacis for Fort William – in other words, it formed part of the defence system of the fort so that in case of attack, this whole area could be raked and swept with artillery fire.

On 6th February 1901, the then Viceroy, Lord Curzon, shortly after the death of Queen Victoria who was also the Empress of India (although she never went there), proposed at a hastily convened meeting as follows: 'Let us therefore have a building stately,

359

spacious, monumental and grand to which every newcomer to Calcutta will turn, to which all the resident population, both European and Native will flock, where all classes will learn the lessons of history and see revived before their eyes, the marvels of the past.' This, of course, was good classic Curzon stuff but he did it, and it was his energy and enthusiasm that carried the day.

Curzon instructed Sir William Emerson the architect to design the monument, and the man appointed to supervise the construction was Vincent Esch, whose son Vivian became enormously interested in our work. The foundation stone was laid by the Prince of Wales in January 1906, but it was not until December 1921 that the monument was formally opened by a successor Prince of Wales. In due course, it was to become the repository of one of the finest collections in the world of works of art over the period 1760–1820, exactly, as it happens, corresponding with the reign of King George III.

Tilly Kettle, who was in India between 1769 and 1776, played an important part in introducing British art into Indian princely society and you can see in the Memorial two of his finest and largest oil paintings which were restored together with their frames by the CTT. One of these paintings, measuring over 9 feet by 8 feet, is of Shuja-ud-Daulah the Nawab of Oudh and four of his sons with General Sir Robert Barker – who it was generally agreed by the restorers I closely resembled – and his military officers.

Now this painting was made for the General when he was provincial Commander-in-Chief in Bengal between 1770 and 1774 and was conducting many negotiations with the Nawab. On 17th June 1772, the General visited Faizabad while Tilly Kettle was there in connection with the offensive and defensive alliance concluded between Shuja-ud-Daula and the Romillas. Tilly Kettle's painting celebrates this event and shows the Nawab holding Barker's hand and standing in an archway together with four of his sons and a group of British officers, all of whose names we know. The negotiations were conducted in Persian (the Nawabs came from Persia originally) and we can see Lieutenant William Davy, the General's Persian interpreter.

You can also see a significant and rare collection of six oil paintings by Zoffany, who was in India between 1783 and 1789, restored by the CTT. These paintings not only include his famous portraits of Warren Hastings and his wife, but also his dramatic and evocative paintings of such events as the *Embassy of Haidar Beg to Lord Cornwallis* and *Prince Jawan Bakht Receiving Hastings at Lucknow*, and also probably his finest and most famous painting, *Colonel Antoine Polier, Claude Martin and John Wombwell with the Artist Zoffany in Lucknow*, with possibly the exception of *Colonel Mordaunt's Cock Match at Lucknow*, in which you can also see Colonel Polier, Colonel Martin and Mr John Wombwell.

These three men were a congenial trio enjoying life in Lucknow and greatly interested in its culture, and who would not have loved life in Lucknow in the eighteenth century and early nineteenth centuries until the British destroyed it during and after the Mutiny? The painting also includes Zoffany himself, looking steadily out at the viewer. Brushes and a palette are in his hand and a large oil painting depicting Indian ascetics under a banyan tree rests on an easel beside him. Two of these ascetics are bearded but the third, a female, is nude. Now it is an interesting commentary on Indian sexual mores in the twenty-first century that this 1786 painting of a nude female in a painting within a painting offended many Indians past and present, and I believe, somewhere along the line, attempts had been made to cover her up.

There are paintings and portraits by Robert Home, who loved India, settled there and died there at the age of 82 in 1834; as well as by William Hodges, James Wales, Arthur William Devis, Thomas Hickey, John Alefounder, Solvyns and many others, but it is particularly the work of Thomas Daniell and his nephew William, whose unique interpretation of the late eighteenth-century Indian landscapes attracted Curzon, and now the Victoria Memorial is the home and proud possessor of the most extensive and important collection of their oil paintings in the world – no less than 39. By the time we left in 2001 we had restored all of them including my favourite, the *Temple of Vishnu at Tirruparavikinram* near Madurai, painted by Thomas Daniell in 1822.

Just as interesting are the many works of art on paper both by professional artists and by the many civil and military, both male and female, amateur artists who produced a prolific amount of material recording the life and landscape of India. There are landscape drawings by Colesworthy Grant, Jacomb Hoad and William Simpson, and the collection also includes groups of work by the highly competent and gifted 'amateurs' Samuel Davis, Sir Charles D'Oyley and George Atkinson. But perhaps the most important group of what are known as 'Company' paintings is the collection of over 200 natural history drawings which were given in 1934 to the Memorial by Maharajah Sir Prodyot Coomar Tagore. The 'Company' is, of course, the Honourable East India Company. These were drawings assembled by John Fleming, a doctor in the Bengal Medical Service around 1785–1811, who had followed in the path of Sir Elijah Impey, a former Chief Justice of Bengal and also the Marquess of Wellesley, the brother of the Duke of Wellington in training and employing Indian artists. This was to assist their research by recording the plants, birds and animals they had assembled in the newly established Botanical Garden across the river from Calcutta and its menageries. And then there are the famous sketches and drawings by Emily Eden, Sister of Lord Auckland, Governor-General 1836–42 – all 193 of them – many of them drawn and painted by her during Lord Auckland's epic journey in 1837 from Calcutta to Simla and back; and who has not read her famous book *Up the Country*.

These collections of paintings and drawings are a cornucopia of outstanding art, with the greatest strength of the collections being paintings from that earlier period when Indian–British relations were much more relaxed and open than they became later, and when what one might call mutual curiosity gave rise to great artistic creativity.

In my many early visits to Calcutta I often used to visit the Memorial, and as a result became infinitely depressed by the sight of all these wonderful paintings neglected and languishing before my eyes. They almost seemed to be begging someone to return them to their former glory and beauty. Many if not all were badly affected by changes in humidity and temperature, the general pollution of Calcutta, the effects of light, especially ultra-violet radiation, by insects and ants, by bird-droppings – pigeons flew freely within the Memorial and often perched on the frames, crapping away – by fungus, by distortion of the canvas supports, and so on. Furthermore, many of the frames of these paintings were rotting and in a state of extreme deterioration and it seemed to me, seeing all this, that something had to be done, because if it was not done, this great collection would be lost for ever to posterity, and one of the most important and historical art collections in the world would vanish.

But how could I, a person virtually unknown in Calcutta and

India, gain access to the necessary political and cultural authorities in Delhi and Calcutta to gain their approval? And just as importantly, how could I raise the necessary funding to restore and conserve these paintings? All I knew was that it was going to be a long and arduous haul, and in fact, in the end, it took 14 years and proved to be a political and financial roller-coaster.

There were two other people apart from myself who were principally involved in the establishment of the Calcutta Tercentenary Trust. One was Patrick (Paddy) Bowring – a director of Sotheby's where he specialised in British art, and who knew India well; the other Philippa Vaughan, an art historian, who had worked as a consultant on Islamic art at Christie's. She also knew India well, and both of them knew the collections.

At the time I did not know that the Government of India (and I use that expression rather loosely) were not enamoured of these two companies' activities in India, and I have to say that one of the greatest difficulties I had – and there were many – was that the Government of India focused their suspicions on both of them, although they were acting entirely voluntarily for the benefit of this charitable trust which was intended to benefit the Victoria Memorial.

It was in October 1987 that Paddy had written an aide-memoire on the need for action at the Memorial. In this aide-memoire, which included sections on the collections themselves and the conservation of paintings in India – he noted that there were hardly any trained Indian restorers in India and very few were experienced in restoring European oil paintings. There were sections on a training scheme for Indian student restorers, studio and laboratory facilities, the display of paintings and so on. But assuming that the authorities had seen this aide-memoire – and I personally had no idea whether they had or not – there was a paragraph on finance which referred to the many paintings in Government offices and institutions in Bengal, which could be restored and conserved at the Memorial. There was also a reference to other paintings in Bengal, not of significance to Indian heritage in Bengal, which he suggested could be sold within India or overseas. He went on to state that a sensitive area was this sale of 'irrelevant' material, but that the proceeds of such sales would enable a fund to be created for the restoration and conservation of the important paintings in Bengal. He went on to state that it would be better for these 'irrelevant' paintings to be sold rather than to allow them to deteriorate further, which so many had.

There was a natural and understandable sensitivity on the part of the Bengalis to the British returning to their old capital, Calcutta, and the Victoria Memorial of all places to restore and conserve British and European paintings of the eighteenth and nineteenth centuries. One could also say that the whole project might be interpreted as one of implied criticism that the Indians did not have the necessary technical experience and finance to restore these paintings. So Indian pride was involved, particularly in the colonial context, and we therefore had to walk extremely delicately. But, of course, there was more to it than that, and this was that there were certain suspicions in the minds of some Indians that the CTT (as we shall now call it for short) was a device to enable paintings to be got out of India, ostensibly for restoration, but possibly ending up in Sotheby's and Christie's auction rooms for sale on the open market. So I had the Indian suspicion of Sotheby's to cope with and perhaps you will know that when Sotheby's did open in India, it was able to hold only two auctions before the authorities found a way of closing it down.

I, naive as I was, had also to contend with a similar Indian suspicion of Christie's, but this centred not only on Christie's itself but also on Philippa Vaughan, although I found this difficult to believe. Interestingly enough, when the Governor of West Bengal gave a great reception at the Victoria Memorial to celebrate the opening of the exhibition of the paintings, which the CTT had restored, there was an explosion of anger from Professor Panda, the Secretary Curator, when he discovered I had invited two members of the staff of Christie's in London to this reception. So you can see quite clearly from all this that some Indians believed that the CTT had a hidden agenda, and were deeply suspicious of our motives. In particular Dr L.P. Sihare, the then Director-General of the National Museum of India in Delhi, now deceased, was vehemently against the CTT project.

Now for this proposed joint British–Indian project to go ahead, we had to get a number of formal British and Indian approvals and agreements. I say British because the Foreign and Commonwealth Office in London, together with the then excellent UK High Commissioner to India, Sir David Goodall, wanted us to be fully aware of the political sensitivities of such a project for relations between the two countries. Sir David, I recall, advised caution and, although this was not an imprimatur, it was also not a ban, so we pressed ahead. And indeed I was ever afterwards at pains to keep the High Commissioner fully informed, also the British Council in Delhi and Calcutta. I remain ever grateful to the Foreign and Commonwealth Office and the Overseas Development Administration for their generous support for the Trust.

At the same time, while groping my way through this maze, I was advised to seek the advice of INTACH, which stands for the Indian National Trust for Art and Cultural Heritage. I therefore went to see Martand Singh – always for some reason known as Mapu – who was the Director-General of the Trust in Delhi and, as it happens, came from a princely family. INTACH also had a UK arm and here my contact was with Dame Jennifer Jenkins, the wife of Sir Roy Jenkins, the Labour Chancellor, who as you will recall cost me £100,000 in estate duty by extending the *inter vivos* period from five to seven years. She was very helpful, and so I developed useful contacts with INTACH both in India and the UK.

Mapu Singh's advice was that the CTT project should be seen as a voluntary and private British contribution to the 1990 Tercentenary celebrations of the founding of Calcutta by Job Charnock in 1690 – hence the insertion of the word 'Tercentenary' in our name.

The next step was to obtain the approval and formal agreement of the Government of India in Delhi, firstly because, as I have mentioned, the project was politically sensitive, and secondly, because the Victoria Memorial was primarily funded from central funds in Delhi and, in particular, from the Secretary of Culture's budget.

Here it is worth recording that since Independence the Trustees of the Victoria Memorial had been more or less entirely passive – for instance, there had been no addition to the collections – and one could almost say that the Memorial was regarded as a colonial embarrassment – certainly the state of the collections seemed to prove that, although there were two small conservation and restoration units in the Memorial.

The then Secretary of Culture was Baskar Ghose – who was, of course, an officer of the Indian Administrative Service (IAS), the successor service to the British ICS, the Indian Civil Service. He was a Bengali, came from, I think, the 1961 Bengali cadre and mercifully for us he expressed an enormous enthusiasm for our project and again, without his unfailing support, sometimes lost in the labyrinths of the Department of Culture and the Government of West Bengal, we would have got nowhere. So we owe him our deepest gratitude.

We needed, of course, agreement and approval of the Chairman and Board of Trustees of the Victoria Memorial, because without that nothing could happen – the Chairman also being the Governor of West Bengal. So once again we entered the political and diplomatic arena.

Here again we struck lucky. The then deputy High Commissioner of India in London was Salman Haidar and he was known to Philippa Vaughan. So we approached him and asked him for his help and support. He willingly agreed and, indeed, he became another enthusiastic supporter of the CTT to the extent of agreeing to become a Trustee.

Salman Haidar was a very talented and able diplomat – he went on from London to be appointed Indian ambassador to China, one of the most sensitive and important diplomatic appointments in the Indian Foreign Service, and then went on to be one of India's two Foreign Secretaries. He and his Hindu wife Kusum, who was the best Shakespearian actress in India, became good friends.

Now the Governor of West Bengal at the time was Professor Nurul Hassan. He had taken a degree at Allahabad University before going up to New College, Oxford. From 1944 to 1954 he taught at the School of Oriental and African Studies in London before going on from there to be appointed Professor of the Muslim Aligarh University. He was nominated to the Rajya Sabha – the equivalent of the House of Lords in India, i.e. the Upper House of the Parliament of India – and after his election was appointed Minister of Education and Social Welfare for the Central Government in Delhi. Subsequently he was appointed Ambassador to Moscow and thereafter Governor of West Bengal, which was then and still is ruled by a Marxist Government, although this Government is much more pragmatic than it used to be.

Salman Haidar had been a history pupil of his at Aligarh University and they had remained friends He very kindly undertook to appraise the Governor of our proposals for the Victoria Memorial and to seek his consent before I formally wrote to him in September 1988, confirming the verbal agreement between him and Salman Haidar. To this letter I never got a reply, and it is interesting to note that until Viren Shah was appointed Governor around about the turn of the century, I never received one single reply to my letters to the Governors.

I must tell you a little of the make-up of the Board of Trustees of the Victoria Memorial. First, of course, there was the Chairman, the Governor of West Bengal. This, as I have mentioned, was an ex-officio appointment. This meant that every time the Governorship changed, and it changed quite frequently, so also did the Chairmanship of the Board of Trustees. Then there was the Executive Committee, all bureaucrats, who included the Principal Accountant-General of the West Bengal Government, the Mayor of the Calcutta Municipal Corporation, the Secretary of the Higher Education Department of the West Bengal Government who was, of course, an IAS officer and then the Secretary Curator of the Victoria Memorial. These were all trustees with the exception of the Secretary Curator. There were two more ex-officio trustees, one being the Secretary of Culture in Delhi, at that time Baskar Ghose, and also the Financial Adviser to the Department of Culture. However it did not stop there because, in addition, there were another four trustees nominated by the trustees who included a Professor of History, the Director of the National Library, a Professor from the Jawant Nehru University and a former Director of the National Museum in Delhi. But the list goes on. There were what the Indians like to call three further seats nominated by the Secretary of Culture in Delhi and during my time these were a Professor of Calcutta University, a member of Parliament, and Bhaskar Mitter who was the Chairman of the Calcutta Electricity Supply Corporation.

Most of these names meant nothing to me, but there were four key figures: the Governor and Chairman, the Secretary Curator Dr Hiren Chakrabarti, the Secretary of Culture and finally the Secretary of the Higher Educational Department of the West Bengal Government. Dr Hiren Chakrabarti was, as most people were, full of enthusiasm for the CTT and once again we were fortunate.

Hiren Chakrabarti was a historian like his second successor, Professor Panda, and was not particularly qualified to act as Secretary Curator except in the historical sense. His problems as Secretary Curator were formidable, and mainly centred around the shortage of money. His immediate successor was Dr Biswas who, I think, had been Director of the Archaeological Survey of India, and he used to tell me with great pride and joy of his restoration of the

367

very fine temples at Bishnupur. Dr Biswas was appointed provisional Secretary Curator at the Victoria Memorial in addition to his full-time duties as Curator of the Indian Museum in Calcutta. Dr Biswas told me that sometimes the shortage of money was so acute that he used to send a member of his staff by air from Calcutta to Delhi to the Department of Culture who would stay there in the Government Secretariat until he was handed a banker's draft drawn on the State Bank of India in Calcutta. Whereupon he flew back to Calcutta and encashed it so that the salaries and wages could be paid.

However, the worst of his problems was his staff, numbering about 300. The staff were heavily unionised – there were no less than four Communist trade unions of which all four were represented by four Communist members in the West Bengal parliament. They engaged in agitations, strikes and litigation at the drop of a hat, so much so that the management represented by the lone Secretary Curator, Dr Hiren Chakrabarti, was often paralysed with fear.

Dr Chakrabarti was a good historian, a kind man, and an academic who found it almost impossible to manage his unruly staff. When we were there, the unions demanded his immediate removal for what they called alleged irregularities in appointments to senior staff positions in the Memorial and in the management of the Memorial's finances. The general secretary of one of the unions by the name of Mr Phani Bhusch Sen went even further – he accused the Curator of nepotism and of furnishing his little retirement house in the university town of Shanti Niketan with marbles stolen from the Memorial. They therefore started an 'agitation' and in the course of this Dr Chakrabarti was 'gheraoed' in his office in the Memorial. This is a particularly nasty Indian torture whereby the victim is locked up in his office and not allowed to leave – not even to go to the toilet – until demands are met. Toilets did not in fact exist in the Memorial – Lady Alexandra Metcalfe, a daughter of Lord Curzon, told me that the architect forgot about them – so that the staff either relieved themselves from the roof or in the gardens. In fact, when I was there, Dr Chakrabarti had a toilet constructed next to his office, so the next time he was gheraoed it was not too painful. Another toilet – the only other one – was constructed outside on the roof adjacent to our conservation studio at our request.

Not only was Dr Chakrabarti gheraoed and hassled, but so also was his acting successor, Dr Biswas from the Indian Museum, so much so that he suffered a heart attack in the Memorial on his first day there and never went back there again. And the same fate happened to his successor, Dr Chitta Panda, who similarly suffered a heart attack while being hassled by the unions. Thus you will see that there was almost a perpetual state of anarchy in the Memorial, and this was the place where we were proposing to carry out our work of restoration and conservation.

But we were getting somewhere. By the end of 1988 we had the agreement of the Board of Trustees of the Victoria Memorial, who stated that they were 'unanimously appreciative of our most generous offer to raise further funds for the development of the Memorial as a gift to Calcutta on the occasion of its Tercentenary'. We had the agreement of the central Government of India in Delhi via Bhaskar Ghose, the Secretary of Culture, and we had a Memorandum of Understanding signed by all parties so that everybody knew more or less where they were, and the UK authorities were aware of what we were doing and although they had misgivings, quite understandably, they raised no objection. However, with the benefit of hindsight, the Memorandum of Understanding was not legally watertight and if I ever had to undertake something like this again I would have had the Memorandum of Understanding drawn up as a legal document.

With all these agreements in place, we were now able to establish a charitable trust, the CTT, and this was dealt with by the Solicitors Monro & Pennyfeather who had experience of charitable trusts for Indian objectives. They had to obtain the approval of the Charity Commissioners and although restoration and conservation was not high on their agenda, nevertheless we informed them that a twin major objective of the trust was the education and training of young Indian students in the techniques of restoration, and this got us through.

So, in due course, we obtained the Charity Commissioners' approval and, of course, the valuable tax exemption. Four trustees were appointed: myself, Paddy Bowring, Philippa Vaughan and Salman Haidar, the latter in his role as Deputy High Commissioner. A London Committee was formed and we were fortunate in that Lady Wade-Gery joined us. Her husband, Sir Robert, had been High Commissioner to India and, as it happened, both her parents had been born in India and, indeed, her grandfather, Sir William Marris, had been Governor of the United Provinces in the 1920s and he had been the author of the Montagu-Chelmsford Report. And for those of you who are not familiar with this Report, it was that Report that would assist India in its steps along the road to complete self-government within the then Empire. In the event, the concept of a self-governing undivided India was sabotaged by the fatal Hindu–Muslim schism.

The other member of this committee was Sir Anthony Hayward who had been knighted in 1978 and whose family had owned a successful business in Calcutta. I think it was called Hayward's Gin. His presence on the committee gave us an entrée to the most influential people in Calcutta and not only was this invaluable, but also he was able to give the committee the benefit of his advice as to how to cope with the bureaucrats in Calcutta. I once asked him what his main advice was, and he told me that on his father's desk, and also latterly on his own, there was a small plaque on which were written the words 'Amiable Persistence', and how right these words were.

So now we had established a charitable trust – we had received all the necessary permissions and approvals both in India and the UK, but we still had to consider how best to establish ourselves in Calcutta. Should we, for instance, have a Calcutta Committee as well as one in London and, if we did, how could I manage two committees so far apart from each other? In the end, we discarded this idea – I simply could not do it. Instead we used the expression Calcutta Advisory Members of which there were three: Dr Hiren Chakrabarti, the Curator and Secretary; the President of the Bengal Chamber of Commerce; and Robert Wright, the Managing Member of the Tollygunge Club in Deshapran Sasmal Road, where the restorers and conservators would be staying and where I always used to stay in Calcutta.

The Bengal Chamber of Commerce was a powerful organisation and I had hoped thereby to influence donations expressed in rupees our way. But I needed a vehicle which had tax exemption. It so happened that the Bengal Chamber of Commerce had established a Tercentenary Trust themselves which had tax exemption under Section 80 G of the Government of India income tax regulations. I had applied myself for such an exemption but had been turned down. The Bengal Chamber of Commerce – and we will be forever grateful to its Managing Secretary, Mr Pradeep Das Gupta – then proposed that all rupee donations should be routed through their

Tercentenary Trust, so that our Calcutta Tercentenary Trust would be effectively a sub-fund within their fund and we would thus gain the benefit of their tax exemption. I agreed this immediately and from then on we developed a close and very useful relationship with the Chamber.

This brings me on to Bob Wright, who worked indefatigably despite ill-health on our behalf, and without his great support and enthusiasm for our project, it would have fallen flat on its face. Bob's father had been Commissioner of Police in Calcutta and Bob had been born in Lal Bazaar. He had joined the Army in England in 1942 when he was just 18, and had been blown up in his tank on D-Day whilst landing on the beaches of Normandy where he was severely wounded in the leg which bothered him all the rest of his life. Later he joined the Sudan Defence Force.

After King's College, Cambridge, he arrived in Calcutta in 1948, just after Independence, to become a 'covenanted overseas assistant', to use that quaint expression, in the well-known managing agency house of Andrew Yule. He married Anne Layard in 1950. Her father Austen, a descendant of the famous Victorian explorer Sir Henry Layard, and himself a scion of the ICS, had brought Anne and her sister Val to Calcutta where they met. Bob was for a long time Chairman of the Board of Management of Dr Graham's Home, the Kalimpong-based school, which had been established originally as a school for the illegitimate children of young Scottish tea planters in Assam who, as Bob put it, were unable to keep their legs crossed when presented with the beautiful local Khasi girls whose sexual techniques are unparalleled. He was also Chairman of the East India Charitable Trust, the umbrella organisation for numerous charities, schools and old people's homes in Calcutta and West Bengal.

In a way he was best known for his management of the Tollygunge Club, which lasted for more than 25 years from the early 1970s to the late 1990s. He was appointed Managing Member at an extremely difficult and dangerous time for the club: the Naxalites were on the rampage and a previous Managing Member had been murdered at his desk in the office. In a way you could say that Tolly survived because of his shrewd negotiating ability and charm – he certainly had charisma, and this charisma grew out of his generosity and his loyalty to his friends and also from an unending capacity to enjoy life. He converted Tolly from just a weekend

371

place to India's premier family and social club. Bob became a wonderful friend, and although he was only five years older than me, he seemed to become a second father to me – extraordinary. So this was Bob, our Calcutta advisory member.

Most charitable trusts seem to like to have a Patron – presumably to add cachet – so via his Private Secretary, we invited Prince Charles to become a Patron. We needed two, one for the UK and one for India. We felt that the historical connection between the Royal Family and the Victoria Memorial might edge him in our direction. However, his Private Secretary said he was full up on patronships so we turned to HRH Princess Alexandra and she very kindly agreed. So also did His Excellency the Governor of West Bengal, Professor Nurul Hassan and now we had our two patrons in place – another achievement.

But, of course, even though we had all the approvals and agreements in the world, patrons and trustees, nothing would happen without money. The bulk of the fundraising effort fell on me, and we started from nowhere. I knew many Indians, not only, of course, in India but also wealthy Indians in the UK, not only personally but also through banking connections. In the late 1980s there had been some sort of boom on the London Stock Exchange and my initial approaches seemed to fall on fertile soil. Indeed I was hoping to raise a capital sum of say £1 million, the income from which would provide for the annual programmes of restoration, conservation and training. Substantial sums were promised, but the downturn in the stock market put paid to most of those promises and I was forced to consider that any money raised would have to be spent as income and not used to establish a capital fund. There was no time to sit around waiting for money to come in because our permissions and approvals were for a limited period and meanwhile, of course, the paintings were deteriorating in front of our eyes and needed to be saved now rather than later.

I cannot now remember the sequence of donations from companies, private individuals and charitable trusts; suffice to say that by the time we had finished our work in 2001, we had raised about £500,000, mostly in sterling but some in rupees. Some charitable trusts were exceptionally generous and among these I would single out the Headley Trust which is the family trust of Tim Sainsbury. We also received money from the Getty grant programme in the sum of $60,000, of which $40,000 was to provide the funds for the restoration and conservation of 13 of the Daniell masterpieces and $20,000 was for the training of Indian student restorers by us. We also received money from the Foreign and Commonwealth Office and the Overseas Aid Administration, but generally we relied on quite small private donations.

It was, of course, quite difficult to raise a substantial sum for the restoration and conservation of paintings in Calcutta because most people except the cognoscenti associated Calcutta with Mother Teresa and her work among the destitute and dying of that city, and therefore her work was a priority for donations, not ours. It was also difficult raising rupee funds because most of the nouveau riche in India preferred modern Indian paintings, some of them excessively overpriced like those of Husein, and hardly related at all to these masterpieces from what was to them a colonial period. The result of all this was that we had generally to rely on the Indian ancien riche who were now nouveau pauvre due to India's then draconian taxation policies.

Still, we were quite successful and here I must single out Russo Modi, the Chairman of the Tata Iron and Steel Company and Vijay Mallya, the Chairman of United Breweries, whose father and mother were from old Calcutta families. Russo Modi, had a luxurious penthouse apartment in the Tisco headquarters in Chowringhee Road, which had a splendid view of the Victoria Memorial which, at night, was illuminated by the son et lumière courtesy of the Bengal Chamber of Commerce. He cooked us dinners himself, beautifully, and here Bob and I would go along and quite often Jyoti Basu, the Chief Minister of West Bengal, would be there with his wife. Jyoti was a Communist but he was also a practical realist and I am glad to say that his successor is an even more practical Marxist. West Bengal is, or could be, the richest state in India, but it has been held back for years – partly because of its geographical position but mainly because of its Marxist policies.

Of course, we needed seed finance to get us going, and here I was extraordinarily lucky. As Napoleon always said, he did not need good generals, he needed lucky ones, and I was lucky. What happened was this. I was one of the bankers to a company called Control Securities whose Chairman and chief executive was Nazmu Virani. He was an Ismaili so he always attended prayers at the Ismaili Mosque opposite the Victoria and Albert Museum. His family had been wealthy business people in Uganda, but like most of the Ugandan Asians he and his family had been kicked out by Idi Amin, the dictator, whereupon the Ugandan economy fell to bits – this was because practically all the businesses in Uganda were owned by the entrepreneurial Indians. He and his family had arrived in the UK in the mid-1960s virtually destitute, but he had started up again and now commanded considerable wealth. He had been hit by the downturn in the stock market to which I have earlier referred, and could not assist me as much as he wanted. However, it so happened that the famous Bollywood super-star Amitabh Bacchan was due to give a concert in Wembley Stadium, with a huge Indian band flown in specially from Bombay together with all their accompanying dancing girls. How the nautch has changed – or has it? Now it had been decided by the Indian committee who were organising this concert that £250,000 of the gate money proceeds would go to charity. Here my friendship with Nazmu and also with the Hinduja family came into good stead, and it was decided that £50,000 of this gate money would be appropriated to the Calcutta Tercentenary Trust.

In due course the great evening at Wembley Stadium arrived. Diana and I were driven out there by Nazmu in his Rolls Royce and we were then ushered to the Chairman's box where refreshments had been laid on. It was an amazing spectacle; about 50,000 young Indians had congregated in the stadium to welcome their Bollywood hero. I had forgotten how many Indians now live in this country, but by now it must be well over 2 million. Suddenly the lights were dimmed. Amitabh Bacchan galloped into the stadium on a white horse, a single spotlight fixed on him. There was a momentary hush, then there was deafening applause and huge enthusiasm as he rode to the stage, and then the huge band and the Indian dancing girls started their intoxicating rhythms. I had never seen anything like this before in my life – it was quite overwhelming. Towards the end of the concert, as Chairman of the Calcutta Tercentenary Trust, I was ushered onto the stage, and in front of this huge number of excited Indians I was presented with a cheque for £50,000, the seedcorn for our work in Calcutta. I could not have been more grateful to all those thousands of London Indians. So this was the story of how we started, and our work could now go ahead.

First of all we had to send out two experts to assess in detail the condition of the paintings and the amount of restoration work which required to be carried out on the oil paintings and, of course,

On Steeple Jason Island, the furthest western island in the Falklands archipelago, looking eastward to Grand Jason.

Mount Paget, the twin peaks of South Georgia's highest mountain (left) form a backdrop to the Harker Glacier and the ice filled waters of Moraine Fjord.   Photograph P & S Lurcock

The Victoria Memorial Hall, Calcutta, view of the north entrance.

Photograph by Kirti Trivedi, 1997.

Equestrian statue of King-Emperor Edward VII by Sir Bertram Mackennal, circa 1905-10, in bronze. The statue stands atop a commemorative arch at the approach to the south entrance, and was erected by public subscription.

Photograph by Rupert Featherstone 1994.

Temple of Vishnu at Tirruparavikinram, near Madurai (after treatment) by Thomas Daniell, signed and dated 1822, oil on canvas, 127.2 x 102 cm. In his later years Thomas Daniell often drew in great detail on the prepared canvas before starting to paint, particularly architectural features as in this image.

Victoria Memorial Hall (c. 977).

Colonel Antoine Polier, Claude Martin and John Wombwell with the Artist (after treatment) by Johann Zoffany, 1786-87, oil on canvas, 138 x 138 cm - an example of Zoffany's finest work.   Victoria Memorial Hall (R 2066).

Shuja-ud-daulah, Nawab of Awadh, with Four Sons, General Barker and Military Officers (after treatment) by Tilly Kettle, signed and dated 1772, oil on canvas, 284 x 243 cm. This is a compelling instance of illusionist portraiture. Victoria Memorial Hall, indefinite loan (R 5636).

Government House, Calcutta (1799-1802). Built for Lord Wellesley by Charles Wyatt, who based the design on Kedleston Hall; a hundred years later, Lord Curzon occupied both.

Photograph by G.H.R. Tillotson 1992.

the works of art on paper. For the first task we found Patrick Lindsay, a distinguished professional restorer. He had, as it happens, been born and brought up in Peshawar, but had never returned since to the Subcontinent. He had been head of the British team of restorers who had been sent out to Florence after the great floods there. He had been so appointed by the Italian Art and Archives Rescue Fund. He had also spent four years at the National Maritime Museum, Greenwich, teaching the techniques and art of restoration, and he had done similar work for the Fogg Museum at Cambridge. Latterly he was the restorer and consultant to the Royal Academy of Arts and was also surveying the collection of paintings at the Dulwich Picture Gallery. His credentials were, therefore, impeccable and he was very keen to undertake the project.

Patrick Lindsay duly went out to Calcutta and on his return he duly produced his report. He considered that it would require five years to carry out the restoration work on the most important pictures in the collection, and that we needed experienced restorers for both lining and retouching to be sent out from England on an annual basis during the so-called winter months in Calcutta.

He considered that the galleries in which the restored paintings would be hung should be properly lit and air-conditioned, although this latter was abandoned following advice from the National Gallery and British Museum. At that time the Calcutta electricity supply was somewhat intermittent and it was considered that air-conditioning, which went on and off depending on the vagaries of this supply, would do more damage to the paintings than if there was none. Furthermore, in a certain sense the Victoria Memorial building was naturally air-conditioned and this is apparent to those who know the building. He reported that as regards pictures that had been restored within the last ten years, although they had not been structurally damaged, nevertheless their varnishes and retouching were not stable. He went on to say that there was a large amount of very skilled work required to clean, line and retouch the greater part of the oil paintings in the collection and he selected 14 of the most important paintings for early restoration. Furthermore he reported that the restoration work at the highest level of skill required the purchasing of special materials and equipment for lining, retouching, photography, research and print restoration, and that most of this would have to be imported from England. It was a long report

Unfortunately Patrick fell ill during his stay in Calcutta and on his return to the UK he felt that he would be unable to lead the restoration team the following year. This was sad, but Calcutta and India do not always agree with everyone's systems.

The second of the experts we sent out to Calcutta, to carry out a survey of the condition of the works of art on paper, was Jane McCausland. Jane was an expert on the conservation of these pictures. After a ten-year apprenticeship with Craddock & Barnard the Old Master print dealers, she set up her own workshop in London. She won a Churchill Fellowship in 1977 and undertook further studies in America. After this she worked for a time in the Royal Library, Windsor Castle, on the Queen's collection of Holbein's drawings. Her clients included major museums in the UK and overseas and she has written and edited *Paper Conservation* – in short she was just the person we needed to send out to Calcutta.

She was also asked to provide us with a conservation plan. Her report was, as to be expected, to the effect that the climate of Calcutta is unsuitable for the display of paper artefacts for any length of time; that the relative humidity levels fluctuate between 40 and 100 degrees; that the temperatures can reach up to 35°C and even higher; that apart from these damaging agents the pollution in Calcutta is increasingly dangerous; and that, again as we knew, birds continually come and go from the display areas through the open windows. She also reported that these problems and poor management had taken their toll on these most delicate works which in about 80 per cent of the cases was demonstrated by extreme darkening and embrittling of the paper.

She particularly reported on Thomas Daniell's *Twelve Views of Calcutta*, the Fleming Collection of Zoological Drawings and the Samuel Davis Watercolours which had been hanging for 60 years and were in a shocking state, and went on to list the materials required for their treatment. She also went on to report that water was vital for these treatments and that this water supply needed to be fresh and clear. Unfortunately there was no water available, and a supply of this needed to be arranged.

So now we knew where we were with both the oil paintings and the works of art on paper, but we also needed an assessment of the building itself, because this was deteriorating and the roof was leaking water into the galleries and therefore onto some of the paintings. Furthermore, this leaking water had rendered the plasterwork of ceilings, cornices and walls extremely unsound and indeed there had been several large plaster falls. Unless these problems of the roof were addressed and solved as a matter of urgency, it would be impossible to display any works of art in the relevant galleries where we hoped the restored paintings would be hung and exhibited.

As it happens Sir Bernard Fielden, a well-known architectural conservation Consultant had been requested by the Trustees of the Victoria Memorial to assess the state of the building at the same time as we were preparing to start work, and we were given a copy of his report. The aspect of his report in which we took the greatest interest was what he wrote about the state of the roof. He described the tar felt roofing as being totally inadequate and said that it needed constant repair and frequent renewal. Furthermore, the work on the roofs was inhibited by the electrical wiring and light fitments freely placed thereon. It was clear that major work needed to be carried out on the roof by the Archaeological Survey of India, which had now taken over responsibility for the building from the Public Works Department.

So we were now in a position to commence the great project, but at this point Dr Sihare, the Director General of the National Museum in Delhi, tried to sabotage it. He was seriously concerned about 'control' of the project. Salman Haidar wrote him a very long letter explaining that we would only be working in the Victoria Memorial at the invitation of the trustees, and control would always ultimately rest with them. Furthermore, he told Dr Sihare that there was no possibility of any outside agency deciding on priorities. Dr Sihare had stated, in his view, that India had the necessary technical expertise for restoring and conserving the paintings and that the only help India needed was financial. I was aware that this was a very delicate issue among Indian restorers and conservators, and that there were sensitivities all round. It was also the case, as Dr Sihare pointed out, that the National Museum had an indirect role in the matter in that funding for the Eastern Region Conservation Centre, located in the Victoria Memorial, was distributed through the National Museum under his control. This aspect was again dealt with very tactfully by Salman Haidar.

However, Dr Sihare's most serious reservation about the CTT project came from his concern that we were a front for Sotheby's and Christie's. I have referred to this earlier, but this concern was now put to us directly and had to be dealt with. Our approach to this was that we had given a formal undertaking that at no stage would any painting or print be taken from the Victoria Memorial, and that all restoration work would be carried out in Calcutta under the control of the Memorial, and that there was a procedure that would prevent any outside agency from taking control of the collection. In fact, as we all knew, the pictures were far too frail to be moved for restoration and conservation elsewhere, so there was no difficulty in our giving such an undertaking. I am not sure whether Dr Sihare was mollified by such an undertaking and I believe that somewhere along the line police files were raised on Christie's and Sotheby's and their activities in India.

In October 1991, the first team of restorers and conservators went out to Calcutta. Before they went out, we briefed them about the difficulties they might face. We told them, for instance, that they were ambassadors for both their profession and their country, and importantly, that they were working in the Victoria Memorial at the invitation of the trustees and the Government of India. We told them that the CTT was a joint project, and also that they should be mindful that the amount of money they were being paid by the CTT was hugely in excess of the salaries of the Indian restorers and conservators. I recall that the salary of the most senior official in the Memorial, the Secretary Curator, was in the region of £2,000 per annum, and the average salary of an Indian restorer was well below £1,000 per annum. Furthermore the CTT restorers were staying at the Tollygunge Club at the Government of India's expense – this was the Government of India's contribution to the project – and a Tollygunge Club room and its facilities represented total luxury to the museum staff. We also reminded them that as we knew already within the Victoria Memorial there were long-standing professional differences of opinion and that they should not get caught up in any of these feuds – in other words, they had to remain neutral at all times.

We also reminded them about the need to take care of their health: for instance, never to drink tap water or any drink containing ice, but always use soda water instead; and that Indian hospitals often seem chaotic and grubby to overseas visitors – perhaps NHS hospitals in the UK now seem the same to visitors. However, Indian doctors were usually excellent as many had had overseas training and experience. I had taken out health insurance for all the restorers and this included emergency evacuation by air if required. As it happens, this was required the very first year when Deidre Mulley, our team leader, was taken seriously ill; she made a complete recovery. We told them to take with them a course of antibiotics of the kind that will cure not just a bad stomach infection but also a disastrous sore throat; that they should take with them Immodium and an anti-nausea pill; that there was a pill available in Calcutta called Basalgham which cures griping stomach pains and which will enable you to keep on your feet if disaster strikes; that they had to have before they left typhoid, anti-tetanus and gamma globulin injections (the latter for hepatitis), and so on, including that they should take malaria pills – which are not so effective now as they once were.

For those of you who are interested in my 30 years of constantly visiting India, I can tell you that only once was I seriously ill, so much so that I ended up in bed at the Rambagh Palace Hotel in Jaipur. Otherwise I remained healthy all the time.

Finally we briefed them on the problem of poverty in India, which is and has always been a major concern for visitors to India. I always used to have at hand some rupees which I used to hand out to beggars, particularly the old and those who had been mutilated by their parents on purpose. I always used to do this when my car was stopped at red lights – I found it impossible to avert my eyes. The street entrance to the Grand Hotel in Chowringhee always greatly upset me. The Grand Hotel is the best hotel in Calcutta and when you enter it you enter an oasis of calm, luxury, tranquillity and air conditioning. Outside there were beggars, bodies lying on the pavement, a terrible human detritus of hopelessness, helplessness and abject poverty, and the contrast for me was usually too much for my conscience. But what could I do? The answer, to all intents and purposes, was nothing.

Now who were the people we were sending out to Calcutta for the first programme of conservation for the season 1991–92 – the season being the winter season in Calcutta? First of all there was Deidre Mulley who worked for the Area Museum Services in Kenwood; Paul Ackroyd who worked for the National Gallery; Carol Willoughby, the Louvre; Samantha Hodge, the Tate Gallery; David Saunders the National Gallery's scientific expert on preventive conservation of works of art with particular emphasis on climatic and lighting; Stewart Meese, a private conservator who had worked for museums in Stuttgart, Zurich, Brussels and Ottawa; and finally Jane McCausland, who I have already mentioned.

They were met at the airport by cars from the British Council and taken to the Tollygunge Club and almost immediately set to work. We had installed at our expense a fairly large air conditioning plant in the restoration studio on the first floor of the south-west wing, but they found it very noisy. They also found the Metro journey very tiring – I found this surprising as the Calcutta Metro is clean, fast and efficient. However, we took the point and arranged for cars to take them from the club to the Memorial, quite a short journey via the backstreets.

The following year I took Diana and Marcia Brocklebank, a friend, to Calcutta. For Diana it was her first trip to Calcutta. While we were in Calcutta Bob Wright kindly arranged for the Governor to agree to our visiting Barrackpore, the Governor's country seat north of Calcutta. We drove in two non-air-conditioned Ambassador cars – hence the windows being open and hence the entry into the car of all Calcutta's obnoxious fumes and hence Diana's asthma. The journey took two hours and our guide was Bunny Gupta, the foremost authority on the history of Calcutta.

Barrackpore was in British times the most unhealthy military station in Bengal. It was, of course, at Barrackpore and on the vast parade ground there that the two famous mutinies took place. The first was in November 1824 and, from the local point of view, the worst. The reason for this first Mutiny was the circumstances created by the first war by the British against the Burmese. These circumstances were the exaggerated accounts of a British military disaster, the sepoys' abhorrence of a sea journey which they believed would destroy their caste (probably the most important factor), recent changes in regimental organisation, higher pay given to low-caste camp followers, fear of the climate in Arakan, and so on. All this drove the sepoys into what was described as a state of stupid desperation, and to mutiny.

The mutiny was described in great detail by Lady Amherst, the wife of the Governor-General who wrote that before the relieving British troops arrived they were in great danger and entirely at the mercy of the mutineers who could have seized both the Governor-General and the Commander-in-Chief who were then at Barrackpore, their country seat. This is now a military hospital, and still a fine but dilapidated building and quite small – not at all the great palace which Lord Wellesley wanted to build there but which was vetoed by the East India Company Court of Directors on the grounds of expense; he had only just completed Government House in Calcutta at vast expense. Bishop Cotton, who used to go to Barrackpore, said that none of the bedrooms were even tolerable in the Bengal climate.

The Mutiny was eventually suppressed but 33 years later what became known as the Great Mutiny took place, once again on the same parade ground. Now the story of what happened here on 29th March 1857 is too well known for me to repeat, but what I would like to do here is to turn from the parade ground to the British barracks. I have here at home some remarkable drawings of the great barracks and the vast parade ground. It was Rudyard Kipling who described the conditions of the old British Volunteer Army in India. He described the sweltering barracks, the red coats, the pipe-clayed belts and the pillbox hats, the beer, the fights, the floggings, the hangings and the crucifixions, the bugle calls, the smell of oats and horse-piss, the bellowing sergeants with their foot-long moustaches, the bloody skirmishes, the crowded troop-ships, the cholera-stricken camps, the 'native concubines' and the ultimate death in the workhouse. It is, of course, a crude picture, but as Kipling said, future generations would be able to gather some idea of what a long-term volunteer army was like and what a life the volunteers had in these huge barracks.

As guests of the Governor, we spent some time walking round the Park. To the north of what was Government House is situated the famous Hall of Fame surrounded by its colonnade of Corinthian columns. Over the outside entrance is a black slab inscribed 'To the Memory of the Brave', and on the walls are four tablets erected by different Governor-Generals to the memory of British officers and soldiers who fell during the conquest of Mauritius and Java in 1811, and who also fell in the Isle of France in 1810, and Maharajpur and Paniar in 1843.

It was both peaceful and evocative to see those tablets in this beautiful colonnaded building in Bengal and to reflect on the lives of those soldiers who had fought and died in these campaigns so far away from England – the imperial urge must have been very strong and compelling.

Close to the Hall of Fame are many of the statues which once adorned the Maidan in Calcutta and adjacent administrative buildings.

Many of these statues found their way near to the Hall of Fame in the 1970s and were erected on new pedestals; here are the equestrian figures of the Earl of Minto, the Earl of Mayo, Lord Napier, Lord Lansdowne and Woodburn – I cannot remember whether he was a Lord, but I expect he was. A marble figure of King George V looks out on to the Hoogli river from beneath the portico of the Hall of Fame, while across the gardens we saw the statues of Montagu, Lawrence, Ronaldshay, Curzon and Northbrook, a veritable Valhalla of great British imperialists. The interesting thing is that someone must have spent a great deal of time and money preparing the new sites and pedestals – the old pedestals remain in Calcutta – and the whole design arrangement of these statues. But the even more interesting thing is that the Indians have now got over their colonial complex and are now thinking about returning these statues to Calcutta. Indeed, in February 2000, when I was in Calcutta, an article appeared in the papers to the effect that 'Calcutta's Marxists Put the Raj Back on a Pedestal', and when the then Public Works Department Minister was asked why, he said it was for artistic rather than political reasons – indeed he said the statues are great works of art.

Moving on we paid our homage to the grave of Charlotte Canning, the wife of 'Clemency' Canning, the Governor-General, with nearby his great equestrian statue overlooking his grave, and we remembered that when Bishop Cotton consecrated this grave he consecrated it only for the families of the Governor-Generals of India. And when the consecration was over, it was reported that Lord Canning walked back slowly and alone to the desolate house nearby.

During the first full season of conservation, the CTT team completed conservation work on some 20 paintings, leaving another five partly treated. A detailed survey was also carried out on the picture frames, many of which were falling apart. However, all was not well within the Memorial itself. What had happened was that a senior Indian restorer by the name of Arun Ghose had become disaffected; I never quite understood whether this disaffection extended to the CTT and its restorers and conservators as his nose had inevitably been put out of joint by our arrival. To cut a long story short, and there were many such stories, Arun Ghose brought the unions out on strike and made various demands for more staff and improved conditions. As I have mentioned earlier they also gheraoed Hiren Chakrabarti, the Secretary Curator, in his office and made various personal accusations against him including corruption and nepotism. Our Indian student restorers were allowed into the museum but were not allowed to work. Furthermore, the museum staff were refusing to pay the agreed Tollygunge bills for the restorers – agreed because this was the Government of India's contribution to this joint project.

One of the keepers in the museum by the name of Pankash Datta was resistant to every suggestion by the CTT team, and because he had recently been made a keeper, this gave him the prime excuse not to part with the keys to the store-cabinets on any pretext – to the extent that the restorers were not allowed to see any of the collections in store for a period of six weeks. Even though he was instructed by the Secretary Curator to open up these cabinets, he refused and generally adopted an attitude of non-cooperation. Later on that year, 1992, we were informed by the Government of India that the Secretary Curator's tenure of office may well not be renewed, as they felt he had lost the confidence of the museum staff. If he went, as appeared likely, then a successor needed to be found, but this would prove extremely difficult as hardly anyone was willing to work in Calcutta and particularly at the Memorial which was by now in a state of permanent anarchy. The Government was aware that Arun Ghose badly wanted the job, but firstly, he did not have a degree, and secondly, he had not published anything, and we were told, therefore, it was unlikely he would get the job. The Secretary Curator did indeed retire at the end of that year 1992. No successor could be found at the time, so there was a total management vacuum and because there was nobody in charge, managing the CTT became extremely difficult. In the end, as I have mentioned earlier, Dr Biswas, the Secretary Curator of the Indian Museum in Calcutta, was appointed acting Secretary Curator of the Victoria Memorial, but that did not work because, on his first visit to the Memorial, he was gheraoed in his office, had a heart attack and refused to go anywhere near the Memorial ever again.

Now I must tell you a little about Dr Biswas, who before he was Curator of the Indian Museum in Calcutta was a senior manager if not the Director of the Archaeological Survey of India. After Calcutta he went on to become the Director of the National Museum of India in Delhi.

When he was with the Archaeological Survey, he spent a lot of his time restoring and conserving the beautiful mediaeval temples at Bishnupur in West Bengal. Bishnupur is about 100 miles from Calcutta, and although the temples are well known in West Bengal, they are far from being well known outside the state – they should be. Bishnupur was once the seat of a powerful family of rulers known as the Mallas. The Mallas were immensely wealthy and used their wealth to build a series of 30 magnificent temples. These are quite beautiful and many of them are richly decorated with ornamental carvings, particularly on the huge pillars of the arched entrances. Most of them were constructed in the seventeenth century. Eventually the Mallas fell on hard times which started with the raids of the Mahrattas and the land expansion of the Zamindars of Bardhaman. In the end the land was sold up by the British East India Company in 1805 for arrears of land revenue, and the Bardhaman Zamindars acquired them. Thus ended the glory and beautiful magnificence of these temples which were left to decay. But now they have nearly all been restored and Dr Biswas was the architect and chief mover of this great work of restoration and conservation. So go and see them – full marks to that great man Dr S.S. Biswas.

Now, while this was going on, I became aware of the Curzon Trust – a fund which had been established by Lord Curzon for the Memorial. As this trust fund was specifically for the benefit of the Memorial and the CTT was, as ever, short of funds, I felt this was a likely source of money. I discovered that the sole trustee was the Governor of West Bengal and he was also the sole signatory on the bank account. The funds were in sterling and I ascertained that they were probably deposited with the State Bank of India in London, but that was all, except that there was a counsel's opinion written in 1977 indicating that these Curzon Trust funds could be used for restoration and conservation. This was confirmed to me by Lady Alexandra Metcalfe (Baba), a daughter of Lord Curzon and who had been married to Fruity Metcalfe, she gave me a copy of the opinion. Again, to cut a long story short, every approach I made to access these funds was met with a wall of impenetrable silence – I was always being told that it would happen, but it never did. The final blow came some time later when I was told that, just as the Governor was about to append his signature to a cheque for £10,000 in our favour, he suffered a heart attack and dropped down dead – so that was the end of that.

While all this was going on a considerable amount of money was being attracted to the CTT and we therefore made plans to carry out a second programme in 1992–93. You will recall that Deidre Mulley, the leader of the previous programme, had fallen ill and had to be flown home with an Indian doctor accompanying her. So now we had to turn our mind to the question of her successor. For this position we lighted on Rupert Featherstone, who was the No. 2 in the Royal Studio and was highly recommended by the head of that studio, namely Viola Pemberton Piggott. He was prepared to spend 4–5 months in Calcutta with Emma, who he was shortly to marry and who was also a painter and potter. Clearly he had to clarify his position with the Royal Studio; I am not sure whether he did this by leave of absence or by resigning temporarily, but anyway he came across to us and with him came Carole Milner from the Louvre in Paris; Andrea Gall from the National Portrait Gallery; Ann Baxter from the Area Museum Service; Annette Rupprecht from the Institute of Fine Arts in New York; Victoria Marshal from the Southampton City Art Gallery, and Samantha Hodge and Ian Rolls both of whom had worked with us in Calcutta the previous season. All were highly qualified and keen to be associated with this increasingly high-profile project – that is to say, the restoration and conservation of one of the finest art collections in the world, hitherto almost unknown. In general, the 1992–93 season went well. There were curfews from time to time due to political disturbances, but nothing serious.

Rupert Featherstone carried out an inspection of all the British and European heritage paintings in the possession of the Asiatic Society in Park Street. These were all wrapped up in newspaper in the cellar. Some of them had been restored by Indian restorers and Rupert was critical of their work – some of them had been restored by Delhi restorers. Unfortunately his report, which was strictly private and confidential, got leaked to the New Delhi newspapers by, presumably the Asiatic Society in Calcutta. There was a furore and that was more or less the end of our relationship with the Society, although they did ask us again some time later to restore their paintings but by this time we had neither the funds nor the inclination. Apart from anything else the society, like most institutions in Calcutta, was prone to litigation – and as an aside here the Secretary Curator of the Memorial had a lot of his time taken up by litigation.

After lengthy and time-consuming negotiations, we arranged for one of the Indian restorers by the name of Shanti Majee to train for a year in the UK and we also similarly arranged for a member of the staff by the name of Annusya Bhattarcharyya to be trained by the Victoria & Albert Museum in London for a curatorship position. All this was expensive and we took a long time finding the necessary grant monies. However, when Annusya Bhattarcharyya returned to Calcutta she never went back to the Memorial and went straight on to Australia where her husband was working, so we were left with egg on our faces and anger in our hearts – indeed so much so that we asked the Indian authorities in Australia to try and trace her with a view to getting our money back, several thousand pounds which we could ill afford. So this element of the joint project fell flat on its face.

We had from the start of this project the desire to see the restored paintings exhibited to the public. We had, we thought, been assigned the first-floor galleries in the south-west wing of the Memorial, adjacent to which is one of the towers where our restoration studio was situated. Unfortunately there were a number of difficulties such as the leaking roof, the amount of money needed to be spent on the refurbishment of the galleries, including preventing the pigeons and other birds getting in. By this time we had discarded the idea of air conditioning following various reports, but the chief difficulty was the Indian National Leaders Portrait Gallery which was adjacent to ours, so to speak, and we needed that one as well. However, the idea of the National Leaders' portraits being displaced by colonial portraits and paintings was offensive to the Indians, and in the end we got nowhere. Only eight years later were we fortunate in getting a new Governor by the name of Viren Shah, a Bombay industrialist but nevertheless somehow acceptable to the Marxist government, who became, of course, Chairman of the Memorial Trust. He was very interested in restoration and conservation and so he took a close interest in our work. So interested was he that he ordered a former Chief Secretary of the Government, Mr Dutt, whom I knew, to provide us with all the support we needed for the paintings to be exhibited.

This was in 2000 so I have run well ahead – but following the death of Nurul Hassan, a new Governor was appointed. I think his name was Raghunatha Reddy, who was a left-wing trade union lawyer. He was very deaf, could hardly speak any English, and more or less declined to speak to me at all. On one occasion I had lunch with him in Delhi at the Indian International Centre before leaving for an important meeting with him and other officials at the West Bengal Governor's Residence in Delhi. Baskar Ghose was with me. The only words the Governor addressed to me during lunch, the car journey and the two-hour meeting were to the effect that he thought the fish at the International Centre was very good.

But worst of all he had a Private Secretary by the name of Mr Chaturvedi who, I am convinced to this day, did everything he could to sabotage the CTT. I greatly distrusted him – so much so that once when I was in Raj Bhavan with Mr Reddy, the Governor, and he asked me which flight I was catching to return to London, I refused to tell him in case I should get arrested at the airport for violation of the Indian foreign exchange regulations – the pretext being that the CTT was keeping out of India monies which should have been remitted to India and, of course, converted to rupees. This was an outrageous accusation which, although it was never put in writing, was nevertheless hinted at from time to time. Later on suspicion of the CTT grew to a fever pitch when the Getty Trust in Los Angeles granted us a donation of $60,000 which resulted in the Marxist government regarding the CTT as a conduit for CIA funds to subvert their powers. All this was nonsense, of course, but the CTT was to Indian eyes an unusual beast and it aroused significant suspicion as to its motives.

Returning to the National Leaders Portrait Gallery, all the work we had carried out to set the exhibition ball rolling came to nothing. Even the proposal which the acting curator, Dr Biswas, and I hatched up whereby the National Leaders portraits would be 'promoted' from the first floor to the ground floor to assuage the nationalist sentiments, fell on stony ground and it was clear that there would be no cooperation from either this Governor or his Secretary.

We had lost a great deal of time as a result of the curfews, the political and communal disturbances, the gheraoing and the general anarchy in the Memorial, so in January 1993 we instructed Rupert not to take time off to prepare a lecture programme, not to work towards an exhibition, to give up training the Indian student restorers and instead to concentrate on the work of restoration only. Despite the difficulties during the 1992–93 programme, the CTT team were able to restore fully 14 paintings, mainly by the Daniells, Tilly

Kettle, A.W. Devis and Thomas Hickey, and a further nine were partially completed including Zoffany's newly discovered *Tiger Hunt* and several works by the Daniells and Hodges. A great deal of progress had been made towards keeping out birds and bats and generally reducing light levels. In addition a lot of work had been done on a hanging plan for the paintings devised by Rupert Featherstone and Charles Greig, preparatory to what we hoped would be the opening of the three CTT galleries in 1995 – although all this work proved abortive and it was to be another six years before the paintings were exhibited. Furthermore, progress had been maintained on the definitive catalogue by Charles Greig's work on the watercolours and portraits, whilst finally the photo-documentation of the collection had gone ahead with new equipment which the CTT had bought. In all the total number of pictures treated or under treatment was 47, and we had raised £180,000 at this stage together with an ODA grant of £10,000. So far so good, and we had some reason to be satisfied.

A very important associated object of the CTT was the training and education of Indian student restorers in the techniques of restoration and conservation, and it was for this particular aspect of our work that we had been able to achieve charitable status. The intention had always been that we should establish a cadre of trained Indian restorers and conservators who would continue to work to complete the trust's primary objectives – the restoration of the paintings.

We had hoped, as I mentioned earlier, to raise a significant capital fund from the income out of which the annual restoration programme, costing us about £50,000, would be financed. Because of my inability to raise this capital sum, we had perforce to live from hand to mouth financially. In any case, as I have mentioned, we had hoped that after 4–5 years' training and education this cadre would have been established formally, which would therefore have enabled us to act in a more consultative and advisory role for the restoration and conservation programmes and, of course, reduce significantly our annual funding requirement.

However, this never occurred – none of the CTT Indian restorers and conservators were ever appointed to the permanent and pensionable staff of the Memorial, with the consequent risk to the programme that they would leave for better pay elsewhere and in particular private practice, so that all our work would therefore be in vain. During the whole time we were in Calcutta we applied great pressure not only on the Memorial management but also on the Secretary of Culture in Delhi as well as the Trustees of the Memorial to so appoint them – but this never happened. We never really knew whether it was unwillingness or inability on the part of the management to do this. Various reasons were given to us including the reservation of jobs for the backward classes and scheduled castes, but at the end of the day, it was more likely that it was union opposition to the promotion of anyone who was working for the CTT in the studios.

Some of the young Indian student restorers and conservators were exceptionally talented, unlike their seniors, in whom we had little faith or confidence and who tended to be careless and sometimes, we thought, deliberately careless. For instance Sujit Ray, a young restorer, had a particular talent in restoring and colour matching, and did some excellent work. But occasionally he had a depressing inertia which was due to the disruptive and bullying nature of the acting head of the studio, by the name of Mainak Sanker Ray, who was not only a maniac in our view but who was a depressive influence on even the best-intentioned. Sujit Ray was married with a family and had been initially appointed as an assistant restorer in the scheduled caste reserved quota in 1989 at a monthly salary of 1400 rupees – say £60 per month – but he had never been appointed to the permanent and therefore pensionable staff. His letters were heartrending:

> Respected Sir, Most respectfully with humble submission I beg to state ... I would therefore earnestly request that you would kindly look into the matter with a sympathetic view and considering the deplorable economic condition of my family, you would kindly favour me with a permanent posting with a view to relieving my mental anxieties. Early action in regard to this matter is highly solicited.

Then there was Subir Dey who had worked in the Paper Conservation Department since the beginning of the CTT project. He worked extremely well and was both diligent and conscientious. He spoke and wrote English perfectly and, in our view, he had quite exceptionally good manual dexterity for paper conservation. He was therefore a young man of very considerable potential but

389

could we get him a permanent pensionable position? The answer was no.

There was also Shanti Majee, who was married and a very good restorer. She had had wide and varied experience over a number of years in studios overseas. She had trained for some years in Poland (she spoke Polish fluently) at the Copernicus University studying conservation and museology. We had also found the money to enable her to study on the conservation training course at Newcastle University, followed by internships at the Area Museum Service for South-East England and also at the Victoria and Albert Museum. We took the view that she was indeed probably one of the best-trained and ablest restorers of paintings in India, but could we get her appointed to the permanent and pensionable staff? Here, once again, the answer was no. It was all immensely frustrating.

Our financial position had always been precarious, so in December 1992 we decided to write to Deborah Marrow, the director of the Getty grant programme in Santa Monica, California, to request financial support in the form of a grant. Essentially we gave her the background to the project, advising her at the same time that we had both a conservation and a training programme; the object of the latter, as I have mentioned earlier, being to make the Memorial self-sufficient in qualified restorers and conservators. We also stated that after three years of research, we fully understood the needs of the collection and had employed top-class restorers to work on it and that furthermore, without this CTT project, the entire collection would soon be damaged beyond recall, because at present India had neither the expertise nor the financial resources to save it for posterity.

We had a reply on 4th February from Deborah Marrow acknowledging our letter and telling us that she had passed it on to Tim Whalen, the Getty programme officer who managed the conservation grants. In March 1993 we had a letter from Tim Whalen enclosing a paper entitled 'Conservation Survey, Treatment and Training Guidelines' which included a section described as 'Application Instructions', setting out the information which he needed to consider a proposal – in other words we had to apply to apply. However the tone of the letter was sympathetic and later in July 1993, we received another letter from Tim Whalen telling us that if the CTT believed a conservation treatment grant was the most appropriate next step, then he would welcome a more detailed inquiry from the CTT regarding the proposal. He went on to say that a proposal for the grant programme would need to be much more specific and he required a list of the individual pictures for which support was requested. So we had to provide a short description of the significance of the paintings to be conserved, information on their current condition, information on the personnel who would be undertaking the conservation work, a description of the proposed treatment, an estimate of the amount of financial support which we would request from the programme, information on the charitable status of the CTT and so on. It was all extremely thorough and presented us with a huge amount of work. They also required details of our costings, which involved a great deal of mathematics and a letter of approval from the Secretary Curator of the Memorial. We mentioned Hiren Chakrabarti's inability to write letters, citing ill health, and asked if a letter of approval from the Secretary of Culture Bhaskar Ghose would suffice. We were told that this would do temporarily, but they still needed a letter for the formal application. In the event we drafted this ourselves and took it to Calcutta where the Secretary Curator signed it just before he formally retired. As it happened Bhaskar Ghose said he could not sign such a letter as he was no longer Secretary of Culture but an officer on special duty at the Ministry of Information and Broadcasting pending him taking over that ministry at the end of the following month.

A year after we had first started we wrote to Tim Whalen applying for permission to submit a formal application for a treatment grant – this application was 15 pages long. In March 1994 Tim Whalen wrote to us to say that our project appeared to be eligible for grant consideration, and enclosed the application instructions in triplicate. We were also told that any treatment grant had to be matched by the CTT which was difficult but not insuperable, although these matching funds had to be guaranteed and so on. By now we had moved on to 1995 when we had to deal with technical conservation questions and points raised by the Getty's outside advisory conservators. But on 25th August 1995, nearly three years after we had started down this Getty route, we were advised that we had been successful: $40,000 by way of a treatment grant and $20,000 for the training programme. Not only did we have a cheque for $60,000, but the CTT now had international recognition for its work.

You may wonder why I have taken you through this lengthy

Getty application process, and there are two points here: the incredible thoroughness of the Getty grant procedure, which I have to say must be greatly commended; and the enormous amount of work we had to carry out ourselves and the required thoroughness of that very detailed work also. But we had got there in the end, mirabile dictu!!

By the middle of 1993 we had raised about £200,000; we had established and equipped to modern international standards two studios in the Memorial, one for restoration and one for conservation; we had had three successful annual programmes; the CTT had the full support of the Government of India, who were paying a significant element of our rupee expenses; the Government had also told us that they attached great importance to this joint project and that they wished to use the CTT as a mechanism for the restoration and conservation of the other European and British art collections in Hyderabad, Madras and Bombay. All this was, of course, music to our ears but it did not add anything to our financial resources which were fast diminishing.

The Government of India then had a bright idea, which we fully supported, and that was that at that time the UK Government's annual grant to India was running at about £90 million, and they therefore suggested that of this figure of £90 million, some £200,000 should be allocated by them to the CTT and that they the Government of India were both quite prepared and willing to write to the UK Government at Ministerial level or even at a higher level, if necessary, requesting such an allocation. I am afraid to say this request to the UK Government fell on stony ground and that was the end of that bright idea initiated by the Government of India, who after all was the Government in receipt of the UK aid monies. However, we did get another cheque from the ODA for £10,000, but it was interesting that the advice note accompanying the cheque specifically stated that these monies were ex-UNESCO funds (the United Nations Educational, Scientific and Cultural Organisation), which seemed curious.

In July 1993 the Governor, our Patron and Chairman of the Victoria Memorial Trust Professor Nurul Hassan, as I have previously mentioned, died of a heart attack with his hand poised to write a cheque to the CTT for £10,000 from the Curzon Trust – so that was the end of that source of funds. Nurul Hassan had been a supporter of the trust and we would not have been there in the

Memorial without his encouragement. I missed our cosy chats in Government House, Raj Bhavan, although I had always to do the running conversationally speaking for about 20 minutes before he opened his mouth not only to speak but also to gobble up the teacakes and sandwiches, which always arrived halfway through the meeting. We were concerned also about Bhaskar Ghose's transfer to run the Ministry of Information and Broadcasting and we were also worried about the probable forthcoming retirement of the Secretary Curator, Dr Hiren Chakrabarti. Suddenly, three of those people who had been greatly supportive of our efforts had gone or were going, and we were now much more on our own with a new Governor, Mr Reddy, formerly the Governor of Orissa, and a new Secretary of Culture, Dr Mahapatra, but no new Secretary Curator. However, there was some good news, and that was that at long last the Archaeological Survey of India had been given the go-ahead, which meant the funds, to start repairing the leaking roof of the Memorial.

At about this time there had been a huge earthquake in Maharashta State and for this the West Bengal Chief Minister Jyoti Basu had established his own Earthquake Relief Fund for the aid of the victims, of which there were thousands and thousands. Jyoti Basu naturally leaned on the Bengal Chamber of Commerce, whose President was our CTT advisory member in Calcutta. He telephoned me to ask whether I would be agreeable to a lakh of our rupee funds, which were lodged with the Chamber's Tercentenary Trust, being made available to the Chief Minister's Fund. Somewhat reluctantly I agreed, silently wondering whether our Indian rupee donors would be aggrieved if they found out that a lakh of their donations for the Memorial's paintings had been diverted to Maharashta, but I felt I could hardly refuse, bearing in mind the importance to us of both the Bengal Chamber of Commerce and the Chief Minister. Also I had to bear in mind that both the Chamber and ourselves were about to launch an appeal for funds in rupees for the refurbishment of what we fondly thought of as our CTT galleries. This never happened, although we had by this time settled the wording of the appeal letter, including the budgeted amount for the galleries, namely 35 lakhs or about £78,000 using the then exchange rate of INR 45 to £1 sterling (a lakh is 100,000 rupees).

Meanwhile, we had started to prepare our 1993–94 programme which we had estimated would cost in the region of £70,000. Many of the restorers going out would be the same as in previous years but, in addition, there would be Adriano Lorenzelli who specialised in restoring gilt frames and Joanna Kosek from the British Museum, who specialised in the conservation of works of art on paper.

It was about this time that we became aware that there was a problem with two of the paintings which we were restoring, and this was over whether these two paintings were on loan to the Memorial from the Royal Collection, or on permanent loan, or whether they had been deemed to have been gifted to the Memorial and, if so, when and why, and whether there was any documentation. The two paintings in question were as follows: a portrait of Mohammed Ali Khan the Nawab of Arcot, by George Willison c 1774–75, which was numbered 1192 in Sir Oliver Millar's Later Georgian Pictures in the Royal Collection, and Ghazi-Ud-Din Haidar, King of Oudh, receiving tributes, by Robert Home – Oliver Millar's No. 832. We never got to the bottom of this except there was a rumour going round that the Memorial was holding them hostage in case the British were unwilling to give up the lease of the High Commissioner's Residence in New Delhi – I think this lease was shortening up.

Charles Greig, who was documenting the collection for us, also became concerned as to the ownership of the Tilly Kettle paintings. The ownership of these magnificent paintings was contested by the Burdwan family, who had been the largest Zamindari family in Bengal and had indeed donated many paintings to the Memorial. As the Burdwan family continued to assert ownership, we felt that we needed an agreement whereby, if their ownership was proved at some future date and the paintings were withdrawn from the Memorial, then we the CTT would need to be reimbursed for the costs of their restoration and conservation. Once again we never got to the bottom of this and as Danny Mahtab, a member of the Burdwan family ,was himself a trustee of the Memorial, we felt we could not insist on such an agreement. It was also the case that Danny and his wife Pussy were always immensely generous to us when we were working in Calcutta, giving us all sorts of parties and providing us with a huge welcome, and also incidentally an insight into the politics of the Memorial. I will always be enormously grateful to them both, and perhaps I could add here that I remain hugely grateful to everybody in Calcutta for their welcome and hospitality and the support they gave us – in such a way that Calcutta almost became a second home to me. I thank them all from the bottom of my heart.

Despite all our trials and tribulations, by the end of our 1993–94 season the CTT with its eleven restorers and conservators in Calcutta had fully restored 15 paintings with eight partially completed, so that the total number of paintings fully restored since the inception of our project stood at 46, with a further eight partially completed and 12 minor treatments – a total of 66 paintings.

Our main concern was still the refurbishment of the south-west wing first-floor galleries, where it was intended at that time the restored paintings would be hung and exhibited. Repairs to the roof undertaken by the Calcutta Public Works Department some years ago had not proved satisfactory, and during the monsoon of 1993 the roof had again begun to leak badly, although fortunately without causing any damage to the paintings. However, falling plaster from the cornices and upper walls had become a hazard. All this was now under the supervision of the Archaeological Survey of India and the problem was now being ameliorated by extensive repairs.

A new problem had however arisen and that was the non-payment by the Memorial to the Tollygunge Club of the restorers' board and lodging charges, which under the agreement between the Memorial and the CTT was the Memorial's responsibility. In fact, since Hiren Chakrabarti's retirement, no bills had been paid at all and the amount had now risen to 3.87 lakhs and even Bob Wright, the Managing Member of the club, was getting restive. At the same time the Bengal Chamber of Commerce, who together with the CTT, was proposing to appeal for funds amounting to 40 lakhs to cover the refurbishment of 'our' galleries had not been paid by the Memorial under its Son et Lumière contract. As a result the Chamber was reluctant to appeal to its members for new funds for the Memorial, when the Memorial was already in default to the Chamber. Furthermore our proposed exhibition following the galleries' refurbishment was dependent on the National Leaders portraits being 'promoted' downstairs to the Durbar Hall. Here, nothing had happened. So what with several senior posts in the Memorial being vacant and unfilled, no supervision of staff, no letters being answered, no Secretary Curator and no cash – it was a difficult position because nobody would take responsibility for anything.

In the end I got into the extraordinary position of being asked by Ashok Vajpeyi, a Joint Secretary of Culture in Delhi and incidentally a famous Indian poet, to draft out a letter addressed to him, Ashok Vajpeyi, to be signed by Dr Biswas the acting Secretary Curator of the Memorial, setting out these problems. Furthermore, I had to clear my draft letter with Ashok Vajpeyi before getting it signed by Dr Biswas.

Following this letter a meeting was held in July 1994, at No. 2 Circular Road, Delhi, the residence of the Governor of West Bengal when he was in Delhi. This meeting was arranged and organised by Salman Haidar, who was by now the Secretary of State for India's external affairs. At this meeting there were present, apart from myself, the Governor of West Bengal, his Private Secretary, Mr Chaturvedi (the man who I never trusted), Mr Sardannah the Resident Commissioner in Delhi of the West Bengal Government, Dr Biswas and, of course, Salman Haidar. At this meeting which I have mentioned earlier the Governor, also of course the Chairman of the Victoria Memorial's Board of Trustees, never uttered a single word.

Before I went to this meeting I went to see Bhaskar Ghose at his offices in Shastri Bhavan. He was, as always, very encouraging and did not think there would be too much of a problem in the Government of India underwriting the costs of the gallery refurbishment spread over two financial years. He also told me that Ashok Vajpeyi was very close to the minister, Arjun Singh, and that Vajpeyi was now the force in the Department of Culture, not the Secretary, Dr Mahapatra. So I had high hopes of the meeting and indeed after it Ashok Vajpeyi came round to have dinner with me at my friend Raman Sidhu's residence. He was in extremely good form and told me not to worry about these problems, and seemed quite confident that there would be no particular difficulties. In the event nothing very much happened, and on my particular point about the status and position of the Indian restorers and conservators who were assisting us at the CTT, a subject very close to our hearts, Dr Biswas advised the meeting that, with the best will in the world, he was unable to comply with our wishes – the reason being that the Memorial had not complied for the last two to three years with the Government of India's regulations on job reservations for the scheduled castes and backward classes, and that until this backlog had been cleared and a balance restored between the various classes and castes, then he could not fill these posts. He also reminded the meeting that he was obliged to deal with no less than four Communist trade unions and that this was no easy matter, so the impasse remained, and it remained until we left Calcutta seven years later.

In the meantime, we had to proceed towards the 1994–95 programme without any progress having been made on the matters referred to earlier. Rupert Featherstone returned to Calcutta in the autumn; there was still no new Curator; no bills had been paid by the Memorial and the new Governor (the silent one) was digging his toes in; Dr Biswas was still continuing to refuse to set foot in the Memorial, and having been physically threatened and gheraoed he had effectively given up any responsibility for the Memorial; the proposed refurbishment had not got anywhere, especially as the designer and contractor for the work was disliked by Dr Biswas; and the Bengal Chamber of Commerce had given up any thoughts of appealing for funds for the galleries refurbishment. All this was very depressing. We even made an approach to Jyoti Basu, the Chief Minister, to help us. He was very aware of the problem and said that he would do all he could to solve it but that, at the end of the day, it was a matter for the Governor of West Bengal in his capacity as Chairman of the Memorial's Board of Trustees. At this stage I went out to Calcutta but before I did so I wrote a long letter to the Minister of Human Resources, Arjun Singh, whose responsibilities included the Department of Culture and therefore the Memorial, setting out my concerns and requesting assistance. Nothing happened, and furthermore I was advised by our proposed designer and contractor for the galleries refurbishment that he would not now enter into any sort of financial arrangement with the Memorial.

For the season 1994–95 we had a total of 12 restorers in Calcutta as against ten the previous year and nine before. Furthermore, some of these restorers were staying longer, as we were in a hurry to complete our work. The question of the reimbursement of their accommodation charges arose again as the estimate for the 1994–95 season had risen to the very large figure of 11.7 lakhs as opposed to 8.67 lakhs for 1993–94. I had never negotiated a fixed charge with the Memorial – I had never negotiated a fixed number of restorers going out to Calcutta – and meanwhile the prices at the Tollygunge Club were rising, so that a single room now cost 1400 rupees – (say £28 per night) and a double room 1500 rupees. This, of course, did not seem very much to us, but put into the context that the monthly salary of an Indian restorer at the Memorial was 1400 rupees and that the monthly salary of one of our restorers was say £2,800, sometimes more, you can see the huge disparity and the ill-feeling that this could lead to. I am afraid I was not too sensitive about all this, because in truth I could not be if, firstly, I had to pay the restorers and conservators the going UK rate with also an enticement to live and work in Calcutta and, secondly, they had to be housed at the Tollygunge Club because they refused to stay anywhere else; and, of course, the project had to proceed. But the Governor, perhaps more understandably, saw large sums of money being taken out of his Memorial budget to pay for these foreign restorers. This impasse waxed and waned during the project, but at least in November 1994 I was able to get a letter out of the Government of India in Delhi instructing the Secretary Curator to make the necessary payment for the accommodation for the restorers, and that this payment should be met from the budget provision of the Memorial. However this, of course, begged the question of whether the Memorial could afford to do this within its budget provision unless this was additionally funded from the Centre, that is, Delhi.

Additional pressure was provided at my request by the Bengal Chamber of Commerce. Pradeep Das Gupta, the Secretary, wrote to Shri Sujit Poddar, the special assistant to the Chief Minister of West Bengal, stating that these inordinate delays were giving some very wrong signals in the UK where a lot of dignitaries, as he put it, were involved who were very favourably disposed towards investment in West Bengal. He asked Shri Poddar to appreciate that when they were going all out to give a positive image of the State of West Bengal for investment purposes, that this matter needed to be sorted out before it went out of control. He asked him to enquire into the real cause and resolve the problem, which he considered could well be the non-cooperation by employees belonging to a certain trade union.

Pradip Das Gupta's letter was dated 14th December 1994; by 4th January 1995 money was beginning to trickle through to the Tollygunge Club. The first cheque was for 3.86 lakhs which had been outstanding for nearly a year. Even then the Memorial's cashier's office raised difficulties, insisting that the Tollygunge send a man to collect the cheque personally, although they did not tell anyone this – this was a new ploy to delay things. Even Rupert Featherstone, our senior restorer-in-charge, was told that he would have to have authorisation from Tolly to collect it personally.

In January 1995, to add to our difficulties, a plague of cockroaches invaded the Memorial and started to eat the glue paste linings, the canvasses and the gum paper tapes of the paintings. There were two types of cockroaches: the big ones were described as 'Americans', although these were felt not to be the culprits, and the smaller ones, the 'Orientals', who presumably were the culprits. They were about half an inch long and came out at night, travelling very quickly along the skirting edges. We consulted Bob Child, an insect expert, and we ordered 50 insect traps which I took out to Calcutta from London with instructions to catch some cockroaches and bring them back to London for positive identification, and from this identification we determined the correct pest control programme. The devised programme worked, and all I would say is that I wish the supposed five-star Ashoka Hotel in Delhi had appropriated our programme.

Meanwhile the war of the Tollygunge bills had reached fever pitch. By now the following people were involved in this war: a Cabinet Minister, the Chief Minister of West Bengal, his special administrative assistant, the Joint Secretaries for Culture in Delhi, the Secretary of State for External Affairs, the Governor of West Bengal as Chairman of the Memorial and the trustees, the Acting Secretary Curator of the Memorial, the Memorial's four unions, the President of the West Bengal Chamber of Commerce and the Managing Secretary of the Chamber, the Managing Member of the Tollygunge Club Bob Wright, and the Chairman and the Committee of the Calcutta Tercentenary Trust.

At this point I was told that the Memorial had lost all the CTT documentation and that they required duplication of everything before a trustees' meeting. I never believed this, but whether or not I believed it, I had to provide the duplicates which ran to several hundred pages. By this time I had come to the conclusion that to all intents and purposes we had come to the end of the road with the Memorial, but I remembered Tony Hayward's dictum that amiable persistence is everything in Calcutta and so we persisted – although worse was to come later.

It was around this time that a new Secretary Curator was at last appointed. His name was Professor Chitta Panda or Pande. He had

399

been a Commonwealth Scholar at St Anthony's College, Oxford and had also been Professor of History at the University of Burdwan. He had, I knew, written a very learned book about the decline of the Bengal zamindars between 1870 and 1920 in Midnapore, who were caught between the high tax demands made on them by the British, with these demands being often forcibly extorted, and their tenants who refused to pay rents commensurate with these tax demands of the British. It is worth reading, and I often wondered when reading it whether Panda's family had been zamindars and had been squeezed out by the British and their tenants.

The word 'zamindar' may be unfamiliar, and perhaps I should explain. The word was first used in Moghul times – it had no precise meaning – but by the eighteenth century it denoted a class of people with proprietary claims over large tracts of land called chaklas, on a hereditary basis subject to the payment of stipulated amounts of money to the then Nawab Subedir of Bengal. This title of zamindar conferred on them the hereditary right to occupy a large tract of land as their own, and from the rest of the land they extracted a produce share as revenue collectors. In effect what this meant was that net of the amount payable to the Nawab's government, the agricultural surplus was their income. In addition they had military, police and civil jurisdiction over their large estates – in effect they were feudal landowners.

When the East India Company came along it changed all this and these landowners were stripped by the British of all their rights and functions except rent collecting. But worse, the British demand of land revenue which the zamindars were liable to pay was fixed in perpetuity at nine-tenths of the jamma, that is to say, the estimated total annual collection of revenue from their estates, and it was this British fixation on a nine-tenths perpetuity which sank the old zamindar families and many of them had to sell up.

Now after this zamindari digression, I asked Kamal Thacker, who was then the officer-in-charge of East India at the British Council in Calcutta, if he could go along to see Professor Panda and give me his impressions. He reported positively and said that he was keen to make a success of his new job. He was, he said, in course of settling down at the Memorial and updating himself with the work of the CTT. He was also, he said, very conscious of the difficulties with the unions and the politics of the Memorial which thus affected the day-to-day running of the Memorial. He also said he was conscious of the problems relating to the peculiar status of the Memorial, which fell somewhere between an autonomous trust, a West Bengal State Institution and a Central Government institution, with all three institutions being involved in policy and decision making. He also reported that the unions had promised him that they would not create difficulties while he was settling in. I also got another line on him from Bob Wright, who told him all about the work of the CTT and got the impression that Panda would try to be cooperative. It also turned out that he thoroughly disliked Dr Biswas, his acting predecessor, who he said had behaved disgracefully towards him, although he did not elaborate.

Accordingly, after hearing all this, I wrote to congratulate him on his appointment, mentioning that I would send him a résumé of the work undertaken by the CTT and also copies of all the relevant reports. There was no reply. I sent a further letter inviting him to join the CTT Committee as a Calcutta member and inviting him to London with a programme to visit the principal museum staff at the Victoria and Albert Museum, the British Museum, the National Gallery and HM the Queen's Collection at Hampton Court and the India Office Library. I also told him that we had, after nearly two years, received a grant from the Getty Trust for $60,000 – only the second Getty grant for India, the first being the restoration of the Nagaur Fort in the former Jodhpur State. A month later I received a response, expressing Panda's deep gratitude for my letter of congratulations; his sincerest apology that he could not respond to my letters earlier; that he had had the privilege of reading through all the various CTT reports; that he wanted to explore all the possibilities to have an opportunity to meet all the honourable members of the CTT; that he was writing to his honourable Chairman about our invitation and hoped to be in London on 16th October 1995, in time for our lecture at the Royal Geographical Society on 17th October; that he needed to know how we had disbursed all our CTT funds to date; that he needed a copy of our trust deed; that he wanted to see a copy of our application to the Getty Trust and a copy of their agreement; that he was required to obtain Government of India approval which was necessary if funding from foreign sources was involved; and so on and so forth. Subsequently he told Kamal Thacker that he wished to stress that he was unwilling to repeat any mistakes which may have been made in the past in view of the Memorial being a public institution; that issues got

29

Travails and Triumph at the Victoria Memorial Hall

One of our greatest difficulties was the infrequency of the meetings of the Board of Trustees of the Victoria Memorial. In fact the trustees hardly ever seemed to meet, with the result that we were always being left up in the air waiting for decisions which never came. In fact I came to believe it was a deliberate policy to frustrate our work, and this could well have been the case.

All of this was extremely unsatisfactory, including the fact that Professor Panda had turned down our invitation to visit London on the grounds that the Secretary Curator of the Memorial, given his status, had to travel business class and not economy class. Clearly the Governor and his secretary had been busy. It was also a great concern to us that we were working to an end of March 1996 deadline for the Getty Trust and that there could be forfeiture or part forfeiture of the grants if the work was not completed by then.

Accordingly we wrote letters to Dr Singhvi, the High Commissioner of India in London, to Salman Haidar, the Secretary of State for external affairs, and to Jyoti Basu, the Chief Minister of West Bengal. Dr Singhvi, the High Commissioner, suggested I wrote yet another letter to the Governor advising that the British government was now seriously concerned that they had provided via the Foreign Office and Overseas Development Administration the sum of £30,000, say 18 lakhs and all this would be wasted, and furthermore that there would be legal complications between Getty, the CCT and the Government of India if the project floundered, particularly as the Government of India had supported the application to the Getty

Trust. If we were refused access to the Memorial, then the CTT would lose £20,000. Of course, I never received a reply so I followed this up with an approach to two of the newly appointed trustees of the Memorial: Mr K.C. Mehra of Tata Iron & Steel Company, and a previous President of the Bengal Chamber of Commerce who, under the terms of our agreement with the Chamber were ex officio Calcutta advisory members of the CTT – and also Mr P.C. Sen, the wealthy Chairman of Peerless. I also wrote to Ashok Vajpeyi in Delhi. Sally Wade-Gery wrote to Sir Nicholas Fenn, the British High Commissioner in Delhi, and also to Dr Gopal Gandhi, the Mahatma's grandson, who was then the Director of the Nehru Centre in London and a great supporter of the CTT. She also called on the Foreign Minister of India who was in London for a brief visit. So all in all we seemed to be heading for a major diplomatic incident.

The next thing I heard was that the Governor, who had never replied to my letter, said that he thought it was too strong and that he had never received any of the CTT's annual reports, although these had always been sent to the Secretary Curator. In the meantime, although we had been able to keep this debacle away from the UK newspapers, it had now been picked up by the Calcutta newspaper the *Statesman* and a reporter of theirs, Manash Ghosh, who had been briefed anonymously. Apparently, as I mentioned earlier, the Governor and a few members of the Memorial Board of Trustees had taken a strong objection to our approaching the Getty Trust for funding our restoration work at the Memorial without seeking the prior approval of the Victoria Memorial trustees. This was, as it happens, incorrect as we had received both the written approval of the Secretary Curator and the Government of India – perhaps the former had not informed the trustees. However they, the trustees, had become apprehensive about the Left Front West Bengal Government's reaction to the American Getty Trust assisting the restoration work financially. Furthermore the Governor was concerned about the ramification of this USA connection as he had been publicly ridiculed a number of times by the State's Marxist leaders for doing his own thing and he did not want to become embroiled in yet another controversy. There was even a rumour circulating in Calcutta that we were a front for the American CIA!

However we did have our supporters in Calcutta, and some trustees of the Victoria Memorial came out of hiding and gave press interviews. They stated that there had been hardly any Indian financial contribution to the work of restoration and conservation, and up to then nobody in India had concerned themselves with the source of our external funding, so it would be quite wrong now to make us accountable to the Victoria Memorial Trust and Calcutta should not spurn our work, particularly as time was beginning to run out if these priceless heritage paintings were to be restored and conserved for posterity.

It had always been a principle of ours that all the sterling and overseas currency funds which we had managed to raise would all be expended on sterling and overseas currency salaries and purchases, so that there was no need for conversion of these funds into rupees. This therefore meant that none of these funds found their way into the accounts of the Victoria Memorial Trust because, if they had, we would have lost financial control of the entire project. But it was this supposed non-conversion that gave rise to the allegation that the Calcutta Tercentenary Trust was in breach of the Indian Foreign Exchange Regulations Act – the dreaded FERA, where the penalties could be severe including imprisonment. This never happened but there was always, at this stage, a lingering implied threat.

A further article appeared at the end of November in the Calcutta *Statesman* which was strongly critical of the Governor and the Victoria Memorial Trust Board. I quote, and I am afraid this quote is lengthy:

The impasse over the restoration of valuable paintings of the Colonial era, which form the bulk of the Collection shows that art is a low priority for our governing class. The paintings are in a lamentable condition because of poor storage and official apathy. This situation is both pathetic and ridiculous. Internationally renowned restorers are being prevented from rescuing the Collection because the Governor of this State has objections to the Getty Foundation funding the Calcutta Tercentenary Trust. Secondly the Governor has never suggested any other alternative source of funding to add credence to his objections. For after all the Chairman of the Victoria Memorial Trust cannot officially hold the position that the paintings be allowed to languish and disintegrate because the only money available for preserving them is of capitalist origin. Going by the same logic one should refuse charitable grants made for disaster relief like the Ford and Rockefeller foundations and others and let people starve or succumb to disease rather than spoil their morals.

The real issue is that there is no time to be lost. Paintings are fragile objects, do not age well and are particularly sensitive to the Calcutta humidity. Paintings do not, like books, come in several interchangeable copies. There is one and only one original and if that is destroyed it is lost. The mind boggles at the thought that a Museum like the Victoria Memorial, itself a work of art of some considerable quality, should not have the wherewithal to restore and store its treasures appropriately or that successive curators should have simply watched them decay, arms folded. The Curator has to manage the Authorities as well as his own subordinates. Neither the authorities nor the subordinates are animated with the same degree of the necessary enthusiasm assuming that the Curator himself has any. It requires men of vision and energy to run these institutions. But the damage having been done, the next best thing is to move quickly in order to save what is irreplaceable. It is not often that the services of internationally renowned art restorers, paid for by a recognised international institution of high repute the CTT are offered on such favourable terms. Get on with it, Your Excellency!

Despite all this, when the Victoria Memorial Trust Board met at long last in early December – the restorers and conservators were still kicking their heels in Calcutta and were prevented from entering the Memorial – the trustees decided as follows:

i) For this season's programme with funds from the Getty Grant, it would be desirable to have an agreement entered upon between the Victoria Memorial Trust, CTT and the Getty Grant Programme within 15 days.

ii) During the current season the CTT restorers may commence the work which should cover the unfinished paintings of the previous season and also the 11–13 paintings to be taken up with the funds obtained by the CTT from the Getty Grant Programme.

iii) Further support of the programme under the Getty Grant

Programme should be based on agreement between the Victoria Memorial Trust and the Getty Grant Programme, avoiding direct contribution of funds to the Victoria Memorial Trust by donor agencies. [I believe he meant indirect contributions.]

Kind regards, Chitta Panda

This letter reached me on Christmas Eve, well past the 15 days mentioned. I therefore telephoned Panda at his home. He was friendly and helpful but he reiterated several times that he was merely a middleman and post-officing so to speak for the Governor etcetera. In other words, he had to do what he was told. He seemed to be worried about the proposed desirable agreement between the Victoria Memorial Trust (VMT), the CTT and the Getty, and I told him that I had no idea what form of agreement this should be and that it was up to the Victoria Memorial Trust to draft this – in other words, there could not be an agreement if no one knew what the proposed terms of such an agreement were.

I then queried him with regard to resolution (iii) as to what he meant by direct contributions. I told him I assumed that he meant indirect contribution; that he must know that if it were not for the CTT there would be no Getty Grant – apart from anything else the Getty Grant had to be matched one for one, and the VMT had no sterling funds and pretty well no rupee funds either. On 3rd January Professor Panda told Rupert Featherstone that he was still not in a position to allow the restorers access to the museum. It was back to square one.

However, nobody gets anywhere by doing nothing and so Sally Wade-Gery, who was in Delhi, called on Madhavrao Scindia, the Minister for Human Resources at the Shastri Bhavan, on 4th January 1996. Before that she had called on B.P. Singh who had been recently appointed Secretary of Culture and to him she poured out all our woes. B.P. Singh was immediately and surprisingly interested; we had been told by Amita Baig of INTACH that he was highly regarded as an effective and efficient Indian Administrative Service (IAS) officer. It was extraordinary – between Sally leaving B.P. Singh and arriving in Scindia's office, the former had telephoned the Governor's secretary, Mr Chaturvedi, the root cause I believed of all our difficulties, and reported that the latter had agreed on the telephone that the restorers should immediately start work on last year's unfinished paintings. However Sally told him that, although this was good news, the financial consequences of this was untenable and that every pound spent on this work would involve the loss of a Getty pound; that this week's delay alone had already lost the VMT about $8,000 worth of CTT restoration. Scindia grasped all this very quickly and said that he would immediately speak to our friend Mr Chaturvedi.

We decided we must press for the urgent go-ahead on the Getty Daniells prior to the signing of the proposed VMT–CTT–Getty memorandum of agreement. The reason for this was that if we waited for it we put ourselves in the diplomatically untenable position of waiting for the Governor's signature on an, as yet, non-existent document before work could start. So more leverage and pressure was required and Sally went back to B.P. Singh who told her that he would telephone the Governor.

Meanwhile Sally went on to Calcutta to meet the Governor, his secretary Chaturvedi and the Secretary Curator. Scindia and B.P. Singh's telephone conversations had clearly worked and she was told by the Secretary that all our requests had been agreed. This was on 13th January 1996, and it had taken six months of protracted negotiations, diplomatic pressure and the threat of a major political incident to get the restorers into the museum to start work on the Daniells' paintings – amiable and not too amiable persistence was necessary to get there.

At the end of January 1996 I was due to go out to Calcutta and elsewhere in India, but at the last minute I put my neck out and I was in such extreme agony that I had to cancel my visit. This was unfortunate as Rupert Featherstone was leaving Calcutta and he was being replaced by Lucia Scalisi from the Victoria and Albert Museum. I must here pay a special tribute to Rupert and his wife Emma. Without him – and he was supported by Emma throughout – we could not have achieved what we did. He spent three long seasons in Calcutta in charge of the programme, and leading the teams throughout what was a very difficult period. He managed the programme brilliantly, in the face of all the unending contention not only in the Memorial itself but also among all the concerned authorities. He lectured in India and London and his great tact and circumspection got us through. Without him and Emma the project would have collapsed, and they both have earned my undying gratitude.

408

Lucia Scalisi was a more volatile character, impatient to get on, and she and Professor Panda did not get on particularly well which sometimes created problems, although this was not her fault. Professor Panda was not a curator, nor was he a museologist; he had no management and administrative skills, and he was caught between the Governor, the Board of Trustees, the Culture Department in Delhi and the CTT. I also got the impression that he had taken a dislike to Philippa Vaughan, who was, in effect, the CTT project director – not only a dislike, but also a suspicion as to her motives – so all this was not particularly helpful.

I did however go out to Calcutta in March, and spent a long time with the Governor who, as usual, never said a word and kept looking at his watch, and with Mr Chaturvedi his secretary who did all the talking. The Professor on these occasions in Raj Bhavan was always excessively servile – far too much so. He entered the Governor's study with his hands clasped together in the namaste greeting and bowed all the time as he was approaching the Governor's chair. At the end of these meetings, he always walked backwards, still facing the Governor, bowing and scraping until his back hit the door, and I felt very embarrassed for him. But at the end of this meeting I got everything I wanted, although I was accused of not preparing the project proposal with due care and was told that if I had, this embarrassing situation would not have arisen – somewhat unfair, I thought, as my main difficulty was that the Governor never once replied to any of my letters. Admittedly, at the end of the meeting, Chaturvedi apologised to me for the wording of the trustees' resolution.

And so the 1995–96 programme limped to an end but, despite all the difficulties, a fair amount of progress had been made and so it was now time to plan the 1996–97 programme. We therefore proposed to Professor Panda the following pictures for restoration (we were getting near the end of the project): the *Blind Vakil* by Hickey; *Lord Minto* by Home; *Warren Hastings* by Stubbs; *Shah Alam* by Tilly Kettle, a wonderful painting measuring 9 feet by 8; and finally *Cornwallis and the Hostage Princes* by Carter. Meanwhile our Indian trainee restorers during the summer had been left to complete the conservation of two major paintings – of which one was *Saadat Ali Khan* by Seton and the other was *Muhi-Ud-Din* by Hickey.

I went out again to Calcutta in October 1996. Before that I had

had a meeting in London with the Chief Minister of West Bengal, Jyoti Basu. There was then some talk about the Queen visiting Calcutta, and if she did the specific *raison d'être* could be her opening of our CTT galleries, on which no work as yet had been carried out. All this came to nothing in the end as Calcutta was not high on the list of the Queen's travel priorities. However, we did have a stroke of luck in that the joint Secretaryship of Culture once again changed and the new appointee was a charming, attractive and highly efficient and intelligent Bengali lady by the name of Kasturi Gupta Menon, whose husband was the Secretary to the Chief Minister. They were both, of course, as IAS officers, immensely capable and I began to cheer up. She lived in Delhi and he in Calcutta and she told me that although they saw each other most weekends, they kept in touch by regular morning telephone conversations. Mrs Menon had, *inter alia* responsibility for the Archaeological Survey of India and also the Asiatic Society, but not at that time the Memorial itself, but nevertheless she was extremely helpful. She was also very interested in the restoration of the Metcalfe Hall in Calcutta and we had a look at it together to see whether it could possibly be used for exhibitions.

Metcalfe Hall – a very fine colonnaded building built to represent the Temple of the Winds at Athens – was erected in memory of Sir Charles Metcalfe, who had been the Governor-General in 1836 and who was also known as the emancipator of the Indian press. It had been occupied by the Calcutta Public Library which was then amalgamated with the Imperial Library; it was once a splendid library and once again it was Lord Curzon who had originated and carried out the scheme, and opened it in early 1903. Now it was grubby, dirty, and was being used as a store by the Post Office. Mrs Menon who was now responsible for Metcalfe Hall wanted to turf out the Post Office, restore it and use it for some other purpose, but that other purpose rather eluded her and hence her coming and asking me whether I thought it was suitable as a picture gallery for some of the Victoria Memorial paintings which we had restored, bearing in mind the difficulties we were having getting them into a place where they could be hung and exhibited to the public. I have to say that it was not ideal, but it was better than nothing, and I said so. She took it all on board, and although we never used it, it has now been restored to its former glory under the aegis of the Archaeological Survey of India (ASI) – a great success for the lovely and capable Mrs Menon.

Professor Panda never replied to my letter dated 30th July 1996, setting out our proposed programme for the end of 1996 and early 1997, and when I was in Calcutta all he said was that he was disappointed that we had reduced the proposed number of restorers coming out to Calcutta – which was partly due to the fact that I had never had a response from him, partly because of our funding problems, and partly because we had problems in finding restorers and conservators who were able and willing to work in Calcutta.

I asked him the present position of the refurbishment of the CTT galleries. His reply was that this expenditure had been budgeted for, namely 35 lakhs, that this money had been paid over to the ASI in Delhi but had not been cleared for payment to the Memorial. Mrs Menon,who was of course responsible for the ASI budget, told me she was not aware of this and she would provide clearance when she got back to Delhi the next day. She also asked me whether there was a problem with the National Leaders portraits, to which I replied yes, but that earlier on Dr Biswas and I had conceived the idea of 'promoting' them to the ground floor. Very few visitors to the Memorial ever ventured up to the first floor, and if they did they often used the stairs as a pissoir on the way up or down, there being no toilets in the Memorial.

While all this was going on Philippa Vaughan had been collecting articles for a volume on the Memorial which was to be published by Marg Publications in Bombay. Of course, there was no money to be made by Marg on this volume so it had to be sponsored by someone for a figure of £7,000. In the end this was kindly provided by Barclays de Zoete Wedd. In my view the publication of this volume was excellent, although it was premature in the sense that we had not finished our work and so there was, in effect, no ending to the book. It was also the case that Professor Panda was very disappointed about this publication, mainly as he felt it represented, as he told me, a renewal of British imperialism and that its publication would cause a very difficult position between the Memorial and the CTT – a scarcely veiled threat. When the publication was eventually brought out, he refused to have the opening Reception at the Memorial and he also refused to attend the reception, the venue of which was changed to the Taj Bengal Hotel.

In early January 1997 we had a visit from Prime Minister John Major who was visiting Calcutta. Two of the restorers, namely Lucia Scalisi and Christine Mackay, who was the Head of the Department of Conservation at the National Gallery of Wales, were 'presented' to him and also to the High Commissioner of the UK, Sir David Gore-Booth and the Deputy High Commissioner, Mr Scaddam, who had suddenly become homosexual and had left his wife and children.

Despite the visit of the Prime Minister – who I believe was prevented from viewing the finest paintings in the Memorial including the self-portrait of Johann Zoffany with his friends Colonel Polier, Claude Martin and John Wombwell because Professor Panda objected to the naked Indian girl in the picture which Zoffany portrayed himself painting – relationships with Professor Panda once again deteriorated. The reason for this was that he denied the conservators access to the stores and it turned out that nobody had been into the store for a year and nobody knew the condition of the pictures in the store. Professor Panda refused to accept responsibility for the store keys, thus negating his prime duty which was to preserve the collection and make it available for display and, I would add, reference. Thus Christine Mackay and Mike Wheeler, both conservators of works of art on paper, were denied access to 98 per cent of the collection which was in store.

However, four days later this all changed due to Danny Mahtab's intervention and suddenly there was all sweetness and light. Another two days later, it was back again to square one. There was a slanging match between the Professor and Lucia Scalisi who was in charge of the restoration programme; he was extremely rude to her and Bob Wright discussed with me whether we should write a formal letter objecting to his behaviour. We never did this but he brought up Getty again and also the CIA, which he had talked about before.

We began to believe that the Professor was having a mental breakdown. The restorers' and conservators' morale was at rock bottom and the stores remained closed – once again there was a complete impasse and I decided that it was necessary to fly out to Calcutta, but I got ill and Paddy Bowring went out instead. I think, reflecting on all this, that the Professor had difficulties coping with strong Western women and that he needed a more emollient and flexible approach. Lucia was quite a volatile lady, although dear

Christine was both firm and emollient at the same time. I suggested all this to Lucia but she replied that he was always entirely different when he was talking to me, and that from her point of view she was always being abused by the staff of the Memorial and that Panda had consistently avoided speaking to her since her arrival in Calcutta.

There were all sorts of conflicting messages about his mental health. One moment he said he had asked the board to relieve him from his post and that he was leaving on an extensive study tour in Europe and America. The next moment the British Council had to withdraw from a concert to be held at the Memorial after failing to agree anything with the Professor. And so on. The 1996–97 programme also limped to an end – the same as the previous season. What were we to do? We had done everything we could, we had interceded with everybody in authority, we had implored their aid, we had raised it all to the diplomatic and political level and even to the international level, and we had written off the sum of 3.5 lakhs made by the CTT by way of advance to the Memorial for the final payment of the restorers' Tollygunge Club bills for 1996.

In July 1997 I received a complaint from the Professor, relayed on to me by the Deputy High Commissioner, that the trustees did not believe we had the best restorers and conservators for the job we were doing at the Memorial. He also complained that Lucia had undermined his authority in front of his own staff in a dispute earlier that year, and that there was no communication between him and the CTT. This was pretty rich, bearing in mind that he never replied to my letters. He had another difficulty, in that he was now required to provide information to the Government Auditors about sources of external financing, but said he had not been able to obtain satisfactory information about this from us. He had in fact never asked for this information, and if he had I would have told him that there was no external financing of the Memorial purse. All that we did was to raise funds in the UK and the USA and these funds were used by us to fund the restoration, conservation and training programme in foreign currency, i.e. sterling and dollars. I also reminded the Deputy High Commissioner that the work of the CTT was an outright gift by the CTT to the Memorial – a gift which all museums would be delighted to accept and cooperate with, except apparently the Professor whose motives or reasons for

413

his attitude to the CTT were unfathomable. I then sent Professor Panda a letter detailing the work and superb CVs of the restorers and conservators who had been described as second-best.

We have moved on to the autumn of 1997. I was in India again both in Delhi and Calcutta. In Delhi I received the good news that the excellent Mrs Menon would be assuming responsibility for the Memorial as Joint Secretary of Culture in place of the poet Ashok Vajpeyi. She then arranged a meeting between herself, her husband, the Professor, Pradeep Das Gupta, the Secretary of the West Bengal Chamber of Commerce, and myself. We agreed to meet at the Tollygunge Club, where I was now staying. Mr Menon told me he had recommended that at State Government level, the responsibility for the Memorial should not lie with the Minister of Education but with Mr Buddhabed Battarcharyya, the Home Minister, also responsible for information and cultural affairs, firstly, because he was the second man in the West Bengal State Government, and secondly, because he was very likely to succeed Jyoti Basu as Chief Minister which, in the event, he did. Nothing which the Professor then said would happen did happen, but at least Mr Menon and Mr Pradeep Das Gupta were there to hear it, so he would not be able to deny it.

Shortly afterward the Professor had a mild stroke when he was in Delhi so he was out of action for some time. It is true to say, however, that by this time – and we are now in 1998 – we had completed the restoration of all 84 oil paintings which we had earmarked for restoration work, so all that remained was the refurbishment of what I termed the CTT Galleries and the exhibition of the restored paintings in those galleries. But nothing ever happened despite repeated intervention with what I used to call the concerned authorities – one of our biggest hopes being Mrs Menon.

We did manage to send out two restorers for a period of two weeks in early January. They were allowed access to the Memorial by the Professor to survey the paintings and most of the prints and drawings in the storeroom, and uniquely the Memorial staff cooperated. While they were there, they gave a series of lectures on 'Caring for Art Collections' at the British Council and these lectures were fully subscribed. They had a meeting with Mr Hirak Ghosh – the new Secretary of Higher Education in the West Bengal Government – who was always extremely helpful, and their meeting with Mr Menon gave them encouragement and support for the CTT.

So although our work had been more or less on hold for two years – that is to say in 1997–98 we only had two restorers and conservators working in Calcutta for a very limited period, and in 1998–99 the same number for two weeks only – nevertheless the climate in Calcutta towards us was changing and changing for the better. The authorities had really got at the Professor, and he had now decided at long last that getting the pictures hung for exhibition to the public had more glory for him than stalling it. He had even been occasionally extraordinarily helpful in the teeth of opposition from Mr and Mrs Arun Ghose, who had always created difficulties, but even they too were perhaps now sensing the climate towards the CTT was warming. Hirak Ghosh, who I have mentioned, the new Secretary of Higher Education, wanted the Memorial turned round during his tenure of office. Mr and Mrs Menon, also at secretary level, were being very helpful and supportive.

But the breakthrough came in December 1999 when a new Governor was appointed in the place of Mr Kidwai, the previous Governor. His name was Viren Shah and he proved to be my saviour and I will be forever grateful to him for the rest of my life. He was a wealthy industrialist from Bombay and was the nominee of the right-wing Hindu nationalist party, the Bharatiya Janata Party, known as BJP for short. In a way one could say that it was a curious appointment – that is to say, a right-wing BJP wealthy industrialist being appointed to the Governorship of West Bengal, a state ruled by left-wing Marxists – but it might also have been a stroke of political genius by the Prime Minister. At any rate his Governorship was a great success, but above all as he wrote to me – the first time a Governor had ever written to me or ever replied to any of my numerous letters – that he was keen about the maintenance and restoration of not only the Victoria Memorial and the Indian Museum, but also other heritage buildings, and that he was studying the means by which this could properly be dealt with. This was music to our ears. Furthermore, he had also appointed in place of the dreaded Chaturvedi a charming and once again attractive and highly efficient, intelligent lady IAS officer, Neera Saggi. Thus with the also charming and efficient Kasturi Gupta Menon, these two ladies changed my Calcutta life. Furthermore, the Governor also appointed a former Chief Secretary of West Bengal by name of Mr T.C. Dutt, who had also been the Director of the West Bengal Development Commission, to have overall responsibility for the proposed exhibition. To add to my joy, I knew him quite well.

In March 2000, Philippa Vaughan accompanied by Danny Mahtab – a Burdwan and who was also a trustee of the Memorial – had a very good meeting with the Governor, Shri Hirak Ghosh, who I have mentioned before was the Secretary for Higher Education in West Bengal, and Dr Pratapchandra Chunder, the Chairman of the Memorial's Paintings Committee. The Professor was in attendance and was put in his place. Various misunderstandings were dealt with, including the original Memorandum of Understanding, which was not the type of formal MOU agreement as was now prepared for similar joint projects.

There was a long discussion about the exhibition of the 84 oil paintings which the CTT had restored, and for the first time to my knowledge it arose that these would now be exhibited in the Durbar Hall, and a provisional date was set for January 2001. A great deal of work had been carried out on the Durbar Hall by the ASI and this work was almost completed, including chemical treatment of the stone and marble and redecoration of the dome. There were still pigeons flying around. A hawk had been recruited and put to work, but the pigeons had turned on him and killed him.

One of the advantages of postponing the exhibition to January 2001 was that it would allow time for the CTT conservators to come out to Calcutta to prepare and, if necessary, retouch the paintings prior to the exhibition, and also time for the installation of solid panels on which to hang them. A postponement was also considered necessary because of all the other work to be done, including the promotion of the National Leaders portraits to a ground-floor gallery, but also because of the many elections in Calcutta and Bengal during the 2000 summer.

The Governor also wished to invite a member of the Royal Family to attend and the name of HRH Princess Alexandra was put forward since she was initially a joint Patron together with the Governor. He also invited Sir Rob Young, the then UK High Commissioner, to attend and indeed he did.

There was a long discussion about the actual exhibition itself and the mechanics to achieve this. A huge amount of work was necessary not only for the exhibition itself but also for the formal opening, the receptions, the lunches and dinners, the invitation lists for all these events and so on. I don't think I ever worked so hard in my life, and it did not help that everything was being done a huge distance away.

By this time, the late autumn of 2000, I seemed to be travelling backwards and forwards to Calcutta and I am not one to enjoy long flights, particularly travelling economy, although sometimes I got upgraded to club class. I used mainly to travel British Airways – by far the best, KLM and occasionally Royal Brunei Airlines, the latter being the cheapest. But for KLM I had to change planes at Amsterdam whilst for Royal Brunei I had to change planes at Dubai with a long wait between flights. Royal Brunei was of course dry, no alcohol was served. Most of the passengers getting on board at Calcutta were Indian migrant workers destined for the Gulf. These, as so many other migrant workers, left their homes, wives and children behind and sometimes, perhaps many times, did not see them again for a year, two years or even three years, but their families were able to live relatively well from the cash remittances. I always remember Tammy, Bob Wright's servant at the Tollygunge Club – a very kind, self-effacing man. He was a Muslim and came, I think, from Hyderabad where his family lived. However, he only saw them twice a year, and this is the horror of the life of economic migrant workers, their detachment from home and family for long periods of time; but this happens everywhere in India.

In early December 2000 I flew out once again to Calcutta and on 4th December I had a long meeting with the Governor to discuss and decide all the detailed arrangements for the exhibition. Present also at the meeting were Neera Saggi, Professor Panda and T.C. Dutt who, as I have mentioned earlier, was formerly the Chief Secretary for the West Bengal government – I suppose in this country he would be called the Cabinet Secretary – a huge job, remembering that the population of West Bengal is in the region of 150 million people or, putting it another way, two and a half times the size of the population of the UK.

It was decided that the exhibition would be declared open and inaugurated at 3 p.m. on Saturday 19th January 2001, at the Memorial. This would be followed by a Reception at the Memorial hosted by the Governor as Chairman of the Board of Trustees. Sir Rob Young, the UK High Commissioner to India, would be the Guest of Honour in place of HRH Princess Alexandra who was unable to come to Calcutta. That evening the Governor would host a dinner party at the Raj Bhavan.

It was also decided that with the agreement of the President of the Bengal Chamber of Commerce, Mr Ganguly, and the Chief Secretary of the Chamber Mr Pradeep Das Gupta, that the President and I, as chairman of the Calcutta Tercentenary Trust, would co-host a reception at the Chamber. This arrangement was very useful to me. I had thought of the CTT hosting a reception at the Bengal Club, but this would have been unbelievably difficult to do on our own and the new arrangement was a great relief. In any case Neera Saggi told me and confirmed it in writing that the Governor had never attended such a reception hosted in a club, the inference being that if he was invited to the Bengal Club, he would decline.

Following this meeting, Victoria Boyer and I met all the concerned staff at the Memorial to discuss and agree the way forward for the mounting of the exhibition and then, at a further meeting which I had with the Professor and Mr T.C. Dutt, (by now a special administrator appointed by the Governor), the latter stated that all the CTT's proposals as put forward by Victoria would receive his full support. Nobody could have worked harder than Victoria for this exhibition, and I owe her and Christine Mackay, our leading conservator, my undying gratitude.

Mr Dutt's full support for us came as a huge relief, as effectively what it meant was what we said went, and not what the Professor said. Thus our design of the screens and their specification were agreed and so was our structural and surface finish requirements. All this was a triumph, as so also were our requirements for the picture barriers and our own proposed pigeon defences, along with the hanging mechanism, the lighting, the hanging plan and the labelling. It was decided that the Professor would report weekly progress to Mr Dutt and that, if Victoria had any concerns about slippage, she would get in touch with Mr Dutt and also, as a long stop, Neera Saggi. The Indian authorities also desired the CTT to keep a continuous conservation watching brief on the collection and that ways and means of carrying this out needed to be considered.

After all our trials and tribulations over the last ten years, all now appeared to be sweetness and light, and indeed it was. I left Calcutta feeling much happier than I had been for a long time, but before I left the Professor invited me to see the Botanical Gardens across the river. We drove there and eventually parked at the entrance after a long altercation between the Professor and the car park attendant, with the Professor saying as Secretary Curator of the Victoria Memorial, he had priority over everybody else, and this was eventually conceded.

Perhaps I could digress here – I seem to have a habit of digressing – and write a little about the Calcutta Botanical Gardens and the sad state to which they have been reduced. These were once the great pride of Calcutta. They have a river face of about a mile long, and in all the gardens extend to 270 acres. As the old guide book put it: 'the avenues of stately palms, the sacred deodars of Bengal, the palm and orchid houses, the picturesque lakes with their water fowl will not fail to delight the eye of even the most ignorant in the science of botany and the arts of the horticulturists. Furthermore the grand banyan tree covering at least a thousand feet in circumference is famous all over the world.' The poet, Bishop Heber, said of the Botanical Gardens: 'It is not only a curious but picturesque and most beautiful scene and more perfectly answers Milton's idea of Paradise than anything I ever saw.' Alas, alas, it is all gone and unkempt and overgrown now, the charming little tea house with its pillars by the river is dilapidated and unused now except as a store, and all that remains are a few stately palms and the great banyan tree. How sad it all is.

On 8th January there was a slight panic. The unions representing the Victoria Memorial's casual workers insisted on displaying their placards in the Durbar Hall. There then needed to be some negotiations between the unions and the construction contractors, and as a result the placards were removed from the screens and placed on the floor leaning against tables in the middle of the Hall. We were all very concerned that this unrest might disrupt all the construction work progress and the hanging of the paintings but, in the event, the unions mercifully laid off.

By the second week in January 2001 I was back in Calcutta, and to my delight everything was moving forward in the right direction and under strict time control. The great day was approaching and after 12 years of hard work and continuous mental anxiety, we were there and there were no hiccups. Everything went according to plan, and for that to happen in Calcutta was quite extraordinary, but it did and for that full praise must be given to everybody involved, particularly Mr Dutt and Neera Saggi and to Victoria and Christine – they were simply wonderful. And full praise must be given to Philippa Vaughan, because she was the linchpin of the CTT and, dare I say it, myself.

The reception at the Bengal Chamber of Commerce co-hosted by the President and myself went well, and at 2 p.m. the next day we started assembling at the Memorial for the formal inauguration of the exhibition, and the reception afterwards. It was all a very long formal affair. All the dignitaries including myself were seated at a table at the north entrance of the Memorial facing the back of Queen Victoria's statue, and we were surrounded by journalists, reporters, photographers and television cameras.

Like such affairs in England, everything was timed to the minute and the protocol was strictly observed. To give you some idea as to how it all went, I will describe it in some detail. At 2.50 p.m. was the arrival of the Honourable Minister-in-Charge Higher Education, Professor Satya Sadhan Chakraborty and he arrived together with Shri Subrata Mukherjee, the Honourable Mayor Calcutta Municipal Corporation. They were followed by His Excellency, the British High Commissioner and promptly at 3 p.m. His Excellency the Governor of West Bengal, Sri Viren Shah.

The first person to kick off was the Professor with a welcome address – three minutes only; followed by me as Chairman of the Calcutta Tercentenary Trust – slightly longer, five minutes. Then there were speeches by the Mayor and the Minister followed by Sir Rob Young and His Excellency the Governor – ten minutes. Finally there was a Vote of Thanks – two minutes only, followed by the formal inauguration of the exhibition by lighting the traditional lamp in front of the Durbar Hall. All of what the Indians called the 'VVIPs' including myself, were formally escorted to the inauguration area where the lamp was lit. I was escorted around my own exhibition – 20 minutes – and all this was followed by tea and cakes in the quadrangle, and at 4.45 p.m. His Excellency, the Governor, departed. It was the culmination of 13 years' work.

In the evening the Governor gave a dinner party for all of what I liked to call the 'concerned persons', in Government House, Raj Bhavan, in the main state dining-room where in days gone past the British Governor-General used to preside. It was what I would call a Gandhi dinner, preceded by orange juice and water, but I had had some whisky beforehand to boost my morale. It was described as non-vegetarian and this word was depicted in large red letters as if it was something unusual – perhaps it was. We

420

sat down to asparagus soup, grilled fish with boiled vegetables, chicken biryanis and chocolate soufflé, with everything washed down with water or fruit juice. It was all a very generous and hospitable gesture on the part of the Governor to give us this large celebratory dinner party but, without alcohol, such dinner parties tend to fall rather flat and, in a sense feeling slightly guilty, I left soon after dinner to go to another party which had been organised by some Indian friends, where I knew there would be plenty of whisky.

The following day was taken up with public lectures at which I had to speak with Philippa Vaughan, and then suddenly it was all over. The Press and TV coverage in India was excellent, particularly, of course, in the Calcutta press and television channels. There was some coverage in the *Daily Telegraph* and what I would describe as 'concerned' magazines, but the article which pleased me most was in *Time Magazine* where four centre pages covered the inauguration under the title 'Victoria's Secret' written by Michael Feathers. He wrote that historians of English paintings say that the collection rivals the best in London's Tate and the Paul Mellon Collection at Yale University. He wrote also, and this I did not know, that during the 1970s and 1980s when Mrs Gandhi was Prime Minister, she and the Government debated whether to sell the whole of the Victoria Memorial collection and almost every other remaining artistic and historical relic, and use the proceeds to buy back 'India's' art that had been taken abroad. And Danny Mahtab – Dr Pronoy Mahtab, a Trustee – stated: 'it was a ridiculous idea – these paintings are part of India's heritage'. He went on to say to Feathers that: 'the paintings will never be loaned for exhibition – they are too fragile and distances are too great. The Collection at the Victoria Memorial is there for one purpose – it represents a part of India's history and it will stay in India.' Amen. Amen, and thank heaven the dreaded Mrs Gandhi did not get her way. But it was a close run thing.

For this work the Queen appointed me a CBE and Lord Camoys, who was then the Lord Chancellor and a friend, read out the citation. It reads as follows: 'For Anglo-Indian relations and the preservation of the cultural heritage of India'. It was the greatest possible honour I could have received.

Finally, perhaps I could return to Professor Chitta Panda. I believe now, although I did not at the time, that many of the difficulties he apparently imposed on the CTT were not of his direct making but that of the previous Governor and his secretary. The Professor was after all only the Secretary Curator and although clearly this was an important position, nevertheless very little authority was delegated down to him from the Chairman of the Board of Trustees, his secretary and the various committees of the trust. I now believe that for virtually everything to do with the CTT, which was an odd animal at the best of times, he had to refer to higher authority and that these were generally their decisions not his. He was also under the necessity of dancing a very delicate role between the Chairman and trustees of the Victoria Memorial, the central Government in Delhi and the Department of Culture who organised the funding and controlled the budget of the Memorial, the Government of West Bengal in Calcutta and the Communist trade unions in the Memorial, who were all represented by a Communist MP in the West Bengal state parliament and, of course, last but not least, the Calcutta Tercentenary trustees who were always putting pressure on him. No wonder perhaps that he suffered a nervous breakdown, like I did myself later on. In all this it has to be remembered that the Professor was an academic historian without any management or museum training. And, of course, within the Memorial he was entirely on his own, subject to being gheraoed and surrounded by a mutinous staff.

Although what we were doing in Calcutta was, we thought, a great benefit and gift to that city, nevertheless everything and anything which is done in that city is highly political and often litigious. The Bengalis are great litigators and the Professor was always endlessly involved in litigation, and all this added to his difficulties. So what I mean by all this is that I feel I should also thank him, and his wife Nandini, for all his efforts on our behalf, efforts which I believe were often negated by his chairman until Shri Viren Shah was appointed Chairman and suddenly dark turned into light both for him and us.

Later I began to understand better his difficult position and, at this distance in time, I feel I should record my sincere appreciation of him and his charming and delightful wife, Nandini.

30

Sundry Activities

Something odd had been happening to me during those last three months or so leading up to the exhibition, and that something was insomnia combined with what seemed to me to be almost an acute mental anxiety. I have always had a horror of insomnia, and I can say that beneath my relatively calm exterior I have generally been a somewhat anxious and nervous person – in other words, I am a worrier. Probably most people are, but possibly I have had in my life more things to worry about, and I do not want to enumerate all these because I think they are in this book and they will have been apparent. It may have been that the huge stress of working in Calcutta and particularly the stress of the exhibition tipped me over the edge, but over the edge I did go and it took the form of acute depression, anxiety and insomnia and I began to find it difficult to manage my affairs.

I went to see my local GP and she gave me some pills, but they did not appear to work – I was hardly sleeping at all, I was hardly eating and I was hardly able to concentrate. In despair I telephoned my London GP, Dr Stuttaford, who for many years had conducted my annual medical check-up both during the time I had been in the bank and afterwards. I had always known that he had written a book on alcoholism, but did not know that he had also written a book entitled *In your Right Mind* two years previously. This was subtitled *Everyday Psychological Problems and Psychiatric Conditions Explored and Explained*.

I told him that I knew something was going wrong when I left the Tollygunge Club in Calcutta at four o'clock in the morning, to catch the British Airways flight to London leaving Dum Dum Airport at nine o'clock (provided it arrived on time from Dacca).

In my defence one never knew what obstacles might be needed to be dealt with in Calcutta such as pujas, bandhs, police roadblocks, road works, floods and so on. Of course, this time there was nothing of the sort and I went straight through to the airport in under an hour. I told Dr Stuttaford that sometimes I woke up in Calcutta wondering what on earth I was doing there, and why I had undertaken voluntarily this huge project of restoration and conservation in the Memorial, lasting over 13 years. I did not really like Calcutta – I hated its poverty, its pollution, its teeming millions, its decay and dilapidation – although I had always enjoyed its vibrant cultural, intellectual and social life. If it had not been for Bob and Annie Wright to come back to at the Tollygunge Club every evening I might very easily have thrown it all in. In truth I had exhausted myself, physically, mentally and financially. I had raised the sum of £500,000 in sterling and in rupees, but that all had gone now. I felt I had come to the end of the road and when I returned to the UK to deal with an avalanche of correspondence and administration together with some unexpected and unbudgeted liabilities of the trust, which I dealt with by way of a large personal loan to the trust, I started to go under.

His advice to me was that I should go to the Priory in West London while I got over this crisis, but the thought of the men in white coats so filled me with horror that I refused. Under his sympathetic and careful medical guidance, I began to improve and started at long last to sleep again and the acute nervous anxiety began to fall away.

The ten years between my retiring from the bank in 1991 and the completion of the Calcutta project were exceptionally busy. In no particular order, I was appointed by the bank to be its Group Adviser for India, but as I was paid very little for this, I set up my own consultancy for Indian business from which I drew some useful commissions. I entitled myself rather grandly as 'Alan Tritton, Adviser for UK Joint Ventures and Investments in India and Indian Joint Ventures and Investments in the UK'. The timing for all this was somewhat premature as it has only been in recent years that India has liberalised, precipitated by its near bankruptcy in 1991, and it is now increasingly prosperous. The greatest difficulty was getting an Indian rupee commission translated into sterling due to the rigidity of the Indian Foreign Exchange regulations, but somehow it was done perfectly properly and in conformity with the regulations.

I continued as Chairman of the Westminster Abbey Investment Committee which position I had inherited as a Director of the Bank from David Vaughan, also a Director when he retired. This appointment continued for something like 20 years from 1976 to 1996, and coincided with the decade-long restoration of the Abbey. I had some hesitation in accepting this appointment as a Catholic, bearing in mind that as a Benedictine monastery it was dissolved by that brute King Henry VIII, when it became a Cathedral Church. It briefly returned to being a monastery again under Queen Mary until Queen Elizabeth took it over herself creating herself its Visitor and releasing it from any episcopal control. She as Supreme Governor of the Church of England took it over from the Pope with jurisdiction vested in her own person.

Westminster Abbey has always been a 'Royal Peculiar' and this needs some explanation, because it meant that it was, of course, independent of the Church Commissioners. By AD 1100 the Abbey owned more than 11,000 acres. The Benedictine community were also Lords of the Manor of Westminster and this in itself not only meant courts and jurisdiction but also a special line with the Crown and, as a mitred churchman the Abbott of Westminster sat in the Upper House of Parliament. So the monastery, being next door, so to speak, to the Royal Palace, the Judiciary and the Houses of Parliament, became very special and therefore peculiar and the monarchy had, I believe, a special power to override the electoral powers of the monks.

It was important that a monastery having a monarchical foundation and also housing the shrine of King Edward the Confessor should be cooperative with the Crown, and it was also important that the Abbey be independent of any episcopal jurisdiction, whether that of the Archbishop of Canterbury or the Bishop of London. This independence was secured by King Henry III. Equally it was important for the monastery – St Edward's Monastery – to be exempted from the jurisdiction of the Provincial of the Benedictine Order. This was also secured, and the monastery came directly under the Pope – so when Queen Elizabeth took over from the Pope as Supreme Governor of the Church of England, Westminster Abbey came directly under the authority of the monarch, hence its 'royal peculiar' status.

When I took over as Chairman I was surprised to find the funds relatively small and I assume this was because King Henry VIII appropriated the land and funds to himself and his cronies in 1540 when the monastery was surrendered to him. And here it is interesting to note that of the 40 monks at the time of this surrender, some were pensioned and paid off, some joined the new so-called Ecclesia Anglicana, while others went off to France where they remained faithful to their monastic vows and eventually gave birth, if that is the right word, to the Benedictine community at Ampleforth, who still elect the Abbott of Westminster.

I must tell you of that day most wondrous to me when Cardinal Basil Hume, who was formerly the Abbott of Ampleforth, brought his Benedictine monks to sing Vespers in the Abbey on the day of his consecration as Archbishop in Westminster Cathedral. It was over 400 years since the Benedictine community at Westminster Abbey had been abolished and here was the 'Abbott' of Westminster leading his monks along the central aisle of their old Abbey. There was a spontaneous and tremendous burst of applause from the congregation and afterwards the Dean told me that he had been quite concerned that the monks having returned to their old abbey should stage a 'sit-in'. A few months later he told me that in the Throne Room of the Archbishop's House, a recording was presented of the 'Imperium Romanum' – a recording of the Archbishop's consecration and enthronement together with the singing of Vespers by the monks in the Abbey. And it was on that occasion that the dear old Duke of Norfolk pronounced that the Reformation had been rubbish. 'The Cecils got all the land and the Howards lost their heads,' he said, and a great gasp went round the Throne Room.

It was a great privilege to be appointed the Chairman of this Committee which included Lord Catto and Lord Remnant, and to whom the Receiver General, the lay administrator of the Abbey, reported.

Unlike cathedral bodies, Westminster Abbey received no grants from the church Commissioners, nor would it be bailed out of any financial difficulty; we were on our own; and we were particularly reliant on entrance charges. There used to be long debates on these and whether they were appropriate. I used to rationalise them on the basis that, prior to the Reformation, there were many wealthy as well as poor pilgrims to the abbey and especially to the shrine of St Edward, King and Confessor, who all gave the abbey donations. Interestingly enough what originally started off the now daily great influx of tourists to the abbey was not the shrine but the unveiling of the Tomb of the Unknown Warrior, after the end of the First World War, and it is this tomb which has become the place of pilgrimage and is where all the Heads of Governments lay their wreaths and pay their respects.

There is one small story in my favour which I must tell you. There had been a financial crash in share prices and property values, but I cannot now remember the year. The Church Commissioners had speculated heavily in property and had even, I think, borrowed against that property portfolio, so that when the collapse came the losses were magnified. Now it so happened that the Church of England set up an Inquiry into the Church Commissioners and during that Inquiry it came out that they had heard that the Abbey had greatly reduced its property portfolio before the crash, so they asked me what I knew which the Church Commissioners did not know. My answer to this was that it was nothing more than that my banker's intuition and caution on this occasion had proved correct. I survived 20 years as chairman and I believe I ended up with a good report. I must have done so because the Dean, who by then was Michael Mayne who had taken over from Edward Carpenter, invited the whole of my family to a farewell dinner in the famous Jerusalem chamber!

I had also continued as Honorary Treasurer of the Royal Geographical Society, a Vice-President and Member of Council, and Chairman of the General Purposes Committee. I had also been elected a member of the Geographical Club. It always surprised me that geography as a subject in the UK was represented by no less than three bodies. First of all there was, of course, the Royal Geographical Society (RGS) itself, whose prime role seemed to be that of supporting expeditions to various parts of the world; then there were the Institute of British Geographers (IBG) and the Geographical Association. Of these latter two the first, the IBG, represented academics and the second, teachers. The Institute of British Geographers had been a breakaway from the RGS some long time ago, I believe, probably pre-war. This did not seem to make sense, particularly as exploratory expeditions had more or less come to an end – there was nothing more to explore, at least on earth. The RGS therefore began to look for a new role; there needed to be a way forward which members could understand and to which they could relate. The obvious way forward was clearly a rapprochement with the academics at the Institute of British Geographers, particularly bearing in mind that many members of the IBG were also Fellows of the RGS. It was also the case that a merger between the two institutions could create a dynamism which was not currently there in either body.

The IBG were naturally hesitant, looking with a certain amount of caution, if not hostility, at the body from which they had broken away some time ago, but when the rapprochement, that is to say a merger, was put to the vote it was carried, and as I had hoped this merger did provide a dynamism and this dynamism came about as a result of a new Director being appointed, Dr Rita Gardner, who was both a member of the IBG and a Fellow of the Royal Geographical Society. I think it is true to say that whereas John Hemming, her predecessor, was moving the Society in the direction of the twenty-first century, Rita Gardner took this up and catapulted it into the new century. The results are there to see and indeed it is now a world-renowned organisation, building on its history and its academic professionalism, supported by its wealth of archival material, its library and its collection of maps, the finest in the world. Although I was coming to the end of my tenure, nevertheless I was very pleased to be associated with what was to be a very successful merger, although it did once again involve me in a lot of work.

From the Royal Geographical Society, I moved seamlessly on to the Council of the Royal Asiatic Society (RAS), which resulted from my being Chairman of the Calcutta Tercentenary Trust. And for those who are not quite familiar with the Society, it was established in 1823 by a group of people led by the Sanskrit scholar Henry Colebrooke, who had worked in Asia and wished to pursue the objectives set out in the Society's Royal Charter of 1824, that is to say, the investigation of subjects connected with and for the encouragement of science, literature and the arts in relation to Asia. Essentially, the Society promotes a number of activities in this area including the publishing of its learned Journal, and providing access to its very extensive collection of books, historical archival material and its paintings, as well as publishing books and monographs on Asian subjects. Like the Royal Geographical Society it was pursuing a gentle course, but in the twenty-first century such a course is no longer tenable. Once again, it was important to have a new invigorating management, which we were lucky enough to find in Dr Alison Ohta.

428

Alison Ohta is a quite remarkable woman. She was brought up in Baghdad and studied Arabic at Durham University. She then taught English in Japan and followed it up by taking a degree in Japanese from the University of Western Australia; she studied for an MA in Islamic art at the School for Oriental and African Studies (SOAS) and then worked full time there. Afterwards she came to us to take up the new post of Curator at the Society. I have the greatest respect for her.

It was also important for us to move away from our dark and rather shabby premises in Queens Gardens and move to Stephenson Way near Euston Station and the university district of Bloomsbury and the British Library. As the RGS was successful in bidding for funds, particularly for the storage and access to its unique archival material, so also now the RAS, with its new management and new premises, must bid for funds to assist the storage of and access to its remarkable library, its unique archival material and collection of paintings.

And, finally on this, I must not let you forget the Society's branch and associate societies, including the original Asiatic Society founded in Calcutta in 1784, the Asiatic societies of Bombay, Ceylon, Malaysia, Burma, Korea, Hong Kong, Shanghai, and finally not only the Madras Literary Society and Auxiliary of the Royal Asiatic Society, but also the Mythic Society of Bangalore – and I have to say I know very little about this last one.

While all this was going on, I was invited to become a non-executive director of a company called Chillington Corporation PLC. The chairman was Konrad Legg and one of the non-executive directors was my friend Selwyn Pryor, whose family had owned tea estates in Ceylon before these were nationalised. I had also known Konrad Legg as the company's banking arrangements were mainly with Barclays. However, I had no detailed knowledge of the company's activities except that they were heavily invested in plantations in Indonesia and Africa; I had always been interested in plantations ever since I patrolled rubber and palm oil estates in Malaya when I was a soldier.

The company's business was much more disparate than I thought and consisted of no less than 40 companies spread over the UK; Brazil; Africa, namely Uganda, Rwanda, Malawi and Zimbabwe; and Indonesia, namely Java, Sumatra and Thailand. Of these 40 companies: eight made things in the UK; seven made agricultural hand tools in Brazil, Thailand and Africa; 12 were involved in what was called tropical agriculture in Indonesia and Africa; and three were trading companies. One of these was called Langdons, and this was engaged in the business of blending, processing and selling coffee and tea in the UK. The second was called Overseas Farmers, and this was the commodity marketing arm of the group, dealing therefore with many of the crops produced by the plantation companies. The last company was called Jacobs, Young & Westbury, which imported wood furniture products and also rattan and bamboo canes. There thus remained ten companies, of which four were dormant businesses.

Plantations are by their very nature long-term businesses and even then, as all agriculturists know, they are subject to volatile commodity prices, volatile weather conditions and volatile exchange rates – in other words plantations are a business for which you need a lot of capital, patience and luck.

The trouble was that the company did not have a great deal of capital and was indeed highly indebted, which meant that there was continuous financial fire-fighting going on which was in its turn a continual distraction to the operating management, who required capital investment in their businesses. It was also the case that Konrad Legg, who had built up the company, had a large shareholding of not far off 20 per cent and liked to run it himself, although Rothschilds had also a shareholding in excess of 15 per cent.

There was a further difficulty, and this was that if the overseas companies made profits, which some of them did, and such profits appeared in the profit and loss account, this did not necessarily mean that they were available to pay the dividends in the UK. Furthermore, this meant that to pay a dividend the company had had to have recourse to selling capital assets overseas, or for that matter in the UK, to get cash. Just by way of illustration, the company either owned or had a large shareholding interest in Anglo-Eastern Plantations, a fine company, but this had to be sold. It was sold just after I arrived for £8.5 million to bring the gearing of Chillington down to below 50 per cent of equity funds. But the valuation of these equity funds was suspect in the sense that nobody could really value, say, an African plantation and, in any case, it entirely depended on the right buyer coming along – and maybe he wouldn't.

This somewhat lengthy introduction should also be prefaced by stating that for the five years before I arrived, profits after tax had fallen by at least two-thirds from their peak, whilst at the same time the share price had fallen by some 80 per cent. So something had to be done and, of course, the shareholders were getting increasingly restive. One of them wrote to the effect that the company was continuing with its eccentric habit of paying even larger dividends which had not been earned, that the shareholders funds were declining and that the performance of the company over the past five years had been appalling – and indeed it had been.

Now a non-executive director, and a non-executive chairman as I became the following year, is always in a difficult position because, of course, he is not himself managing the company – and in this case not managing a company in which the managing director had close on 20 per cent of the shares and had himself built up the company, although it was now on the way down.

The result was that there were interminable discussions as to what to do, but it was very difficult to reach a consensus *ad idem* on the way forward. My view was that we should be a seller of all the UK and overseas manufacturing interests and get the cash and not retain any minority interest; that we should reduce our direct investment exposure to Africa and repatriate what capital we could by floating our business in Zimbabwe, Malawi and Tanzania, probably on the Harare Stock Exchange, and expand this business with local cash; that we should float the Indonesian business and expand it with local cash and possibly some UK cash; and that we should sell the Langdon business. In all this what I wanted to do was to have cash and marketable stock exchange investments in the UK and concentrate on the plantations, preferably financed by local cash to reduce the exchange risk at the same time. I was particularly concerned about the financing of the company's large new rubber estate in the Bengkulu province of Sumatra, extending to 6,000 hectares, say 15,000 acres, where we were in negotiations to increase this concession by a further 6,000 hectares – that is to say 30,000 acres, a large concession which needed to be tightly managed and controlled.

Interestingly enough Bencoolen as it used to be called by the British was a trading post and garrison established there in 1685 by the Honourable East India Company's traders and soldiers. What had happened here was that the growing market for spices in Europe led the Company to expand its activities in the east, and this trading post at Bencoolen was established for the acquisition of pepper. This post was known as the Fort Marlborough establishment and the fortifications as York Fort, Marlborough Fort and Fort Anne further up the coast at Muko Muko.

The British remained at Bencoolen for 140 years, and during that time hundreds and thousands of soldiers died of cholera, malaria and dysentery. Living conditions were extremely poor compared with those in India and there was constant friction between the civil administrators and the military officers. There were also numerous minor skirmishes with the hostile local natives, and in 1760 there was the shameful capitulation to a French expeditionary force when the British surrendered to the French without a fight. The French occupation lasted only a few months, during which time most of the French and British soldiers died of disease, so much so that Comte d'Estaing, the leader of the French force – or what was left of it – decided to evacuate the settlement. I often wonder whether this Comte d'Estaing was an ancestor of the French President Valery Giscard d'Estaing.

It was during the period 1811–14 that the Honourable East India Company became involved in the operation to secure Java from the Dutch. An expedition sailed from Malacca, which at the time was under British control, consisting of foot regiments of the British army, detachments of the Bengal and Madras artillery and volunteer battalions of the Bengal Native Infantry. As I have mentioned earlier, they had to be volunteers as it was against their caste to cross seas. This expeditionary force defeated the Dutch and the French, the terms of the surrender by the General Jansens being that he agreed 'to surrender himself and his army, to resign the sovereignty of Java and all Dutch and French possessions in the East Indies into the hands of Great Britain, who therefore should be left free with regard to the future administration of the islands'.

As a result Mr Stamford Raffles (who later became Sir Stamford Raffles and was appointed Lieutenant Governor of the Settlements on the west coast of Sumatra where Bencoolen was situated) was appointed Governor of the Island. Soon after he took over, three of his children died from one of the Bencoolen epidemics and the only surviving child, Ella, was sent back to England – just before their infant daughter Flora also died two months after she was born in September 1873. The loss of four children was a tragedy for the Raffles family.

During this time the British and Dutch governments were negotiating this question of territory and commerce in the East Indies, and as a result the British gave up all rights to colonisation on the island of Sumatra in exchange for the settlement at Malacca. In August 1824 Raffles left for England and later for Singapore, but that is another story. But Fort Marlborough has now been fully restored and so also has the Christian burial ground so you can go and see it. It is now a museum, and when it was formally opened in 1994, the pipes and drums of the Black Watch played, and that night there was a huge spectacular dance and music staged by the citizens of Bengkulu nearby where our 30,000 acres were situated.

I decided I also needed to pay a visit to Indonesia with Diana to inspect what the Scots would call 'the policies', in this case the plantations, and form my own view. Such a visit would need to fit in with a meeting of the Council of the Foundation of Aviation and Tourism in Delhi, of which I was the only British member. Associated with this meeting was a seminar on 'Emerging Trends in Aviation Tourism in South and South East Asia'. From Delhi we would go on to Calcutta where I had some important work to carry out in connection with the Calcutta Tercentenary Trust. From Calcutta we would fly down to Madras and then catch an Indian Airlines flight to Kuala Lumpur where we would stay with our friends the Carruthers. From Kuala Lumpur we would fly down to Jakarta and go into the interior of Java to inspect the plantations. I would have liked to have gone on to Bengkulu in south-west Sumatra, but as it was looking like a fairly extended trip I unfortunately did not have the time available, and I only had time to visit a tea estate in Central Java called Cukul.

So we set off in early February and arrived in Delhi where, because we were guests of the Government of India, we had to stay at the Ashoka Hotel which, as you will know by now, is not my favourite hotel in India and should have been privatised years ago. The Ashoka lived up to its reputation, as we saw cockroaches scurrying across our hotel bedroom floor. Unfortunately, also during our stay in Delhi, Diana fell down visiting a shop and badly sprained her ankle, so she was in great pain and hardly able to walk. The night of our arrival we attended what the Indians call a

Welcome Reception at the Ashoka Hotel given by Mr Bhardwan and his wife – he being an IAS officer and also the Chairman of the International Airports Authority of India. These Welcome Receptions, and I have attended many of them, were never the most cheerful of affairs, so there was always a tendency on my part to drink too many whiskies and soda. The Council Meeting and seminar went well, there was the usual run of parties, and on Sunday as was my wont we had a large lunch party with our friends at the Delhi Golf Club, which on most days, and particularly on Sundays, is always the social hub of Delhi and was always my favourite watering hole in Delhi.

From Delhi we flew to Calcutta to stay at the Tollygunge Club with our friends Bob and Annie Wright where, as it happens, Tony and Jennifer Hayward were also staying. Tony Hayward, who had been at my prep school Stone House with me, was pretty well the last 'Koi Hai' in Calcutta apart from Bob Wright, and for those not familiar with the expression it means 'Anyone about', the call made to summon servants. The expression metamorphosed into meaning a sahib. Tony and Jennifer Hayward had a large house, I believe in Alipore, and there was no lack of servants there – the last count being 35.

The Wrights gave a huge party on the terrace of the clubhouse in the evening and there were masses of interesting people here. The following day at breakfast with the Wrights on the first-floor terrace of the clubhouse where they lived, Diana suddenly went down with the dreaded Delhi belly – not a good omen as we were flying down to Madras the following day where we were due to have dinner with some Parsee friends and stay with them until we caught the early morning India Airlines flight to Kuala Lumpur. We did fly down but Diana had to lie down when she arrived, so no dinner party for her, and then it was off to KL.

We stayed a few days with John Carruthers and his wife Rocky (short for Rukiah), a high-born Thai Malay girl. She was his second wife and much younger than he was. He had been married before to an English girl. He had once been an ADC to the last British Governor of Singapore – by name Sir William Goode – and there is a historic newsreel clip often shown on television in Singapore showing him descending the steps of City Hall together with the Governor after the swearing in of Lee Kuan Yew as Singapore's first Prime Minister in 1959. The clip shows the Governor speaking to John Carruthers, but of course nobody knew what he was saying – they thought probably something about the end of the Empire. However John confirmed to me that what the Governor was saying was, 'What the hell have you done with the Rolls, John?'

As it happens John Carruthers's grandfather had been General Manager of the Anglo-Egyptian Bank which, as I have mentioned, was one of the founding components of Barclays Bank (DCO) in 1925, and of which my grandfather became a Director in that year. His father had also worked for the Anglo-Egyptian Bank and Barclays. There was no doubt that John was in many ways an ideal Representative of the Bank: discreet, diplomatic, charming and extraordinarily knowledgeable about local policies and the wealthy Malay and Chinese. He originally had a large house in the city's most exclusive residential district, Kenny Hill, later called Bukit Tunku after Tunku Abdul Rahman, the first Prime Minister of Malaysia. Later he had moved to a charming colonial bungalow on the outskirts of the city with a swimming pool, and it was here that we stayed and refreshed ourselves while Diana recovered from her sprained ankle.

Later John moved to Labuan, although Rukiah mainly stayed in Kuala Lumpur, and later on in this book I will tell you a story about Labuan, an island close to Brunei. Labuan had become British territory in 1846 when it was uninhabited, and this was as a result of a treaty signed on board HMS *Iris*, then lying off Labuan, by a certain Captain Mundy, Royal Navy, representing Queen Victoria and by a certain Malay nobleman, one Pangiran Munim, deputising for his cousin the weak-minded, ugly old Sultan of Brunei who had pleaded that sea-sickness prevented his coming to Labuan to sign the Treaty himself. In the Malay language Labuan means 'Beautiful Harbour', but the subjects of the Sultan of Brunei were well aware at that time that Labuan was a beautiful but pestilential swamp. Now it is an offshore financing centre and this is where John Carruthers now lives. He has become one of our greatest friends.

From Kuala Lumpur we flew down to Jakarta after a short visit to my old stamping ground at Kuantan on the East Coast, and this time there were no ambushes. It was a short flight, but with wonderful views of the Malacca and Singapore Straits, Sumatra, and then the north coast of Java. Jakarta is not an attractive city and after a night at the Hilton we were met and taken up by road

435

to the Cukul Tea Estate by the General Manager. He had been a tea planter in north-east India and he was now in Java. Unfortunately, Diana took an immediate dislike to him and I was not surprised – he had a rather odd appearance.

The journey up took several hours. There was thick fog and the road twisted and turned on its way up to the mountainous area of Central Java. Diana is not good on twisting and turning roads and was feeling sick again. Eventually we arrived at the top to see a beautiful Tudor-style house, where we were to stay for the next day or so whilst I inspected the policies. From the top there were stunning views of Central Java down to the south of the island and the sea, and it was all unbelievably beautiful and green.

The Cukul Tea Estate extended to 1,300 hectares, of which 832 hectares were planted with tea, and of this hectarage 590 hectares were what were regarded as mature, with 242 hectares being immature. It was one of the most beautiful places I have ever visited, apart from, of course, the Antarctic. This was lush, verdant green, with hills and lakes, but also as a reminder of war, remains of the gun emplacements of the Japanese who had occupied the territory for about two and a half years. It is an interesting fact that following the surrender of Japan in 1945, the Indonesians fought the incoming Dutch administrators, but of course the Dutch had no armed forces, so the British were sent to fight the Indonesian insurgents and among the British forces was my battalion of Seaforth Highlanders, which I joined a few years later. The British suffered quite severe casualties, and finding it difficult to get the country under control, decided to enlist the support of the Japanese forces who had been disarmed, and rearmed them. No less than 65,000 Japanese troops in Java were incorporated into the British and Gurkha command structure to defeat the Indonesians. But it is interesting to note that when in Java my battalion of Seaforth Highlanders boarded their departing ship, they began to mock the disembarking fresh recruits from the Netherlands, shouting: 'Merdeka' or 'Freedom for the Indonesians'.

The first night we spent in the Tudor mansion at Cukul was a nightmare for Diana. I have already mentioned her immediate dislike of the General Manager, but when during the night he began what we thought was goose-stepping along the corridors surrounding the three sides of our bedroom she became frantic with terror and I had to hold her tight all night to try and calm her down. All this

436

was not helped by there being no water in the lavatory, and as the electricity had been switched off, I had to set forth in the middle of the night in total darkness to find a bucket in the external kitchen quarters in an entirely strange house. I did in the end find a candle and lit, it but in a sense that made the remaining darkness and shadows even more menacing.

Thus a somewhat bedraggled and sleepless pair arrived down for breakfast in the morning, but as I was the visiting Chairman I could not let the side down and shortly afterwards we set forth in a Land Rover to tour and inspect the policies.

First of all we looked at the tea factory, which seemed in quite good working order. Secondly we inspected the houses and housing conditions of the Indonesian tea estate workers, and we were impressed by these. For the rest of the day we drove slowly and at times very precariously round the estate, with steep drops on one side of the track and sometimes on both sides. I was not overly impressed with the state of the plantation and what was apparent to me was that the general shortage of investment was inhibiting the potential yield of the estate.

There was very little sign of fertilisers being applied, and sure enough it had been a year since this had been done. There were large amounts of infilling and replanting required and there was a lot of weed about, and I think my exam report would have reached the conclusion that 'he could have done better'. That may or not have been true, but there is no doubt that the general shortage of cash and capital in the group was inhibiting the necessary investment and this was having its effect. And of course, once again, so was the weather. There had been a severe drought in Indonesia in 1994, and partly because of this all the tea estates in Indonesia lost money, although these losses were partially set off by good profits from the rubber estates. Overall, however, the Indonesian business made little or no contribution to group profits in London.

We stayed one more day and we then had to leave to catch the British Airways direct flight to London from Jakarta the following day. Diana, however, refused to tackle the hairpin bends of the road to Jakarta, which drops down from some 6,000 feet to sea level in constant twists and turns. We therefore drove down to Bandung, an attractive town full of art deco architecture built by the Dutch, which again had a modern, attractive railway station. Here we were welcomed aboard the Jakarta Express by two very

437

attractive and smartly uniformed Javanese stewardesses in charge of our first class carriage, and we set off on what was truly an amazing railway journey through the most lovely countryside. It was well worth it.

I returned to Chillington PLC, now renamed Plantation & General Investments PLC. Despite there being no consensus *ad idem* on the way forward, it was decided to float Eastern Highland Plantations on the Harare Stock Exchange so that 30 per cent of the shares would be held by the public and 70 per cent retained by Plantation & General Investments. Now the Eastern Highland Plantations was the jewel in the crown of the company. It was a successful producer of tea, coffee and timber situated in the Honde Valley in Eastern Zimbabwe, in fact right on the Zimbabwe–Mozambique border where, in the latter country, a civil war was then raging. Most of the tea and coffee crop was exported, so the company was almost entirely dependent on international tea and coffee prices, which were, as always, highly volatile. However, at that time, 1994 coffee prices were increasing and in 1993 there was a substantial increase in profits, although what was happening to these profits when converted into sterling, I cannot now remember. The purpose of the issue was to raise local capital for the expansion of the business.

The altitude in the Honde Valley was ideally suited for tea production. The average rainfall in the valley was higher than elsewhere and there was very little frost. The estate also had a well-developed infrastructure and housed 1,500 workers and their families. It maintained four schools, three medical clinics, three trading stores, two staff clubs and, last but not least, three beer halls. So, as I have mentioned, it was very much a jewel in the crown. I decided to go out to Zimbabwe and not only inspect the plantation, but also help to get the issue away to the investing institutions in Harare – and furthermore to help establish a new board of Directors, and particularly African non-executive Directors.

So I left on the British Airways flight to Harare in August 1994. It was an uneventful flight except for a spectacular electrical display over what I assumed to be Mount Kilimanjaro. At Harare I was met and taken straight to the plantation. The journey took about four and a half hours, most of which was on a good road.

The farming then looked prosperous, and as we moved into the Eastern Highlands the scenery changed but I was appalled at the poverty of the Africans themselves in their little round huts with

438

thatched roofs, and it all looked very much like a subsistence economy. In due course, we drove up to the estate office which was attractively situated on a hill overlooking the Honde Valley.

Here I was welcomed by the Managing Director Malcolm Johnstone and his wife. He was a Scot and had been a tea planter for most of his life in India, during which he spent four years in Assam before moving first to Kenya and then to Zimbabwe. It is probable that the Indianisation of the tea estate managements in north-east India precipitated his move to Africa.

The estate office and house had been fortified during the troubles and I believe had been besieged at one time so, in that sense, it was all familiar to me from my Malayan days. It was very comfortable. I toured the estate – it extended to about 4,500 acres and one could easily see why it was known as the Jewel in the Crown. We also toured the adjacent Aberfoyle Plantation which was again magnificent, but clearly not as well managed as Eastern Highlands. The owner was, I think, an Indian called Mr Harpel Ranhawa but it was leased to a Mr Bellingham whom I never met. He had constructed an airstrip for light aircraft nearby but, from time to time, the unfriendly natives used to block it with boulders so that he could neither land nor take off. Also at Aberfoyle was a European Country Club with a swimming pool and a nine-hole golf course with a magnificent westerly view to the tree-covered mountains, an area which I believe was called Rhodes Inyanga National Park, although whether the name Rhodes has survived I do not know. Although we had lunch at the clubhouse, it was clear that it was a victim of unfriendly activity by the natives and it looked rather sad, shabby and shoddy. I cast covetous eyes over that Aberfoyle Plantation – it would have been a superb add-on to the Eastern Highlands Plantation.

Later that night I was given a reception by the African middle management and their wives in one of their staff clubs. They were all extraordinarily polite, well mannered and well educated, but the wives were very shy and I hardly spoke to any of them.

Some fairly long time after I left, an Australian who had just been appointed finance director of Eastern Highland Plantations was confronted by some African terrorists who forced him to drink sulphuric acid in front of his wife and three children. He died in agony. I have no wish to return to the Eastern Highlands.

But now it was time to return to Harare after my three-day visit to the Honde Valley and here I spent most of my time talking to the principal bankers and the issuing bank, namely the Merchant Bank of Central Africa, and also the sponsoring brokers. In the event the issue got away successfully in November 1994. I also took the opportunity to talk to Isaac Takawira, the Managing Director of Barclays Bank Zimbabwe, to ascertain his views on possible non-executive African Directors and in all this he was extremely helpful. I have to say I was not very impressed with Harare, a modern town with unattractive buildings, and I sensed tension between the poor Africans and the affluent Europeans wherever I went and I felt uncomfortable with this and was glad to leave.

On my last night I had dinner with a South African friend to whom I said I could not understand why Africa was so backward compared with say India, which of course I knew well. I said that in India there were settled communities going back hundreds of years if not thousands, and these communities developed a merchant middle class and an upper class which became wealthy, and because of this accumulating wealth built the great forts, castles, palaces, temples and monuments of India. Why, I asked was it that there was nothing in Africa? His answer was that historically when the African peasant or farmer exhausted the fertility of his soil, he moved on, and because of this incessant movement there never developed settled communities and therefore a prosperous middle and upper class and therefore no palaces, castles, forts, temples which are everywhere in India. I suppose he was right, but there must be more to it than that and I remembered V.S. Naipaul's novel entitled *A Bend in the River* which chronicles the collapse of a small European and Indian trading town in the middle of Africa after it was overrun by the natives. Someone once told me the story about the difference between an African and an Indian businessman: 'The Indian businessman takes a 10 per cent commission, has a nice house, a nice new Mercedes and a nice new road outside his house; the African takes a 100 per cent commission, has a nice house, ten new Mercedes cars, but there is no road outside his house.' Africa is indeed very different from India, and I remembered an old retired British Colonial service officer who had served in Africa for most of his working life, weeping over his pink gin at the East India Club in London, telling me that it had taken the British 50 or so years to drag Africa out of barbarianism and now 50 years after the British had left, it appears to all intents and

440

purposes to have reverted to its original condition. In contrast India is moving to become a major world economic power. So all this requires careful thought, but I have never been back to Africa.

I had been invited as a member of Council of the Delhi-based Foundation for Civil Aviation and Tourism to participate in a Council meeting and conference in Mauritius, and I was also to be a guest of the Indian Chairman of Air Mauritius who was hosting the conference. It was therefore with some relief that, after fighting my way through the Zimbabwean passport control officers at Harare Airport, I boarded a brand new Air Mauritius Airbus and was greeted with great courtesy and charming smiles by the lovely Air Mauritius stewardesses who had been advised that I was the Chairman's guest. Suddenly I seemed to be back in an orderly world, and I do not think I have ever relished any flight so much as that flight to Mauritius, a four-hour journey overflying Madagascar – an unattractive island which was once offered to the Jews to settle there instead of Palestine, but they did not accept it – a pity.

It was an interesting conference held at the Maritime Hotel just outside the capital St Louis. Some of the attendees were Indian, but lucky for me most of these were friends so I had a thoroughly good time, not only attending the conference but also visiting and lunching with some friends who owned large sugar plantations in the south of the island. They had a lovely house overlooking the sea, and after landlocked Zimbabwe, it was a great pleasure to sit with a glass in one hand and gaze over the blue sea of the southern Indian Ocean and listen to the booming of the great breakers on the basalt cliffs. It was idyllic, but I was beginning to get homesick.

Before I go home, I must digress once again. Yes, once again and I am as conscious as you are of these many historical digressions, but they are what to me brings a place alive. It is not the hotels, the restaurants, shops and cafes that interest me, it is the history of the people, the architecture and the geography – an island geography in the case of Mauritius – which matters.

Now I must tell you a little bit about Sir John Pope-Hennessy who was Governor of the Island from 1883 to 1887. Mauritius was his last Governorship, and depending on which way you look at it, it was either his most successful or his most disastrous. He had been successively Governor of Labuan, the West African Settlements, the Bahamas, Barbados, Hong Kong, and now finally Mauritius.

It was in Labuan – hardly a prestigious appointment – that shortly after his arrival there the bachelor Governor met his future wife Kitty and married her six weeks later – she being 17 and he 34. Kitty was the only daughter of Hugh Low who, as Colonial Treasurer, had administered the Colony no less than three times as a stand-in for absent Governors. He therefore felt he should have been appointed Governor, and here he was once again being passed over by a man who had obtained his appointment through an exercise of political patronage of the most blatant kind. However, later on he was instrumental in creating the Federated Malay States, but that is another story.

Kitty had come out to Labuan to join her father who was now a widower, although he had a native mistress, a Sarawak lady by whom he had another daughter. Kitty's mother was the Eurasian daughter of William Napier, the first Governor of the Island, who had married a Malay and it was from her that Kitty had inherited her beautiful dark looks.

Moving from Labuan to Mauritius, you will see a fine statue of Sir John Pope-Hennessy situated in the Place d'Armes outside the Hotel de Ville in Port Louis, a statue erected by public subscription 20 years after he had left the island, and indeed long after he had died in 1891. Sir John was a devout southern Irish Catholic who, naturally enough, resented British Protestant rule over Ireland and who therefore sympathised greatly with the natives of the six British colonies he successively administered. It is interesting to read his lengthy obituary in *The Times* in 1891. The obituarist declared that:

> his Colonial career says little for the intelligence or the discretion with which the Colonial Office exercises its patronage. He ought never to have been placed in charge of such colonies as Hong Kong and Mauritius where the pretensions of the natives threatened to make trouble. The sympathiser with the down-trodden Catholics of West Ireland was an enthusiast with regard to the equal rights of men.

And indeed he was, and for many years he was remembered with affection by the inhabitants of the West African Settlements, Hong Kong, Barbados and, of course, Mauritius. In fact the natives of these colonies believed that here, at long last, they were being represented by a Governor who was actually on their side, and put their welfare and interests first and in many cases before that of the British (usually Protestant) colonial administration.

In fact the people and the problems of this French-speaking Crown Colony reminded him of those of his native Ireland. This went straight to his heart, and the islanders returned his affection with gratitude. He was the first British Governor to take a positive interest in the plight of the poor Mauritians and those of poor Euro-African and Asiatic origin. Of course, this attitude of his led to all sorts of disputes and animosities and eventually to his suspension as Governor, although he was later reinstated. This reinstatement the Mauritians regarded as a victory for liberalism over bureaucracy, for the Irish over the English and in a sense, more than anything else, as a brave and successful challenge to the colonial power, although as Governor he represented that colonial power.

This is a brief introduction to that man represented by that statue outside the Hotel de Ville in Port Louis, and there is a cafe close by where you can sit and sip your cup of coffee. Here you can think of Sir John and Kitty – she of the beautiful dark Eurasian looks – arriving in Mauritius in 1883, only 13 years after my grandfather had been born, and recall that he had only been appointed to Mauritius because he had been turned down as Governor of Queensland, Australia, by its inhabitants because of his Irish Catholicism, and maybe because Kitty's mother had been a Malay native.

One can also, while sipping that cup of coffee in the Place d'Armes, reflect on the miscellany of life and religion – Mauritius has every religion – and on the attractive metisse of blood in Mauritius as one watches the beautiful Eurasian girls step by past the cafe in their high-heeled shoes, and as one does so one thinks of that beautiful but sad poem by Horace: 'Eheu Fugaces, Postume, Postume, anni labuntur' – and for those who do not understand Latin: 'Alas, Postume, Postume, how the fleeting years slip by'.

I flew back on a direct Air Mauritius flight to London which took far longer than I had expected.

I remained as Chairman of Plantation & General Investments for the next two and a half years or so. During this time there were endless discussions as to how to restructure the company to bring in local cash, and many of these proposals seemed perfectly

443

sensible to me, particularly the proposals to float locally the plantation and agricultural tool business in East Africa. These proposals were put forward by Sebastian Hobhouse, a very capable Cambridge economist responsible for the company's African interests, but whilst I was there very little became of them.

Another estate called Kalimas, this time in Indonesia, was sold for £6.5 million, realising a profit just in excess of £4 million. It was essentially a sale to raise cash. Unbeknown to me, however, there was a loan of £1.8 million to PT Tatar Anyar, the Indonesian company, by the Commonwealth Development Corporation (CDC) and technically and quite correctly to me as a banker under the terms and conditions of the loan, this loan should have been repaid from the sale proceeds of Kalimas. This did not happen, however, and the cash was directed elsewhere. It was therefore a shock to me when I received a letter from the General Manager of the CDC threatening legal proceedings if repayment was not undertaken forthwith.

It was at about this time that the non-executive directors wrote a note to the executive directors, drafted by myself, to the effect that we were concerned and dissatisfied with both the financial performance of the company and its management. It was not only the non-repayment of the CDC loan which upset us, it was also because the provisional half-year's figures for 1996 were showing a loss as compared with a budgeted profit of £1.2 million; and furthermore because of the deferral apparently *sine die* of the strategy to float the African plantation business, resulting in losing some potentially valuable worthwhile plantation acquisitions in Africa. I ended the note by saying that waiting and hoping for something to turn up was not a policy, and that in any case we did not have the luxury of waiting for something to turn up given our cash position, and that lastly we were extremely concerned that the business was neither profitable nor cash positive and that we wanted the necessary management steps taken to rectify this as soon as possible.

This letter showed clearly – as I was the instigator – that I had lost confidence in the Managing Director, although the other two executive directors were doing an excellent job given the circumstances, so it was not well received, but nor did I expect it to be.

In 1993 a certain Mr Roditi had become a shareholder of the company, although before that he had, as he told me, been watching the company for a good deal longer. He was a Rhodesian by birth and had become the right-hand man of George Soros – this was the Hungarian who had become famous by heavily speculating against sterling when it entered the European Exchange Rate Mechanism. Soros's speculation was a considerable factor in ejecting sterling from the mechanism and, in so doing, it was rumoured he had made a fortune – somewhere, I was told, in the region of £1 billion – when he closed his positions. It may be recalled that those two bank clerks, John Major the Prime Minister, and Norman Lamont the Chancellor, had entered sterling into the mechanism at what they should have known was at an unsustainably high rate, hence its later ejection – and hence the later rejection by the Electorate at the 1997 general election of the Conservative government. Essentially it was just poor financial mismanagement and incompetence on the part of the Conservative government, and they paid the price.

Roditi and I used to meet from time to time, mainly at the Farmers' Club in Whitehall. It was clear that as a Rhodesian and therefore a white African he was mainly interested in the African business, and it may be recalled that at that time there was some sort of feeling that an African political and economic renaissance was in the air. I told him, as he well knew, that we had some magnificent assets, but the problem was that they were neither showing a satisfactory return nor creating cash. I also told him I was concerned about the loan stocks amounting to some £15 million of which £5.5 million was due within one year and £9 million due after one year. I told him my feeling was that we needed to run for cash by selling off the Indonesian estates and all the UK manufacturing businesses so that we had sufficient and more to deal with the liabilities, and perhaps concentrate on Africa, where there appeared to be acquisition possibilities, which we could finance locally and not from London. Nick Roditi agreed with all this.

In fact there were some good acquisition possibilities about at that time including Aberfoyle, the adjacent estate to Eastern Highlands in Zimbabwe, with which we had a common border. It is always possible to bid up for what I would call contiguity, because of the ability to spread costs over a wider area. The two estates combined could produce something like 5 million kilograms of tea annually. However, nobody was sure whether the owners could deliver a clear title or indeed were actually interested in selling.

And just to illustrate further these possible acquisitions, it came to our notice that Unilever were selling their Malawi tea plantation interests. The Lujeri Tea Plantations were and presumably still are a high-yielding compact tea estate producing something like 5 million kilograms – very similar to a combined Eastern Highland and Aberfoyle yield. Unilever were selling for about $4–5 million, which we thought was a fair price, well below replacement cost. My chief concern, assuming we were in a financial position to bid, was of course the world price of tea, but over and above that was the problem of the relative value of the Malawi kwacha currency against the US dollar. Essentially what was happening here was that historically the kwacha devalued at a speed materially different to the rate of Malawi price inflation, at least in the short term, and this misalignment could well destroy profitability.

To cut a long story short, it was clear that the Managing Director seemed unwilling to dismantle some of his disparate businesses, and it was also clear to me that if he could not do it, or was unwilling to do it, then somebody else had to do it for him, and this is exactly what happened after I resigned. Here I think that what happened was that Roditi and his colleagues had been willing to stand back while I was still Chairman and trying to get the company going in the right direction, but once I had retired there seemed no point in holding back any longer and accordingly Roditi bid for the company, succeeded, and it was taken private. For me it would be interesting to know what happened subsequently and, in particular, to know what happened to Eastern Highland Plantations under Mugabe, who has collapsed the economy, thus confirming the views of my old retired district officer friend sadly sipping his pink gin at the East India Club.

31

South Georgia Revisited

While everything else was going on, in 1996 I was invited to join some old polar friends visiting the Falkland Islands and South Georgia – my old haunts. It seemed to be too good an opportunity to miss and having re-equipped myself with some polar clothing, together with a new ice-axe and rucksack, I set off for RAF Brize Norton where I had booked a seat on one of the twice-weekly RAF Transport Command Tristar flights to Mount Pleasant on East Falkland, about one hour's drive on the new road to Port Stanley. About 10 per cent of the accommodation on these military flights was reserved for civilians, except in the case of emergencies, and I had booked it at the Falklands Islands Government Office by St James's Park underground station. I was to get to know these offices very well because that was where the Falkland Islands Conservation Trust to which I was later appointed a trustee and Director, had their regular meetings.

The security at Brize Norton was very tight but by midnight the plane was ready for departure, crammed full of squaddies, and I was equally crammed into a small cramped seat for the eight-and-a-half-hour flight to Ascension Island. An ageing Tristar is not my favourite aircraft at the best of times. The last time I had been on one was on one of my regular flights to Delhi when a technical fault developed in one of the engines over the Mediterranean and we had to return to London, jettisoning most of our fuel on the way back. The inside of the aircraft was very spartan as you would expect, but there was some refreshment in the form of a cheese bun and an apple and, quite surprisingly, half a bottle of wine – I thought these flights were dry.

There were no difficulties with the long flight to Ascension except the realisation that Ascension was only halfway to the Falklands. At Ascension, which is an RAF and USAF station, we were allowed off the plane but we were kept under control in a small space surrounded by a barbed-wire perimeter fence. Inside this fence was a small bar, a small restroom and a small shop. Naturally, the squaddies filled up with lager while the plane filled up with fuel. The night was warm and balmy but there was something surreal about walking round and round for those two hours on a little patch, eyeing the great bulk of the Tristar crouching like some huge beast on the tarmac, floodlit, with little men, or so they seemed, servicing the aircraft. The equatorial dawn arrived swiftly and soon we were back on board and taking off along a runway with a disconcerting bump in the middle. Wheeling, we once again turned south for the long haul down and across the South Atlantic. It was a curious feeling flying down the middle of the South Atlantic, as we had previously flown down the middle of the North Atlantic, and flying over the sea the entire time, thousands of miles from land and theoretical safety. It was, however, a great joy observing the cloud formations and flying over a large South Atlantic depression and seeing the familiar cirrostratus developing into the great cumulus. The second eight and half hours went as slowly as all flights go, but then suddenly a trio of RAF Tornado aircraft arrived as an escort into Mount Pleasant – we had arrived. After a lecture on unexploded ordnance left by the Argentinians during the 1982 conflict – the lecture was twice as long for any visiting Argentinians – I boarded the bus, drove into Stanley and found my way to the Islas Malvinas Hotel at the west end of the town not far from Government House. I was last there 42 years before, but it was all very much the same and familiar except for a small supermarket and a plenitude of four-wheeled cars and trucks.

I had a day or so to kill before the MS *Explorer* arrived to take us to some of the outlying islands and then on down to South Georgia via the Shag Rocks. Also a number of Americans who were arriving via a chartered flight from Santiago. So we decided to visit Goose Green and Darwin, which I had last visited so many years ago and where the fierce battle took place between the Argentinian invaders and the British paratroops under the command of Colonel Jones, who was awarded a posthumous Victoria Cross. I visited the memorial where he was shot, apparently in the back.

As an infantry officer I was very surprised that he took the risk that he did, bearing in mind that he had not secured his right flank before advancing: it was the Argentinians on his open right flank who shot and killed him.

Goose Green was a shadow of its former self – many of the houses were empty and boarded up, a long way from the bustling Goose Green I had known 42 years before, when we loaded up all those sheep carcasses for the whaling stations in South Georgia.

The following day we went by Land Rover to Darwin and then on the rough track to Camilla Creek, to Port Sussex with Grantham Sound opening up to the west, on to Falkland Sound and then over the hill down to San Carlos where again, forty-two years earlier, I had stayed as a guest of the Bonner family. It was, of course, here that in 1982 the British troops had landed to retake the islands from the Argentinians, and it is here that there is now situated a circular stone cemetery with the names of those who had been killed in the conflict, among them that of Colonel Jones VC. Above the cemetery, in the strong Falkland wind whistling across San Carlos Sound, fluttered a Union Jack, standing out brilliantly and defiantly against the bright blue of the Falkland sky. It was wonderful to be back here but it was sad that all the warnings we had given to the British government had been ignored, and had led to this cemetery. I said a prayer for these brave men and then walked slowly back to the old Bonner house, where I had stayed all those years ago. Nothing had changed except for the cemetery and the unkemptness of the old garden. We returned to Stanley.

The following day the Americans arrived and we boarded the *Explorer* and then it was full away to what I have always considered some of the most beautiful of all the Falkland Islands, namely the Jasons. The Jasons are a chain of reef-strewn, tide-ripped islands which stretch to the north and west of West Falkland towards Patagonia. They had been called the Jasons in 1786 by Captain John McBride, who had been sent out by the British Admiralty to survey the islands in the frigate HMS *Jason*. Steeple Jason is the most dramatic of all the islands in this archipelago and it used to support an enormous number of birds, but many of these, including thousands of penguins, were rounded up, clubbed to death and rendered down for oil in the eighteenth and nineteenth centuries. Sheep were grazed on this island but declining wool markets brought this to an end and by 1968 there were no more but you can still see, as I did, the small old shearing shed and the hut for the shearers, which looked as if they had left it not all that long ago, but in reality 30 years before.

We anchored off the north neck of the island and went ashore, myself on my own to climb the steep west crag, about 1,000 feet high, with several pairs of striated caracaras keeping their beady eyes on this interloper. The view from the summit was magnificent, but in an entirely different way so was the view of the world's largest colony of black-browed albatrosses, containing something like 150,000 breeding pairs and stretching for a staggering almost 3 miles along the south coast below me. Not only were the black-browed albatrosses' nests there, but so also were thousands and thousands of rockhopper penguins – the latest estimate by Falklands Conservation is about 90,000 – and many Falkland skuas and king cormorants, plus of course the striated caracaras nearby. I descended into the tussock, outnumbered by 250,000 to one. The tussock grass was very high, about 6 feet, and it was difficult to see where I was going. I carried my ice-axe above my head, but even so I was attacked on the head by an aggressive caracara, and I started to bleed quite badly. I tied my head up with a handkerchief which stopped the bleeding, and beat a slow retreat. As I could not see where I was going, all I could do was try and go uphill, and after what seemed an interminable time – probably not long, but all the time being attacked by the caracaras – I managed to gain ground and eventually emerged on the high slopes of the crag, safe at last. The last time I had been attacked like this was by Antarctic skuas, but then I had the protection of a long ski-stick, not a short ice-axe.

By now recovered, I crossed the neck of the island to the crags of Steeple Jason East, circled it, and returned via the sheep shearing shed which was located by the only stream I saw on the island. I could have stayed there for days, but the Captain of our ship was anxious to get away in the evening for Carcass Island, which is to the west of Byron Sound.

Carcass Island takes its name from HMS *Carcass* which visited it and may have discovered it in the late eighteenth century. It is now owned by Rob and Lorraine McGill who have lived on the island for 30 years, but although the island supports about 1,000 sheep, their main income is from tourism. We landed at Dyke Bay, where I was greeted by all those tussock birds, who always seem so tame. I climbed up to the top of Jason Hill, with below me colonies of gentoo and Magellanic penguins. I passed by a charming cottage called Valley Cottage, built in the 1870s and now used as rented accommodation, and entered the Settlement Gardens. These were a joy, and apart from anything else are a living testament that trees can grow in the Falklands. There were some beautiful Monterey cypress trees and cabbage palms introduced from New Zealand, while all around seemed to be fields of gorse in full yellow bloom. It was warm in the sun; the settlement is very shielded, and protected from the westerly winds.

Rob gave us a huge tea – his teas are famous – and we reminisced about life in the Falklands in the 1950s, before embarking for Sanders Island. It was a glorious day – a day in which it was the greatest joy to be alive and to thank God for his great blessings and his creation. There was a cloudless bright blue sky; the sea was a magnificent Mediterranean blue, flecked with small white caps; there was a stiff westerly breeze; and all around us were the beautiful mauve green islands, islets and mainland of West Falkland all bathed in the most glorious summer sunshine. And everywhere there was a teeming life of penguins, porpoises, terns, gulls, ducks, geese, and the black-browed albatrosses wheeling and soaring above the ship.

We anchored not far from the south shore of The Neck which links Elephant Point to the main part of the island. We landed to be greeted by gentoos and Magellanics, rockhoppers, oystercatchers, kelp geese, king cormorants and Falkland steamer ducks. I wandered off as usual on my own and nearly came to grief on the steep, slippery slopes leading down to the sea below, booming and breaking on the sea-cliffs in a thunderous, foaming roar. As dusk descended we re-embarked and set sail for the Sea Lion Islands some distance off the south-east coast of East Falkland.

We made a surprisingly easy landing; the weather was still perfect and we walked to Sea Lion Lodge, which has several bedrooms with bathrooms and telephones, a dining-room, a bar and a small shop. Once again I detached myself from the group and set off for the north-west coast of the island where, having penetrated through the tussock, I found myself completely alone on a most beautiful white sandy beach where gentoo penguins were bathing and disporting themselves. I moved no further and lay down in a sheltered spot, sunbathing and drinking in the peace and the

451

tranquillity of this island paradise. Once again I found it difficult to detach myself but, after about two hours, time was running short and it was time to get back to the lodge and re-embark – this time en route for South Georgia. We weighed anchor and shortly afterwards sailed past Beauchene Island, home to 100,000 black-browed albatrosses and something like 70,000 rockhopper penguins. Beauchene had been home to many fur seals, but they were virtually wiped out by sealers during the nineteenth century and, indeed, you can see their names carved on the flat rocks at the old boat landing place on the east coast of this tussock-covered island.

So now we were en route to South Georgia, the weather good but the ship rolling as usual. Now you will know already a fair amount about South Georgia from the description of my first three visits there in 1953 and 1954, but this time there were several huge differences. In no particular order: the reduction in the snow cover and the retreat of the glaciers was very significant and noticeable; all the whaling stations had been closed down; the huge increase in the number of fur seals made it sometimes very difficult to land – we had particular difficulty at Elsehul; South Georgia is now on the tourist map with cruise ships visiting the island – in 2004 there were something like 4,000 cruise passengers who landed at Grytviken; the restoration of the Whalers' Church in which Sir Ernest Shackleton's funeral was held; the conversion of the manager's villa into a superb whaling museum – it was in this house that I had drinks with the Manager both in 1953 and 1954. Now there is a Commissioner responsible for South Georgia and the South Sandwich Islands who also doubles up as the Governor of the Falkland Islands. Finally, although this is not a difference, it was here at Leith on 23rd March 1982 that the Argentinian naval vessel the *Bahia Paradiso*, later to become infamous for spilling fuel oil off the Antarctic Peninsula, arrived. A few days later this ship and another, and their helicopters, landed 200 Argentine forces at King Edward Point at Grytviken and after a two-hour battle overpowered the 22 Royal Marines stationed there. However, mercifully Mrs Thatcher came to the rescue and later that same month British forces, in a side-play to the Falklands War, retook South Georgia, sank the Argentinian submarine *Santa Fe*, which was commanded by a real war criminal, Captain Astiz, and took 185 Argentinians prisoners.

We visited various bays and harbours, most of which I had

visited before, namely the Bay of Isles, Right Whale Bay, Possession Bay, St Andrew's Bay, Coopers Bay and so on; also Ocean Harbour, Cold Harbour, Moltke Harbour and the spectacular and magnificent Drygalski Fjord and Larsen Harbour. But it was not so much all these bays and harbours on the north-east coast which interested me, but the bays and glaciers on the south-west coast, particularly King Haakon Bay where Shackleton landed after his epic open boat voyage from Elephant Island in 1916.

I was on the bridge as we entered the Bay. There is a jagged reef in the middle of the entrance and many others in the approaches, so we came in very carefully and cautiously. There is a small cove close to the entrance of the bay on its south side, which has a boulder-strewn beach guarded by a reef and it was here that Shackleton landed and it was here we landed also – it is called Cape Cove. It was a beautiful place with magnificent views to the Range Mountains northwest of the bay and above the cove there was a mass of tussock grass with here and there tarns and ponds with albatrosses nesting all around. I climbed the nearest mountain on my own – it was not dangerous – and at the top looked over to Queen Maud Bay to the south and to the west to Cape Rosa. I returned surrounded by aggressive skuas, but I had an ice-axe with me so I was not unduly perturbed.

It is interesting that Shackleton counted 12 glaciers descending into the bay, and every few minutes heard the roar caused by masses of ice calving into the sea. But what about now, 80 years later? Now there were only two glaciers – ten had gone as a result of increasing temperatures, and all in such a short time. It was dispiriting. The next day we sailed up to a point about a mile and a half west of the north-east corner of the bay and it was here we landed as Shackleton had landed those 80 years before – it was called Peggoty Camp, after the Peggoty family in Charles Dickens's novel *David Copperfield*, who sheltered in a home fashioned out of an upturned boat on the beach.

Once again I set off on my own, cramponed up, and this time using my ice-axe up the glacier, which had greatly receded since Shackleton's time. There were only a few crevasses and these were not dangerous, but two things militated against my upward climb: the first was the cloud which started to come down, and the second was the ship's siren, which was summoning me back. The crew knew from the tag system that I was the only passenger still ashore and they did not want to leave me behind – nor for that matter did I want to be left behind – so sadly and with much regret I retraced my steps to the shore, where a boat came out from the ship to fetch me and the ship immediately weighed anchor and departed.

A few days later we left South Georgia, although not before carrying out a splendid walk in glorious sunshine – a calm, cloudless blue sky, so unlike South Georgia – between two whaling stations, namely Leith and Stromness. Of course, it was at Stromness where Shackleton eventually arrived after his epic crossing of the island from King Haaka Bay.

Stromness, like all the whaling stations, is now abandoned with most (although not all) of the buildings now in disrepair. But I paid my respects to the manager's villa where Shackleton arrived with his companions, all with long beards and matted hair, unwashed and in clothes that they had worn for a year without a change. They were unrecognisable, but when the manager, Mr Sorlle came to the door, Shackleton asked whether he knew him. Sorlle said no, but added that he knew his voice thinking he was the mate of the *Brig Daisy* on which Robert Cushman Murphy, the greatest Southern Ocean ornithologist, was working. Shackleton put out his hand and told him who he was, and the Norwegians' hospitality knew no bounds. Now there is a plaque marking this historic meeting, and I went round this villa, which is in a good state of preservation. It has recently come to light, 90 years later, that it was the adjacent villa and not the one where the plaque has been placed.

So now to all intents and purposes my return journey to South Georgia was over, and we set sail for Stanley in the teeth of a north-westerly gale and from there to Brize Norton via Ascension, and so home.

32

The Equitable Life Assurance Society: Litigation from 1999 to 2005 as Experienced by a Non-Executive Director

It was just before midnight on 14th December 2001 when I was woken up by footsteps on the gravel outside our house. I went downstairs to find a courier with a large bundle of papers addressed to me from the Equitable. I signed for them and the courier disappeared into the night on his motorcycle. His visit at such a time and just before Christmas smacked of the midnight visits and arrests of the Gestapo.

By the time I had read the contents it was nearly three o'clock in the morning and I went back to bed – not to sleep, but to lie awake with my mind in turmoil and anxiety, which was to persist for the next four years. The package contained a formal eight-page letter from the solicitors, Herbert Smith, who unknown to me were regarded in the legal profession as the Rottweilers of litigation. This letter said that they had been instructed by the Equitable Life Assurance Society to advise on such claims as it may have against its former Directors, advisors and Regulatory Authorities, arising out of the policy adopted by the Society in 1993 and in certain subsequent years to declare differential terminal bonuses, and so on.

They went on to state that the purpose of the letter and the accompanying particulars of claim against me were to set out the grounds on which the Society was considering bringing a claim against me as a former director of the Society, and all this was to comply with the Professional Negligence Pre-Action Protocol; something I had never heard of before, but I believe it was also described as a Letter before Action. I was given six weeks to reply to the 24 pages of claims.

These stated in outline that as a former director of the Society I owed it a number of duties: firstly, a duty to comply with the terms of the Society's Articles of Association – and, of course I had; secondly, a duty not to exercise the powers conferred on me as a director of the Society for purposes other than those for which they were conferred – of course I had not; thirdly, a duty not to distribute the Society's assets in a manner contrary to the Articles of Association – of course I had not; fourthly, a duty to exercise reasonable skill, care and diligence in my conduct of the Society's affairs – of course I had. So what was all this about?

Herbert Smith then went on to tell me that they considered I had breached each of those duties; that the Society had suffered loss and damage as a result; and that they therefore believed I was liable to repay to the Society such amounts which would not have been paid out but for my breaches of duty; and that I should pay damages and compensation in respect of the Society's losses which were estimated to be in the region of £1.5 billion, to which they had thoughtfully added interest.

And so began four years of unceasing nightmarish Kafkaesque litigation in which the only certainty was uncertainty. It was a litigation totally divorced from any sort of reality or truth, and because of this there was always a temptation to consider that all this must really be a joke – admittedly a joke in the worst possible taste, but nevertheless a joke. It sometimes took a major effort to remind oneself that it was all actually deadly serious and that the consequence of not winning was bankruptcy, with all that that entailed in human and family misery.

Indeed the new chairman of the Society, a certain Mr Vanni Treves, who was conducting the litigation against us, emphasized this in the press by stating that he was very unwillingly ruining our lives. Yet at the same time, he asked us to imagine what it would be like to spend Christmas with our families knowing that we risked losing every penny we had earned. Against what he was saying in the press, he was also saying in certain private conversations that there was no intention to bankrupt us; but after years of this and other similar utterances, we no longer believed a word he said.

The litigation thus took over my life and that of my wife and family to the exclusion of almost everything else. I had only recently recovered from a bout of depression and nervous anxiety caused in the main by my monumental effort in staging the exhibition of the restored paintings in Calcutta. Now I returned for three long years to the depths of depression. It was a horrible experience, made ever worse by the fact that the charges against me appeared to be trumped up, reminiscent of those trumped up against innocent men and women by the Nazi and Soviet regimes. Litigation is to my mind rather like the HIV virus: first of all it takes on a life of its own, and secondly it constantly mutates, like the HIV virus. Thus the claims against me were altered no less than five or six times and there were constant and numerous shifts in the Society's position as Herbert Smith cast around for some sort of credible basis on which to put forward claims against us – claims which were all based on hindsight, i.e. the House of Lords' totally unexpected and aberrational judgment and a series of hypothetical assumptions based on this assumed hindsight. It was indeed a trumped-up case, but it took four years to defeat it.

The Equitable Life Assurance Society was founded in 1762 and was therefore the world's oldest mutual life assuror until it was killed off by the House of Lords – that is to say, on the morning of their judgment it was a thriving Society with free assets of around £5 billion, but by the evening the House of Lords created a black hole in the balance sheet by implying a term into the Articles of Association which was not there, and by Lord Steyn contradicting his own judgment in the *Bratton Seymour* case of 1992 when he ruled that it was not possible in his judgment to imply a term into the Articles of Association (I will explain all this a little later). Nowadays, many life assurors are companies with shareholders and the return on the funds must be distributed between shareholders and policyholders. A mutual is owned by its policyholders. When a policyholder's pension matures, the basic idea is that he should receive his share of the mutual's assets, namely the with-profits fund.

Now in my book and also in all the dictionaries I have looked up, the word 'mutual' is stated as 'sharing in common', meaning in the world of life assurance, that the policyholders share in common the profits and expenses of the society. 'Equitable' means dealing fairly and equally with all concerned, and in this context the policyholders of the Society. Unfortunately, Lord Steyn in his

House of Lords judgment disregarded these fundamental aims and objectives of the Society.

Back in 1956 the introduction of a new statutory pension regime caused the Society to design a new form of with-profits pension contract for the self-employed. Although the specific details of each class of policy differed, they all provided policyholders with the right to take the benefits of the policy either in the guaranteed annuity rate (GAR) form or benefit written into the policy, or in 'fund' form to purchase an annuity at current market rates from either the Society or another provider. A GAR policy meant that when the pension matured, the owner of the pension would receive an annuity on the pension fund at a guaranteed percentage. The Society regarded its GAR provision as providing a 'floor' below which the pension provided by the policy could not fall. Now all this may sound arcane and boring, but a pension is of the utmost importance and concern to everybody, not only to the self-employed to whom these pension policies were sold. Most other offices provided GARs. However, as I eventually discovered, no extra premium was charged by the Society for this guarantee. Unfortunately, as it also became apparent, the interest rate underlying the guarantee started off at a sensible 2.5 per cent in 1957, but was then gradually raised to 7 per cent in 1975 which with the benefit of hindsight was too high. Nowadays, it is recognised that any financial guarantee gives rise to certain financial risks and should, as a matter of insurance, be hedged in the financial markets or the risk otherwise offloaded.

In any case, because the GAR premiums were both single and variable – after all anybody who is self-employed has variable earnings – the amount to be hedged against downward movements in interest rates was to all intents and purposes unknown. This was unlike other insurance houses whose GAR premiums were regular and fixed and who therefore had much greater control.

There was a further problem, which was that, although the Society ceased writing these GAR policies in 1988, nevertheless GAR policyholders were entitled to continue to pay recurrent and variable single premiums into these policies until their maturity and obtain the GAR thereon.

In the life assurance business there are two types of bonus: the first is the reversionary bonus which is now generally allocated every year and once allocated is guaranteed by the life assurance company until the policy matures; the second is a bonus allocated when the policy matures, which is neither guaranteed nor contractual until the maturity of the policy, when it is only allocated if there are sufficient free assets to support its payment. In general terms, as said above, the idea is that when a policyholder's pension matures, he receives his appropriate asset share of the Society's With-Profits Fund when the amount of the terminal bonus is adjusted to ensure that such occurs.

Up until 1993 the actual rate that one would get in the market, the current annuity rate (CAR), exceeded the guaranteed annuity rate (GAR), but in 1993 the GAR started to exceed the CAR. As a result of this the Society amended the terminal bonus arrangement so as to equalize (so far as was possible) the benefits taken by departing policyholders in GAR form with those benefits taken in fund form, all this in line with the principles of equity and mutuality for which the Society had been established. In short, the arrangement was that those departing GAR policyholders who sought to exercise their right to a guaranteed annuity, had the terminal bonus reduced by the cost of the purchase of the guaranteed annuity, so that in financial terms their asset share was the same as all other policyholders. Thus, the overriding principle was of fair and even distribution of assets of the with-profits fund. The introduction of this arrangement which was later to be described as the differential terminal bonus policy (DTBP) was included in a Bonus amendment paper to the Board but was not mentioned or highlighted as a policy. It was merely an amendment to the previous year's terminal bonus rates, a small thing which turned out to have a devastating effect, as we shall see.

It was in 1976 that I was invited to join the board of the Society. What happened here, is that the then President of the Society Robert Henderson, who was also chairman of Kleinwort Benson, went along to see Anthony Tuke who was the then Chairman of Barclays Bank and asked him if he could recommend a youngish Director of the Bank to be a non-executive director of the Society, who could make a contribution to the increasing commercial banking demands on the Society which was beginning to expand. The Chairman alighted on my name; I was then the youngest member of the group board of the Bank. So in due course I was elected to the board and stayed there until my retirement in 1999. By then I had been appointed the Senior Vice-President of the Society and was appointed to chair not only the subsidiary companies but also, very importantly, the Audit Committee. This had been established at the request of the non-executive directors and was to feature prominently in the litigation. My career with the Equitable was regarded as a success, and after I retired I was given a farewell dinner at Claridges.

In late 1998 shortly before my retirement and following complaints about the DTBP by a number of GAR policyholders, which was the first time the DTBP had been brought to the attention of the non-executive directors, the Society decided to seek guidance from the Courts as to whether this practice was in fact legitimate, although the Articles of Association were quite clear and stated that the directors of the Society had an absolute discretion with regard to the awarding of bonuses and that the directors' decision in this regard was final and conclusive, and that in any case a terminal bonus was non-contractual and non-guaranteed, as it had to be. To me all this was quite clear, and the meaning of the Articles was perfectly straightforward.

When I retired in early 1999, the Society seemed to me to be in good financial shape, although I have to say that the solvency margin (that is, the difference between the assets of the Society and the funds allocated and guaranteed to policyholders) was not as high as I would like it to have been, and indeed on several occasions I had written to the executive management expressing my concerns on this. Nevertheless at that time, admittedly on a rising stock market, the position had improved and the Fund for Future Appropriations (FFA) – that is to say the free unallocated assets of the Society – had risen to £3 billion and the following year to almost £5 billion. At the same time the key expense ratio had declined from 8.5 per cent in 1989 to 4 per cent in 1998, and this was the lowest in the business. Furthermore, guaranteed reversionary bonuses had been steadily reduced ahead of the pack since 1989 in line with declining gilt yields, and given that in most policies there was a GIR (guaranteed investment return) of 3.5 per cent, the guaranteed reversionary bonus for 1998, my last year, was only 1.5 per cent. This was a reduction of 50 per cent on the previous year's rate of 3 per cent. Going from there, looking at the period 1989 to 1999, which was the year I retired, the accumulated return on the With-Profits Fund was 146 per cent whilst the return allocated to policy holders was 132 per cent, a margin in favour of the FFA of 14 per cent. Perhaps it should have been higher, but it did mean to me as a non-executive director that there had been no over-bonusing – one of the main allegations levelled against me.

This was one of the first mysteries of the later litigation. I, and all the other directors, were accused of over-bonusing, and to the extent that we were deemed to have over-bonused – several hundreds of million pounds each year – we were told by Herbert Smith to repay these amounts to the Society, a tall order for a retired pensioner! But during the course of the litigation, in October 2004 to be exact, the Society under its new management together with its friendly solicitors, Herbert Smith, announced in a press release entitled 'Penrose Report: policy value reductions and alleged over-bonusing' that there had been no over-bonusing. Quite simply, Lord Penrose had got it wrong, and I will come back to this later.

Before we embarked on the original litigation to determine the validity of the differential terminal bonus policy within the GAR class of policyholders, we took advice from two eminent Queen's Counsels, namely Mr Grabiner, who was later ennobled, and Mr Green, who were both experts in this sort of thing, together with the Society's solicitors Denton Hall. They all advised us that the board did indeed have discretion to apply the DTBP; there was virtually no serious qualification, except that some of the documentation was not quite clear. However, they advised that our discretion was absolute. They went on to say that the board's decision to seek to achieve a result under which all persons holding similar policies got the same investment return irrespective of whether some had the benefit of guaranteed annuity rates was, and I quote, 'perfectly legitimate'. Furthermore they were of the opinion that the DTBP was and had always been wholly within the discretion of the directors, conferred on them by Article 65 of the Articles of Association, which I repeat also stated that the decision of the directors was both final and conclusive.

The purpose of the original lawsuit was to discover whether the Society was allowed to differentiate between GAR policyholders choosing to take a market annuity and those choosing the guaranteed annuity, which as it happens was an unattractive option as it was single-life only (that is, it did not provide for a widow or widower's pension), and very few people would take that route. In fact, despite all the furore in my last year at the Society only about ten or eleven policyholders elected to take a guaranteed annuity. It was

461

never intended to have anything to do with the policyholders who did not have guarantee options, now to be called the non-GARS, whose policies because they were a different contract class had necessarily to be segregated from the GAR contract class. In other words, as far as everyone was concerned, any extra liability caused by GAR policyholders exercising their right to a guaranteed annuity could be kept within the GAR policyholder class.

In the winter of 1998–99 before the first lawsuit was fully under way I, as chairman of the Audit Committee, together with the executive management, the accountants and the auditors, started working our way through the Report and Accounts for the year ending 31 December 1998 in order that we should get into a position to recommend them to the board and thus the policyholders.

Now, there were two main concerns about these guaranteed annuity options. The first was the extent to which we needed to provide for them; the second was whether a contingent liability arose in respect of the litigation relating to the GAR contract class – and here, just to make it quite clear again, this litigation had nothing whatsoever to do with the non-GAR policy classes and all this was reflected in the Originating Summons, as I understand it.

In the case of the former, to me as a non-executive director there seemed to be a bewildering number of choices and opinions. The view of the actuaries was that the commercial cost of these options to the whole Society would never exceed £50 million, and they never changed this figure. This figure became known as the 'Z factor', because in certain financial circumstances, it represented a leak out of the GAR class into the overall With-Profits Fund, after having taken into account the operation of the DTBP. The reason that it could leak out of the GAR class was because in certain circumstances the difference between the CAR and GAR might be so significant that it could not be satisfied by adjusting the terminal bonus to zero. It should be remembered that policyholders had guaranteed reversionary bonuses to which guaranteed annuity rates would be applied. As said above, the GAR option was very unattractive, being single-life only. Only a very few GAR policyholders had gone down this route, and the total 'cost' of this was just £240,000 for the year ending 31 December 1998. Nevertheless it seemed to us that what perhaps we needed was some sort of precautionary provision, so the actuaries delved into the Society's entrails and came up with a figure of £350 million, which to me seemed way over the top, bearing in mind that the total cost to date was only £240,000. This figure was later reduced to £200 million.

Now, at about this time, the Regulator awoke like Abou Ben Adem ('may his tribe increase'), from his 'deep dream of peace' to realise that they might have a problem with these GAR options and, in particular, as to how they should be reserved for. I recall that the main thrust of their thinking was that we should reserve at a take-up rate of something like 82.5 per cent when the actual take-up rate was 0.1 per cent. The 'actual' cost was, as I have mentioned earlier, about £240,000 for the 1998 year, but the regulator wanted us to reserve at this 82.5 per cent rate, which produced a figure of nearly £2 billion. Here I must make the assumption that this figure presupposed that all the GAR policyholders would flee at one and the same time and that interest rates would remain unchanged, an absurd scenario. So we entered a sort of regulator's *Alice in Wonderland* world where reality went out of the window. This imaginary take-up rate placed a great strain on our solvency position so the regulator, to get us off the hook, suggested we reinsure out half of what, to my mind, was a wholly mythical liability, and this is what we did.

Now my other main concern as chairman of the Audit Committee was this question of a contingent liability relating to the now ongoing litigation, and whether a Note to the Accounts was required to put the policyholders on notice. We discussed all this at great length and took into account the Financial Reporting Standard 12, which dealt with the necessity or otherwise of producing a Note relating to contingent liabilities. This Note defined a contingent liability as a possible obligation that arises from past events and whose existence will only be confirmed by the occurrence of one or more uncertain future events not wholly within the control of the entity – the entity being the society; or a present obligation that arises from past events but is not recognised because it is not probable that a transfer of economic benefits will result. Thus to my mind this FRS was attempting to deal with the circumstance where a company is undertaking legal action, but where there is uncertainty as to whether the entity has any liability at all. It went on to say that a company need not and should not disclose a contingent liability if the possibility of any transfer of economic benefit was remote.

It was the case that all our Queen's Counsels had opined that we had acted entirely correctly and properly and within the powers conferred on us in the articles of association, which just to remind you yet again, stated that the directors had an absolute discretion and that their decision was both final and conclusive. We, therefore, came to the conclusion that no Note was required and Ernst & Young, who had presumably seen Counsel's opinion, agreed with us on this. The chance of losing the litigation was remote.

Now, I mention all this because one of the main charges levelled against us by our friends Herbert Smith was that apparently we should have anticipated the eventual House of Lords adverse judgment and accordingly inserted a Note into the Accounts. But this was one of the charges they seemed to have dreamt up, because for some reason they construed the legal advice that we had received which stated, in effect, we had only a very remote chance of losing the Hyman litigation, if any, into one where we had a real risk of losing. I was surprised when I was in the box that Mr Milligan kept on about this, when he must have known that 'remote' does not mean a 20 per cent risk of losing. Or perhaps it does to a lawyer.

By now we were in the hands of the lawyers and a whole new world of litigation opened up for me. It was indeed legal *terra incognita*. The Queen's Counsel and solicitors opined on various esoterica and a wonderful cornucopic feast of fees opened up before them, culminating in a grand slam for them of something in the region of £100 million, all of course to be paid for by the policyholders. Expressions like 'Without Prejudice' and 'Privileged' and similar such minutiae deluged us in never-ending cascades. Endless conferences were held. The litigation took on a life of its own, apparently divorced from any sort of reality, and all this because we wanted to clarify our position on the DTBP – something which to me seemed eminently fair and sensible and for which, moreover, we had the necessary authority. The Articles of Association stated in perfect English that the directors had an absolute discretion and that our decision was both final and conclusive. Only a Law Lord could imply that this English did not mean what it said.

After I retired, the case went to the Vice-Chancellor of the Head of Chancery Division in the High Court of Justice. He confirmed that we had discretion 'well wide enough' to grant a final bonus of an amount dependent upon the form in which the benefits were taken. He also held that there was nothing contractually improper in the allotment of differential final bonuses and he confirmed that the Society's approach did not deprive policyholders of any part of their asset share. Hurray, hurray, at least he understood the originating summons. Unfortunately, he gave leave for the plaintiff, whose legal fees we were paying, to appeal to the Court of Appeal.

I am not sure whether the Court of Appeal judges, unlike the Vice-Chancellor, really understood the purpose of the Originating Summons. They ruled against the Society by a margin of two to one, but they got there in different ways, and rumour has it that one of them admitted that he did not really understand the case. Now, if the case had stopped there, the Society would have still been alive today, but the then board felt that the Appeal Court did not give it the certainty which the Society was seeking. In other words, did the directors have the discretion to effect the DTBP or not? Here, please, may I remind you again that the Originating Summons was solely to do with the GARS and nothing whatsoever to do with the non-GARS, who were not a party to the action. In short, no one had any dispute that any liability was 'ring-fenced' to the GAR class of policyholders. If they had been, the Society could still have been thriving today. People ask why they were not represented. The answer is the lawyers did not think it necessary as the action had nothing to do with them. With hindsight, this was a catastrophic error, but then how were the lawyers to know what aberration lay before them?

So the Society appealed to the House of Lords, which meant in effect to one of its ad hoc Appellate Committees. The leader of this committee was a certain Lord Steyn, who came from South Africa. He and the other four members of this committee decided that what we had done was wrong, that is to say illegal, but they got there in the most peculiar way, effectively by stating that the English of the Articles of Association did not mean what it said. The English was, of course, perfectly clear, but they stated that there was somehow an implication that it did not mean what it said. Because we had disregarded this implication, which nobody had heard about before, we had therefore committed an illegal act in approving the DTBP. Furthermore, they disregarded the Originating Summons by disallowing ring-fencing.

Now, as I have stated, the Originating Summons had nothing to do with the non-GARS, but by disallowing ring-fencing, they rode roughshod over the contracts of the non-GARS, in effect forcing them to subsidise the GAR contract classes. This was the torpedo that ultimately sunk the Society. In doing so they failed to take on board that the GAR policyholders under the terms of their contracts were allowed to pay recurrent and variable premiums into their policy pots, and continue to obtain the benefit of the GAR on those monies until the maturity of their policies, which could be anything up to 30 years in the future. The effect of the judgment was to create a colossal black hole of a billion pounds or so in the Society's books, because these amounts were unknown and, of course, unquantifiable. This unknown liability would rise as interest rates fell, and fall as interest rates rose. It might, of course, disappear altogether if the current annuity rates went above the guaranteed annuity rate. For me, the judgment was devastating, because they had judged that I had committed an illegal act, although the full import of this took a long time to percolate through and did not really come home to roost until the midnight knock on the door just before Christmas in 2001.

Now going back to this so-called implication in the language of the Articles of Association, here Lord Steyn contradicted himself on a previous judgment of his, which Peter Martin discovered during the course of the litigation. This case known as the *Bratton Seymour* case, which I believe took place in 1992, similarly concerned articles of association and here Lord Steyn ruled that it was simply not possible to imply a term into the articles, because if you did so, no company director would ever know where he stood again. I understand that Lord Steyn and other judges were not aware of the consequences that their decision would cause to the Society. Indeed, I understand that counsel for the Society did not spell that out. Thus, the House of Lords may have thought that this was a simple case of discrimination. This shows the dangers of legal intervention in complex financial matters. I understand that Jonathan Sumption QC who represented the GAR policyholder class was very surprised at the result.

The effect of this judgment was a catastrophe for the Society and for that matter most of the British life insurance industry, and it destroyed in one fell swoop the oldest and most successful mutual life assuror in the world. The only thing that can be said in defence of their Lordships is that they did not really understand what they were being asked to judge, because if they had, they could never have come to the conclusion they did, and perhaps the culpability associated with this decision should be shared by the Society's lawyers in not explaining to their Lordships that the case and its Originating Summons had nothing at all to do with the non-GARs.

Now let us take this a little further, because one of the most baleful effects of this judgment was that the government actuaries – who never in their wildest nightmares ever thought that the House of Lords would come up with such an aberrational judgment, as our later enemy Mr Treves, the man who became the chairman of the society, described it – panicked and started bringing in even more stringent solvency regulations. The result of these tighter regulations was that many of the life and pension funds, which for a long time had been investing their funds in a range of 60 to 65 per cent in equities and property, which is where you obtain the best long-term total returns, were in effect forced to divest themselves of say 30–35 per cent of these equity investments – as it happened more or less at the bottom of the then bear market – and invest the proceeds into fixed-interest securities. The effect of this reversal was the death or near death of many of these wonderful with-profits funds which had served so many policyholders so well over so many years.

Now in all this I feel I must mention our beloved Chancellor Gordon Brown's raid on the Equitable and other gross pension funds. This weakened the Society just as it weakened everybody else. What he did was to remove the long-standing dividend tax credit for these funds, thus netting for his Treasury something like £5 billion in the first year (1997) and subsequent years so that the total mount estimated to date is to the order of £100 billion, this figure being provided by Christopher Fildes in the *Spectator* magazine of February 2006. The withdrawal of this tax credit has been one of the main contributors to the pension crisis in this country along with, of course, increasing longevity. It also had the effect that instead of valuing the portfolio on a gross-of-tax basis, it had to be valued on a net-of-tax basis, which meant that in the case of the Equitable, the Chancellor removed the sum of £660 million from the free assets and therefore from the policyholders.

Another pertinent fact to my trial is this whole question of regulation which changed fundamentally while I was a non-executive director of the Society. What happened here, as far as I remember, was that before we got tangled up with our friends across the Channel, the regulatory system was both benign and flexible. For instance, when I joined the Society in 1976, the banking system was in chaos and a liquidity crisis was leading into a solvency crisis, which as the director of Barclays Bank in central London, I had to manage. At that time, interest rates were rapidly rising, the stock market was rapidly falling and property valuations were collapsing. As a result, all the life companies became more or less technically insolvent, including the Equitable. At that time, we were not constrained by the much tighter European regulations, mercifully and an important factor – very important to my mind – was that valuations were only carried out on a triennial basis. The Equitable was the last to join this annual rat-race and this brought a very unsatisfactory immediacy to a long-term fund, which everybody has had great difficulty in managing, because the swings can be so large. As a side comment here, these immediate snapshots had the effect of confusing income with capital, as the capital swings were taken through the income account. In the event, the Institutions led by the Prudential decided to buy the market. Asset values increased accordingly and this enabled the Funds to become solvent again.

Unfortunately our friends across the Channel were beginning to flex their harmonising muscles and the UK was whipped into line. The European funds were by and large almost entirely invested in fixed interest securities, whereas the UK was mainly invested in equities. Thus these new tighter regulations together with the fall in interest rates greatly reduced the flexibility of the UK actuaries in managing their books, and as it happens put greater pressure on their solvency margins. To be reluctantly fair to the Europeans, they did understand the UK position and, as what I would describe as an emollient, they 'allowed' us three escape valves. The first of these was the right, subject to the approval of the Regulator, to take in future profits to bolster the solvency margin, the reason behind this is that when you have a steady stream of premium income, which contains a profit element, you can bring this forward. The second of these escape valves, again subject to the prior approval of the Regulator, was the ability to issue subordinated loan stock, which again boosted the solvency margin. The third, I have already mentioned, which was to reinsure out some of the liabilities, and indeed in this case this was suggested to us by the Regulator.

Now the reason why I am mentioning all this is because all

three of these mechanisms, all of which had to be approved by the Regulator, were used as ammunition against us in the litigation by the Society under its new management and their acolytes Herbert Smith. They said that their use by us meant that we were mismanaging the business.

Now after this little European divertissement, we need to come back to Lord Steyn and his non-mutual and non-equitable misjudgment. Effectively, not only did he destroy confidence in a large pension Fund of around £30 billion, thus setting off a run on the Fund as everybody started looking for the exit, but his other great achievement was to set policyholder against policyholder, and this in a mutual Society. The non-GARS were outraged that Lord Steyn had forced them to subsidise the GARS to the tune of £1 billion or so, and the GARS were outraged that they had been denied by reason of the DTBP the GAR on their terminal bonuses, now guaranteed and contractual by order of Lord Steyn and his Appellate Committee.

If we look even more closely at Lord Steyn's judgment, we find the law of unintended consequences operating in no uncertain fashion. And here let me say that I adopt with both approval and respect the sentiments of Mr Justice Felix Frankfurter, who was one of the most famous Supreme Court justices, in the *Bridges* v. *California* case in, I believe 1941. He was the one who stated that:

Although it may be regarded as presumptuous to criticise our Court of Final Appeal, it is indeed wholly proper to do so. Judges as persons and Courts as institutions are entitled to no greater immunity from criticism than other persons or institutions. Judges must be mindful of their limitations and of their ultimate public responsibility by a rigorous stream of criticism expressed with candour however blunt.

And to that I say amen, amen.

I have already mentioned that the authorities were apparently completely taken aback by this totally unexpected judgment, and as a result brought in even more stringent solvency requirements. This in effect forced many of the life and pension funds to divest themselves of a goodly proportion of their equities in a falling market, and invest the proceeds into fixed-interest instruments, mainly gilt-edged. This, of course, forced down equity values even more and at the same time forced down gilt yields, almost to the floor; but because gilt yields are used to discount future liabilities, the lower the interest rate, the higher the liabilities. The gilt bubble arising from this totally unnecessary misallocation of capital not only reduced economic growth but also led to a severe undervaluation of equities, which left many companies vulnerable to foreign predators. I believe that it was also the case that these very low interest rates, to which mortgage rates were aligned, were to some extent responsible for the huge inflation in house values. So, whichever way you look at it, Lord Steyn's judgment, engineered on the basis of an implication in our articles of association, created a gross distortion in the economic life of this country. Of course it must be the case that Lord Steyn did not intend for all this to happen, but it did happen and it occurs to me that as a lawyer, he should have been aware of the law of unintended consequences when he was applying his mind to implications.

So now I think we will have to leave Lord Steyn and his Appellate Committee for the time being and start dwelling on the furore which followed his judgment. The government naturally launched an inquiry into the reasons for the near collapse of the Society, although of course the answer was staring everyone in the face. The main inquiry was launched in August 2001, more than two years after I retired, and was undertaken by a Scottish Law Lord, Lord Penrose, who produced a report of great thoroughness and meticulous attention to detail as to what he thought had gone wrong. It is sometimes the case that a report of such length – something like 800 pages – and detail misses the main point, encapsulated in the expression of 'not being able to see the wood for the trees'. I personally believe that he got his main conclusion wrong. It is perhaps also the case that as a Law Lord himself, he felt unable to criticise his fellow Law Lord. Be that as it may, his main conclusions, eventually refuted by the Society itself under its new management, were that by disregarding 'accrued' terminal bonuses, we had over-allocated bonuses beyond our available assets at market value, and that we had also made payments on claims that exceeded the relative available assets at the time.

Now this notion of 'accrued' terminal bonus – and I emphasise the word 'accrued' – was a complete misunderstanding of the nature of terminal bonus. If you look at the dictionary, you will see that 'accrued' means the coming into existence of a legally enforceable claim. There never was such a legal claim and, of course, there could not be, because if there were, there would be no free estate – in our case called the Fund for Future Appropriations. By contending that there were 'accrued' legal claims on this fund, when there were not and could not be, I think got Penrose off to a false start. However, he did state on page 355 of his report on terminal bonus that: 'in my view, the Society was not required by Statute, nor by any recognised accounting or actuarial principle or practice to value or set up reserves for accrued terminal bonus payments that are likely to be made in the future, notwithstanding the "accrual" of those future benefits in its Office Valuation.' He then went on to say quite incorrectly that the Society exploited the freedom from disclosure that this afforded, not only by withholding publication of the accrued value or rolled-up future terminal bonus to policyholders, but also by progressively reducing guaranteed benefits.

You will, I am sure, notice the continual use of the word 'accrued', which is entirely incorrect both legally and practically. A much better adjective to me would have been 'notional' or 'indicative' as it was indeed notional until paid, or for that matter not paid, on maturity. It had to be thus, because it could alter at any time depending on stock market values, and it had to be at the directors' absolute discretion, because otherwise they could not manage the business.

Now indeed in all this the executive management did have an office valuation, which was not disclosed to the non-executive directors, and this office valuation did include notional or rather indicative terminal bonus, but in no sense was it 'accrued' and therefore because it was not accrued, it was not reserved for. If it had been reserved for, the Fund for Future Appropriations would have disappeared. But it was this office valuation that Penrose seized on, and it was this valuation which sometimes did show indicative values in excess of asset values, but all this would come out in the smoothing process. As for his assertion that this enabled the Society progressively to reduce guaranteed benefits, this was altogether in a different world. Surely he must have known that the fewer guarantees you provide the better, and as interest rates fell this was precisely what we did. The fewer guarantees you provide, the more flexibly can the business be managed.

The litigation against us had already started when Lord Penrose was gathering together his papers. I was asked to give evidence to the Inquiry sort of voluntarily, so to speak. I was very much in two minds whether to go along or not, and the reason for this was, of course, my desire not to provide ammunition to our dear friends Herbert Smith, and for this reason many of us did not. But my elder son, Guy, who is a barrister, suggested to me that it could be sensible and so I agreed, provided he came along to hold my hand.

So one day I went along to his chambers and we set off for the long, hot walk to the Inquiry's office in a dingy, dirty building south of the river. In the event, we were greeted most courteously and pleasantly by a charming lady by the name of Gillian Glass, late of the Serious Fraud Office (which was disconcerting) and also by a South African accountant. I was questioned without any froideur for the best part of three hours, by which time I was beginning to wilt, partly from the heat and partly because an interrogation is an unpleasant experience and I was not at all sure where all this was going to lead.

Their most unsettling questions were those to do with policy and asset values, and in particular the office valuation, which I had never seen. The import of what they were saying was that with aggregate policy values including 'accrued' terminal bonus exceeding asset values, the Society was continuing to trade while it was technically insolvent. In other words its liabilities exceeded its assets. Clearly they also were confused by the nature of terminal bonus, so I had, as a non-executive director, to try and put them right on this. However, I did tell them that in 1994, one of those harmonising European Life Directives stated quite clearly that their regulations did not require recognition of liabilities based on the quantification of 'accrued' terminal bonus either absolutely or as a reflection of the management of a life assurance company or as a reflection of policyholders' 'reasonable expectations', an expression which everybody seemed to get very excited about, particularly the lawyers. So we were back to this question of whether terminal bonus was a liability or not, and the answer is that it is not and cannot be. Overall, Guy and I judged that the interrogation had gone well and afterwards we repaired to El Vinos for a bottle of champagne.

In March 2004 when the litigation was in full swing – it had started in December 2001 and seemed, like *Jarndyce* v. *Jarndyce*, to go on interminably – the great Penrose report came out and was delivered to the House of Commons, where Ruth Kelly, who was then the Financial Secretary to the Treasury, issued a Statement to the House accusing us of concealment and manipulation. She ended up by saying that it was now up to the Serious Fraud Office and the DTI to decide whether we should be prosecuted. Mercifully this never happened. In any case, who was supposed to be defrauding whom? The only people who could say they had been defrauded were the non-GARs, and they had been defrauded (perhaps dispossessed is a better word) by the House of Lords!

Now just before we leave Lord Penrose and his accusations that we had over-bonused, I would like to refer you to the Society's own press release in October 2004, entitled 'The Penrose Report: policy value reduction and alleged over-bonusing'. In this press release the Society stated that the Penrose Report gave rise to highly complex, factual, legal and actuarial issues, but went on to say that Lord Penrose freely admitted that some of his calculations were 'necessarily crude' and that he had considered matters with the benefit of hindsight. Furthermore, his Report stated that the Financial Services Authority in its representations to the inquiry had maintained that there had been no over-allocation or over-bonusing. Later on in Paragraph 3.7 of the press release, it stated that the entire adjustments in July 2001 could be explained by market events after 1999, and that as a result there was no case for claiming that any material component of the bonus cuts could be attributable to any alleged over-payments in the 1990s.

Despite the Society and the FSA stating that there had been no over-bonusing, nevertheless this was still one of the central planks in their claims against us in the High Court. Lord Penrose maintained that we had over-bonused, but he only got there by interpreting indicative terminal bonus as accrued terminal bonus, which we all know by now was not and could not be. The Society continued to press its claims against us for over-bonusing, but gradually they began to reduce them steadily and ended up by dropping them altogether and abandoning the case. But it took four years of virulent litigation and an eight-month trial to force them to back down.

We need now to go back to the night of 14th December 2001, midnight to be exact, when I had read briefly the Pre-Action protocol – an expression which to me resembled the 'standing to' in the trenches in the First World War before the whistle blew and you scrambled up the ladders and into action. I also read the particulars of claim, which made no sense to me; in any case, I had no knowledge of the intricacies and minutiae of the litigation process. This litigation process was truly unnerving because one felt that at the age of 70 one was entering a Kafkaesque nightmare, full of half-truths, subtleties, niceties even downright lies, twisted evidence and, yes, what seemed to me an extraordinary naiveté on the part of the claimant's solicitors and barristers. How on earth could they have cooked all this up? Had they been instructed to do so? Did they really actually believe there was a case against us? Did they really get legal advice that there was such a case? After the trial was over, we were told and, of course, one does not know this for sure, that both Herbert Smith and Ian Milligan QC had told the Society that there was no case against us. Yet the Society's board were saying that they were obliged to bring this action again the ex-directors because of legal advice. All I know for sure was that when we continually asked for this legal advice to be shown to us, the Society always pleaded privilege. Therefore the suspicion must remain that the legal advice might well have not been in favour of proceeding – it remains a mystery only known to the Society.

Now the reason why I have highlighted this mystery of the legal advice is that when the then directors lost the original litigation case in the House of Lords, much to everybody's amazement including that of Jonathan Sumption QC who was leading for Mr Hyman, the policyholder who wanted his GAR rights extended to his non-guaranteed terminal bonus, the directors took advice from a certain Mr Terence Mowschenson QC as to whether he believed that the Society could and should bring proceedings against any current or former director in relation to the GAR dispute.

He advised more or less as follows: that having considered the circumstances applicable, he believed that as we had acted entirely honestly and reasonably throughout, it was absolutely inconceivable that we would not be relieved under Section 727 of the Companies Act; he regarded it as clear that the court would not make a finding of breach of duty on our part in failing to take legal advice in 1993 and that there had been no breach of duty; and that any attempt to sue the Society's former directors would be seen by the Court as naked opportunism. Expressions like 'absolutely inconceivable' and 'naked opportunism' presumably do not come lightly from an eminent Queen's Counsel, so given that advice, what was the advice, if any, being given by Herbert Smith and Mr Milligan to the Society? Both advices were at the opposite end of the legal spectrum, so something was very odd, unless the case was trumped up against us regardless of legal advice.

Now what do you do when you receive a Pre-Action Protocol letter like that to which you are told to reply within six weeks? And told that to avoid any argument as to time-bar (what was time-bar? I wondered) it may well be that the Society would have to issue claim forms in February 2002, in order to preserve the possibility of pursuing legal proceedings against other defendants. In other words, it seemed to me that regardless of what I was going to say in response to the Pre-Action Protocol letter, they were going to sue me anyway. That hardly seemed fair and, of course, was not.

In the event Peter Martin,who like me had been on the Transglobe Expedition committee and was also a non-executive director of the Society, came to my rescue along with my eldest son, Guy. Peter Martin had been a senior litigation partner with the solicitors Frere Cholmeley, so he knew all about Pre-Action Protocols. He it was who began to seize the reins and started to put everything into some form of understandable legal context, as it was, of course, all *terra incognita* to me.

Of course the first thing was to engage the best lawyers but again, of course, I was a retired pensioner and my cash resources were very limited. However, I summoned up courage to engage the law firm Allen & Overy, and I have to say here right at the outset that they steered me successfully over the next four years to what the lawyers call 'finality', and finality in this case was when we won, the Society having abandoned its case against us. I owe our team of litigation solicitors a debt of great gratitude not only for their litigation skills but also for their human navigation skills; not only were they dealing with us as defendants, but they were also dealing with our wives and families, who had decided views of their own. I also owe my son Guy a debt of great gratitude, who, full of filial piety like Aeneas, supported me, encouraged me, comforted me and indeed acted as my McKenzie friend when I was no longer able to pay Allen & Overy's costs. For the record, the names of the Allen & Overy team were: Tim House, a senior partner in charge of the case: Andrew Denny, a New Zealander:

475

Matt Bower, at age 28 one of the best brains in the business and a junior, Joanna Powell. And here I think it would be appropriate to introduce you to the Allen & Overy Six because all six of us – all non-executive directors – went through the ordeal together and just as importantly stuck together throughout.

I think I need now no introduction so I will start off with John Sclater, who became President of the Society while I was there and to whom I became senior vice-President. When he was young John had been torn between the Church and finance, but Mammon won, and having joined Glyn Mills as a cadet in 1964 he worked his way up to become a director in 1970. I had never heard of the expression 'cadet' in banking circles. I knew there were army and naval cadets, I had been one myself, but banking cadets – no. He had been on the boards of various enterprises and for seven years had been chairman of the Foreign & Colonial Investment Trust as well as Guinness Mahon and Hill Samuel, so he had plenty of experience. He was also a trustee of the Grosvenor Estate and had been a Church Commissioner. He had also been in line to be appointed High Sheriff of Sussex, but from this he had to withdraw when the litigation came along. The collapse of the Equitable and the subsequent litigation unnerved him, not surprisingly, and he was always tending to look on the gloomy side of affairs. However he was very fortunate in having a strong wife behind (or perhaps nearly in front of) him, and she helped him through. John is a very kind, thoughtful and conscientious man, highly intelligent, but not perhaps cut out for leading a company through such a bruising experience; but then not many people are.

Next, and these are in no particular order, was Peter Sedgwick, who like me was appointed a vice-president of the society and succeeded me as chairman of the Audit Committee. He joined a commercial bank as a clerk but in 1970 he moved to Schroders where he ended up as Chairman – a huge success story. Peter was an outstanding non-executive director, very capable, sensible and practical and unlike some of us he kept his feet firmly on the ground throughout the litigation and trial. In all this he was once again supported very firmly by his wife, and my goodness, we all needed strong wives when we were facing bankruptcy throughout those four long years of uncertainty.

The third, again in no particular order, was Peter Davis, whom we all regarded as our anchorman – a job he took on voluntarily.

He it was who undertook the huge burden of our administration: that is to say, he negotiated with our solicitors and barristers; he prepared all the agendas for our endless meetings and conferences calls, prepared all the papers for these meetings and wrote the minutes; he carried out all our budgeting exercises and cash reconciliation, and remember he was dealing with millions of pounds; and so on. In all this he was brilliant and he kept his nerve throughout, and once again he was ably supported by his wife. Peter had been a senior partner of PricewaterhouseCooper, a deputy chairman of Sturge Holdings, an insurance company, a deputy chairman of Abbey National and the first Director General of the National Lottery. Again he had served on the Council of the Institute of Chartered Accountants. I sincerely believe that without him we may well have floundered, at least administratively. In many ways he was the unsung hero of the Allen & Overy Six, and I salute him.

The fourth was David Price, who was an investment man. He had been deputy chairman of Warburg Investment Management which became Mercury Asset Management, where he was responsible for the group's financial, personnel, compliance and administrative functions as well as the company's global custody arrangements and services. David was and is a Catholic and was extremely able and shrewd, particularly on investment matters, such that he became chairman of the Society's Investment Committee. He stood up well to the pressure but by the time the trial came along, he started to go downhill and eventually had to be hospitalised and was therefore unable to be cross-examined in the box. But once again he had a wonderful wife, Shervie, who took the greatest care of him and in a sense us as well, because she made cushions for us all to sit on in the courtroom. I believe she made one for the Judge, but whether he accepted it, I do not know.

And finally, there was Jonathan Taylor, who had been chief executive of Booker and then non-executive chairman of that company, but besides this he had been on the boards of various large companies like MEPC. He had another side to him, and that was literary and academic: he had been chairman of the Booker Prize Foundation, chairman of the governing body of the School of Oriental and African Studies at the University of London and Chairman of the Bodleian Library Development Board at Oxford. Jonathan Taylor had the great misfortune to know Mr Treves, and he used to have this disconcerting habit of supping, so to speak, with the devil, who used, I believe, to murmur comforting but cynical words to him about the litigation.

So these including myself were the Allen & Overy Six. Of the other three non-executive directors, one was David Wilson, chairman of the family building company Wilson Bowden, who was separately represented by his Barrister Jules Sher QC, who presumably retired on his fees from the case. It was rumoured that the legal costs of David Wilson who settled, unlike us, on a 'drop hands' basis amounted to something in the region of £6 million. Then there was my friend Peter Martin, a lawyer and former senior partner of Frere Cholmeley and an ace litigator himself and a litigant in person. And finally there was Jennie Page, also a litigant in person who had moved from the Civil Service to manage the Greenwich Dome and who had been driven mad by the meddling interference by government ministers in establishing it. Jennie also had the bad luck of having been a non-executive drector of Network Rail, and she experienced therefore the woes of not only the Dome and Network Rail but also now the Equitable – three poisoned chalices. Jennie was immensely intelligent, extremely hardworking and conscientious, and also had a very attractive verve about her. She was the last to settle – she stood out to the end for her very considerable costs and in the end she got them. Well done her.

The cost of defending oneself was, of course, the greatest worry and the first thing we did was to contact a solicitor by the name of Nick Rochez, a partner with the firm of Leboeuf, Lamb, Greene & MacRae who represented the Royal Sun Alliance with whom the directors had taken out a Directors and Officers Insurance for what turned out to be the very meagre sum of £5 million. Spread around the defendants, this only amounted to about £330,000 per person. Peter Martin advised him that we would be claiming under this policy.

Now the Royal Sun Alliance (RSA) like most insurance companies initially turned us down, having had, as they stated, written advice from a leading counsel who opined that there was a clause in the policy – always be careful of the fine print – excluding any claims arising out of or under insurance contracts. As the whole of the Society's business was related to insurance contracts, it seemed to me that there had been absolutely no point in paying premiums into a policy which excluded everything to do with the Society's business – in other words the policy was a commercial absurdity and therefore a sham. However, the RSA did agree that the claim could go to arbitration, and although I had no particularly high hopes of being successful in the arbitration (although my son was confident) nevertheless we instructed Allen & Overy to act on our behalf.

The stakes were, of course, exceptionally high. If we lost the arbitration, we would lose not only our individual £330,000-worth of cover, but also we would have to pay both their costs and ours, and bankruptcy loomed before the main case was a few months old. So I signed the first of many of Allen & Overy's terrifying engagement letters. I signed it with extreme reluctance and not only with this, but in fear and trembling, although I knew I had no alternative. It was, of course, a complete gamble and the odds seem stacked against us, but we were desperate and sometimes desperate men do desperate things.

Now somewhere along the line, I think it was in May 2002, Allen & Overy withdrew on the basis of a conflict of interest. Why had this not been raised at the beginning? I believe the reason for this was because RSA were their clients and so we had to cast about for another firm of solicitors to represent us. In the end we alighted on a firm called Cameron McKenna, who were, we were told, one of the best specialist insurance lawyers. We signed up with them and their advice was to take the RSA up to the wire if necessary – another curious military legal expression. We were also told that our costs on a paper arbitration would be in the region of £30,000–£50,000, but if it went to a full hearing costs would be to the order of £75,000–£100,000. I decided to cap my share of the costs at £10,000 which allowed me to sleep slightly better at night. In fact I was told that the costs for the whole arbitration worked out at around a £250,000.

In due course our arbitrator was eventually agreed and appointed – his name was Adrian Hamilton QC,and in December 2002, nearly a year after the litigation had commenced and we had approached Royal Sun Alliance to honour its obligation to us, he the arbitrator concluded that we the claimants had proved our case, and that what we had done was not excluded by the policy's exclusion clause and that therefore we had won. Mercifully the RSA decided not to appeal (although I am told that it is very difficult to appeal against the decision of an arbitrator). The gamble had paid off and we now had, so to speak, the sum of £330,000 to each defend ourselves. Not much, but better than nothing.

Of course, while all this legal shuffling was going on with RSA, the main case was wending along its wearisome way. Discovery of documents came early on in the agenda in February 2002, as I recollect, and a disclosure questionnaire was issued to all of us. We had to disclose all emails. I have never had an email-machine or CD Rom and I remember thinking at the time, what are they? Electronic diaries, floppy discs, documents on servers, microfiche, tapes, back-up audio tapes and so on – I was told to search my desk area, my filing cabinets, my drawers, my bookshelves, even my attic. I was asked if I owned a Palm Pilot – what is that? I did this and it was all quite simple, as I had retained relatively few papers. I gave all my papers to Guy, who had the laborious job of copying and cataloguing everything. In the end the total number of documents disclosed must have amounted to something like a million, enough to fill a warehouse. One had to ask oneself whether all this was necessary – after all, it was not a Nuremberg trial. Or perhaps it was.

I remember in January 2004 that our co-defendant Jennifer Page, who had had a distinguished Civil Service career and who was a litigant in person – that is to say she was representing herself – was repeatedly rebuffed by Herbert Smith when she repeatedly requested documentation concerning Denton Hall, the Society's previous lawyers. Herbert Smith stated that this documentation was not in the Society's control, without revealing that Denton Hall had in fact extended a standing offer to provide any documents that anybody involved in the litigation required. This was the bad boy being found out, and it also transpired during the course of the trial that some further important documentation had also been withheld by Herbert Smith and not disclosed. But it should not be up to the defendants to try and guess what important documentation was being suppressed and not disclosed, so there must be a question mark on the efficacy of disclosure, if documents can be suppressed.

In April 2002 the Society informed us that they wished for an early resolution of the dispute on a mutually cost-effective basis as they recognised that, firstly, costs were running out of control, and secondly, too much time and energy was being spent on the case. They went on to say that they had no wish for a trial. This resulted in some fairly desultory discussions about a settlement with Sir Philip Otton, a retired Court of Appeal judge and a director of the Society, telling us that the board was in the hands of Herbert Smith who were emphasising the risks to the present board of directors if they did not pursue us. The board, of course, was not in the hands of Herbert Smith because it was the board who were instructing Herbert Smith. In the event these discussions came to nothing. Moreover, this is strange if Herbert Smith had advised them that they had no prospects of success against us. An example of the tail wagging the dog.

Sometime in May 2002 there was a meeting between Herbert Smith and Allen & Overy. The former wanted to assess the state of our confidence in our legal case. They wanted to know the likelihood of a settlement offer from us and, in particular, they wanted to assess the extent to which we would support their case against Ernst & Young, the Society's auditors with whom we were now joined together in the case. Ernst & Young were regarded as a deep pocket, and, astonishingly, we were supposed to be the conduit to this deep pocket. And finally, they wanted to know if there were going to be any more litigants in person, which they said they would find a major irritant. Apparently they were already exasperated by having to deal individually with a number of law firms and Queen's Counsel and, of course, the litigants in person. Their belief at the outset had been that we should all be represented by one law firm. This was a naive belief; after all we all had different positions and they should have realised that from the start. As it was, they were now being daily and even hourly bombarded with letters, emails, telephone calls and faxes from every director and every defendant, including Ernst & Young. It was indeed a war of attrition, and we all made it a deliberate policy to carry out this guerrilla war. Marshall Kutuzov would have been proud of us – and of course both he and we won, and I suppose the costs the Society had to pay in the end were their Beresina.

The Society's requests set out earlier were treated with the contempt they deserved, but even during the course of the trial they were assuming we would support their case against Ernst & Young – an astonishing assumption when they were suing us at the same time. Indeed when their case against Ernst & Young was abandoned, the Society actually had the temerity to blame us, even though they must have known all along what our reactions would be.

In July 2002 (and you will know that it was not until December 2002 that we knew we were going to get our D&O Insurance monies), Herbert Smith decided they would need a full-scale case management conference in front of Mr Justice Langley, a judge for whom I developed a very high regard. So in October 2002 Diana and I went along to the High Court, which was packed full of lawyers busying themselves like bees in a nest with what I could only describe as periphera.

We were sitting at the back of the court but I was unable to hear anything – there were no microphones. Nothing very much seemed to happen. There was something about disclosure of documents, but we had been through that exercise already; there was something about the defendants trying to agree amongst themselves what questions we should ask the plaintiffs, but, of course, this was pie in the sky as everybody was in a different position and had different questions. It all seemed to be a complete waste of time and money. There were more case management conferences to come, which irritated the Judge so much that he asked the parties to liaise with one another to avoid them, but in this I do not think he was successful.

So we all went home, none the wiser – in any case I had not heard anything. Afterwards Ian Milligan QC for the Society opined to Peter Martin that the case would never go to trial. In this he was wrong as he was overridden, as I suspected would be the case. In any case it appeared to us that the law was being used to blackmail us into a settlement, but as I had no money to provide towards a settlement the whole thing was not only hopeless but also pointless. We were also beginning to feel that as this was really turning out to be some sort of blackmail case, then we had to stand up to it, defeat it, and also at the same time clear our names and reputations. But, of course, the costs of this were beginning to scare us rigid.

Throughout the litigation, there was a steady stream of witness statements, position statements, defences, amended defences, re-amended defences, we even got up to re-re-re-re-amended defences and claims. There was an equal stream of case memoranda, summaries, responses to questions, case documents, further information on case documents, skeleton arguments, submissions – a flow of never-ending paper going backwards and forwards with intermittent case management conferences and, finally, a pre-trial review. One has to ask oneself whether all this was in any sense a sensible and cost-efficient way of settling a dispute, and of course, the answer is no.

At the same time there were all sorts of inquiries going on: the Lord Penrose inquiry, the Treasury Committee inquiry, the Parliamentary Ombudsman inquiry, the Institute of Actuaries inquiry; there was a Baird inquiry, and several more whose titles I cannot now remember. All these inquiries were the result of the wholly manifest error of judgment made by Lord Steyn. What did intrigue me and at times amuse me was that none of these intelligent and erudite professionals were able to bring themselves to admit openly that Lord Steyn was wrong, and that the answer, despite all their contortions, was staring them in the face. Surely they must have known that Lord Steyn's judgment was not only fatally flawed, but also was a contradiction of his own previous judgment in a similar case.

Meanwhile another case management conference was looming in February 2003 – the trial, in the event, was to be over two years later. As I could not hear I did not attend; in any case I was now myself a litigant in person. In the event we asked for more information, Herbert Smith amended their particulars of claim for the third time, we had to file a third defence and I think a third witness statement by a certain date; we requested disclosure of the legal advice afforded the Society in their action against us, but this was once again declined with the Society claiming lawyer–client privilege. Although I understand the need to encourage clients to be able to speak to their lawyers without fear of their discussions being used against them, in this case I and others had a real suspicion that we were being pursued contrary to the advice of their lawyers.

During the summer nothing very much was happening but in the hope of putting an end to all this legal travail and anxiety it was decided we should go for a strike-out of the claims against us. Ernst & Young were doing the same but they were slightly ahead of us, which turned out to be somewhat unfortunate. Their strike-out application was heard by the same judge, Mr Justice Langley, and seemed to go well – that is to say, in favour of Ernst & Young. However, the Society appealed and Ernst & Young lost their appeal – although one Appeal Court judge apparently admitted that he was basically lost in the case. Herbert Smith and the society went into triumphant mode.

To my mind, of course, Mr Justice Langley was right and the Appeal Court was wrong. I suppose I would say that, but no judge presumably likes to have his judgment overturned. Thus there was increasing apprehension in our camp that our strike-out application would also be turned aside. However we had gone too far to turn back and if we retreated, so to speak, we would be liable for the Society's costs as well as our own.

For this strike-out application I had given up temporarily being a litigant in person but represented by Guy, and rejoined the Allen & Overy fold and was now liable for their costs. *Ab initio*, the estimate for the fees seemed reasonable, but in the event they doubled to something like £90,000 just for me alone. Despite this, having been as prudent as I could and with Guy as my McKenzie friend, I still had a good sum in my D&O pot as a reserve for a trial if it took place, or for a settlement.

In the event we did lose, but Mr Justice Langley had mercy on us and deferred any recovery of the Society's costs from us until the end of the trial. Of course these costs did hang up there in the sky over our heads, so to speak, but at least bankruptcy was deferred. I cannot remember now the reasons for our losing, but by this time Judge Langley may have felt it was too complex a case to resolve there and then by a summary judgment, and I personally believe that he was right in this, although I was bitterly disappointed. In court, Ian Milligan QC said that it was a case which cried out for cross-examination at trial. In the end, and ironically, it was his cross-examination of the defendants which defeated him.

We therefore began to resign ourselves to a trial, and not a short trial either – in the event it lasted eight months and achieved nothing. Now an eight-month trial does cost defendants a lot of money, and estimates started to emerge which were truly terrifying. But we decided it was now a fight to the finish and we had to fight down these trumped-up charges.

After the strike-out application was turned down, there was a lull during which the two opposing factions regrouped and brought up reinforcements. It was indeed a long war of attrition, with the campaign being conducted on both a strategic and a tactical basis by both sides. The military analogy was apt throughout this war of litigation, which lasted as long as the First World War.

Nearly all of us became litigants in person – we had to, in order to preserve our D&O pots. But this meant that Herbert Smith had now to deal separately with no less than 15 defendants while of course conducting their own litigation war against Ernst & Young – the main charge against them being that they had missed a liability of £1.5 billion while auditing the books of the Society. The case against Ernst & Young was, of course, a nonsense, like that against us, because it was Lord Steyn and his Appellate Committee in the House of Lords who created this liability which was not there before they came to their judgment decision. I repeat that on the morning of the judgment the Society was, although wounded by the media, financially in no difficulty, but by the afternoon it had been torpedoed below the waterline and began to sink. Quite an achievement by the House of Lords, if one can put it that way, but a disaster of Titanic proportions for the policy-holders.

A temporary truce was now called, and during this truce the possibility of a mediation of the dispute began to be seriously considered, although it had been on the cards for some time. Most of us were in favour of such a course. Having decided on this, negotiations began to get under way against the backdrop of the usual bellicose statements from the Society and Herbert Smith. For instance, Charles Plant, a litigation partner of Herbert Smith, said he had been heartened by the findings of the Penrose inquiry, although we all knew and he knew that the Society had admitted that Penrose had got it wrong. He went on to say that he was determined to press on with the litigation, which he said had now every chance of success, and that he had so advised the Society. Of course Herbert Smith were on the biggest gravy train of all time and every month the fees came rolling in. Mr Treves stated that he believed the Society's 'targets' (so we were back in the front line) would be forced to settle out of court by as early as the end of 2004, three years after the litigation started, and that he was in absolutely no doubt that we would settle. But what with? It was about this time that the Society hinted that they might settle for a minimum of £30 million from the defendant directors. By saying this we assumed that their 'target' was David Wilson, who was admittedly a wealthy man, but had only served a short time on the board as a non-executive director. We were also told that the Society might settle with Ernst & Young for a figure of £100 million. Here Charles Plant of Herbert Smith opined that their expert witnesses would demonstrate that there had been a massive audit failure on the part of Ernst & Young, and so on.

I think it took the lawyers nearly a year to limber up to the mediation front line; why it took so long I do not now recall. There seemed to be endless legal minutiae, position statements, indemnity negotiations – what would happen if the mediation was successful – unlikely but one had one's hopes. There were equally endless discussions as to who should be the mediators, one or two? Various names were proposed and discarded, but eventually after months and months the name of Lord Alexander of Weedon emerged, a former chairman of the National Westminster Bank. In the event he suffered a stroke from which some time later he died, so it was back to the drawing board. Eventually the names of Presiley Baxendale QC and Sir Anthony Evans QC emerged, and two days at the end of July were agreed. The mediation would be at the offices of the solicitors Baker MacKenzie in New Bridge Street. It had taken a year to set up.

Thus it was that on the morning of 29th July all participants gathered together. There were a lot of sideways glances – this was the first time we had seen the enemy – and an atmosphere of total unreality surrounded the proceedings. After all here were the director defendants, each being sued for billions of pounds, and each of them except perhaps for one or two living on their retirement pensions.

It was the first time that one or two directors of the Society and also Charles Plant and his support staff had emerged out of their trenches and had become visible. I did not particularly like what I saw. There was a Mr Shedden who combed his hair forward – always a bad sign – whilst Mr Plant arrived in one of those dreadful black trench coats with buttons and overlaps everywhere. They looked like KGB apparatchiks. Any optimism I had more or less evaporated immediately, and after this truce mediation I never saw them again until the trial.

There were approximately 30 people in the room. Presiley Baxendale took the chair and set out the objectives of the mediation, which was, of course to extort money out of us, but the question was how much. I had previously written a position statement – yet another one – and gave it to Sir Anthony Evans, to whom I took an instant liking. I was, like all of us, privately interviewed by him; he was very gentlemanly and understanding and the interview was entirely amicable. He became very interested in my career in the Bank, the Antarctic, India and so on, and we talked so much about the Antarctic that by the end of the interview I had signed him up for the South Georgia Association – my favourite island in the Antarctic, which he had visited recently as a tourist. Like King Agag, as a mediator, he had, of course to walk 'delicately' as the Bible says, but I did tell him that I thought the charges against us were absolutely outrageous and that all this had resulted from a totally unexpected and flawed judgment in the House of Lords. He did not demur from this, but of course his job was to find a *via media* between us not wanting to pay anything and the Society's wish to obtain amounts from us collectively in excess of £30 million.

For two whole days we sat confined in the little offices allocated to us. We were allowed water, tea, coffee and some sandwiches and cake. Hopes rose and fell. Guy joined us from time to time. Once I went out for eggs and bacon. It was becoming interminable, and the tension was almost tangible. A great deal of pressure was applied to David Wilson, the main target, to ante up and I think in the end he came up with a figure of £750,000 which seemed very high bearing in mind he had done nothing wrong. In the end we came up with a collective figure of around £4 million – I was never told the exact figure. Charles Plant and Herbert Smith and the Society then opined that the offer was inappropriate and that was that. It was a complete waste of time, money and effort.

While the mediation was in its death throes, I sat with Guy in the graveyard of a local church, dispirited and depressed, but afterwards most of us repaired to a local hostelry and consoled ourselves with numerous bottles of Vin Rose. I then discovered that most of us were relieved that the mediation had been a failure, because if we had settled it would be tantamount to admitting to the world that we were partly guilty, and that we were not. So much, therefore, for a mediation which took a year to crank up, lasted two days and failed, but thank heavens, looking back with the benefit of hindsight, that it did fail.

Following the collapse of the mediation – and I suppose it was inevitable it would collapse bearing in mind that they, the Society, wanted in excess of £30 million mainly by blackmailing David Wilson, and our offer was under £5 million – we put ourselves on a war footing to prepare for the great Armageddon of the trial.

The date for this was now fixed for 11th April 2005, three and a half years after the litigation had started. Why is it that lawyers take so long in cranking themselves up – unless it is that the longer the crank, the bigger the fees? The proposal now was for a trial lasting eight months with a holiday break in August, and one asked oneself how such an open and shut case could last eight months. But, of course, a case built on an edifice of hypothetical assumptions which were in their turn based on the benefit of hindsight (that is to say, we should have been aware of the likelihood of the totally unexpected House of Lords judgment), meant that most of the trial was spent exploring a hypothetical world which did not exist. None of this made any sense to me.

Of course, none of us with the exception of David Wilson could by now afford legal representation. By now our legal D&O pots were mostly exhausted and one kept on coming back to this legal absurdity whereby if we could not afford to pay our own costs, why were we being sued for billions of pounds? The only answer we could come up with was that all this was some sort of vendetta against us by Mr Treves. In the event, he kept the litigation going against us even after he had abandoned the case against Ernst & Young.

So, as I have said earlier, we mobilised and put ourselves on a war footing and geared up accordingly. We could only do this because Allen & Overy offered first me and then the others something called a conditional fee agreement, which I had never heard of before. This CFA, if I can call it that for short, was negotiated for me by Guy and later on the other Allen & Overy five followed suit.

Thus we were all presented with some formidable documents as well as engagement letters, in which you sign your life away – lawyers like doing this. In essence the CFA agreement was one in which if we lost, we would have to pay no fees. In a sense one could say this was entirely academic, because if we lost we would all be bankrupt anyway. The other side of the coin was that if we won, Allen & Overy were entitled to a success fee of 50 per cent. However, the difficulty was that a settlement between the two parties would be construed as a win, but it was by no means certain that the plaintiff, i.e. the Society, would pay our costs plus a 50 per cent fee in addition. In effect this meant we could not settle unless we had full or virtually full reimbursement of all our costs, including the 50 per cent success fee. Here it is worth commenting on the fact, if it was a fact, that Allen & Overy must have been very sure we would win because without this relative certainty they would not have offered us a CFA.

One could say that, looking at it from my point of view, it was a mechanism of dealing with a cashflow problem engendered by the case, because without the CFA I could not have had the benefit of legal representation. So, of course, it was a gamble for Allen & Overy and less of a gamble for me, because if it failed I would be bankrupt anyway. However, try as we could, the benefit of this CFA largesse did not extend itself to our redoubtable barristers, namely Lawrence Rabinowitz QC and Richard Handyside, so we were forced to agree a fee account for these two gentlemen of around £1.2 million, of which my one-sixth share was £200,000. In addition there were expert witness fees and all sorts of other fees which started floating in, including copying fees, transcript fees, hire of room fees, and so on and so forth. Once the legal machinery gets its claws into your flesh, there is no way of stopping it, and every additional fee was greeted with a cry of despair from my wife and me. But we were always told there was no alternative but to pay up.

The mobilisation, and now the war footing – and there was no doubt that this was a legal but of course totally unnecessary fight to the finish – took the following form. Steering committees were established – these met fortnightly. There were full agendas and minutes covering every aspect of the case – the 'great case' as it was becoming known in legal circles – including all stances, positions and position shifts on the part of the Society, Herbert Smith, Ernst & Young, their solicitors, Barlow Lyde & Gilbert, Ince & Co. representing David Wilson, also his barrister Jules Sher QC, an intelligent but rather long-winded man, and all the other lawyers representing other individual directors. And finally the positions of the litigants in persons were analysed and discussed in great depth.

Our position vis-à-vis the media was always on the agenda, as well of course as the budgets and the budget variances against actuals. With regard to the media there was no doubt that they were baying for our blood, but as the trial got under way and the true case as opposed to the imagined case of the media started to emerge, the media started to swing in our direction, with Nikki

Tait of the *Financial Times* who was the court correspondent of this paper and who attended court most days, leading the way.

These regular War Cabinet meetings enabled us to discuss tactics and strategies at length – nothing, we decided, had to be left to chance, although litigation seems to be a very chancy business. I always remember one Labour Member of Parliament saying to me that he could not for the life of him understand why the Society went to the House of Lords, because he said if ever there was a gamble, going to the House of Lords was a gamble. This remark saddened me – even at the age of 70, I had never become that cynical – but I am afraid that following Lord Steyn's judgment I have to agree with that Labour MP. The real sadness was that I was being sued by lawyers, and I felt that lawyers were the ones who had brought down the Society.

The financial work and all the accounting was carried out by Peter Davis, a former senior Partner of PricewaterhouseCooper, like me a defendant, and I and we owe him a depth of gratitude for the huge amount of work he undertook for us, not only in respect of the financials, but also for his work in keeping the group together when we could no longer afford the fees and therefore became litigants in person (LIPs), much to the irritation of our dear friends Herbert Smith. Of course, when we were LIPs as the expression goes, Herbert Smith wrote endless formal legal letters to us apropos of nothing in particular, but throughout these four years they never once addressed me correctly and always deliberately or otherwise omitted titles. Considering that they were suing four CBEs namely Roy Ranson, Jennie Page, myself and later Jonathan Taylor, and considering that lawyers always or nearly always are very correct and formal – for instance always calling Mr Justice Langley his Lordship – it seemed to me just plain bad manners and disrespect.

We prepared ourselves for the ordeal of the eight-month trial. It was just like planning a military operation except that they were on the offensive and we were on the defensive. Our main objective, therefore, was to mount such a massive in-depth defensive exercise that they would themselves be forced on the defensive, and this is in effect what happened. Their gamble had been that the case would never come to trial, that it would be settled as Mr Treves himself stated, and I have mentioned this earlier that this is what he anticipated. But he got it wrong, and the main reason he got it wrong was that we refused to be blackmailed through a legal process.

We were obliged by the lawyers to read a huge amount – a monthly schedule was provided of such tasks and as I completed them I carefully ticked them off against the schedule. In all, I calculated that after I had finished I had read something over 10,000 pages. These reading tasks included reading all the board papers and minutes going back to 1993, likewise all the Investment Committee and Audit Committee papers and minutes. I had to read all the defence papers of each individual defendant, their witness statements, their position statements, the opening position statements, all the particulars of claim, the skeleton statements, two volumes of papers entitled 'Exhibits to the Witness Statements of Alan Tritton', four volumes of summary judgment application bundles each running to about 300 pages, various summaries including an Allen & Overy 'Case Map of Evidential Issues', draft proofs of evidence, the Penrose inquiry report running to 800 pages, and so on and so forth – it was interminable. However at the end of all this, my self-confidence started to return. It quite evidently was a trumped-up case and I had all the facts, figures and evidence at more or less my fingertips to demonstrate in cross-examination that this was the case. Above all, I was able to commit to memory some of the most useful and important statements, such as Lord Woolf in the Appeal Court stating that what we had done, in his opinion, was entirely reasonable and fair.

Somewhere along the line we were sent to a certain Anthony Temple QC to be inculcated in the art of expressing and conducting oneself during cross-examination in the box – in my view a very expensive and not entirely necessary experience. I was told to listen to the questions (this seemed fairly obvious). I was told to take my time. I was told to speak up – as I have a loud voice this was not necessary and in any case there were microphones. I was told to tell the truth – this also seemed fairly obvious. I was told to be short and to the point – for example 'I agree' and 'I disagree'. This latter advice was completely impossible: there were far too many hypothetical questions based on hypothetical assumptions being asked of me, and there were a multitude of misunderstandings on the part of the Society's barristers which had to be cleared up as I went along. You could not say 'I agree' or 'I disagree' when the whole case against me seemed to me nothing more than an edifice of conjecture (I was almost going to say creative fiction), the alleged losses being based on a hypothetical test case in the

House of Lords, leading to a hypothetical outcome, leading to a need to make a hypothetical change in final bonuses, with that change being hypothesised to be defective in some way.

I was told I should try and recollect documents and not try to reconstruct events – this was emphasised. I was told that my attitude in the box was very important as the Judge would be watching me all the time, as indeed he did. At the end he suddenly asked me whether I had been in the Army, to which I replied yes and that I had fought in the Far East. He then said I had a very forceful attitude in my response to his advice and questions, with some sort of implication that I should be less so in the box. In the end I am not sure how useful this all was. The best advice came from my wife, who told me to sit up in the chair and not lean backwards.

By the autumn of 2004, the cold war started to warm up. There were endless meetings, case management conferences, pre-trial reviews, discussions, tactical and strategic manoeuvrings. Expert witnesses produced learned reports on actuarial, audit and investment banking matters at vast expense; most of them disagreed with each other. There were negotiations about this and that, claims were re-re-re-amended as Herbert Smith constantly shifted their position, claims were reduced or abandoned altogether, and so on. We even considered insuring Mr Justice Langley's life for the duration of the trial, but the premium was so prohibitive that we backed off. Mr Treves wrote and said he was looking for a global and realistic offer of settlement from all the directors and we were asked to talk to David Wilson to move the discussion forward, as he put it, in a positive way and that was the hope (indeed expectation) of the board. Peter Martin continued his daily guerrilla tactics against Herbert Smith. Calderbank offers were made to Herbert Smith but they never bothered to reply either to our letters or to our offers. A trial timetable was established and a seating plan was prepared by Herbert Smith in courtroom 76. EMAG – the Equitable Members Action Group – continued its daily musings on its website. All this and very much more. All correspondence was conducted by the email and every day my wife presented herself to me with lengthy emails as I had still not mastered the mysteries of the machine, or 'crouching beast' as I called it, after my outboard engine in the Antarctic which constantly broke down. It was all a Kafkaesque farce, but all the lawyers took it extremely seriously as, of course, they had to; and, of course we took it extremely seriously, farcical as indeed it was.

One day before the trial, I went along to courtroom 76 in the High Court of Justice, armed with my seating plan. It was all very ordinary, in fact it looked like a classroom with the teacher – that is, the Judge – on his raised podium at one end of the room with below him the touch typists and office clerks, the latter not having very much to do. On his left was the raised box where I would have to sit and be cross-examined. Below the podium and the box were several rows of desks with microphones and computer screens where the plaintiffs' and the defendants' barristers and solicitors would sit surrounded by boxes of files. As for the defendants themselves, there was virtually no room for them so we had to sit in the public gallery. The rest of the courtroom was packed with files and documentation, all carefully tagged for use during the Great Trial. It was all light and airy, being on the third floor of the High Court building, but for me looking around it for the first time, it reminded me of my school room, except that, firstly, I was not going to squeak cherry stones under my shoes and, secondly, that here it would be determined whether I would be made bankrupt or not.

It was in November 2004 that Herbert Smith let it be known that Equitable would be prepared to settle with Ernst & Young for a payment of £400 million or so, to which the answer was, as you can naturally imagine, no. Mr Plant also raised the question of settling with us, and by that I mean the Allen & Overy group of six. He told us that he believed that he had a case which would succeed against Ernst & Young on liability, but what was bothering him was causation. Here he believed that the evidence which he hoped and expected would be forthcoming from us, the non-executive directors, would be crucial to Equitable's case against Ernst & Young.

This was a quite astonishing remark, bearing in mind that he was also suing us for billions of pounds and to me it made absolutely no sense and, if anything, showed an extraordinary naiveté. To me it seemed a totally preposterous proposition on his part to believe that Herbert Smith could cross-examine the non-executive directors on a series of hypothetical permutations and that in so doing they would elicit evidence which would assist their case against Ernst & Young. Did they really think we would, so to speak, incriminate

Ernst & Young on the basis that they should have made us make a substantially greater provision for the GAR liabilities in relation to the GAR guaranteed benefits, when it was Lord Steyn who had created these liabilities himself with his own fair hand?

Clearly they did, because Plant was explicit in his suggestions that the settlement dynamics between the Society and Ernst & Young would be materially altered if we gave an indication of the likely evidence we would give against Ernst & Young and thus assist Herbert Smith's causation case against them. In other words, he was asking us the defendants to help him out, and he even went on to say that we and Herbert Smith had a common interest in so doing! I am afraid that all this left a very nasty taste in the mouth, and I began to wonder whether this was all part of the dirty tricks of litigation.

Here once again I would like to set out my position vis-à-vis Ernst & Young. I had worked closely with them for over 20 years and I had gone through all the accounts with a toothcomb. We had had numerous debates and discussion about provisions and reserves, contingent liabilities and everything else. I personally associated myself strongly with their defence. Did they really think I was about to be a turncoat and say that all my work had been flawed in some way? Of course not. But this response seemed to take Herbert Smith very much by surprise, and it was not long after my cross-examination in the witness box that they abandoned their case against Ernst & Young.

By now, spring 2005, we were getting ready to go over the top. The ladders were in position, bayonets had been fixed and the whistle was about to be blown. It was hailed in the press as the biggest ever civil suit and the most expensive case in legal history. Mr Thomson – the newly appointed actuary for the Equitable (who wrote his own reference for the job), opined that if the Society lost the case it would cost the policyholders in the region of £100 million. And so it was that on the morning of 11th April 2005, at the age of 73, I started commuting again.

33

The Equitable Trial 2005

On that morning of 11th April 2005 the courtroom was packed with well over 100 people. There were about four dozen Queen's Counsel, barristers and solicitors, defendants, plaintiffs, press and three rather expensive-looking people from the Treasury and the Financial Services Authority. The top Queen's Counsel were all seated at their desks immediately below the Judge. These were Ian Milligan and Robert Miles for the Society, Jules Sher for David Wilson, and Mark Hapgood and Jonathan Gaisman for Ernst & Young. Behind this top drawer so to speak were Charles Plant and Julian Copeman for Herbert Smith. These two were not very impressive – were they the best Herbert Smith could produce? Going to the right were David Wilson's team of solicitors from Ince & Co; and further to the right the solicitors of Barlow Lyde & Gilbert acting for Ernst & Young, headed by the formidable and most attractive Clare Canning, the belle of the court. Behind all these were our Queen's Counsel Laurence Rabinowitz and Richard Handyside, both of whom inspired much confidence; behind them our team from Allen & Overy crouching behind their screens with Jennie Page and her husband Jeremy Orde next door; with in front of them Peter Leaver, Queen's Counsel and Mr Vaughan, barrister and solicitor respectively, acting for them. Finally, moving to the right again, was David Mumford, a young barrister acting for Roy Ranson who impressed everybody with his intellectual acumen – so much so that I reported very favourably on him to the head of his chambers, a certain Mr Aldous. It was all quite jolly in a way, with a lot of chat and conversation going on, except that we were not allowed to speak to the Society's barristers or their Herbert Smith solicitors. Naturally, I did not want to talk to Charles Plant, but I did want to and did eventually have a short talk with Ian Milligan, as I knew his father who was in the Scots Guards and came back from the War to take over a house at Eton. We all wondered why he had taken on this case, and whether his advice had been to the Society's new management to sue us all indiscriminately and to include Ernst & Young in the same lawsuit.

Promptly at 10.30 a.m. Mr Justice Langley arrived. Everybody stood to attention and bowed. Then he signalled to Milligan to go over the top and commence the proceedings. I must say here, before I embark on the case, that over the months I formed the highest opinion of Mr Justice Langley. He was immensely intelligent, scrupulously fair, extremely percipient, and above all he had a good sense of humour. I formed the highest regard for him.

Milligan now got up and after shuffling his papers around for a bit, set forth. I was expecting all sorts of salvos, but instead of these, he appeared to conduct a sort of *tour d'horizon*. He wandered around addressing the Judge on various background topics, and never once responded to our defence submissions. He went on for several hours on these background topics, by which time most of the Press had got bored and left. He then suddenly sat down and that was that for the day.

The following day, Milligan was still touring the horizon. He wandered through the regulatory guidelines, the actuarial valuation of liabilities, the Society's free asset ratio, future profits, contingent liabilities – all still background material, which I would have thought could have been taken as read. However, he did fall into our big trap and that was encouraging. He started to quote extensively from the Penrose report on our so-called over-bonusing, without apparently realising that the Society itself had quite recently issued a press release stating that there had been no over-bonusing and that Penrose had got it wrong. I think it was somewhere here that Herbert Smith tried to amend their case against us yet again. They had had three and a half years to sort themselves out, but by this time everybody including the Judge was fed up with their constant amendments and re-amendments.

After Milligan had sat down, Rabinowitz, our QC, rose to his feet and poured scorn on the Society's revised claim against us, which was lodged only the previous day. He correctly described it as being re-re-re-re-re-amended. He told the Judge that he regarded all this as cloud cuckoo land, even 'Alice in Wonderland', and that

496

as a result the defendants (that's us) no longer understood what was now being alleged against them. All this had Milligan on the ropes and as he could not answer the questions, he was reduced to saying that he would take instructions overnight and provide the answers the following day. So it appeared we had drawn first blood. Then Rabinowitz went on to say that the logic of the new claim against us was that *'in essentia'* the Judge was being invited to try the original Hyman litigation all over again, to which the Judge somewhat mischievously replied that he had 'never been dealt a more attractive hand'. At that, for the first time, the court room exploded with laughter.

So the third day came along and I now realise that I cannot in this memoir go through every day of an eight-month trial – I can only try to describe some of the highlights, although I have to say to do even that is very difficult. So on the third day our redoubtable QC rose and delivered what the lawyers call his opening submission. He was extraordinarily effective and rubbished Herbert Smith's edifice of creative fiction. In particular he told the Judge that we had acted consistently with the advice given to us by the lawyers and QCs all the way along the line. You will recall that these QCs had told us that what we were doing was 'perfectly legitimate', and so on.

The following day – day 4 – started off well for us when Milligan confirmed that the Society was no longer bringing a claim for negligence against us due to the board's approval of the differential terminal bonus policy in February 2000. I was not there, of course, but Milligan agreed that the Society would bear our costs and that we were to submit our estimates as to these costs – so second blood to us. Later there followed more opening oral submissions on behalf of other directors, and then Chris Headdon, the former appointed actuary, a litigant in person, got up to deliver his own opening submission. He was excellent. He suggested that Milligan and Herbert Smith were making up the case as they went along. He quite rightly attacked Lord Penrose, pointing out the basic errors in his financial tables as well as his comparisons between total assets and policy values, which he had got completely wrong and arose from a basic misunderstanding about the nature of terminal bonus. In particular he noted that in every year the board reserved the right subsequently to vary their bonus declaration, and that a decision in any one year did not bind the board for the future. At this, which was of course quite true, our lawyers looked at each other and opined cheerfully that this was catastrophic for the Society's claim on bonus cuts. He also addressed the case against him in respect of the additional guaranteed annuity rate (GAR) liability, noting that there was a sharp distinction between the existence of a liability and the need to make a provision for that liability. The latter depends on the application of actual historical experience in order to determine whether the liability is likely to crystallise within the relevant accounting period. When he finished, I almost felt like throwing my non-existent hat into the air and cheering, and it was very noticeable how closely the Judge followed his reasoning and logic. Almost certainly this was our third blood, and all this in the first five days of the trial of the century!

After Christopher Headdon came Peter Martin, a litigant in person and a lawyer. His view, and I agreed with him, was that Lord Steyn and the House of Lords Appellate Committee quite simply had got the Hyman case wrong, and therefore it was the House of Lords that had precipitated the crisis, not the directors. It was the case, he said, that Lord Penrose failed to review the House of Lords decision, implying that constitutionally any review of a Court of Final Appeal judgment would be impermissible. But why would it be impermissible if there was a consensus of legal opinion that he had got it wrong? Perhaps lawyers would jeopardise their legal careers if they were brave enough to challenge the House of Lords Appellate Committee. Peter Martin then referred to the case called the *Bratton Seymour* v. *Oxborough* case of 1992, which was taken to the Court of Appeal where Lord Steyn as a Lord Justice was one of the judges.

I am afraid that I will have to set out what Lord Steyn said in his judgment. He stated that there was an implication in the articles of association that the directors' decision was limited in some way; in other words, although the articles clearly stated that the directors had an absolute discretion and that their decision (on bonuses) was final and conclusive, this did not necessarily mean what it said. In his judgment on this earlier *Bratton Seymour* case, however, Lord Steyn stated that:

Here the Company puts forward an implication to be derived not from the language in the Articles of Association but purely from extrinsic circumstances. That, in my judgement, is a type

498

of implication, which, as a matter of law, can never succeed in the case of Articles of Association. After all, if it were permitted, it would involve the position that different implications would notionally be possible between the Company and different subscribers. It is not permitted to seek a rectification; neither the Company nor any member can seek to add or to subtract from the terms of the Articles by way of implying a term. If it were permitted, it would be equally permissible over the whole spectrum of company law cases.

But that is precisely what he did to Equitable. He implied a term into the Society's articles of association which simply was not there, and in the process ruined the Society.

Finally Jules Sher, the rather long-winded QC, submitted his opening case for David Wilson, and that was that for the directors, both executive and non-executive. We now started on the seventh day with Jonathan Gaisman QC leading for Ernst & Young on the liability case against them. He performed brilliantly, and to my mind he totally rubbished the society's claims against Ernst & Young and like all the defence barristers he poked fun at Herbert Smith's constant re-re-amending its claims. At one point he said that it all felt like 'litigation by divination', and this caused a good laugh on our side of the fence. His first heavy body blow – and you can see that we have moved out of the trenches into the boxing ring – came at the end of the seventh day. He said that the new Equitable board had been considering since they had taken over, restating the 1999 Accounts to increase the £200 million provision for GAR liabilities on a different set of assumptions – you will recall that these were the provisions which Lord Steyn by sleight of hand had managed to increase to over £1.5 billion by not ring-fencing the GAR liabilities from the non-GAR policy classes. In the event the new board did not do this. Thus the Accounts for 2000 and 2001 continued to show this provision of £200 million although the new board claimed that it was wrong and that it was all Ernst & Young's fault. However, Gaisman went on to reveal that on the same day, 15th April 2002, Thomson had both signed off the 2001 Accounts – thereby representing that the 1999 Accounts, which had not been restated, continued to give a true and fair view of the Society's business at the relevant time – and at the same time signed off the statement of claim against Ernst & Young seeking over £3 billion-worth of damages on the directly contradictory assertion that the 1999 accounts did not give a true and fair view.

So this was the third contradiction; the first was Lord Steyn's contradicting himself on the articles of association and implying that there was something there which wasn't; the second was the claim against us for over-bonusing with the Society contradicting itself by issuing a press release on 15th November 2004 to the effect that there had been no over-bonusing. And now here was Thomson's contradiction. With so many contradictions flying around, it seemed to be possible to start enjoying the trial despite the inevitable and continuous anxiety.

On the eighth day of the trial, 21st April 2005, the Judge gave his views on the Society's trying again to amend its claim yet again, and this in the middle of a trial. What Herbert Smith wanted to do was to introduce a new alternative case against us claiming damages in the hypothetical circumstances of a 'hypothetically successful Hyman test case'. This the Judge described as moving from a hypothetical world to a new solar system. This was all good news, and we needed good news.

Jonathan Gaisman sat down, and if I could have applauded him, I would have done so – instead I invited him out to lunch when the case was over and presumably we had won. Mark Hapgood QC then took off where Gaisman had ended. He described the 'hornets' nest' which the Society's claim had moved into even if it was able to overcome all Gaisman's objections on liability. This 'hornets' nest' included factual causation, legal causation, scope of duty, and contributory fault, as he made the point that between the Society and Ernst & Young the issue was not what the directors should have done, but what the directors would have done. In particular he stated that the substantial bonus reduction of the type the Society was saying should have occurred would have conflicted with what was described in the trade as policyholders' reasonable expectations, and departed from the Society's smoothing policy and our desire to avoid discontinuities in our approach to bonuses. All this quite apart from the fact that the Society – and here I would remind you of this – had stated that there had been no over-bonusing. Mark Hapgood finished on the ninth day of the trial. One had to keep reminding oneself that he was there to defend Ernst & Young and not us, although generally I would say his submissions were very helpful. I was, of course, particularly concerned as I had been chairman of the Audit Committee, and I was concerned that nothing would come out which was detrimental to my defence. In the event it did not, and in fact my position was very similar to that of Ernst & Young. And here I would just like to remind you that the central case against Ernst & Young depended on the suggestion that the additional GAR provisions would have been a matter of great concern to us, but of course these additional provisions only came into being as a result of Lord Steyn disallowing ring-fencing as between GARs and non-GARs, against whom he discriminated. So once again it all came back to Lord Steyn. Mark Hapgood had a formidable intellect, he was very precise and clear and knew his case backwards, and I did not entirely look forward to being cross-examined by him later on in the trial.

I did not attend every day of the trial, although I think that if I had lived in London, I would have done. I was never bored, and I enjoyed the camaraderie of it all – I have always been a somewhat social person. When the trial first started Allen & Overy had rented a room on the same floor as courtroom 76, and after the morning was over we repaired to this little room together with our lawyers and wives, if they were present, and discussed the morning proceedings. It was in a sense our strategic headquarters, and we all analysed every shade and nuance of the trial, the enemy's tactics, our tactics, the enemy's strategy, our strategy. We grasped at straws, trying to bolster up our self-confidence, and anxiety was written all over our faces. I am not really one to eat sandwiches in a small confined space, talking endlessly over our chances, so in the end I decided to go out to a small pub frequented by Guy called the Seven Sisters, in Carey Street of all places. Most days therefore Guy and I had lunch there, and the lunches were excellent. I had two glasses of wine and two cigarettes, and this put me in a good mood for the afternoon. The mistress of the pub, called Roxy, was well known to Guy who frequently went there, and one day she asked me why I came so often. I said that I was involved in a court case over the road in the High Court, and that I was being sued. 'For how much?' she asked, and I replied, 'Three billion,' and she roared with laughter. Occasionally I was joined by Christina and Charles, so that together with Guy we had a real family lunch. It is astonishing looking back on that terrible and unnecessary case, how it brought me much closer to the children, or perhaps them much closer to me in my tribulations. I remain profoundly grateful for their loving support during all that dreadful time when Mr Treves was trying to ruin me, and I would remind you again what he said: 'Just imagine what it is like spending Christmas with your family knowing that you risk losing every penny you have earned.'

So now we are on the tenth day, and Mr Charles Thomson went into the box to be cross-examined by Jonathan Gaisman QC for Ernst & Young. Charles Thomson was the key witness in the Society's case against the director defendants and Ernst & Young, and if their case against us was going to succeed then his evidence was going to be crucial. Mr Thomson was a lowland Scot with a pronounced Scottish accent, and sometimes one found it difficult to understand him. Now of course it was part of Gaisman's job to undermine his integrity, and this he set out to do with gusto, and he had the ammunition to do this. It emerged at the outset that Thomson, who had been brought in as chief executive to save the Society after the House of Lords had collapsed it and the former chief executive Chris Headdon had resigned, had written his own reference for the job and had even threatened to sue his former chief executive. He freely admitted that he had 'largely' written a glowing testimonial for himself and that he had purported that this had been written by Michael Ross, who was then the chief executive of Scottish Widows. The reference that he wrote about himself claimed that he had enjoyed an 'exceptional level of success' at Scottish Widows. It went on to say that 'we will miss his intellect, integrity and energy and feel sure that he will bring great value to other organisations at the highest levels'. All this was written by himself, but after he had submitted this reference he later withdrew it because Michael Ross having seen the document for the first time, refused to sign it. A twist to this story is that Michael Ross, with whom he had fallen out, had been asked to appear as an expert witness for Ernst & Young. All this was good exciting preliminary stuff, helped by a photograph in one of the daily tabloids showing him with a lady not his wife, and a young baby.

Gaisman's cross-examination of Thomson took a whole day. Thomson came over as a shifty man and nobody was at all impressed by him. Frequently he resisted answering straightforward key questions, which he knew were likely to cause him difficulty. Just as frequently he sought to excuse what appeared to be inadequacies in his own performance as a director by hiding behind advice of professionals or colleagues, or by explaining that pressure of work stopped him from giving some important matters the attention they required. Frequently he emerged as someone willing to adopt inconsistent views simultaneously if it suited his purpose to do so, and his credibility as a result was seriously damaged. Essentially, all through the day he was on the ropes, constantly conceding this or that, and by the end of the day it was difficult to say whether he or Herbert Smith came out of the cross-examination worse – the latter because they had initially failed to disclose some very important documents and had done so only after strong and sustained objections. And when these documents were disclosed, large sections had been redacted for privilege reasons, confidentiality, and so on. All this left a very nasty taste in the mouth because the assumption had to be that not only had these documents not initially been disclosed, but also that large sections had been adapted before they were disclosed.

As an example of Thomson's shiftiness, he repeatedly hid behind his claim that he 'believed it to be the case at the time and on the basis of the advice I was given', always with the implied caveat that, of course, he subsequently learnt that he had been misinformed and that with the benefit of hindsight he had been wrong. And here it has to be remembered that the whole case against us had been constructed with the benefit of hindsight, based on the hypothetical assumption that we should have had a premonition of Lord Steyn's catastrophic misjudgment, which Thomson himself had described as aberrational and unpredicted.

The next day Mark Hapgood QC took up the cudgels and went for him on causation. His cross-examination was extremely effective and once again Thomson was back on the ropes. Hapgood managed to obtain a number of concessions from him which were directly contradictory either to the Society's case against Ernst & Young or their own expert witness's evidence. As a result Thomson's credibility had been steadily compromised.

After Gaisman and Hapgood it was now the turn of our QC Laurence Rabinowitz to cross-examine Thomson, who was now back on the ropes. First of all he admitted that he was not certain that he had ever looked at any of the documents in the Society's £1.7 billion claim against the directors, before signing the claim as a statement of truth. He was then asked if he had ever read the documents supporting the pleading, to which he replied he 'could not recall'. He was further asked if he had ever read any of these documents signed by him as a statement of truth. To this he admitted that he could not recall: 'I cannot give you a cast-iron guarantee as to what I would have looked at.' Rabinowitz then, shooting from the hip, said, 'Mr Thomson are you not very good with detail?' To which Thomson, a trained actuary, replied, 'I'm not sure I am very good at detail. I have a good overview.'

There were two particular points which came out during cross-examination, of which I was not previously aware. The first of these was what I can only describe as hypocrisy in the original ridiculous claim against us of several billion. This was that the Financial Ombudsman relied on the pleaded claims against us for determining the mis-selling claims of policyholders against the Society. The Ombudsman was not shown our very strong defences and this meant that he or she saw only one side of the case which he or she relied on. Now of course this was very deleterious to the Society in their defences against the mis-selling claim, so for a long time the Society together with its solicitors tried desperately to get the Ombudsman to consider our evidence, with the result that the Society had perforce to take our standpoint in defending their actions, thus hopelessly compromising themselves. As someone put it, it was an incontrovertible example of the Society talking out of both sides of its mouth at the same time. The hypocrisy of this action was brought fully to the attention of the Judge and was not denied by Thomson.

The second point which was put to Thomson, and which seemed to me to be more of a *coup de grâce* than anything else, is that Thomson had done exactly what he was accusing us of doing, and that was in making his bonus declaration in March 2001 for the year 2000. He declared an annualised bonus of 8 per cent against an investment return of only 2.7 per cent, and that on a closed fund. Without therefore at that time a market value adjustment, there was a huge run for the exit by policyholders, and it is estimated that this run amounted to a billion pounds or even more.

Over the next day or so Thomson was cross-examined by other lawyers and litigants in person, particularly Chris Headdon, who immediately demonstrated who was the most able actuary and chief executive. Then Hapgood came temporarily back into the fray, stating that Herbert Smith had never carried out a proper disclosure of the society's 2000 and 2001 documents, and had even stated that they were not relevant. But, of course, they were, and this caught our friend Milligan on the hop. This meant that he again had to request the Judge if he could take instructions overnight.

At last Thomson stood down from the box. It seemed to me that he had been thoroughly discredited. He had been the Society's key witness, and if that was the best he could do, it did not amount to very much. Once again we wondered why the case had been brought in the first place. Perhaps it really was the case that Mr Treves and Sir Philip Otton had never expected it to go to trial and that the whole legal exercise to date had been an attempt to force us into some sort of settlement. Both were lawyers: Mr Treves had been a senior partner of Mcfarlanes, whilst Sir Philip Otton had been a judge in the Court of Appeal. In fact, although I know little about the etiquette of the law, I found it strange, to say the least, to find a former Court of Appeal judge instigating litigation against me. (He resigned before the case came to trial.) They both must have known that the case against us was largely hypothetical and based on hindsight, and stemmed from the House of Lords judgment. Even Mr Treves said it was aberrational. He further went on to say that we had behaved perfectly correctly and properly, which is exactly what our QCs had told us. So why were we in that courtroom and what, again, was the legal advice which had propelled them to litigate? They never disclosed it, pleading privilege. It was also interesting to me to note that Mr Treves never once came to the courtroom. There is no doubt that given the atmosphere in there, he would have been made to feel extremely uncomfortable, and as somebody in the public gallery said to me, there most certainly would have been an audible reaction if he had appeared! So it all remains a mystery to me today.

On the thirteenth day Mr Mumford, the young and very able barrister for Roy Ranson, began his cross-examination of Thomson. The first of his main points was that Scottish Widows, for which he had been appointed actuary, had been doing exactly the same as what we were being accused of. Mr Thomson agreed with this and conceded that our policy of a differential terminal bonus and that of Scottish Widows not only had the same economic effect, but was arrived at by the same philosophical approach. So it was back to Lord Steyn again. Secondly, Mr Mumford took Mr Thomson to the Faculty of Actuaries 'Position Paper on Guaranteed Annuities', which Thomson had said did not support our position. Mumford used this paper, and a letter from the regulator which had been endorsed by the faculty's position paper, to show Thomson that, on the contrary, they did indeed support our policy of reducing terminal bonuses on GAR policies. I did not hear Thomson's response, but he could have only agreed with Mumford.

It was now Chris Headdon's turn to cross-examine Thomson. It was one actuary against another and it was clearly no contest. Chris Headdon showed himself as being actuarially far more able and intellectually far superior to Thomson. This is what we expected, and our confidence grew. So far there had been 13 days in court, and everything seemed to have gone in our favour. The solicitors were cautiously optimistic, but still worried about future developments; after all there was still something like seven and a half months to go and matters could still go wrong.

On the fourteenth day of the trial Mr Brian McGeough, a retired partner of the Society's solicitors Denton Hall, was brought in for cross-examination as a witness for the prosecution. Most of us knew him very well. I certainly did, having known him for nearly 30 years, and during that time he had been very helpful to my Calcutta Tercentenary Trust. I found it very odd that he had been asked to, or perhaps told to, testify against us, and I did truly wonder what he was doing there. After all, he was the lawyer who had told us that the DTBP was entirely within our discretion under the powers given us under article 65 of the articles of association. This was the article which stated that the directors had an absolute discretion with regard to the awarding of bonuses, and that their decision was both final and conclusive. What could be plainer than that? He had also confirmed to us that in his opinion this enabled the directors to take a differential approach between classes of policies, and between benefits within a policy. So what was he going to say that contradicted all this? Well, the answer was nothing. He did not contradict anything he had told us and therefore this prosecution witness supported us, the defendants. So what were Herbert Smith on about?

The last witness was Cindy Leslie, who had succeeded Brian McGeough as Denton's lawyer for the Equitable, just before I retired. It came as a bit of a surprise to me to learn that the new board had intended to sue Denton's, but had apparently agreed not to do this as a quid pro quo for their witness statements. Having agreed this, I was told by somebody that Herbert Smith had drafted part of their witness statements and had also deleted parts which they felt did not help their cause. I do not know whether this is a normal feature of litigation practice, to play around with solicitors' witness statements, but perhaps it is. Cindy Leslie was also in some difficulty when she tried to explain to the Judge why a number of documents relevant to the case in Denton's possession had not been disclosed by Herbert Smith. She told the Judge that when she was drafting her witness statement, she could not shut her eyes to certain documents which Denton's had retained. She explained to the Judge that she had made it known to Herbert Smith that she had this material, and thought she ought to use it in preparing her statement. However, in the final draft, she did not include comments from two particular documents because Herbert Smith apparently had told her not to. She then referred to a letter which she had received from Herbert Smith alleging that Denton's had not advised us properly about the risks of the original litigation, even though the risk was considered to be minimal, if not non-existent.

She said that this was a 'terrible letter' to receive and that this had coloured her statement; and that even after Denton's had been told Equitable would not sue them, nevertheless this threat remained in her memory. So what was going on here? Cindy Leslie's cross-examination started to grind to a halt, but before she stood down, our QC rose to say that there were three major concerns regarding the Society's mis-selling claim against us. The first was that the pleaded case was totally inadequate, given that Cindy Leslie's evidence against us was about as weak as any evidence could be. Secondly, Denton's had retained documents which were clearly relevant to this issue, and not only was it highly objectionable not to have all the relevant documents before the court in a claim for several billion pounds, but it was also highly objectionable for Herbert Smith not to reveal it had access to these documents. Thirdly Herbert Smith had told Cindy Leslie to remove material relating to mis-selling from her witness statement. Thus, he concluded, real prejudice had been caused to the defendants and furthermore the Society should seriously consider whether it should continue with its claim against us for mis-selling. However, Robert Miles, who was Milligan's sidekick, tried to refute all this, unsuccessfully as it turned out. I personally hoped the Judge would intervene here but he did not. Anyway it was all a useful exposition of Herbert Smith's skulduggery.

So that was the end of the witnesses for the prosecution. If I had been the plaintiff, I would have regarded them as an unmitigated disaster. First of all, there was Mr Thomson, who contradicted himself and who could not remember whether he had ever looked at any of the documents claiming vast amounts from us before signing them off as statements of truth. Then there was Brian McGeough, extremely uncomfortable and embarrassed, who was supposed to testify against us but didn't. He was presumably there because of Herbert Smith's undertaking not to sue Denton's provided he took the witness stand. And finally there was Cindy Leslie, also there for the same reason. What I believe is that Herbert Smith wanted her to tell the court that during the original Hyman litigation she had advised the Society that there was a real risk of losing, and that because of that, we should have taken precautions. But of course, she had done no such thing, at least when I was there, and in any case all the QCs had told us that what we were doing was perfectly legitimate. So once again, it all came back to Lord Steyn and his aberrational judgment. Once again the only conclusion I could draw from all this was that it could never have been expected by Mr Treves and Sir Philip Otton that their litigation would end up in an eight-month trial, during the course of which their bluff would be called. So the lesson is never, ever submit to intimidation by lawyers.

Roy Ranson was the first of the executive directors to bat and he was in the box for several days as, of course, he had been the architect of the differential terminal bonus policy and had been both the appointed actuary and managing director during most of the relevant period. He was quite good in the box but I think it is fair to say that he was not as good as I had hoped and expected. Like Thomson he seemed initially to come across as somewhat evasive and detached. Like Thomson he did not appear to answer questions directly but rather obliquely, and I became somewhat discouraged. There are, of course, constant ebbs and flows in any trial. There were, as one would expect, numerous actuarial questions, so clearly Milligan had had to mug up on the business of actuaries. Roy Ranson refused to agree with most of the questions that were put to him, often taking issue with the way questions were put, but he faced some very difficult questions about why the DTBP was not clearly put to policyholders, let alone to us the non-executive directors, and he seemed uncomfortable a lot of the time.

I thought he was generally a less than cooperative witness but nothing he said hurt us in any way. However, as was reported, we did not look happy when he was being cross-examined whilst on the other hand Thomson, who was there with Herbert Smith, appeared for the first time to be very pleased with the way things had gone; so this was all somewhat disconcerting.

I have to say at this stage, long after the trial, that I believe strongly that Roy Ranson should have told us and explained to the non-executive directors exactly what he was doing, and just as importantly the implications of what he was doing. He never did, and this was the reason why all the non-executive directors were so disconcerted when the balloon went up in September 1998. We did not know, and we were caught completely unawares. I had always liked Ranson, but he was a complex man and his technical actuarial expertise coupled with a certain amount of what I have to call arrogance was not helpful. Did I trust him when I was a non-executive director? The answer is, I am afraid, not entirely. However the lucidity of his thought process was always exemplary and I always found myself agreeing – sometimes against my will – with his philosophical actuarial reasoning. When being cross-examined by Jules Sher acting for David Wilson he agreed that throughout the relevant period he knew of the additional GAR 'liability' but he did not take it into account as a relevant factor; nor, he agreed, did he refer it to the board when making bonus recommendations. So this was helpful for the non-executive directors (if not himself). There were further cross-examinations of him by Gaisman and Hapgood who, I would remind you, were acting for Ernst & Young, but nothing detrimental to us came out of there.

Now it was the turn of our star witness, Chris Headdon, in my book the best actuary in the UK whose great misfortune it was to be destroyed in his exceptionally promising career by Lord Steyn. The vindictive Financial Services Authority had barred him from being a director of a financial services company despite his undoubted abilities, and this it did because he had been involved in a financial reinsurance arrangement to bolster the Society's reserves and a financial reinsurance arrangement which had been suggested by no less than the Financial Services Authority itself – what do you make of that?

Chris Headdon, who was acting as a litigant in person, had prepared himself exceptionally well for his ordeal and he came across, as we knew he would, as a particularly articulate and convincing witness. He was in command of all the practical and methodological actuarial issues which were relevant to him as appointed actuary. His answers to the questions were very precise and clear, and Allen & Overy opined to us that his evidence raised the threshold the Society had to reach to prove that it would have been bizarre for a non-executive director not to have accepted his recommendations for bonus decision in the applicable years.

Milligan QC started off with a good deal of assertion and self-confidence – after all this should have been his finest hour, or rather day – but as time went on, it was Chris Headdon who looked increasingly self-confident and assertive. Not only that, he even appeared to be enjoying himself as he methodically and meticulously parried Milligan's blows and gradually got him on the ropes. It was an astonishing performance. Chris Headdon was in his actuarial realm and Milligan, who I admit did try very hard, was simply not up to this actuarial tour de force and was never allowed to plant any actuarial punches on Chris Headdon's head.

Chris was in the box for several days and he came out as a hero, not only for us but also for Ernst & Young. Now I do not think it necessary for me to go into any of the technical detail, although I personally found the debate between him and Milligan absolutely fascinating. However, one sentence of his evidence summed up for us what was wrong in this case. He said, and I quote:

> In the case of the earlier years, i.e. prior to 2000 the argument seems to be nothing more than an edifice of conjecture [I would say creative fiction] – the alleged losses being based on a hypothetical test case – leading to a hypothetical outcome, leading to the need to make a hypothetical change in final bonuses – with that change now hypothesised to be defective in some way.

Well said, Chris. He was right – it was all hypothetical.

On Wednesday, 18th May 2005, the Society under the chairmanship of Mr Treves held its annual general meeting and it was at this meeting that he came out with a series of almost unbelievably offensive statements about the former directors. As it seemed to me, he had a particular animus against the former non-executive directors. Let me explain.

510

A policyholder got up to ask him about the trial proceedings, which were now in their sixth week. Mr Treves told the assembled policyholders that, 'The question as to whether or not there was fraud or any other misfeasance on the part of our predecessors is central to this litigation.' He then went on to say, 'As I have said many times before and I stress again today, we were advised by leading counsel on several occasions that we had and have a duty to bring these actions, and not to do so would have been a dereliction of fiduciary duty on our part.' At the same meeting, he was asked whether or not he told the former president John Sclater that the reason he was being sued was as a means of getting at the deep pockets of Ernst & Young. Recognising that the question related to matters being raised in the trial, he responded as follows: 'I am not prepared for obvious reasons to comment on what has been said or presently unsaid in the court of litigation, but what I would say as a matter of generalisation that if you were to believe everything that is said in court, you would be living permanently in a world of fiction.'

This was too much and we instructed our solicitors to write to Mr Treves on the following lines:

> If you have said that fraud is central to this case, you should have known that there is no allegation of fraud, misfeasance or want of probity whatsoever in this case and the Society's pleaded case makes plain that there is no allegation of dishonesty. If you even had a rudimentary knowledge of the claims the Society has so unwisely brought, you would have appreciated the falsity of your remarks when you made them. Whatever the state of your knowledge, the remark was gravely defamatory and very hurtful to our clients.

On 23rd May, the Society's leading counsel got wearily to his feet and acknowledged that if such a remark had been made then plainly it should not have been made. The Society's solicitors, Herbert Smith, had written to them to say that they understood 'that Mr Treves has acknowledged that the comment was not accurate'. Our solicitors then wrote again, stating we had seen no such acknowledgement, no retraction and no apology in the newspapers, and neither had the policyholders to whom this falsehood was communicated.

Our solicitor's letter covered the Society being advised to bring these actions:

We find it very hard to believe that any leading Counsel, properly instructed, would have advised the Society had a duty to sue indiscriminately all members of the previous Board. It is just not credible that this advice could have been given by any Counsel familiar with the facts, our clients' pre-action protocol response and most particularly Mr Mowschenson QC's opinion that it was absolutely inconceivable that the Directors would be found liable. As we see it, there are only two options, either you did receive advice that the Society had a duty to sue or you did not receive any such advice at all. If you as an experienced lawyer did receive such advice then it is inconceivable, you would have accepted it without challenge. If you did not receive advice in these terms, then you have consistently misled policyholders.

The letter covered Mr Sclater's note:

Mr Sclater's contemporaneous note of a conversation with Mr Treves at 7 p.m. on the 20th May 2001 has been referred to in Court by Mr Rabinowitz QC and is referred to in our client's written opening submission. It records Mr Treves as saying that Herbert Smith's objective in investigating claims against Mr Sclater and by implication the other Directors is to 'see if there is a deep pocket which can be made to pay up, e.g. especially Ernst and Young.' The note has been put to Mr Sclater under oath and he has testified as to its accuracy. The Society has made absolutely no attempt to challenge this evidence. Mr Treves' remark at the Annual General Meeting was a disingenuous attempt to avoid embarrassment for himself at the expense of a gratuitous attack on Mr Sclater's integrity and I would add honesty under oath.

And so the letter went on.

It was poor Mr Miles QC who had to get up in court to retract and apologise for Mr Treves's remarks. However, he offered no explanation as to how Mr Treves, an experienced lawyer, could have made such an obvious and offensive error, except to say that his remarks were made in the 'heat of the moment' – about as flimsy an excuse as one has ever heard. I personally would have expected him to be man enough to come to the court to apologise, but he did not, so I suppose there were some feathers flying around.

Now for the last time, I would like to come back to this question of the Society's legal advice. Did it or did it not exist? If it did, why was it not disclosed and why did the Society claim privilege in not disclosing it? After all, we disclosed all our legal advice. If privilege can override disclosure, then what does that say about disclosure? It renders it meaningless. Disclosure must override privilege; otherwise the defendants are placed on an unequal footing. In any case, it should not be up to the defendants to try and find out what documents have not been disclosed, as happened with the apparent suppression of the Denton papers. As I have mentioned earlier, theirs must have been very peculiar advice, if indeed it did exist, as it must have been the exact opposite of ours. All this left me feeling very uncomfortable. Lawyers, in my opinion, should think long and hard about the efficacy of disclosure and this question of privilege.

But now we must get back to the trial, and we are now on day 27 and Mr Nash is in the box, Alan Nash being the managing director who took over when Roy Ranson retired whilst Chris Headdon took over as appointed actuary. As a side comment here, it was clear that with the benefit of hindsight Roy Ranson should not have combined those two exceptionally important roles, as in corporate governance terms he became too powerful and perhaps a whiff of arrogance attached itself to him, not only in his dealing with the board but also with the regulator, whose views he often used to dismiss airily.

Alan Nash did not do so well in the box as Chris Headdon, but nevertheless he put up a stout defence. The Equitable disaster had been a personal disaster for him. He was highly intelligent and imbued with all the ethos of the Equitable, that of mutual benefit. He had only recently taken over from Roy Ranson as managing director and everything seemed set fair. But then greed destroyed this ideal of mutual equitable benefit when some of the GARs, led by Stuart Bayliss of Annuity Direct, decided that the guaranteed annuity rate should not only be applied to the total of the premiums they had paid and the guaranteed reversionary bonuses allocated to their policies, but also to their non-contractual terminal bonuses.

In a mutual equitable Society, this extra money could, as I have mentioned, only come from other policyholders, who would thus be disadvantaged. It was this, which Lord Steyn apparently never understood, that destroyed the Equitable. All this and the process of disintegration was a ghastly traumatic experience for this relatively young man. The aberrational decision of Lord Steyn forced his resignation and now he was being sued in a court of law for several billions. It was as Kafkaesque for him as it was for us, but of course he had been the managing director during the relevant period. Personally I think he did very well; he had his wobbles of course, as we all did. I used to sit next to him during the trial and I found him remarkably equable and sanguine. Alan Nash is a good man and he was unlucky, just like all the other policyholders were unlucky with Lord Steyn decreeing the Society's demise. Again, as with Chris Headdon, most of the points put to him were framed with the benefit of hindsight – always a difficult position for the recipient of such questions, but he did well and I congratulated him at the end.

After Alan Nash left the box, Mark Hapgood QC got up for Ernst & Young as he wished to make a submission with regard to what he called the rapidly disintegrating case brought by the Society. He made a number of points, which Milligan in his usual way said he would reflect on overnight and perhaps take instruction as necessary. The following day after his period of reflection, he stood up to say that the Society was still going ahead with its various claims. At this point Mark Hapgood said the lost sale claim was hopeless, and on the assumption that the claim failed, Ernst & Young would be claiming costs on an indemnity basis. The Judge, who only intervened occasionally, commented in relation to the bonus cuts claim that there was a dilemma facing the Society in that large cuts would be self-defeating, whilst small cuts would achieve nothing. How right he was, and how interesting it was to observe that he was always well ahead of the game and always absolutely on top of the case. As I have said before, I formed a very high opinion of Mr Justice Langley and his intellectual acumen and perspicacity.

The next witness to go into the box was David Thomas, the Society's very able investment director. He was cross-examined by Robert Miles QC who put his questions in such an agonisingly slow way that one felt like jumping up and finishing them off for him. He also had a disconcerting habit of looking vaguely round the courtroom as if he had momentarily forgotten where he was, but perhaps that was because he needed so much time not only to frame the next question but also to get it out. In any case he made no headway against David; nor did he make any headway against the two remaining former executive directors, Roger Bowley and Shaun Kinnis, whose appearance in the box was his first and only visit to the courtroom.

One evening Robert Miles was invited to an 80th birthday dinner party in Skye to which my sister was also invited. He was placed next to her. For some 20 minutes he rambled on to her about the Equitable case he was on. After all this time my sister could not stand it any longer and told him that he was in court acting against her brother. He was suitably abashed, went quite quiet, and then appropriately apologised!

Now it was my turn to go over the top and face Milligan's machine gun. It was Tuesday, 14th of June. After nearly four long years, I was finally on trial and in the box. I was nearly 74 years old and here was I, a former senior director of Barclays Bank, defending myself against bankruptcy. Diana and Guy were in the public gallery and they were there to hang on my every word. For the last six months I had prepared myself for this astonishing, almost unreal ordeal. I recall that my greatest concern was not to be led by Milligan's cross-examination expertise and sophistry into agreeing with him to the point of incriminating myself. This is what I understood is the practice of barristers, that is to say they go round and round every point, so much so that you are led irretrievably into saying something which you should not have, and thereby are made to look and feel guilty. I resolved therefore to ignore most of Anthony Temple QC's advice, and go for it.

I had been chosen as the first non-executive director to go into the box and in fact I believe I volunteered to do this, not only because I had been the longest-serving non-executive director but also because John Sclater, the former president of the society, was not as physically strong as we would have wished in these particular circumstances of cross-examination and interrogation. There was no doubt in my mind that this was a show trial, but was it politically inspired?

I stepped up into the box. Every eye in the courtroom was staring up at me and I was sworn in by the Court Clerk. Our QC Lawrence

Rabinowitz then introduced me and I was asked to state my full name and home address. I was then asked to confirm my signature on my witness statement, and off we went.

Milligan's first question seemed very wide of the mark. He asked me whether I would agree that unlike a proprietary company, a mutual has no shareholders to influence the conduct of its business and that in reality policyholders have no effective powers, and that therefore the non-executive directors had a particularly important role to play in protecting the interests of the policyholders. Put like that, of course, the answer was yes, but the duties of a non-executive director of a company and a mutual are almost identical, so why did he ask the question?

His next question was about the introduction of the differential terminal bonus policy 12 years ago in 1993. My answer to this was that it was not a policy – it only became referred to as such very much later – and that all it was then was part of an actuarial amendment to the previous actuarial amendments made a year previously. Later on he asked me whether I had read in the board papers from November 1993 the paragraph which later on transmogrified itself into the differential terminal bonus policy (DTBP). I said I would have, but it would have meant nothing to me because it was an actuarial amendment in respect of policy classes, and without knowing the detail of every policy class and contract it would have meant nothing to me. I felt somewhat uncomfortable here, particularly when Milligan said it was incumbent on me as a non-executive director to read everything placed in front of me by the management and to have understood everything. To this I replied quite truthfully that I had no recollection 12 years later, but that I would have asked the management, as I always did, whether there was anything in these actuarial amendment statements which the management felt that they should specifically draw our attention to. I also said that if, as Peter Martin alleged, I had asked the management whether we were all right on contract with regard to that particular amendment, that is the sort of thing I would have asked.

I went on to say, and here I quoted from Mr Ranson's witness statement, that if he had been asked that question, he would have replied that: 'As I understood the policies as appointed actuary, there are no contractual issues'. To this Milligan responded by saying that Mr Ranson was not a lawyer, and knowing that, I should have asked if we had taken legal advice. This was one of the big claims against me, that I had been negligent in not seeking legal advice about what became known as the DTBP. To this my response was that when we did take legal advice in 1998 – as opposed to 1993 – all the Queen's Counsels had told us that what we had done was perfectly legitimate. And so it went on, backwards and forwards, and here I was being pressed hard, but then Milligan abruptly changed his attack and got on to this question of the terminal bonus.

I am convinced to this day that Lord Steyn, Lord Penrose and now Milligan never truly understood the real nature of a terminal bonus, or alternatively did not want to. I still believe this misconception, if it was one, arose from the practice of the Society to tot up all the indicative fund values of each policy and arrive at a certain figure. This indicative fund value illustrated as on one particular date, that is to say 31st December, consisted of the guaranteed fund value, plus the guaranteed interest and bonus for the preceding year, giving a new guaranteed fund value. On top of that there was an indicative final bonus addition, giving a total fund value of x. Now the mistake of the Equitable management was not to show on the front page of the policy statement that the final bonus was indicative, although if one turned over the statement page you could see it stated, loud and clear, that the final bonus was not guaranteed – nor of course could it be.

However, Milligan's point was that a policyholder seeing his total fund value on his statement sheet would have considered that his guaranteed annuity rate would apply to the total fund value and not just the guaranteed fund value. This was, of course, not the case. The terminal bonus was at the director's discretion; it was not guaranteed, it was not contractual and it was not consolidated in the company's accounts. The differential terminal bonus policy was used to ensure that the outgoing policyholder was delivered his personal asset share of the with-profits fund, no more and no less. When I said this to Milligan, I asked him what was wrong with that, to which his reply was that he was going to explore what was wrong with that in a moment. I was amazed – what could be wrong in a mutual and equitable Society providing an outgoing policyholder with his fair share of the with-profits fund?

But, of course, I then remembered that this was the genesis of the whole DTBP problem. Some GAR policyholders, egged on by

Mr Bayliss of Annuity Direct, felt that they should have more than their fair share of the equitable and mutual with-profits fund. The corollary being that if they got more than their fair share, then other policyholders would get less than theirs. How inequitable and unmutual can that be? The sad thing, of course, is that Lord Steyn went down the inequitable route.

Milligan then asked whether I would not agree that a GAR policyholder might be surprised to find that terminal bonus rates were being manipulated to deprive him of the GAR in his policy. No, I said, there was no manipulation, which was an outrageous suggestion anyway; because what we were doing was to give the outgoing policyholder his fair share of the with-profits fund. All this went backwards and forwards. Milligan then went on to ask me to agree with him that the with-profits fund as a whole should be used to subsidise the outgoing GAR policyholder. No, I said, that was impossible, because all profits and losses in any one particular class of policy had to be held within that particular class and not used to subsidise another policy class. I put it to him that why should the GAR policy class be preferred at the expense of another policy class in an equitable and mutual society?

Putting all this another way, I said that a non-GAR policyholder would be outraged if his savings were diverted by the Society to subsidise another policy class. And I went on to say later, warming to my theme, that it was Lord Steyn's edict to disallow ring-fencing between policy classes that sank the Equitable. This was his torpedo, as I have stated before. Milligan then got on to the intention of the DTBP, so I referred him to the last page of my witness statement and asked him to read it out in court, adding that it was most unfortunate that Lord Steyn did not see it that way – which may have been the understatement of the year.

Milligan then wandered back to his old theme that we should have taken legal advice and that perhaps a compromise scheme between the GARs and non-GARS might have been advisable, which could have been taken to court. Well, I said, it might have ended up in court, but all this had to be put into some sort of context and the context was the original reason why we had gone to court in the first place. We had simply asked the court whether we were allowed to differentiate between GAR policyholders choosing to take fund form benefits and those choosing to take the guaranteed annuity. The issue, said Elizabeth Gloster QC, who succeeded Lord Grabiner, was nothing to do with whether the society was allowed to differentiate between final bonuses to GAR and non-GAR policyholders. But, of course, what happened in the House of Lords was that Lord Steyn disregarded the terms of the originating summons, so that his judgment had everything to do with the poor unfortunate non-GAR policyholders, who were obliged to hand over £1 billion or so of their money to the now privileged GAR policyholders. It was one of the most inequitable judgments ever made by the House of Lords.

So that was that, and Milligan now moved over to the regulatory returns, which came before the Audit Committee. Here it had always been recognised that the basis on which these returns were compiled was significantly more stringent than the Companies Act accounts. We then got on to the subject of future profits.

When I was a bank manager, I disapproved of future profits. To my mind profits were either there or not there, but as I have mentioned earlier on, if you have an insurance book into which regular premiums are being paid over many years and these premiums contain an element of profit, then the profit embedded in these future contracted premiums can be anticipated, and thus you arrive at the embedded value of an insurance business. We then finally agreed that the Companies Act accounts showed a true, fair and realistic position, unlike the regulatory returns, which did not. I later asked myself why he had asked that question, and came to the conclusion that he wanted me to agree with him on something.

So ended my first day in the dock. The Judge rose and we all rose. He bowed. We all bowed. After he had gone, everybody started talking to each other – except me, as I was now in legal purdah.

It was one of the peculiar features of this very peculiar trial that whilst, on the one hand, I was being sued for several billion pounds, I was at one and the same time also apparently being cross-examined as an independent witness in the prosecution case against Ernst & Young. My difficulty was that I never really knew during this cross-examination, which went on for four days, which particular stance I was supposed to be adopting. In other words, like Janus, it seemed I was supposed to be facing in two directions at the same time!

After we had bowed ourselves out, Diana and I commuted back to Chelmsford on the train. I had a couple of strong drinks. In a way, I felt quite pleased with myself, but it was still almost impossible to really believe this was happening. Luckily, with the aid of some valerian hops, I slept quite soundly, but the next night was going to be very different.

At 10.30 a.m. the next morning, I was back in the box. Milligan was once again going on about the genesis of the DTBP and whether this time it had been discussed at a board meeting in 1996. I told him that was nine years ago, and I could not remember. Once again, I repeated that this detailed statement of terminal bonus was a technical paper for the actuaries and that this sort of technical minutiae could not possibly be the formal responsibility of a non-executive director who was not and could not be fully cognisant of the detail of each policy contract. After he had gone backwards and forwards on this for some time, he once again reverted to this question of legal advice with the implication that if we had not taken it, then we were negligent. He seemed very fixated on this legal advice and I had to remind him that when we did take legal advice, we were told that what we had done was perfectly legitimate. So it if was perfectly legitimate in 1999, then I had no doubt that it was perfectly legitimate in 1996. I also added that in my view the DTBP was equal and fair, and I told him that with the greatest respect to him as a lawyer, if being equal and fair was legally wrong, then I was living on the wrong planet.

Milligan continued to try and trip me up on this question of ring-fencing, that is, the requirement to keep the liabilities of one policy contract class within that class in the with-profits fund. But then he changed direction and we were now into a hypothetical Hyman test case in 1996, and an assumption that this hypothetical case had already started. I have to say here that I had huge difficulty with these endless assumptions based on hypotheses and I felt I had to remind Milligan that the dictionary definition of an hypothesis was that it was a groundless assumption!

My heart sank when he said, 'I am now going to ask you to make four assumptions. I know by now that you hate assumptions and four may be pushing my luck.' To this, I asked him to produce one assumption at a time, to which he replied, 'I appreciate that, Mr Tritton, but unfortunately I have to combine all four assumptions in order to get the point which interests me.' To this I said that I would have to write all four down and then try and wrap up my answer at the end. By the time I had scribbled down some of these assumptions, I had begun to lose track, and a further difficulty was that each assumption begged a number of questions in itself. Thus I entered a maze of hypotheses and assumptions and I began to lose patience with Milligan, something I was told never to do.

One of the oddities of this very peculiar trial was that Milligan's cross-examination did not seem to be entirely real. For instance, he seemed quite content to engage in philosophical excursions, digressions, detours and debates, so much so that one ended up discussing all sorts of questions and topics. Perhaps this is how all trials go. I had never been to one before. Certainly it was a novel experience for me and was far removed from Mr Anthony Temple's strictures to keep my answers as short as possible. So we wandered around the effects of the Common Market Life Directives, the history of the introduction of the DTBP in 1993, the philosophy of 'smoothing', and so on.

Then Mr Milligan started to talk about notional litigation, which I suppose was marginally removed from hypotheses and assumptions. What he was trying to say was that given this notional litigation, I should have been a little more cautious in allocating notional growth rates to policies. My reply to this was that if we had notionally reduced the growth rate at that declaration by say 1 per cent, and thus had notionally saved £18 million, then this was entirely marginal in the context of a fund of £30 billion. I said that on the contrary, my great concern was to reduce guaranteed liabilities, meaning by that guaranteed reversionary bonuses. These were real live liabilities as opposed to the notional and indicative final bonuses, which could be altered at any time. Mr Milligan responded to this by saying we were now going around in circles, to which quick as a flash I replied that at least it was a hypothetical circle. Mercifully, he smiled at this and agreed with me. So that was a relief. One needs such oases during a long drawn-out cross-examination.

He then got on to policy values and asset values, and here I knew we were going to disagree. Once again, I disputed his calculation of policy values, because his included a notional terminal bonus, which was neither contractual nor guaranteed, nor consolidated in the Accounts. I also asked him whether he knew that we had consistently under-allocated returns to policyholders over the last ten years with the exception of 1990 and 1994, which as we all knew had been poor years for investment returns. I went on to say that over the past ten years, cumulative investment returns of 146 per cent had exceeded allocated returns of 132 per cent, a net retention of some 14 per cent in the Fund for Future Appropriations. That can hardly be described as an over-allocation.

Nevertheless, he did return to what he described as over-allocation, and therefore the need to adopt a more cautious approach to growth rates. He reminded me of my awareness of the relative narrowness of the solvency margin and of the letters that I had written to the executive management about this. He then was kind enough to read excerpts from these letters to the Judge, which fortunately showed quite a considerable degree of prescience on my part. These also showed that I had put in a great deal of time and effort in focusing on the management of actual and potential risks to the Society. All this work now stood me in good stead.

Still moving along, we began discussing the CAR–GAR rate divergence, which I knew nothing about until September 1998. However, the assumption for the purpose of the trial was that I did know about this divergence. All this was in connection with taking a more cautious approach to the growth rate. I told Mr Milligan that I would not necessarily have looked at the widening of the divergence his way even if I had known about it. I told him that I would have looked at it in percentage terms, that the divergence was only marginal, and that in a long-term fund you only had to have a relatively small increase in interest rates and the divergence would disappear.

We were moving up to the lunch adjournment and now Mr Milligan was discussing with me the 1998 bonus decision and also Gordon Brown's raid on the pension funds when he abolished the dividend tax credit. This had the effect of removing £660 million from the pockets of the policyholders as the assets now had to be valued on a net-of-tax basis. Prior to that we had fortunately, as it happens, raised a subordinated loan stock of £346 million net, which assisted our solvency margin. However, like future profits, this raising was a source of deep suspicion to Mr Milligan as it might have been a marker in regulatory terms that the Society's capital was becoming constrained. In a sense this was partly true, but I told him that I was particularly glad we had done it as it partly offset the cost of Gordon Brown's raid. However, Mr Milligan did point out that this episode showed the problems of operating the Society without a large free estate. Well, you can say that, I replied, but the free estate in 1998 amounted to approximately £3 billion and in 1999, it was £5 billion, significant figures. Mr Milligan than asked me whether these figures referred to the Fund for Future Appropriations, to which I replied, 'Of course.'

At long last the lunch break arrived and I was off to the Seven Stars for a glass of wine and a cigarette and some cured herrings.

On my return, we got on to managing regulatory solvency; although it had always been a concern to me, it was not until we started receiving Chris Headdon's monthly solvency matrices that I had begun to feel uneasy. Accordingly, I had addressed my concerns to Alan Nash, who was now the managing director, in a letter and Mr Milligan read it out in court. If I say so myself, it was a good letter. We discussed his reply, and then we were back again to smoothing, asset values, policy values, and what was meant by policy values. This took us back again to the Fund for Future Appropriations, which as we all know by now represented the free assets of the Society, from which terminal bonus was paid when a policy came to maturity. There ensued a long discussion about the nature of this fund. All this seemed somewhat odd to me because it was perfectly obvious what it was, but Mr Milligan seemed suspicious about it and all this stemmed from our disagreement about policy values. Here I was in some difficulty, as unbeknownst to me till my Penrose interrogation, I was not aware that the Society added up all the fund values presented to policyholders, including the indicative or notional terminal bonus values. Sometimes these total fund values exceeded total asset values. I told Mr Milligan that the notional terminal bonus available could never be greater than the Fund for Future Appropriations, because in a sense the one was a reflector of the other. This discussion went round and round until Mr Milligan suddenly said he would like to have a ten-minute break, which the Judge kindly granted. This was not construed as a good sign in my favour, because it showed that Mr Milligan was losing patience with me as I was with him, but then he could and I, as the defendant, could not.

After the short break, Mr Milligan said that we were going to be re-entering the world of hypothesis, but this time it was to relate to Ernst & Young's position. Now I was supposed to mutate into an independent witness and theoretically forget about being a defendant. What a muddle. What Mr Milligan was trying to do with all his hypothetical assumptions was to find out what I, as a non-executive director and chairman of the Audit Committee, would have done if Ernst & Young had come along and said to me, 'Sorry, but we need to make a provision of a billion pounds or so in the audited accounts for these GAR liabilities.'

My reply to this was that I would not have believed it. Apart from anything else, how do you get from £245,000, which was the actual cost of the GARs in 1998, to over £1 billion in the same year? Furthermore, this latter figure presupposed that, firstly, interest rates would remain the same over the remaining period of the GAR book, say 30 years, and secondly, that every GAR would leave the fund at the same time. This made absolutely no sense at all. If one suddenly made a provision of £1 billion, it would not give a true and fair view of the Society's financial position.

Then I had the bright idea of giving an analogy of the Governor of the Bank of England (who was then responsible for the regulatory supervision of the commercial banks, until this responsibility was removed from him by Gordon Brown with catastrophic results vis-à-vis Northern Rock) telling himself that he had forgotten that all the deposits of the commercial banks are guaranteed repayable on demand or on maturity, and are therefore liabilities in the true sense of the word. Should he, I asked Mr Milligan, have made all the banks reserve fully for all those liabilities? No, of course not, because if he did so then the banks would not have had a business. In any case, I told Mr Milligan that all you would need to do if interest rates went lower would be to increase the precautionary provision; if interest rates went higher, you would decrease the provision; and if they went higher still then the need for a provision would disappear altogether. It would be quite wrong, I said, to provide fully for a liability which could disappear if interest rates went higher and, in any case, it would be grossly inequitable to out-going policyholders.

I then said that if Ernst & Young had insisted on such an absurd provision, then I would want to change the auditors. At this the whole court burst into laughter, although I had no intention of being amusing. I realised subsequently that this was the last thing I had been expected to say! And so it went backwards and forwards, with Mr Milligan trying to get me to agree with his assumptions. In the end, Mr Milligan gave up, saying that he was extremely tired of battling with me, and that was the end of the second day.

I was very concerned that evening about how to deal with these hypothetical assumptions when I could not agree with their basis. For instance, I said to myself, if Mr Milligan asked me to assume that God was dead, how on earth could I deal with that, when I believed the opposite? Furthermore, it occurred to me that my apparent non-cooperation might be proving counterproductive, so I resolved to say something to the Judge the following day. That evening I noted some adverse comment in the online EMAG *Motley Fool* about me possibly suffering from Alzheimer's.

The next morning I stood up in the dock, and delivered myself of the following words: 'My Lord, before we return to Mr Milligan's hypothetical world, can I just say two things about yesterday. First, I was under the impressic ᷎ that Mr Milligan was asking me to agree with his hypothetical assumptions. I think we rather got at cross-purposes on that. Secondly, on the basis that he is not asking me to agree with his hypothetical assumptions, then I will do my best to answer his questions.'

This seemed to clear the air. The Judge leaned over and said, 'That was very helpful, Mr Tritton.'

So now we were back in the world of hypothesis, with Mr Milligan telling me that he was grateful for the indication I had given to His Lordship. We then had a long discussion on the notional effect on the Society's finances of the sudden appearance of a GAR liability of £1 billion or so, and what we would have done to offset the effect. Together we explored what we might have done, or could have done and as it happens we generally agreed. Then I said that although we had been discussing the tools needed to ameliorate the apparent capital constraints, which would have arisen as a result of the appearance of this mythical liability, I myself would have looked at the position somewhat differently.

My position was that I had become increasingly aware that there were capital constraints, but that I believed this was quite separate from this supposed GAR liability. In that sort of situation, you could tinker around the edges, so to speak, but something more needed to be done and that should take the form of a capital injection. The best way to provide for this was by way of a demutualization, although I said this would be anathema both to the management and probably to most of the board. Mercifully this demutualization view of mine had been minuted in the board papers. This was picked up by Mr Milligan, who said that given a hypothetical additional GAR provision, I would have been particularly keen to have a capital injection, to which I replied, 'Yes, indeed.'

Mr Milligan then launched into a new set of assumptions regarding smoothing, which became circular. I told him once again that I got very confused with all his hypothetical assumptions, to which he replied, 'I know it is extremely wearying answering these questions, but I have to say it is extremely wearing asking them, too.'

I replied to this by saying, 'I am sure it is, but you are younger than I.'

To which he replied, 'At times, I feel I am catching you up fast.'

To give you some idea of this questioning process, let me set out one of our short assumptive dialogues.

M So if you could make this assumption for a moment. [The assumption being an eighty per cent chance of winning or a twenty per cent chance of losing the original Hyman litigation.]

AGT Yes, 80 per cent. No, 20 per cent.

M Yes, an 80 per cent chance of success or looked at the other way round, there is a 20 per cent risk of losing. The consequences are horrible if you lose.

RABINOWITZ QC Is that an assumption or an assertion?

M Take it as an assumption for now. We are still a while earlier in 1998, when you are making your bonus decision.

AGT Yes.

M So perhaps I could just ask you to assume for a moment that the same Hyman litigation has started, all right? [I hated his 'all rights'.]

AGT Yes. [I was on my best behaviour.]

M And that you have been told there is a 20 per cent risk of losing. [We had actually been told that what we had done was perfectly legitimate, so it was difficult for me to translate this into a 20 per cent risk of losing.]

AGT Losing in House of Lords terms or Court of Appeal terms?

M Well, I am going to break it into two parts. Of losing in the sense that the DTBP is inappropriate, all right?

AGT Within that policy class?

M Well, can I just add that extra bit now; but if you do lose it will be a House of Lords answer that you cannot ring-fence. Do you understand?

AGT Well that goes against every principle of the life insurance industry.

M Well that may be so, but could you just make that assumption. I am not going to hold you to that assumption.

AGT We are now again on assumptions. Yes?

M It is just an assumption. On that assumption, I would be right to understand that you would have wanted to be more cautious and gone for the twelve per cent growth rate rather than the 13 per cent actually agreed?

AGT In your hypothetical assumptive world, the answer is obviously yes.

M Would you have gone lower?

AGT No, I do not think so. The House of Lords decision was so utterly removed from the reality of the position, that you simply do not start wrecking a business on the offchance that the House of Lords will make that sort of decision. [That decision was nothing to do with the originating summons, which was solely confined to the GAR class.]

And so it went on and on – hypotheses, assumptions, notional values. All these eventually dribbled away and we were back in the real world of 1998 when the GAR crisis blew up.

We discussed the legal advice we had been given and, pleading deafness, which can be useful at times, I asked Mr Milligan to read it out:

Mr Headdon reported that the Society's lawyers, Denton Hall, are satisfied that the Directors have discretion regarding bonuses which are allocated to policies. Brian McGeough confirmed this latter point and referred to the wide powers given to the Society's Directors regarding declaring bonus. [This referred to Article 65, which the House of Lords decreed did not mean what it said.] He confirmed that in his opinion this enabled the Directors to take a differential approach between classes of policy and between benefits with a policy. He referred to the requirements that the Directors must do justice between different classes of policy holders and that is what they had done.

The next half-hour was so boring that I wondered whether Mr Milligan was going through the motions just for the sake of them. Mainly, we agreed with each other about events, discussions and debates following the emergence of the GAR problem. There were no particular polemics; everything, or more or less everything, had been disclosed. Then Mr Milligan started ruminating – that was his word not mine – on this question whether *the problem* could be confined to the GAR policy class. He said that in the light of what the former Appointed Actuary had said to me earlier, it was clearly my view that in the ordinary course of business, bonuses had to be kept within their own policy class. So, I thought, he had now got that message loud and clear: the House of Lords had got it wrong.

He then read out the management notes written after my group risk management meeting: 'Free assets/solvency – AGT thinks we need a higher margin – perhaps we need to reconsider our full distribution policy.' We discussed this and Mr Milligan said this was an example of me calling into question whether we should be proceeding as before. I asked him if I had done something wrong, and Mr Milligan gave me his highest praise and said what I had suggested was laudable! Why did he say that?

After that, we were back onto the Society's capital position and the decision to proceed with the Hyman litigation. Once again he reverted to this question of legal advice and I asked him to read out Lord Grabiner's advice, which effectively destroyed his case against me. This is what Lord Grabiner wrote:

> This low take up rate of GARs will have been very substantially influenced by the Society's practice, over the period, of adjusting the final bonuses of any given policyholder so as to ensure, in as far as it is possible, that the value of the benefits if taken in guaranteed annuity form is no greater than the cash fund available to provide for an annuity on current rates. This practice is and has always been wholly within the discretion of the Board exercising the wide discretions conferred on them by Article 65 of the Society's Articles of Association. Policyholders have no contractual right to have final bonuses allotted or otherwise made available in advance of the Board exercising such discretion in their favour and it has been made abundantly clear throughout the Society's literature, including the annual statements issued to policyholders, that any illustrated final bonuses are entirely non-guaranteed prior to their actual allotment to the policy in fact and not the subject of any right or entitlement in advance of such allocation.

Amen, amen, and now it was time for lunch.

During this break, Mr Milligan dug out of his files Mr Green QC's opinion and read it out in court for the benefit of the transcript. It said: 'The Board's decision to seek to achieve a result under which all persons holding similar policies achieve the same investment return, irrespective of whether some policyholders had the benefit of guaranteed annuity rates applicable to guaranteed benefits is perfectly legitimate.' So how could that be transmuted into a 20 per cent risk of losing? Mr Milligan said he entirely understood what I was saying and that what we had done according to Queen's Counsel was perfectly legitimate. If it was, then why was I in the dock? The trial was a sham and a put-up job.

Then there was a sort of toing and froing: nothing awkward or difficult about my request to the Managing Director to be careful about going forward with the litigation in the first place; about my establishment of a special committee to deal with the GAR problem; my writing to Jonathan Taylor, another non-executive director, to inform him that I had 'bitten the bullet', in the sense that I had hopefully got to grips with the problem. This was a nice nineteenth-century expression, as I put it, to which Mr Milligan responded, quick as a flash, 'not unconnected with 1857', referring to the main cause, as I was, of the Indian Mutiny in that year. We then got on to my proposals for demutualization, all of which were minuted and which clearly found favour with him. Perhaps he was trying to do me a good turn?

He also read out a letter which I had written to the President about his draft statement to policyholders in respect of 1998. I had forgotten all about this, but I quote:

> Bearing in mind the present position, I just wonder whether it is sensible to re-iterate the philosophy of distributing profits fully and fairly without building up unnecessary reserves, now that we need to strengthen our reserve position. We have been through this countless times, but I query we should emphasise this, when you could say that this full distribution of profits and consequent lack of internal reserves have led to our solvency problem.

All this was music to my ears. Perhaps Milligan's heart was not really in it. It seemed curious that a prosecuting Queen's Counsel should extol a defendant's cautious and prudential virtues.

After this Mr Milligan asked me to re-enter the hypothetical world, presupposing that the auditors had insisted on a contingent liability note concerning the original Hyman litigation and the possibility of an additional liability amounting to some £1.5 billion if we lost the litigation, and also the ability to ring-fence. It was a curious hypothetical world we were in; a precautionary provision of £50 million, which we had prudently increased to £200 million or the Government Actuary Department figure of £1.5 billion. My response was that the Institute of Actuaries had apparently told the management that what we were doing was perfectly valid, so had the Government Actuary's Department (originally in their letter to us dated 18 December 1998), all our QCs and even the auditors, who had said that under the Standard Accounting Practice rules (I think it was number 17) it would have been positively misleading to have inserted such a note in the accounts, because the possibility of any economic transfer was remote.

Now Mr Milligan said we were going to re-enter the real world again and he again reverted to this matter of ring-fencing and the keeping of policy classes separate, which I had been told was a fundamental principle of the life insurance industry, and which in any case made perfect sense. We then discussed discrimination, and I told him that Lord Steyn did indeed discriminate against the non-GARS. First of all he landed them with a fine of £1 billion or so, and secondly, because he did not seem to be aware that under the terms of their contract the GARS could continue to pay variable premiums into their policies and continue to gain the benefit of the GAR, he thus created with his own fair hand a massive black hole in the accounts which had made the Society unsaleable. The reason for this was that nobody would buy a business which had an unknown and unquantifiable liability imposed on it by the House of Lords! There was dead silence at this blasphemy from all the assembled lawyers, but it was of course true, and as the Equitable Members Action Group put it that night in their online newsletter: 'it was now perfectly obvious that the no ring-fencing judgement of Lord Steyn was totally idiotic'. Their words, not mine.

Mr Milligan then continued at some length as to whether we should have taken legal advice on this subject of ring-fencing. To this I replied that the originating summons was nothing to do with the non-GARS. It was solely to do with the GARS, and nobody in their wildest nightmares thought that the House of Lords would disregard the summons and involve the non-GARS. As a final blast, I told Mr Milligan that in any case Lord Steyn had only got there by implying something in the articles of association which was not there.

This seemed to finish off Mr Milligan, and that was the end of his cross-examination. He told me that I had been very patient and courteous and I in my turn thanked him very much for his patience and courtesy. It had been a very curious four days of cross-examination, not to be recommended for someone in their seventy-fifth year. I had had enormous difficulty with all his hypotheses and assumptions. I thought, presumably in my ignorance, that lawyers were supposed to deal with the facts and not theories made up with the benefit of hindsight, so it was all a very novel experience for me. The main thought which kept on recurring to me throughout my time in the box was, did Mr Milligan really advise or think there was a case against us, or was he just going through the motions? He must have known that it was not us but the House of Lords who torpedoed the society.

After my cross-examination was over, the EMAG online reporters wrote that Tritton had all his marbles, no trace of Alzheimer's; that he had had an interesting discussion with Mr Milligan and that he had come across as a very astute, cultured, retired commercial banker with an independent mind. Not only that, they opined that if Tritton had been an executive director, things might have been different, and that it was a pity he had retired in 1999. That was a real clap on the back, but the supreme accolade came from my son, Guy, who said that I had been magnificent, charismatic and magisterial – wonderful words for a father to hear from his son.

I had now to be cross-examined by the other lawyers, and first of all came Mr Sher, the Queen's Counsel for David Wilson, another non-executive director. I think it was now 3.45 p.m.

Mr Justice Langley leant over and said, 'Mr Tritton, do you want to take on Mr Sher for a quarter of an hour, or do you want to go home?' I said that I would quite like to take on Mr Sher, to which he replied, 'Very good', and up jumped Mr Sher, who said that 'sounds ominous to me Mr Tritton', and I replied ,'I am bigger than you.'

So Mr Sher set off, but it was all quite easy and in a quarter of an hour he had finished. At the end he said, like Mr Milligan,

'Mr Tritton, you have been very patient, it was not too bad, was it. Thank you very much.'

To which I replied, 'I will go home quite happy.'

It was now Monday, 20th June and Mr Leaver, the QC for Jennie Page was cross-examining me. It was friendly fire. Unbeknown to me Guy had given him the excerpt from the judgment of Lord Woolf in the Court of Appeal which during my cross-examination by Milligan I could not quite point to, so Mr Leaver read it out for my benefit and that of the court.

It read: 'In my judgement no criticism of the management or the Policyholders of the Society is justified. If the Society is entitled to adopt the course, which it has then having regard to its responsibility for *all* the policyholders it seems to me that what it is seeking to achieve is perfectly reasonable.'

He later read out a part of my Witness Statement. In it I said:

It is said that I ought to have considered whether the GAR had any purpose if the Society was entitled to award GARs and non-GARs policyholders' benefits of the same value. If a GAR policyholder exercised his right to take a guaranteed annuity, the guarantee rate applied to the composite sum of the basic sum assured, the guaranteed reversionary bonuses and the adjusted terminal bonus. Upon a policy maturing, his policy would have benefited from substantial guaranteed reversionary bonuses. On those sums he was entitled to receive a guaranteed rate, without any adjustment of these amounts. Plainly there was considerable value to a GAR.

It is said by the Society that the effect of the DTBP was to benefit those with-profits policyholders not exercising a GAR at the expense of those that did exercise a GAR. That is simply not correct. A GAR policyholder who exercised his right to a GAR was never worse off than a non-GAR policyholder. The purpose of the DTBP was to ensure that a GAR policyholder who exercised his right was not substantially better off than a non-GAR policyholder or a GAR policyholder who did not exercise his right. The reason for this was to ensure that those who exercised their rights did not take more than their fair share of their contribution to the Society's funds.

At that Mr Leaver sat down and Mr Mumford the lawyer for

Mr Ranson got up, and we got on to the divergence between the GAR rates and the CAR rates, which was of course changing all the time – the GAR rate being fixed, and the CAR rate variable. At one point Milligan jumped up querying the rates – Milligan said one thing, Mumford said another and in the end I got lost, as did the Judge, who told me not to worry. Finally it had to be put to Chris Headdon, the fount of all actuarial wisdom and knowledge, who produced the right answer, and so we proceeded.

I don't think I want to take you through my Mumford and Headdon cross-examination, which was all friendly fire and easily disposed of. The cross-examination by Mark Hapgood QC for Ernst & Young however was different, as it had to be, because I was not being cross-examined as a defendant now but as a witness and it was, of course, my evidence and also that of the other non-executive directors which Herbert Smith thought would bring Ernst & Young down; having even observed, as I have mentioned earlier, that it was in our interests so to do.

Although Hapgood's cross-examination was intensely interesting to me, particularly as I had been chairman of the Audit Committee during most of the relevant period and as such had worked closely with Ernst & Young, nevertheless the greater part of it was highly technical.

Suffice it to say that we discoursed on demutualisation, flotation, rights issues, the distribution policy of the Society, viable sale structures, technical provisions, the commercial cost of GARs, the possibility or impossibility to my mind of spreading the GAR costs over all with-profits policy values, the Hyman case, the 1998 bonus decision, the absurdity of the Government Actuary's Department's position on reserving for GARs as opposed to the commercial true and fair position, disclosure notes about the Hyman litigation, contingent liabilities, the returns on the with-profits fund and the allocation of those returns to policyholders, changes in the actuarial basis of the valuation of liabilities, the variation between the GAR rate (fixed) and the CAR rate (variable), and so on.

I cannot recall that there was any disagreement between Hapgood and myself. What he said made good sense to me, particularly as we were discussing the real world and not the hypothetical world inhabited by Milligan, in which I quite often got lost. Mark Hapgood told me later that he had been very impressed with my evidence, and it was my evidence that had been the swing factor in the case against Ernst & Young. I think it was four months later that the Society quit their case against Ernst & Young, blaming in the process both the executive and the non-executive directors.

It was now Rabinowitz's turn to re-examine me and he used that opportunity, *inter alia*, to read out some of the legal advice we had been given by the lawyers. Brian McGeough, our Denton's lawyer, had confirmed and referred to the wide powers given to the Society's directors regarding declaring bonus (article 65 of the articles of association). He confirmed that in his opinion this enabled directors to take a different approach between classes of policies and between benefits within a policy. He then went on to Mr Green QC and the attendance note of a conference with him in September 1998.

Mr Green was asked, 'Does the board's discretion permit it to award different bonuses to different classes of policyholders and within any class, to different policyholders depending on the policyholder's choice of benefits?' Mr Green's answer was yes.

Rabinowitz went on further, reading out Mr Green QC's advice: 'Does Counsel agree with instructing solicitors that under Article 65 of the Society's Articles of Association, the Board of the Society has a complete discretion as to the allotment of bonuses amongst policyholders? Counsel agreed and stated that the Court will *not* interfere with the bona fide exercise of discretion by the Trustees i.e. the Board.' Mr Green had then gone on to say:

In particular I confirmed that the Society was *justified* in law in adopting the approach of declaring different final bonuses in order to ensure (so far as was possible having regard to the operation of guaranteed annuities on previously guaranteed values) that the ultimate cash value of any given policy would be a single sum irrespective of whether the policyholder took the guaranteed benefits under his policy or elected to take an alternative annuity based on an application of current annuity rates.

With a few more questions Rabinowitz came to a stop, and that was the end of my ordeal in the box. Of course I was glad it was all over, but in a curious way I had enjoyed battling with the QCs and I found it all quite stimulating and exciting. As far as I knew, I had been the first non-executive director of a major company ever to have been taken to trial, let alone sued for billions of pounds. But what gave me the self-confidence, sometimes even the ill-concealed impatience I had displayed in the box, albeit from time to time somewhat incoherently? Well, the short answer to this is that I had prepared myself exceptionally thoroughly for the case, had my own view on all the major issues, and I had no hesitation in expressing them. I also had most of the facts, figures and details at my fingertips. Fortunately I have a good retentive memory and this served me in good stead. As somebody once said to me, 'Bankers, like elephants, never forget.'

We were not quite at the end though, because there were still Jennie Page and Peter Martin to take their turns in the tumbril. Jennie Page excelled herself, but Peter, who had been a litigant in person for several years and had waged an unceasing guerrilla war against Herbert Smith, began to take a somewhat one-off line. We had originally been content for him to bring up the rear, so to speak, because as a lawyer we felt he would be able to bring all our defences together and thus deliver the knockout blow. But we felt less confident as time went on that he would do this. To my mind this was because he felt he was going on trial as a lawyer first and a non-executive director second. The whole litigation had been an appalling experience for him as a lawyer, and I sensed that he felt very badly let down by his own profession, particularly as the whole case against us had no merit at all. Here he was, a retired senior partner of a respected law firm, being accused by colleagues of breach of duty, negligence and everything else they could throw at him. It was unthinkable and very hurtful to him.

Thus it was that we felt we should take some precautions. This meant that we instructed our two barristers to be present in court when Peter was being cross-examined, in case he took a different line not wholly in accordance with ours. As it happens, it was fortunate that we did so. However all's well that ends well, and there was no harm done in the end. I count myself very fortunate to have Peter as a friend, particularly in the early dark days of this terrible legal experience when he held my hand and gave me hope. Thank you, Peter.

After Peter had been cross-examined, Mr Hapgood got up and informed the Judge that he did not propose to advance any factual evidence and that they had made this decision following their assessment of the directors' evidence. He said that the case against Ernst & Young was now hopeless. Now why did he do this? Presumably the answer is that they were now more or less sure of winning the case based on our evidence, and did not want the waters muddied by any cross-examination of their witnesses.

All this elicited a very curious nine-page letter from our friends Herbert Smith. First of all, they stated that it was in their experience unprecedented for professional persons charged with negligence not to defend their professional conduct when that conduct remains an issue. What all this really meant, they said, was that Ernst & Young had finally recognised that their audit of the society's accounts was indefensible and that they had chosen not to call any factual evidence so as to avoid their audit work being ridiculed in cross-examination; that this decision was a tacit admission of negligence; and that their defence to the allegations of negligence was hopeless. Furthermore they opined that much of the hypothesis on which Hapgood cross-examined us was false; that our evidence highlighted a problem in the evidence of all the directors; that at the pre-trial review in February 2005 they had raised this question of friendly cross-examination; that all our evidence had been obtained by leading us down carefully constructed paths, on occasions adducing evidence directly contradictory to that which we had given when being cross-examined by Herbert Smith's counsel; that this should never have been permissible and that, therefore, little if any weight should be given to the evidence of all the directors; that it was apparent from the way we had given our evidence that we were palpably hostile to the Society's case against Ernst & Young and that therefore our evidence was unreliable, and so on. All this was good Herbert Smith stuff. Clearly they had deluded themselves into thinking that we were bound to incriminate Ernst & Young in the hope of saving our necks.

It was about this time that Mr Treves and the Equitable dropped their lost sale claim against Ernst & Young for £1.3 billion. Ernst & Young's solicitor, the beautiful Clare Canning of Barlow Lyde & Gilbert, claimed that, 'Equitable has had finally to face the obvious. It's no surprise to us given that from day one, we said that the claim was rubbish.' She went on to say, 'This is one of the worst examples ever seen of the disreputable tactic of making a hugely inflated claim, now admittedly hopeless, against a deep pocket in the hope of forcing a settlement out of fear of litigation risk.'

536

The Equitable had been equally scathing in public about the last-minute withdrawal of the Ernst & Young partners due to be defence witnesses. Mr Treves in his inimitable style went on the record to state that: 'E&Y must now recognise that their defence to this allegation in the claim for negligence still on the table is bleak, fruitless and doomed to failure and we call on them to admit negligence.'

By this time nobody knew where they were, and this seemed to include the Judge. He looked at Milligan and said: 'It is all different now. We have finished the factual evidence, but we have, as you rightly pointed out, a considerable amount of expert evidence to come. What are you seriously aiming at and it would be helpful to everybody to know the answer to that.' He then went on to say 'what are you going to put to this Court that enables it to disbelieve the Directors? The response I have read is one which I do not think has been suggested to any Director in the course of these proceedings and there has been ample opportunity so to do. You are entitled, Mr Milligan, to say wait and see the closing submission but it would be helpful to at least know where you are coming from in a little more detail'.

It was on that note that the court adjourned to 19th September, a legal vacation of something like seven weeks. It seemed that not even the Judge knew where we were, because if he had, he would not have asked all those questions of Milligan and he seemed to be as frustrated as we were. So there we were: we were in a muddle; the Judge seemed to be in a muddle; Herbert Smith was certainly in a muddle; Milligan was in a muddle because he could not answer the Judge's criticism; and Ernst & Young were in a muddle because there were glaring inconsistencies in the case which had been put to us and to them – so perhaps it was true that Mr Treves and Herbert Smith had never expected the litigation to go to trial and their bluff had been called. It was at this moment that Herbert Smith, with their usual delicacy, sent us a revised timetable of the trial, starting on 19th September and going all the way through to just short of Christmas, and we reminded ourselves of Mr Treves's earlier remarks about Christmas.

The following day we had a meeting at Allen & Overy to consider the trial so far. I was there with Guy, the most supportive son I could ever hope for. It was felt that generally matters had gone very well. It was thought that we had impressed the Judge and that we represented a good board of directors. It was felt that Milligan now realised he was in a weak position, and that the case against Ernst & Young was hopeless. Equally the Ernst & Young barristers had reported that they thought the case against us as directors was also hopeless. It was also considered that if he could have, the Judge would have halted the proceedings. So all this sounded hopeful.

Meanwhile Peter Davis was constantly monitoring our legal costs against budget. He was exceptionally thorough in all this and very detailed, as perhaps befitted a former senior partner of Price Waterhouse. We all owe him our deepest gratitude. The figures he produced monthly were of course in respect only of the Allen & Overy Six. So far we had spent something like a £1 million between us on two excellent barristers, and this had had to come out of our own pockets. For Allen & Overy the figure was just under £3 million I recall, but because we were all on a conditional fee agreement, the figures were totted up and did not have to be paid. It was always a worry that under the terms of the agreement a settlement was regarded as a win, in which case a 50 per cent success fee would be levied. Adding everything up, I recall our overall costs had reached the dizzy height of about £5.5 million, of which my share was around £800,000. Clearly there could be no settlement unless the Society agreed to pay our costs. If they did not, we would be bankrupt, and if they won we would be bankrupt anyway – not a nice choice, and strong nerves were needed.

Towards the end of August 2005, Allen & Overy received a letter from Herbert Smith purporting to make an offer of settlement on a 'drop hands' basis, conditional on all the directors agreeing, and a settlement with Ernst & Young. The first condition could, of course, not be fulfilled – everybody's position was different – and the second condition was up in the air and outside our control. So the offer was rejected and Herbert Smith were reminded that costs were still running at a very significant rate, particularly in connection with the closing written submissions and the forthcoming cross-examination of the expert witnesses.

The next thing we heard was that Ernst & Young had originally in July offered to settle on a drop hands basis, but this had been rejected by Herbert Smith who were holding out now for £30 million – a far cry from their claim for billions. This had now changed and Herbert Smith were now offering to settle with Ernst & Young on a drop hands basis. There seemed a good chance of a settlement between the Society and Ernst & Young in which both sides paid their costs.

By now, in early September, Ernst & Young were beginning to feel rather bullish in the sense that rather than drop hands, they were interested in getting some of their costs back from the Society. The negotiations with Herbert Smith were becoming difficult, firstly because Charles Plant kept on changing his mind, and secondly because he had chosen this time of all times to disappear off on holiday and nobody seemed to quite know where he was. Our position had not changed, of course. We had to get our costs, and these were rising quickly and had now reached the figure of £5.8 million, and if indemnity costs were included the figure rose to £6,237,000.

On Friday, 16th September, three days before the trial was due to restart, we heard that Ernst & Young had agreed a settlement in principle with the Society. Although we were not told that it was on a drop hands basis, we assumed it was. Clare Canning for Barlow Lyde & Gilbert, as she described it, had been beating her head against a brick wall with Herbert Smith, as with Mr Plant away she was dealing with a junior partner, Julian Copeman, and she felt he was out of his depth, or alternatively was receiving conflicting instructions. She told us that Herbert Smith had said that they meant to take a strong line on costs with us. To this Clare Canning replied that she had told them that they would have to pay our costs. There appeared to be some movement, but not enough to stop the trial starting off again on the 19th, and this it duly did.

I did not attend the court because from now on it would be expert witness against expert witness until the time came – and we hoped it would not – for the closing submissions. Jonathan Gaisman, for E&Y, cross-examined Mr Law, a partner of PricewaterhouseCoopers who had been called by the Society as their expert witness. He was, of course, not an independent witness as PricewaterhouseCoopers were the new auditors to the society, having taken over from Ernst & Young. Even Mr Justice Langley expressed incredulity at some of his answers. When Jonathan Gaisman said to the poor Mr Law at one point that he simply could not believe they were having this conversation, the Judge interrupted and said that neither could he. Apparently, however, it was all not one way, and although he came under intense cross-examination, in the end he did not in fact resile from his report conclusions concerning Ernst & Young's audits of the Society's books.

The following day the Society decided to abandon its claims amounting to £2.6 billion against Ernst & Young, and they did so without any admission of liability or concession by Ernst & Young. In fact the Society had to pay a substantial amount to Ernst & Young in respect of the latter's costs. The Senior Partner of Ernst & Young stated in a press release that the past four years since the legal proceedings began had been a scandalous waste of money, time and resources. He went on to say that the management of the Society's sole strategy had been to bully them into settlement by bringing a hugely inflated claim against them, and the whole matter had been a disastrous misjudgement which had wasted tens of millions of pounds of policyholders' monies. Similarly, he continued, the claim against former directors had caused considerable and unwarranted distress and cost to a group of individuals who were seeking to discharge their responsibilities in a conscientious and responsible way.

Mr Treves's statement was that:

> The Society launched this hugely technical and complex litigation having taken expert audit and actuarial guidance and having received clear legal advice. But now having received firm advice from our legal team, the Board has now decided to settle. We remained confident of proving that Ernst & Young's audit was negligent; indeed even its own independent financial witnesses were unable to fully support the basis of the Audit. But the evidence given by the former Directors in Court has persuaded us that there is too great a risk that the Judge would find as a matter of fact that the former Directors would not have done anything differently whatever Ernst & Young would have done or said. Or alternatively that they would have taken steps to mitigate the problems but not ones which would allow the Society to claim losses from Ernst & Young. We have therefore concluded that the risk of establishing audit failure but not establishing a recoverable loss to the Society is too high to justify continuing the litigation.

So we were to blame for the failure of the Society's action against Ernst & Young, and because of that Mr Treves had clearly decided to continue his litigation against us, despite having said he was only going to sue us to get at the deep financial pocket of Ernst & Young. Well, he had lost their deep pocket, but why continue against us when to all intents and purposes we had no money? Except David Wilson, and in any case he was the least culpable, if there indeed was any culpability at all. To all of us there seemed to be a nasty smell of vindictiveness about continuing a totally pointless trial.

Ernst & Young's lawyers were not unnaturally cock-a-hoop. Mark Hapgood condemned the action as: 'this very long, costly and utterly pointless litigation which has culminated in the biggest climb-down in English legal history. It started at £3.6 billion, came down to £2.3 billion, down again further to £2 billion then to £700,000 and now it was down to zero.'

Jonathan Gaisman had stated that: 'it must be unique in a claim against an auditor, which depends on factual causation, that a company does not adduce a single piece of evidence from the relevant managers or directors that they would have done what the Society now say. On the contrary the claimant has to advance its case directly in the teeth of the cogent and unequivocal evidence of the Society's management and Board that they would in fact have done no such thing.'

As an aside here on my part, I thought it was pretty clear in our Witness Statements as to what we would have done or not done, and for the Society to claim that our evidence was a surprise to them, when I believe it was in our witness statements, showed either that they had never bothered to read our witness statements or that they never expected the case to come to trial. My guess is both. I had always had the feeling that Herbert Smith never seriously read any of my successive witness statements or defence statements because they continually repeated mistakes which I continually pointed out to them.

But once again I would refer to Mr Treves's statement that he had clear legal advice to litigate in the first instance. But whose legal advice was it and why was it never disclosed? It would have saved a huge amount of time and policyholders' money, if it had been. I remain convinced that it never existed as advice per se, and that it was all made up. And you have to remember that this advice, if it did indeed exist, must have been exactly the opposite of our very clear legal advice, and we disclosed our legal advice. To us, it still remains a mystery.

Coincidentally with all this, we received a letter from Herbert Smith repeating that their drop hands offer was still on the table and it was negotiable, but that the Society would not contemplate the payment of any of the directors' costs. Nobody knew quite what was meant by this letter, as to all intents and purposes only David Wilson could pay his costs and the rumour was that these had now risen to the dizzy height of £6 million.

Peter Martin chose this time to write an open letter to Herbert Smith, which he copied to the Attorney General, about the letter Mr Treves had written to the policyholders explaining why they had backed down in their litigation case against Ernst & Young. He said that the Society had had upwards of four years to investigate in correspondence what the former directors would have done vis-à-vis Ernst & Young, and in any case it had been set out in our witness statements. Why, therefore, was the Society taken aback by our oral evidence, with the innuendo that the directors had lied on oath to protect Ernst & Young? He wrote that what Treves's letter was clearly trying to do was to mislead the policyholders into believing that in some way the Society was entitled to evidence from us that would make good the wholly preposterous case against Ernst & Young, while at the same time suing the former directors. He regarded the Treves letter as a contempt issue, which should give rise to a defamation claim. He concluded by saying that everybody knew that the House of Lords bore the real responsibility for the Equitable demise. Whether or not he received a reply to this letter I do not know.

Meanwhile there were calls for the resignation of the present board, particularly Mr Treves and Charles Thomson, whilst the Equitable Members Action Group wrote to say that Milligan should waive his fee in the light of the most inept and embarrassingly incompetent performance ever seen in a British court of law. This was to my mind somewhat unfair to Milligan, because he did not have a case. Therefore the question is why did he take on the case when he must have known that there was no case? Another member of the action group wrote that it was his belief that the four days of Charles Thomson's testimony in the witness box hopelessly holed any possibility of success below the waterline, and that he was the weakest of all the witnesses who took the stand.

The next day we received another letter from Herbert Smith written to all the legal representatives of the defendants and the litigants in person, in answer to a suggestion by one of the lawyers that we should all meet to discuss a settlement. They did not want to attend such a meeting, but they suggested we should all meet without them. They then went to say that they thought we ought to bear in mind this question of the separate representation of the various director defendants and that they, Herbert Smith, had always taken the view that there was no justification for this. Now this sort of comment, coming from a law firm who was suing each director defendant individually, all of whom had different positions (some were executive directors, most were non-executive directors, some had retired at different dates, and so on), was ludicrous in the extreme. In a sense it may have shown their frustration at being harassed throughout the litigation by seven different law firms all representing different director defendants, and also two litigants in person who were exceptionally active, and of course, at one remove, all the lawyers representing Ernst & Young.

On 24th September 2005 we had a meeting to decide on tactics with regard to settlement. We decided to do nothing and await developments from both Herbert Smith and the solicitors for David Wilson, because if he settled, that removed the remaining economic purpose of the litigation. Meanwhile we heard that both Peter Martin and Shaun Kinnis had settled on a drop hands basis. As a litigant in person, Peter Martin had not run through his Directors and Officers Insurance pot of £330,000, whilst Shaun Kinnis had exhausted his pot but, as I understood, with little overhang of his own money.

While all this was going on and continuing to go on, our personal tension levels were rising. Mine had always been at a high level but now they were going even higher. There was a feeling of 'so near but yet so far', and I did not like the drop hands settlements which Peter Martin and Shaun Kinnis had concluded and David Wilson was probably about to conclude. We could not possibly afford to settle on such a basis. Every hour of the day and often at night, as had been the case for the past four years, we could not think of anything else, although we had to try and carry on our lives. Our lives were dominated by emails, the telephone and articles in the press. It is extraordinarily difficult to cope with continuous uncertainty, and the litigation and trial was similar to a mental cancer which gnawed on us all the time. Every morning when we woke up (at least I was able to sleep with the help of my valerian hops), Diana and I reviewed the position in bed before we got up and discussed the odds. Every morning we read the papers searching for clues, and we conferred constantly with Guy for reassurance and hope. It was a terrible time we were living through, and our position demanded a mental stamina which I do not think I really possessed. There were also wild swings between depression and hope as the litigation moved through to its climax.

On 7th October 2005, our senior lawyer Tim House wrote to Herbert Smith on behalf of the Allen & Overy Six stating that our costs including the uplift under the conditional fee agreement now amounted to £7.2 million and estimated that our costs to the end of the trial would be to the order of £6,300,000. Of this figure £1,980,000 could be deducted, representing our pots under the Directors and Officers Insurance arrangements. Having done some sums Tim House told Herbert Smith that subject to the formal consent of the D&O insurers we would settle at a figure of just over £5 million, and that we required an answer by that evening.

This was followed by a meeting on 10th October between Tim House, Charles Plant – who had at long last returned from holiday – and his underling Julian Copeman. Herbert Smith at the end of the meeting stated that the Society was prepared to offer £1 million in respect of our costs of £7 million gross and Jennie Page's costs, which I recollect were roughly to the order of £2 million. To this our answer was that they had already lost the case. They had now settled with David Wilson, the only director with any substantial assets. Treves and Thompson would not survive the attack the Judge was likely to make in his judgment on the Society's motives and their conduct of the litigation.

In particular, Tim House said that Herbert Smith were very exposed for three reasons. Firstly, because Julian Copeman's witness statement served in response to Tim House's evidence in the summary judgement application would come under intense scrutiny in the context of an application for indemnity costs. The reason for this was because his witness statement contained material for which we thought there was no basis, and this had been demonstrated as the trial unfolded. Secondly, because Herbert Smith had deliberately removed relevant material from Cindy Leslie's witness statement concerning communications with policyholders. And thirdly, because Herbert Smith had 'spun' the legal advice given in relation to the original Hyman litigation for the purposes of attacking the directors and in doing so they had exposed the Society to mis-selling claims quite needlessly. As an aside here, you will remember that in their dealings with the Ombudsman they had only given this person the particulars of their claims against us and not our defences, so the Ombudsman relied on the former to the Society's detriment, although Herbert Smith had made some last-ditch attempts to try and reverse this, thus hopelessly compromising themselves.

Tim House went on to say: that the Society had had every opportunity to settle the litigation, firstly at the mediation, and secondly when Calderbank letters were sent in 2004, which Herbert Smith ignored and left unanswered; that Plant and Copeman should appreciate that we regarded them and their clients as bearing a personal responsibility for destroying the last four years of the directors' lives which had cost them a fortune; that Plant and Copeman had tried at every turn to bully us into submission but that they should appreciate that we were principled, courageous and determined people, who intended to stand up to these bullying tactics (I would have used the words 'intimidatory tactics'); that we wanted proper payment for our legal costs that we were prepared to fight on and thus achieve vindication through Langley's judgment, and so on. Charles Plant responded to this attack without much vigour or conviction and stated that he would go back to the Society and seek further instructions.

So the pressure was on, and it was a relief that the Society had for the first time abandoned its previous 'non-negotiable' stance. Perhaps the best thing to do was to do nothing, just like the tactics of Marshal Kutuzov during Napoleon's invasion of Russia in 1812. So we did nothing. Herbert Smith came back with an offer of £2.5 million and we immediately rejected it, stating that we had offered the Society the opportunity to reduce its exposure to costs from £8 million to £5 million, a reduction as a result of our not insisting on costs reimbursed by the D&O insurers and costs which we had all incurred as litigants in person. Once again we stated we would settle at £5.2 million.

Herbert Smith came back with a letter dated 13th October 2005, stating that the reality was that it was the conditional fee agreements which we had entered upon with Allen & Overy that were the cause of the present difficulties, and there was obviously some truth in this. The offer of £2.5 million was proposed again and we rejected it. This elicited a telephone call from Charles Plant to Tim House, from which Tim House got the impression that they now seriously wanted a settlement and wanted to avoid the settlement negotiation becoming personal. Charles Plant did not seem to understand that when 15 directors are sued for several billions of pounds, this is seen as personal; once again an astonishing naiveté on the part of Herbert Smith. Tim House told Charles Plant that the litigation was in fact exceedingly personal, and that Herbert Smith was approaching the negotiations as if they were acting for an investment bank who was trying to settle some difficult financial litigation. So Tim House put the screws on Charles Plant and after a time he became more conciliatory, although he brought up Peter Martin's evidence once again, which purported to weaken our position.

By this time we were all getting fed up with this legal soap opera, for that is what it was, and quite frankly we were astonished that the law was being used once again to bully us into a settlement which was to our huge financial disadvantage. That day the Society put out a press release to the effect that they had withdrawn its lost sale claim against the directors, but that the other claims against us still continued. The ineffable Charles Thomson said that as they had taken this pragmatic decision to withdraw the lost sale claim, this would speed up the process and reduce overall costs. This meant that the Society would have to pay our costs relating to this claim which had now been withdrawn. The Society advised us of this in writing and added that our current offer was unrealistic, leaving Herbert Smith with no option but to continue the proceedings. All this meant that the case moved out of court and into preparations for the written closing submissions.

Nobody could understand what the Equitable and Herbert Smith meant by all this, and as usual we brought out our diagnostic equipment – that is to say our brains – to try and fathom their tactics. Was it really the case that they preferred to deconstruct their case piecemeal, picking off individual directors as and when they could in individual settlements, whilst also at the same time disclosing a running programme of concessions, or what? My view was that Mr Treves was trying to save as much face as he could and that a gentle collapse was better than a precipitate collapse, but who knows. We were softening him up in order for him to make a more realistic offer.

On Tuesday, 18th October 2005 we heard that Alan Nash had settled on a drop hands basis. However there was no movement from Herbert Smith and we decided to do nothing, although we had a good look as to how our costs were stacking up. Alan Nash's settlement was followed by that of Roy Ranson, his predecessor as managing director. In a trial statement Ranson said: 'I sincerely regret both the changed prospects for all with-profits policyholders following the House of Lords judgment and the loss of policyholders' money wasted on the litigation against the directors and Auditors. The present Board should be held to account for this appalling waste of policyholders' money.'

On 2nd November 2005 Tim House had a long conversation on the telephone with Charles Plant. He said that he had noted the settlement with Roy Ranson, and went on to say that everybody now knew that the Society and Herbert Smith were going to lose this action; that they had already abandoned their claims against all categories of defendants, both executive and non-executive directors, early leavers, late joiners, lawyers and non-lawyers; that they had abandoned their claims against the former two chief executives, Roy Ranson and Alan Nash, and so on. There was no particular response from Herbert Smith except that we were told that their closing written submissions were powerful documents.

So the date was now 4th November 2005 and we gave Herbert Smith an ultimatum to get back to us by 4 p.m., 7th November on this question of a settlement. It was at this point that Guy came up with an email letter addressed to all six of us. We were, of course, floundering in this litigation quagmire and his letter endeavoured and to my mind entirely succeeded in giving us legal outsiders a realistic view as to where we really stood in these tortuous settlement negotiations – a refined form of torture.

His view was that whereas at that stage we were offering some significant personal write-offs of our personal costs in order to achieve a settlement, this was not the case with Allen & Overy who were offering only a small discount on their success fee, which for the six of us amounted to something like £1.25 million. What better proof of their confidence in our case could we ask for? Guy's view was that the case was extremely unlikely to go to a judgment – a view obviously shared by Tim House and the Allen & Overy team – and that the Society would have to settle with us, even on substantially worse terms than we had then been offered. The problem for us was that under the terms of the conditional fee agreement a settlement was a win, so that it was imperative for us to stand firm on this matter of recovery of our costs. He recalled that we were in the same position as the Bank of England in the case brought against them by the liquidators of the Bank of Credit & Commerce International. For 12 years the Bank of England stood firm and refused even to negotiate on damages and costs, and were therefore likely to get every penny back. So his advice to us was to hold firm like the Bank of England and not be bludgeoned into a less than satisfactory settlement. He went on to say that if the case actually got to judgment, the Society would very likely have to pay us considerably more than the costs which were currently being offered to us. He also pointed out how embarrassing it would be for them to win the case now, having settled with the richest director, David Wilson. Think how they would be pilloried for having done so. This barrage stiffened our wavering resolve. We went back to Allen & Overy and said that Herbert Smith's most recent offer of £3.5 million was unacceptable and that for every week the trial continued we required another £200,000 in costs (that was our weekly expenditure on the lawyers); and I withdrew my proposed personal write-off of £75,000 which I could ill afford anyway.

So like Marshal Kutuzov we waited and waited. We were both distressed and infuriated at the same time by the Society's cynical approach; perhaps as a final act of vendetta they did indeed want to torture us. To give us some further comfort Tim House said that when the closing submissions were published, they would not be at all complimentary either about the Society or its lawyers; that the press could not understand why the Society would want to resume in court, as it would be a purposeless and pointless exercise; and that if the case did start again, it was likely that Mr Justice Langley, who had been quite reticent in the courtroom, would take his gloves off and lay into Milligan in no uncertain fashion.

So we sat and waited for the enemy to show his face above the parapet and peer around. And he did, and it was Mr Copeman, and he was told that he would have to make a serious and significantly improved offer. He was further told that our latest offer of £4.7 million including certain concessions was now withdrawn. These concessions had been made to achieve some sort of finality – a word which lawyers like to use – and to avoid the unpleasant necessity of having to deal with the preparation of detailed closings, which added immeasurably to the personal and family pain involved in these proceedings and, of course, the cost.

Tim House went on to state that the Society had deliberately chosen to put us all through this quite unnecessarily; that we now wanted 100 per cent of our costs back; that foregoing a judgment impacted on all of us in reputational and economic terms; and that in any case the Society's position was weakening day by day. The figure we now wanted stood at £5.55 million but we, the six of us, were prepared to settle at £5.2 million.

Copeman came back with a figure of £4.7 million and over the weekend we discussed this amount ourselves and decided to stand firm. Tim House accelerated the closing submissions so that they would be on the court file, and therefore as I understood it in the public domain as a public vindication of our stewardship of the Society and a refutation of the misleading impression given by Lord Penrose in his lengthy inquiry report.

Monday morning came, 28th November 2005, and the news was that they had settled at our figure of £5.2 million, and we immediately issued a press release. It said:

> The former Board did its level best to steer the Society through impossibly difficult times [not said, of course, was that these impossibly difficult times were engineered by Lord Steyn in his wholly unexpected and destructive judgment]. Painful though this whole episode has been for everyone involved, not least the policyholders, we were not prepared to give in to these claims. Nor were we prepared to let the current Board skulk away from this litigation, leaving us to pay for the privilege. We have had our personal and professional lives ruined by this misguided litigation for almost four years and we are pleased to be rid of it.

Allen & Overy litigation partner Tim House said:

> This case should never have seen the light of day. This action

against the non-executive Directors, involving them, as it did, in an attempt to make them scapegoats for what happened to the Society was from the outset totally heartless, utterly pointless and wholly misconceived.

If it was true that the current Board of the Equitable was advised that it had a duty to bring this case, then serious questions need to be asked of the Society's advisers and about the Board's judgement in accepting that advice. If it is not true, then serious questions need to be asked about the motives for pursuing the litigation – no Director (least of all a non-executive Director) who is doing his or her honest best attempting to manage a difficult situation and who has to make difficult commercial judgements in the process, should face the threat of ruin simply because they could not avert the consequences of aberrational events.

This settlement is a clear acknowledgement that the Society now accepts that it was entirely wrong to bring this action and that it indeed had no justification for so damaging the lives and reputations of these former non-executive Directors.

Mr Treves of course had another view, and this was that : 'They started these claims with the full support of policyholders and action groups; that the risk of litigation is obvious as are the potential costs. However having had the best legal and other expert advice available, we concluded we had a duty to pursue these claims against the former Directors while they were cost effective.' But once again what was this best legal advice, which was diametrically opposite to our best legal advice? Ours was disclosed, theirs never, and for this apparent suppression they claimed privilege. One can only deduce from this that the only purpose of privilege in this context is not to disclose something detrimental to your own case – something that needs to be changed, in my view.

So it all ended, and spluttered into a Settlement Agreement which we all signed. Congratulations came in from all quarters, every non-executive director in the country heaved a deep sigh of relief. We all thanked Tim House and his legal team at Allen & Overy profusely. They had been superb, and Tim House had been exceptional with his navigational skills. Steering six independent directors and six concerned wives through the litigation cataracts was no mean feat.

Tim House replied to the effect that we had been exceedingly courageous and determined clients with whom it had been a great pleasure to work. He congratulated us on our 'deserved and long overdue victory'.

And so we emerged from the darkness of our legal bunker in which we had lived for the past four years. We stood outside, our eyes blinking in the unaccustomed sunshine, and we looked at the ruins of that monstrous edifice of legal fiction, built at a cost to the policyholders of £100 million which now lay shattered at our feet.

There was a feeling of relief, but there was no joy. After all, everybody had suffered from Lord Steyn's aberrational judgment – the hundreds of thousands of policyholders, pensioners, with-profit annuitants, the staff, management, the Directors, everybody. And a fine institution which prided itself on being equitable and fair to all its policyholders had been sunk by an implication. How very, very sad and painful it all was, but the worst of it was that it was all totally unnecessary.

34

The Half-Closed Door

And so the long legal blackmail came to an end, and for those of us who had already retired, we were free to resume our retirement, but for those who had not retired, their careers had been blighted. Two of the actuaries were admonished by the Institute of Actuaries and Roy Ranson, the appointed actuary, who had been awarded a CBE for his services to the insurance profession, was expelled from the Institute.

As for myself, now in my 75th year, my life did resume and with the threat of bankruptcy removed we decided to make over Lyons Hall to the next generation and move back to our old farmhouse on the estate. I continued as a council member of the Royal Asiatic Society; I was appointed to the new Committee of Honour of the Calcutta Tercentenary Trust; I remained a trustee at Brentwood Cathedral; and I became involved with the world of academia through the Royal Asiatic Society. I enjoyed it all very much.

But now, as the shadows lengthen, the opening lines of that old familiar Horace ode come back to haunt me, *Eheu fugaces Postume Postume anni labuntur*, 'Alas, Postume, Postume, how the fleeting years slip by', and I find myself like many old men remembering my vanished years. Once again I hear that sweet sad silvery echo of the trumpets, now metamorphosed into the bugles, pipes and drums of my Regiment, when I was a serving officer just like my Baillie great-uncles had been so many years before.

And then I think of my men who served and fought with me during those interminable patrols in the jungle, and I hear again the crackling of the musketry, the chatter of the machine-guns, and occasionally the explosions of the rifle grenade mortars, and I feel again too close to those six live grenades tucked into my Army belt.

And I start to recall my long voyages in that great Southern Ocean where the waves were sometimes 40 or so feet high with something like a mile between them, so that our little research ship ran up the side of the wave, tottered for a few moments on the crest, crashed down the far side and then wallowed in the comparative calm of the trough; and then as we edged our way south, I see again the great icebergs looming out of the mist and fog, drifting forlorn and lonely up from the ice-shelves in the south, and I see again the pack ice and the mountains and the glaciers; I feel again those blizzards sweeping across the ice and the searing cold on my face, and again the snow drifting and swirling and forming those long sastrugi. And I hear again my huskies singing in the silent moonlight when they were filled with happiness and joy, and their songs call to me still, just like that sweet sad silvery echo of the trumpets.

And then I am back in the high Himalayas and see again the plumes of snow streaming from the mountain peaks, the prayer-flags flying in the wind, the lammergeyers soaring and wheeling overhead, the stupas standing sentinel, the Buddhist monks chanting their incomprehensible mantras, and I hear again the tinkling of the bells of the yaks as they come down from the high passes and once again those bells call to me still just like that old sweet sad silvery echo. And I think again of that great poem of Kipling, 'On the Road to Mandalay': 'By the old Moulmein pagoda looking lazy at the sea, There's a Burma gel a'settin' and I know she thinks of me; For the wind is in the palm trees and the temple bells they say Come you back you British soldier come you back to Mandalay'.

And then, closer to home, I am high up on Ben Wyvis walking up the grouse with my pointers, close to the snowline and the ptarmigan, and looking south across the Moray Firth towards Cawdor, Daviot and Clava, and if I look hard enough perhaps I can even see Lochloy. I think again of those long-lost days as we gathered round the fire listening to the old wind-up gramophone, and walk again along those beautiful Old Bar sands and see the big grey battleships steaming up the Firth to Cromarty and the Loch itself where in summer we picnicked and in winter we skated on the frozen ice. And the fairies – they have long since gone.

And now I sometimes sit in the garden at Lyons Hall with my

gin and cigarette looking westward as the sun sets across the park, and see the mile-long sweep of trees along the river bank. And I watch the wagtails and the house martins in their evening passagio and listen to the calling of the cock pheasants and the chatter of the partridges, the cooing of the collar doves, and I think of old Jolyon in the *Forsyte Saga* dying in his garden chair, and as the diurnal breeze springs up I listen to the souching of the wind in the old Scots pine.

And in the mornings of the autumn I look at the gossamer, as if there had been a midnight shower of jewels, the condensing dew of that 'season of mists and mellow fruitfulness' that causes each thread to glisten with silvery light.

As I do so I think of my children and grandchildren, those miracles of birth and Creation, and I give thanks for the preservation of all this beauty and life and the estate, which three times was so nearly torn away from me. And I think again of my grandfather, his two sons dead, the onset of his Second World War, evicted from his home and dying just after Dunkirk, and wondering about the future of the family estate and his only grandson.

Then I come back to my old preparatory school, evacuated at the beginning of the War to Ingleborough Hall, and sitting with the boys on the spiral staircase in the Hall where JLR the headmaster used to stand in front of the fire in the evening with his left hand as always clutching his left lapel, intoning that old familiar prayer: 'O Lord, support us all day long of this troublesome life until the shades lengthen, the evening comes, the busy world is hushed, the fever of life is over and our work is done; Then Lord in thy Mercy grant us a safe lodging a holy rest and peace at the last.' Amen, Amen. And then we used to sing that great hymn, 'The day thou gavest, Lord, is ended, the darkness falls at they behest'. And occasionally, if we were lucky, we would sing that great psalm, 'I will lift up my eyes unto the hills from whence cometh my help'. And through all my years I have loved the hills and mountains and sometimes mourn that I live in flat old Essex.

And now at last, I come back to that little ice-cap on Galindez Island where, after a long day's work on our new scientific station, I used to sit alone and wonder at the great panorama of mountains and glaciers, pack ice and icebergs, stretching seemingly hundreds of miles towards the Pole, all suffused in those wonderful evening colours of green, mauve, purple and pink, and marvel in the serenity

Index

The index uses the initials A.T. when referring to Alan Tritton.